AMERICAN ERAS

CIVIL WAR AND RECONSTRUCTION

1 8 5 0 - 1 8 7 7

AMERICAN ERAS

CIVIL WAR AND RECONSTRUCTION

1850 - 1877

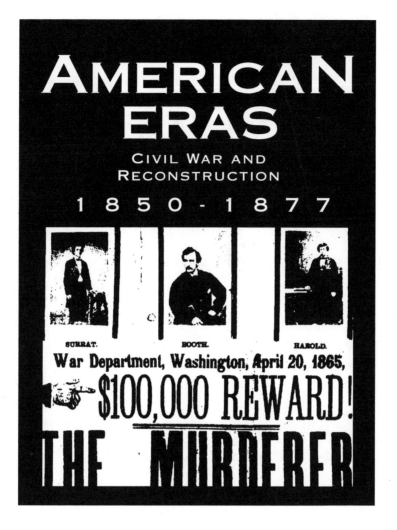

EDITED BY
THOMAS J. BROWN

A MANLY, INC. BOOK

GALE

DETROIT   NEW YORK   TORONTO   LONDON

AMERICAN ERAS

1850–1877

Matthew J. Bruccoli and Richard Layman, Editorial Directors
Karen L. Rood, Senior Editor

ADVISORY BOARD

LIBRARY OF CONGRESS CATALOGING-IN-PUBLICATION DATA

American Eras: civil war and reconstruction, 1850–1877/
    edited by Thomas J. Brown.
    p. Cm.
    A Manly, Inc. book
    Includes bibliographical references (p.) and index.
    Printed in the United States of America
1. United States—Civilization—1783–1865. 2. United States—Civilization—1865–1918.
I. Brown, Thomas J., 1960–   .
E166.A48 1997   97–16011 CIP\
973—dc21

Copyright ©1997 by Gale Research
ISBN 0-7876-1484-X

10 9 8 7 6 5 4 3 2

CONTENTS

INTRODUCTION

American Era. The years from 1850 to 1877 comprise not merely one coherent segment of the American past but the very cornerstone of national identity. Markets for popular books, films, television productions, and tourism steadily confirm the observation of the poet Robert Penn Warren that "the Civil War is our only 'felt' history—history lived in the national imagination." None of the other vital topics in the American experience can compare with the fascination exerted by the dramatic myth of national self-destruction and rebirth, centered on the ordeal of slavery and the elusive promise of equal rights. The period from 1850 to 1877 is scarcely less central to the canon of American literature, opening with Nathaniel Hawthorne's *The Scarlet Letter* (1850), Herman Melville's *Moby-Dick* (1851), Harriet Beecher Stowe's *Uncle Tom's Cabin* (1852), and Henry David Thoreau's *Walden* (1854), and continuing through the poetry of Walt Whitman and Emily Dickinson to the publication at the end of the era of major works by Henry James, Henry Adams, and Mark Twain. It is probably no coincidence that this most distinctively American era is not usually connected to simultaneous developments elsewhere in the world. Unlike the periods before 1815 and since 1914, little attention is devoted to international context in tracing the course of U.S. history from 1850 to 1877; the mythic focus of the Civil War era is relentlessly inward looking.

Global Era. One of the most striking features of the period, however, is that it comprised a distinct phase not only of American history but of world history, in which the United States participated fully. To be sure, special circumstances and unique contingencies helped to shape the American experience. But like earlier and later chapters of history, the Civil War and Reconstruction era cannot be wrenched from its global context. The starting point of the period is a case in point. It was the discovery of gold in California in 1848 and the resulting influx of settlers that obliged the United States to confront immediately the status of slavery in the lands wrested from Mexico, the key issue in the Compromise of 1850. But the gold rush was not merely the opening of a chapter in American history; it also provided bullion for a rapid growth of international trade and drew upon an unprecedented migration from China that marked California from the outset as an extraordinary crossroads of world cultures. Similarly, the European upheavals of 1848 had no direct counterpart in the United States, but they profoundly affected American development by prompting British investors to shift investments away from the Continent and by adding a stream of German immigrants to the Irish refugees of the potato famine.

Economic Integration. The flows of investment and migration in the late 1840s and early 1850s point to the central theme of world history during the third quarter of the nineteenth century and the primary connection between American developments and their international context. As the historian Eric Hobsbawm has written, the fundamental framework for the period is "the global triumph of capitalism." The integration of separate markets forged connections between areas of the world that had previously had virtually no contact, as when Comm. Matthew Perry sailed into Yedo Bay (later Tokyo Bay) in July 1853 on instructions of President Millard Fillmore to open Japan for trade with the West. In addition to providing new opportunities for commerce, the expansion of capitalism brought more areas of the world into similar patterns of development and spread shared values emphasizing reason, political liberalism, and faith in material and moral progress. The westernizing Meiji Restoration of 1868 in Japan was perhaps the most remarkable example of the exportation of European cultures, but events in the United States similarly reflected powerful influences from abroad. Mark Twain once remarked, only half-facetiously, that the novels of Sir Walter Scott caused the American Civil War. Economically, although the United States had emerged from a colonial dependence on Europe, the reintegration taking place during the mid nineteenth century substituted new ties between domestic politics and the vicissitudes of the international business cycle. For example, the worldwide boom of the early 1850s played an important part in undermining the Whig-Democratic party system that had peacefully resolved slavery issues for twenty years. At the other end of the period, the economic crisis that shook Vienna, Austria, in early 1873 converged with weaknesses in the domestic economy to produce a financial panic in the United States that contributed to the end of Reconstruction and inaugurated a long depression, reorienting politics around agrarian and industrial discontent.

Slavery. The decline of various forms of "unfree labor" was the logical counterpart to an emerging world order based in large part on the expansion of markets in which individuals exchanged labor for money. This economic pressure and the widespread appeal of more broadly representative government, both intensified by the urgency of mobilizing resources in support of the nation-state, spelled the doom of serfdom and slavery. The European uprisings of 1848, like the French Revolution on which they were modeled, swept away serfdom wherever they reached. Within little more than a decade the institution was ended even in Russia. Similarly, the enslavement of Africans, long the most powerful thread unifying the Atlantic world, had retreated dramatically by 1850. Slavery remained vital in only three areas of the western world: Brazil, Cuba, and the southern United States. Within the parts of the United States that still permitted slavery, moreover, attentive observers recognized that economic development had almost entirely driven the institution out of Delaware and was perceptibly turning Kentucky, Maryland, and Missouri into free states. Similar transformations were foreseeable in Virginia, North Carolina, and Tennessee. These trends pointed toward an eventual abolition of slavery resembling the process that took place throughout the rest of the western world, including the northern United States—a peaceful, if unconscionably protracted, transition. But although free labor did triumph in the United States, as elsewhere, emancipation came through a violent convulsion that deeply affected the permanent structure of American life.

Cotton. The distinctiveness of the American transition to free labor partly reflected the specialized role that the country had played in the international economy. The industrial revolution that provided the momentum for the integration of a world economy after midcentury had also provided unique reinforcement for the institution of slavery in the lower South. Both in England, where it began during the late eighteenth century, and in the United States, where it began during the early nineteenth century, the Industrial Revolution had been based on the manufacture of cotton textiles. The southern United States supplied over three-fourths of the world production of cotton, which accounted for well over one-half of the entire revenue earned by the country in international trade. The cotton-growing districts, particularly along the Mississippi River and in East Texas, drew slaves from the upper South in large numbers. And unlike the wealthiest slaveholders of the eighteenth century, the sugar planters of the Caribbean, American cotton producers typically lived near their slaves in a region that mixed relatively few large plantations with large numbers of modest-sized farms; unlike the situation elsewhere in the New World, whites in the American South could find safety in the fact that they outnumbered blacks by a margin of two to one. Although interests in cotton and slaveholding faced significant political rivals in every state except South Carolina, the lower South afforded a large, prosperous, self-confident area that could provide the geographic basis for a counterattack against the decline of slavery. Besieged by condemnation from England as well as the northern United States, troubled by the loss of political influence as free labor expanded, American slaveholders lashed out against the flow of history.

Southern Expansionism. Southerners recognized that their increasingly peculiar institution could survive only by expanding. This conclusion had little to do with soil exhaustion in the region but resulted instead from the need of slavery-based societies for a buffer against the expansion of free labor. The southward progress of emancipation in the late eighteenth century had been halted in the nineteenth century by the growth of the cotton kingdom. Similarly, Southerners would conclude in the 1840s that the continued expansion of slavery into Texas was essential to the defense of slavery in the old Southwest and would conclude in the 1850s that the expansion of slavery into Kansas was essential to the defense of slavery in Missouri. As American slaveholders came to identify themselves as guardians of conservatism in an age of liberalism, the strategy of expansionism expressed a self-appointed world mission. Southerners sought to refute their critics by arguing that slavery was not an unfortunate vestige but a better basis for society than free labor. The rise of a slavery-based Caribbean empire, centered on the acquisition of Cuba, was among the fondest wishes of American slaveholders.

Northern Expansionism. As one of the fundamental institutions of American life, slavery presented many issues for public consideration, but it is no coincidence that Southern expansionism was the aspect that most effectively unified the North into an antislavery political force. Moderate Northerners regarded slavery as a stain on the United States, but they believed that if contained within its current boundaries the institution would be, in the words of Abraham Lincoln, on a "course of ultimate extinction." The resistance of Northerners to the extension of slavery reflected many things, including a mortification and repugnance for a reversal of moral progress, disgust with a slowing of material progress, and indignation at the dictation of national policy by slaveholding interests. Moreover, Southern expansionism collided with Northern expansionism. Free labor was spreading not only into the upper South but was also settling the West, where the dream of landownership was helping Kansas, Minnesota, and Nebraska to become states during the period. Not all of the conflicts between slavery and free labor took place in what is now the United States, for Northern expansionism, like Southern expansionism, also tended toward a more far-flung imperialism. This impulse would be expressed after the Civil War in such events as the acquisition of Alaska and in the dispute over the proposed acquisition of Santo Domingo that proved to be one of the crucial turning points of Reconstruction. Before the war, the Southern dream of a slaveholding empire collided with Northern goals of commercial expansion not only on the plains of Kansas but also in such places as Nicaragua, where William Walker's reinstitution of slavery won applause from Southerners but ran afoul of Cornelius Vanderbilt's recognition that the narrow passage between the Atlantic and Pacific Oceans was now a critical juncture in the shifting patterns of international trade. Vanderbilt prevailed in part because he was able to ally himself with local desire for self-determination. Such incidents underscored that the contest between North and South was not merely a family quarrel within the United States but a struggle shaped by a rapidly changing world.

Costs of Insularity. One of the several reasons for the defeat of the Confederacy illustrates the consequences of failure to appreciate American events in international context. Southerners' confidence in their ability to take a stand against the progress of emancipation drew on an outdated and narrow understanding of the way the American situation looked from abroad. The chief foreign implication of the sectional conflict, Southerners believed, was that it would endanger the supply of cotton to England. Sen. James Henry Hammond of South Carolina boasted in 1858 that "England would topple headlong and carry the whole civilized world with her, save the South. No, you dare not make war on cotton. No power on earth dares to make war upon it. Cotton is king." When the Union did in fact dare to make war on the cotton-growing states, the South looked to support from England comparable to the European intervention that had transformed the American Revolution into a world war and ensured the independence of the United States. But this expectation was sadly misinformed. Just as the North was no longer an economic appendage to the South, as it had been in the colonial period, Britain and the rest of Europe no longer regarded the United States merely as a supply of cotton. Although self-interest had hardly disappeared from diplomacy, England now invested a significant part of its national identity in its own abolition of a profitable slave empire; even textile workers who suffered from the closing of factories rallied to support the Union after the Emancipation Proclamation. And before that point, England and the rest of Europe looked upon the situation less simplistically than Hammond had projected. The reign of King Cotton was ending. The primary cause for Southern poverty after the war, the imminent decline in the world demand for cotton would have adversely affected the South even if no war had taken place, and the increasing economic importance of iron tied Britain more closely to the North. Moreover, active support for the Confederacy made no sense for Britain, France, or Russia in the crucial terms of the balance of power in Europe. Britain and France welcomed the weakening of a potentially power-ful American rival, aided the Confederacy usefully in some ways, and stood prepared to accept a Southern victory that was still certainly possible. But the hope for decisive military intervention from Europe was a chimera born from an insular American understanding of its place in the world.

Nationalism. No word is more important to the enduring fascination of the years from 1850 to 1877 than *nation,* and no word better explains the tendency of Americans to lose sight of the rest of the world in thinking about the period. History offers a basis for collective identity by focusing on details particular to the country. Ironically, however, the developing concept of nationhood was one of the points on which the American experience can only be understood as a product of pressures and ideas manifested elsewhere around the same time by the unification of Germany and Italy, the establishment of Hungarian autonomy, the increasing consolidation and independence of Canada and Australia, the Meiji Restoration in Japan, and the failure of Buenos Aires to secede from Argentina. To be sure, nationalism was not a new concept for America or the world in 1850–1877. The United States remained influenced by the Puritan vision of nationhood that had taken root in New England and continued to reflect the Enlightenment principles of national existence embedded in the structure of the country during the Revolutionary era. But both materially and intellectually, the nationalism of the mid nineteenth century was a new force.

War. Like the outward thrust of the slaveholding South and the northern United States, the effort to build large political units organized to compete in an integrated world was the universal quintessence of nationalism in the years after 1850. The Italian nationalist Giuseppe Mazzini doubted that all of Europe had room for more than twelve countries large enough to be viable in the modern age. Similarly, Lincoln argued that "that portion of the earth's surface which is owned and inhabited by the people of the United States, is well adapted to be the home of one national family; and it is not well adapted for two, or more." As in the case of the United States, the establishment of these large political units often meant war, and the two decades after 1850 comprised a violent age that contrasted sharply with the relative peace which had prevailed since 1815 and would resume from 1871 until 1914. Nationalist sentiment was the child of war in the nineteenth century, as it had been in Calvinist Holland in the seventeenth century and revolutionary France in the eighteenth century. Thus, Southern nationalism was before 1861 limited mostly to a small circle of intellectuals and political agitators, but in the crucible of the Civil War it became a dynamic culture that turned events in unexpected ways: for example, by fostering a movement to reform slavery. American nationalism similarly achieved a new power in the course of the struggle to preserve the Union. When a group of Northerners founded a magazine in 1865 to carry on the ideas for which so much had been sacrificed, they inevitably named their publication *The Nation*.

History. Intellectually, the nationalism at the heart of the period from 1850 to 1877 involved a new approach to time as well as space, a rethinking of the structure of history as well as a redrawing of the map of the world. The two major sources of ideas about nationhood, Puritanism and the Enlightenment, had not pinned American identity to specific events taking place at particular times. To the contrary, these patterns of thought adapted from biblical and classical sources a common view of nationhood as a transcendence of history, a universal consummation of civilization that John Winthrop summarized in his famous vision of a "city set upon a hill" and that the cosmopolitans of the Revolutionary era reflected by drawing indiscriminately on models ranging from classical Greece and Sparta to modern Denmark and Poland in their debates over the United States Constitution. The dominant theme of nineteenth-century intellectual history, in contrast, was the rise of historical self-consciousness. The so-called higher criticism of the Bible placed Scripture for the first time in the context of the times and places of composition. Charles Darwin similarly transformed nature into a product of history, the current stage of ongoing evolution. The continuities and discontinuities created by the passage of time were a central motif of romanticism from William Wordsworth to Hawthorne to Richard Wagner to Marcel Proust. In this setting the concept of nationalism shifted from the realization of a universal ideal to the embodiment of distinctive values forged in individual countries at specific moments. Alert Americans recognized during the mid nineteenth century that the contingency of events unfolding during the crisis would harden into the core of the nation. "We cannot escape history," Lincoln reminded his generation. Subsequent generations have been equally unable to escape the history made during this American era.

ACKNOWLEDGMENTS

This book was produced by Manly, Inc. Anthony J. Scotti and Karen L. Rood were the in-house editors.

Production manager is Samuel W. Bruce.

Office manager is Kathy Lawler Merlette.

Administrative support was provided by Ann M. Cheschi and Brenda A. Gillie. Bookkeeper is Joyce Fowler.

Copyediting supervisor is Jeff Miller. The copyediting staff includes Phyllis A. Avant, Patricia Coate, Christine Copeland, Thom Harman, Rebecca Mayo, and William L. Thomas Jr.

Editorial associates are L. Kay Webster and Judith E. McCray.

Layout and graphics staff includes Marie L. Parker and Janet E. Hill.

Photography editors are Julie E. Frick and Margaret Meriwether. Photographic copy work was performed by Joseph M. Bruccoli.

Software specialist is Marie L. Parker. Systems manager is Chris Elmore.

Typesetting supervisor is Kathleen M. Flanagan. The typesetting staff includes Pamela D. Norton and Patricia Flanagan Salisbury.

Walter W. Ross, Steven Gross, and Mark McEwan did library research. They were assisted by the following librarians at the Thomas Cooper Library of the University of South Carolina: Linda Holderfield and the interlibrary-loan staff; reference-department head Virginia Weathers; reference librarians Marilee Birchfield, Stefanie Buck, Stefanie DuBose, Rebecca Feind, Karen Joseph, Donna Lehman, Charlene Loope, Anthony McKissick, Jean Rhyne, Kwamine Simpson, and Virginia Weathers; circulation-department head Caroline Taylor; and acquisitions-searching supervisor David Haggard.

Special thanks are due to Kenneth Graham and William L. Thomas Jr. for their help with the Arts chapter and Hugh Norton for his help with the Business chapter. Dirk Killen provided a draft of the chronology and an entry on music for the Arts chapter.

AMERICAN ERAS

1850–1877

WORLD EVENTS:

SELECTED OCCURRENCES OUTSIDE THE UNITED STATES

CONFLICTS

1850–1864—T'aiping Rebellion

1852—Second British-Burmese War

1853–1856—Crimean War

1859—Franco-Austrian War

1863–1864—Second Polish Revolution

1866—Austrian Seven Weeks' War against Italy, Germany, and Bohemia

1870–1871—Franco-Prussian War

1873–1874—Second Ashanti War

1877—Russian-Turkish War

1877—War between Britain and Afghanistan

1877–1878—Kaffir War

NEW NATIONS

1852—South African Republic (Transvaal) is declared.

1861—United Italy

1871—German Empire

MAJOR POWERS AND LEADERS

Austria-Hungary—Emperor Francis Joseph I (1848–1916)

China—Emperors Hsüan Tsung (1821–1850), Hsien Feng (1851–1861), T'ung Chih (1862–1874), and Kwang Hsü (1875–1908)

France—President, Prince Louis-Napoleon (1848–1851); proclaimed himself Emperor Napoleon III (1852–1870); presidents Adolphe Thiers (1870–1873) and Marie Edmé MacMahon (1873–1879)

German Empire—Chancellor Otto von Bismarck (1871–1890); Emperor William I (1871–1888)

Great Britain—Queen Victoria (1837–1901); prime ministers Lord Palmerston (1846–1865), Lord John Russell (1865–1868), Benjamin Disraeli (1868, 1874–1880), and William Gladstone (1868–1874)

Italy—King Victor Emmanuel II (1861–1878); premiers Baron Bettino Ricasoli (1861–1862, 1866–1867), Giovanni Lanza (1869–1873), Marco Minghetti (1863–1864, 1873–1876), and Agostino Depretis (1876–1879, 1881–1887)

Japan—Shoguns Ieyoshi (1838–1853), Iesada (1853–1858), Iemochi (1858–1866), Keiki (1867); and Meiji (1867–1912)

The Ottoman Empire—Sultans Abdul Mejid (1839–1861), Abdul Aziz (1861–1876), Murad V (1876), and Abdul Hamid II (1876–1909)

Russia—Czars Nicholas I (1825–1855) and Alexander II (1855–1881)

1850

20 Mar.	The Erfurt parliament meets; it has been summoned by King Frederick William IV of Prussia to form a new confederation opposing Austria.
12 Apr.	French troops restore Pope Pius IX, who had fled to Gaeta after a popular insurrection in 1848, to power in Rome; Pius revokes the liberal 1848 Roman constitution.
19 Apr.	Britain and the United States agree to the Clayton-Bulwer Treaty, which provides that neither country will assert exclusive control of any canal built across the Isthmus of Panama.
31 May	Universal suffrage is abolished in France; henceforth, in order to vote one must show that one has lived in the same place for three years. The measure is aimed mainly at industrial workers, who tend to move frequently and to have radical political views.
2 July	Prussia and Denmark agree to the Treaty of Berlin, providing for Denmark to govern Schleswig and for an administrator to govern Holstein.
5 Aug.	The British Parliament passes the Australian Colonies Government Act, providing for self-government for the Australian states.
18 Aug.	The French novelist Honoré de Balzac dies.
26 Aug.	Louis Philippe, who had abdicated as king of France in 1848, dies; his grandson, Louis Philippe, the comte de Paris, succeeds to the Orléanist claim to the throne.
30 Sept.	A papal bull sets up a hierarchy of Roman Catholic bishops in England in Great Britain; the bishops are to take their titles from sees created by the bull.
Oct.	The Taiping Rebellion breaks out in China; it is led by the mystic Hung Hsiuch'üan, who takes Nanking and Shanghai, declares himself emperor, and attacks Beijing.
11 Oct.	Count Camillo Benso di Cavour is appointed minister of agriculture and commerce in Piedmont.
29 Nov.	Germany and Austria agree to the Punctuation of Olmutz, providing for Prussia to recognize the Frankfurt Diet.

1851

•	The English philosopher Herbert Spencer publishes *Social Statics*.
•	In response to the papal bull of the year before, Parliament passes the Ecclesiastical Titles Bill; it bars Catholic bishops from accepting titles from areas within Britain.
•	Gold is discovered in Australia.
16 Mar.	Spain enters into a concordat with the papacy, providing for Catholicism to be the only authorized faith in Spain.
1 May–15 Oct.	The London Great Exhibition, known as the Crystal Palace Exhibition, inaugurates the era of world's fairs.
24 July	The British window tax is eliminated, leading to the construction of buildings with more windows.
18 Nov.	King Ernest Augustus of Hannover dies and is succeeded by George V.

	2 Dec.	President Louis Napoleon leads a coup d'état in France.

1852

17 Jan.	The British government signs the Sand River Convention, recognizing the independence of the Boer territory of the Transvaal in South Africa.
22 Jan.	The Orléans family is banned from France.
1 Apr.	The second British-Burmese War begins.
8 May	Britain, France, Russia, Prussia, Austria, Sweden, and Denmark conclude the London Protocol, in which Denmark agrees to preserve a special status for the colonies of Schleswig and Holstein, and the other powers guarantee the territorial integrity of Denmark.
30 June	Britain promulgates a new constitution for New Zealand, dividing it into six provinces and granting it self-government.
4 Nov.	Count Cavour is named prime minister of Piedmont.
2 Dec.	The Second Empire is proclaimed in France; Louis Napoleon becomes emperor as Napoleon III.

1853

•	Baron Georges Haussmann, named prefect of the Seine by Napoleon III, begins the reconstruction of Paris by laying out the Bois de Boulogne.
•	The Italian composer Giuseppe Verdi writes the operas *La Traviata* and *Il Travatore*.
30 Jan.	Napoleon III marries the Spanish countess Eugénie de Montijo.
18 Apr.	British chancellor of the Exchequer William Ewart Gladstone proposes a budget that eliminates import duties on most foods and partially manufactured goods and cuts most duties on manufactured goods in half.
19 Apr.	The Russian emissary to Constantinople, Prince Alexander Menshikov, asserts a Russian protectorate over Christians in the Ottoman Empire.
2 July	The Russian army invades the Danubian principalities of Wallachia and Moldavia.
4 Oct.	The Ottoman Empire declares war on Russia.
15 Nov.	Pedro V succeeds to the Portuguese throne on the death of Maria II.
30 Nov.	Russian shelling destroys the wooden Ottoman fleet at Sinope, demonstrating the importance of armor plating.

1854

•	The newspaper *Le Figaro* begins publication in Paris as a weekly.
12 Mar.	Britain and France form an alliance with the Ottoman Empire against Russia.
28 Mar.	France and Britain declare war on Russia.
13 July	Abbas I, Ottoman viceroy of Egypt, is assassinated; he is succeeded by his uncle, Mohammed Said.

14 Sept.	The Allied Powers land in the Crimea.
20 Sept.	French and British troops prevail over the Russian army at the Battle of the Alma River.
17 Oct.	French and British troops begin the siege of Sebastopol.
25 Oct.	The Allies prevail in the Battle of Balaclava after heavy losses; the disastrous Charge of the Light Brigade will be immortalized this year in the poem by Alfred, Lord Tennyson.
8 Dec.	Pope Pius IX proclaims that belief in the Immaculate Conception of the Virgin Mary is an article of faith in the Roman Catholic Church.

1855

20 Jan.	Discontent over the Crimean War causes George Hamilton-Gordon, fourth earl of Aberdeen, to resign as prime minister of Britain; he will be succeeded on 5 February by Henry John Temple, third viscount of Palmerston.
26 Jan.	Piedmont enters the Crimean War alliance against Russia, hoping to earn goodwill for Italian unification.
2 Mar.	Czar Nicholas I dies; he is succeeded by Alexander II.
11 Sept.	The Russians abandon Sebastopol after blowing up their forts and sinking their ships to keep them from falling into Allied hands.
Nov.	The Scottish missionary and explorer David Livingstone discovers Victoria Falls on the Zambezi River in Africa.

1856

•	The skull of Neanderthal man is discovered in Germany by Johann C. Fruhott.
•	The French statesman and author Alexis de Tocqueville publishes *L'Ancien Régime et la révolution*.
1 Feb.	The Crimean War ends when Russia yields to an Austrian ultimatum and agrees to preliminary peace terms at Vienna.
30 Mar.	The Treaty of Paris is signed: the Allies recognize the integrity of the Ottoman Empire and guarantee the independence of the Danubian principalities; Russia agrees to the neutrality of the Black Sea and free navigation of the Danube.
6 May	The Austrian psychiatrist Sigmund Freud, the founder of psychoanalysis, is born in Freiburg, Moravia.
12 July	Austria grants amnesty to participants in the Hungarian rebellion of 1848–1849.
26 July	The Irish playwright George Bernard Shaw is born in Dublin.
8 Oct.	War breaks out between Britain and China after Chinese sailors board the British ship *Arrow* at Canton and arrest its crew.
1 Nov.	The Persian occupation of Herat in Afghanistan prompts a war with Britain.

1857

•	Gustave Flaubert publishes *Madame Bovary*.

- Parliament passes the Matrimonial Causes Act, creating divorce courts in England and Wales and ordering the world's first alimony payments.

- The National Portrait Gallery opens in London.

- The French artist Jean François Millet paints *The Gleaners.*

- The French poet Charles Baudelaire publishes *Les Fleurs du mal.*

4 Mar.	The Treaty of Paris ends the Anglo-Persian War; the shah acknowledges the independence of Afghanistan.
10 May	The Indian Mutiny against British rule begins with a revolt of sepoys (Indian soldiers in the Bengal army of the British East India Company) at Meerut.
26 May	Prussia renounces its authority over the Swiss canton of Neuchâtel, which had declared itself a republic in 1848.
Aug.	Giuseppe Garibaldi forms the Italian National Association, seeking unification of Italy under the leadership of Piedmont.
5 Sept.	The French philosopher Auguste Comte, exponent of positivism, dies.
29 Dec.	French and British forces capture Canton, China.

1858

- Bernadette Soubirous reports seeing the Virgin Mary at Lourdes, which begins to attract pilgrims.

- The Covent Garden Opera House opens in London.

- Construction begins on the Ringstrasse in Vienna.

- The British explorers Richard Francis Burton and John Hanning Speke, seeking the source of the Nile, discover Lake Tanganyika; Speke goes on alone and discovers Victoria Nyanza, the largest lake in Africa.

June	The property requirement for members of the British Parliament is abolished.
26–29 June	The Anglo-Chinese War ends with the Treaties of Tientsin between China and Great Britain, France, the United States, and Russia, which open eleven additional Chinese ports; a further agreement in November will legalize the opium trade.
8 July	Britain declares that the Indian Mutiny has been suppressed.
23 July	Civil disabilities of Jews in Britain are removed by an act of Parliament; Baron Lionel de Rothschild becomes the first Jewish member of Parliament.
2 Aug.	British Columbia is removed from the jurisdiction of Hudson's Bay Company and organized as a colony.
7 Oct.	Prince William of Prussia is named regent for the insane King Frederick William IV.
10 Dec.	France and Piedmont enter into an alliance.

1859

- John Stuart Mill publishes *On Liberty.*

- Karl Marx publishes *Zur Kritik der politischen Oekonomie.*

- Charles Darwin publishes *On the Origin of Species by Means of Natural Selection, or, The Preservation of Favoured Races in the Struggle for Life.*

- Charles Dickens publishes *A Tale of Two Cities.*

27 Apr. Tuscan rebels call on the House of Lorraine to declare allegiance to Austria or Italy; similar peaceful uprisings follow in Modena and Parma in May.

29 Apr. Austria invades Piedmont.

12 May France declares war on Austria.

4 June The French defeat the Austrians at Magenta and liberate Milan.

24 June France and Piedmont defeat Austria at Solferino.

8 July Charles XV takes the Swedish throne on the death of Oscar I.

11 July The Peace of Villafranca provides for Austria to transfer Parma and Lombardy to France for subsequent cession to Piedmont, but authorities in Tuscany and Modena are restored, and Venice remains under the control of Austria. Count Cavour resigns as prime minister of Piedmont in protest.

Sept. Rudolf von Benningsen forms the German National Association to promote German unification under the leadership of Prussia.

22 Oct. Spain declares war on Moors in Morocco.

10 Nov. Buenos Aires, which had seceded from the Argentine Confederation in 1853, agrees to reunion after defeat by federal troops.

10 Nov. The Treaty of Zurich confirms the preliminary Peace of Villafranca.

1860

- *The Cornhill Magazine* is founded in London, with William Makepeace Thackeray as its first editor.

- The first British Open golf championship is won by W. Park.

20 Jan. Count Cavour is recalled to office as the prime minister of Piedmont.

13–15 Mar. Citizens in Tuscany, Emilia, Parma, Modena, and Romagna vote in plebiscites in favor of union with Piedmont.

17 Mar. The second Maori War breaks out in New Zealand.

24 Mar. Under the Treaty of Turin, Piedmont transfers Nice and Savoy to France.

2 Apr. The first Italian parliament meets in Turin.

3 Apr. Transvaal establishes its capital at Pretoria.

26 Apr. The war between Spain and the Moors in Morocco ends, with Spain victorious.

27 May Giuseppe Garibaldi and his Redshirts conquer Palermo.

July The city of Vladivostok is founded in Russia.

7 July The Austrian composer Gustav Mahler is born.

7 Sept. Francis II of Naples flees as Garibaldi's troops enter the city.

10 Sept. Piedmont attacks the Papal States.

| 21–22 Oct. | Naples and Sicily vote in favor of union with Piedmont. |
| 26 Oct. | Garibaldi meets Victor Emmanuel II, king of Piedmont, and declares him king of Italy. |

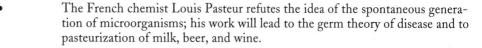

1861

- The French chemist Louis Pasteur refutes the idea of the spontaneous generation of microorganisms; his work will lead to the germ theory of disease and to pasteurization of milk, beer, and wine.

- William Siemens in Britain and Pierre Émile Martin in France independently introduce the open-hearth process, which will permit increased production of steel.

- Construction begins on the Paris Opéra; it will be completed in 1875.

- Charles Dickens publishes *Great Expectations*.

- The Russian novelist Ivan Turgenev publishes *Fathers and Sons*.

2 Jan.	Frederick William IV of Prussia dies and is succeeded by William I.
3 Mar.	Czar Alexander II proclaims the emancipation of the serfs in Russia.
17 Mar.	Victor Emmanuel II is proclaimed king of a united Italy by the Italian parliament.
18 Mar.	At its own request, Santo Domingo is annexed by Spain.
10 Apr.	Russia grants a constitution to Finland.
6 June	Count Cavour dies.
25 June	Sultan Abdul Mejid of the Ottoman Empire dies and is succeeded by his brother, Abdul Aziz.
11 Nov.	Pedro V of Portugal dies and is succeeded by Louis I.
14 Dec.	Albert, prince consort of Queen Victoria, dies.
23 Dec.	The Ottoman sultan acquiesces in the unification of Moldavia and Walachia as Romania.

1862

- Verdi's opera *La forza del destino* (The Power of Destiny) premieres.

- The actress Sarah Bernhardt makes her debut at the Comédie Française in Paris.

5 Feb.	Delegations from Moldavia and Walachia meet in Bucharest for the formation of Romania.
10 Mar.	Britain and France acknowledge the independence of Zanzibar.
5 June	France and Annam agree to the Treaty of Saigon, whereby France annexes the three eastern provinces of Cochin China.
Sept.	Otto von Bismarck becomes premier of Prussia.

| Oct. | The Prussian Diet is dismissed, beginning four years of rule by Bismarck without a legislature. |

1863

	•	The French historian Ernst Renan publishes *Vie de Jesus* (*The Life of Jesus*).
•	The French artist Édouard Manet paints *Déjeuner sur l'herbe* (Luncheon on the Grass).
•	The first running of the Grand Prix de Paris is held at Longchamp.
22 Jan.	The Polish insurrection begins.
8 Feb.	Prussia joins with Russia to suppress the Polish insurrection.
Mar.	Russia divides Poland into provinces.
Mar.	Denmark incorporates Schleswig.
30 Mar.	A seventeen-year-old Danish prince becomes king of Greece under the name George I.
June	Civil war breaks out in Afghanistan.
11 Aug.	France establishes a protectorate over Cambodia.
15 Nov.	Frederick VII of Denmark dies and is succeeded by his cousin, Christian IX.
24 Dec.	The English author William Makepeace Thackeray dies.

1864

	•	The Geneva Convention calls for wartime immunity for the Red Cross, founded by Henri Dunant.
1 Feb.	Austrian and Prussian troops enter Schleswig.
Mar.	The Taiping Rebellion ends in China.
18 Apr.	Germany invades Denmark.
25 Apr.	Lord John Russell calls the London Conference of Britain, Russia, France, Austria, and Prussia to address affairs in Denmark.
26 June	War resumes in Denmark following the end of the London Conference.
15 Sept.	In a treaty with France, Italy renounces its claim to Rome and agrees to make Florence its capital.
30 Oct.	In the Peace of Vienna, Denmark cedes Schleswig, Holstein, and Lauenburg to Austria and Prussia.
8 Dec.	Pope Pius IX promulgates the Syllabus of Errors, asserting the authority of the Roman Catholic Church over science and culture.

1865

| | • | Lewis Carroll (Charles Lutwidge Dodgson) publishes *Alice's Adventures in Wonderland*. |
| 27 Jan. | The independence of Peru is established in a treaty with Spain. |

18 Mar.	War breaks out, pitting Paraguay against Argentina, Brazil, and Uruguay.
1 May	A revolt in Santo Domingo causes Spain to relinquish sovereignty.
13 July	The English mountaineer Edward Whymper is the first to scale the Matterhorn.
14 Aug.	The Convention of Gastein divides the fruits of the war against Denmark: Austria annexes Holstein; Prussia receives Schleswig and Kiel and buys Lauenburg from Austria.
4 Oct.	Bismarck and Napoleon III meet at Biarritz, France; the French emperor agrees to a united Italy and to Prussian supremacy in Germany.
18 Oct.	Lord Palmerston dies and is succeeded as prime minister of Great Britain by Lord John Russell.
Dec.	New Zealand moves its capital from Auckland to Wellington.

1866

- The German composer Johannes Brahms writes *Ein deutsches Requiem* (*A German Requiem*).

- The Austrian monk and botanist Gregor Mendel publishes the results of his research into the principles of heredity; his work will be ignored until 1900.

- The Swedish chemist Alfred Bernhard Nobel invents dynamite.

- The Russian novelist Fyodor Dostoyevsky publishes *Prestupleniye i nakazaniye (Crime and Punishment)*.

14 Jan.	Peru declares war on Spain.
17 Feb.	Disturbances in Ireland lead Britain to suspend the writ of habeas corpus.
12 May	Italy forms an alliance with Prussia against Austria.
7 June	Prussia invades Holstein.
14 June	The German federal diet calls for mobilization against the Prussian invasion of Holstein; the Prussian delegates declare the German Confederation ended.
20 June	Italy declares war on Austria.
3 July	Prussia defeats Austria at Sadová (Königgrätz), Bohemia.
10 Aug.	Bolivia cedes the territory between the Andes Mountains and the Pacific Ocean to Chile.
23 Aug.	The Treaty of Prague ends the war between Austria and Prussia; Prussia is to annex Hannover, Electoral Hesse, Nassau, and Frankfurt am Main.
2 Sept.	Crete revolts against the Ottoman Empire and declares union with Greece.
12 Oct.	The Treaty of Vienna ends the war between Austria and Italy.
Dec.	Napoleon III withdraws French backing for Emperor Maximilian in Mexico.

24 Dec.	Prussia annexes Schleswig, Holstein, and Lauenburg as the province of Schleswig-Holstein.

1867

- Karl Marx publishes the first volume of *Das Kapital*.

- The British athlete John Graham Chambers formulates the rules of boxing; they are called the Marquis of Queensberry Rules after John Sholto Douglas, eighth marquis and earl of Queensberry, the sponsor of Chambers's amateur club.

- The English surgeon Joseph Lister describes the procedure for antiseptic surgery aided by use of phenol (carbolic acid).

- Paris World's Fair introduces Japanese art to the Western world.

17 Feb.	The Hungarian Diet opens; it will lead to the creation of the Dual Monarchy, whereby the Magyars will rule Hungary, the Germans will control the rest of Austria, and a single foreign policy will be established.
29 Mar.	The British North America Act establishes the Dominion of Canada, with provinces of Quebec, Ontario, Nova Scotia, and New Brunswick.
16 Apr.	The North German Confederation, headed by Prussia, is organized.
8 June	Emperor Francis Joseph I of Austria is crowned king of Hungary.
19 June	Emperor Maximilian is executed in Mexico.
15 Aug.	The British Parliamentary Reform Bill extends the franchise and redistributes seats.
21 Aug.	An act of Parliament establishes working hours and conditions for women and children in British factories.
Dec.	Diamonds are discovered in the Orange Free State in South Africa.
21 Dec.	The Austrian constitution recognizes the Dual Monarchy.

1868

3 Jan.	The Meiji dynasty is restored in Japan on the abolition of the shogunate.
29 Feb.	Benjamin Disraeli becomes prime minister of Great Britain.
30 Sept.	Queen Isabella flees Spain after revolution breaks out.
Nov.	Liberals defeat Conservatives in British elections; William Gladstone will replace Disraeli as prime minister.

1869

- John Stuart Mill publishes *The Subjection of Women*.

- The Russian chemist Dmitry Mendeleyev publishes the periodic table of the elements.

- Richard Wagner composes *The Rhinegold*.

6 Feb.	Greece defers to a Turkish ultimatum to leave Crete.

6 June	A new constitution is announced for Spain.
12 July	Napoleon III adopts a parliamentary system of government in France.
2 Oct.	The Indian political and spiritual leader Mohandas Gandhi is born in Porbandar.
17 Nov.	The Suez Canal opens.
8 Dec.	The Vatican Council begins.
31 Dec.	The French painter Henri Matisse is born.

1870

•	The German archaeologist Heinrich Schliemann begins excavations in Asia Minor at what he believes to be the site of Troy.
1 Mar.	The war between Paraguay and the alliance of Brazil, Argentina, and Uruguay ends.
9 Apr.	Vladimir Ilyich Ulyanov, the future Russian Communist leader Vladimir Lenin, is born.
4 June	The British Civil Service is reformed to open most domestic offices to competitive examinations.
9 June	Charles Dickens dies.
19 June	Prince Leopold von Hohenzollern-Sigmaringen of Prussia accepts the offer of the Spanish throne.
25 June	Queen Isabella of Spain, in exile in Paris, abdicates the throne in favor of Alfonso XII.
12 July	Leopold's claim to the Spanish throne is withdrawn on his behalf by his father, Prince Charles Anthony.
13 July	King William, at Ems, rejects a French demand that Prussia apologize for trying to claim the Spanish throne and promise not to renew the claim; Bismarck publishes the telegram in which the rejection was reported to him.
15 July	Manitoba becomes a province of Canada.
18 July	The Vatican Council proclaims the dogma of papal infallibility in matters of faith and morals.
19 July	France declares war on Prussia.
4–6 Aug.	Defeats at Wörth and Weissenburg begin a string of reverses for France.
1 Sept.	The French are defeated at the Battle of Sedan; Napoleon III surrenders the following day.
4 Sept.	Revolt breaks out in Paris; France is proclaimed a republic.
19 Sept.	Two German armies besiege Paris.
20 Sept.	Italy attacks Rome, which had previously been protected by France.
2 Oct.	Rome is incorporated into Italy and declared the capital.
30 Dec.	The duke of Aosta becomes king of Spain as Amadeus I.

1871

• Charles Darwin publishes *The Descent of Man, and Selection in Relation to Sex,* applying his theory of evolution through natural selection to the human species.

• The English novelist George Eliot (Mary Anne Evans) begins serial publication of *Middlemarch.*

18 Jan. William I of Prussia is crowned German emperor at Versailles.

28 Jan. Paris surrenders to Germany.

26 Mar. The Paris Commune is established.

14 Apr. A constitution is issued for the German Empire, modeled on the constitution of the North German Confederation.

10 May The Peace of Frankfurt transfers Alsace and part of Lorraine from France to Germany and provides for German military occupation of France until a large indemnity is paid.

13 May Italy passes the Law of Guarantees, promising protection for the Pope and leaving him in control of the Vatican.

28 May The Paris Commune falls after a week of bloodshed.

25 June The Jesuits are expelled from Germany; Bismarck, chancellor of the German Empire, launches the *Kulturkampf* (Cultural Struggle) to suppress the influence of the Roman Catholic Church in Germany.

29 June The Trade Union Act grants legal recognition to unions in Britain.

1 July British Columbia is added to the Dominion of Canada.

10 July The French novelist Marcel Proust is born.

18 July Britain adopts voting by secret ballot.

31 Aug. Adolphe Thiers becomes president of the French republic.

10 Nov. The Anglo-British explorer and journalist Henry Morton Stanley meets David Livingstone at Ujiji on Lake Tanganyika, greeting him with the words "Dr. Livingstone, I presume?"

1872

• France and Japan establish compulsory military service.

• Rebellion against Spanish authority takes place in the Philippines.

26 Apr. Coronation of Charles VII in Spain leads to civil war.

4 May Charles VII flees to Spain upon defeat of supporters.

25 June Germany expels Jesuit order.

18 July Britian adopts the Ballot Act, providing for voting by secret ballot.

1873

• The Scottish physicist James Clerk Maxwell publishes *A Treatise on Electricity and Magnetism.*

• The Russian novelist Leo Tolstoy begins serial publication of *Anna Karenina.*

•	The French science-fiction writer Jules Verne publishes *Le Tour du monde en quatre-vingts jours* (*Around the World in 80 Days*).
9 Jan.	Napoleon III dies in England.
12 Feb.	The radical majority in the Cortes proclaims Spain a republic; Amadeus I abdicates.
May	A financial crisis begins in Vienna; it will spread throughout Europe and, by September, will reach the United States.
5 June	Under pressure from the British government, Sultan Barghash Sayyid of Zanzibar abolishes slave markets.
6–12 Sept.	The emperors of Germany, Russia, and Austria-Hungary meet in Berlin, leading to formation of an entente.
16 Sept.	The last German troops are withdrawn from France.
Nov.	The cities of Buda and Pesth are combined to create the capital city of Hungary.
20 Nov.	Marshal Marie Edmé MacMahon is named president of France for a term of seven years.

1874

•	A group of painters rejected by the Salon holds an independent exhibition in Paris; Claude Monet's *Impression: Sunrise* inspires the critic Louis Leroy to ridicule the entire group as "Impressionists."
•	Richard Wagner completes the opera *Götterdämmerung (The Twilight of the Gods)*.
•	The Russian composer Modest Mussorgsky's opera *Boris Godunov* is produced in Saint Petersburg.
•	The British sportsman Walter Clopton Wingfield patents the rules of lawn tennis.
15 Mar.	France asserts a protectorate over Annam.
July	Denmark permits limited self-government for Iceland.
30 Nov.	The British statesman Winston Churchill is born.

1875

25 Feb.	Kuang Hsü becomes emperor of China.
May	The Socialist Workingmen's Party is formed at an international congress held in Gotha, Germany.
8 May	Prussia abolishes religious orders.
July	Bosnia and Herzegovina rebel against the Ottoman Empire.
16 July	France adopts a republican constitution.
24 Aug.	The Englishman Capt. Matthew Webb becomes the first person to swim across the English Channel.
12 Dec.	The Ottoman sultan offers reforms in response to the rebellion.

1876

•	The anarchist Michael Bakunin is among the organizers of a Russian secret society, Land and Liberty, that becomes the basis for the Populist movement.
26 Feb.	Japan recognizes the independence of Korea from China by signing a treaty opening Korean ports to Japanese trade and allowing Japan to have a resident at Seoul; China does not protest.
30 May	Sultan Abdul Aziz of the Ottoman Empire is deposed; his nephew is proclaimed Murad V.
30 June	Serbia declares war on the Ottoman Empire.
July	The Spanish Cortes adopts a new constitution, providing for the election of members of a bicameral legislature.
2 July	Montenegro declares war on the Ottoman Empire.
13–16 Aug.	The Bayreuth Festspielhaus holds the first complete performance of Wagner's *Der Ring des Nibelungen* (The Ring of the Nibelungs), which consists of *Das Rheingold, Die Walküre* (*The Valkyrie*), *Siegfried,* and *Götterdämmerung.*
31 Aug.	Murad V is deposed as sultan of the Ottoman Empire on grounds of insanity; he is succeeded by Abdul Hamid II.
12 Dec.	The Constantinople Conference meets to address rebellions in the Ottoman Empire.
23 Dec.	A new constitution is issued for the Ottoman Empire, providing for parliamentary government and freedom of expression.

1877

•	The Norwegian dramatist Henrik Ibsen writes the play *Pillars of Society.*
•	Spencer Gore wins the first All-England Lawn Tennis championships, played at Wimbledon.
1 Jan.	Queen Victoria of Great Britain is proclaimed empress of India in a ceremony at Delhi.
20 Jan.	The Constantinople Conference dissolves without resolving disputes in the Ottoman Empire.
28 Feb.	A peace treaty is signed between the Ottoman Empire and Serbia.
19 Mar.	The first Ottoman Empire parliament opens.
24 Apr.	Russia declares war on the Ottoman Empire and invades Romania.
May	Romania joins the war against the Ottoman Empire.
Oct.	In a commercial treaty with Britain, Madagascar agrees to emancipate its slaves.
14 Dec.	Serbia joins Russia in the war against the Ottoman Empire.

THE ARTS

by
MICHAEL McLOUGHLIN, ROBERT MOSS, ANTHONY J. SCOTTI, and CAROLYN SHAFER

CONTENTS

Sidebars and tables are listed in italics.

1850

Literature	Ralph Waldo Emerson, *Representative Men;* Nathaniel Hawthorne, *The Scarlet Letter;* Herman Melville, *White-Jacket; or the World in a Man-of-War.*
Music	"Camptown Races," by Stephen Foster; "Carol (It Came upon a Midnight Clear)," by Richard S. Willis; "Santa Lucia," by Thomas Oliphant and Teodoro Cottrau.

- Thomas Cole's *The Voyage of Life* is exhibited for the first time; the artist had died in 1848.

- Popular singer Jenny Lind, "The Swedish Nightingale," undertakes an American tour sponsored by the showman P. T. Barnum.

- The earliest known poems of Emily Dickinson are written. Her most prolific period of composition is the early 1860s, but her first book of poems, edited by Mabel Loomis Todd and Thomas Wentworth Higginson, is not published until 1890.

- Throughout the 1850s and 1860s Mathew Brady establishes himself as the premier photographer in America.

19 July	Transcendentalist literary critic Margaret Fuller, Marchioness D'Ossoli, dies in a shipwreck off Fire Island, New York.

1851

Literature	Nathaniel Hawthorne, *The House of the Seven Gables;* Francis Parkman Jr., *The History of the Conspiracy of Pontiac;* Henry Wadsworth Longfellow, *The Golden Legend;* Herman Melville, *Moby-Dick; or, The Whale;* William Gilmore Simms, *Katharine Walton.*
Music	"Old Folks at Home (Way Down upon the Swanee River)," by Stephen Foster.

- Jasper Cropsey paints *Eagle Cliff, New Hampshire.*

- John Notman designs Emmanuel Church in Cumberland, Maryland.

- *The Photographic Art Journal* begins publication.

13 Jan.	William Niblo launches the lavish musical "spectacle" *Faustus; or, the Demon of the Dragonfels* at his Niblo's Garden theater in New York City.
7 Apr.	Niblo produces another musical spectacle, *Vision of the Sun,* at Niblo's Garden.
14 Sept.	The novelist James Fenimore Cooper dies in Cooperstown, New York.

1852

Literature	Nathaniel Hawthorne, *The Blithedale Romance;* Herman Melville, *Pierre;* William Gilmore Simms, *The Sword and the Distaff;* Harriet Beecher Stowe, *Uncle Tom's Cabin; or, Life among the Lowly.*
Music	"Massa's in de Cold, Cold Ground," by Stephen Foster.

- Richard Upjohn designs the Church of Saint John in the Wilderness in Copake Falls, New York.

27 Sept.	George L. Aiken's dramatization of Harriet Beecher Stowe's novel *Uncle Tom's Cabin,* in which Aiken appears, premieres in Troy, New York.

1853

Literature	Joseph Glover Baldwin, *The Flush Times of Alabama and Mississippi;* Nathaniel Hawthorne, *Tanglewood Tales, for Girls and Boys; Being a Second Wonder-Book.*
Music	"My Old Kentucky Home" and "Old Dog Tray," by Stephen Foster.
•	Richard Upjohn designs Saint John Chrysostom Church in Delafield, Wisconsin.
•	*Putnam's Monthly Magazine* is founded.
8 Oct.	The *Musical World* reports that six companies of blackface minstrels will be performing in New York City.

1854

Literature	Timothy Shay Arthur, *Ten Nights in a Bar-Room and What I Saw There;* John Esten Cooke, *Leather Stocking and Silk;* Maria Susanna Cummins, *The Lamplighter;* Henry David Thoreau, *Walden; or, Life in the Woods.*
Music	*Le Banjo,* by Louis Moreau Gottschalk.
•	Leopold Eidlitz designs The Chalet in Newport, Rhode Island.
•	Francis D. Lee designs the Unitarian Church in Charleston, South Carolina.

1855

Literature	Henry Wadsworth Longfellow, *The Song of Hiawatha;* Walt Whitman, *Leaves of Grass.*
Music	"Come Where My Love Lies Dreaming," by Stephen Foster; "Listen to the Mockingbird," music by Richard Millburn, lyrics by Alice Hawthorne (Septimus Winner).
•	Frederic Church paints *The Andes of Ecuador,* often considered his first major painting.
•	James Goodwin Clonney completes his genre painting *What a Catch!*
•	Artist Asher Brown Durand publishes nine "Letters on Landscape Painting" in the art journal *The Crayon.*
•	The Smithsonian Institution, designed by James Renwick, is completed in Washington, D.C.; construction began in 1848.
•	Charles Heard designs the Old Stone Church in Cleveland.
•	Jacob Wrey Mould designs the All Soul's Unitarian Church in New York City.
24 Dec.	James Robinson Planché's *King Charming* opens on Broadway in New York City.

1856

Literature	Herman Melville, *The Piazza Tales;* John Lothrop Motley, *The Rise of the Dutch Republic;* William Gilmore Simms, *Eutaw;* Harriet Beecher Stowe, *Dred: A Tale of the Great Dismal Swamp;* John Greenleaf Whittier, "The Barefoot Boy."

| 18 Aug. | Congress passes a copyright law to protect playwrights. |
| 25 Dec. | Charles M. Walcot's *Hiawatha; or, Ardent Spirits and Laughing Water* opens on Broadway with Walcot in the title role. |

1857

Literature	Herman Melville, *The Confidence-Man: His Masquerade.*
Music	The Philadelphia Academy of Music is established and built.
•	The landscape architect Frederick Law Olmsted becomes superintendent of New York's Central Park, which is under construction.
•	*The Atlantic Monthly* and *Harper's Weekly* are founded.
•	John P. Gaynor designs the Haughwort Store building in New York City.
•	Ammi Burnham Young designs the Customs House in the District of Columbia.
•	Alexander Jackson Davis designs the Gate House, Llewellyn Park, in Orange, New Jersey.
8 Dec.	Dion Boucicault's play *The Poor of New York* opens in New York City.

1858

Literature	Oliver Wendell Holmes, *The Autocrat of the Breakfast-Table;* Henry Wadsworth Longfellow, *The Courtship of Myles Standish and Other Poems.*
Music	"Down in Alabam' (The Old Gray Mare)," by J. Warner; "The Yellow Rose of Texas (The Song of the Texas Rangers)," by J. K.
•	James Renwick begins construction of Saint Patrick's Cathedral in New York City; it is completed in 1879.

1859

Literature	William Gilmore Simms, *The Cassique of Kiawah;* Harriet Beecher Stowe, *The Minister's Wooing.*
Music	"Dixie," by Daniel Decatur Emmett.
•	Frederic Church paints *Floating Icebergs.*
•	George Henry Durrie paints *Winter Landscape: Gathering Wood.*
•	James McNeill Whistler paints *At the Piano.*
•	Patrick S. Gilmore becomes the director of the Boston Brigade Band.
28 Jan.	The historian William Hickling Prescott dies in Boston.
24 Nov.	The American-trained coloratura soprano Adelina Patti debuts in Gaetano Donizetti's *Lucia di Lammermoor* in New York City.
28 Nov.	The author Washington Irving dies in Irvington, New York.

1860

Literature   Ralph Waldo Emerson , *The Conduct of Life*; Nathaniel Hawthorne, *The Marble Faun; or, The Romance of Monte Beni*; John Greenleaf Whittier, *Home Ballads and Poems.*

Music   "Old Black Joe," by Stephen Foster.

* Martin Johnson Heade paints *Approaching Storm.*

* The first "dime novel," *Malaeska*, by Ann Sophia Stephens, is published.

26 Nov.   The musical spectacle *Seven Sisters* opens on Broadway with Laura Keane in the lead role.

1861

Literature   Oliver Wendell Holmes, *Elsie Venner: A Romance of Destiny*; Henry Timrod, "Ethnogenesis"; Henry Wadsworth Longfellow, "Paul Revere's Ride."

Music   "The Bonnie Blue Flag," by Harry McCarthy; "Our Willie Dear Is Dying," by Stephen Foster.

* The American painter and sculptor William Rimmer's *The Falling Gladiator* is exhibited in plaster form in the Paris Salon.

* Asher Brown Durand resigns as president of the National Academy of Design.

* Albert Bierstadt completes his *Indians Traveling near Fort Laramie*, based on sketches he made while traveling with a government survey team in 1859.

* The actor Antonio (Tony) Pastor opens the first vaudeville theater at 444 Broadway in New York City.

1862

Literature   Charles Farrar Browne, *Artemus Ward, His Book*; Harriet Beecher Stowe, *The Pearl of Orr's Island: A Story of the Coast of Maine.*

Music   "The Battle Cry of Freedom," by George F. Root; "The Battle Hymn of the Republic," by Julia Ward Howe.

* Fitz Hugh Lane paints *Owl's Head, Penobscot Bay, Maine.*

7 Apr.   Julius Eichberg and B. E. Woolf's musical play *The Doctor of Alcantara* premieres in Boston.

6 May   Henry David Thoreau dies in Concord, Massachusetts.

1863

Literature   Edward Everett Hale, "The Man without a Country"; Henry Wadsworth Longfellow, *Tales of a Wayside Inn.*

Music   "Bring My Brother Back to Me," by Stephen Foster; "Tenting on the Old Camp Ground," by Walter Kittredge; "When Johnny Comes Marching Home," by Patrick S. Gilmore.

* James McNeill Whistler exhibits *The White Girl* (1862) — which was rejected by the Royal Academy and by the Paris Salon — at the Salon des Refusés, where it is ridiculed.

1864

- Henry Austin completes the Morse-Libby House in Portland, Maine.

Literature William Cullen Bryant, *Thirty Poems;* David Ross Locke, *The Nasby Papers;* James Russell Lowell, *Fireside Travels.*

Music "Beautiful Dreamer," by Stephen Foster; "Der Deitcher's Dog (Where ish mine little dog gone?)," by Septimus Winner; "Goober Peas," by Johnny Reb; "Tramp! Tramp! Tramp!," by George F. Root.

- Elihu Vedder paints *The Lair of the Sea Serpent.*

19 May The author Nathaniel Hawthorne dies in Plymouth, New Hampshire.

26 Dec. P. T. Barnum's "musical fairy romance," *The Ring of Fate,* is first performed.

1865

Literature Dion Boucicault and Joseph Jefferson, *Rip van Winkle;* Charles Farrar Browne, *Artemus Ward; His Travels;* Samuel Langhorne Clemens (Mark Twain), "Jim Smiley and His Jumping Frog (The Celebrated Jumping Frog of Calaveras County)"; Henry Wheeler Shaw, *Josh Billings: Hiz Sayings;* Francis Parkman Jr., *Pioneers of France in the New World;* Walt Whitman, *Drum-Taps.*

Music "Marching through Georgia," by Henry Clay Work.

- George Innes paints *Peace and Plenty.*

- Winslow Homer paints *Prisoners from the Front.*

- Dr. William Halliwell draws *The Peaceable Kingdom* in pen and ink.

- Peter B. Wight completes the National Academy of Design in New York City.

- Thomas Ustick Walter completes the dome of the U.S. Capitol in Washington, D.C.

- The San Francisco Minstrels open on Broadway.

8 May Arthur D. Gilman and Gridley Bryant complete the Boston City Hall.

1866

Literature Harry Brownell, *War-Lyrics and Other Poems;* Herman Melville, *Battle-Pieces and Aspects of the War;* John Greenleaf Whittier, *Snow-Bound. A Winter Idyl.*

Music "Come Back to Erin," by Claribel (Charlotte Barnard); "Now I Lay Me Down to Sleep," by Hattie Fox and A. D. Waldridge; "When You and I Were Young, Maggie," by James A. Butterfield.

- Winslow Homer paints *Croquet Scene.*

- John La Farge paints *The Greek Love Token.*

- Work on Memorial Hall, Harvard University, is begun by William R. Ware and Henry Van Brunt; it is completed in 1878.

12 Sept. Charles M. Barras's *The Black Crook* is produced at Niblo's Garden in New York City.

1867

Literature Augustin Daly, *Under the Gaslight;* John William De Forest, *Miss Ravenel's Conversion from Secession to Loyalty;* George Washington Harris, *Sut Lovingood Yarns;* James Russell Lowell, *Biglow Papers: Second Series;* Francis Parkman Jr., *The Jesuits in North America;* Henry Timrod, "Ode."

Music *Slave Songs of the United States,* edited by William Francis Allen, Charles Pickard Ware, and Lucy McKim Garrison.

- Alexander Jackson Davis completes renovations to Lyndhurst in Tarrytown, New York.

1868

Literature Louisa May Alcott, *Little Women;* Bret Harte, "The Luck of Roaring Camp."

- John Rogers sculpts *The Council of War.*

- *Lippincott's Magazine, Overland Monthly,* and *Vanity Fair* begin publication.

10 Mar. *Humpty Dumpty,* a pantomime starring George Lafayette Fox, opens in New York City.

1869

Literature Samuel Langhorne Clemens, *The Innocents Abroad;* Bret Harte, "The Outcasts of Poker Flat"; Francis Parkman Jr., *LaSalle and the Great West;* Harriet Beecher Stowe, *Oldtown Folks.*

- John B. Snook designs Grand Central Depot in New York City, completed in 1871.

18 May George Lafayette Fox opens in the pantomime *Hiccory Diccory Dock* on Broadway.

1870

Literature Ralph Waldo Emerson, *Society and Solitude.*

Music "Frankie and Johnny," anonymous.

- John F. Kensett paints *Thunderstorm, Lake George.*

7 Feb. J. C. Foster's *The Twelve Temptations* opens on Broadway.

11 July Dan Emmett's *Fritz, Our Cousin German* opens at Wallack's Theatre in New York City.

5 Oct. George Lafayette Fox opens in the pantomime *Wee Willie Winkie.*

1871

Literature Henry Adams and Charles Francis Adams Jr., *Chapters of Erie and Other Essays;* Edward Eggleston, *The Hoosier School-Master;* John Hay, *Pike County Ballads and Other Pieces;* Henry James, "A Passionate Pilgrim"; Joachim Miller, *Songs of the Sierras;* Walt Whitman, *Democratic Vistas.*

- Alfred B. Mullett designs the War and Navy Building in Washington, D.C.

- Winslow Homer paints *The Country School.*

- William Rimmer sculpts *The Dying Centaur.*

1872

Literature   Samuel Langhorne Clemens, *Roughing It;* William Dean Howells, *Their Wedding Journey;* Clarence King, *Mountaineering in the Sierra Nevada.*

Music   "Silver Threads among the Gold," by Hart Pease Danks and Eben Rexford.

- H. H. Richardson begins work on Trinity Church, Boston; construction is completed five years later.

- William Rimmer paints *Flight and Pursuit.*

- James McNeill Whistler paints *Arrangement in Gray and Black, No. 1 (The Artist's Mother).*

9 Sept.   James Barnes and W. H. Brinkworth's *Chow Chow, or A Tale of Pekin* opens at Wood's Museum theater in New York City.

25 Nov.   Augustin Daly produces *Round the Clock, or New York by Dark* at the Grand Opera House in New York City.

1873

Literature   Samuel Langhorne Clemens and Charles Dudley Warner, *The Gilded Age;* William Dean Howells, *A Chance Acquaintance;* Henry Timrod, *The Cotton Boll.*

- Winslow Homer paints *The Berry Pickers.*

- George Innes paints *The Monk.*

- Leopold Eidlitz designs the Church of the Holy Trinity in New York City.

- *The Delineator, St. Nicholas,* and *Woman's Home Companion* begin publication.

1874

Literature   Ambrose Bierce, *Cobwebs from an Empty Skull;* Hjalmar Hjorth Boyesen, *Gunnar: A Tale of Norway;* William Dean Howells, *A Foregone Conclusion.*

Music   "La Reine d'Amour Waltzes," by John Philip Sousa; "The Skidmore Guard," by David Braham and Edward Harrigan.

- Thomas Eakins paints *Starting Out After Rail.*

27 July   A musical version of Henry Wadsworth Longfellow's *Evangeline* opens at Niblo's Garden in New York City.

1875

Literature   Samuel Langhorne Clemens, *Mark Twain's Sketches;* John William De Forest, *Honest John Vane;* Bret Harte, *Echoes of the Foot-Hills* and *Tales of the Argonauts;* Henry James, *Transatlantic Sketches.*

Music   "Grandfather's Clock," by Henry Clay Work; "The Phoenix," by John Philip Sousa.

- John H. Sturgis and Charles Brigham design the Museum of Fine Arts in Boston.
- Richard H. Hunt designs the Lenox Library and the Tribune Building in New York City.
- George B. Post designs the Western Union Building in New York City.
- Thomas Eakins paints *The Gross Clinic.*

31 May Edward Harrigan and Tony Hart's *The Donovans* opens in New York City.

28 Aug. The dancers Haniola, Imre, and Bolossy Kiralfy produce a musical version of Jules Verne's *Around the World in Eighty Days* at the Academy of Music in New York City.

1876

Literature Samuel Langhorne Clemens, *The Adventures of Tom Sawyer;* Henry James, *Roderick Hudson;* Herman Melville, *Clarel;* Walt Whitman, *Leaves of Grass,* Centennial Edition.

Music "The Honored Dead March," by John Philip Sousa; "The Rose of Killarney," by Thomas P. Westendorf.

- The Pennsylvania Academy of the Fine Arts in Philadelphia, designed by Frank Furness, is completed.

May–Nov. The Centennial Exposition is held in Philadelphia.

27 Sept. Augustin Daly's *Life* opens in New York City.

1877

Literature Henry James, *The American;* Sarah Orne Jewett, *Deephaven;* Sidney Lanier, *Poems;* Francis Parkman Jr., *Count Frontenac and New France.*

Music "Abdulla Bulbul Ameer," by Percy French; "In the Gloaming," by Annie F. Harrison.

- James W. McLaughlin designs the John Shillito store in Cincinnati.
- Thomas Eakins paints *William Rush Carving the Allegorical Figure of the Schuylkill River.*
- Winslow Homer paints *The Cotton Pickers.*
- Currier & Ives publish the engraving *The Great East River Suspension Bridge.*
- The humor magazine *Puck* begins publication.

3 Sept. Edward Harrigan's *Old Lavender* opens in New York.

OVERVIEW

An American Renaissance. The 1850s were a watershed decade for American literature. Nathaniel Hawthorne's *The Scarlet Letter* (1850) and Herman Melville's *Moby-Dick* (1851) are widely acknowledged as the first true masterpieces of the American novel. Henry David Thoreau's *Walden* (1854) received similar acclaim as a classic of American nonfiction, while Walt Whitman's long poem *Song of Myself,* published in his *Leaves of Grass* (1855), is still regarded by many as the great epic celebration of American democracy. Harriet Beecher Stowe's best-selling novel *Uncle Tom's Cabin* (1852) profoundly influenced the nation's attitude toward slavery.

New American Art. American artists were also coming into their own. Frederic Church and Albert Bierstadt—known as luminists for their emphasis on atmosphere and light—were turning away from the Old World romanticism of their predecessors, the Hudson River School, in favor of a new realism based on a nearly scientific attention to detail.

Music and Drama. To a lesser extent American musicians and playwrights were beginning to make their mark in the 1850s. Stephen Foster was writing his extraordinarily popular songs, including the enduring favorite "Old Folks at Home" (1852). At the same time Americans were taking an interest in the folk music that lies at the roots of American jazz, blues, country and western music, and rock and roll. While in most cases Americans still seemed to prefer plays from abroad, the most popular play of the era was George Aiken's stage adaptation of *Uncle Tom's Cabin,* which opened in 1852. It was still playing to packed houses nationwide in 1880.

American Voice, American Vision. What all these works had in common was their American-ness. Earlier American writers and artists had employed New World subjects and themes but had presented them through imitations of Old World styles. Hawthorne, Melville, Thoreau, and Whitman spoke of America with American voices, saw the nation with American eyes, and created distinctly American literary forms. Though her great contribution to American letters is marred by old-fashioned melodrama, Stowe infused *Uncle Tom's Cabin* with the manners and speech of a region. She was in fact an early contributor to the genre of local-color fiction

that became popular after the Civil War, portraying New England life in *Oldtown Folks* (1869). Foster's songs share the attention to regional dialect as well as the nostalgic tone apparent in much local-color writing. In the 1850s Church traveled to Maine while Bierstadt spent time in the West. Into the 1870s they—and fellow luminist Thomas Moran, who first saw the West in the early 1870s—celebrated the unspoiled beauty of the American wilderness, painting panoramic landscapes that conveyed their sense of the endless possibilities of American life. Their artistic vision has sometimes been compared to the Transcendentalists' belief in the existence of a perfect higher truth that may be glimpsed through intuition, the mind's "inner eye."

Disillusionment. Yet American optimism was already waning. Debates over slavery became increasingly heated as the 1850s progressed and the nation headed toward war. One great Transcendentalist, Ralph Waldo Emerson, the prophet of America's literary declaration of independence, was writing less and less. While Thoreau and Whitman professed allegiance to his Transcendental optimism, their views were tempered by current events. By the time he published *Drum-Taps* in 1865, Whitman, who had been profoundly influenced by the suffering he saw as a volunteer nurse during the Civil War, was taking a more somber view of his nation's destiny. Hawthorne and Melville had never shared the Transcendentalists' optimism. What Melville admired and identified with in the writings of his friend and mentor Hawthorne was a "great power of blackness" that owed its strength "to that Calvinistic sense of Innate Depravity and Original Sin." Both men saw human existence as essentially tragic, and as war tore the nation apart, their vision began to predominate.

Regionalism. By the end of the war grand visions of American destiny had gone out of fashion. The most popular works of fiction were novels and short stories that focused on a particular region, not on the nation as a unified whole, as Whitman, for one, had done in *Song of Myself.* Local-color fiction was often infused with a sentimental longing for a rural past that had been lost forever with rapid industrialization that had accompanied the war or for the southern way of life that the war had destroyed. In place of Whitman's heroic American were smaller-than-life characters who were sometimes treated with condescending humor, as in the western local-color fiction of Bret Harte or Samuel Langhorne Clemens (Mark Twain). A similar trend could be detected in art. While the luminists were still active and had an admiring audience, public taste began shifting toward the romanticized genre painting, which—like local-color fiction—was often infused with sentimentality and nostalgia for the past.

The Rise of Realism. At the same time, however, a new literary movement was arising in America. Though they did not reach the heights of their artistry until the 1880s and after, three major American realists produced novels in the 1870s that displayed the promise of future greatness. These books included *The Adventures of Tom Sawyer* (1876) by Samuel Langhorne Clemens, *The American* (1877) by Henry James, and *Their Wedding Journey* (1872) by William Dean Howells. These writers offered no visions of American heroism. Instead they looked at life as it was really lived, and in portraying the American character they found much to criticize as well as much to admire. In art Winslow Homer, who had started out as a war illustrator for *Harper's Weekly*, was beginning to paint in a style that Henry James called in 1875 a "perfect realism" that sometimes produced "damnably ugly" results. Homer's realism, and that of his contemporary Thomas Eakins, shocked many viewers in the 1870s, but by the 1880s it was clear that, in art as well as fiction, realism was the style of the future.

TOPICS IN THE NEWS

ART: LANDSCAPE PAINTING

The Hudson River School. Landscape painting became the first major art movement to emerge in America after the Revolutionary War. Around 1820 a group of artists living and working in the Catskill Mountain region of New York began producing large-scale, dramatic scenes of the American wilderness. Profoundly influenced by contemporary writers such as Washington Irving, James Fenimore Cooper, and William Cullen Bryant, the Hudson River artists expressed pride and awe for the unspoiled American landscape. Far from being "pure landscape" artists, the Hudson River School excelled at romantic depictions of nature and often infused their paintings with moral and literary themes. Thomas Cole (1801–1848), a self-taught artist and the leading member of the group, combined allegory with his magnificent outdoor settings. The paintings of Cole and his colleagues Asher B. Durand (1796–1886), J. F. Cropsey (1823–1900), and Thomas Doughty (1793–1856) revealed their spiritual reverence for nature.

Intrepid Luminists. Working between 1850 and 1870, the generation of artists that followed the Hudson River School downplayed the romanticism of their predecessors in favor of more-precise realism. Working in a style known as "luminism" because of their emphasis on the effects of atmosphere and light, these second-generation painters produced meticulously detailed works. Cole's only student, Frederic E. Church (1826–1900), along with Thomas Moran (1837–1926) and Albert Bierstadt (1830–1902), took the Hudson River legacy westward to the expanding American frontier.

Bierstadt and Moran. Bierstadt joined a survey team mapping the American West in 1859. On this trip he first saw the dramatic, unspoiled mountain vistas that he later immortalized in paintings such as *The Rocky Mountains* (1863), *The Sierra Nevada in California* (1868), and *Rainbow over Jenny Lake* (circa 1870). To capture effectively the immense grandeur of the western landscapes he had seen, Bierstadt painted vast canvases—some up to nine feet high and twelve feet long—that overwhelm the viewer with their sheer size. During his lifetime, Bierstadt experienced wide public acclaim and financial success, often selling a single painting for $20,000 or more. Like Bierstadt, Thomas Moran was instrumental in bringing the images of the western frontier to people on the East Coast. In 1870 he was commissioned by *Scribner's Monthly* to illustrate their reports on the first scientific expedition to Yellowstone, and his lithographic illustrations from subsequent trips were also widely published. Moran's devotion to the American West led him to campaign for Congress to establish of Yellowstone National Park. In appreciation Congress purchased two of his paintings, *The Grand Canyon of the Yellowstone* (1872) and *Chasm of the Colorado* (1873). Mount Moran in the Grand Teton Mountains was named after him.

Marine Painting. The mountainous panoramas of the West were not the only popular subjects for American

The Grand Canyon of the Yellowstone (1872), by Thomas Moran (National Museum of American Art, Smithsonian Institution, lent by the Department of the Interior, Office of the Secretary [L. 1968.84.I])

artists at midcentury. Ship portraiture and seascapes were also common specializations. To many writers and artists of the nineteenth century, the sea was a mysterious force, a metaphor for God's omnipresent power, as evidenced in *Thunderstorm Over Narragansett Bay* (1868) by Martin J. Heade (1819–1904). Yet the sea was also a source of livelihood, a thriving avenue of commerce on which man depended. The steamboat and the clipper ship cemented man's ties to the sea and were lauded in works such as *Brother Jonathan* (1871) by painter James Bard (1815–1897) and in Fitz Hugh Lane's luminist paintings of New England harbors. Musing about the combination of technology and nature, Ralph Waldo Emerson said, "When its errands are noble and adequate, a steamboat bridging the Atlantic between Old and New England and arriving at its ports with the punctuality of a planet, is a step of man into harmony with nature." The Atlantic coast was the focus of much early marine painting, but by the second half of the century, American lakes and rivers, the Gulf of Mexico, and finally the Pacific Ocean took their places as subjects of marine paintings.

Sources:

Gordon Hendricks, *Albert Bierstadt, Painter of the American West* (New York: Abrams, 1974);

John Wilmerding, *Paintings by Fitz Hugh Lane* (Washington, D.C.: National Gallery of Art / New York: Abrams, 1988);

Michael David Zellman, *300 Years of American Art*, volume 1 (Secaucus, N.J.: Wellfleet Press, 1987).

ART: ROMANTICISM AND GENRE ART

Celebrating the Common Man. Genre painting, which focuses on scenes from everyday life, was a strong force in American art during the nineteenth century. By the 1840s it rivaled portrait and landscape painting in popularity. Its practitioners ignored specific names and

THE BIRTH OF PHOTOGRAPHY

Photography was born in France in 1826, when a chemist made the first surviving photograph by exposing a pewter plate for eight hours. Soon after and with great excitement, Louis J. M. Daguerre (1789–1851) introduced the daguerrotype, a more practical photographic process that required exposure times of ten to fifteen minutes. The invention of the photo negative came in 1839, followed in 1851 by a wet-plate process that Civil War photographer Mathew Brady used successfully to take more than seven thousand photographs of the American conflict. By the 1850s photography had established itself as a legitimate commercial enterprise. The tintype, introduced in 1855, was a fast and cheap method of making portraits. Although tintypes often produced poor-quality images, they were extremely popular and readily available to the masses.

Another large market for photography was travel pictures. Nineteenth-century audiences hungered for the exotic, and scenes of foreign countries and the American West were in constant demand. Timothy O'Sullivan (1840–1882), who had worked with Brady during the war, became one of the first leading travel photographers, documenting his journeys to Arizona, Nevada, and Panama.

Sources: George M. Craven, *Object and Image: An Introduction to Photography* (Englewood Cliffs, N.J.: Prentice-Hall, 1975);

Phil Davis, *Photography* (Dubuque, Iowa: William C. Brown, 1982);

Carol Strickland, *The Annotated Mona Lisa* (Kansas City, Mo.: Andrews & McMeel, 1994).

Boston Harbor (1854), by Fitz Hugh Lane (White House Collection)

places in favor of depicting general, everyday occurrences. While there were exceptions, most genre scenes conveyed an optimistic or sympathetic view of American life. A particularly favored subject was rural America, especially the hardworking, rustic lifestyle of the farmer. With industrialization slowly changing the face of America, genre artists nostalgically captured the fading heritage of rural America. William Sidney Mount (1807–1868) preserved one country tradition in *The Banjo Player* (1858), while Eastman Johnson's *The Old Stage Coach* (1871) was painted as railroads expanded nationwide, replacing that older mode of travel. George Caleb Bingham (1811–1879) was the first important genre painter of the American West. In frontier scenes such as *Fur Traders Descending the Missouri* (1845) and *The Wood Boat* (1850), he heroicized the grizzled traders, riverboat men, and pioneers who ventured into unknown territories.

The Rise of Printmaking. The popularity of genre subjects increased dramatically with technological developments in the field of printing. Industrial growth had spawned a large, literate middle class, which demanded printed news, books, and eventually graphic arts. Metal engraving, which used strong steel plates, enabled images to be mass-produced at affordable prices. The introduction of lithography in 1818 provided another efficient medium for reproduction. Perhaps the most notable lithographers of the second half of the nineteenth century were Nathaniel Currier and Merritt Ives, who formed Currier & Ives in 1857. Covering almost every subject imaginable to suit a wide range of tastes, the firm created more than four thousand images during its production life. Their pictures of ships and prairies, cities and farms, firefighters and fisherman chronicled American life and endeared Currier & Ives to the American

public. Their series of prints depicting battles of the Civil War was overwhelmingly successful.

The Civil War. In his 1859 painting *Old Kentucky Home* Eastman Johnson (1824–1906) compared a grand southern manor with less-than-ideal quarters for slaves. Depicting southern slavery in a poignant way, Johnson recorded the nation's bloodiest conflict. The devastation of the South and the repercussions following the Civil War were not lost on genre painters. *We Both Must Fade (Mrs. Fithian)* (1869), a portrait by Lilly Martin Spencer (1822–1902), shows a southern belle looking in a mirror while clutching a crumbling rose in her fingertips. Not just a commentary on the fragility of life, the work also seems to suggest the fading away of genteel southern life. Spencer, a child prodigy born to intellectual parents, was the first American woman painter to be acknowledged

The Wood-Boat (1850), by George Caleb Bingham (The Saint Louis Art Museum)

Rounding a Bend (1866), a popular lithograph by Currier & Ives

on an equal footing with her male peers, setting an important precedent for women artists of future generations.

Sources:

Daniel M. Mendelowitz, *A History of American Art* (New York: Holt, Rinehart & Winston, 1970);

John Lowell Pratt, ed., *Currier & Ives, Chronicles of America* (New York: Promontory Press, 1968);

Michael David Zellman, *300 Years of American Art,* volume 1 (Secaucus, N.J.: Wellfleet Press, 1987).

LITERATURE: AN AMERICAN RENAISSANCE

American Literature for an American People. In the early years of the nineteenth century American authors such as William Cullen Bryant (1794–1878), Washington Irving (1783–1759), and James Fenimore Cooper (1789–1851) achieved critical recognition in America and England for their literary merits. While they saw the need for an American literature that treated issues and depicted scenes that were distinctively American, these writers modeled their own poetry or fiction after that of Sir Walter Scott (1771–1832) and other well-known British writers of the time. Yet by 1837, the year in which Ralph Waldo Emerson (1803–1882) published his "American Scholar" address, the United States was well on its way to having its own national voice in literature. In "The American Scholar" Emerson proclaimed that "our day of dependence, our long apprenticeship to the learning of other lands, draws to a close," expressing a sentiment widely shared by Americans of his time. With the population of the United States more than doubling from nearly 13 million in 1830 to nearly 39.9 million 1870, there had developed an audience of American readers that could sustain a significant number of professional authors, many of whom achieved fame and fortune by responding to Americans' desire to read about their own country.

Transcendentalism on the Wane. New England Transcendentalism originated in the area around Concord, Massachusetts. Never a fully organized movement, the Transcendentalists were a group of highly individualistic writers—including Ralph Waldo Emerson, Henry David Thoreau (1817–1862), Bronson Alcott (1799–1888), and George Ripley (1802–1880)—with a loosely related set of principles. Though they often disagreed, they shared the belief that people can "transcend" the limits of the senses and discover higher truths directly through intuition, rather than through participation in a conventional church. From 1836 through 1855 Transcendentalism developed into a full-scale rejection of the established order. Its message was in accord with the frontier spirit of the young United States, whose citizens shared the conviction that through self-reliance and determination, Americans could create a new and improved society for themselves. By 1850, however, Transcendentalism was in decline. Margaret Fuller (1810–1850), an early American feminist and co-editor of the Transcendentalist periodical *The Dial,* died in that year, and Emerson, though still active as a lecturer, had gradually become less productive as a writer since the death of his five-year-old son, Waldo, in 1842. During the 1850s, as the debate over the extension of slavery to new states and territories became more and more heated, Americans increasingly lost patience with the naive optimism generally associated with Transcendentalist

THOREAU IN THE WOODS

Henry David Thoreau's *Walden* (1854) has been called the finest example of American nature writing and the first great example of modern American prose. Readers still enjoy Thoreau's account of self-sufficiency and solitude in the woods and long for the simple communion with nature that the book celebrates. Yet during his two years in a cabin by Walden Pond (1846–1847), Thoreau was never as independent or as alone as his book suggests. Living only a mile or two from the village of Concord, Massachusetts, he visited his neighbors there nearly every day. He often arrived at the Emersons' or Alcotts' home in time to be invited for dinner. Though *Walden* gives the impression that he grew or caught most of his own food, the meals he ate in his cabin came mainly from the fresh provisions that his mother and sister brought him every Saturday.

One incident alone must have convinced the people of Concord that Thoreau lacked the necessary skills to be a self-sufficient woodsman. One day, planning to cook some fish he had caught, Thoreau started a fire in a hollowed-out tree stump and accidentally burned three hundred acres of woods.

Source: Karen L. Rood, ed., *American Literary Almanac, from 1608 to the Present* (New York & Oxford: Facts on File, 1988).

Nathaniel Hawthorne and Herman Melville (left: portrait by George P. A. Healey [1852], New Hampshire Historical Society; right: photograph by R. Dewey)

thought. The best-known Transcendentalist literary work, Thoreau's *Walden, or Life in the Woods* (1854), an account of his two-year sojourn at Walden Pond, near Concord, is also one of the last significant literary productions to come from the group.

Hawthorne's Power of Darkness. During the second third of the nineteenth century, Nathaniel Hawthorne (1804–1864), a native of Salem, Massachusetts, explored complex moral and psychological conflicts in his highly symbolic fiction. After writing an unsuccessful first novel, *Fanshawe* (1829), and the tales collected in *Twice-Told Tales* (1837) and *Mosses from an Old Manse* (1846), he produced *The Scarlet Letter* (1850), the novel that is widely regarded as his masterpiece. In this novel and his next, *The House of the Seven Gables* (1851), he examined the gloomy, brooding spirit of Puritanism and the moral consequences of sin. In his next novel, *The Blithedale Romance* (1852), Hawthorne satirized Transcendentalist ideas, drawing on his own experiences as a member of the Transcendental commune Brook Farm from less than a year in 1841. His final published novel, *The Marble Faun* (1860), set in Italy, is an early example

of the international novel, a genre that American realist Henry James (1843–1916) later employed to compare the cultures of America and Europe. Also widely respected for his short fiction, Hawthorne—along with Edgar Allan Poe (1809–1849)—helped establish the American short story as a distinctive, important art form.

An Artist in the Rigging. Born in New York City, Herman Melville (1819–1891) wrote his first great books at the same time that Hawthorne published *Mosses From an Old Manse* and his last in the same decade that Stephen Crane published *The Red Badge of Courage* (1895). Melville's grappling with moral issues was as profound as Hawthorne's, and his view of life was darker and more realistic. Melville's youthful experiences on a whaling ship (1841–1842) and ashore in the Marquesas (where he was captured by cannibals) and other South Sea islands led him to write *Typee* (1846), *Omoo* (1847), and other popular romances. Melville's masterpiece, *Moby-Dick; or, The Whale* (1851), the tale of a whaling captain's obsessive search for the white whale that had dismembered him, is at once a gripping adventure story, a deeply philosophical inquiry into the human condition, an allegory about evil, and one of the most challenging and impenetrable novels ever written. Both *Moby-Dick* and Melville's next novel, *Pierre; or, The Ambiguities* (1852), were misunderstood and poorly received by his contemporaries. Though ill, deeply in debt, and disheartened by his failure to win an audience, Melville continued to write, producing such important works as *The Piazza Tales* (1856)—a short-story collection including "Benito Cereno" and "Bartleby, the Scrivener"—*The Confidence Man* (1857), and the novella *Billy Budd* (published posthumously in 1924). After working as a customs inspector in New York City for nineteen years, Melville died poor and obscure. He did not receive the recognition he deserved until more than thirty years after his death, but he has now become the most remarkable example of an author who was forgotten during his lifetime and elevated to the highest rank of American writers after his death.

A Barbaric Yawp. At thirty Walt Whitman (1819–1892), who was born in West Hills, Long Island, New York, began to travel America to record in poetry his impressions of the nation and its people. Whitman printed the first edition of *Leaves of Grass* (1855) himself, and throughout his life he continued to publish expansions and revisions of the work. He sent copies of the first edition to well-known literary men, including Emerson, who wrote back, "I greet you at the beginning of a great career" and called the book "the most extraordinary piece of wit and wisdom yet contributed to American literature." Whitman published Emerson's letter of praise in the 1856 edition of *Leaves of Grass*.

Sources:

Lawrence Buell, *Literary Transcendentalism: Style and Vision in the American Renaissance* (Ithaca, N.Y.: Cornell University Press, 1973);

Richard Chase, *The American Novel and Its Tradition* (Garden City, N.Y.: Doubleday, 1957);

F. O. Matthiessen, *American Renaisance: Art and Expression in the Age of Emerson and Whitman* (New York: Oxford University Press, 1941).

LITERATURE: CIVIL WAR AND AMERICAN LETTERS

A Nation Divided. The Civil War sharply interrupted American literary activity. Although several major authors of the American Renaissance continued to write after the war ended, most had done their best work by 1860. The Civil War was traumatic, and the debate over slavery that preceded it challenged the notion that America was founded on the democratic ideal set forth in the Declaration of Independence: that "all men are created equal." The widely held idea of America as a nation free of European immorality and excess was further undermined by widespread political corruption in Washington, D.C.; by the growing industrialism that moved people from farms to cities and led to bitter quarrels between workers and employers; by increased immigration, which spawned ethnic animosities; and by westward expansion, which triggered conflicts with Native Ameri-

Walt Whitman in 1862 (photograph by Mathew Brady)

cans. No longer could Americans look to the future with optimism; the events surrounding the Civil War prompted them to assess their world directly and honestly.

The Little Lady Who Started the War. The daughter of renowned preacher Lyman Beecher, Harriet Beecher Stowe (1811–1896) was born in Litchfield, Connecticut. She was first a student and later a teacher at Hartford Female Seminary. After Stowe and her husband, seminary professor Calvin Ellis Stowe (1802–1886), moved to Brunswick, Maine, in 1850, her sister-in-law challenged her to "write something that would make this whole nation feel what an accursed thing slavery is." Stowe responded with *Uncle Tom's Cabin; or, Life Among the Lowly*, which was published serially in 1851 and 1852 in the *National Era*, an antislavery periodical. Though her novel depicts some of the benign aspects of slavery of the relationship between master and slave, it emphasizes the inequities and cruelty of slavery. Published in book form in 1852, *Uncle Tom's Cabin* was a major best-seller. By the outbreak of the Civil War Americans had bought some three million copies. Many scholars maintain that

The best-known novel about the Civil War is *The Red Badge of Courage* (1895) by Stephen Crane, whose descriptions of battle were so realistic that some veterans of the war were convinced that Crane must have fought beside him. In fact, Crane was born in 1871, some six years after the war ended. Some actual veterans of the Civil War did write fiction in which they drew on their battle experiences, most notably Ambrose Bierce, John Esten Cooke, and John William De Forest.

Ambrose Bierce, who served in the Union army for most of the Civil War probably had more first-hand battle experience in that war than any other American writer. He fought in several major battles in Tennessee, some of the bloodiest of the war, including the battles of Shiloh (April 1862), after which he was commended for bravery; Stones River (December 1862), where he rescued his commanding officer from the field ; Chickamauga (September 1863); Missionary Ridge (November 1863); and Kennesaw Mountain (June 1864), where he received a serious head wound. After returning to active duty in autumn 1864, he fought in two more major battles in Tennessee before accompanying Gen. William Tecumseh Sherman on his March to the Sea. Long after the war Bierce remained obsessed by his battle experiences, commenting in 1887, "I never hear a rifle-shot without a thrill in my veins. I never catch the peculiar odor of gunpowder without having visions of the dead or dying." He used his war experiences in about twenty-five short stories, including "One of the Missing," "A Son of the Gods," "A Tough Tussle," "Chickamauga," "One Affair at Coulter's Notch," "An Occurrence at Owl Creek Bridge,"

and "Parker Addison, Philosopher." Many of these stories were written more than twenty years after the end of the war and were collected in his *Tales of Soldiers and Civilians* (1892) and *Can Such Things Be* (1893). He also wrote nonfiction and poetry about the war.

John Esten Cooke, who served in the Confederate army, fought in a howitzer brigade at the first battle of Bull Run (July 1861) before being commissioned a lieutenant in Gen. Jeb Stuart's cavalry, serving until the end of the war. He drew on his war experiences for the popular romantic novel *Surry of Eagle's Nest* (1866), the first published novel about the war, and four other works of fiction: *Fairfax* (1868), *Mohun* (1869), *Hilt to Hilt* (1869), and *Hammer and Rapier* (1870). He also wrote nonfiction about the war as well as biographies of Stonewall Jackson (1863) and Robert E. Lee (1871).

John William De Forest, served in the Louisiana campaign of early 1862 and fought in the Shenandoah Valley campaign (autumn 1864), spending a total of forty-five days under fire. Though it was published after *Surry of Eagle's Nest*, De Forest's *Miss Ravenel's Conversion from Secession to Loyalty* (1867) was written before Cooke's novel and is generally considered the first novel written in English to be based on the author's firsthand battle experiences. De Forest's novel is also considered a pioneering work of American realism. During the Reconstruction period De Forest worked for the Freedmen's Bureau in Greenville, South Carolina, and later used his experiences there as background for his 1881 novel, *The Bloody Chasm*.

Source: Karen L. Rood, ed., *American Literary Almanac, from 1608 to the Present* (New York & Oxford: Facts on File, 1988).

no book has ever had a more direct and powerful influence on American history than Stowe's novel, which inflamed opposition to slavery in the North and thus became a force in bringing about the Civil War. When Stowe visited the White House in 1862, President Lincoln exclaimed, "So this is the little lady who made this big war!"

Honest Abe and the Gettysburg Address. The political achievements of President Abraham Lincoln (1809–1865) assured his lasting fame. He also made no small contribution to American letters with his extraordinary eloquence, which was best exemplified by his Gettysburg Address, the famous speech in which defined the war as a national rededication to the egalitarian ideals of the Declaration of Independence. Lincoln delivered

the address on 19 November 1863, at the dedication of a national cemetery on the battlefield at Gettysburg, Pennsylvania, where the Union armies had driven back Confederate forces in the only battle fought on northern soil, a decisive and costly engagement. The chief speaker was Edward Everett (1794–1865), a noted orator and former Harvard professor, who regaled those present with two hours of extravagant oratory. President Lincoln, who had been invited to make only a few appropriate remarks, delivered his Gettysburg Address in just a few minutes, so quickly that a photographer taking his picture barely finished his preparations on time to catch the president as he left the platform. Lincoln thought his speech was a failure, as did most of the newspapers, but even then a few recognized it as one of the most historically important speeches ever delivered by an American.

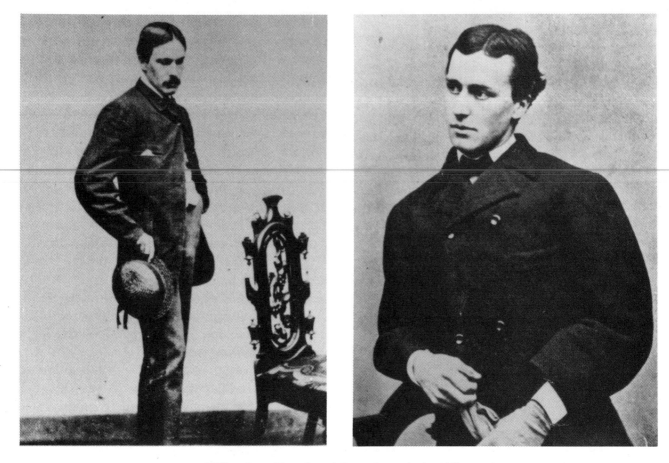

William Dean Howells and Henry James in the 1860s

Whitman with the Troops. Early in the Civil War Walt Whitman learned that his brother George was wounded and had been hospitalized in Washington, D.C. He found George nearly recovered but saw other soldiers badly in need of care. He stayed in Washington, working as a government clerk and serving as a hospital volunteer. The suffering he saw had a lasting influence on his poetry, directly inspiring the volume of poetry he called *Drum-Taps*. In 1871 he published "Democratic Vistas." In this work, instead of the exuberantly praising American democracy, as he had in 1855, Whitman urged Americans to look critically at their society and to work hard to keep it healthy. After the war Whitman's books began to sell well. In 1873 he became ill, suffering the first of several paralytic attacks. He retired to Camden, New Jersey, where he lived out the remainder of his life as an invalid and was frequently visited by literary pilgrims seeking out the "good, gray poet."

Sources:

Van Wyck Brooks, *The Times of Melville and Whitman* (New York: Dutton, 1947);

Marcus Cunliffe, *The Literature of the United States* (Harmondsworth, U.K.: Penguin, 1954);

Benjamin T. Spencer, *The Quest for Nationality: An American Literary Campaign* (Syracuse, N.Y.: Syracuse University Press, 1957).

LITERATURE: LOCAL COLOR AND REALISM

Regional Fiction. After the Civil War local-color fiction gained widespread popularity in America. Bret Harte (1836–1902) acquainted the country with the western miner in stories such as "The Luck of Roaring Camp" (1868) and "The Outcasts of Poker Flats" (1869), while in the late 1870s the *Atlanta Constitution* began publishing the dialect stories of plantation life in the Deep South that Joel Chandler Harris (1848–1908) later collected as *Uncle Remus, His Songs and His Sayings* (1880). George Washington Cable (1844–1925) wrote of Creoles and the bayou country near New Orleans in popular magazine stories, later collected in *Old Creole Days* (1879). Harriet Beecher Stowe (1811–1896) wrote *Oldtown Folks* (1869), a representative portrayal of life in New England. Later New England also figured prominently in the stories of Sarah Orne Jewett (1849–1909) and Mary E. Wilkins Freeman (1852–1930). Local-color writers depicted nearly every region of America, lending realism to their stories by describing customs and manners and re-creating dialects. Because these authors usually set their stories in their regions as they remembered them from their own youth, however, they often blended realism with nostalgic sentiment. Many Americans found this mixture appealing, and local-color

If members of the mid nineteenth-century American reading public were alive today, they would most likely be shocked to discover that by twentieth-century standards one of the greatest American poets of their time, is someone they never heard of: Emily Dickinson (1830–1886). It is also likely that most of Dickinson's contemporaries would have hated her poems if they had read them. The few people who did see them considered them incompetent and amateurish. Yet today most scholars consider only Walt Whitman to be Dickinson's equal and relegate nineteenth-century favorites such as Henry Wadsworth Longfellow, John Greenleaf Whittier, and Sidney Lanier to the second rank.

Dickinson's life is wrapped in a mystery that may never be solved. Some time between 1858 and 1862 she had a traumatic experience. No one knows what happened, but many believe that she was in love with a married man who did not return her affection. Suffering profound psychological distress, Dickinson withdrew from the world and spent the rest of her life at family home in Amherst, Massachusetts. She dressed only in white and devoted most of her time to writing more than fifteen hundred poems, polishing nearly nine hundred of them to what she considered finished form and tying them together in forty-three little manuscript books.

Dickinson sent some fifty of her poems to a family friend, Samuel Bowles, editor of the *Springfield Republican*. Bowles thought women should write light, sentimental poems , and he disliked Dickinson's irreverence in regard to religious and social orthodoxies and her uncompromising approach to fears of madness and death. Eventually, however, he published in his newspaper five of the seven Dickinson poems, all unsigned, that appeared in print during her lifetime. Dickinson also sent more than one hundred poems to Thomas Wentworth Higginson, literary editor of *The Atlantic Monthly*. He told her they were unpublishable. He considered her rhyme and meter too rough and unmelodic, her word choice far too eccentric, and her punctuation exceedingly strange.

After Dickinson's death, Higginson helped a friend of her family edited some of her poems for publication. They "cleaned up" her writing, making it more "graceful" and conventional, but even then most critics considered them peculiar and even "ungrammatical." Yet the reading public was fascinated. Three collections of Dickinson's poems were published in the 1890s, and all sold well. An edition of the poems based on the original manuscripts was published in 1955. By then Dickinson was already held in high esteem by critics and readers alike. Tastes in poetry had changed dramatically. Dickinson was praised for her original images, her spare language, and her modern, skeptical point of view—all the things Higginson and others had disliked in her poems.

Dickinson's personal life continues to fascinate. She is the subject of a popular one-woman show. Writers continue to speculate about what happened to turn her into the mysterious recluse of Amherst, always gowned in white, the poet who wrote:

The Soul selects her own Society—

Then—shuts the Door—

To her divine Majority—

Present no more—

Source: Richard B. Sewall, *The Life of Emily Dickinson*, 2 volumes (New York: Farrar, Straus & Giroux, 1974).

stories filled the pages of the leading magazines until the end of the nineteenth century.

Drawn From Life. Realism as a literary movement began in the mid nineteenth century as a reaction against romanticism. Whereas romantic literature presented an idealized vision of human existence, realistic works were intended to be accurate portrayals of life, depictions of the world based on careful observation. As such, realism was a literary response to the development of the modern scientific method, substituting experimentation for philosophical speculation and recognizing the flawed nature of the real world instead of aspiring to transcendental perfection. This new literary creed emerged primarily in the novel. The three major American realists began their careers in this period. They stand in interesting relationship to each other. At one extreme is the self-educated Samuel Langhorne Clemens (1835–1910), who wrote under the pen name Mark Twain, a product and a chronicler of the frontier. At the other is the educated, cosmopolitan Henry James (1843–1916), whose novels usually portray Americans in Europe who confront an old, rigid, and traditional society. Clemens and James were not personally acquainted, but each was a good friend of the third realist, William Dean Howells (1837–1920), who as a native of rural Ohio and a part of the Boston literary establishment embodied both the provincial and the cosmopolitan literary bents of his two friends.

An opera performance at Niblo's Gardens theater in New York City, 1855

Lighting Out for New Territory. Born in the small town of Florida, Missouri, Clemens moved with his family to Hannibal, Missouri, on the Mississippi River, when he was four years old, and it was in this river town that he grew up, gathering the material for his most famous stories. After the Civil War cut short his career as a riverboat pilot, Clemens went west to Nevada, where he became a reporter on the Virginia City newspaper and wrote the humorous sketches collected in *The Celebrated Jumping Frog of Calaveras County* (1867). He next combined personal anecdotes and humorous commentary in two travel books: *The Innocents Abroad* (1869), a bestseller about his 1867 tour of Europe and the Holy Land with a group of his fellow Americans, and the less successful *Roughing It* (1872), which drew on his experiences in Nevada. After he and his neighbor Charles Dudley Warner wrote *The Gilded Age* (1873), a satire on political corruption, Clemens turned to his childhood on the Mississippi, writing his classic novel *The Adventures of Tom Sawyer* (1876) and the autobiographical *Old Times on the Mississippi* (1876), later expanded as *Life on the Mississippi* (1883). During the 1880s and 1890s Clemens's output included *Adventures of Huckleberry Finn* (1884), his masterpiece, which expanded the literary possibilities of common, everyday American speech, and the historical novels *The Prince and the Pauper* (1882), *A Connecticut Yankee in King Arthur's Court* (1889), and

Personal Recollections of Joan of Arc (1896), which he considered his best work.

A Timely Man. Howells was not only the author of important realistic fiction but also a literary critic, who as assistant editor (1865–1871) and then editor of *The Atlantic Monthly* used his considerable influence to promote realism in American fiction. While working as a reporter and editor for the *Ohio State Journal* in Columbus (1857–1861), Howells wrote the poems collected in *Poems of Two Friends* (1860). In that same year his campaign biography of Abraham Lincoln (1860) launched his career. After Lincoln took office in 1861, he named Howells American consul at Venice. While Howells wrote the sketches he revised and collected in *Venetian Life* (1866) after settling in Boston in 1865. After receiving positive reviews for this book, he drew again on his experiences abroad for *Italian Journeys* (1867) and collected his sketches of life in Cambridge, Massachusetts, in *Suburban Sketches* (1871). The following year he published his first novel, *Their Wedding Journey*. This and his next two novels, *A Chance Acquaintance* (1873) and *A Foregone Conclusion* (1874), are sometimes called steps toward the realism of Howell's finest mature fiction. By the end of the 1870s Howells had found his true literary voice in *The Lady of the Aroostook* (1879), which, like his previous two, portrays an American girl in Europe—the

Stephen Foster

Roderick Hudson (1876), about a young American sculptor in Rome. Having established his international theme, James wrote several novels in quick succession—*The American* (1877), about a wealthy Civil War veteran who goes to Paris in search of a wife, and *The Europeans* (1878), about two young, Europeanized Americans who visit cousins in New England. His next book, the short novel *Daisy Miller* (1878), became one of his biggest popular successes. The story of a young American girl who falls prey to a corrupt Italian gigolo, the book introduces a theme that appears in much of his writing: the clash between the innocence and exuberance of the New World with the corruption and wisdom of the Old. Known for his skill in portraying the complex psychology of his characters, James wrote some of his best fiction in the 1880s, including *The Portrait of a Lady* (1881), *Washington Square* (1881), *The Bostonians* (1886), and *The Princess Casamassima* (1886). His later works include *The Tragic Muse* (1890), *What Maisie Knew* (1897), *The Turn of the Screw* (1898), *The Awkward Age* (1899), *The Wings of the Dove* (1902), *The Ambassadors* (1903), and *The Golden Bowl* (1904).

Sources:

Josephine Donovan, *New England Local Color Literature: A Woman's Tradition* (New York: Ungar, 1983);

Leon Howard, *Literature and the American Tradition* (Garden City, N.Y.: Doubleday, 1960);

Eric Sundquist, ed., *American Realism: New Essays* (Baltimore: Johns Hopkins University Press, 1982).

international theme developed most successfully by his friend Henry James. Howells wrote his finest realistic fiction during the 1880s, portraying character types and treating social questions of American life in his times in *Dr. Breen's Practice* (1881), *A Modern Instance* (1882), *The Rise of Silas Lapham* (1885), *Annie Kilburn* (1889), and *A Hazard of New Fortunes* (1889). Taken together, Howells's novels give a full picture of American life in the last years of the nineteenth century.

The Complex Fate of Being an American. One of the most productive and influential American novelists, Henry James was a master of fiction. Marked by a highly individual method and style, his innovative writings enlarged the possibilities of the novel. The younger brother of philosopher William James (1842–1910), James was born in New York City and educated by private teachers before entering Harvard Law School in 1862. Dropping out at the end of one academic year, he began writing short fiction and reviews. His first published story appeared in the March 1865 issue of *The Atlantic Monthly*. After much travel, he decided in 1875 to live in Europe, going first to Paris but settling in London in 1876. By the time he arrived in Paris he had collected some of his short fiction in *A Passionate Pilgrim, and Other Tales* (1875) and some travel essays in *Transatlantic Sketches* (1875). He had also completed his first published novel,

MUSIC

Two Traditions. The United States in the mid nineteenth century was home to two separate and distinct traditions in music, which historian H. Wiley Hitchcock has labeled "cultivated" and "vernacular." The cultivated tradition had its origins in European, especially German, classical music. Its concert-hall repertoire included Johann Sebastian Bach, Joseph Haydn, Ludwig van Beethoven, and other standard European masters. Its famous conductors and popular virtuoso performers were almost invariably born and trained in Europe. Audiences attending a concert or an opera in nineteenth-century America expected to find a specimen of the best that European high culture had to offer, and they were rarely disappointed. The influx of immigrants from Germany, Scandinavia, and Italy helped to assure a flourishing of the cultivated tradition. In addition to bolstering the numbers of discerning listeners and talented performers in large urban areas along the Eastern Seaboard, they provided a large number of music instructors to smaller towns in the interior. The main goal of the cultivated tradition was aesthetic enlightenment and moral uplift.

A Developing American Idiom. The vernacular tradition, as its name implies, drew on native materials for inspiration. New England psalmody, African American work songs, country fiddling based on traditional folk dancing tunes, patriotic songs on military themes, and the sentimental songs of talented songwriters such as

Stephen Foster entered a mainstream of popular music whose worth was judged largely by its entertainment value and rarely, if ever, as high artistry. Yet the practitioners of this vernacular music were beginning to establish an American musical vocabulary that later defined an indigenous American musical tradition in blues, jazz, country and western, and rock and roll. By the turn of the twentieth century composers such as Aaron Copland and Charles Ives were mining American vernacular music in search of a modern cultivated tradition that was both sophisticated and accessible to wide audiences. Though the cultivated and vernacular traditions seemed like divergent streams in the nineteenth century, they were marked for a merger by the start of the twentieth.

Common Ground. One place where the high and the low met in the nineteenth century was in the American musical theater. At establishments such as Niblo's Garden and the Olympic Theatre in New York City, audiences were treated to a variety of acts that ranged from plays and operas to sentimental or satirical songs, comic dancing of hornpipes and jigs, and pantomimes and burlesques, often all on the same bill. Prominent producers in the musical theater typically lightened the high tone of featured operas or melodramas with interludes of comic song and dance. Carrying over the miscellaneous comic spectacle of the minstrel show, which had been firmly entrenched in American popular entertainment since the 1820s, and combining these lighter touches with some attempt at serious virtuoso performance, the founders of American musical theater created a form of entertainment at once old and new, cultivated and vernacular. The origin of the American musical is usually located in *The Black Crook,* a musical extravaganza mounted at Niblo's by William Wheatley, Henry Jarrett, and Harry Palmer on 12 September of 1866. The trio combined elements of a melodrama by Charles M. Barras with the dancing of Jarrett and Palmer's French ballet troupe and some of the sentimental ballad-opera songs of the day to produce a five-and-one-half-hour-long spectacle, which became an immediate sensation in post–Civil War New York. *The Black Crook* set the stage for dozens of similar performances in the ensuing decades, and it established one of the most universally recognized American genres—the musical. Some other successful "musicals" of the period include J. C. Foster's *The Twelve Temptations* (1870), Dan Emmett's *Fritz, Our Cousin German* (1870), Augustin Daly's *Round the Clock, or New York by Dark* (1872), and Ned Harrigan's *Old Lavender* (1877).

Minstrel Days. As early as the 1820s Americans had attended performances of comic songs and dances by entertainers such as George Washington Dixon (1808–1861) and Thomas Dartmouth Rice (1808–1860), white men who blacked their faces with burnt cork and pretended to be reenacting authentic scenes from southern plantation life. Such performances, known as minstrel shows, remained popular throughout the country for the remainder of the nineteenth century.

Troupes of performers, including the famous E. P. Christy's Minstrels (organized in 1842), performed an increasingly standardized repertoire of jokes, songs, dances, and comic sketches to audiences in large cities and small towns. They accompanied their performances with instruments such as castanets, tambourines, banjos, and fiddles. The two most famous composers of minstrel songs were Dan Emmett (1815–1904) and Stephen Foster (1826–1864). The grand finale of most minstrel shows was something called the "Walk Around," an ensemble piece involving singing, dancing, and a parade of the performers around the stage. The most famous walk-around song before the Civil War was Dan Emmett's "Dixie," first performed in 1859 and destined to become the anthem of the Confederacy. After the war black minstrel troupes, such as Brooker and Clayton's Georgia Minstrels, also toured the northern states and found some success and popularity with white audiences. Although the comic routines of blackface minstrels going by the stage names of "Mr. Bones" and "Mr. Tambo" were perhaps intended mostly for laughs, they were travesties of the culture they pretended to represent, and they perpetuated hurtful stereotypes of African Americans. William Francis Allen, Charles P. Ware, and Lucy McKim Garrison made a more sympathetic attempt to collect and preserve the so-called Negro spiritual songs as evidence of a people's sorrows and its struggles, publishing the songs they had gathered in 1867 as *Slave Songs of the United States.*

An American Original. In the course of his short life Stephen Foster (1826–1864) had probably as great an influence on American popular music as any songwriter who has ever lived. Unlike his contemporary Dan Emmett, Foster never took the stage as a performer. In fact, even his first successful minstrel songs, such as "Oh, Susannah!" and "Uncle Ned," were published without attribution in a collection called *Songs of the Sable Harmonists* (1848). Born and raised in western Pennsylvania, Foster moved to Cincinnati in 1846 and took a job as a bookkeeper in his brother Dunning's office, while beginning to churn out songs in the sentimental genteel tradition in which he was immersed. His catchy tunes became almost immediately popular with minstrel performers and managers such as Thomas D. Rice and G. N. Christy. In his lifetime Foster wrote more than two hundred songs, some of the best known of which are "Lou'siana Belle," "Camptown Races," "Away Down South," "My Old Kentucky Home," "Nelly Bly," "Jeanie with the Light Brown Hair," "Beautiful Dreamer," and "Old Folks at Home" (also known as "Swanee River"). Although his songs have often been taken as representative of a distinctly southern way of life, Foster did not travel to the South until 1852, when he took a brief trip to New Orleans. In that same year his best-known work, "Old Folks at Home," was published (with Foster's knowledge and agreement) with Christy's name on the title page. The song eventually sold more than forty thousand copies, a

Actor-playwright Dion Boucicault and actress Charlotte Cushman

phenomenal success for a piece of sheet music in the 1850s. Foster's last years were darkened by poverty, loneliness, and alcohol, but his songs have continued to resonate down the years for generations of Americans.

Operatic Heights. The American poet Walt Whitman once claimed that, "But for Opera, I could never have written *Leaves of Grass.*" Whitman's particular favorites were the Italian operas of Gioacchino Rossini, Gaetano Donizetti, Vincenzo Bellini, and Giuseppe Verdi. In Manhattan during the 1840s and 1850s, an aficionado of good opera had ample opportunity to hear the standard repertoire of European opera, sung by some of the best opera singers of the day. In the years before the Civil War Jenny Lind, Adelina Patti, and Whitman's favorite, Marietta Alboni, were among the divas who toured the United States and remained for extended periods in New York City, where they performed on local stages. The famous showman Phineas T. Barnum sponsored and directed Jenny Lind's tour, which began in September 1850 and lasted until the spring of 1852. The Swedish-born soprano took the country by storm, earning an enormous amount of money for herself and for Barnum and endearing herself to the American public along the way. In 1859 a young Italian diva and professed admirer of Jenny Lind, Adelina Patti, had a similar triumph with her debut performance in Doniúetti's *Lucia di Lammermoor.* She made a brilliant success in New York during the 1860–1861 season, but soon thereafter she chose to pursue her career in the capitals of Europe. From the summer of 1852 through the spring of 1853, Whitman went to hear each one of Marietta Alboni's celebrated performances in Manhattan. Whitman's greatest tribute to Alboni's magnificent voice may be seen in the opening line of one of his best-known "chants" in *Song of Myself* (1855): "The pure contralto sings in the organ loft." In the catalogue of laborers in Whitman's democratic vineyard, the great diva finds herself side by side with the carpenters, slaves, omnibus drivers, and rivermen of Whitman's America, underscoring the attempt by the great American poet to bridge the gap between the cultivated and the vernacular in the American tradition.

Sources:
Gerald Bordman, *American Musical Theatre: A Chronicle* (New York: Oxford University Press, 1978);

Gilbert Chase, *America's Music: From the Pilgrims to the Present*, third edition, revised (Urbana: University of Illinois Press, 1987);

John Dizikes, *Opera in America: A Cultural History* (New Haven: Yale University Press, 1993);

H. Wiley Hitchcock, *Music in the United States: A Historical Introduction* (Englewood Cliffs, N.J.: Prentice-Hall, 1974).

THEATER

A New Theater Capital. By 1850 New York City, with a population of 500,000, had become the center of theatrical activity in the United States, a position formerly held by Philadelphia. The largest New York theater was the New Bowery Theater, featuring a large proscenium stage and four thousand seats. Twice as large as the largest theater of twenty years earlier, the New Bowery reflected not only the dynamic growth of American cities and their increasingly urbanized, middle-class populations, but also the democratic spirit that Walt Whitman was celebrating in the 1850s. Other cities with major theaters were Boston, Charleston, and New Orleans. At a first-class theater, ticket prices averaged from fifty to seventy-five cents for seats in the orchestra section, twenty-five cents for box seats, and twelve cents for seats in the galleries. Over the next two decades top ticket prices rose to a dollar and then to $1.50. Nearly all flourishing theaters had their own companies of actors, and by midcentury fifty resident theater companies were actively performing plays in the large and smaller cities of the United States. As a rule actors and actresses were paid poorly. Only stars such as Edwin Forrest (1806–1872) and Charlotte Cushman (1817–1876) commanded large salaries. African American actors did not perform in legitimate theaters during these years. The predominantly white theatergoing public refused to accept them, and, when a play called for a black character—whether in *Othello* or *Uncle Tom's Cabin* (1852)—the role was performed by a white actor. Most theaters were located in the East, but San Francisco opened its first professional theater in 1850, and in the following decades western and midwestern cities such as Saint Louis and Chicago built theaters and paid salaries that rivaled those at the established theaters in the East. In addition to resident companies, there were also touring theatrical companies that—aided by the growth and convenience of railroad travel—carried their productions to small towns.

The Great American Blockbuster. The dramatic version of Harriet Beecher Stowe's best-selling novel *Uncle Tom's Cabin* (1852) was a theatrical phenomenon unparallelled in American theater history. In 1852, the same year the novel was published, George L. Aiken (1830–1876) adapted Stowe's antislavery story for the stage, and the first performances of *Uncle Tom's Cabin* were held in Troy, New York. After breaking theater records by running for 100 nights there , the play moved to Purdy's National Theater in New York City, where it opened on 18 July 1853 and ran for 325 performances. By 1854 traveling companies performing this melodrama in tents were traveling across the United States; at one point *Uncle Tom's Cabin* was running in five New York theaters simultaneously. The play became the most popular of its era, and by the end of the 1870s, forty-nine theater companies were performing it nationwide. In 1878, twenty-six years after the premiere of *Uncle Tom's Cabin*, Sam Lucas became the first African American actor to play the role of Uncle Tom.

Melodrama and Gradual Americanization. As in the earlier decades of the century, the plays of William Shakespeare and the other great British dramatists continued to be popular on American stages. Edwin Booth (1833–1893), often considered the finest actor of the American theater, made his reputation by performing the title role in *Hamlet* in New York in 1864. Yet melodrama became the reigning theatrical genre in the United States during the 1850s, 1860s, and 1870s, partly because of the extraordinary success of *Uncle Tom's Cabin* and partly because melodramas imported from Europe won the enthusiastic applause of the theatergoing public. These melodramas typically featured stereotypical characters, improbable plots leading to dramatic climaxes, simplistic moral messages, happy endings, and sensational stage effects, such as storms or earthquakes. Meanwhile, the percentage of plays by American playwrights produced in the United States had risen from 2 percent at the beginning of the century to 19 percent by 1850. This trend continued over the next quarter-century, though slowly, as American playwrights began writing their own melodramas with American characters in American settings. These plays provided star vehicles for such celebrated American actors as Joseph Jefferson (1829–1905). Actor-playwright Dion Boucicault (1820?–1890) set *The Octoroon* (1859) in New Orleans. The play, which examines racial prejudices, opened at the Winter Garden Theater in New York and was one of Boucicault's first successes, which also included *Rip Van Winkle* (1866), his adaptation of the story by Washington Irving (1783–1859), and *Belle Lamar* (1874), one of the first important Civil War plays. A firm believer in the sensationalism of melodrama, Boucicault noted: "Sensation is what the public wants and you cannot give them too much of it." Another successful American playwright—renowned also as a producer and director—was Augustin Daly (1838–1899), whose *Under the Gaslight* (1867) featured a character tied to railroad tracks in the path of an oncoming train; Daly's highly improbable but effective theatricality inspired many imitators. Still, in the 1869–1870 season, only a half-dozen of the eighty plays produced in the first-class New York playhouses were American works. In 1869 William Dean Howells wrote sardonically in *The Atlantic Monthly*, "There is nothing American on the American stage."

Sources:

Gerald Bordman, *American Theater: A Chronicle of Comedy and Drama, 1869–1914* (New York: Oxford University Press, 1994);

Garff B. Wilson, *Three Hundred Years of American Drama and Theater: From* Ye Bare and Ye Cubb *to* Hair (Englewood Cliffs, N.J.: Prentice-Hall, 1973).

HEADLINE MAKERS

HENRY ADAMS

1838-1918
HISTORIAN, WRITER

Illustrious Family. Born in Massachusetts in 1838, Henry Adams was descended from a long line of distinguished American statesmen. His great-grandfather John Adams and grandfather John Quincy Adams had both served as president of the United States, and his father, Charles Francis Adams, was a congressman and diplomat. His childhood instilled in him a belief in the virtues of public duty and political service, and as a youth he had little reason to doubt that he, too, would advance to national public office as an adult. Adams graduated from Harvard College in 1858, traveled and studied in Europe for two years, then served as his father's private secretary, first in Washington, D.C., and then in London following Charles Francis Adams's appointment as ambassador to the Court of St. James's.

A Passion for History. In 1868 Henry Adams returned to Washington and, appalled by the corruption and incompetence of the Grant administration, wrote scathing essays in the *North American Review* and *The Nation* that condemned the crass ambitions of the new American capitalism and called for civil-service reform. These articles and other efforts to organize political reform proved ineffectual, and in 1870 Adams left Washington and accepted an instructorship at Harvard. For seven years he taught courses in medieval and American history and began the research and writing that would earn him a reputation as the foremost American historian of the nineteenth century. In 1879 he published his first major book, a biography of Albert Gallatin, Thomas Jefferson's secretary of the treasury, then began working on the monumental *History of the United States of America During the Administrations of Thomas Jefferson and James Madison*, which would be published in nine volumes between 1889 and 1891. A classic of American historical writing, the work was an early model of

"scientific" historiography. Rather than telling an entertaining narrative, Adams elected to arrange the facts of the two administrations in sequence and to invite his readers to form their own conclusions. The objectivity of such a method was not absolute, and Adams's history portrays Jefferson's and Madison's efforts as an admirable experiment in popular democracy that failed because of the incompatibility of its ideals with America's geographic immensity and its fragmentation of culture and identity into sectionalism. The work ends with questions that Henry Adams saw his own generation struggling to answer: What path will the country take? What common ideals and culture will unite a vast society? What goals will the nation seek to attain?

Later Work. Following the suicide of his wife in 1885, Adams withdrew even further from the public sphere. His last two major works, *Mont-Saint-Michel and Chartres* (1904) and *The Education of Henry Adams* (1907), were initially privately published and not intended for a commercial audience. The first, which takes the form of a travel guidebook addressed from an uncle to his nieces, is a meditation on two wonders of medieval French architecture, the cathedral at Chartres and the monastery on the island of Mont-Saint-Michel, and the moral lessons they offer about the society that produced them. In eleventh-century Norman culture, Adams found a desirable image of unity: a society that through common passion and faith triumphed over hardship to create the enduring art of the cathedrals. Adams saw no such unity in his own time, and his masterpiece, *The Education of Henry Adams,* documents his struggles to come to terms with the changing political and cultural character of mid-nineteenth-century America. He perceived a degenerative moral movement in the country from the optimistic democratic vision of Thomas Jefferson to the crassness and decadence of the administration of Ulysses S. Grant. In the process Adams found himself dispossessed of the traditional role of his statesmen forbears and alienated from a world that seemed to have lost the virtues of culture, civility, and public service. Against the Virgin Mary, an older symbol of unity and feminine wisdom, he contrasts the image of the dynamo, a masculine force of energy, power, and motion that he saw as characteristic of his own age. Adams's works are read today primarily as reflecting the philosophical and social concerns of his generation and class at a time when American cultural and political authority was passing from the Colonial-era patricians of New England and Virginia to the capitalists and party-machine newcomers of the Gilded Age. A year after his death in 1918, Adams received the Pulitzer Prize for *The Education of Henry Adams*.

Source:
Elizabeth Stevenson, *Henry Adams: A Biography* (New York: Macmillan, 1955).

MATHEW B. BRADY

1823?-1896

PHOTOGRAPHER

An Odd Little Man. Union soldiers on the way to Bull Run in July 1861 were surprised to see following their column a small, bespectacled civilian with a goatee. He wore a long, white duster coat and a straw hat, and drove a black-curtained wagon. Not knowing what to make of the mysterious stranger, they shrugged him off and dubbed his odd-looking wagon the "Whatisit." This man was Mathew B. Brady, the leading portrait photographer of Washington, D.C.—one of his subjects had been President Abraham Lincoln. Brady was now about to try something that few had ever attempted: to record on film the actual sights of war. Swept up in the Federal retreat following Bull Run, Brady failed at his first effort. Nevertheless, he persisted and went on to form several photographic teams to cover the Civil War. Today the pictures taken by Brady and his assistants represent landmark achievements in the history of photography.

Background. Brady was born in Warren County, New York, and although the exact year of his birth is not known, historians surmise it was around 1823. In the early 1840s he became interested in photography and was introduced to the daguerreotype process by the inventor Samuel B. Morse. (A daguerreotype was a photograph produced on a silver or silver-covered copper plate). Brady opened his own photography studio in New York City in 1844. Six years later he published his *Gallery of Illustrious Americans*, which confirmed his reputation as one of the foremost portrait photographers in the nation. In 1855 he experimented successfully with the wet-plate process of photography. When the Civil War began in 1861, he owned a gallery in the nation's capital, and President Lincoln authorized him to accompany and photograph the armies so that a visual record of the conflict could be preserved. To the consternation of family and friends, Brady took the assignment. As he later explained: "A spirit in my feet said go, and I went."

In the Field. In the 1860s action photographs were impossible to take because the exposure time (up to ten seconds) required by the wet-plate process blurred all movement. Brady, however, took many static pictures at the First Battle of Bull Run (21 July 1861), and in doing so inadvertently contributed to the rout of Union forces. A newspaper later reported that some of the Northern troops fled after mistaking the huge brass-barreled lens of Brady's camera for the enemy's rumored rapid-firing steam cannon. Thereafter Brady and his specially built darkroom wagon were seen on battlefields throughout the war. Brady and his assistants took many memorable scenes of the war, but their views of dead and wounded soldiers did not meet with public approval when they exhibited them in New York and Washington. For the general public, the stark reality of the pictures destroyed all romantic images of the war.

Legacy. The pictures of Brady and other photographers, such as Alexander Gardner and Timothy O'Sullivan, could not be reproduced in newspapers because the technology necessary to do so did not exist. Many of the photos, however, became the basis of line engravings in illustrated publications. When the conflict ended in 1865, war-weary Americans had little interest in buying Brady's pictures. By that time Brady was in dire financial straits because he had paid for most of his travels and equipment with his own money. In 1875 the government alleviated some of his monetary woes by purchasing part of Brady's collection. Although private collectors eventually paid high prices for his pictures, Brady never recouped his losses and died in poverty in New York in 1896. Today many of Brady's photographs are still used in history books, and a large collection of them is housed in the Library of Congress.

Source:
Roy Meredith, *Mr. Lincoln's Camera Man: Mathew B. Brady*, second revised edition (New York: Dover, 1974).

FREDERIC CHURCH

1826-1900

LANDSCAPE ARTIST

Hudson River School. During the middle decades of the nineteenth century there emerged a group of American painters influenced by the currents of European Romanticism and inspired by the natural grandeur of their homeland. Several of these landscape painters came to be known collectively as the Hudson River School.

In the 1870s the landscapes of Albert Bierstadt and Thomas Moran brought the grandeur of the American West into the popular imagination. But in the genre of landscape painting Frederic Church became its most famous and admired exponent.

Early Years. Born on 4 May 1826 in Hartford, Connecticut, to Joseph Church, a prominent and wealthy businessman, and Eliza Janes Church, Frederic studied art briefly in Hartford and displayed considerable ability. In 1844 he became the first pupil accepted by Thomas Cole, the artist considered to be most representative of the Hudson River School. From Cole he derived much of his philosophy of landscape painting, especially the notion that the artist's role was to express not only the physical aspect of the external world but also observations about the human condition.

Style. At age nineteen Church began exhibiting works at the National Academy of Design. His first success, *Rev. Thomas Hooker and Company Journeying through the Wilderness from Plymouth to Hartford, in 1636,* is a historical landscape celebrating the founding of his hometown. This work and others, such as *July Sunset* (1847), show the influence of Cole but display Church's trademark attention to detail and precise rendering of light.

Success. Church established a studio in New York City in 1847, where he worked in winters painting finished pictures from oil and graphite sketches. Summers were spent close to nature. In 1850 he made his first trip to Maine, whose landscapes were to figure in many of his paintings, such as *Beacon, off Mount Desert Island* (1851). Around this time he also began reading German naturalist Alexander von Humboldt's *Cosmos* (1845–1862), which led him to produce paintings that combined panoramic vistas with scientifically correct detail, as in his *New England Scenery* (1851). Inspired by Humboldt, Church made his first trip to South America in the spring of 1853, returning to New York with many sketches of the scenery. The first finished work based on these sketches, *La Magdalena* (1854), appeared at the National Academy of Design in spring of 1855 and was highly acclaimed, as was *View on the Magdalena River* (1857).

Return to Latin America. But greater adulation was still to come. *Niagara,* first displayed at the National Academy in 1857, captured the grandeur of the falls as no other painting had before and was seen by thousands in American and England. In spring of that year he returned to South America, this time staying in Ecuador. The first painting from these sketches was *Heart of the Andes* (1859), regarded by many as his masterpiece. During this period Church produced signature pieces such as *Twilight in the Wilderness* (1860), *The Icebergs* (1861), and *Cotopaxi* (1862).

Crisis of Spirit. The year that Church displayed *Heart of the Andes* was also when Charles Darwin published *On the Origin of Species.* The implications of Darwin, and of the accumulation of scientific knowledge in general, seemed to provoke in Church a crisis of spirit. For the Transcendentalist-influenced Church, nature was the theater of man's mystic regeneration, a phenomenon of providential design. He saw his art was a means of bringing mankind into harmony with God's universe. But perhaps there was no grand design in nature, and his confident, optimistic renderings of nature came to seem out of place as times changed.

Later Years. After the Civil War Church continued to travel and sketch, visiting Jamaica in 1865 and Europe and the Middle East in 1867–1869. Questioning his own ideal of the union of science, religion, nature, and art, he appeared to be turning to the Holy Land for answers. One painting to result from this journey was *Jerusalem* (1870), considered one of his better later works. His paintings from this trip show the influence of English landscape painter J. M. W. Turner in a greater emphasis on visionary atmospheric effects and the transient effects of light and climate. Church's paintings, however, fell from favor during the last decades of his life, as collectors discovered Impressionism and as artists began to favor less sublime portrayals of nature. He spent his later years at Olana, his house overlooking the Hudson River, producing oil sketches and continuing to travel, especially to Maine and Mexico. At the time of his death on 7 April 1900 in New York City, his art was unappreciated by critics and unknown to younger artists. But with a renewed appreciation in the twentieth-century for nineteenth-century landscape painting, Frederic Church is again recognized as its preeminent artist.

Sources:

Frederic E. Church: *Under Changing Skies: Oil Sketches and Drawings from the Collection of the Cooper-Hewitt, National Museum of Design, Smithsonian Institution* (Philadelphia: Smith Edwards Dunlap, 1992);

David C. Huntington, *The Landscapes of Frederic Edwin Church: Vision of an American Era* (New York: Braziller, 1966);

Frances P. Smyth, ed., *American Paintings from the Manoogian Collection* (Washington, D.C.: National Gallery of Art, 1989).

BRET HARTE

1836-1902
WRITER

Western Legacy. Bret Harte, the first American writer from the West Coast to gain an international reputation, was instrumental in introducing frontier literature to eastern audiences. His stories established many of the basic characteristics of the western genre: rough, sarcastic humor, rustic dialect, and character types such as good-natured gamblers, greedy bankers, and prostitutes with hearts of gold. His literary fame was brief, lasting less than a decade, but it helped make possible the success of other frontier writers, including Ambrose Bierce, Robert Newell (Orpheus C. Kerr), Charles Farrar Browne (Artemus Ward), and Samuel Langhorne Clemens (Mark Twain).

Success. Harte was born in Albany, New York, on 25 August 1836. His father died in 1845, and at the age of thirteen Harte was forced to leave school and work to support his family. His mother remarried in 1853 and moved to California, where Harte joined her a year later. He drifted from job to job at first—schoolteacher, gold prospector, drugstore clerk, stagecoach guard—before deciding to become a printer. He worked for the *Northern Californian* in Union, California, then moved to San Francisco and became a compositor for *The Golden Era*, a respected literary magazine. He began making friends in the city's growing literary and artistic circles, contributed a column titled "Talk of Town and Table" to the magazine, and began writing the stories and poems that would make him famous. He received his first big break in 1868 when he was appointed editor of *The Overland Monthly*, a newly established regional magazine with ambitions of national circulation. His short story "The Luck of Roaring Camp" was published in the August 1868 issue and brought him immediate national fame. A second story, "The Outcasts of Poker Flats" (January 1869), and a prose poem, "Plain Language from Truthful James" (September 1870), cemented his reputation. The poem, better known as "The Heathen Chinee," became so popular that it was quoted in the streets, dramatized, set to music, and repeatedly pirated.

Writer's Block. In 1870 Fields, Osgood, and Company published Harte's collection *The Luck of Roaring Camp and Other Sketches,* and the firm purchased the exclusive rights to print his stories and poems in their magazines *The Atlantic Monthly* and *Every Saturday.* Buoyed by his success, Harte left California in 1871 and came east, where he was lionized by the literary society of Boston and New York. At the peak of his fame, however, Harte found himself unable to produce new works. He was six months late in fulfilling his contract with Fields, Osgood, and Company, and the agreement was not renewed for the following year. Between 1873 and 1876 Harte published only seven stories and soon was deeply in debt. He made lecture tours through the Eastern Seaboard, Midwest, and the South, and his first novel, *Gabriel Conroy* (1876), was a commercial success, but his financial troubles continued. In 1878 he accepted an appointment as the U.S. commercial agent at Krefeld, Germany, then served as U.S. consul in Glasgow, Scotland, from 1880 to 1885. Harte lived in London for the remainder of his life and resumed his writing career, but he never matched his success of the 1870s. He died of throat cancer in London on 5 May 1902.

Impact. In Harte's best stories he balances realistic description, dialect, and characterization with sentimental plots and narration. His tales rely heavily on local color, and the Humboldt River, Nevada, about which he wrote became known as "Bret Harte Country." Harte used a detached, third-person point of view, and his sophisticated, highly polished narration made palatable to genteel eastern readers the rough-and-tumble characters, dialogue, and events in his stories. Though his vogue was brief and he never attained the lasting reputation of his friend Samuel Clemens, Bret Harte's writing was instrumental in popularizing stories of the western frontier and in establishing the characteristics of the western genre that survive in books and movies today.

Sources:

Alvin F. Harlow, *Bret Harte of the Old West* (New York: Messner, 1943);

Richard O'Connor, *Bret Harte: A Biography* (Boston & Toronto: Little, Brown, 1966).

OLIVER WENDELL HOLMES

1809-1894
AUTHOR, PHYSICIAN

Popularity. According to one of his students, when Dr. Oliver Wendell Holmes entered his classroom at Harvard College to lecture on anatomy, he was greeted "by a mighty shout and stamp of applause. Then silence, and there begins a charming hour of description, analysis, simile, anecdote [and] harmless pun, which clothes the dry bones with poetic imagery. . . ." Holmes's fame, however, went far beyond his medical lectures, for he also gained renown as a poet, novelist, biographer, and essayist. Indeed for more than half a century Holmes was a dominating force in the intellectual life of New England. His novels were much admired for their wit and humor, shrewd observations, originality of prose, and inventiveness of created characters. Furthermore, his writings exhibited an independent intellectual attitude, aversion to any restraint on free thought, and a scientific habit of mind.

Doctor. Oliver Wendell Holmes was born on 29 August 1809 in Cambridge, Massachusetts. His father, the Rev. Abiel Holmes was a Congregationalist minister. The young Holmes received his initial education at Phillips Academy. Between 1833 and 1835 he studied medicine in Paris. When he returned to America, he quickly wrote an essay on heart inflammation in order to fulfill a requirement for the Harvard Medical School and received the M.D. degree in February 1836. Over the course of the next two years

Holmes won three Boylston prizes—an unprecedented feat—for medical essays on various topics. This achievement undoubtedly helped Holmes earn a professorship at Dartmouth Medical College in 1839. On 15 June 1840 he married Amelia Jackson and then settled in Boston to practice medicine. Holmes gained further recognition by publishing a landmark study on puerperal, or childbirth, fever. In 1847 he joined the faculty of Harvard Medical School, where he served as professor of anatomy and physiology for the next thirty-five years. (He also served a brief stint as medical school dean between 1847 and 1853).

Literary Interests. The work of being a physician did not detract from Holmes's interests in the literary arts. He was an intimate friend with some of the leading New England writers of his day—Ralph Waldo Emerson, Nathaniel Hawthorne, James Russell Lowell, and John Greenleaf Whittier. In this circle of writers Holmes quickly became recognized as a brilliant conversationalist and poet. When Lowell became the editor of a new literary magazine in Boston, it was inevitable that Holmes was asked to submit contributions. Holmes suggested the name for the publication, *The Atlantic Monthly*, and its first issue in November 1857 had the opening installment of Holmes's "The Autocrat of the Breakfast-Table," a series of essays detailing the daily conversations of residents at a Boston boardinghouse. (In 1858 the twelve essays would appear in book form.) The essays included some of Holmes's best poems and reflected the author's ideas on the limitations of the human will, art, youth and age, and love. Holmes capitalized on his success with the publication of *The Professor at the Breakfast-Table* (1860), a book that followed the same conversational pattern but which dealt with the conflict between religion and science. In 1861 Holmes wrote his first major novel, *Elsie Venner: A Romance of Destiny*, in which he treats the life of a young girl as an allegory of original sin and moral responsibility.

Later Years. In 1872 Holmes published *The Poet at the Breakfast-Table*, bringing to a close his trilogy. He retired from Harvard Medical School in 1882 in order to devote more time to his active literary career. Four years later he toured England and wrote a book recounting his travels. In 1891 the Boston publishing house Houghton, Mifflin produced a thirteen-volume edition of *The Writings of Oliver Wendell Holmes*, a tribute to more than sixty years of observations on life, science, art, and philosophy. Among his other writings were *The Guardian Angel* (1867), *Pages from an Old Volume of Life* (1883), *Ralph Waldo Emerson* (1885), and *Over the Teacups* (1891). Holmes died at his home in Boston on 10 October 1894. He was the father of the eminent U.S. Supreme Court justice Oliver Wendell Holmes Jr.

Sources:
Miriam Rossiter Small, *Oliver Wendell Holmes* (New York: Twayne, 1962);
Eleanor M. Tilton, *Amiable Autocrat: A Biography of Dr. Oliver Wendell Holmes* (New York: Henry Schuman, 1947).

SIDNEY LANIER

1842-1881
POET

Verse. Though his career was shortened by his death at the age of thirty-nine, Sidney Lanier wrote poetry that attempted to adapt and respond to a world disrupted by the violence of the Civil War, the unsettling advances of science, and the social upheaval of industrialization. He recognized the unsuitability of traditional forms—particularly those of the English Romantics—for dealing with modern realities, and he experimented with new rationales for the construction of verse based on sound. Along with his precursors Walt Whitman and Edgar Allan Poe and his contemporary Emily Dickinson, Lanier helped pave the way for the revolution in poetic forms and content that took place in the early twentieth century.

Civil War. Lanier was born in Macon, Georgia, on 3 February 1842. The son of a successful lawyer, he was raised in an atmosphere that mixed strict Presbyterian morality with the Southern gentleman's ideal of social graces and intellectual refinement. He attended Oglethorpe University near Milledgeville, Georgia, where he was inspired by recent advances in science and instilled with a desire for serious scholarly study. Charles Darwin's *On the Origin of Species* (1859) was published while Lanier was still an undergraduate and convinced him of the need to reconcile the claims of modern science with a traditional respect for religion and the arts. He graduated in 1860 and hoped to study abroad in Germany, but after the shelling of Fort Sumter he enlisted in the Confederate army. In 1864 he was captured and imprisoned for four months, and during his confinement he was stricken with tuberculosis.

Devoted Intellectual. For the remainder of his life Lanier struggled with his health and poverty. He worked a variety of jobs—hotel clerk, teacher, lawyer—before deciding to devote himself to a career in music and literature. His first novel, *Tiger Lilies*, was published in 1867, and in 1873 he began playing flute for the Peabody Orchestra in Baltimore. In 1875 the first of his important poems, "Corn" and "The Symphony," appeared in *Lippincott's Magazine*. His lectures on Shakespeare and Elizabethan literature caught the eye of the faculty at Johns Hopkins University, and in 1879 he accepted a position as a lecturer in English literature. Though he continued to produce poems and scholarly essays, Lanier's health rapidly declined. He died from tuberculosis on 2 September 1881.

Nature and Music. For his poetic material, Lanier drew primarily on the landscape of his native state, and his series of poems on the marshes of Georgia remain his best-known works. He had great distrust of the increasingly commercial nature of American society, and his verses condemn industrialism and trade for stifling life and civilization. As a corrective he offered the abstractions of music and art and expressed an almost-religious admiration for nature. More important than his themes, however, are his experiments in sound and verse forms. A talented musician since his childhood, Lanier increasingly emphasized the musical elements in his poetry and experimented with repetition, alliteration, rhyme, and irregular meter and line lengths. From these experimentations he developed a theory, expressed in his book *The Science of English Verse* (1880), that the laws of music and verse are identical. Both, he argued, are based on "a set of specifically related sounds," and the form and technique of poetry can be reduced to a science, broken down and classified in the same manner as musical pitch, tone, and duration. Lanier's ideas were well-received but seldom imitated. His experiments, nevertheless, both indicated a growing awareness of the need for more-vigorous and relevant verse forms and laid the groundwork for the future American reassessment of the rules of poetic composition.

Source:
Aubrey H. Starke, *Sidney Lanier: A Biographical and Critical Study* (Chapel Hill: University of North Carolina Press, 1933).

JAMES RENWICK JR.

1818-1895

ARCHITECT

Influence. Like his contemporaries Richard Upjohn and Alexander Jackson Davis, James Renwick Jr. was a champion of the Gothic revival style in architecture. He sought to make American architecture reflect the styles of the Middle Ages, with massive, turreted, castle- and cathedral-like structures. His success at pleasing rich clients made him a wealthy man at a young age, the owner of an extensive art collection and two steam yachts.

Making a Reputation. James Renwick was born on 3 November 1818 in Bloomingdale, New York, the second son of James and Margaret Brevoort Renwick. His father was a prominent Columbia College science professor who had a love for architecture. James Renwick Jr. inherited his father's taste and was given every opportunity to develop his genius. At age fourteen Renwick entered Columbia College, where he studied engineering. After his graduation in 1836, he became an assistant engineer on the Croton aqueduct in New York City, supervising the building of a distribution reservoir between Fortieth and Forty-second streets. During this period he also designed and supervised the erection of a fountain in Union Square. Appointed to construct Grace Church on Broadway and Tenth Street (1843–1846), Renwick won praise for his elegant neo-Gothic design with its rich ornamentation and decorative scrollwork.

Accomplishments. His reputation established, Renwick soon acquired a large and lucrative architectural business. He was architect of Calvary Church, Fourth Avenue, the Church of the Puritans, Union Square, and many businesses and private residences in New York City. In 1847 Renwick embarked upon his most ambitious project to date, the Smithsonian Institution in Washington, D.C. Two years before the Smithsonian was completed in 1855, Renwick entered plans in competition for a Roman Catholic cathedral in New York City. He received the appointment, and between 1858 and 1879 he supervised the construction of St. Patrick's Cathedral, probably his best-known work. The monumental structure occupied the entire block bounded by Fifth and Madison Avenues, and Fiftieth and Fifty-first Streets; it remains one of the most imposing churches in the country.

Other Work. Among Renwick's other accomplishments are the Corcoran Art Gallery, Washington, D.C. (1859); the first Vassar College building in Poughkeepsie, New York (1865); and Booth Theater, New York City (1869). Until 1874 Renwick served as chief architect to the board of charities and correction of the city of New York, supervising the building of the City Hospital, Smallpox Hospital, Workhouse, Lunatic and Inebriate asylums on Ward's Island, the Catholic archbishop's residence on Madison Avenue, and the Young Men's Christian Association. He also loved fine art and collected paintings from all over Europe. He was known as one of the best art connoisseurs in the nation, and many of his paintings were masterpieces. Renwick married Anna Aspinwall in 1852; he died in his native city on 23 June 1895.

Sources:
John Burchard and Albert Bush-Brown, *The Architecture of America: A Social and Cultural History* (Boston: Little, Brown, 1961);

David P. Handlin, *American Architecture* (London: Thames & Hudson, 1985);

Vincent Scully, *American Architecture and Urbanism*, revised edition (New York: Holt, 1988).

WILLIAM WETMORE STORY

1819-1895
SCULPTOR

Legal Profession. As the son of a respected Supreme Court justice, William Wetmore Story appeared to be headed toward a distinguished career in law. But he became side-tracked from that profession and chose to seek fame in the arts, publishing several literary works and becoming the most celebrated American sculptor of his time, patronized by European royalty, American businessmen, and Pope Pius IX. Born on 12 February 1819 in Salem, Massachusetts, Story earned his law degree in 1840 from Harvard College and began practicing law in Boston. Here he became part of an intellectual coterie that included Ralph Waldo Emerson, Washington Allston, and James Russell Lowell. In addition to publishing two legal treatises, he served as an art critic and literary editor. His two collections of poetry from this period (published in 1847 and 1856) were undistinguished.

New Career. When his father died in 1845, Story was commissioned, somewhat unexpectedly, to design a statue for the tomb. Having already displayed some talent with sculpting, he sailed to Italy in 1847 to gain the necessary technical proficiency to complete the task. His marble portrait, *Joseph Story* (1854), was well-received when it was placed in Mount Auburn Cemetery, which further encouraged his artistic ambitions. By 1856 he had settled permanently in Rome, his salon in the Palazzo Barberini becoming a great social and intellectual center, where he entertained lavishly. With his affable manner and considerable social skills he attracted a distinguished group of friends that included Margaret Fuller, Nathaniel Hawthorne, and Robert and Elizabeth Barrett Browning.

Fame. Story's sculpture first earned widespread public admiration at the London International Exhibition in 1862, where his *Cleopatra* (1858) and *Libyan Sibyl* (1861) were the highlight of the show. Hawthorne contributed much to Story's success by his lavish praise of *Cleopatra* in *The Marble Faun* (1860). Indeed his work was admired by many, as Story attracted a steady series of commissions. He followed with several esteemed sculptures, most depicting mythological or biblical characters, and portrait statues of prominent contemporaries. Typical of these works are *Sappho* (1863), *Medea Contemplating the Murder of Her Children* (1864), and *Saul, When the Evil Spirits Were Upon Him* (1868). The dramatic themes and psychological approach of his later works were notably influenced by the theories of his close friend Robert Browning. Story's best known portrait statue, of Boston

orator Edward Everett, was a critical failure when it was unveiled in 1867, helping to mark the shift in public taste from the Italiante neoclassicism of Story to the newer realistic style emanating from Paris.

Writings. Possessed of many talents, Story also received some recognition for his belletristic efforts: *Roba di Roma* (1862), a collection of essays with Story's commentary on Roman art, history, and culture; *Graffiti d'Italia* (1868), considered his best collection of poems; and *Fiametta; A Summer Idyl* (1885), his only novel. He died on 7 October 1895 in Vallombrosa, Italy. Though his artistic reputation declined precipitously after his death, he achieved a measure of lasting renown through the publication of Henry James's biography, *William Wetmore Story and His Friends* (1903).

Source:
Henry James, *William Wetmore Story and His Friends* (Boston: Houghton, Mifflin, 1903).

HARRIET BEECHER STOWE

1811-1896
WRITER

Impact. Harriet Beecher Stowe's first novel, *Uncle Tom's Cabin* (1852), not only was the best-selling novel before the Civil War but also became a highly effective instrument in the movement to abolish slavery in the 1850s. Abraham Lincoln is reported to have commented upon meeting Stowe, "So this is the little lady who made this big war!" The remark is certainly an overstatement, but it indicates Stowe's fame and the extent to which her writing was seen as influencing the moral attitudes of the nation.

Early Years. Stowe was born in Litchfield, Connecticut, the daughter of the respected Congregational minister Lyman Beecher and Roxana Foote. She was raised in an environment that emphasized strict moral principles and intellectual energy, elements that shaped her future writing. She attended the Hartford Female Seminary, which was run by her sister Catharine, and later taught there. In 1832 Lyman Beecher was appointed president of the Lane Theological Seminary, and the family moved to Cincinnati, Ohio. Stowe continued schoolteaching until 1836, when she married Calvin Stowe, a professor at the seminary. She began writing stories both as an escape from the drudgery of raising her seven children and as a way to earn extra income for the family. In 1843 *The Mayflower*, her first collection of sketches and stories, was published by Harper.

Uncle Tom's Cabin. The Stowes moved to Brunswick, Maine, in 1850, and the passage of the Fugitive Slave

Act the same year caused her to begin writing *Uncle Tom's Cabin*. The novel was printed in forty installments by *The National Era* between June 1851 and April 1852, then published in book form by John P. Jewett of Boston in March 1852. It was an immediate success. By May, 50,000 copies had been sold. Within a year the total had reached 300,000. The book was widely pirated in Europe, and 1.5 million copies were printed in London alone. The story and its characters were written into plays, featured in songs, and incorporated into souvenir and keepsake items, making it the most popular book of its time.

A National Lesson. Much of the appeal of *Uncle Tom's Cabin* was due less to its moralistic message than to the emotional force behind the story. Stowe argued that Christian feeling and human compassion, not cold reason, should be the guide for moral behavior and society's laws. Accordingly, she tells her story in compelling episodes with strongly defined characters and sharp melodramatic and sentimental language. The novel's two main plots—the flight of Eliza, George, and Harry Harris northward to freedom and the descent of pious Uncle Tom southward to suffering and death—move swiftly and are skillfully charged with suspense. In the process, Stowe explores the complicity of both North and South in the evils of slavery and calls for a renewed moral effort to abolish the institution.

Other Books. Though *Uncle Tom's Cabin* remains her best-known work, Stowe wrote prolifically for the rest of her career. In 1853, as an attempt to rebut criticism of her portrayal of slavery, Stowe published *A Key to Uncle Tom's Cabin*, which contained the court records, handbills, eyewitness reports, and other documents that she had used as sources while writing the novel. She treated the antislavery theme again in *Dred* (1856), then began a series of novels dealing first with colonial New England life and, later, post-Civil War society. In 1870 she again caused a literary sensation when she published *Lady Byron Vindicated*, which revealed Lord Byron's incestuous relationship with his half-sister and defended Byron's wife, Anne, who had been Stowe's friend. At her death in 1896, Stowe's collected works filled sixteen volumes.

Sources:
Noel B. Gerson, *Harriet Beecher Stowe: A Biography* (New York: Praeger, 1976);

Forrest Wilson, *Crusader in Crinoline: The Life of Harriet Beecher Stowe* (Philadelphia: Lippincott, 1941).

PUBLICATIONS

Washington Allston, *Lectures on Art and Poems* (New York: Baker & Scribner, 1850)—a posthumously published collection that includes four discourses on aesthetics and the philosophy of art by an American romantic painter whose career spanned the years 1810–1840;

William Cullen Bryant, *A Discourse on the Life, Character and Genius of Washington Irving* (New York: Putnam, 1860)—the first major biography of the author of "Rip Van Winkle," written by a respected American poet;

William Ellery Channing, *Thoreau, the Poet-Naturalist* (Boston: Roberts, 1873)—a literary biography of the author of *Walden*, written by a friend and fellow Transcendentalist;

Andrew Jackson Downing, *The Architecture of Country Houses* (New York: Appleton, 1850)—a widely read work by the influential horticulturist and landscape architect who designed the grounds of the Capitol, the White House, and the Smithsonian Institution in Washington, D.C.;

Evert Duyckinck, ed., *Cyclopedia of American Literature*, 2 volumes (New York: Scribner, 1855)—a groundbreaking biographical dictionary of American authors;

William Morris Hunt, *Talks About Art*, 2 volumes (London: Macmillan, 1875, 1883)—thoughts on art education by an influential American painter;

Cornelius Mathews, *A Pen-and-Ink Panorama of New York City* (New York: J. S. Taylor, 1853)—a cultural analysis of New York City by an American critic and scholar;

Alexander Beaufort Meek, *Songs and Poems of the South* (New York: S. H. Goetzel, 1857)—an early collection of Southern literature;

Anna Cora Mowatt, *Autobiography of an Actress* (Boston: Ticknor, Reed & Fields, 1854)—a memoir by an accomplished actress, playwright, and novelist;

Solomon Franklin Smith, *The Theatrical Journey—Work and Anecdotical Recollections of Sol Smith* (Philadelphia: T. B. Peterson, 1854)—an autobiography of a leading figures in American theater.

Source: Karen L. Rood, ed., *American Literary Almanac, from 1608 to the Present* (New York & Oxford: Facts on File, 1988).

BUSINESS AND THE ECONOMY

by FREDERICK DALZELL

CONTENTS

Sidebars and tables are listed in italics.

1850

- Isaac Singer, an illiterate machinist, redesigns a sewing machine and, over the next several years, begins manufacturing them.

- Allan Pinkerton starts a detective agency in Chicago, a business that becomes the largest of its kind and, in the late nineteenth century, a notorious means of breaking strikes.

19 Apr. Great Britain and the United States sign the Clayton-Bulwer Treaty, agreeing to joint use of a canal across the Isthmus of Panama .

20 Sept. Congress grants public lands to the states of Illinois, Mississippi, and Alabama to help fund railroad construction—the first federal railroad land grants.

1851

1 Apr. Hiram Sibley incorporates the New York and Mississippi Valley Printing and Telegraph Company (which eventually becomes Western Union).

15 May Trains begin running on the Erie Railroad between Lake Erie and New York City. The 483-mile line is the world's longest railroad.

1852

- Massachusetts establishes safety standards for steam engines, the first of their kind.

- In the Crystal Palace Exhibition in London, American manufacturers exhibit various industrial products, including the McCormick reaper, Borden meat biscuits, and the Colt revolver.

- The Pennsylvania Railroad connects Pittsburgh and Philadelphia.

- Potter Palmer opens a dry-goods store in Chicago.

- Boston businessmen form the Boston Board of Trade.

- Henry Heinz begins peddling food to Pittsburgh grocers.

- Paul Masson, a French immigrant, plants a vineyard near Santa Clara, California.

5 Jan. Delegates from eleven Southern states convene in New Orleans to discuss the region's economic development.

20 Feb. The first train reaches Chicago from the East Coast, on the Michigan Southern.

3 July Congress establishes a San Francisco branch of the U.S. Mint.

1853

- Prominent New York banks form a clearinghouse to facilitate east-west interbank transfers and loans.

- Gail Borden invents condensed milk.

- Samuel Colt builds an armory at Hartford, Connecticut, to make small arms. He trains employees in the "American System" of interchangeable parts, made by machines.

- Levi Strauss immigrates to San Francisco from Bavaria with a stock of heavy canvas, to sell to prospectors as tents, wagon covers, and, as need emerges, work pants.

4 Mar. In appropriation legislation for the army, Congress provides funds for surveying routes for transcontinental railroads.

1854

- Elisha Otis demonstrates his safety elevator, patented the year before, at the New York World's Fair, and sets up a company to manufacture them.

- Dry-goods merchant Junius Spencer Morgan joins the investment banking firm of George Peabody & Co. in London.

- R. H. Macy, in an effort to cope with the large number of sales clerks working in his dry-goods store in Haverhill, Massachusetts, adopts a one-price policy.

- Minneapolis's first commercial flour mill opens. In the post–Civil War decades, Minneapolis mills will come to dominate the nation's flour industry.

31 Mar. Commodore Matthew C. Perry forces Japanese signing of the Treaty of Kanagawa, opening two Japanese ports to U.S. trade and establishing relations between the two nations.

1855

- A railroad across the Isthmus of Panama is completed.

1 Jan. The first American oil company, the Pennsylvania Rock Oil Company, is formed.

1856

- Fruit of the Loom, a clothing firm founded by Benjamin and Robert Knight in 1851 in Providence, Rhode Island, adopts a red apple label to identify its fabrics—the first clothing trademark.

- Borden patents condensed milk.

- A streetcar line begins running in Boston, the first of its kind in the United States.

- The Eagle Pencil Company starts in New York City.

- The German Mills American Oatmeal Factory opens in Akron, Ohio, under Ferdinand Schumacher, and begins marketing oatmeal as a foodstuff.

- Cadwallader C. Washburn forms the Minneapolis Mill Company and begins experimenting with new milling processes.

21 Apr. The first railroad bridge spanning the Mississippi River opens.

1857

- Massachusetts law grants interstate commerce rights to all manufacturing and mining companies.

- Augustus Wolle starts the Saucona Iron Company, which will become Bethlehem Iron in 1861 and, later, Bethlehem Steel.

21 Feb. Congress abolishes legal-tender status for foreign coins.

24 Aug. The failure of the New York branch of the Ohio Life Insurance & Trust Company sets off widespread commercial and financial panic. The national economy settles into a prolonged depression.

1858

- R. H. Macy opens a fancy dry-goods store in New York City—a retail establishment that grows to become one of the earliest American department stores.

- Isaac Singer starts selling a lightweight sewing machine for "family" use.

1859

- A Philadelphia convention of machinist and blacksmith union workers articulates one of the first organized-labor demands for an eight-hour day.

- The State of New York creates a state agency to regulate insurance companies.

- Ebenezer Butterick, a tailor, begins using patterns to manufacture clothing in large batches.

- Edwin Drake drills the first U.S. oil well, in Pennsylvania.

1 Sept. George Pullman tests a model sleeping car on the railroad line between Chicago and Bloomington, Illinois.

1860

- Francis A. Pratt and Amos Whitney form a business to make precision machinery.

- Charles H. Morgan invents the first commercial paper-bag machine.

- Illinois charters the Chicago Board of Trade as a "body politic and corporate," in effect recognizing its quasi-regulatory function in grading grains so that they can be handled en masse by grain elevators and railroads.

16 Mar. Some six thousand shoemakers march in protest in Lynn, Massachusetts, at the high point of the largest strike of the pre–Civil War period. The strike fails to secure union recognition, though it does win higher wages.

1861

- Elisha Otis patents the steam elevator.

- Factory production of Borden's condensed milk begins.

- The American Miners' Association forms, becoming one of the first industry-wide unions.

- Jay Cooke & Co. is formed, a banking house that dominates the sale of government bonds during the war, and government securities and railroad finance after the war.

5 August   Congress passes the first federal income tax, levying 3 percent on all income over $800.

1862

- The federal government issues currency called "greenbacks"—the first national paper money.
- F. A. O. Schwarz opens a fancy toy store in New York.
- The invention of the McKay stitcher revolutionizes shoe manufacturing, enabling the industry to move from outwork to centralized, in-factory production.

1 July   Congress passes the Pacific Railway Act, chartering the Union Pacific Railroad.

1863

- Ebenezer Butterick begins selling clothing patterns commercially.
- Pennsylvania Railroad becomes the first American railroad to use steel rails.
- John D. Rockefeller starts an oil refinery in Cleveland with Maurice Clark.

25 Feb.   Congress passes the National Banking Act, establishing a network of national banks.

3 Dec.   At Omaha, Nebraska, ground is broken for the Union Pacific Railroad.

1864

- The U.S. Mint begins engraving "In God We Trust" on coins.
- C. P. Barber, a match salesman, starts the Barber Match Company, forerunner of the Diamond Match Company (which controls 85 percent of the U.S. market by the late 1800s).
- Milton Bradley, railroad businessman and parlor-game designer, starts a business to manufacture and market board games.

4 July   To encourage importation of foreign workers, Congress passes a labor law permitting employers to contract workers abroad to work in the United States.

1865

- George Westinghouse patents a rotary steam engine.
- The U.S. Treasury Department creates the Secret Service Agency to battle counterfeiting.
- John B. Stetson starts a hat-making business in Philadelphia.
- The North Chicago Rolling Mill is built, where the first steel rails are manufactured.

25 Dec.   The Union Stockyards open in Chicago. Within a few years, several million head of livestock would pass through the stockyards every year.

1866

- Workers in several cities try to coordinate a general strike for an eight-hour workday.

- Congress passes the Mineral Land Act, the first federal law regulating mining industries.

- The Pacific Mail Steamship Company opens a regular steamship line between San Francisco and Hong Kong.

- Massachusetts becomes the first state to pass a factory-inspection law.

1 July   Congress enacts a 10 percent tax on state bank notes, in an effort to drive the state banks out of business.

20 Aug.   A National Labor Congress convenes at Baltimore.

1867

- Miners at the Comstock Lode form a union to protest wage cuts.

- Francis W. Ayer starts an advertising business in Philadelphia, N. W. Ayer & Son, that pioneers modern advertising techniques (including market research) and grows to become the largest advertising firm in the country.

- George Pullman incorporates the Pullman Palace Car Co. in Chicago to manufacture sleeping cars and, eventually, dining cars.

- Armour and Company opens its first packing plant in Chicago, with an annual butchering capacity of thirty thousand hogs.

4 Dec.   The Patrons of Husbandry, or Grangers, organize at a national convention in Washington, D.C.

1868

- In the "Erie War," Cornelius Vanderbilt squares off against Jay Gould and Jim Fisk for financial control over the Erie Railroad.

- Massachusetts creates a state labor bureau.

- Oliver W. Norton begins manufacturing tin cans in a small company in Chicago and promoting their use in preserving foods. Campbell Soup and Heinz become two important early customers.

- Boston businessmen form a lobbying group, the National Board of Trade.

- Deere & Company starts, manufacturing farm implements.

1869

- In San Francisco whites riot against Chinese workers.

- The Colored National Labor Union forms, the first national black labor organization.

- The Knights of Labor organizes, initially as a small craft union of garment cutters.

- Massachusetts establishes a Board of Railroad Commissioners, a pioneer state regulatory agency.

- Joseph Campbell, a fruit merchant, joins with icebox manufacturer Abram Anderson in a business canning tomatoes, vegetables, and preserves—the beginning of the Campbell Soup Company.

- Marcus Goldman, a Philadelphia retailer, moves to New York City and starts an investment banking firm—the beginning of Goldman Sachs & Co.

- In Manhattan retailer R. H. Macy adds toys, silver, and house furnishings to his stock of clothing and dry goods.

- Henry J. Heinz launches his first business, making and selling horseradish. (The business fails, but Heinz starts again with his brother and cousin, this time making prepared foods.)

- A schooner carries a cargo of Honduran bananas to New Orleans, inaugurating the tropical fruit trade with Central America.

18 Mar. The Public Credit Act provides for repayment of the government's Civil War obligations in gold.

Sept. A refrigerated railroad car makes the first shipment of fresh meat from Chicago to the East Coast.

24 Sept. On "Black Friday," an effort by Jay Gould and Jim Fisk to corner the gold market collapses, ruining many investors.

1870

- Congress passes the first national trademark law. The first trademark granted is to William Underwood & Co., for their "Deviled Entrements."

- Sherwin-Williams begins manufacturing prepared paints.

10 Jan. John D. Rockefeller and associates incorporate the Standard Oil Company, establishing what quickly becomes the world's largest oil refinery complex.

1871

- Ebenezer Butterick launches a promotional magazine.

- The U.S. Supreme Court rules that greenbacks are legal tender.

- J. P. Morgan and Anthony J. Drexel join forces to create Drexel, Morgan & Co. in a bid to cut into Jay Cooke's monopoly of U.S. securities finance.

- Aaron Montgomery Ward starts a small retail business in Chicago. The following year, Ward's becomes the official supply house of the National Grange, and issues its first mail-order "catalog," a one-page handbill.

7 Apr. Illinois passes the Railroad Act—the first of its kind—establishing a commission to set maximum shipping rates and prohibit railroads from favoring large corporations with low rates.

1872

- Montgomery Ward and Company opens the nation's first mail-order house in Chicago.

- Enos M. Barton and a partner start up the Western Electric Manufacturing Company in Chicago, making electrical materials and appliances.

- Andrew Carnegie starts building a steel-rail rolling mill, later named the Edgar Thomson Works.

- Frederick Weyerhauser starts the Mississippi River Boom & Logging Company.

4 Sept. The *New York Sun* exposes political corruption in the Crédit Mobilier scandal, in which a construction company organized by the promoters of the Union Pacific Railroad Company had skimmed profits.

1873

- E. Remington & Sons, a firearms company, begins manufacturing and selling typewriters.

- Lydia Pinkham begins marketing a remedy for female complaints, made of a vegetable compound laced with 19 percent alcohol.

- Singer Sewing Machine centralizes its manufacturing in a large new plant in Elizabethtown, New Jersey, that makes standardized machines with interchangeable parts in a continuous-assembly process.

- Minor C. Keith begins buying up banana plantations in Central America—the start of a business that grows and merges with competitors to become United Fruit in 1899.

- Cornelius Vanderbilt builds the New York Union Depot.

18 Sept. The financial collapse of Jay Cooke's Northern Pacific Railroad sets off a five-year depression.

1874

- Montgomery Ward expands its mail-order catalogue to a one-hundred page circular, measuring 3 ½ by 7 inches. The company's sales pass $100,000 by the end of the year; by 1878 they exceed $400,000.

- R. H. Macy in New York creates a mail-order department.

13 Jan. In Tompkins Square, New York City, a crowd of seven thousand unemployed workers demonstrates for public works, under the slogan "Work or Bread." City police crack down on the gathering, dispersing the crowds and arresting scores of demonstrators.

11 Mar. Wisconsin passes the Potter law, regulating railroad rates.

23 Mar. Iowa passes a law regulating railroad rates.

8 May Massachusetts passes first effective ten-hour workday for women.

Nov. The Greenback Party forms on a platform of looser federal currency policy.

24 Nov. Joseph F. Glidden patents barbed wire—an invention that transforms western ranching.

1875

- Fourteen members of the "Molly Maguires"—a secret organization of Irish mine workers—are tried for murdering mine owners. Meanwhile, the "long strike" shuts down anthracite coal fields in Pennsylvania for several months.

- The Widows and Orphans Friendly Society reorganizes as the Prudential Friendly Society, which provides the first U.S. industrial insurance.

- In an effort to curb crippling rate wars, twenty-four Southern railroads found the Southern Railroad and Steamship Association.

- R. J. Reynolds starts a chewing tobacco factory in Winston-Salem, North Carolina.

- Gustavus Swift, a Massachusetts wholesale butcher, starts a meatpacking business.

14 Jan. Congress passes the Specie Resumption Act, arranging the exchange of legal tender for gold in 1879.

30 Jan. A U.S.-Hawaiian treaty admits duty-free importation of Hawaiian sugar and other produce.

1876

- Henry J. Heinz starts a new business making pickles, condiments, and prepared foods.

- Albert G. Spalding, a baseball player and manager, starts a sporting-goods business with his brother.

- John Wanamaker starts a retail store in Philadelphia, in an old freight depot, that becomes an early, trend-setting department store.

1877

- Gustavus Swift begins shipping dressed beef east; several years later, he will begin experimenting with refrigerated beef shipments.

- Quaker Mill trademarks Quaker Oats Cereal—the first breakfast cereal registered.

- Eastern railroad lines form the Eastern Trunk Line Association, in an effort to stabilize rates.

- Asa Candler begins a drug business in Atlanta. Ten years later, he will buy a part interest in Coca-Cola, a patent medicine.

- The Smith Brothers begin selling their cough drops in packages bearing their trademark, in an effort to prevent druggists from substituting cheaper cough drops in open jars.

- The Colgate Company begins marketing Colgate Dental Cream, which rises on a tide of heavy advertising to become the world's largest seller.

1 Mar. The U.S. Supreme Court rules in *Peik* v. *Chicago and Northwestern Railroad Company* that the states have the authority to regulate not only intrastate traffic, but also interstate traffic originating within their boundaries.

1 Mar.   The U.S. Supreme Court rules in *Munn* v. *Illinois* that the states have the authority to regulate warehouse and intrastate railroad shipping rates.

21 June   Ten "Molly Maguires" are hanged.

16 July   The first nationwide strike erupts when railroad workers in six cities refuse to work and try to shut down train traffic. Violent confrontations draw in federal troops and National Guard units.

OVERVIEW

The Midst of Change. The Civil War caught Americans in various stages of a profound economic transformation. Pockets of the nation, particularly in the Northeast and Midwest, had begun to industrialize and to lay the foundations for centralized, national market structures. In other regions, rural, local patterns of economic life still prevailed. And of course in the South, an economy built around slave labor and the export of agricultural commodities had taken deep root. Still, above the Mason-Dixon Line the pace of change began accelerating rapidly over the 1850s, driven above all by the railroads, which opened possibilities of enterprise on an unprecedented scale. The war itself checked some aspects of this change temporarily; others it intensified, especially as it destroyed Southern slavery and the economy it had supported. By 1877 it was becoming clear that the entire nation was being drawn into a new, recognizably modern economic system of making, earning, spending, and living.

Infrastructure. From a business viewpoint, the most important development of the mid 1800s was the laying down of a new infrastructure that was highly efficient, usable year-round, relatively inexpensive, and increasingly national in scope. Over earlier decades steamships and canals had begun the process. But it was railroads and the telegraph that would radically reshape the contours of American economic life. The first lines of rail transport and electronic communication were laid down in New England and the Middle Atlantic states in the 1830s and 1840s. Over the 1850s, 1860s, and 1870s rail corridors spread across the continent, into the Midwest, the Far West and the South. This shipping network in turn set off rapid, radical economic restructuring. Without the railroads, mass production, distribution, and consumption—the fundamental features of our modern economy—would have been inconceivable. With the railroads, they not only became workable, they happened with blazing speed.

Railroads as Business Pioneers. As the railroad network expanded, the scale of individual railroads' business and financial structures grew apace. Starting in the 1850s, they became the biggest businesses the country had ever known—enterprises capitalized in the tens, then hundreds of millions of dollars, and employing thousands, then tens of thousands of workers. As shippers the railroads untapped vast new entrepreneurial possibilities; as businesses they presented the United States with its first taste of the challenges that big business in an industrialized, centralized economy would create. The railroads, in other words, posed new and important problems, in finance, in management, in labor relations, and in public policy.

Livelihoods. The signs of industrial development were clear by midcentury, but industrialization did not dislocate American agriculture. In 1880 as in 1850, over half of American workers worked on farms, and only one in twenty worked in manufacturing. Farmers easily outnumbered factory workers, and while the number of those employed in manufacturing climbed steadily, doubling between 1850 and 1870 and reaching 3.3 million by 1880, the number of agricultural workers grew at just about the same rate, reaching nearly 9 million by 1880. While factories, mines, and steel mills burgeoned, new farmers began cultivating vast stretches of the prairies in the Midwest. Even in the South, where forceful emancipation necessitated structural economic change, and where wartime destruction abruptly cut off economic growth, broad macroeconomic patterns—export commodity agriculture, especially the cultivation of cotton—remained intact.

Urbanization. Most Americans, then, continued to live and work in the countryside through and in fact well past 1877, on farms and plantations, or in small rural towns. Still, the pace of urbanization was mounting by midcentury. As factories grew in size and spread across the landscape they tended to gather workforces in clustered, urban locations. And as railroads centralized production and distribution, they centralized settlement, too. Thus between 1850 and 1860, while U.S. population as a whole grew 36 percent, the country's urban population grew 75 percent—more than twice as fast. By 1880, the population of Manhattan had reached 1 million, nineteen other cities held populations of over 100,000, and more than half of the Americans living in the Northeast lived in cities.

Immigration. The expanding economy drew, and also drew on, waves of immigration. Over the late 1840s and 1850s, famine in western Europe drove hundreds of thousands of families to the United States, principally from Ireland and Germany. Some two million immigrants came through the Port of New York over the 1850s alone. Employers actively promoted immigration: companies such as the American Emigrant Company, established in New York, dispatched agents abroad to recruit foreign workers for American factories, railroads, and mining companies. On the West Coast, a parallel system developed to bring over Chinese immigrant labor. Congress endorsed the practice in 1864 in the Contract Labor Law, which authorized businesses to set up contracts abroad paying for passage in exchange for labor once an immigrant arrived. Immigration, in other words, tied in directly with economic growth; it represented a response to expansion, and it contributed to expansion too, by providing employers with a continuous stream of cheap labor.

Getting and Spending. In 1851 Horace Greeley's *New York Tribune* published a weekly budget of $10.37 for an urban working-class family of five, allotting $3 for rent, 54 cents for fuel and candles, $2 for clothing, 25 cents for "wear and tear" of "household articles," 12 cents for newspapers, and the remainder for foodstuffs: flour, sugar, butter, milk, butcher's meat, potatoes, coffee and tea. But $10 was a weekly rate only an elite segment of New York's skilled workmen could hope to earn; smiths and wheelwrights, for example, earned closer to $7.50. Common laborers and factory workers, lower on the social scale, earned substantially less: when workers in Lynn, Massachusetts, went on strike in 1860, male factory hands earned weekly wages of $3, and female workers $1, for workdays up to sixteen-hours long. Moreover, industrial and unskilled employment was frequently erratic, and wages tended to shrink during periods of economic downturn. In the depression of 1877 railroad brakemen (ranking near the bottom of the railroad salary scale) earned an average of $1.75 a day for a twelve hour day. Firemen (who shoveled coal and worked tender brakes) earned slightly more, $1.90 per day, while conductors commanded salaries of $2.78 per day.

Child Labor. American children worked not just on farms and in households, but in mills and factories in large numbers in the mid 1800s. The Civil War actually exacerbated the trend by draining the supply of adult male labor. By the end of the war as many as 13 percent of Massachusetts textile-mill workers were under sixteen; in Pennsylvania the proportion was closer to one-quarter. And the end of the war did not release children from working. By 1872 more than 10,000 children toiled in Philadelphia's industrial workplaces. A year later, reformer Charles Loring Brace surveyed New York City factories and estimated that they employed 100,000 children, including boys and girls as young as four years old toiling in tobacco factories in New York neighbor-hoods. Mill, factory, and sweatshop owners hired boys and girls because they earned less than adult workers—as little as a dollar a week. Advocates like Brace agitated against child labor, pushing for the formation of state investigations and regulations. Enacting legislation prohibiting child labor also became a major goal for emerging labor political movements. But even in those states that passed child labor laws, commitment to change was slow in taking hold, partly because lower-class families often desperately needed the extra income their children's labor earned.

Sectional Trends. Industrialization, urbanization, and immigration occured throughout the country, but they concentrated especially strongly in the northern states. In New England manufacturing investment, broken down per capita, had topped $80 by 1860; while in the South as a whole the figure barely exceeded $10, and in the cotton South specifically it came in at $7.20. Antebellum Southern entrepreneurs tended overwhelmingly to sink their capital into agriculture—into plantations and slaves—while their Northern countrymen were investing in railroads, mines, and factories. Southern settlement patterns were correspondingly rural: whereas over 35 percent of New Englanders and residents of the Middle Atlantic states lived in cities in 1860 (including more than half of those living in Massachusetts and Rhode Island), less than 12 percent of southerners did. Pockets of urban and industrial activity had emerged in the South—in cities such as Richmond, for example, where slaves worked in iron forges, tobacco factories, and flour mills. But these pockets remained isolated. The changes transforming economy and society in the Northern states were not taking hold in the South, and as a result the two sections were growing more and more different, economically speaking.

"Robber Barrons" and the Republic. As industrialization worked its way into the American economy, it set off profound social changes—changes that stirred powerful popular concerns about where the nation was going. From diverse quarters, sharp protest resisted the new economy. Antebellum proslavery spokesmen, laboring to deflect criticism of conditions on Southern plantations, fulminated against conditions in the nation's new cities and factories. Workers in many of the industries drawn into the factory system issued searching and impassioned denunciations of "wage slavery" and the power of the new industrial capitalists: as the *National Labor Tribune* put matters in 1874, "the working people of this country . . . suddenly find capital as rigid as any absolute monarchy." In the countryside, farmers also felt their loss of autonomy keenly. These various critics spoke from sharply different perspectives, and for sharply different agendas. Yet all of them were concerned with how the new industrial economy could be made compatible with American institutions of government and ideology? This concern grew more pointed over the wartime and postbellum years, as the excesses of financial speculation surrounding and supporting railroad construction became lurid spectacles. It was an age that stirred profound anxiety—an age that made men such as Cornelius Vanderbilt and Jay Gould wildly rich, and made them infamous, too, as "Robber Barons." Exposing the corrupt lobbying and influence-buying that underlay the struggle between these two titans over financial control of the Erie Railroad, Charles Francis Adams came to realize that the emergence of the railroads, the nation's first big businesses, presented the United States with a situation it had never before encountered. Striving to express the situation, Adams groped for terms, and resorted an older image he knew his countrymen and his Revolutionary ancestors would appreciate: "It is a new power for which our language contains no name," he warned Americans. "We know what aristocracy, autocracy, democracy are; but we have no word to express government by monied corporations."

TOPICS IN THE NEWS

BUSINESS CYCLES

Prosperity. At the start of the 1850s, a tide of prosperity buoyed the U.S. economy. The discovery of gold in California in 1848 generated dramatic developments and windfall earnings. Moreover, a few years later, the outbreak of the Crimean War created strong European demand for American wheat, a demand nicely timed with the opening of the railroad and rapid cultivation of the Midwest. During the 1850s American farmers exported some $420 million worth of wheat, mainly to European markets. Meanwhile, immigrants continued to pour into the country, looking for work or to buy land or both. These developments drew European investors back to American investments (which had become suspect after several American states had repudiated their debts in the late 1830s). These sources of capital played a prominent role in financing the 1850s boom in railroad construction: European investors fed close to $200 million in capital into the U.S. economy over the 1850s, most of it into railroad securities.

Collapse: 1857. Growth could not continue indefinitely, however, particularly growth as superheated as that of the early 1850s. Crisis erupted on 24 August 1857, when the New York office of the Ohio Life Insurance and Trust Company closed its doors, unable to pay its obligations—news that "struck on the public like a cannon shot," *Hunts Merchant Magazine* reported. Ohio Life, like other Western firms and banks, had been issuing drafts (paper that circulated among merchants as currency) and meanwhile borrowing heavily from a series of New York banks; when it went under, it threatened to drag many of these banks with it. Severe financial constriction resulted as the New York banks, operating without any central bank or lender of last resort, frantically tried to call in their outstanding loans and notes to meet suddenly pressing demand from their depositors for hard currency. A partner wrote to Jay Cooke, then a young investment banker, "Money is *not tight—it is not to be had at all*. There is no money, no confidence and value to anything." On 13 October the New York banks suspended specie payments and closed their doors, forcing other banks across the country to follow suit. Businesses began failing, and the pace of failures mounted rapidly. Within a few months the chaos spread to Great Britain and Europe, as plunging stock prices dragged down investors holding American railroad and municipal securities.

Into and Through the War. The economic downturn proved steep but relatively short-lived. Within a couple of years the cycle swung back; prices recovered; and prosperity returned to much of the country. Over the course of the war, though, the economic fortunes of the two sides diverged sharply. In the North, despite war-related resource dislocations, heavy government spending and inflationary prices drove a war boom. In the South, on the other hand, the collapse of the Confederacy's currency and finances, coupled with military defeat and the disintegration of slavery, left economic chaos, hunger, and a landscape of ruined farms, plantations, railroads, and cities. While Southerners picked through the postwar ruins, northern industrial expansion largely picked up where it left off, with redoubled railroad construction, fueled by intense speculation.

Collapse. Once again, however, speculative energies overheated. This time the crisis came from abroad: prominent business failures broke out in Vienna in May 1873, then spread to Germany. German investors made up an important part of the European financial base for American railroads and western lands, and when that support weakened, American finances tottered dangerously. They fell on 18 September, when the collapse of Jay Cooke's various bank-

Painting by H. Cafferty, "Wall Street at Half Past Two O'Clock," depicting the chaotic scene in the financial center of Manhattan at the height of the Panic of 1857

ing firms (comprising a string of brokerages and banks in Washington, Philadelphia, and New York) set off a panic that quickly spread through the nation's banking centers. After two days of severe financial spasms, the New York Stock Exchange closed for ten days in an effort to cool off the crisis, but long-term economic malaise had already begun to set in: the nation spent the next sixty-five months in depression—the longest spell the nation had known.

Hard Times. The depression of the mid 1870s created unprecedented levels of misery. As more Americans became enmeshed in national market and economic conditions—working in factories or on railroads for wages, for example, rather than on farms that might be at least semi-self-sufficient—less of the population remained insulated from economic contractions. By 1873 financial contraction

meant that some one million workers had been thrown out of work, and millions more had suffered sharp wage cuts. Hundreds of thousands of tramps migrated around the country looking for work, food, and shelter. In New York City, where an estimated quarter of the workforce lost their jobs, soup kitchens overflowed and city police dumped hundreds of unemployed and homeless men on Blackwell's Island. In Boston, so many families applied to the Overseers of the Poor that it seemed to besieged officials as if "some great fire or more ferocious calamity" had struck.

Riots. Not only did depressions hit harder, they seemed to stir up greater levels of social tension and anxiety. The Panic of 1857 provoked bitter recriminations against bankers and stockbrokers. Conditions in the mid 1870s grew more highly charged, setting off incendiary confrontations be-

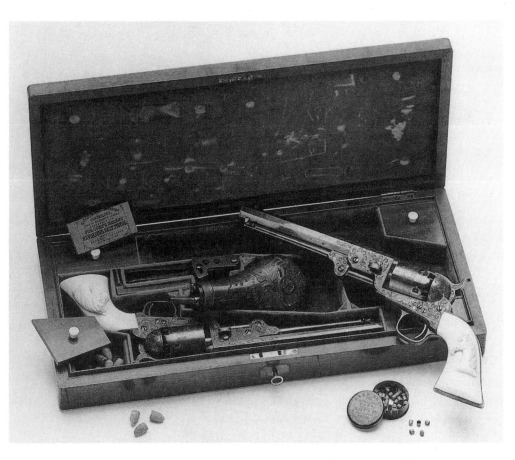

Colt Model 1851 revolvers

tween organized labor and local municipal authorities. In New York City the mood became especially confrontational over the winter of 1873–1874, with mounting protests and processions demanding public relief. Tensions eventually erupted in the Tompkins Square Riot on 13 January 1874. A group of organized-labor representatives and reform politicians styling itself the Committee of Safety had planned a demonstration at the square and applied for permits, but the city's police board and parks commission denied the applications. Organizers then canceled some of the proceedings, but word of the cancellations did not circulate widely, and some seven thousand men and women gathered at the site anyway. A force of sixteen hundred police mustered and ordered the crowd to disperse; when protesters refused, the police charged, setting off a mélée in which many participants and bystanders were seriously injured. The incident was foretaste of what was to come in the approaching decades, as social tensions continued to escalate and financial contractions periodically crippled the new industrial economy.

Sources:

Charles P. Kindleberger, *Manias, Panics and Crashes: A History of Financial Crises*, third edition (New York: John Wiley, 1996);

Samuel Rezneck, *Business Depressions and Financial Panics* (New York: Greenwood Press, 1968).

COAL, IRON, GUNS, STEEL

Anthracite Coal and Pig Iron. The industrialization of the Northern states was fueled, literally, by rich supplies of key raw materials. In the 1820s substantial anthracite coal fields opened in eastern Pennsylvania, and as canals and eventually railroads reached into the region, substantial supplies became available to the nation's burgeoning mills, forges, factories, and railways. By the mid 1840s annual production of the Pennsylvania mines topped two million tons, and the price had dropped to three dollars a ton. This output in turn supplied American manufacturers and railroads not only with inexpensive fuel for steam power, but also with plentiful domestic stocks of iron. In the 1840s and 1850s the number of anthracite coal blast furnaces proliferated, rising from 60 to 121 between 1849 and 1853 alone. With average workforces of eighty and capital assets typically close to $100,000, these operations were not especially large, but their impact on the industrializing northern states was disproportionately enormous.

Metalworking. The development of coal mines and iron furnaces and forges encouraged substantial expansion in the American metal-working industry. Firearms manufacturers, bolstered by army contracts, had pioneered increasingly specialized production methods and the use of interchangeable parts—called "the American System of manufacturing." Starting in the late 1840s, these methods spread to factories making locks, safes, clocks, and watches. Meanwhile, new small-arms manufacturers built formidable factories and businesses, including Christian Sharps, Eliphalet Remington, and Samuel Colt.

Colt. The rise of Samuel Colt's firearms manufacturing company demonstrated the prowess and potential of American industrial methods not just to the nation, but to the world. As a young man in the 1830s Colt had invented a revolver and, after securing a patent, immediately set up a business to manufacture and market it. Business got off to a slow start, but picked up once Colt secured profitable government contracts during the Mexican-American War, enabling him to build a factory in Hartford, Connecticut, to expand production. Colt aggressively mechanized and streamlined production, undermining the process control and prerogatives of traditional, skilled gunsmiths, but achieving impressive efficiencies. In 1855 he built a second, larger factory, and within several years his company was making 150 guns a day. Meanwhile, Colt's revolvers were attracting worldwide notice. A display at the Crystal Palace of 1851 was a triumph, generating many orders from clients. Several years later a visiting member of the British Parliament toured Colt's plant and found the production methods equally striking. Commenting as much on the industrial culture of the workplace as on its equipment, he remarked: "In those American tools there is a common

Henry Bessemer

sense way of going to the point at once, that I was quite struck with; there is great simplicity, almost a Quaker-like rigidity of form, given to the machinery; no ornamentation, no rubbing away of corners, or polishing; but the precise, accurate and correct results. It was that which gratified me so much at Colonel Colt's, to see the spirit that pervaded the machines."

An International Arms Trade. Colt eagerly courted just this kind of testimony. He promoted international sales vigorously, sending agents abroad to dispense gifts of custom-made weapons, ornately engraved, to kings and ministers throughout Europe. In the wake of his Crystal Palace success, he set up a factory in England (a first for American manufacturers). Elsewhere he licensed the manufacture of his revolvers to foreign companies and armories, including those equipping the Russian army. These efforts were matched by Colt's competitors, especially in the post–Civil War years, after factories had expanded production capacities. Remington, for example, began shipping rifles to Sweden, Denmark, France, Spain, and Egypt. When France went to war with Prussia in 1870, the company secured more than $11 million in contracts from the French military. These kinds of successes firmly established American small arms in the European marketplace. Between 1868 and 1878, U.S. manufacturers exported over $4 million of

REMINGTON DURING THE CIVIL WAR

Of course, the firearm industry boomed during the Civil War, when government contracts kept factories going full throttle. Industry grew frantic at places such as Illion, New York, where workers at E. Remington and Sons churned out revolvers and rifles in response to government orders numbering in the tens of thousands. In an effort to meet demand, the company threw up a temporary production facility and a steam generator to increase power. In peak periods, it was reported, every man and boy in the town worked day and night for weeks at a time to fill contracts. All told, the company (and the town) made nearly $3 million worth of rifles. The pace of production may have contributed to founder Eliphalet Remington's death in the first few months of the war. But the company pressed on, passing to Remington's sons and, in the midst of the urgent press of wartime production, developing a rifle that was breach- rather than muzzle-loaded, a product that would buttress his company's growth through and beyond the war years.

Source: Warren E. Schulz, *Illion: The Town Remington Made* (Hicksville, N.Y.: Exposition Press, 1977).

firearms annually, prompting one Russian to observe, "Just as European factories had earlier supplied America with arms, so America, in turn, is now the great industrial power. Its products are capable of glutting all the European arms markets and with little strain filling the enormous orders of European governments."

Metal. Notable as it was, however, American success in metalworking industries would eventually be overshadowed by the more basic industry of making the metal that was coming to symbolize the age: steel. Industrial demand, particularly from the railroads, encouraged substantial expansion in ironmaking over the 1850s, at the same time as mounting coal production and spreading railroad transportation made expansion feasible. By the eve of the Civil War, the largest ironmakers ran plants that integrated blast furnaces, forges, rolling mills, and finishing mills. These operations included three major Pennsylvania mills—the Mountour Iron Works of Danville, the Cambria Iron Works at Johnstown, and the Phoenix Company of Phoenixville—along with the Trenton Iron Works in New Jersey. They were capital-intensive (more than $1 million each), and labor-intensive as well, with workforces of one thousand or more—three thousand at Mountour. Maintaining industrial capacity on this scale might have proven difficult, especially given the vulnerability of the mills' most important customers, the railroads, to financial vicissitudes. But the Civil War bolstered production, and during the war years the mills grew in number, though not appreciably in size.

The Bessemer Process and the Engineered Steel Plant. In the years immediately following the war, an important new technology of steel manufacture swept through the industry, the Bessemer process. Achieved by blasting air into hot pig iron (consuming the carbon in the iron and so producing a metal that was less brittle and therefore more malleable—steel), the technology was perfected in the late 1850s and the 1860s. American mills began to introduce Bessemer converters in the late 1860s, setting them up alongside traditional puddling mills. It was a plastic moment, when the possibilities of new, more efficient technologies of production met up against the existing plant investments and structures, and Andrew Carnegie, a rising Pittsburgh steel magnate, seized it aggressively. While other mill owners tried to fit Bessemer converters into existing plants, Carnegie overhauled or built new ones, custom-designed to integrate the new technologies into a streamlined flow of production. His masterwork was the 1875 Edgar Thompson Works, engineered by Alexander Lyman Holley to run like a machine. With the completion of the E.T. Works, Carnegie was positioned to lead Americans to the forefront of world steel production in the closing decades of the nineteenth century.

Sources:

Joseph Bradley, *Guns for the Tsar: American Technology and the Small Arms Industry in Nineteenth Century Russia* (Dekalb: Northern Illinois University Press, 1990);

"KING COTTON" AND THE WAR

Southern secessionists boasted at the outbreak of the war that "King Cotton" would force Great Britain to recognize the Confederacy and bring the North to terms. The British textile industry depended on Southern cotton, the theory ran, and once the supply was cut off and the mills ground to a halt, popular opinion would compel the British government to mediate and the North to negotiate. It proved to be a disastrous miscalculation. At the outset of the war Southern planters embargoed cotton shipments and waited for Britain to act, but bumper crops and record exports in 1857–1860 allowed the British mills to wait out the first stages of the conflict; textile manufacturers did not feel a serious pinch until 1862. Meanwhile, European governments, reluctant to antagonize the Union, waited to see how the war developed. By the time British mills had consumed their stockpiles of cotton, the Confederacy, starved for supplies and funds, had itself abandoned the embargo. British public opinion did not prove as mercenary as secessionists had expected; especially after Lincoln issued his Emancipation Proclamation, a strong anti-slavery movement in England resisted Confederate recognition. Finally, as the price of cotton climbed to new highs, cotton planting and exporting developed in Egypt and India to fill the need. As Confederate military initiatives flagged, hopes of British recognition died. "King Cotton" had proved to be an empty figurehead.

Source: James M. McPherson, *Battle Cry of Freedom: The Civil War Era* (New York: Oxford University Press, 1988).

Alfred D. Chandler Jr., *The Visible Hand: The Managerial Revolution in American Business* (Cambridge, Mass.: Harvard University Press, 1977);

Robert Laurence Wilson, *The Colt Heritage* (New York: Simon & Schuster, 1979).

THE COTTON ECONOMY IN THE SOUTH

The Cotton Boom. While the pace of industrialization picked up in the North in the 1850s, the agricultural economy of the slave South grew, if anything, more entrenched. In the decade before the Civil War cotton prices rose more than 50 percent, to 11.5 cents a pound. Booming cotton prices stimulated new western cultivation and actually checked modest initiatives in economic diversification of the previous decade. The U.S. cotton crop nearly doubled, from 2.1 million bales in 1850 to 3.8 million bales ten years later. Not surprisingly, given these figures, the southern economy remained overwhelmingly agricultural. Southern capitalists sank

Slaves at work on Pope's Plantation, near Hilton Head, South Carolina, circa 1860

money into cotton rather than factories or land. More precisely, they invested in slaves; the average slave owner held almost two-thirds of his wealth in slaves in 1860, much less than he held in land. Economic historians have concluded that returns on capital in antebellum Southern manufacturing were reasonable and sometimes lucrative, but they simply failed to attract investors in any numbers. By 1860, while northeastern states such as Massachusetts and Pennsylvania had nearly $100 million each invested in manufacturing enterprises, even Virginia, the most industrialized of the Southern states, had invested less than $20 million, and the figure dropped below $5 million elsewhere in the South. A comparison of the value of goods manufactured in each region is similarly lopsided: more than $150 million each for Massachusetts and Pennsylvania, less than $30 million for Virginia, and less than $5 million for Alabama.

Antebellum Railroads. The South did participate in the boom in railroad construction of the 1850s, more than quadrupling its total mileage. Results were less impressive and, more important, less transformative than they proved in the North and Midwest, however. By 1860 the railroad mileage per thousand square miles in the seven most populous Northern states had reached sixty-two; in the seven most populous southern states, the figure was twenty-two. In other words, the southern rail network was less developed by a factor of nearly three. Moreover, Southern railroads tended to run fewer trains and make fewer stops than Northern ones. In addition, most Southern lines were built to connect plantation districts to southern ports; that is, they did not open new territories or serve new industries, as railroads did in the North.

Preindustrial Structures. The dominance of the slave plantation in the southern economic landscape had multifaceted consequences for Southern economic development, including key social and cultural ramifications. As businesses, the plantations channeled economic functions that went well beyond cotton (or sugar or tobacco) cultivation. For example, larger plantation owners either procured or produced on site goods and services that, in the free-labor economy of the Northern states, were produced and exchanged as part of the wider economy. Thus, few towns or villages emerged in the South. Much of the region's commercial exchange operated through the larger plantation owners or through businessmen known as cotton factors, usually agents of Northern or British firms, set up at river landings to market crops and provide planters with imported manufactured goods. The ideology of slaveownership probably inhibited key industrial values, fostering a fiercely defensive agrarianism and a sharp distaste for Yankee commercialism, industry, and wage labor, particularly as proslavery advocacy grew more insistent in the late-antebellum period. More tangibly, slavery cut off the potential immigration of free labor; while strong immigrant flows were feeding into the Northern economy in the 1850s, the South remained a largely closed society. Whether or not slaveowners can be called profit-minded entrepreneurs and capitalists (a question still under debate), the world they made was distinctly preindustrial, even anti-industrial.

POCKETS OF INDUSTRY: LYNCHBURG

The antebellum South was not all cotton plantations and riverboats. Small-scale industry did emerge in Southern towns such as Lynchburg, Virginia. By 1858 three railroad lines intersected there, and like railroad connections in the Midwest, the industrial infrastructure boosted manufacturing in the town. On the eve of the Civil War, Lynchburg held eleven grist mills, several coppersmiths, a fertilizer manufacturer, and four coachmakers—one of which employed twenty-five workers making freight and passenger railroad cars for the Virginia and Tennessee Railroad. Lynchburg's most important industry, though, was tobacco manufacturing: in 1860 more than one thousand slaves and free blacks worked in tobacco factories—steaming, stemming, and dipping leaves in syrup, then spicing the tobacco, molding it into plugs, and packaging it for delivery to the North. Most slaves were "hired," or rented from their masters, on an annual basis. Some of these slave workers managed to negotiate with employers on their own behalf; lucky ones earned cash incentives for "overwork." During the war the curtailment of tobacco planting in the surrounding countryside shut down the industry, and postwar conditions fluctuated wildly. Freed workers tested their autonomy in several strikes during this period and wrested modest concessions from factory owners (all of whom were white). Meanwhile, in the wake of emancipation small black businesses proliferated in the town: by 1880 African Americans owned and operated groceries, liveries, produce stalls at the city market, saloons, bathhouses, and artisinal shops.

Source: Steven Elliott Tripp, *Yankee Town, Southern City: Race and Class Relations in Civil War Lynchburg* (New York: New York University Press,1997).

Exports. The Southern economy was not undynamic or unproductive, though. During the period before the Civil War, Southern staples made up three-fifths of total American exports, and cotton was by far the country's largest export. Southern plantations and farms supplied three-fourths of the world cotton crop—the mainstay of textile manufacturing in both Great Britain (the world's leading economic superpower) and the United States. Southern planters saw themselves, and accurately so, as a key component in the Industrial Revolution and a critical part of an international economic system. As one planter bragged in 1853, "Our Cotton is the most wonderful talisman in the world. By its power we are transmuting whatever we choose into whatever we want." James Hammond, speaking in the U.S. Senate five years later, was even more trenchant: "The slaveholding South is now the controlling power of the world. Cotton, rice, tobacco, and naval stores command the world. . . . No power on earth dares . . . to make war on cotton. Cotton is king."

Cotton Farms and Plantations. The image of the large cotton plantation dominates popular impressions of the antebellum South and Southern economy, and to be sure it was the preeminent economic unit of the region, but it was hardly the norm. Nearly three-fourths of free families in the South did not own slaves. The typical Southern white was a small farmer. Many of these families grew cotton, which unlike sugar or rice did not require heavy capital to cultivate. The crop was basically nonperishable and survived relatively rough handling, so it tended to survive transportation to distant markets in better shape than other crops. Small farmers often devoted at least part of their acreage to cotton, and small slaveowners could be found working alongside their slaves in the field throughout the region. Still, most slaves lived on—and the bulk of the cotton crop came from—plantations worked by twenty or more slaves. On the largest plantations, fifty or more slaves were divided into gangs, run by drivers and sometimes, though not always, by overseers. On these large plantations, complex divisions of labor evolved. The most developed plantations came to resemble village economies: one Virginia planter in 1854, for example, owned and managed eight plowmen, ten hoe hands, two wagoners, four oxcart drivers, a carriage driver, a hostler, a stable boy, and various craftspeople, including two carpenters, five masons, two smiths, a miller, two shoemakers, five spinners, a weaver, and the owners' household staff.

Wartime. The Civil War destroyed this economic world. Emancipation (coupled with Union victory) formally dismantled slavery, of course, but even before the Union army liberated slaves in a particular region, plantation and farm discipline eroded rapidly as African Americans, taking advantage of wartime conditions, began asserting control over their labor and, once Northern armies approached, ran away in large numbers. Whatever the mechanism of abolition, the war left the South devastated. Military destruction cut deep gouges into the region's infrastructure, farms, and white population. More basically, emancipation wiped out the bulk of Southern capital and the basis of its economy and society. In the decades that followed, the central facts of Southern economic life were social turmoil, a dearth of capital, and poverty.

Postwar Development. In aftermath of the war, the Southern economy began slowly to diversify and commercialize. Agriculturally, land-use patterns grew even more cotton-intensive as new stretches of upcountry shifted from food production, such as corn and pork, to cotton. But the region (like other parts of the nation) also underwent a boom in railroad construction, and enthusiastic boosters and carpetbaggers also started manufacturing enterprises in the 1860s. The rate of manufacturing growth leveled off in the following decade but redoubled in the 1880s and 1890s. These enterprises included cotton mills, commercial fertilizer manufacturing plants (by 1877 South Carolina phosphate mines were shipping more than 100,000 tons to foreign markets), and iron forges. Whereas antebellum Southern ironmakers had relied on outdated and inefficient charcoal-burning operations, their postwar counterparts ran modernized coal mines, coke ovens, and blast furnaces. The town of Birmingham, for example, became an industrial center during this period. Organized in 1871 as part of a land speculation project by the Louisville and Nashville Railroad, the town rapidly developed substantial iron- and eventually steelworks, contributing to a statewide coal output of nearly 200,000 tons in 1877 and pig-iron production of nearly 37,000 tons.

Stores, Towns, Cities: A "New South." Other changes, equally far-reaching and much more widely distributed, overhauled southern demographics and commercial patterns. Within a few years after the end of the war, a network of stores and towns began to spread through the region. "We have stores at almost every crossroad," a South Carolina correspondent reported, "and at the railway stations and villages they have multiplied beyond precedent." Indeed, the number of towns in that state doubled in the 1860s, then tripled in the 1870s. By 1880 more than eight thousand stores had sprouted across the South. Railroad connections made larger towns such as Selma and Macon key market connections, channelling the flow of commercial goods from the North out to the country stores. Atlanta, which proclaimed itself the capital of the "New South," grew even more dramatically, prompting a visitor in 1870 to report that the city contained "more of the life and stir of business than in all the other Southern cities." Capital and the credit on which the new commercial enterprises operated traced back to Northern sources, but even so, the transformation profoundly reoriented southern habits of buying and selling, tying the region into new, national commercial markets.

Free Labor. As they adjusted to new commercial structures and infrastructures, Southerners—white and black—began to hammer out new systems of labor. The most radical economic change of the postwar period was the elimination of slavery and the necessary definition of what free labor would mean in the cotton economy. The transition was not smooth, uniform, or peaceful. Former slaveowners retained their land, for the most part, and struggled to impose as much control as possible over the people who worked it. The freedmen, for their part, bargained for higher wages, insisted on the freedom to shop their labor, and refused to work in gangs as they had on the plantations. Plantation owners were forced to either pay wages (though few had money or access to it, in the postwar economic chaos) or, increasingly, to break their

landholdings into family-sized plots and let African Americans farm it on a share basis.

The Emergence of Sharecropping. By the early 1870s the sharecropping system was solidifying. From the point of view of the freedmen, sharecropping permitted them to operate as family-sized economic units and to function with some measure of economic autonomy, but their measure of autonomy soon began to shrink. As they entered the new marketplace and began purchasing clothing, farming supplies, and other store goods, blacks put themselves under the control of storekeepers and former planters, who took out liens on future crops and thus bound the freedmen ever more tightly to cotton farming. One Alabama merchant gloated, "I have sold Jack Peters' negroes more goods this year than ever I sold Peters, and he owned 450 negroes." Ultimately in the postwar South, the entrenchment of a "free market" undid much of the gains of freedom itself.

Sources:

Eric Foner, *Reconstruction: America's Unfinished Revolution, 1863–1877* (New York: Harper & Row, 1988);

Gavin Wright, *Old South, New South: Revolutions in the Southern Economy Since the Civil War* (New York: Basic Books, 1986).

INDUSTRIALIZATION: THE SPREAD OF THE FACTORY SYSTEM

The Conversion to Factory Production. In 1880 Census official Carroll D. Wright reported that of the nearly three million Americans working "in the mechanical industries of this country," at least four-fifths were working "under the factory system." Large-scale factories, in other words, were replacing artisanal shops and handicraft production. The trend had begun in the early 1800s in the textile industry. Over the 1850s, 1860s, and 1870s the transformation rippled outward to a host of other industries. Surveying the economic landscape, Wright found that factory production methods had overhauled "the manufacture of boots and shoes, of watches, musical instruments, clothing, agricultural implements, metallic goods generally, fire-arms, carriages and wagons, wooden goods, rubber goods, and even the slaughtering of hogs."

The Scale of Production. These factories did not yet operate on the scale of modern national and multinational industrial complexes. Even the largest operations, the textile mills of Waltham and Lowell, Massachusetts, were still contained in size and fixed to single locations. The new businesses tended to be privately held: larger factories, mills, or mines were often owned by partnerships or groups of associates, but they were not yet public companies owned by stockholders or run by boards, and capital was generally raised locally, by local entrepreneurs using local banks. Nevertheless, these factories represented manufacturing enterprise on an unprecedented scale. They were new kinds of businesses, structured along new lines: they required substantial capitalization (several hundred thousand dollars for the larger factories, up to as much as $500,000); they employed hundreds of workers, paying them cash or company "scrip," at hourly, weekly, or piece-rate wages; and they usually operated under the direction of salaried middle managers. Manufacturing, in other words, was starting to become "big business."

Shoe Manufacturing. The conversion of the shoe and boot manufacturing industry that emerged in Lynn, Massachusetts, and other New England towns was fairly typical. Over the early decades of the nineteenth century this industry had taken shape as a series of scattered, small-scale manufacturing operations that combined initial preparation (cutting soles and leather uppers) in numerous small shops with outsourcing of stitching and binding: shop owners would dispatch wagons to make the rounds among local farm families, dropping off materials and picking up finished work. Much of the labor, in other words, was performed in family homes, between the household tasks and farm chores. The spread of sewing machines in the 1850s (which dropped in price over this decade from $75-100 to about $20) began to tranform the industry, encouraging manufacturers to bring stitching into their shops, where they could oversee the labor and increase and regularize their rate of production. By 1860, what the U.S. Census of that year called "a silent revolution" was unmistakably overhauling shoemaking in Lynn, Natick, and a dozen smaller New England towns. Manufacturers now ran larger shops, several stories high, with cutters and sorters working on ground floors and stitchers (usually women) working on upper floors, as many as three or four dozen in a shop. Steam engines powered the sewing machines; carts on wheeled rails carried materials to and from elevators. Workers labored under the watchful eyes of managers, at regular hours marked by time clocks. Shoemaking had become an industrial business.

The "Great Strike." Industrialization established not only a new kind of manufactory, but a new kind of workplace, with sharply different labor conditions and relations. Here too Lynn's shoe and boot industry signaled general trends—trends that became sharply clear in 1860 when workers set off the largest strike the nation had ever seen. The Panic of 1857 hit Lynn as it had elsewhere, driving factory owners to make drastic cuts in business, employment levels, and wages. Tensions simmered for a few years, then boiled over in the winter of 1860, when the workers of Lynn and other shoe-manufacturing centers in Massachusetts and New Hampshire struck for higher wages. The workers commenced the strike on Washington's birthday—a gesture attempting to tie their protests to the traditional, artisinal economic ideals of the early republic. Over the next six weeks, processions repeatedly marched through the city streets, drawing thousands of workers and sympathetic members of the community. On 16 March, at the climax of these processions, a parade of six thousand protesters assembled, including companies of firemen, brass bands, mili-

tiamen, and several worker delegations from other towns. Women workers and family members played a prominent role in several of the demonstrations.

The Owners Respond. The manufacturers rounded up replacement labor, and when strikers tried to intimidate incoming "scabs," or strikebreaking workers, owners prevailed on the mayor to call up the state militia and police forces from outside Lynn. As these forces entered the city in late February, skirmishes erupted, eventually forcing the militiamen and police officers to withdraw. Through March the strikers' resolve remained firm, but into April the movement lost momentum. Some manufacturers agreed to pay higher wages, though they resisted signing new bills of wages, refusing to countenance worker negotiation in setting wage levels. It was a tense kind of truce and, for onlookers, an ominous portent of things to come, as American employers and workers began to adjust to assembly lines, factory wages, industrial capitalist ownership, and organized labor.

Sources:

Alan Dawley, *Class and Community: The Industrial Revolution in Lynn* (Cambridge, Mass.: Harvard University Press, 1976);

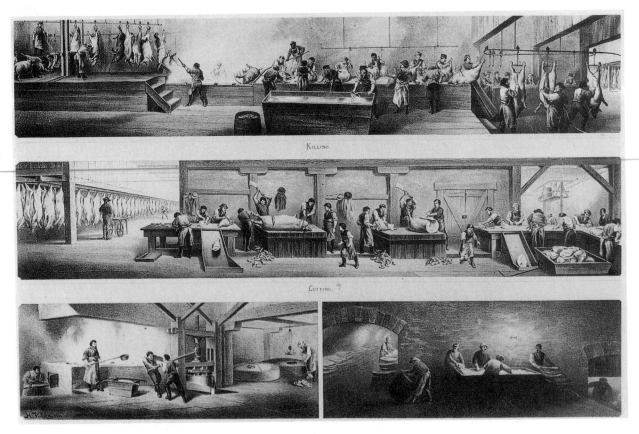

Illustrations of a Cincinnati pork-packing plant, 1873, showing workers extracting everything possible from the carcass

Edward Chase Kirkland, *Industry Comes of Age: Business, Labor and Public Policy, 1860–1897* (New York: Holt, Rinehart & Winston, 1961).

THE RAILROADS: EXPANSION AND ECONOMIC TRANSFORMATION IN THE MIDWEST

Wider Markets. Before the middle of the nineteenth century, the economic highways of the nation lay along its waterways: the coastlines and rivers, and, after 1810, the artificial rivers carved into the land in the form of canals. But by 1850 the railroads were beginning to redraw the economic map, connecting regions along radically new lines, opening overland channels of buying and selling. As the U.S. Senate observed in an 1852 report analyzing the profound impact of the railroads, the cost of overland transportation confined prerailroad, landlocked farmers to tight circles of distribution: estimating the cost of wagon transportation at 15 cents per ton per mile, and the value of wheat at $1.50 per bushel, the Senate calculated that a farmer transporting his crop "with only a common earth road as an avenue" would spend its entire sale value getting it to a market 330 miles away. The railroad, however, could carry a ton of wheat for 1.5 cents per mile—a tenth of the cost. Suddenly the farmer's potential market orbit leapt outward by a factor of ten.

Midwestern Development. The implications of railroad transportation proved especially significant for settlement and development in the Midwest. Initial settlement over this region had followed riverine paths south—clustering along the water routes that carried ultimately to the Mississippi and the Gulf of Mexico. The great entrepot of the West up until about 1850 was New Orleans, which channeled produce from thousands of river flatboats and steamboats to ocean-going ships bound for Atlantic and European markets. But in the 1840s, the northern midwestern states began building canal and railroad linkage eastward, opening direct connections to the metropolitan markets of the urban Atlantic. In the 1850s the total railroad mileage in Indiana, Missouri, and Iowa climbed from 339 to 6,635 miles. Illinois laid down 2,500 miles of track over this same, pivotal decade. These new lines of transportation quickly rerouted the traffic of midwestern produce to flow east, rather than south. By 1850 Chicago was handling as much grain as Saint Louis, and by 1854 more grain was moving along the Great Lakes than through New Orleans. It was moving in different forms, too: grain traveled through river ports such as Saint Louis in burlap sacks, crossing the levee on the backs of men and mules, to be loaded into flatboats and steamships. Grain flowed through the rising cities of the Midwest, through Buffalo, Milwaukee, and above all Chicago, in railroad cars carrying 325 bushels each, to be sorted, graded, and loaded onto steam-powered conveyor belts to be borne up into grain elevators—into numbered bins where it

Directors of the Union Pacific confer in a private railroad car, circa 1860

waited to be dropped through chutes into other railroad cars or the holds of oceangoing ships.

Chicago. This transformation quickly made Chicago the nerve center and metropolitan hub of the northern Midwest. As the new map of railroad transportation unfolded, the city became a key terminal. In 1852 two lines, the Michigan Southern and the Michigan Central, first linked Chicago to New York, the most important eastern market and Atlantic shipping center. Meanwhile, to the west, a spreading web of smaller railroad lines began drawing in the produce of not only northern Illinois, but Wisconsin, Michigan, Indiana, and Iowa as well. These railroads formed a powerful circulating system with Chicago at its heart: a western network of capillary lines that assembled the products of western farms in bits and pieces, to form the bulk shipments that flowed east along the thicker arteries of the trunk lines. By 1857, only five years after linking itself to New York, Chicago was channeling millions of bushels of grain annually through a

dozen grain elevators. By 1877 the New York Central Railroad was running sixteen miles of freight cars daily from Chicago.

New Relations. But the changes wrought by the railroads went well beyond geography. The transformation was also, in economic terms, structural. The key figure in the earlier, prerailroad economic system had been the local storekeeper of a given region, who received produce from area farmers in exchange for food, seed, and manufactured goods (clothing, farming tools and implements, medicines). Typically, little cash changed hands in these transactions; more often, the exchange was effected via barter or store credit. Thus while the farmer operated within a larger market economy—ultimately much of his produce went to distant buyers and sellers—transactions were mediated on a microeconomic scale by personal, face-to-face dealings. In other words, this was still a world of personal connections and ties. With the rise of Chicago and the other urban centers of the Midwest, a

Golden spike ceremony at Promontory, Utah, on 10 May 1869, marking the completion of the first transcontinental rail line

new economic order and a new world of business relations began to form. Farmers getting their crops to market now began to deal, at least implicitly, with a host of faceless figures: railroad managers, grain elevator warehouse men, urban grain merchants, wholesalers and dealers, food processors, and manufacturers. The new path to market was more efficient (railroad transportation and handling by grain elevator sharply reduced the labor costs of shipment, for example), but it was also much more distant and depersonalized.

Commodity Trading. Meanwhile, as the scale of handling, shipment, and storage grew, grain elevator receipts began to trade hands, replacing actual sacks or grain samples and becoming an instrument of exchange that functioned much like currency. In Chicago a new agency, the Board of Trade, became a central way to coordinate and oversee the buying and selling of grain in bulk. The Board, called the Change (or Exchange), quickly assumed the quasi-regulatory authority to grade grain so that it could be stored in common bins (regardless of who originally sold or owned a given bushel). And that transformation in turn facilitated the growth of futures trading—that is, the buying and selling not of grain itself, but of "to arrive" contracts agreeing to supply grain at set future dates at an agreed-on price. So grain trading at the Board became a speculative market, with

"bulls" and "bears" betting, alternatively, that prices of a given commodity would rise or fall. The opening of telegraph communication fueled these speculative fires, rapidly flashing long-distance information about the prospects of western crop conditions and the prices at eastern markets.

Railroads and Prairie Consumption. The new channels of production and distribution worked both ways: farmers not only sold to distant, urban markets, they bought from those same markets too. Trains carrying crops to market in Chicago returned to the agricultural heartland of the Midwest carrying lumber, furniture, clothing, toys, musical instruments, newspapers—a wide assortment of consumer goods. Among other items, Midwestern farmers invested heavily in new kinds of farm machinery. By 1851 Cyrus McCormick's Chicago factory was making over a thousand mechanical reapers a year, and most of them were being bought and used in the Midwest—one-fourth in northern Illinois alone. John Deere was manufacturing more than ten thousand plows annually by the eve of the Civil War. By the 1870s Midwestern farmers were becoming accustomed to using mechanical reapers, harvesters, and binders, as well as increasingly sophisticated plows, mowers, and spreaders. Within a few decades farmers had come to depend on such implements and, by implication, the manufacturers and sellers of this machinery.

The fiercest and most notorious of the financial railroad struggles pitted Jay Gould against shipping magnate Cornelius Vanderbilt, "the Commodore." Over the 1860s Vanderbilt had invested heavily in railroads, securing financial control over the New York Central, which carried a lucrative traffic between Buffalo and New York City. The main competitive threat to the New York Central came from the Erie, a railroad Gould and his allies had bailed out of financial difficulties in the depression of 1857, then joined the board in order to manipulate its stock price on the New York Stock Exchange. When Vanderbilt moved on the Erie in 1867, Gould (together with Daniel Drew and Big Jim Fisk) maneuvered slyly, issuing thousands of shares of watered-down stock. Once Vanderbilt's unsuspecting agents bought up the largely worthless certificates, the Commodore was trapped; Gould printed thousands more that Vanderbilt was forced to buy in order to hold up the value of his earlier purchases. Vanderbilt obtained a court injunction and arrest warrants for the Erie gang, driving Drew, Fisk, and Gould across the Hudson to New Jersey, beyond the reach of New York law, carrying $7 million. Both sides lobbied (and freely bribed) the New York legislature in dueling efforts for legislative relief. Eventually the parties negotiated a settlement, in which Vanderbilt swallowed significant losses. When Charles Francis Adams exposed the tawdry affair in a series of articles titled "Chapters of Erie," he generated a good deal of momentum for reform.

McCormick: Rural Distribution. It was the railroads that enabled manufacturers like Cyrus McCormick not only to set up shop, but also to build up a national and ultimately an international network of customers. Reliable year-round transportation permitted factory managers to set up smooth inflows of raw material and outflows of manufactured products, regularizing production itself. On the consumption end, McCormick learned through trial and error how to make the new possibilities of national marketing work. Initially the company relied on territorial agents, each overseeing a district and hiring subagents or dealers to make sales, service and repair machines, and handle credit arrangements for local customers. By the late 1870s McCormick was refining this marketing structure, centralizing control, replacing regional agents with salaried managers, and converting subagents into franchised dealers; competitors soon followed suit.

Source:

William Cronon, *Nature's Metropolis: Chicago and the Great West* (New York: Norton, 1991).

THE RAILROADS: FINANCE

"The Most Developing Force." Charles Francis Adams decided to devote his public career to studying and writing about railroads because over the middle decades of the nineteenth century they became, as he put it, "the most developing force and largest field of the day." After a burst of construction over the 1850s, in which the nation's railroad mileage grew from 8,879 to 30,626, the railroads emerged as a key industrial infrastructure, and at the same time as the country's biggest business and one of the era's most pressing public policy issues. In other words, the new economy was not only carried by railroads; it was driven by railroads. As sources of transportation they pinned together the new agricultural and industrial landscape, and as businesses they themselves led many of the transformations reworking the national economy. By the time of the Civil War the railroads dwarfed other American businesses in capital, labor, and geographic scale of operation. Thus the development of a rail network required the pioneering of new business methods of finance and management.

Federal Land Grants. Up to 1850 federal construction or funding of internal improvements such as roads and canals remained politically controversial. But federal policy shifted in 1850, when Congress authorized a federal grant of some 3.7 million acres of public land to the states of Illinois, Mississippi, and Alabama to help promote and finance railroad construction. Specifically, the grant allocated a two-hundred-foot right-of-way corridor, and alternating parcels of land on either side of that corridor. This grant, converted into mortgages secured by the land, became the chief source of capital for the Illinois Central and other railroads. It was the first grant of its kind, and it set a precedent; other federal land grants followed in 1852, 1853, 1856, and 1857—grants that dispensed land totaling close to 18 million acres.

The Appetite for Capital. Congress started committing federal assistance for railroad construction in the 1850s in part because the railroads then being projected from the eastern seaboard into the continent were substantially larger than earlier railroads, and they needed huge amounts of capital—more than American businesses had ever raised before. In 1850 the nation's largest railroad, connecting Worcester and Albany, cost $8 million. This figure far surpassed the investment required to capitalize the factories of this period: by comparison, all but the largest textile mills and ironmaking or metalworking factories were less than $1 million each. But even the Worcester and Albany's price tag paled in comparison to the money needed to finance the east-west trunk lines of the early 1850s. Railroads such as the Erie or the Pennsylvania cost tens of millions of dollars, and the smaller new western railroads in the Northwest still ate up substantial amounts of capital—over $10 million apiece.

New Financial Markets. Earlier railroads had survived by drawing largely on local sources of capital;

Stock certificate issued to the Union Pacific Railroad for shares in the dummy construction company Crédit Mobilier.

most of the money that built a line came from farmers and other businesspeople up and down the route or at either terminus. But local sources could not satisfy the intensive capital requirements of constructing, maintaining, and operating the new railroads. New sources of capital had to be found, and new ways of mobilizing that capital. In the 1850s railroad finance came to rely on bond issues marketed in the eastern cities of the United States and abroad in Europe. By 1859 American railroad corporations had floated bonds worth more than $1.1 billion—$700 million of it from the previous decade alone.

New York. It was over this decade, in response to these financial pressures, that New York City became the financial capital of the nation and the New York Stock Exchange assumed essentially its modern form. Organized in 1817, the New York Stock and Exchange Board (as it was originally called) remained for decades a small-scale operation attended by a few dozen brokers, handling a few hundred trades a week. But as the investment market in railroad and municipality securities multiplied, activity at the Board accelerated. Soon the weekly volume of trade was registering not in the hundreds, but in the hundreds of thousands. In 1863 it took on its modern name—the New York Stock Exchange—and in 1865 it opened its first permanent headquarters at the corner of Broad and Wall streets, making the term "Wall Street" synonymous with high finance. Certain investment-banking partnerships began to specialize in railroad finance. Brokers began to develop

modern speculative techniques: selling "long" and "short" positions in stocks, and dealing in puts and calls. Some speculators proved espcially adept at manipulating this new marketplace, acquiring (and sometimes losing) vast sums, as well as notorious reputations. A generation of "Robber Barons," businessmen who became wealthy through exploitation, came to the forefront—men such as Daniel Drew, Jim Fisk, and Jay Gould, the "Mephistopheles of Wall Street."

Postwar. The Civil War checked the pace of railroad building, but only temporarily; the coming of peace released a burst of pent-up construction. Between the end of the war and the depression of 1873, thirty-five thousand miles of track were laid—more than doubling the nation's total railroad mileage. Some of this new construction reached into new territories, but other projects paralleled existing railroads, competing for traffic or financial leverage. Railroad construction became a dangerous, high-stakes game as speculators contended with each other and with railroad managers for control. Still, over this period the railroad network pushed deeply into the western and southern parts of the country. By the middle of the 1870s railroads were beginning to explore ways to check increasingly destructive rate wars. Meanwhile, two of the largest railroads, the Pennsylvania and the Baltimore and Ohio, had assembled the nation's first self-contained trunk and feeder systems on a regional scale.

Sources:

Alfred D. Chandler Jr., *The Visible Hand: The Managerial Revolution in American Business* (Cambridge, Mass.: Harvard University Press, 1977);

The growth of the Pennsylvania Railroad—the largest U.S. railroad in the 1870s—gives a good impression of how large the scale of railroad business was starting to become. It was not yet typical, but it was a sign of things to come. After an aggressive five-year program of expansion beginning in 1869, the Pennsylvania owned or controlled railroads and canals capitalized at $398 million, earning net profits (in 1873) of $25 million. The company owned almost one thousand miles of railroad outright and, through financial leverage, controlled another five thousand miles. Outside of the United States, only two other *countries*—Britain and France—contained more mileage than the Pennsylvania. The system as a whole encompassed a transportation empire extending from the Hudson River to Massachusetts, and from the Great Lakes to the Potomac. Moreover, for a short period of time, the Pennsylvania organized overseas shipping and steamship lines, mining operations, and steelworks; though the company eventually pulled back to concentrate on running its vast railroad operations. Over this period the company employed more than 50,000 workers, and needed over 1,000 managers to supervise them.

Julius Grodinsky, *Jay Gould: His Business Career* (Philadelphia: University of Pennsylvania Press, 1957);

George Rogers Taylor, *The Transportation Revolution, 1815-1860* (New York: Rinehart, 1951).

SELLING IN THE NEW MARKETPLACE

Toward Mass Distribution. With the spread of the railroads, shipments of goods began crisscrossing the country more swiftly, in larger volumes, and on steadier schedules than ever before—a development that rapidly worked structural commercial change. Mass distribution, in short, accompanied the rise of mass production; the new landscape of railroads, factories, and industrial cities grew a new commercial network of distributors, department stores, and mail-order houses. It was a far-reaching transformation, and it would take decades longer to complete, but it was well underway by the end of the 1870s. Already the nascent outlines of a modern consumer economy were growing clear.

Pre-Railroad. In the early nineteenthth century, few Americans were plugged into anything like a consumer-goods economy. Most clothing was made in family households, and products such as tools, shoes, furniture, and even firearms were usually made by local craftspeople and acquired by means of barter or book credit.

Those goods that came from beyond the village or surrounding countryside typically came by way of traveling peddlers or through country stores. Keeping a country store during this period meant stocking a general assortment of goods, accepting farmers' crops and produce in payment, and extending long credits to local customers to get them through harvest times. It also required making annual buying trips to a commercial entrepot like New York City, Philadelphia, or Baltimore, to stock up for each coming year.

Wholesaling. The railroads undid this world in several stages. The first stage of change happened behind the counter, in the wholesaling of goods. As manufactured goods began to flow out of American factories, a new group of middlemen—"jobbers"—positioned themselves to buy them up in bulk and distribute them to country stores. The jobbers first infiltrated the northern and middle Atlantic states, then developed midwestern territories as rail connections hooked hinterlands into cities such as Cincinnati, Saint Louis, and above all Chicago. By 1866 Chicago, at the railroad hub of the Midwest, had fifty-nine jobbers handling sales of more than $1 million. After the war, Southern systems proliferated along much the same lines, networking the country stores that were then forming (in the wake of the dismantling of the plantations) as the region's rural commercial nodes. With the coming of the wholesalers, storekeepers left off their annual buying trips; now the jobbers dispatched traveling salesmen to them, men called "drummers," who carried trunks full of samples and catalogues, and telegraphed a storekeeper's orders into the home office. The largest of the jobbers was A. T. Stewart, who by 1870 had amassed a business with sales of $50 million ($42 million wholesale, $8 million retail) and a workforce of two thousand drummers, clerks, managers, and other employees.

Department Stores. Meanwhile, in urban areas, denser market concentrations permitted even more direct connections between manufacturers and customers. Here innovation happened at the retail level, in the form of the department store. Rowland H. Macy was an important early example. His early career was checkered: four times he started stores; four times he went under, the last failure (in Haverhill, Massachusetts) forcing him into bankruptcy. But when he moved his efforts to New York City, the largest urban market in the country, Macy's fortunes turned. He set up his fifth store in 1858 on Sixth Avenue near Fourteenth Street, and business quickly thrived. Like other successful department stores, Macy's sold a widening assortment of goods at low prices, maintaining low profit margins and counting on high volume to make profits. It also sold its products at set prices, clearly labeled on affixed tags; earlier retail establishments had tended to set prices in negotiations with customers, but for the department stores, where dozens or even hundreds of clerks handled customers'

THE GREAT QUESTION SETTLED!!
SEWING BY MACHINERY, ONCE DEEMED IMPOSSIBLE, IS NOW AN ESTABLISHED FACT.

Seven Gold and Silver Medals awarded at public Fairs in different States, to

I. M. SINGER,
FOR THE BEST
SEWING MACHINE,
Prove conclusively the immense superiority of this Labor-saving Instrument.

SINGER'S PATENT
Straight Needle, Perpendicular Action
SEWING MACHINE,
Secured by two distinct Patents in the U. S.

No. 323 Broadway, New York.
BRANCH OFFICES:
57 South Fourth Street, Philadelphia,   159 Baltimore Street, Baltimore,
251 Washington Street, Boston,   197 Elm Street, Cincinnati.
I. M. SINGER & CO.

An 1853 advertisement for the Singer Sewing Machine. Singer was the first U.S. corporation to spend $1 million a year for advertising.

purchases, uniform price systems became the rule. Macy's operated on a cash-only basis, both in its sales and its stock purchases, enabling the company to more easily weather the economy's periodic financial panics. By 1870 the store was stocking an impressive array of goods—including dry goods, men's hosiery and ties, linens and towels, costume jewelry, silver, and clocks—and was doing more than $1 million worth of business.

Merchandise. The department stores depended on their urban locations to concentrate client bases. But their impact was ultimately felt beyond the cities, for they prefigured an even wider dispersal of mass retailing via the mail-order houses and the chain stores such as Woolworth's that emerged later in the nineteenth century. The department stores represented not just new kinds of commercial establishments, but new patterns of selling and of buying—indeed, new concepts of consumer goods as store merchandise, arrayed in windows and advertisements, priced and tagged. Department stores competed in creating lavish displays and environ-

ments that stimulated customers' appetites. Wanamakers, for example, Philadelphia's grandest department store, erected a huge silk tent in the center of the store and created within it a luxurious, carpeted, and chandeliered ballroom setting where ladies could shop for evening gowns.

Brand Names and Packaging. It was during this period that trademarks and brand names appeared and quickly began to be a critical part of doing business on a national scale. One early manufacturer to adopt these techniques was the Smith Brothers, who concocted cough drops at their factory in Poughkeepsie, New York, and shipped them to general stores and drugstores nationwide. Finding in the late 1860s that competitors were releasing imitations under names such as "Schmitt Brothers" and "Smythe Brothers," the Smiths responded by registering their portraits as a trademark and emblazoning the images on the glass bowls in which the cough drops were sold. But this measure still left the company vulnerable to unscrupulous retailers who filled the bowls with cheaper imitations, so in 1872 Smith Brothers began packaging their cough drops in "factory-filled"

MARGARET GETCHELL

One of the key figures in Macy's early years was Margaret Getchell, who rose to become a central manager and, very possibly, one of the first woman business executives in America. Originally a schoolteacher, she came into the company (she was Macy's cousin) as a cashier and was quickly promoted to the position of bookkeeper. As her management potential became clear, Macy elevated her again in 1866, to the job of superintendent, which put her in a position directly under his own in the store's managerial hierarchy. Three years later, she married Abiel LaForge, a salesman with the company. Initially after marrying she kept her position at the company, working alongside her husband, running the store while he focused on merchandising. But when the couple had their first child, Getchell's status within the company shifted: while LaForge became a partner in the firm, Getchell gave up her job as superintendent. She continued sporadically to assist in managing the store; for one three-month period while Macy and LaForge traveled to Europe on a buying trip she ran operations single-handedly (and pregnant with her third child). But she received only token presents from Macy for this work. Executive business responsibilities remained the domain of men during this period, even when women displayed unmistakable managerial competence.

Source: Bruce Levine and others, *Who Built America?*, 2 volumes (New York: Pantheon, 1989, 1992).

Farmers adjusted uneasily to being enmeshed in distant markets. Tensions flared over railroad and grain elevator rates, grain price fluctuations, banks and interest rates. Agrarian politics grew especially heated in the decades following the Civil War, when falling grain prices and deflationary pressures squeezed farmers who had to repay loans with currency that was worth substantially more than it had been when they borrowed it. Late in 1867, these impulses found organized political expression in the Patrons of Husbandry, a secret association organizing in Washington, D.C. The Grangers, as they were popularly known, quickly grew in numbers and spread across the agricultural heartland. A Farmers' Convention held in Springfield, Illinois, adopted typical resolutions, including a denouncement of "all chartered monopolies" and a call for legislation "fixing reasonable maximum rates" for railroad freights and passengers. In the same vein, the Declaration of Purpose of the National Grange in 1874 advocated cooperative marketing and purchasing ventures among farmers, the elimination of the middlemen who seemed to stand between farmers and their ultimate customers, and the establishment of agricultural and technical colleges. Meanwhile, calls for state regulation of railroad and warehouse rates first came to fruition in Illinois in 1871, followed by Wisconsin and Iowa several years later. Intrastate railroad regulation proved ineffective, however, and by the 1880s the agrarians were turning their attention to Congress.

boxes, each bearing the company's trademark. (Smith Brothers employed families in Poughkeepsie to fill the boxes, each with sixteen cough drops; every evening a wagon would drop off five-gallon cans of cough drops and stacks of boxes, and pick up the boxes that had been filled the previous day.) The first cough drops to be marketed, Smith Brothers joined a growing number of factory-packaged, trademarked products on store shelves.

Mail Order: Montgomery Ward. The man who devised the nation's first mail-order company had experienced business at each step in the commercial chain on the path to market. As a young man Aaron Montgomery Ward ran a general store in Saint Joseph, Michigan, then worked for Field, Palmer, and Leiter, Chicago's largest wholesale dry-goods house, then traveled as a drummer for another jobber based in Saint Louis. He thus developed a working sense of both how goods moved through the modern economy and how they were received by customers in the countryside. At some point in his early career, Ward conceived of a new way of marketing goods that cut out the jobber and the country store, namely, doing business by connecting directly with customers through the mails. It was a radical stroke, and it fit neatly with the spirit of the times: just as Ward opened his business in 1872, rural, agrarian hostility toward "parasitic middlemen" such as jobbers and grain warehouse men was driving farmers to organize marketing and purchasing cooperatives of their own. Ward started off with one partner, capital of only $2,400, and a "catalogue" that consisted of a single sheet listing 163 items. Within a few years, the purchasing agencies of the National Grange endorsed the company and began placing orders. Ward emblazoned the endorsement, advertising his firm as "THE ORIGINAL WHOLESALE GRANGE SUPPLY HOUSE" and vowing to sell to "Patrons of Husbandry, Farmers and Mechanics at Wholesale Prices." His prices were low, and business boomed. Within two years the catalogue had grown to eight pages; two years after that it was 150 pages and illustrated with woodcut engravings. By the end of the 1880s the company was doing more than $1 million worth of business a year.

Sources:

William Cronon, *Nature's Metropolis: Chicago and the Great West* (New York: Norton, 1991);

Robert Hendrickson, *The Grand Emporiums: The Illustrated History of America's Great Department Stores* (New York: Stein & Day, 1979);

Glenn Porter and Harold C. Livesay, *Merchants and Manufacturers: Studies in the Changing Structure of Nineteenth-Century Marketing* (Baltimore: Johns Hopkins University Press, 1971).

CHARLES FRANCIS ADAMS JR.

1835-1915

RAILROAD COMMISSIONER AND EXECUTIVE

An Adams and the Railroads. Charles Francis Adams Jr. was born in patrician circumstances, into a line that stretched back to two presidents: his grandfather was John Quincy Adams and his great-grandfather John Adams. Yet for Charles's generation, the responsibilities of leadership and public service would be not only heavy burdens, but vexing challenges. Charles Francis Adams took on an especially daunting task when, well into his career, he set out to reform the most dynamic force in American business at the time: the railroads.

Youth and Early Career. Adams spent his early years ensconced in elite Boston circles, attending the Boston Public Latin School, then Harvard, and, upon graduating, reading law at the prominent Boston firm of Dana and Parker. For several years after passing the bar Adams practiced in Boston, but half-heartedly—a purpose in life, he felt, was eluding him. When the Civil War broke out, things took an exhilarating turn. Adams promptly enlisted in the Union army, leading a black regiment, seeing action at Antietam and Gettysburg, and rising to the rank of colonel. With the coming of peace, he determined to fashion a public career for himself by developing an expertise in railroad policy.

Essayist. He first made his mark, in true Adams style, with his pen, publishing articles on the railroads beginning in 1867. Early general essays such as the "The Railroad System," published in the *North American Review,* gained him some notice, but Adams's most effective and popular piece was "A Chapter of Erie," which chronicled the outrageous and politically corrupt antics of Cornelius Vanderbilt, Jay Gould, Daniel Drew, and Jim Fisk as they contested for financial control of the Erie Railroad. By the time Adams started this piece, he had become convinced that the proper way to exert public regulatory control over the railroads was by means of commissions—expert, apolitical bodies armed with general mandates to represent the public interest. Adams lobbied hard for the creation of a Massachusetts commission, and in 1869 these efforts bore fruit when the state legislature established the Massachusetts Board of Railroad Commissioners and the governor appointed Adams to one of its three seats. Adams spent the next ten years running the commission, de facto until he became chairman in 1872.

Commissioner. Armed with a brief but broad charge, the commission suited Adams's initial instinct to effect change by, on the one hand, educating the public about the business of running railroads and, on the other, persuading the railroads to act responsibly in the public interest. The commission enjoyed prestige among both the public and the Massachusetts railroads, and little effective power. Early commission accomplishments included arbitrating labor disagreements, investigating accidents and promulgating safety recommendations (including the use of telegraphs to coordinate traffic and prevent accidents), and codifying existing railroad regulations. Adams grew increasingly frustrated with the limits of the commission and its lack of enforcement powers, however, and in 1878 he left.

Executive. The following year, Adams crossed over, in effect, to the ranks of railroad executives. From 1879 to 1884 he served in Albert Fink's Eastern Trunk Line Association, which the railroads themselves had set up in an effort to end the crippling rate wars that were breaking out between competing lines. The experience dampened Adams's enthusiasm for interrailroad cooperation, as the lines more often than not ignored their association's agreements and judgements. In 1884 Adams assumed the presidency of the Union Pacific, which was reeling under the weight of heavy debt and public censure because of its involvement in the Crédit Mobilier scandal. If Adams's unimpeachable public reputation lent the troubled railroad some measure of respectability, though, he proved ill-suited to day-to-day railroad management. The Union Pacific paid off its debt but then embarked on an ill-advised campaign of expansion. In 1890 Adams was forced out when Gould (whom Adams had deftly castigated in Erie reportage) secured financial power. Adams spent his remaining years much as he had begun his career: in writing, public advocacy, and travel.

Sources:

Edward Chase Kirkland, *Charles Francis Adams, Jr., 1835-1915: The Patrician at Bay* (Cambridge, Mass.: Harvard University Press, 1965);

Thomas K. McCraw, *Prophets of Regulation: Charles Francis Adams, Louis D. Brandeis, James M. Landis, Alfred E. Kahn* (Cambridge, Mass.: Harvard University Press, 1984).

GAIL BORDEN JR.

1801-1874
INVENTOR; INDUSTRIAL ENTREPRENEUR

Condensed Milk. It was not meteoric or sensational, but the rise of Gail Borden Jr.'s business selling condensed milk was emblematic of the transformations overtaking the American economy. Ultimately the emergence of products like Borden's cans of condensed milk signaled how profoundly new industrial processes would alter not just production and distribution, but the fundamental patterns and expectations of everyday life in American kitchens and at American tables.

Go West. Borden was born in 1801 in rural, upstate New York. Like so many others, his family moved west, first to Kentucky, then to the Indiana Territory. As a young man Borden taught school and surveyed land in Mississippi. Shortly after marrying, he picked up and moved again, further west, to join his family in Texas. Here he performed more surveys and served as an agent for the Galveston City Company, which was developing and selling the properties that eventually made up the city of Galveston. Along the way, he devised several inventions, including the prairie schooner (a wagon powered by sails), and the lazy Susan, a revolving tray used for serving food. Thus Borden played a key and varied role in western expansion and settlement. Indeed, as editor of the *Telegraph and Texas Register,* he is credited with writing the headline that became a rallying cry in the war against Mexico: "Remember the Alamo."

Trial and Error. To this point, Borden had lived a life of some local civic accomplishment and solid respectability. But he made his most lasting mark in his forties and fifties, when he began to experiment with food-processing techniques. As an agent and promoter of western settlement in frontier conditions, he had recognized the utility of preparing food in concentrated, portable forms, and he now turned his knack for invention in this direction. First he concocted the "meat biscuit," which was nonperishable (if less than savory). Borden invested heavily in this venture, but it sank commercially, in part because of opposition from competitors vying for army contracts. Still, the meat biscuit earned him international recognition, including a trip to London where Queen Victoria conferred the Great Council Medal on Borden in 1851.

Inspiration. It was on the passage back to the United States, Borden later recalled, that inspiration struck for the product that would make him literally a household name. When several children died on board the ship from drinking contaminated milk, Borden set about finding a way to preserve milk. Eventually he succeeded, by evaporating the milk in a vacuum pan over slow heat. (Though he called the product "condensed milk," what kept it from spoiling was not the evaporation, but the heat, which killed the bacteria.) This accomplishment did not readily or easily translate into commercial success, however. Borden did not manage to persuade the U.S. Patent Office to confer a patent on his technique until 1856. And the resulting business struggled to attract customers for its new product. After several early efforts, Borden formed a partnership in 1858 with wholesale grocer, banker, and railroad financier Jeremiah Milbank. This enterprise, called the New York Condensed Milk Company, began to do business in earnest after one of its advertisements appeared in an issue of *Leslie's Illustrated Weekly* that happened to contain an article exposing the unsanitary conditions of New York's dairies (including the fact that many city dairy men added chalk and eggs to their product). Local sales grew quickly, and soon the company was delivering to a network of customers in New York City and Jersey City.

Success. Borden's eventual early success was therefore tied closely to several key aspects of doing business in the new economy: advertising and an urban market. The business took another leap forward (or in market terms, outward) at the outbreak of the Civil War, when the U.S. government began to order condensed milk for its troops. As the scale of the war grew, so did Borden's business, and with the coming of peacetime, the company enjoyed an established market of Civil War veterans. Business continued to thrive through 1874, when Borden died and management of the company passed along to his sons.

Significance. The expansion of Borden's market hinged directly on the experience of the war. Appropriately, the company emblazoned its product with an American bald eagle—an early example of the business trademarks that were beginning to label the products that moved through this new, national marketplace. The mark symbolized not only a new market, but ultimately a new kind of consumer good and a new pattern of consumption: originally designed for frontier portability and wartime durability, products such as Borden's condensed milk adapted readily to centralized, industrial production and distribution across a national scale. Though Borden himself may not have fully realized it, what he had done was to transform milk from an agricultural commodity that circulated in local networks (particularly before the spread of pasteurization) into a brand-name and a packaged product, well-suited for railroad transportation and ready-made for grocery shelves. It was not only a new kind of food, it was an altogether new sense of what food was and where it came from.

Source:

Alfred D. Chandler Jr., *The Visible Hand: The Managerial Revolution in American Business* (Cambridge, Mass.: Harvard University Press, 1977).

JAY COOKE

1821-1905
FINANCIER

Background. The Union's preeminent financier through the Civil War and into the 1870s was born on the western frontier. His father, Eleutheros Cooke, was a prominent lawyer and eventually congressman in Ohio, but the "Western Reserve" (which eventually became the state of Ohio) was during the period of Cooke's youth rugged and isolated. Cooke received his training in "high finance" by working at a series of commercial apprenticeships that took him gradually east, to the money markets he would one day dominate. He entered business at the age of fourteen as a clerk in his hometown of Sandusky, then moved to Saint Louis in 1836. When his employers there went under in the Panic of 1837, he relocated again, to Philadelphia where he found a clerkship with a canal packet line.

Philadelphia Banker. When he reached Philadelphia, Cooke had arrived at what was then still the financial capital of the country. In 1839 he changed jobs and put himself right at the heart of the money market when he joined the firm of E. W. Clark & Company, an unincorporated bank that functioned (like others in the city) as a kind of currency clearinghouse, buying up the notes of other, often distant banks at a discount and sending them back to the home institution for redemption. The work required a keen eye for counterfeits and an ability to keep track of which banknotes from where had what values—a complicated business in an economy that circulated innumerable currencies, notes, and other forms of money. After the Panic of 1857, Cooke retired from the firm.

Union Finance. By the time Cooke reentered business in 1861, new financial challenges and opportunities were forming. The outbreak of the Civil War caught the federal government at a bad time, fiscally speaking. The country had run deficits for four years since 1857—the longest stretch of deficit finance since the War of 1812. Secession intensified the pressure, draining gold from the treasury and undercutting the government's credit rating. Soon the government was having trouble meeting even its ordinary peacetime expenses. The incoming secretary of the treasury, former Ohio governor Salmon Chase, had worked with Cooke's brother, Henry, in Ohio politics and quickly adopted Cooke as an informal financial adviser. Initial issues of short-term bonds yielded lackluster results, but when Union defeat at the first Bull Run in July 1861 began to make the scale of the upcoming war clearer, Cooke first secured a $2 million infusion from Philadelphia bankers, on the security of three-year notes bearing interest of 7.3 percent ("seven-thirties"), then together with Chase brokered an agreement from the Associated Banks (a New York group) for $50 million more, again in seven-thirties. Thereupon Cooke returned to Philadelphia and converted his office into an agency promoting and subscribing the public securities of the Union.

Marketing the War Effort. Salmon Chase was determined to make war finance a broad, democratic, and propagandistic campaign, and Cooke adapted his financial promotions to this end. Anticipating twentieth-century war finance, Chase and Cooke (to borrow an anachronistic phrase) not only used the war to sell the bonds, but used the bonds to sell the war. Cooke orchestrated a massive public-relations campaign that ultimately enlisted more than 600,000 subscribers, perhaps as many as a million, and sold over $1 billion worth of securities. He grossed commissions of about $4 million for this service, though he also paid heavy advertising expenses and ran the agents himself; net profit probably came to about $700,000.

Postbellum Expansion and Bust. After the war Cooke converted his operations back to a general banking business, based in Philadelphia and opening branches in New York in 1866 (by which time the latter city had supplanted Philadelphia as the nation's financial capital), and in London in 1870. He became involved in many enterprises during this period of heady national economic expansion, most notably (and disastrously) the Northern Pacific Railroad. Construction on this railroad, projected to link Duluth on Lake Superior to Tacoma on the Washington coast, reached as far as the Missouri River from the east before Cooke's finances collapsed on 18 September 1873— in part because of unrelated failures in European financial markets. As Cooke went under, he pulled down enough affiliates with him to set off a general economic panic. In later years he managed to recover some of his holdings, and to develop a second fortune in western mining and other investments. The 1873 collapse, however, gave J. P. Morgan, his chief rival, the opportunity to supplant Cooke as the high financier of the federal government.

Source:
Henrietta M. Larson, *Jay Cooke: Private Banker* (Cambridge, Mass.: Harvard University Press, 1936).

LYDIA ESTES PINKHAM

1819-1883
SOCIAL REFORMER, PATENT-MEDICINE ENTREPRENEUR

A Household Name. Over the late nineteenth century, in the booming patent medicine industry, the most popular brand was "Lydia Pinkham's Vegetable Compound." Her name and likeness integral parts of the product's packaging, Pinkham became a household name and one of the best-known women of the period. And yet, she entered the business world late in her life, after spending thirty years as a housewife and mother, in a desperate effort to save her family from poverty.

Background. Pinkham's father was a shoemaker in Lynn, Massachusetts, where she lived virtually all her life. She went to school at the local academy and after graduating became a schoolteacher. In the decades before the Civil War she joined a number of the reform movements that emerged in northern antebellum middle-class circles, including abolitionism, temperance, Swedenborgianism, and women's rights. In 1843, at the age of twenty-four, she married Isaac Pinkham and settled into the traditional Victorian roles of wife and mother, rearing five children. She may well have remained in these roles all her life, but in 1873 her husband's real estate speculations collapsed amid the general financial panic, throwing the Pinkhams onto hard times.

Remedies. It was at this point that Lydia Pinkham made herself into an entrepreneur and her family into a business, when she began bottling and selling the home remedies she had been concocting for years and dispensing to neighbors and kin. Made principally from unicorn root and pleurisy root, with a healthy dose of alcohol (a "solvent and preservative"), they were popular in Lynn because they were thought to treat "female complaints" that many women were reluctant to discuss with their male doctors. The family put it on the market in 1875, starting in Lynn and beginning to widen their customer base. Business got off to a slow start, but the famly worked assiduously at promotion: Pinkham dispatched her sons through the area, and eventually across New England and New York to drum up sales. The family printed handbills and pamphlets, and solicited testimonials from customers and druggists. In 1876 the product began to circulate more widely when New York's major patent medicine broker, Charles N. Crittenden, took his first cash order. Newspaper advertisements in the *Boston Herald* cultivated the Boston market at around the same time. By her death in 1883, Lydia Pinkham's medicine was grossing $300,000 a year, and sales were still growing. The product remained popular well into the twentieth century, in part because the company continued to spend heavily on advertising.

"Homemade" in the Mass Marketplace. What ultimately put "Mrs. Pinkham's" across was the image the company built around their product. At the suggestion of Daniel, who had a good feel for the market, they began using Mrs. Pinkham's image on labels in 1879. They also adopted a general pitch that Daniel first suggested while traveling in New York and Brooklyn, trying to persuade druggists to sell the product. "If we should hitch on to the medicine somehow 'The Great New England Remedy,'" he predicted, "and then after awhile have our Trade Mark picture some New England Scenery with a humble cottage, these 'golds' would consider it homemade and rush for it, as they seem to be all tore out on homemade goods." It was a shrewd assessment, and a telling insight into Americans' ambivalence over the economic transformations happening all around them. Even if they were going to be mass-produced and distributed, it would be those goods that managed to create an aura of being "homemade" would attract customers in the new marketplace.

Source:
Robert Collyer Washburn, *The Life and Times of Lydia E. Pinkham* (New York: Putnam, 1931).

CORNELIUS VANDERBILT

1794-1877
SHIPPING MAGNATE, RAILROAD TYCOON

Beginnings. Fittingly, the man who built America's largest Civil War–era shipping and railroad empire was raised on the edge of the Narrows below New York —on the threshold of the city that would, over the course of his lifetime, become the financial capital and commercial center of the nation. Cornelius Vanderbilt was born in 1794 and moved with his family the following year to Stapleton, New York, between the Upper and Lower Bays. He embarked on his career as a shipper at a young age, purchasing a small sailboat when he was sixteen and immediately going into business ferrying passengers and freight between Staten Island and Manhattan. Over the course of his career, Vanderbilt's vessels grew progressively larger and grander, and eventually they would travel transoceanic routes, but his business would remain essentially the same until he made a decisive shift to railroads and multiplied his fortune several times over.

Growth. Vanderbilt's initial foray—the Staten Island ferrying service—launched his career fortuitously. Charging as little as 25 cents per round trip, Vanderbilt amassed $1,000 in his first year in business. During the War of 1812 he landed a government contract supplying six of the forts lining the Upper Bay. By 1817 he had compiled working capital of $10,000 and a fleet of five coasting vessels which he ran on trips from Boston to Delaware Bay, along with the ferry business. In 1818 Vanderbilt tied his fortunes to the new technology transforming shipping when he went to work for Thomas Gibbons operating a steamboat between New Jersey and New York. It was dicey work at first, since Gibbons operated in violation of a state monopoly Robert Fulton and Robert Livingston had secured from the New York legislature (and leased in turn to Aaron Ogden). But in 1824 Gibbons, with Vanderbilt as his lieutenant, managed to put the case before the U.S. Supreme Court, where John Marshall broke the monopoly in a famous decision, *Gibbons* v. *Ogden*, which reserved the regulation of interstate commerce for the federal government. By the time Gibbons died three years later, the Union Line under Vanderbilt's stewardship was earning an annual profit of $40,000. Unable to buy the line and unwilling to join Gibbons's son as a partner, Vanderbilt pulled out (buying several boats from the line as he left) and set up the Dispatch Line, which ran between New York City and Philadelphia and coordinated several steamboat legs with interim stage service. Competing directly with the Union Line, Vanderbilt forced his rival to buy him out in 1830.

The "Commodore." The transaction set a pattern Vanderbilt repeated several times as the scope of his shipping interests expanded: invest in modern, upscale facilities, build profitable lines, and eventually either sell out to or buy out competing lines. From the mid-Atlantic coastal routes, Vanderbilt shifted to the Hudson River, where he went head-to-head with Daniel Drew (who would become an occasional ally as well as an archrival) and then with the Hudson River Steamboat Association. The former he bought out; the latter he forced to buy him out for the lucrative sum of $100,000 plus annual payments of $5,000. In 1835 he turned back to the sea, to the Long Island Sound route between New York and Providence. By the early 1840s the "Commodore," as Vanderbilt was starting to be known, was worth more than $1 million.

The Transit. Vanderbilt's most ambitious projects lay ahead of him. With the discovery of gold in California and the explosion of development on the Pacific Coast,

Vanderbilt set up the Transit Company running steamships down to the Central American isthmus on the Atlantic side and up to San Francisco on the Pacific side. To connect the overland link, Vanderbilt explored the possibility of bisecting the isthmus with a canal. Though the Panama Canal in fact took more than half a century to realize, Vanderbilt managed to sell most of his holdings in the Transit at a considerable profit in 1852, when he took a hiatus from business.

New Shipping Ventures. On returning to business several years later, Vanderbilt developed several grand projects. He returned to the Central American/West Coast line, first setting up a line competing with the Transit Company, then buying up enough stock in his old company to take it over. Eventually in 1859 he formed the Atlantic & Pacific Steamship Company and built a railroad across Panama. Meanwhile, he had begun running steamships on a transatlantic route between New York and Le Havre, France (which earned only modest profits). During the Civil War he turned his larger ships over the Union navy (while continuing to run smaller vessels in the Atlantic & Pacific). In 1864, at the age of seventy, Vanderbilt retired from shipping with a fortune of nearly $30 million.

Railroads. He did not, however, retire from business altogether. Indeed, the scale of Vanderbilt's financial empire-building increased considerably in his last dozen years, as he plunged more deeply into the world of railroad finance. This involvement dated back to the 1840s, when Vanderbilt had begun investing in the New York & Harlem and other New York lines. In 1865 he built up his stake and buttressed his competitive position, when he engineered the consolidation of the New York & Harlem and the Hudson Line (which ran along the line of the Erie Canal to Buffalo). Several years later, he moved against the New York Central, which connected the Vanderbilt lines to western points, by refusing to accept the Central's passengers or freight and thereby cutting it off from its port connections (a maneuver Vanderbilt carefully timed for the winter, when freezing conditions had shut down the Erie Canal). Forced to capitulate, the Central relinquished control of its board to Vanderbilt, consolidating his hold on rail traffic from the West to New York City. Only the Erie Railroad eluded the Commodore's grasp, when speculators Daniel Drew, Jay Gould, and Jim Fisk successfully thwarted Vanderbilt's bid for control in 1867–1868.

Grand Central. Perhaps Vanderbilt's most enduring monument to posterity was Grand Central Station, which he had constructed in 1871 as the terminus for the Central. He had already built an impressive freight terminal for the Hudson—a monumental structure three stories high, with a facade 150 feet long and 30 feet high, decorated with a bas-relief depicting the various stages of Vanderbilt's business career, framing a huge statue of the Commodore himself. The Grand Central passenger terminal was executed in even grander style, running 250 feet along Forty-second Street. The New York City public was suitably impressed, but was determined to force Vanderbilt to put the tracks below street level, which the city eventually required him to do (softening the blow by paying for half the cost).

Legacies. Vanderbilt died in 1877, passing along most of his $100 million estate to his son William, in the form of New York Central and Hudson River Railroad stock. His less tangible and more public legacy was an early taste of empire building, railroad style. As Charles Francis Adams put it, Vanderbilt "involuntarily excites feelings of admiration for himself and alarm for the public. His ambition is a great one. It seems to be nothing less than to make himself master in his own right of the great channels of communication which connect the city of New York with the interior of the continent, and to control them as his private property." To a striking extent, he had succeded.

Source:

Wheaton J. Lane, *Commodore Vanderbilt: An Epic of the Steam Age* (New York: Knopf, 1942).

PUBLICATIONS

Charles Francis Adams Jr., *A Chapter of Erie* (Boston: Fields, Osgood, 1869)—exposes the shady financial dealings of Jay Gould, Jim Fisk, and Daniel Drew in seizing control of the Erie Railroad from Cornelius Vanderbilt;

Adams, *Railroad Legislation* (Boston: Little, Brown, 1868)—a comprehensive study of the industry and its laws, recommending the confederation of lines and government regulation;

David Christy, *Cotton Is King* (Cincinnati: Moore, Wilstach, Keys, 1855)—the author, who was neither a Southerner nor a proslavery advocate, argues that the Southern slave system formed a key component in the nation's larger economic system of agriculture, commerce, and manufacturing, and that it thereby contributed to prosperity in both the North and South;

Jay Cooke, *The Pacific Railroads as the Relations Existing between Them and the Government of the United States* (New York, 1879)—a promotional tract extolling the financial potential of a project in which Cooke had invested heavily, a railroad running from Duluth, Minnesota, to Tacoma, Washington;

William H. Maher, *On the Road to Riches* (Toledo: T. J. Brown, Eager & Company, 1876)—hints for clerks and young businessmen on such subjects as buying goods, business correspondence, selling goods on the road, duties of clerks, partners, etc;

New York Life Insurance Company, *Cable-Cipher and Crytograph for Economical and Confidential Correspondence by Letter or Telegraph* (New York: Hart, 1877)—a handbook suggesting a secure method of business communication using telegraphy;

Henry Varnum Poor, *Money and Its Laws* (New York: H. V. and H. W. Poor, 1877)—a financial history of the United States;

A Practical Guide to Business (Philadelphia: J. G. Fergus & Co., 1872)—A handbook for the American farmer, merchant, mechanic, and investor, with advice about earning and saving money;

Abraham Ritter, *Philadelphia And Her Merchants As Constituted Fifty to Seventy Years Ago* (Philadelphia: The Author, 1860)—an anecdotal history of business in Philadelphia, illustrated with diagrams of the riverfront and portraits of some of the prominent occupants;

William Leete Stone, *History of New York City from the Discovery to the Present Day* (New York: E. Cleave, 1868)—an early history of New York City, valuable for its account of the development of business interests;

Mark Twain [Samuel Langhorne Clemens] and Charles Dudley Warner, *The Gilded Age: A Tale of Today* (Hartford, Conn.: American Publishing Company, 1873)—a satiric novel which lampooned, among other subjects, the period's mania for economic speculation in railroads and land deals, as well as the political corruption this economic activity engendered;

Amasa Walker, *The Science of Wealth: A Manual of Political Economy* (Boston: Little, Brown, 1866)—an analysis by a lecturer on economics at Amherst College of various aspects of the emerging industrial economy. Among other topics, Walker examines the structuring of manufacturing operations so that "each workman confine himself to a single operation," maximizing efficiency and productivity.

Iron mining in Idaho

THE CIVIL WAR

by ROBERT ZALIMAS

CONTENTS

Sidebars and tables are listed in italics.

1861

12 Apr. South Carolina artillerymen fire upon Fort Sumter, a Union stronghold located in Charleston Harbor.

13 Apr. After forty thousand shells hit the fort, Union Maj. Robert Anderson surrenders Fort Sumter to Confederate forces.

15 Apr. President of the United States Abraham Lincoln issues a call for seventy-five thousand three-month volunteers; African Americans are rejected.

19 Apr. Lincoln orders a naval blockade of all Confederate ports. Southern sympathizers attack Massachusetts militiamen in Baltimore.

19 Apr. Dorothea Dix volunteers to supervise women nurses for the Federal army.

20 Apr. Robert E. Lee resigns his commission in the Federal army and sides with the Confederacy.

27 Apr. Lincoln suspends the writ of habeas corpus from Philadelphia to Washington.

3 May Union General-in-Chief Winfield Scott announces his "Anaconda Plan," a naval blockade of the Southern coastline in conjunction with a land attack along the Mississippi River. Lincoln calls for forty-two thousand additional volunteers as well as eighteen thousand sailors.

6 May Confederate president Jefferson Davis approves a bill declaring a state of war between the United States and the Confederate States.

13 May Queen Victoria declares English neutrality and grants each side in the American conflict the status of belligerent.

24 May While removing a Confederate flag from a hotel roof in Alexandria, Virginia, Union officer Elmer Ellsworth becomes the first combat casualty of the war after he is killed by the innkeeper, James T. Jackson; Union troops then shoot and kill Jackson. Both men are recognized as martyrs by their respective regions.

31 May Confederate general P. G. T. Beauregard is given command over all Confederate troops in northern Virginia.

4 July Lincoln sends out a call for an additional four hundred thousand recruits.

13 July Union forces defeat Southern troops at Carrickford, Virginia, and take control of the entire area known as West Virginia. Union casualties are fifty-three, while the Confederates lose twenty.

21 July In the first major battle of the war, Confederate troops defeat Federal soldiers at the First Battle of Bull Run near Manassas, Virginia. Southern losses equal 387 dead as opposed to 460 for the Union.

25 July Congress passes the Crittenden Resolution, which states that the war will be fought to preserve the Union, not to destroy slavery.

27 July Lincoln removes Gen. Irvin McDowell as commander of the Army of the Potomac and replaces him with Gen. George B. McClellan.

10 Aug. At Wilson's Creek, Missouri, Confederate troops defeat Union forces in the second major battle between the two adversaries.

30 Aug. Gen. John Frémont places Missouri under martial law and authorizes Federal troops to confiscate all Confederate property. Frémont also frees all slaves in the state who belong to Confederate sympathizers.

2 Sept.   Abraham Lincoln notifies Frémont that his edict may move the border states toward secession.

1 Oct.   Confederate president Jefferson Davis and his military staff decide to wait until the spring before attacking the Northern states.

3 Oct.   Louisiana governor Thomas O. Moore bans the shipment of cotton to Europe. Moore hopes to pressure England and France into recognizing Southern independence.

14 Oct.   Lincoln suspends the writ of habeas corpus from Maine to Washington, D.C.

21 Oct.   Union troops are defeated at the Battle of Ball's Bluff near Leesburg, Virginia. Sen. Edward Baker, one of Lincoln's close friends, is killed during the fighting. Northern casualties are more than a thousand compared to less than one hundred for Southern forces.

24 Oct.   Lincoln signs orders replacing Frémont with Gen. David Hunter.

1 Nov.   Union General-in-Chief Winfield Scott, a veteran of both the War of 1812 and the Mexican War, resigns his post because of his age and personality clashes with younger subordinates. Lincoln promotes George B. McClellan to become Scott's replacement.

8 Nov.   In the Caribbean the captain of the U.S.S. *San Jacinto* stops the British frigate *Trent* and arrests two Confederate diplomats, James Mason and John Slidell, who are on their way to Europe. This incident, known as the *Trent* Affair, sparks a diplomatic crisis between the United States and Great Britain and almost leads to war.

9 Dec.   The United States Senate establishes the Joint Committee on the Conduct of the War to address rumors of military incompetence at First Bull Run and Ball's Bluff.

1862

11 Jan.   Under criticism that his office suffers from corruption and mismanagement, Secretary of War Simon Cameron submits his resignation. Lincoln chooses Edwin Stanton, former attorney general and personal friend of General-in-Chief George McClellan, to fill the post.

27 Jan.   Lincoln releases *General War Order No. 1,* calling for a Union offensive by 22 February.

6–16 Feb.   Confederate forces at Fort Henry and Fort Donelson, Tennessee, surrender to Union troops under Gen. Ulysses S. Grant. As a result of his victories Grant is promoted to major general.

24 Feb.   Nashville becomes the first major city in the South to fall to Union forces.

27 Feb.   Confederate president Jefferson Davis suspends the writ of habeas corpus.

9 Mar.   In the world's first clash between ironclad warships, the U.S.S. *Monitor* and the C.S.S. *Virginia* fight to a draw off the coast of Hampton Roads, Virginia.

11 Mar.   Due to a lack of initiative on the part of McClellan, Lincoln removes his title as general-in-chief, but retains his services as commander of the Army of the Potomac.

13 Mar.   Lincoln approves General McClellan's plan for operations along the coast of Virginia.

4 Apr.	General McClellan moves against Yorktown, Virginia, in order to establish a base between the James and York Rivers on the peninsula.
6–7 Apr.	Union forces win a costly victory at Shiloh, Tennessee.
16 Apr.	Confederate president Jefferson Davis approves a bill instituting the first military draft in American history.
25 Apr.	New Orleans falls to Union commander David Farragut.
9 May	Union general David Hunter, commander of the Department of the South, frees slaves in Georgia, South Carolina, and Florida without congressional approval; Lincoln countermands the order several days later.
13 May	Robert Smalls, a slave working for the Confederate navy, steals the steamer *Planter* from Charleston Harbor, South Carolina, and surrenders the ship to Union blockading forces.
20 May	Gen. George McClellan stops his advance toward Richmond, eight miles outside the Confederate capitol.
25 May	Lincoln orders McClellan to attack Richmond or return to Washington.
31 May	Confederate general Joseph Johnston is wounded at the Battle of Seven Pines. Robert E. Lee replaces Johnston the following day as commander of the Army of Northern Virginia.
6 June	Memphis, Tennessee, surrenders to Union naval forces.
25 June–2 July	During the Seven Days' Battle, Virginia, Confederate forces under Robert E. Lee push Federal troops back to the peninsula between the James and York Rivers.
11 July	Abraham Lincoln names Henry W. Halleck as Union general-in-chief.
17 July	Lincoln signs the Second Confiscation Act, which frees slaves that flee to Union lines.
22 July	Lincoln informs his cabinet about his intention to issue the Emancipation Proclamation.
4 Aug.	Lincoln institutes a military draft calling for 300,000 new enlistees. The act, however, does not go into effect because 421,000 Northerners volunteer to join the Union army for three years.
28–30 Aug.	At the Second Battle of Bull Run , Virginia, Confederate troops once again defeat Union forces.
17 Sept.	At Antietam Creek, Maryland, Gen. George McClellan forces Gen. Robert E. Lee to retreat into Virginia in the bloodiest day of both the war and American history.
22 Sept.	Lincoln publishes the preliminary Emancipation Proclamation.
27 Sept.	In New Orleans, Union general Benjamin F. "The Beast" Butler musters the first official African American regiment into the Union army, the First Louisiana Native Guard Infantry.

11 Oct.	Southern critics label the war "a rich man's war and a poor man's fight" after Confederate president Jefferson Davis amends his draft law to exempt anyone owning twenty or more slaves.
5 Nov.	Lincoln retires McClellan as commander of the Army of the Potomac and replaces him with Ambrose E. Burnside.
13 Dec.	At the Battle of Fredericksburg, Virginia, Lee turns back an offensive by Burnside.
17 Dec.	In the Western theater, Ulysses S. Grant issues *General Order No. 11* expelling Jews from his area of operation. Grant rescinds the order a few weeks later.

1863

1 Jan.	President Abraham Lincoln of the United States issues the Emancipation Proclamation. Except for the border states (Missouri, Kentucky, Maryland, and Delaware) and those enemy areas already under Union control, the proclamation frees all slaves located in the Southern states.
25 Jan.	Lincoln replaces Ambrose E. Burnside with Joseph Hooker as commander of the Army of the Potomac. Meanwhile John A. ›Andrew, the governor of Massachusetts, receives permission to recruit African Americans, and the Fifty-Fourth Massachusetts Infantry becomes the first black regiment from the North.
3 Mar.	Lincoln signs the Union's first Conscription Act, calling for the enlistment of all male citizens between the ages of twenty and forty-five. The bill allows chapters to hire a substitute for $300.
1–4 May	At the Battle of Chancellorsville, Virginia, Lee repels another Union offensive, but the South suffers a blow when Gen. Thomas "Stonewall" Jackson is wounded by friendly fire.
10 May	"Stonewall" Jackson dies from pneumonia.
22 May	In Mississippi, Grant places Vicksburg, the last Confederate stronghold on the Mississippi River, under siege.
23 May	The Battle of Port Hudson, Louisiana, leads to a prolonged siege; it is the first major engagement in which African American troops participate.
3 June	Confederate general Robert E. Lee decides to invade the North and moves his army from Fredericksburg, Virginia, toward the Maryland border.
16 June	Lee moves the Army of Northern Virginia across the Potomac River into Maryland.
27 June	Abraham Lincoln removes Joseph Hooker as commander of the Army of the Potomac and replaces him with George Meade.
1–3 July	At Gettysburg, Pennsylvania, in some of the fiercest fighting of the war, Meade inflicts a decisive defeat upon Lee, forcing the Southern army to retreat into Virginia. Both sides suffer a total of fifty thousand casualties. Lee's army, having lost seventeen generals and one-third of its strength, never attempts to invade the North again.
4 July	After a six-week siege, Vicksburg, Mississippi, falls to Federal forces under Gen. Ulysses S. Grant and over twenty-nine thousand Confederates become prisoners.

8 July	Port Hudson, Louisiana, surrenders to Union forces, who now control the entire Mississippi River. Confederate cavalry commander John H. Morgan crosses the Ohio River and begins his raids into Indiana and southern Ohio.
13–16 July	A draft riot occurs in New York City in which approximately one thousand people are killed or wounded before Federal troops restore order.
18 July	The all-black Fifty-Fourth Massachusetts Infantry attacks and suffers heavy losses at Battery Wagner, South Carolina. Journalists on the scene later immortalize the assault in magazines and newspapers.
26 July	Militiamen capture John Morgan and his Confederate cavalry at New Lisbon, Ohio.
8 Aug.	Gen. Robert E. Lee offers his resignation. Confederate president Jefferson Davis refuses to accept it, noting that the Confederacy cannot afford to lose his leadership capabilities.
21 Aug.	Confederate guerrilla fighter William Quantrill burns Lawrence, Kansas, and murders more than 150 men and boys. The raid alienates many Southerners who see the war as a moral crusade.
19–20 Sept.	In a major battle at Chickamauga, Georgia, Confederate troops force Federal troops to retreat into Tennessee. The number of casualties on both sides reaches thirty-five thousand, including Lincoln's brother-in-law, Confederate general Ben Hardin Helm.
16 Oct.	Lincoln chooses Ulysses S. Grant to command all Union forces in the west.
19 Nov.	Lincoln delivers the Gettysburg Address.
23–25 Nov.	A Union victory at Chattanooga, Tennessee, forces the Confederates to retreat into Georgia, abandoning Knoxville and leaving Tennessee under Union control.
8 Dec.	Lincoln presents his Proclamation of Amnesty and Reconstruction, offering a full pardon to Confederates who take an oath of allegiance.
12 Dec.	The Confederate government refuses to accept supplies sent from the Northern states to Union prisoners of war.

1864

18 Jan.	Confederate president Jefferson Davis issues a conscription law enlisting all white males between the ages of eighteen and forty-five (later seventeen and fifty) into the Confederate army.
1 Feb.	Lincoln calls for an additional five hundred thousand enlistees for the Union army.
3–14 Feb.	During operations in Mississippi, Union general William T. Sherman occupies the town of Meridian. Sherman destroys buildings, supplies, and railroads in his path, a tactic that he will later implement in his infamous "March to the Sea."
27 Feb.	At Andersonville, Georgia, Union prisoners arrive at an unfinished, sixteen-and-one-half-acre log stockade. The prison quickly gains notoriety for its uninhabitable conditions.
9 Mar.	Lincoln promotes Ulysses S. Grant to lieutenant general and general-in-chief of all Union armies.

12 Apr.	Confederate cavalry under Nathan Bedford Forrest capture Fort Pillow, Tennessee, in the process murdering black soldiers who are trying to surrender. "Remember Fort Pillow!" becomes a rallying cry for African American troops.
3 May	The Army of the Potomac (122,000 men) advances toward Richmond and the Army of Northern Virginia (66,000 men).
4 May	In the west Gen. William T. Sherman leaves Chattanooga with 110,000 men and advances toward Atlanta.
5–6 May	The armies of Grant and Lee fight an inconclusive battle in thick woods at Wilderness, Virginia. Casualties are heavy, more than twenty-five thousand for both sides, as brush fires in the forest kill many wounded soldiers.
8–12 May	Unlike his predecessors who failed to keep pressure on the enemy, Ulysses S. Grant pursues Robert E. Lee after Wilderness and fights the Confederate army for five days at Spotsylvania Courthouse, Virginia; the battle ends in a draw.
12 May	The Confederate cavalry general Jeb Stuart dies from wounds suffered the previous day at Yellow Tavern, outside Richmond.
1–3 June	At Cold Harbor, Virginia, Grant attempts to outflank Lee in another inconclusive battle which produces heavy casualties on both sides. After one month of continual fighting the Union casualties reach 50,000 (41 percent of their original strength) while Southern losses equal 32,000 (46 percent of their original strength).
15–18 June	Lee repulses several assaults by Grant upon Petersburg, Virginia, an important railroad center. Grant places the city under siege.
25 June	The Forty-Eighth Pennsylvania Regiment, a unit of former coal miners, begins digging a mine underneath the Confederate breastworks at Petersburg.
27 June	At Kennesaw Mountain, Georgia, Confederate forces repel an assault by Gen. William T. Sherman, resulting in heavy losses for the Federals.
12 July	After maneuvering to the outskirts of Washington, D.C., Confederate cavalry general Jubal Early retreats into Virginia rather than face newly arrived Union reinforcements.
17 July	Confederate president Jefferson Davis replaces Gen. Joseph E. Johnston with Gen. John Bell Hood after Johnston fails to stop Sherman's advance.
20–28 July	In a series of assaults, Hood attacks Sherman's forces on the outskirts of Atlanta. Hood's men fail to dislodge the Federals and suffer heavy losses.
30 July	Union forces blow up the mine under Confederate fortifications at Petersburg, but fail to take the city.
5 Aug.	Union admiral David Farragut captures Mobile, Alabama. During the battle Farragut utters his famous cry, "Damn the torpedoes. Full speed ahead!"
2 Sept.	Atlanta falls to Union general William T. Sherman.
19 Sept.– 9 Oct.	Union cavalry general Philip Sheridan drives Confederate cavalry leader Jubal Early from the Shenandoah Valley, Virginia.
16 Nov.	Sherman leaves Atlanta and begins his "March to the Sea."

30 Nov.	Gen. John B. Hood attacks Union forces at Franklin, Tennessee, and suffers heavy losses, including the death of six generals. Union general John M. Schofield withdraws to Nashville to reinforce Gen. George H. Thomas.
15–17 Dec.	Thomas attacks Hood outside Nashville and nearly annihilates the Southern force. This is the last major battle fought by the Confederate Army of Tennessee.
21 Dec.	Gen. William T. Sherman takes Savannah, Georgia, without a fight.

1865

15 Jan.	A joint assault by Union army and navy forces capture Fort Fisher, a Confederate stronghold protecting Wilmington, North Carolina.
16 Jan.	Sherman issues his *Special Field Order No. 15,* which sets aside land along the Georgia coast for the exclusive settlement of African American refugees.
17 Feb.	Sherman captures Columbia, South Carolina. Fires set by fleeing Confederate soldiers as well as by some of Sherman's men nearly destroy the capital city.
22 Feb.	Union forces capture Wilmington, North Carolina, the last open Confederate port.
3 Mar.	U.S. president Abraham Lincoln orders Ulysses S. Grant to reject Robert E. Lee's request for peace negotiations unless Lee intends to surrender first.
13 Mar.	Confederate president Jefferson Davis signs a bill allowing African Americans to enlist in the Confederate army.
27–28 Mar.	Lincoln meets with Gen. Ulysses S. Grant, Gen. William T. Sherman, and Adm. David D. Porter, directing each of them to offer Southerners generous terms of surrender to avoid postwar guerrilla activity.
1 Apr.	In one of the last battles of the war, Union cavalry general Philip Sheridan and a force of fifty thousand rout ten thousand Confederates at Five Forks, Virginia.
2 Apr.	Robert E. Lee abandons Petersburg and notifies President Jefferson Davis to move the Confederate government from Richmond.
3 Apr.	Union forces take Richmond without a fight; Lincoln arrives the following day.
6 Apr.	In the last battle between the Army of Northern Virginia and the Army of the Potomac, Southern troops lose one-third of their total strength at Sayler's Creek, Virginia.
9 Apr.	Robert E. Lee formally surrenders at Appomattox Courthouse, Virginia.
14 Apr.	John Wilkes Booth assassinates President Abraham Lincoln.
18 Apr.	Confederate general Joseph E. Johnston formally surrenders to Union general William T. Sherman at Durham Station, North Carolina, to end hostilities between the North and South officially.

OVERVIEW

The Modern War. In comparison to other nineteenth-century conflicts, the American Civil War was a modern war. This is not surprising for, as historian James McPherson states, "every war is more modern than the previous one." Before 1861, wars, especially in Europe, were won by outmaneuvering enemy forces. Casualties were not excessive and efforts were made to respect private property and civilians. During the Civil War, however, enemy forces attacked each other in frontal assaults in which the victors suffered just as much as the losers. For the first time in American history, armies of more than one hundred thousand men fought in major battles ending in extremely high casualty rates. Confiscation of private property and uprooting civilians from their private residences also became common practice. In addition, innovations in weapons and military tactics forced Civil War commanders to revolutionize battlefield strategy; trench warfare, for example, moved the Civil War into a stalemate during the final campaign in Virginia.

The Traditional War. Although modern in many ways, America's Civil War was also a "traditional" conflict that mirrored many of the battles, weapons, and military tactics of the Napoleonic Wars fought in Europe (1793–1815). Despite revolutionary changes in arms and combat strategy, aggressive infantry assaults across treacherous fields of fire accounted for more battlefield victories than modern weaponry. Similarly, mounted cavalrymen and fixed bayonets played a more prominent role than the new repeating rifles or experimental machine guns. In their attempt to resupply forces, quartermaster personnel continued to favor horse-drawn wagons over logistical innovations such as the steamboat and railroad. Finally, both governments still depended upon inexperienced state militiamen, not professional soldiers, to fill their manpower needs.

The Balance Sheet. When the war began, the North dominated the South in manpower and resources. The population of the North was 2.5 times larger than that of the South, 22,300,000 to 9,100,000 (3,500,000 of whom were slaves). Moreover, the Union outnumbered the Confederacy in white males ages eighteen to forty-five, the main age group to fight the war, by a margin of 4.2 to 1. The North outproduced the South in textiles, firearms, iron, coal, corn, wheat, draft animals, shipping tonnage, and railroad mileage. Overall the North had 90 percent of all U.S. industrial capacity and two-thirds of its railroad track. The only resource advantage for the South was its cotton production, which was 96 percent of the national output. Due to this lopsided edge in men and materials, many Union observers boldly predicted that the Southern rebellion would crumble after one battle.

Southern Advantages. Although the Union appeared superior on paper, Southern strategists were confident that the Confederacy would win. Many observers at home and abroad felt that the Union would not be able to conquer a region larger than all of western Europe. The military analyst for the London *Times* commented: "Just as England during the revolution had to give up conquering the colonies so the North will have to give up conquering the South." Psychologically as well, the advantage clearly lay with the South, which defended land, homes, and families against Northern aggression. This fact strengthened Southern morale and was a strong motivation to fight. Southerners also argued that they held a superiority in martial qualities. As a rural people, many hunted and rode horses, in contrast to the Northern city dwellers and shopkeepers who did neither. In addition, more Southerners attended West Point and other military academies, fought in the Mexican War, and served in the Federal army. Southerners were also more likely to join or form a local militia unit as part of their community culture. The prevalence of these regional companies allowed the South to prepare for war long before the North mobilized in large numbers. When each Southern state seceded, local governments called up these militiamen, allowing the Confederacy to field sixty thousand troops before Lincoln's call for seventy-five thousand ninety-day enlistments. Southern troops were more familiar with southern topography and were aided by a civilian population that actively spied on Union troop movements. These martial advantages, however, were not strong enough to repel the Northern onslaught, as Union commanders devised plans to protect their supply lines within enemy territory and deployed enough men to occupy more than five hundred thousand square miles of Southern land.

Union and Confederate Armies. Both sides had to raise armies from scratch—the federal army in 1860 numbered only sixteen thousand men, many of whom were located in small units scattered west of the Mississippi River. After four years of war, more than two million men fought for the Union and almost another million for the Confederacy. These figures represent half of the Northern male population of military age (eighteen to forty-five) and three-quarters of the comparable Southern white male population. During the first two years of the war, most of these soldiers were volunteers. Later, both sides implemented drafts to fill regimental ranks, and although these drafts produced few recruits they did spark additional volunteer enlistments. When war broke out neither side was prepared to enlist African Americans. The North eventually recruited 180,000 black men while the South refused to acknowledge this untapped manpower source until late in the war. Most Civil War soldiers were young; more than 40 percent fell into the eighteen to twenty-one age bracket. The majority were farmers or farm laborers. By the end of the war, approximately 618,000 would lose their lives, two out of three dying from diseases that festered in camps, hospitals, and prisons.

Organizing Regiments. The bulk of these volunteers were organized in state militia units. The units first organized by company (one hundred men) and usually drew recruits from a county, town, or city neighborhood. A company elected its own officers (a captain and two lieutenants), and ten companies formed a regiment. The colonel and majors of a regiment were appointed by the state governor. Each regiment was named for the state that organized it and were numbered sequentially following their completion, for example: the Fifty-Fourth Massachusetts Infantry, First Louisiana Native Guard Infantry, Fifth Virginia Cavalry, and so on. Some regiments were organized by ethnicity such as Irish, German, Scandinavian, or African. Cavalry regiments mirrored infantry regimental organization while artillery units were arranged in "batteries." Each battery was composed of four to six cannon along with ammunition wagons, 155 artillerymen, and seventy-two horses. The infantry comprised the major fighting component in both armies, accounting for 80 percent of all Civil War regiments. As the war progressed and combat, desertion, and disease took their tolls, and regimental combat strength decreased, with most units averaging five hundred men or less. Many times new recruits preferred to organize their own companies rather than fill the ranks of existing ones.

Discipline. For the most part, Civil War volunteers were not professional soldiers. As citizen soldiers, many lacked military discipline and displayed contempt toward officers. Early in the war, this unprofessional disregard for authority led to many battlefield disasters. This problem was particularly evident in Confederate regiments since rural individualism dominated Southern society.

Unruly soldiers were known to threaten or physically assault officers, discard equipment on long marches, and leave the ranks to loot and pillage. Desertion was a major problem for both sides, and during the course of the war, Union forces had a total of 200,000 cases while Confederate armies had 104,000. While Northern authorities caught and returned 80,000 to their regiments, Southern officials were only able to locate and return 21,000.

Weapons. Although both sides utilized cavalry regiments and artillery firepower, infantry rifles accounted for 80 to 90 percent of all battlefield casualties. The greater reliance on infantry regiments was due to an innovation in nineteenth-century muskets. Before the Civil War, the primary infantry weapon was the smoothbore musket. The maximum range of this weapon was 250 yards, but its accuracy was closer to eighty yards. As the musket ball left the smooth barrel, it did not spin and, as historian James McPherson notes, "might behave as erratically as a knuckleball in baseball." By cutting spiraled grooves inside a musket barrel, a bullet would spin and provide better accuracy and range. Designed in 1849, the "minié ball," a cone-shaped lead bullet named after its designer, French army Captain Claude Étienne Minié, gave infantrymen greater accuracy and range in their firepower. When an American designer made a cheaper version of the minié ball that was less likely to malfunction, both Confederate and Union armies abandoned the old smoothbore muskets and embraced the new "rifled" muskets. The rifled musket was accurate up to four hundred yards and had a maximum range of one thousand yards.

Tactics. Though cavalry and artillery tactics changed following this wartime innovation, the longer range and greater accuracy of the new rifles did not force Civil War commanders to alter infantry operations drastically. Many West Point graduates on both sides clung to lessons learned at the academy which emphasized linear tactics (long lines of opposing infantrymen exchanging musket fire at close range). Military theoreticians also advocated close-order frontal assaults. Taken from the Napoleonic era, this offensive movement was designed to overrun enemy positions with overwhelming numbers. When fired from strong defensive positions such as a trench or breastwork, however, the new rifles cut down onrushing infantrymen long before they reached the fortifications. Infantry advances across open fields resulted in enormous casualties, as incurred by Union forces at Fredericksburg, Virginia, in 1862 and Confederate troops at Gettysburg, Pennsylvania, in 1863. By war's end, soldiers had mastered the art of firing a weapon from behind cover in a prone position while their commanders learned to save regimental strength by skillfully outmaneuvering their opponents and attacking the enemy's flank.

Confederate Supply Shortages. In addition to raising an army, the ability to support and supply regiments also played a major role in the war. To function efficiently, armies require a dependable flow of food, weapons, clothing, ammunition, medical equipment and other war matériels. From the outset, food and clothing shortages plagued the Confederate army. A lack of railroad tracks, inflation, and inefficient government bureaucracy hindered quartermaster and commissary personnel from meeting supply demands. Southern soldiers often marched and fought on empty stomachs and many suffered from scurvy during the winter months. At one point, supplies were so low that Confederate general Robert E. Lee ordered daily rations reduced to four ounces of bacon, eighteen ounces of cornmeal, and a handful of rice or black-eyed peas. Southern industries suffered from inadequate raw materials, and this also affected the fighting ability of Southern soldiers. Throughout the war, many Southerners fought in ragged uniforms and marched in bare feet. Although he lacked food and clothing, the Confederate soldier was usually well stocked in weapons and ammunition. Ordinance Bureau chief Josiah Gorgas used crafty measures to recycle lead and iron to manufacture bullets and cannon balls. This Herculean effort to keep Confederate weapons loaded was not enough, however, to offset the weakened fighting ability of hungry and ragged soldiers.

Union Production and Supply. For most of the war Union soldiers were adequately supplied. Northern textile mills ran at full production capacity and kept Federal troops well stocked with overcoats, shoes, and uniforms. Since Northern farmers grew more crops and raised more livestock than their Southern counterparts, food shortages did not inhibit troop movements as Northern infantrymen feasted on pork, vegetables, coffee, and bread (known commonly as "hardtack"). With a strong logistic edge in supplies and men, the Union army kept most of the fighting contained within the Southern states and hampered Confederate efforts to resupply their own soldiers. Thus the Federal advantage in modern technology and production kept Northern soldiers in the field while supply shortages in the Confederate army compelled many Southerners to abandon the cause and return home.

TOPICS IN THE NEWS

ADJUSTING EXPECTATIONS

"Forward to Richmond." After the fall of Fort Sumter, South Carolina, on 13 April 1861, the Confederate government transferred its capital from Montgomery, Alabama, to Richmond, Virginia. Located a hundred miles from Washington, D.C., Richmond now became the focal point of the war. Northern newspapers advocated a quick strike against the Southern capital city and printed inflammatory slogans like "Forward to Richmond" at the top of each daily edition. Union recruits stationed in Washington embraced the war hysteria and also clamored for a battle. Many joined the Union army under ninety-day enlistments which would soon expire, and they feared going home without heroic tales of battlefield glory.

The First Battle of Bull Run. Moved by pressures from Northern civilians and President Abraham Lincoln, Union General-in-Chief Winfield Scott ordered Gen. Irvin McDowell and thirty-five thousand troops to advance toward Richmond. Many civilians anticipated that the ensuing battle would be the war's only one, and as a result they followed McDowell's army. On 21 July 1861 McDowell, who did not believe his raw recruits were ready for battle, confronted twenty thousand screaming Confederates (the famous "rebel yell" was first heard here) under the command of the hero of Fort Sumter, P. G. T. Beauregard. The armies clashed twenty-five miles southwest of Washington at a creek named Bull Run, near the important rail junction of Manassas, Virginia. The Northern soldiers appeared to be close to victory when a Virginia brigade under the command of Gen. Thomas J. Jackson unexpectedly arrived from the Shenandoah Valley by train. Jackson and his men reinforced the Confederate line and, standing "like a stone wall," repulsed multiple Federal frontal assaults. The Southerners then counterattacked and forced the frightened Union troops to drop their rifles and retreat wildly to Washington. Although casualties on both sides were light compared to later Civil War battles, the Battle of Bull Run made a strong impression on both home fronts. On the one hand, Southerners quickly grew overconfident of their fighting ability and proclaimed that one Rebel soldier was equal to ten Northern bluecoats. On the other hand, Northerners took the Confederate threat more seriously than before and quickly woke up to the fact that most civil wars are not won or lost in the first ninety days.

First Confiscation Act. Southerners basked in the first major victory of the war and many felt that the disheartened Northerners would quit after one defeat. Instead of giving up, however, young white males in the North flooded recruiting stations. Congress promptly authorized a new army to include up to a million volunteers signed to three-year enlistments. In addition, the Republicans in Congress sought to weaken Southern labor reserves by issuing the First Confiscation Act on 6 August 1861. Confederate commanders used slaves instead of white soldiers to perform rear-echelon details, saving every available white soldier for battle. The policy of confiscation allowed Union commanders to seize slaves within reach of Northern forces, but did not specifically emancipate them.

McClellan Takes Command. More important to the Union cause at this time, President Lincoln replaced Irvin McDowell with Maj. Gen. George B. McClellan, the

Gen. George B. McClellan (second from left) with members of his staff

By late 1862 Civil War soldiers recognized each other by the color of their uniforms: blue for Federals and gray for Confederates. At the beginning of the war, however, uniforms varied significantly in both armies. Both Union and Confederate governments did not enter contract negotiations with American and/or European textile manufacturers until after Fort Sumter fell in April 1861. As a result many state militiamen wore flashy regalia reserved for ceremonial parades that turned early Civil War battlefields into multicolored affairs. The Emerald Greens of Mobile, Alabama, a unit composed of Irish immigrants, marched to Richmond dressed in dark green outfits. The Yellow Jackets of East Tennessee arrived in yellow uniforms while the Granville Rifles of North Carolina wore black and flaming red flannel shirts. The most gaudy and most creative uniforms were worn by Zouave regiments. Organized in both Southern and Northern states, these regiments patterned their combat ensemble after the French infantry stationed in Algiers, Africa. The Zouave uniform included red, baggy trousers banded at the ankles by white gaiters; a blue sash for a belt; a short, tight jacket trimmed with lace; a blue shirt cut low; and a short, brown fez.

Ironically at the beginning of the war gray was more popular in Northern militia units while some Southern regiments wore blue, which caused confusion and tragedy in early battles. At First Bull Run, Virginia, the gray-clad Second Wisconsin Infantry were shot at by their confused Northern comrades. Likewise, in a later engagement, several Indiana soldiers wearing gray were killed by friendly fire after an Ohio regiment mistook them for the enemy. On the Southern side, blue-clad Louisiana infantrymen were shot at by friendly troops shortly after they arrived at Shiloh, Tennessee. In some cases, however, wearing enemy colors proved to be an advantage. At Wilson's Creek, Missouri, Union soldiers did not fire upon advancing Louisiana and Arkansas forces dressed in blue. This allowed the Confederates to easily outflank the unsuspecting Federals and force them to retreat. By the summer of 1862, with the exception of a few units, the deviations in uniforms had disappeared and both sides had adopted their respective colors.

Sources: Larry M. Logue, *To Appomattox and Beyond: The Civil War Soldier in War and Peace* (Chicago: Ivan R. Dee, 1996);

Bell I. Wiley, *The Life of Billy Yank: The Common Soldier of the Union,* revised edition (Baton Rouge: Louisiana State University Press, 1978);

Wiley, *The Life of Johnny Reb: The Common Soldier of the Confederacy,* revised edition (Baton Rouge: Louisiana State University Press, 1978).

North's first military hero. Prior to this new assignment, Union forces under "Little Mac" had swept Confederate troops from the pro-Union western counties of Virginia, an area later admitted to the Union as West Virginia. Lincoln called on McClellan to organize his new troops into the Army of the Potomac. A perfectionist by nature, McClellan molded the new army into a strong, fully equipped, and well-disciplined fighting force. However, McClellan's penchant for moving at a slow, careful pace drew criticism from Northern observers and politicians as he continually missed good opportunities to strike vulnerable Confederate forces.

Missouri. If Southerners were convinced that Northerners would soon sue for peace, the war in Missouri reaffirmed this conviction. Union general John C. Frémont, former explorer of the Rocky Mountains and the first Republican presidential candidate, confronted an unwinnable situation in Missouri. Guerrilla warfare weakened his control over the area and impeded reinforcements from resupplying Union forces on the state's southern border. On 10 August 1861 ten thousand Southern troops met six thousand Northern soldiers at Wilson's Creek and quickly overpowered their positions,

exposing southern and western Missouri to Confederate control. Frémont would lose nearly half of Missouri unless he acted quickly, and in desperation he turned to drastic measures. On 30 August he issued an order which placed Missouri under martial law, promised field executions for captured guerrillas, and freed slaves owned by Confederate sympathizers. Lincoln immediately countermanded the order. Although he was willing to hurt the Confederate war machine by removing part of its labor pool, the president was not willing to change the conflict into an abolitionist crusade. In addition, Lincoln feared that Union slaveholding states such as Kentucky and Maryland would secede following Frémont's revolutionary edict. "To lose Kentucky is nearly the same as to lose the whole game," Lincoln prophesied; with "Kentucky gone, we cannot hold Missouri, nor . . . Maryland."

Ball's Bluff. While things heated up in the West, the war slowed to a standstill in the East. McClellan continued to drill methodically and organize the Army of the Potomac while waiting for the right moment to attack. To quiet critics McClellan pointed to exaggerated estimates of the size of his Confederate opponent to justify

THE MONITOR AND THE VIRGINIA

On 19 April 1861 Union President Abraham Lincoln declared a naval blockade on all Confederate ports. Lincoln hoped to block British imports, particularly weapons and ammunition, from reaching the Confederate nation. To break the blockade, the Confederate navy built ironclad "rams," ships protected by iron armor and designed to puncture large holes into old-fashioned wooden ships. Although the rams were modeled after the French and British prototypes, the Confederate government became the world's first belligerent to use them in naval warfare. The ten-gun C.S.S. *Virginia* moved against the Union blockade on 8 March 1862 at Hampton Roads, Virginia. (The ship was actually the converted U.S.S. *Merrimac*, a federal steamer captured by the Confederates after they seized the federal naval base at Norfolk, Virginia in April 1861). The *Virginia* quickly sank one Union ship by charging into it with its iron ram and another with cannon fire. The *Virginia* seemed unstoppable as cannon balls fired from the wooden ships bounced harmlessly off its iron plates. Attempting to escape, the remaining Union frigates ran aground and helplessly awaited for the *Virginia* to sink them the next day.

The carnage might have been worse except for the timely arrival of the U.S.S. *Monitor*, a Union ironclad. Docked at Hampton Roads, the *Monitor* sailed into action and saved the day. Smaller than the *Virginia*, the Federal iron ship was armed with two eleven-inch guns mounted in a revolving turret. Since its deck was flush with the water, the *Monitor* offered a small target which could easily maneuver into close firing range. On 9 March the *Virginia* and the *Monitor* fought to a draw in history's first conflict between ironclads. Afterwards, the *Virginia* staggered home and Confederate ironclads never again threatened the Union blockade. Conversely, the smaller size and better maneuverability of its ironclad compelled the North to build fifty-eight *Monitor*-class ships, effectively ending the era of wooden warships.

Source: Allan Nevins, *The War for the Union*, volume 2 (New York: Charles Scribner's Sons, 1960), 50–56.

his failure to advance. By October 1861 he began to draw the ire of congressional Republicans who suspected that McClellan, a Democrat, was unwilling to attack the Confederates aggressively. On 21 October these suspicions were heightened when a Rebel brigade ambushed a Union reconnaissance force at Ball's Bluff, Virginia. The Rebels captured more than seven hundred Yankees and killed more than two hundred, including the mission's commander, Col. Edward Baker, a Republican senator from Oregon and one of Lincoln's close friends. Despite this tragic news and McClellan's public distaste for Republican policies, Lincoln elevated him to general-in-chief in November after Winfield Scott stepped down.

Investigation. Unfortunately for McClellan and his subordinates, congressional Republicans were not so forgiving. In December they created the Joint Committee on the Conduct of the War to investigate the actions of Union field officers, especially at Bull Run and Ball's Bluff. Their first target was Gen. Charles P. Stone, the divisional commander of Colonel Baker's doomed reconnaissance force. Like McClellan, Stone was a Democrat and opposed emancipation. During the war he returned slaves to their owners and reportedly was in contact with Confederate friends before the Ball's Bluff expedition. The congressmen used Stone as a scapegoat for early Union setbacks and sent him to jail. By the end of the year Federal military authorities started to make changes in how they conducted the war, but these early losses did not yet force Lincoln to rethink Union war strategy altogether.

Sources:

Bruce Catton, *Mr. Lincoln's Army* (Garden City, N.Y.: Doubleday, 1951);

James M. McPherson, *Ordeal by Fire: The Civil War and Reconstruction*, second edition (New York: McGraw-Hill, 1992);

Brooks D. Simpson, *America's Civil War* (Wheeling, Ill.: Harlan Davidson, 1996).

FIGHTING IN THE WEST, WAITING IN THE EAST

The Emergence of Grant. While Gen. George McClellan brooded over Gen. Charles Stone's arrest and continued to rehearse his impending assault upon Richmond, heavy fighting and a new Union war hero emerged in the west. Ohioan Ulysses S. Grant led a combined force of infantrymen and ironclad gunboats in February 1862 to victory at Fort Henry and Fort Donelson, Confederate strongholds on the Tennessee and Cumberland Rivers just below the Kentucky-Tennessee border. An unlikely hero, Grant had left the army eight years earlier after a discouraging post on the Pacific coast. Following a succession of civilian occupations, Grant returned to the army in 1861 and quickly rose in rank and fame. During the battle of Fort Donelson, Grant refused to negotiate terms with the Confederate commander and sent a formal reply: "No terms except an immediate and unconditional surrender can be accepted." The Northern press quickly picked up the famous lines and "unconditional surrender" soon became both a slogan and nickname for Grant. With the victories, Grant gave the Union control of both rivers and cleared the way for occupation of Nashville, the first Confederate state capital to surrender, on 24 February 1862.

The Battle of Shiloh. Grant confidently moved southward with thirty-five thousand men and established a base at Pittsburg Landing on the Tennessee

Union general Ulysses S. Grant

Shiloh. Casualties were high on both sides, accounting for more American dead than in all battles of the Revolutionary War, the War of 1812, and the Mexican War combined. Although he again proved his ability to defeat Southern commanders, Grant's reputation suffered immeasurably. Some Northern politicians and military leaders called for his removal due to the high casualty rate coupled with rumors that Grant had a drinking problem. Following Shiloh, many Americans, Southern and Northern, began to reject the romantic view of the war so prevalent during the first year of fighting.

Winning the West. More Union victories in the Western theater occurred during the spring and summer of 1862. In late April New Orleans fell to Gen. Benjamin F. Butler and Adm. David G. Farragut. In May Grant and Gen. Don Carlos Buell regrouped their battered troops and pushed the Confederates out of Corinth. In June Memphis fell to Federal naval forces after a spectacular battle between Union and Confederate gunboats.

The Peninsula Campaign. Back in Virginia, McClellan finally moved against Richmond in May. Avoiding an overland trek across difficult terrain, McClellan moved his men from Washington, D.C., by naval transports and landed at the tip of the peninsula formed by the York and James Rivers. In an iniative known as the Peninsula Campaign, McClellan sought to capture Richmond from the southeast. With an army numbering over one hundred thousand men and more in reserve, he moved cautiously after several victories and established a base at White House Landing, a point less than twenty-five miles from the Confederate capital. McClellan's renewed campaign, coupled with the springtime success in the west, convinced Northern newspapers that the war was nearly over. Many Northerners eagerly awaited news detailing the doomed fate of the Confederate nation.

Sources:

Bruce Catton, *Mr. Lincoln's Army* (Garden City, N.Y.: Doubleday, 1951);

James M. McPherson, *Ordeal by Fire: The Civil War and Reconstruction*, second edition (New York: McGraw-Hill, 1992);

Brooks D. Simpson, *America's Civil War* (Wheeling, Ill.: Harlan Davidson, 1996).

INTERNATIONAL CONTEXT OF THE WAR

England. At the beginning of the war, the Confederate government eagerly anticipated European assistance. France and England viewed the war with keen interest due to the large amount of cotton both countries imported from Southern plantations. In addition, ruling classes from both world powers hoped the war would weaken American business interests since the United States had emerged as a viable competitor in the world market. On 13 May 1861 England raised the Confederacy's hopes by proclaiming its neutrality in the conflict following Lincoln's decision to blockade the Southern coastline. The neutrality declaration did not grant recognition to the seceded states as an independent nation. It

River just north of the Mississippi-Tennessee border. On Palm Sunday, 6 April, Confederate general Albert Sidney Johnston and a force of forty thousand attacked unexpectedly at dawn near Shiloh Church. Surprising many Union soldiers who were still half dressed and brewing coffee, the Southerners drove the bluecoats back toward the Tennessee River. After Union reinforcements rushed to the area during the night, Grant's men recovered the next day and forced the Confederates to retreat to Corinth, Mississippi, twenty miles south of

Confederate diplomats James Mason and John Slidell, whose forcible removal from a British ship by the Union navy almost brought England into the war on the side of the South

did, however, identify the Confederacy as a legitimate and equal belligerent, ignoring Union claims that the conflict merely represented a domestic insurrection. For the Confederacy, England's declaration meant that it was one step away from acknowledging Southern independence. Moreover, the status of legitimate belligerent gave the Confederate government bargaining power overseas to negotiate loans and purchase military supplies. In addition, the status granted its navy international recognition and protection as a belligerent under international maritime law.

Disappointments. Unfortunately for the Confederate government, European powers would never intervene to secure Southern independence unless the Confederate army appeared likely to win. Although early Southern victories kept Europe interested, Northern resolve to keep fighting held England and France back. Without assurances of a possible Union surrender, European nations wanted to avoid antagonizing the Union government and jeopardizing diplomatic relations with the United States following the war. Furthermore, Europe looked upon the Civil War in terms of its impact on the European balance of power. England and France were reluctant to intervene without the approval of Russia, which strongly supported the Union. Nevertheless, the Confederate government looked to apply economic pressure on England to coax it to side with the Southern revolutionaries.

King Cotton Diplomacy. Southern leaders hoped to counter European hesitancy by disrupting English and French textile production. In 1861 Southern newspapers called upon plantation owners to hold their cotton from

export for one year. Confederate officials reasoned that the ensuing cotton shortage overseas would depress the British economy and force England to side with the South. "King Cotton diplomacy," as it was called, failed miserably. Southern officials did not recognize that large cotton harvests in 1859 and 1860 had produced a surplus of American cotton in France and England. Both countries could withstand a temporary decline in Southern imports. When the surplus did run out, European textile manufacturers turned to Egyptian and Indian planters to keep their cotton mills open. Thus, as the war progressed, Europeans saw no incentive to recognize the Confederacy. In addition, English antislavery societies moved popular support behind the Union cause, forcing Parliament to keep British soldiers at home. England also maintained trade relations with the Union and risked hurting other British industries, such as the export of iron rails, if it entered on the Southern side. The maturing industrialization of England placed these industries at the forefront of British prosperity, relegating the textile industry to a secondary status in British economic affairs.

The *Trent* Affair. Confederate frustration in obtaining European recognition was highlighted by the *Trent* Affair. In early November 1861, two Confederate diplomats, James Mason and John Slidell, sailed to Cuba and boarded a British steamer, the *Trent*. They planned to sail to Europe to request diplomatic recognition for their new nation. As the ship sailed from Cuba to Saint Thomas, Virgin Islands, a boarding party from a Union naval frigate, the U.S.S. *San Jacinto,* stopped the *Trent,* arrested the diplomats, and carried them to Boston. Furious, England prepared for war. The British navy strengthened its North Atlantic fleet while the British army readied for an overseas landing in Canada. Since a war between England and the United States was not in the best interests of either country, both sought to end the crisis peacefully. President Abraham Lincoln released the two diplomats and stated that the naval commander acted without proper authority. England accepted this indirect apology, and relations between the two countries remained intact. As a result the Union averted war with a second country while thwarting the Confederacy's best and perhaps only opportunity to bring a European power into the war.

Sources:

Howard Jones, *Union in Peril: The Crisis over British Intervention in the Civil War* (Chapel Hill: University of North Carolina Press, 1992);

Robert E. May, *The Union, the Confederacy, and the Atlantic Rim* (West Lafayette, Indiana: Purdue University Press, 1995).

MOBILIZATION OF THE CONFEDERACY

The Battle of Seven Pines. Gen. George McClellan came within six miles of Richmond by the end of May 1862. Relying on inaccurate intelligence reports, McClellan claimed that his Confederate counterpart outnumbered his massive army, and as a result he stopped his advance toward the Confederate capitol in order to await reinforcements from Washington. President Abraham Lincoln denied McClellan's pleas, stating that he needed a strong military presence along the Potomac River to thwart a possible Confederate counterattack upon the Union capital city. Lincoln also bluntly reminded his general-in-chief that the Army of the Potomac had the advantages of size, manpower, and resources over any enemy army. While McClellan hesitated in the face of his adversary, the Confederate commander guarding Richmond, Joseph E. Johnston, attacked. The Battle of Seven Pines (31 May–1 June 1862) produced no strategic advantage for either side. To McClellan the surprise attack was enough to confirm his suspicions and delay a counterattack. For the Confederates the battle

Confederate general Robert E. Lee on Traveller

was a turning point as a wounded Johnston was taken from the field and replaced by Robert E. Lee.

Lee Takes Command. The change in command ended the string of Union victories in 1862. During the first year of the war, Lee served as a military advisor to Confederate president Jefferson Davis. Before secession he was a high-ranking officer in the United States Army, graduating second in his class at West Point and gaining distinction as a field officer in the Mexican War. Recognized as one of the best officers in the U.S. military, Lee turned down an offer to command Union forces in April 1861 and resigned his commission in order to fight for his native Virginia. Unlike McClellan, Lee possessed the qualities of a great general. Throughout the war he boldly took risks in anticipation of Union advances and displayed a fearlessness to attack stronger enemy forces. Lee's superior leadership skills first became evident a

The Battle of Antietam, 17 September 1862: the bloodiest single day of the war (photograph by Mathew Brady)

Union president Abraham Lincoln visiting the Antietam battlefield, with Secret Service head Allan Pinkerton and Maj. Gen. John A. McClernand (photograph by Mathew Brady)

month following the Seven Pines conflict. While McClellan lobbied Lincoln for reinforcements, Lee attacked McClellan's right flank on 26 June, engaging "Little Mac" in a series of battles called the Seven Days' Battles. Lee's 80,000-man army pressured McClellan's 100,000 and by 1 July drove them to a point on the James River twenty miles from the capital city. Casualties on both sides were high (the South lost 20,000 to the North's 16,000). The staggering death rate, coupled with McClellan's failure to counterattack and take Richmond, swung the momentum of the war back to the Confederacy. In a year when Nashville, Memphis, and New Orleans fell into Union hands and many eagerly anticipated Richmond's capitulation, Northern morale took a severe blow.

The First Military Draft. Meanwhile, Jefferson Davis and the Confederate government instituted measures designed to intensify Southern commitment to the war. The defeats at Fort Henry and Fort Donelson shook Southern confidence and convinced Davis to move beyond the euphoria following Bull Run and mobilize for a longer struggle. In April 1862 Davis issued a conscription edict, the first military draft in American history. All able-bodied white males between the ages of eighteen and thirty-five were to be inducted into the Confederate army for three years. The draft immediately produced resentment from the yeoman class (small landowning farmers) that later intensified when the government exempted planters holding twenty or more slaves. In addition, those who could afford it were given the option to hire a substitute from the lower classes until the next call for men. Although it drew criticisms from some Southerners, the draft did spark volunteer enlistments as many young men opted to organize units from their local communities and pick their own officers.

Internal Conflicts. Davis also strengthened Confederate commitment by imposing martial law and suspending the writ of habeas corpus (requiring specific charges in order to hold an individual in jail), especially in areas threatened by immediate Union attack such as Richmond. Many Southern leaders rejected these measures as an attempt by Davis to strengthen the central government and encroach upon sovereign rights. The measures revealed the internal conflicts within the Confederate nation as some leaders worked against Davis. For example, Gov. Joseph E. Brown of Georgia fought conscription at every step and refused to fill the state's manpower quota. Nevertheless, these conflicts in and of themselves would not halt the Southern independence movement as long as Lee and his subordinates continued to master their Union counterparts on the battlefield.

Counteroffensive. By the spring of 1862 Union forces controlled fifty thousand square miles of Confederate territory in the West. At this point in the war, the Union army was not prepared to occupy the confiscated lands with a strong force. Conversely small Northern detachments found themselves deep in enemy territory far from Federal supply trains and the main fighting force; these isolated units were vulnerable to Confederate cavalry raids. During the summer and fall of 1862 Confederate cavalry assaults led by Nathan Bedford Forrest and John Hunt Morgan played havoc with Union occupation troops in Kentucky and Tennessee. They destroyed bridges, tunnels, and railroad tracks while seizing supply bases and capturing Northern garrisons. By August these cavalry raids weakened the Union stranglehold over the

Confederate president Jefferson Davis

western lands and opened the West to a spirited Confederate counterattack. Southern troops moved northward through east Tennessee and Kentucky before reaching the Ohio River in September. If they crossed the Ohio River and invaded Indiana or Ohio, then a Union advance in the West would be delayed.

Antietam. In the East, Lee's war machine pressed forward its counteroffensive in Virginia. By the end of August, Lee and Stonewall Jackson moved north to defeat Union forces for a second time at Bull Run Creek. A week later Lee's men reached the Potomac River and moved into Maryland, just forty miles from Washington, D.C. Lee hoped to split Maryland from Washington in order to weaken Lincoln's political strength and convince Northerners to sue for peace. France and England watched from the wings, anticipating one more Southern victory as a sign of Confederate military superiority. The foreign powers might then side with the South and support the Confederacy as an independent nation. As with many events during this Civil War, a surprising twist of fate turned the tide at a critical moment in history. A Union infantryman found Lee's invasion plans wrapped around three cigars that were dropped earlier by a Confederate officer. This time McClellan acted with uncharacteristic speed and blocked Lee's advance at Antietam Creek near the town of Sharpsburg, Maryland. On 17 September, in the bloodiest day of the war, McClellan

Known as the "Thunderbolt of the Confederacy," Confederate cavalry commander John Hunt Morgan played a prominent role in the Western counteroffensive of 1862 by conducting raids into Kentucky. A year later in June 1863, Morgan again moved toward the Ohio River Valley to raid Union supply lines and simultaneously divert Federal reinforcements from reaching Tennessee, where Confederate General Braxton Bragg and his Army of Tennessee were retreating in the face of a stronger Union force.

Morgan, a veteran of the Mexican War and a businessman by trade, decided to move his two cavalry brigades into Indiana and Ohio. He surmised that a trek across the southern counties of those two states would be more effective in relieving the pressure on Bragg. Morgan planned to raid Cincinnati, move east to the Ohio River, and then ride through Pennsylvania to join Lee's army. Although Bragg ordered him not to undertake such a risky venture, Morgan disobeyed his superior officer. After several small skirmishes in Kentucky delayed their advance, Morgan's 2,400 raiders entered Indiana on 8 July 1863. There the invaders battled a local militia unit, scattering them with cannon fire from two rifled Parrott artillery pieces.

As they progressed through enemy territory, Morgan's men continued to tussle with small militia units. The Confederate cavalrymen decided to make these civilian soldiers "feel the war" and began to live off the land, stealing food, horses, and household goods. In some places, they burned farmsteads used by Ohio militiamen as hiding places. Pressured by Federal cavalry, Morgan decided to race non-stop across Ohio and ford the Ohio River into West Virginia. Morgan did not anticipate, however, the mobilization of 50,000 militiamen who slowed his men with small arms fire. Riding hard for sixteen consecutive days and nights, Morgan reached Ohio's eastern border on 18 July. Stranded on Buffington Island and surrounded by Union river gunboats, half of the Confederates surrendered. Morgan escaped with over a thousand Southern horsemen but finally surrendered at New Lisbon, Ohio, on 26 July after failing to secure safe passage across the river. Although the South lost two cavalry brigades, Morgan's raid did delay the advancement of the Union Twenty-third Army Corps into Tennessee. More importantly, by bringing the war to civilians, Morgan assisted Lee in scaring unsuspecting civilians and damaging their will to continue supporting the war effort.

Source: Shelby Foote, *The Civil War, a Narrative: Fredericksburg to Meridian* (New York: Vintage Books, 1986), pp.678–683.

---

forced Lee back into Virginia. In less than seven hours, both sides had six thousand men killed and over seventeen thousand wounded. Claiming that overwhelming enemy reinforcements awaited his advance, McClellan refused to finish Lee and allowed the invading Southerners to escape back to Virginia.

Lee Survives. A month later, in October 1862, the Confederate cavalry raiders in the West were turned back at Perryville, Kentucky. Thus the failed invasions denied the Southern government propaganda material to win coveted European assistance. Despite these setbacks, Lee's army survived and repulsed two Northern offensives at Fredericksburg in December 1862 and Chancellorsville in May 1863. The Battle of Chancellorsville proved costly, however, as Lee's ablest general, Stonewall Jackson, was mortally wounded by friendly fire. By the end of May, Lee looked northward one more time. In the West, Union armies were moving closer to another victory. Lee planned to invade the Northern states for a second time in an attempt to divert troops from the Mississippi. This time it would be more of a gamble as the Confederate general decided to cut his supply lines and live off the land. Lee would bypass Maryland and move into Pennsylvania in order to frighten civilians and weaken Northern resolve. At the same time, he also wanted to revive European interest and sway foreign powers to intervene on behalf of Southern independence.

Sources:

Douglass S. Freeman, *R. E. Lee,* 4 volumes (New York: Scribners, 1934–1935);

Allan Nevins, *The War for the Union,* volume 2 (New York: Scribners, 1960);

Emory M. Thomas, *The Confederate Nation 1861–1865* (New York: Harper & Row, 1979).

MOBILIZATION OF THE UNION

A Dismissal. Gen. George McClellan's Peninsula campaign mirrored the rise and fall of Northern morale during the spring and early summer of 1862. Northerners sensed victory in May when McClellan's force camped six miles outside Richmond, but morale collapsed in July as Lee drove a hesitant McClellan twenty miles backward to the James River in seven days. Once again claiming that he and his men were outnumbered, McClellan called for reinforcements and planned a second march to Richmond. Lincoln responded by replacing McClellan as general-in-chief of the army with Henry W. Halleck and ordered "Little Mac" back to Washington.

Confederate dead after Gettysburg

Militia Act. Unlike a year earlier, when Northern resolve hardened after the first defeat at Bull Run, the Northern response wavered after Lee's counteroffensive in 1862. New recruits trickled into Union recruiting offices after the Seven Days' fiasco. Congress then passed a Militia Act in July authorizing the president to institute a draft in order to force state governments to meet recruiting quotas. The following month Lincoln made plans to conscript 300,000 men, but before the draft could be implemented, Federal military forces received 421,000 three-year volunteers and 87,000 nine-month militiamen. Lincoln thus avoided a national draft and deflated civilian resentment, but the message was clear: Northern support for the war waxed and waned in direct correlation to Union success or failure on the battlefield.

Decision for Emancipation. In July Lincoln moved to escalate the war beyond preserving the Union. From the beginning, Radical Republicans and abolitionists pushed for emancipation as a war aim. Swayed by their arguments and the recent Union retreat from Virginia, Congress passed a Second Confiscation Act in July 1862 authorizing Union commanders to free all slaves that came within Union lines. Acknowledging the growing sentiment that to fight slaveholders without attacking slavery was a "half-hearted" business, Lincoln informed his cabinet at a 22 July meeting that he planned to issue an emancipation proclamation. The revolutionary edict would abolish slavery in the seceded states. Union soldiers would not only fight to save the Constitution, but also to free the slaves, turning the rebellion into a war of liberation. Lincoln hoped not only to hurt the South militarily but also to undermine renewed Confederate efforts to obtain European recognition. The president decided to wait for a Union victory on the battlefield before signing the proclamation into law after Secretary of State William Seward convinced Lincoln that to do otherwise would make emancipation appear to be an act of mere desperation.

Preliminary Proclamation. Following the Union victory at Antietam, Lincoln released a preliminary Emancipation Proclamation on 22 September 1862. It stated that unless the seceded Confederate states voluntarily returned to the Union by 1 January 1863, all slaves within those states would be free. The act specifically excluded the Union slave states (Maryland, Delaware, Missouri, and Kentucky) and Southern territory under Union control. Approximately 830,000 slaves out of a total of four million were excluded under the provisions of this decree. On paper the Proclamation liberated all enslaved persons south of the Mason-Dixon line, but in reality they were not liberated until the arrival of Northern troops. Opposition to Lincoln's policy grew nevertheless in the North as Peace Democrats agitated for an immediate cessation of hostilities without destroying slavery. To prevent criticism from undermining recruitment, Lincoln suspended the writ of habeas corpus throughout the Northern states in September 1862. This gave Union authorities the power to arrest anyone suspected of disloyal or antiwar activism and hold them indefinitely without trial.

Gettysburg. In November 1862 Lincoln fired McClellan as commander of the Army of the Potomac because he failed to follow his victory at Antietam with a vigorous pursuit of Lee's army. He replaced McClellan with Gen. Ambrose E. Burnside, who suffered defeat at Fredericksburg, Virginia, in December. An exasperated Lincoln then replaced Burnside with Gen. Joseph Hooker, who nearly lost the entire Army of the Potomac at Chancellorsville, Virginia, in May 1863. One month later Lee moved north into Pennsylvania. George G. Meade, the latest commander of the Army of the Potomac, positioned the Union army between Lee and the nation's capital to check the Confederate advance. On 1–3 July, Union and Confederate forces fought the war's most famous battle after reconnaissance teams from both armies accidentally collided at the small town of Gettysburg. Following two days of failed assaults, Lee sent thirteen thousand screaming infantrymen, under the command of George Pickett, to assault the center of Meade's forces, entrenched on Cemetery Ridge. "Pickett's Charge" was Lee's greatest mistake, be-

The Fifty-Fourth Massachusetts Infantry Regiment attempting to capture Battery Wagner at Charleston Harbor

cause Union defenders killed or wounded more than half of the charging Confederates and forced Lee to retreat once again into Virginia on 4 July. Lee's defeated Army of Northern Virginia lost nearly a third of its men at Gettysburg, and the severely weakened Confederate army never again threatened the Northern states with invasion.

Vicksburg. Independence Day 1863 also marked a turning point in the war because of the dramatic news that came from the Western theater. After a prolonged siege, Vicksburg, a Confederate stronghold on the Mississippi River, fell to Gen. Ulysses S. Grant. Four days later, the last Confederate fort on the Mississippi, Port Hudson, fell to Union troops. These stunning victories now placed the entire Mississippi River under Union control and split the Confederate nation geographically, as Texas, Louisiana, and Arkansas were cut off from other Southern states.

Draft Riots. The summer of 1863 also signified a stronger Union commitment to the war. In March Congress had turned to a national draft which included a clause allowing men to hire substitutes for $300 (a year's wage for a worker or ordinary farmer) to take their places. Not surprisingly, the draft produced much resentment, raising cries that the conflict was a "rich man's war, but a poor man's fight." Soon antidraft protests turned into antidraft violence. The worst incident oc-

curred on 13 July in New York City when mobs of Irish workingmen and women took to the streets. After four days of rioting and more than a hundred deaths, the rioters were stopped by Federal troops fresh from Gettysburg. It was the worst riot in American history and represented one of the last acts of public defiance against the Union war efforts. Afterward, antiwar sentiment declined, especially following the victories at Gettysburg and Vicksburg.

Battery Wagner. Inspiring news from South Carolina brought further criticism upon the rioters. On 18 July African American soldiers attempted to take Battery Wagner, a Confederate stronghold at the entrance of Charleston Harbor. (Lincoln's Emancipation Proclamation had called for the enlistment of African Americans into Union ranks). Led by Col. Robert Gould Shaw, a product of Boston's high society, the Fifty-Fourth Massachusetts Regiment became the first Northern black unit to engage Confederate soldiers in a major battle. At Battery Wagner the regiment unsuccessfully charged the enemy defenses and lost 40 percent of its strength, but the defeat was hailed as a moral victory throughout the North. Eradicating popular myths of black inferiority, the African Americans under Shaw proved they could fight aggressively for their freedom. Before the war was over, some 180,000 blacks would fight for the Union.

THE LOUISIANA NATIVE GUARDS

Organized in April 1861, the Louisiana Native Guards, an African American regiment, served in both the Confederate and Union armies. After the fall of Fort Sumter, the free black community of New Orleans answered Jefferson Davis' call to arms and formed an all-black militia unit. The regiment numbered 35 officers and 870 enlisted men; more than 80 percent were mulattoes, individuals having both white and black ancestry.

Ignoring the unit's requests to fight, Southern military leaders relegated the regiment to parades and other public displays. When New Orleans fell in April 1862, Confederate authorities quickly disbanded the unit before Northern soldiers occupied the port. Union General Benjamin F. Butler took control of the city in May. Attempting to gain political favor with Republican officials, Butler mustered the African Americans, including many runaway slaves, into the Union army in September 1862, several months before the Emancipation Proclamation would officially sanction the enlistment of black soldiers. They were formed into three regiments, designated the First, Second, and Third Louisiana Native Guard Infantry. In May 1863 the regiments fought at the battle of Port Hudson, a Confederate stronghold on the Mississippi River. Although they fought bravely, the attack was repelled by the Confederate defenders and the Union commander placed the fort under siege. Nevertheless the Louisiana Native Guards became the first black regiment to fight in a major Civil War engagement. Afterward, like so many other African American regiments, the Louisiana Native Guards were relegated to rear echelon details.

Source: James G. Hollandsworth, *The Louisiana Native Guards: The Black Military Experience During the Civil War* (Baton Rouge: Louisiana State University Press, 1995).

Sources:

Dudley Taylor Cornish, *The Sable Arm: Black Troops in the Union Army, 1861–1865* (Lawrence: University Press of Kansas, 1987);

Shelby Foote, *The Civil War, a Narrative: Fredericksburg to Meridian* (New York: Random House, 1963);

Mark E. Neely Jr., *Fate of Liberty: Abraham Lincoln and Civil Liberties* (New York: Oxford University Press, 1991).

THE NEW WAR OF ATTRITION

Virginia. By the end of 1863 Northern hopes for a quick end to the war faded after Union troops failed to capitalize on their July victories. Union general George G. Meade and his Army of the Potomac followed Robert E. Lee's army into Virginia, but, like his predecessors, Meade failed to strike a crushing blow against the Confederate commander's crippled force. For the rest of the year both armies jockeyed for position in Virginia with no results. In the West the war also slowed, as Confederate and Union troops parried from June to November 1863 in Tennessee. At the end of November, Gen. Ulysses S. Grant finally drove Southern forces back to Georgia. Although Georgia was now open to Union invasion, the long campaign in East Tennessee once again confirmed Confederate resiliency to check Northern invasion. Many Northerners now accepted the fact that strategic victories alone, such as the capitulation of important cities, would not compel Confederate forces to lay down arms. Federal commanders would have to destroy the Southern army.

Southern Strategy. Other events in 1863 also affected Confederate strategy on the battlefield. Defeats at Gettysburg and Chattanooga, Tennessee (23–25 November), shattered Southern hopes for a knockout blow through invasion of the North or European intervention. Moreover, staggering casualties took their toll on the Confederate army, and the South found it increasingly difficult to secure new recruits. By the end of 1863 Confederate officials hoped to defeat the Union at the ballot box. They implemented a defensive strategy, hoping to prolong the war and break the Northerners' will to continue fighting. If this strategy worked, Southern leaders were convinced that in the November 1864 elections the North would elect a Democrat who would enter into immediate peace negotiations to end the war and leave the Confederate nation intact.

Grant Takes Command. In 1864 Union president Abraham Lincoln faced an election year. Although fighting slowed down by January 1864, military successes during the previous summer and fall fed Northern expectations for a quick victory. To meet this demand, Lincoln turned to Grant and named him general-in-chief in March. The new commander of Union armies planned to wage a war of attrition, wearing down enemy forces with his superior numbers in troops and supplies. Grant designed a plan to coordinate movements in the Eastern and Western theaters: two armies would strike Confederate forces simultaneously to prevent Lee from moving reinforcements from one region to the other. While Grant himself launched an offensive against Lee in Virginia, Gen. William T. Sherman, Grant's replacement in the West, would attack Confederate defenses in Georgia. With 115,000 troops under his command, Grant moved against Lee's 75,000-man army in May. Over the next six weeks, Lee continually checked Grant's advance in Virginia. Unlike previous Union commanders and despite an astonishingly high casualty rate, Grant refused to retreat and kept moving his force south toward Richmond. The series of battles (the Wilderness, 5–6 May; Spotsylvania Courthouse, 8–12 May; and Cold Harbor, 1–3 June) produced the war's heaviest casualties. Grant lost 60,000 men compared with 30,000 for Lee. By mid June, Grant changed strategies and decided to bypass Richmond and strike farther south.

The Crater at Petersburg, Virginia

Petersburg. Grant planned to hit the railroad junction at Petersburg, a town located twenty miles south of Richmond which guarded the rail link to other Southern states. If it fell Grant could isolate the Confederate capital and cut its communications to Southern armies in other seceded states. Lee again challenged Grant's assault, however, and this time Grant viewed the high casualties as a sign to settle down for a siege against the Confederate trenches that stretched from Petersburg to Richmond.

The Battle of the Crater. The frustration of the Union invaders trying to break through Confederate defenses at Petersburg was highlighted at the end of July. Lt. Col. Henry Pleasants, the commander of the Forty-Eighth Pennsylvania Infantry, a regiment of former coal miners, received permission to dig a mine under the enemy entrenchments and fill it with gunpowder. After detonating the explosives and blowing a hole in the Confederate line, Union infantry would sweep around the abyss and attack the enemy flanks and rear. On 30 July 1864 the miners detonated the gunpowder and blew a huge crater in the Confederate fortifications. However, instead of sweeping around the hole and attacking the rattled enemy flanks, Brig. Gen. James H. Ledlie sent his men into the crater. The Federals quickly found themselves trapped, and they became easy prey for Southern sharpshooters. As he watched his men die like ducks in a shooting gallery, Grant lamented that the battle was "the saddest affair I have witnessed" and ordered a retreat. He finally settled down to a prolonged nine-month siege. In addition to this fiasco, news from Georgia mirrored the stalled operations in Virginia—Sherman's troops were stalled at the outskirts of Atlanta. With Northern elections only a few months away, the Confederate strategy of weakening Northern resolve seemed to be working as the conflict drew to an apparent stalemate.

Sources:

Bruce Catton, *A Stillness at Appomattox* (Garden City, N.Y.: Doubleday, 1953);

William S. McFeely, *Grant: A Biography* (New York: Norton, 1981).

SOLDIERS IN CAMP

Waiting. Following Gettysburg both sides settled into camps or defensive fortifications during the long, monotonous stretch from July 1863 to August 1864. As in any war, boredom filled the everyday life of Civil War soldiers. Union and Confederate fighting men averaged fifty days in camp for every day in battle. Lulls in the fighting allowed men to bond and build up morale before the next frontal assaults decimated regimental strength and destroyed small-unit cohesion.

Northern Camps. Reveille woke Union soldiers every morning at five o'clock (six in the winter). After roll call and breakfast, the soldiers spent the rest of the day drilling and marching. The daily drills were designed to break resistance to military authority and to make soldiers work as a cohesive unit. The Northern enlisted men hated it. "The first thing in the morning is drill, then drill, then drill again," wrote one frustrated bluecoat. "Then drill, a little more drill . . . Between drills, we drill and sometimes stop to eat a little and have rollcall." In the afternoon the men spent most of their time preparing their uniforms for the evening dress parade. The troops

Examples of Union and Confederate uniforms

polished boots and brass buckles and mended clothing in order to pass inspection and move on to supper call. By summer 1862 the Union army had standardized the Northern uniform. Each soldier wore a blue cap with black visor; a long, dark blue dress coat with stand-up collar; light blue trousers; and rough black shoes. The uniforms were made of wool and worn year-round. The blue coats and trousers were trimmed with stripes to signify a particular combat branch: blue for infantry, scarlet for artillery, and yellow for cavalry. Brass insignia sewn into caps also designated branch: a bugle for infantry, crossed sabres for cavalry, and crossed cannons for artillery. Unlike their Confederate counterparts, Federal uniforms were of high quality; long campaigns, rather than shortage in stock, led to brief instances of raggedness.

Northern Food. The Union enlisted man's diet consisted of three main staples: bread, meat, and coffee; fresh fruits and vegetables were available depending on the season. Throughout the war, Northern soldiers bitterly complained about the bread, commonly known as "hardtack." It was a hard, stale cracker that soldiers soaked in water or coffee in order to eat; ten or twelve crackers equaled a full ration. Despite the lack of variety or texture in their diet, the Union army was well fed and, by the end of the war, the Northern soldier ate better and received more food than contemporary soldiers in the British, French, or Russian armies.

Off-Duty. After supper call, soldiers relaxed and engaged in activities that helped them to escape camp routine. They wrote letters, sang songs, and played games. The average age of the Northern soldier (by July 1863)

PRISONERS OF WAR

In the beginning of the Civil War, the Union and Confederate governments agreed to exchange an equal number of captured soldiers immediately following a battle. This practice left detention centers virtually empty and kept precious resources such as food and medical supplies reserved for the soldiers in the field. In 1863 the exchange policy stopped when the Confederate government refused to exchange captured black soldiers and instead re-enslaved them. By December 1863 Confederate prisons held 13,000 Federals while Northern prisons kept 26,000 Southerners under guard. Following the May–July 1864 battles in Virginia, the prison population exploded for both sides, leaving many captured men without adequate shelter, food, and medical care. The results were tragic.

Although most captured soldiers exaggerate the conditions of their captivity, Civil War prisons were indeed ghastly places. The overcrowded stockades, coupled with poor sanitation and bad water, became death traps. Some prison camps offered no shelter from the elements and men were forced to build makeshift tents from rags, blankets, and uniforms. The worst conditions were at Andersonville, Georgia. At this site the Confederates housed 33,000 Northerners in a stockade built to hold 15,000. One hundred prisoners died every day, and gangs of thieves ruled the overcrowded conditions. Disease thrived in the confined area since a small stream used for drinking water also doubled as a sewer. Similar conditions like these in other prisoner of war camps produced high mortality rates: by 1865 over 30,000 Federals died in Southern prisons while 25,000 Confederates died in Northern detention stockades.

Sources: Larry M. Logue, *To Appomattox and Beyond: The Civil War Soldier in War and Peace* (Chicago: Ivan R. Dee, 1996);

William Marvel, *Andersonville: The Last Depot* (Chapel Hill: University of North Carolina Press, 1994).

Columbia, South Carolina, after the departure of Gen. William T. Sherman

ern counterpart, the Southern soldier usually did not receive a full supper ration. Poor distribution, lack of salt and preservatives, and limited access to transportation facilities restricted the Southern diet to cornbread and beef. Complaints about the bleak Southern diet dominated letters home. "If any person offers me cornbread after this war comes to a close," one exasperated Southerner wrote. "I shall *probably* tell him to —— go to hell!" Men under the age of twenty-five also dominated Confederate ranks, and they turned to songs, hunting, gambling, and alcohol as diversions from the war. To avoid using ammunition, the soldiers often hunted with clubs and competed with each other for extra rations. Since the Southern soldier received only eleven Confederate dollars a month (by the end of the war they were worth only half their value), troops gambled for food and used the extra rations to trade for tobacco and stationery. In addition to a lack of food, the Southern army lacked consistency in its uniforms. Although the standard issue was a gray coat and trousers, many units did not have enough uniforms in stock, and a homespun, ragged appearance became rampant in the ranks. Moreover, the Union naval blockade forced the Confederate army to use homemade dye to color uniforms. The dye was made from copperas (a green sulfate) and walnut shells which gave the Confederate uniform a yellowish brown color that soldiers called "butternut." As both armies standardized their uniforms by 1862, Northern soldiers were commonly called "bluecoats" while Southern soldiers were labeled "butternuts."

Sources:
Larry M. Logue, *To Appomattox and Beyond: The Civil War Soldier in War and Peace* (Chicago: Ivan R. Dee, 1996);

James I. Robertson Jr., *Soldiers Blue and Gray* (Columbia: University of South Carolina Press, 1988);

Bell I. Wiley, *The Life of Billy Yank: The Common Soldier of the Union* (Baton Rouge: Louisiana State University Press, 1978);

Wiley, *The Life of Johnny Reb: The Common Soldier of the Confederacy* (Baton Rouge: Louisiana State University Press, 1978).

was twenty-five, and with the arrival of payday (once every other month), the tired bluecoats turned to hedonistic pleasures such as alcohol consumption, gambling, or visiting a prostitute. Gambling was particularly hard on the losers since white Northern soldiers made only thirteen dollars a month while black soldiers received ten. By the end of the war, pay was raised to sixteen dollars a month for both races.

Confederate Camps. For the most part, Confederate camp life mirrored the Union routine. Unlike his North-

Union soldiers outside the Wilmer McLean home at Appomattox Court House, Virginia, where Lee surrendered to Grant

TRIUMPH OF THE NORTH

Deadlock. The stalemates at Petersburg and Atlanta spread despair throughout the North. Many felt Gen. Ulysses S. Grant's strategies had turned the war into a draw. The high Union death rate in all theaters (110,000 in three months), coupled with reports that Northern prisoners at Andersonville, Georgia, were dying at a rate of one hundred a day, combined to revive antiwar sentiments. Even faithful Republicans became swept along by Northern discontent; some called for President Abraham Lincoln to drop emancipation as a war aim. Many Republicans became convinced that the president would lose in the upcoming November 1864 elections to his Democrat opponent, former Union general-in-chief George B. McClellan.

Atlanta. Nevertheless, the war still raged, and Northern morale continued to swing in response to reports from the battlefield. A glimmer of optimism first emerged in August when Adm. David Farragut's wooden fleet maneuvered around underwater mines and took Mobile Bay, an important Confederate port located in the Gulf of Mexico on the Alabama coast. A month later the tide turned again. In September 1864 Northern sentiment swung back to the side of the president as Gen. William T. Sherman sent good news from Georgia. On 2 September Sherman's men captured the last rail link into Atlanta, forcing Confederate general John Bell Hood to abandon the city to save his army. The victory restored Northern faith in Lincoln as a leader, while Democrat claims that the war was a failure fell on deaf ears. Additional reports from the Shenandoah Valley, Virginia, secured Lincoln's reelection bid. There, in October, Union cavalry general Philip Sheridan swept Jubal Early and his Confederate horsemen from the area. Twice before, the valley had served as an invasion route north for the Confederate army, and its farms continued to supply the Army of Northern Vir-

ginia. Now, Union control of the area denied Southern forces precious foodstuffs. In the November elections, Lincoln easily beat McClellan; 80 percent of soldiers in the field voted to retain their commander-in-chief in office.

March to the Sea. In response to Lincoln's reelection, Confederate president Jefferson Davis declared that his nation stood "defiant as ever" and would continue to persist wholeheartedly against Northern aggression. Determined to break Southern will, Sherman decided to march through the eastern Georgia countryside. Sending half his army to Tennessee to check Hood's impending counterattack at Nashville, Sherman abandoned his supply lines in November to begin his famous "March to the Sea." After three years of fighting Confederate soldiers, Sherman now turned his attention to the civilian will to fight. Moving unopposed and living off the land, Sherman had his men cut a sixty-mile swath across Georgia, demolishing everything in their path. Not only did Sherman want to hurt the Confederate army by destroying war matériel and railroads, but he also sought to make the Southern civilian population feel the war by burning towns, plantations, and anything else within his army's reach. "We cannot change the hearts of those people of the South," he said, "but we can make war so terrible and make them so sick of war that generations would pass away before they would again appeal to it." By 20 December he reached Savannah and presented the port to Lincoln as a Christmas gift. Moving with an air of invincibility, Sherman moved into South Carolina in February and took Columbia before finally stopping his destructive path in North Carolina. Sherman's five-month crusade spread terror and despair throughout the South. "All is gloom, despondency, and inactivity," wrote one South Carolinian. "Our army is demoralized and the people panic stricken. To fight longer seems to be madness."

Conclusion. As Sherman conquered the Southern coastline, the war slowly moved to a close. In December 1864, Union general George H. Thomas defeated and nearly annihilated Hood's forces at Nashville. By February, Sherman's march and Grant's suffocating siege at Petersburg convinced many Confederate soldiers to return home. On 1 April 1865 Gen. Philip Sheridan's cavalry broke Robert E. Lee's right flank and cut the last rail link into Petersburg. The next day, in a desperate attempt to join Gen. Joseph E. Johnston in North Carolina, Lee's army set fire to all military supplies in Richmond and retreated west. Sensing victory at hand, Grant pressed forward and blocked Lee's escape route at Appomattox Court House, ninety miles from Petersburg on 8 April. The following morning, Palm Sunday, Lee formally surrendered to Grant in the parlor of a private residence. Nine days later, Johnston surrendered in North Carolina, officially ending hostilities between North and South.

Sources:

Bruce Catton, *A Stillness at Appomattox* (Garden City, N.Y.: Doubleday, 1953);

Shelby Foote, *The Civil War, a Narrative: Red River to Appomattox* (New York: Random House, 1974).

HEADLINE MAKERS

CLARA BARTON

1821–1912

FOUNDER OF THE AMERICAN RED CROSS

Responsibility. With her indomitable will, limitless energy, and sense of mission, Clara Barton was ideally suited to work on the battlefront during the Civil War and in disaster relief as the head of the American Red Cross, whose founding was largely a personal achievement. Born on Christmas Day 1821 to prosperous farmers Stephen Barton and Sarah Stone Barton in Oxford, Massachusetts, Clarissa Harlowe Barton was a shy and sensitive child with a quick temper. Born ten years later than her youngest sibling, Clara grew up with no playmates but with a good education. Her mother, troubled by Clara's shyness, consulted phrenologist Lorenzo Fowler, who offered the advice, "Throw responsibility upon her. . . . As soon as her age will permit, give her a school to teach." So, at age fifteen, Clara Barton began a career as a teacher.

Teacher. Despite her youth and inexperience, she was immediately successful and gained self-confidence as well as initiative. After running several district schools, she moved to North Oxford and for ten years oversaw the education of local children and workers of a mill owned by her brothers. After completing a course at the Liberal Institute in Clinton, New York, she accepted a teaching position in Bordentown, New Jersey, where she displayed the qualities that would make her both a powerful and controversial figure. At the time, free public schools were a rarity, and Barton offered to serve three months without pay if the town would make the school free for all the town's children. Overcoming powerful opposition, she personally persuaded the town's leaders to support her experiment. It was such a success that a larger schoolhouse had to be built and an assistant teacher hired. But when opposition to a woman heading so large a school caused the town to appoint a male principal, Barton resigned rather than accept a subordinate role, thus ending her eighteen-year career in education.

An Angel. In 1854 Barton moved to Washington, finding employment as a clerk in the Patent Office. In 1861 she began her war service by supplying the needs of the Sixth Massachusetts Regiment, which en route to Washington had had to fight its way through Baltimore (many of whose residents sympathized with the South) and whose soldiers had lost much of their baggage. Moved by stories of soldiers' suffering during the Battle of Bull Run, she took the initiative to advertise in the *Worcester Spy* for supplies for the wounded. As donated provisions accumulated, she established a distributing agency. During the remainder of the war she displayed great courage and perseverance in getting supplies to the front. The horrors of battle did not faze her. Thousands of soldiers remembered fondly this slight, seemingly frail woman ministering to the wounded during battle, applying to her the sobriquet "Angel of the Battlefield." Rather than as a field nurse, her greatest service was in securing provisions for the relief of suffering and in getting them to where they were needed promptly.

Mission. Her health failing, Barton went abroad in 1869, but soon found herself in the midst of the Franco-Prussian War. It was here that she began her association with the International Red Cross, which had been established in 1864, distributing relief in the French cities of Strasbourg, Paris, Lyons, Belfort, and Montpellier. Honored with the Iron Cross of Merit by the emperor of Germany, she returned home in 1873 determined to establish an American Red Cross. She initiated a crusade almost single-handedly and began an educational campaign, personally visiting the secretaries of state and war as well as influential congressmen and publishing a pamphlet titled "The Red Cross of the Geneva Convention, What Is It?" (1878). In 1881 she persuaded President James Garfield to adopt the treaty bringing the United States into the International Red Cross. After Garfield was assassinated, President Chester A. Arthur secured Senate confirmation of the treaty. In March 1882, after a four-year struggle, the American Red Cross became a reality, almost entirely due to Barton's efforts.

American Red Cross. For the next twenty-three years she directed the activities of the organization, personally supervising its relief work during the various natural disasters of the period and during the Spanish-American War. She ran the Red Cross largely as her personal fiefdom, which was both its strength and its weakness: its strength because of the energy and zeal with which she directed the organization, and its weakness because her domineering role inhibited its growth and failed to inspire public confidence. While she was perfectly suited for the relief work itself, she was not as well qualified to run a large, bureaucratic organization. Her unwillingness to delegate responsibility and her arbitrary governance (she often acted without consulting the Red Cross's executive committee) offended members and potential supporters. Public confidence waned as the organization's accounting practices came under question, finally resulting in a congressional investigation. After a bitter fight she resigned the presidency, making possible a thorough reorganization of the society. Embittered by the affair, she briefly entertained the idea of going to Mexico to establish a Red Cross there but was finally dissuaded. She spent her remaining years at her home just outside Washington and died on Good Friday, 12 April 1912.

Sources:

David H. Burton, *Clara Barton: In the Service of Humanity* (Westport, Conn. & London: Greenwood Press, 1995);

Elizabeth Brown Pryor, *Clara Barton: Professional Angel* (Philadelphia: University of Pennsylvania Press, 1987);

Ishbel Ross, *Angel of the Battlefield* (New York: Harper, 1956).

NATHAN BEDFORD FORREST

1821-1877

CONFEDERATE CAVALRY

COMMANDER

Raider. One of the best cavalry commanders during the Civil War was Confederate general Nathan Bedford Forrest. For four years Forrest and his men frustrated Union military leaders with aggressive raids behind Federal lines. Time and again these Southern raiders appeared out of nowhere and thwarted Union advances. At various skirmishes Forrest was successful in overpowering enemy forces by fighting from a dismounted position and using such irregular weapons as shotguns, squirrel rifles, and flintlock muskets. These tactics allowed Forrest to rout Northern cavalry units which fought in a conventional manner and relied on the cavalry saber as a battle weapon. Throughout the war Forrest operated an independent command that wreaked havoc upon Union forces and at times created controversy by stepping outside the traditional lines of nineteenth-century warfare.

Background. Forrest was born in a secluded Tennessee frontier cabin during the summer of 1821. When he turned sixteen his father, a blacksmith, died, leaving Nathan as the sole family provider. Although he did not receive a formal education, Forrest worked as a real estate broker and slave trader and eventually amassed a large fortune, buying several cotton plantations in Arkansas and Mississippi. At the time of the outbreak of war between the North and the South, he was living in Memphis. Since he did not have a college degree or military training, Forrest enlisted as a private in a cavalry regiment that he raised and equipped himself. By October 1861 the new unit elected him as its commander with the rank of lieutenant colonel. The regiment's first assignment was at Fort Donelson on the Kentucky-Tennessee border, the site of Union general Ulysses S. Grant's early victory. Informed that the Confederate commander would surrender the stronghold to Grant, Forrest led his cavalrymen through Union lines by fording flooded rivers.

A Clever Opponent. Forrest soon gained a reputation as a military genius. In April 1862 his men fought at Shiloh, Mississippi, where Forrest was seriously wounded. After he recovered, Forrest and his cavalrymen fought at Murfreesboro, Tennessee. His surprise attack captured a thousand Union soldiers, destroyed supplies valued at a million dollars, and wrecked a portion of the railroad. For the next year and a half Forrest conducted raids from west Tennessee and moved as far as the Ohio River. He hit Union supply lines and at one point severely impeded Grant's drive to Vicksburg, Mississippi. In the spring of 1863 Forrest displayed his tactical genius by tricking a Union commander into surrendering his fifteen hundred soldiers to Forrest's battalion of five hundred.

Fort Pillow. One of the most controversial events of the Civil War involved Forrest and his cavalrymen at Fort Pillow, Tennessee, in April 1864. In an attack known as the "Fort Pillow Massacre," the Southern raiders reportedly murdered black Union troops who were trying to surrender. Forrest denied the charge that his men killed African American soldiers in cold blood. On previous occasions, however, Forrest sought to terrorize Union garrisons and force them to give up by raising the threat of no quarter. At Fort Pillow, his men apparently carried out the threat and were not ordered to stop the carnage. In his report written three days after the event, Forrest seemed to take delight in the death of enemy troops who were shot in the Mississippi River trying to escape. He noted that their blood "dyed" the river red and he hoped that their death "will demonstrate to the Northern people that negro soldiers cannot cope with Southerners." Whether he ordered the massacre or not, the event followed Forrest for the rest of the war and, coupled with his leadership role in the Ku Klux Klan during the Reconstruction era, clearly showed his belief in white supremacy.

Final Stages. From June to November 1864 Forrest conducted a series of raids against Union general William T. Sherman's supply lines. On several occasions

Forrest beat Union forces nearly twice the size of his unit. On 10 June he captured two thousand Federals along with sixteen guns and 250 wagons at Brices Cross Roads, Mississippi. Later, while operating in west Tennessee in October and November 1864, Forrest destroyed four Union gunboats, fourteen river transports, and $7 million worth of property. After serving with Confederate general John Bell Hood during the latter's catastrophic Tennessee campaign, Forrest returned to his independent operations in 1865 and received a promotion to lieutenant general in February. However, his command grew ineffective as hunger and Forrest's aggressive tactics finally took its toll on his men. Failing to stop Union forces from capturing Selma, Alabama, in April 1865, Forrest finally surrendered to Northern troops in May. Following the war, many military historians recognized Forrest as the best tactician to fight for the Confederacy.

Sources:

John S. Bowman, ed., *Who Was Who in the Civil War* (New York: Crescent Books, 1994);

Dudley T. Cornish, *The Sable Arm: Black Troops in the Union Army, 1861–1865* (Lawrence: University Press of Kansas, 1987).

THOMAS J. "STONEWALL" JACKSON

1824-1863

CONFEDERATE GENERAL

Hero. Confederate general Thomas J. Jackson was arguably the first military hero of the Civil War, gaining a national reputation as a winner and tough warrior. During the First Battle of Bull Run in July 1861, when Federal troops appeared close to victory, Jackson suddenly arrived with his fellow Virginians to shore up the weakened Confederate line. Jackson's men firmly held their positions and turned back several enemy assaults. Trying to rally his own troops among the confusion, Gen. Bernard Bee pointed toward Jackson's men on his left and yelled: "Look at Jackson's brigade! It stands there like a stone wall!" The Southerners finally regrouped and counterattacked, forcing the Northerners to retreat. For his heroic stand, Jackson gained celebrity status and, until his untimely death, he was simply recognized as "Stonewall."

Early Years. Thomas Jackson was born on 21 January 1824, in Clarksburg (now Clarksville), Virginia. Orphaned at age six, Jackson was raised by his aunt and uncle in one of Virginia's poorest regions (this area would later become the state of West Virginia). Although he lacked a formal education, Jackson received an appointment to West Point in 1842. He was known for his strong ambition and disciplined study

habits. He graduated seventeenth out of forty-three in a class that would send twenty-four general officers to the Union and Confederate armies. Like many Civil War officers, Jackson fought in the Mexican War. Following that conflict, he resigned his commission in 1852 in order to teach physics at the Virginia Military Institute in Lexington. During his tenure, he was not liked by the students and many ridiculed him and his rigid teaching habits behind his back. When the War Between the States broke out, Jackson resigned his post and accepted a commission as a colonel in the Virginia militia.

Reputation. Jackson was first sent to Harper's Ferry to organize recruits. After Joseph E. Johnston took command of all forces in the area, Jackson was given command over the First Brigade (later known as "The Stonewall Brigade"). Adhering to his reputation as a strict disciplinarian, Jackson trained his men hard and prepared them to hold their ground during fierce fighting, a tactic that won fame for the unit at First Bull Run. In October 1861 the Confederate War Department promoted Jackson to major general and gave him command of the entire Shenandoah Valley. That winter Jackson revealed his strength of character when he submitted his resignation after a subordinate broke the chain of command and sent a complaint directly to the Confederate secretary of war. Recognizing Jackson's talent as a field commander and his reputation as a hero, Confederate president Jefferson Davis was forced to apologize formally in order to keep Jackson in uniform.

Lee's Lieutenant. Jackson soon gained a reputation as Gen. Robert E. Lee's right-hand man. In order to counter the superior numbers of the Northern army, Lee brilliantly planned massive flanking movements to catch his opponent off-guard and sweep them from the battlefield. To execute these bold offensives, Lee turned to Jackson. Although constantly outnumbered, Jackson struck unsuspecting Northern troops hard and carried many battles with his strong determination to win. Jackson fought in every major battle in the Eastern theater including Second Bull Run, Antietam, and Fredericksburg (all in 1862). The successful partnership achieved its most daring victory at the Battle of Chancellorsville, Virginia, in May 1863. Facing more than ninety thousand Federal troops, Lee split his command and sent Jackson with twenty-six thousand men on a wide-flanking movement against the Union's right. Once again, Jackson caught the Federals off guard and the right flank quickly collapsed, forcing the Northern army to retreat. That night, as he conducted a reconnaissance at the front, Confederate pickets shot Jackson by mistake. Two bullets hit Jackson in his left arm, which Southern doctors amputated immediately. He survived for a few days before succumbing to pneumonia. Upon hearing the news, Lee wept openly and lamented: "He has lost his left arm, but I have lost my right." Over twenty thousand Southerners paid their respects to Jackson as his body lay in the executive mansion in Richmond; he was later put to rest in Lexington. The Confederate army never recovered after Jackson's death as Lee failed to find a general with his combat confidence and aggressive fighting ability.

Sources:
Joseph T. Glatthaar, *Partners in Command: The Relationship Between Leaders in the Civil War* (New York: Free Press, 1994);

Bill Sell, *Leaders of the North and South* (New York: Metro Books, 1996).

WILLIAM T. SHERMAN

1820-1891
UNION GENERAL

"War is Hell." Near the end of the Civil War, Union general William Tecumseh Sherman perfected an offensive strategy that foreshadowed twentieth-century total war. Marching from Atlanta to Savannah, Georgia, in the fall of 1864, Sherman directed his army to destroy everything of military significance. Sherman hoped to break civilian support for the war by marching through the Georgia countryside and instilling an air of insecurity among the inhabitants. Scorching a sixty-mile swath across Georgia, Sherman's army of sixty thousand men leveled almost everything in their path while being careful not to abuse the rural people physically. Major cities such as Atlanta and Columbia, South Carolina, went up in flames. In Columbia the anticipated fear of Sherman's arrival caused fleeing Confederate soldiers to burn cotton bales in the streets and, subsequently, start the fire which nearly burnt the entire capital to the ground. The events instituted a psychological warfare in which the mere mention of his name caused panic. Sherman's marauders focused their attention on destroying the Southern infrastructure to impede enemy troop movements. Their main target was railroad tracks, which they heated and then twisted around trees. Even though his orders called for restraint, some Northern troops known as "bummers" (so named because they straggled from the line of march) looted and burned plantations, farms, and fields, effectively forcing many white and black Southerners to flee their lands. As a result Southern morale broke and Sherman's scorched-earth strategy facilitated a faster end to the war. Although many Southerners hated Sherman for his "march to the sea" and viewed him as a brute, the native Ohioan insisted that he only sought a quick end to the war. Indeed, during a graduation address at the Michigan Military Academy in 1879, the general publicly mocked those who glorified his de-

structive strategy. "War is at best barbarism . . . . Its glory is all moonshine," he despondently remarked. "It is only those who have neither fired a shot nor heard the shrieks and groans of the wounded who cry aloud for blood, more vengeance, more desolation. War is hell."

Early Life. Sherman was born on 8 February 1820 in Lancaster, Ohio. His father, an Ohio Supreme Court justice and local politician, named him Tecumseh after the famous Shawnee tribal leader. Sherman was orphaned in 1829 when his father died unexpectedly. Thomas Ewing, a close friend of the elder Sherman and a national political figure, took the young Sherman into his home. Ewing's wife named the boy William, preferring an Anglican name over the Indian cognomen. In 1836, Ewing, now a U.S. senator, used his influence to provide the sixteen-year-old Sherman an appointment at West Point. Sherman graduated sixth in a class of forty-three in 1840.

Military Career. For the next six years Sherman served in duty stations in the South. During the Mexican War he was sent to California but saw no action. When the war ended in 1848 Sherman ridiculed the lenient terms handed to the Mexican government and proposed that the United States burn Mexico City and other key towns to teach America's southern neighbor the futility of any future confrontation with the United States. Sherman resigned his commission in 1853 and failed miserably at various civilian jobs. In 1859 he returned to the South to head a military academy (later Louisiana State University). The Ohioan basked in the Southern lifestyle and shined in his role as superintendent. When secession divided the nation, however, Sherman clung to his Northern heritage and accepted a commission as a colonel in the Union army.

The War. Sherman saw action at the First Battle of Bull Run in July 1861, commanding a brigade that suffered heavy casualties. Shocked by the experience, he submitted his resignation. President Abraham Lincoln refused his request and instead sent him to Kentucky, where he was promoted to brigadier general. While in the Western theater he suffered from depression over conflicting emotions about his failure at Bull Run, his decision to leave the South to fight against his friends, and the North's underestimation of a highly motivated and united Southern army. To add to his woes, unwarranted rumors that Sherman was insane and incompetent spread throughout the Northern states and deeply hurt his reputation as a commander. On the brink of losing his command and suffering another failure, Sherman was sent to assist Ulysses S. Grant to help prepare the offensive against Forts Henry and Donelson. The two Ohioans instantly developed a strong friendship that would carry beyond the war. Despite suffering several setbacks, Sherman distinguished himself under Grant and participated in many key western engagements, including the Battle of Shiloh (1862) and the siege of Vicksburg (1863). After Grant moved east to command all Union armies in 1864, Sherman assumed command of the entire Western theater.

March to the Sea. Three years of fighting Confederates in the west influenced Sherman's strategy to break the Southern determination to fight. After facing tenacious enemy guerrillas in Tennessee and Missouri, Sherman surmised that Southerners would never accept defeat as long as civilians kept sending soldiers into battle and supporting irregulars at home. Thus, as he proposed in Mexico, Sherman was determined to make Southerners "feel the war" in order to crush civilian resistance. He abandoned his supply lines in the fall of 1864 and boldly marched on Atlanta and then Savannah. He remarked upon leaving Atlanta: "We don't want your negroes, or your horses, or your houses, or your lands, or anything you have, but we do want and will have just obedience to the laws of the United States." By making war so terrible, Sherman terrorized the populace. In the end his strategy of psychological warfare worked, as the destructive trek changed the hearts and minds of the Confederate civilian population and shattered their will to fight. The fear of destruction caused many mothers and wives to call their men back home, and many deserted.

Postwar Years. Following the Civil War, Sherman rose to celebrity status in the North and turned down several invitations to run for president. However, he did stay in the military, becoming general and commander of the army in 1869. He retired in 1884 and died seven years later. In the South, Sherman was hated well into the twentieth century as the embodiment of Northern aggression and brutality.

Sources:

Henry Hitchcock, *Marching With Sherman*, edited by M. A. DeWolfe Howe, revised edition (Lincoln: University of Nebraska Press, 1995);

John F. Marszalek, *Sherman: A Soldier's Passion for Order* (New York: Free Press, 1993);

Bill Sell, *Leaders of the North and South* (New York: Metro Books, 1996).

ROBERT SMALLS

1839-1915
AFRICAN AMERICAN SAILOR

The Escape. While their white officers slept peacefully in Charleston, the slave crew aboard the Confederate gunboat *Planter* made a daring run for Northern vessels anchored off the coast of South Carolina. During the predawn hours of 13 May 1862, the ship's pilot, Robert Smalls, and his crew sailed the vessel from its dock in Charleston Harbor, discreetly slipped past Confederate cannons at Fort Sumter, and surrendered the ship to the Union blockading squadron. Startled by the fast approaching ship, Northern seamen prepared their guns to fire, but quickly stopped after a sailor spotted a white flag. The astonished Northerners seized the ship with its four unmounted guns and crew of eight African American males (five women and three children were also aboard). The remarkable tale of the *Planter* quickly spread throughout the divided nation, making Smalls a hero in the North and an outlaw in the South.

Early Life. Robert Smalls was born a slave on 5 April 1839 in Beaufort, South Carolina. His mother worked as a house servant for her master John K. McKee, a wealthy plantation owner. McKee was probably Smalls's father. After McKee died in 1848, his son Henry inherited Smalls and his mother. In 1851 McKee hired Smalls out as a laborer in Charleston. There he worked as a waiter, lamplighter, and stevedore. Eventually he secured employment on a commercial ship docked in Charleston. After gaining experience as a sailor, Smalls hired on to pilot the *Planter* in March 1861, a cotton steamer converted into a gunboat by the Confederate government in order to move supplies between forts in Charleston Harbor.

A Contraband of War. Like all slaves who fled to Union lines, Smalls was received by the Union navy as a contraband of war. Although the *Planter* and its crew represented a propaganda coup for the North, Smalls' knowledge of local waters and enemy encampments proved more valuable. Piloting the ship for over a year before his defection, Smalls had traveled along the coast of South Carolina, Georgia, and Florida laying mines, transporting men and supplies, and surveying local rivers. His intelligence reports convinced Union naval officers to attack Rebel strongholds on Cole's Island on the Stono River immediately. Smalls had informed the Union naval commander for the area that the Confederates recently disarmed the fort and sent its cannons to Charleston because of a weapons shortage. On 20 May 1862 Union gunboats seized the fort without a fight, and the Northern navy used the river inlet as a base of operations for the rest of the war. Shortly afterward Smalls became a pilot for a Federal naval ship. Due to navy restrictions, however, Smalls served the Union navy as an army volunteer since the navy only enlisted blacks as ship laborers.

National Hero. The story of Robert Smalls and the *Planter* became a national phenomenon. *Harper's Weekly* published a celebrated article about the great escape along with pictures of Smalls and the Confederate gunboat. To honor the feat, Congress passed a bill bestowing a cash prize to Smalls and the other crew members; Smalls received $1,500 while the crew received $400–$450 each. After a brief stint as pilot for the U.S.S. *Wabash*, Smalls traveled to New York and embarked on a speaking tour designed to generate excitement for the Union cause. Following the tour, Smalls returned to South Carolina and was appointed captain of the *Planter* (now in service with the Union army), an unprecedented promotion for an African American during the Civil War. Smalls fought in seventeen engagements before docking the *Planter* in Philadelphia for an overhaul and repairs. He spent seven months in the city and afterward returned to Charleston, where the *Planter* was primarily engaged in ferrying men and supplies across the harbor for the remainder of the war. During the Reconstruction era Smalls used his national reputation to gain political office in South Carolina, first as a state representative and later as a congressman in the U.S. House of Representatives. He died in 1915.

Source:
Edward A. Miller Jr., *Gullah Statesman: Robert Smalls from Slavery to Congress, 1839–1915* (Columbia: University of South Carolina Press, 1995).

SUSIE KING TAYLOR

1848-1912
AFRICAN AMERICAN EDUCATOR
AND NURSE

Enslavement. Susie King Taylor was one of many African American Southern women who served the Union army as a laundress, nurse, and teacher. She was born a slave on 6 August 1848 on one of the Sea Islands located thirty-five miles off the coast of Georgia. For most of her childhood she lived with her grandmother in Savannah. With the aid of white acquaintances and free African Americans, Taylor broke Southern laws regulating the activity of slaves and learned to read and write, an accomplishment that would help her find employment in the Northern army.

Contraband of War. When the war broke out Taylor was sent to the Georgia coast by her owners. Shortly after she arrived a combined Union naval and army expedition attacked Fort Pulaski, a Confederate stronghold near her current home, and drove the Southern defenders into the Georgia interior. Taylor, along with her uncle and eight cousins, fled to the Union lines and were immediately declared by Federal military authorities as "contraband" of war. As contraband, Taylor and her family were expected to work for the Union army in some capacity, usually as field laborers. Consequently, the Northern liberators moved them to the Sea Islands off the South Carolina coast to operate captured cotton plantations. Because Taylor could read and write, army officials asked her to run a school for former slave children.

Off to War. As more and more contraband males found their way to the Sea Islands, military commanders began to organize them into infantry regiments. Although only fourteen years old at the time, Taylor immediately offered her services to the First South Carolina Volunteers, later known as the Thirty-Third United States Colored Troops (U.S.C.T.). The army initially employed her as a laundress, a thankless and unpaid assignment. Taylor, however, rarely served in that capacity. For most of the war, the teenager ministered to soldiers as a nurse. During her off-duty hours, she ran an impromptu school for African American soldiers, teaching many of them how to read and write.

Field Duty. Taylor often traveled with the regiment as a medical orderly. During several small engagements she worked close enough to the fighting to hear the whistle of artillery shells over her head. Although assigned to the Thirty-Third U.S.C.T., she served for a brief time with the all–African American Fifty-Fourth Massachusetts Infantry during their operations in South Carolina. In July 1863 Taylor assisted the famous Civil War nurse Clara Barton, future founder of the American Red Cross, in treating the heavy casualties following the Fifty-Fourth's legendary assault upon Fort Wagner. Taylor continued to assist Barton for the next eight months before returning to her original unit. For the rest of the war she continued to move with the regiment on small skirmishes, but most of her time was spent on rear-echelon duty. When the army disbanded the unit in February 1866, Taylor and her husband, a sergeant in the Thirty-Third U.S.C.T., returned to Georgia. Later, she moved to Boston and became active in a veterans' organization. One of many African American women to serve the Union army without pay or complaint, Taylor in 1902 wrote her memoirs, the first documentation of duties performed by an African American nurse in the Civil War. She died in 1912 at age sixty-four.

Source:
Susie King Taylor, *A Black Woman's Civil War Memoirs: Reminiscences of My Life in Camp with the 33rd U.S. Colored Troops, Late 1st South Carolina Volunteers,* edited by Patricia W. Romano (New York: Markus Wiener, 1988).

PUBLICATIONS

A. S. Abrams, *A Full and Detailed History of the Siege of Vicksburg* (Atlanta: Intelligencer Steam Power Presses, 1863);

Markinfield Addey, *"Old Jack" and His Foot-Cavalry; or, A Virginian Boy's Progress to Renown* (New York: J. Bradburn, 1864)—one of the first biographies about Confederate general Thomas J. "Stonewall" Jackson;

Battle-Fields of the South, from Bull Run to Fredericksburg; with sketches of Confederate Commanders, and Gossip of the Camps (New York: J. Bradburn, 1864)—written by an Englishman who served as an artillery officer in the Confederate army. His good observations make the book one of the best Southern sources covering the early battles;

P. G. T. Beauregard, *Principles and Maxims of the Art of War; Outpost Service; General Instructions for Battle; Reviews* (Charleston: Press of Evans & Cogswell, 1863)—stresses the value of fortifications as well as flanking movements. Beauregard, a West Point graduate and Confederate general, also translated Antoine-Henri Jomini's *The Art of War* (1838);

William D. Bickham, *Rosecrans' Campaign with the Fourteenth Army Corps, or the Army of the Cumberland: A Narrative of Personal Observations with . . . Official Reports of the Battle of Stone River* (Cincinnati: Moore, Wilstach, Keys, 1863)—written by a newspaper correspondent from the Cincinnati *Commercial*;

Montgomery Blair, *Speech of the Hon. Montgomery Blair on the Revolutionary Schemes of the Ultra Abolitionists, and in Defense of the Policy of the President* (New York: D. W. Lee, 1863)—Blair served as postmaster general in the Lincoln administration;

Henry N. Blake, *Three Years in the Army of the Potomac* (Boston: Lee & Shepard, 1865)—written by a former captain of the Eleventh Regiment of Massachusetts Volunteers;

John Minor Botts, *The Great Rebellion: Its Secret History, Rise, Progress and Diastrous Failure* (New York: Harper & Brothers, 1866);

J. F. J. Caldwell, *The History of a Brigade of South Carolinians, Known First as "Gregg's" and Subsequently as "McGowan's Brigade"* (Philadelphia: King & Baird, 1866)—a typical unit history to come out at the end of the war. It is surprisingly objective in view of its publication date;

David Power Conygham, *Sherman's March through the South. With Sketches and Incidents of the Campaign* (New York: Sheldon and Co., 1865)—one of the first personal accounts about the march written by a New York *Herald* war correspondent;

Joel Cook, *The Siege of Richmond; A Narrative of the Military Operations of Major-General George B. McClellan during the Months of May and June, 1862* (Philadelphia: G. W. Childs, 1862)—excellent account written by a Philadelphia *Press* war correspondent;

Nicholas A. Davis, *The Campaign from Texas to Maryland* (Richmond: Office of the Presbyterian Committee of Publication of the Confederate States, 1863)—narrative written by a Confederate army chaplain attached to Confederate general John B. Hood's Texas Brigade;

William S. Dodge, *History of the Old Second Division, Army of the Cumberland* (Chicago: Church & Goodman, 1864)—one of the first historical accounts about a Civil War division;

Frederick Douglass, *Men of Color, To Arms!* (Rochester, N.Y., 1863)—recruiting pamphlet for the 54th Massachusetts;

George W. Driggs, *Opening of the Mississippi; or Two Years' Campaigning in the South-West* (Madison: W. J. Park, 1864)—witty account of the war in the west. The account was taken from letters written by a sergeant in the 8th Wisconsin Infantry;

James Dugan, *History of Hurlbut's Fighting Fourth Division: And Especially the Marches, Toils, Privations, Adventures, Skirmishes and Battles of the Fourteenth Illinois Infantry* (Cincinnati: E. Morgan, 1863)—study of the war in Missouri and Mississippi;

Sarah Emma Edmundson, *Unsexed: or, The Female Soldier. The Thrilling Adventures, Experiences and Escapes of a Woman, as Nurse, Spy and Scout, in Hospitals, Camps and Battle-Fields* (Philadelphia: Philadelphia Publishing, 1860)—personal account of a woman who disguised herself and served in the Union army for two years;

Sir Arthur James Lyon Fremantle, *Three Months in the Southern States: April–June 1863* (New York: J. Bradburn, 1864)—classic account of wartime South by English army observer;

Richard F. Fuller, *Chaplain Fuller: Being a Life Sketch of a New England Clergyman and Army Chaplain* (Boston: Walker, Wise, 1863)—good behind-the-lines account of the 16th Massachusetts Infantry;

Henry W. Halleck, *Elements of Military Art and Science; or, Course of Instruction in Strategy, Fortification, Tactics of Battles, etc., Embracing the Duties of Staff, Infantry, Cavalry, Artillery, and Engineers,* third edition (New York & London: D. Appleton, 1863)—Halleck, a general in the Union army, emphasizes the value of fortifications in battle. As it was written in English and contained a good bibliography citing works in military history, Halleck's book bypassed Jomini's work as the standard text on military strategy read at West Point;

Ward Hill Lamon, *The Life of Abraham Lincoln* (Boston: James R. Osgood, 1872);

Dennis Hart Mahan, *Advanced-guard, Out-post, and Detachment Service of Troops, with the Essential Principles of Strategy, and Grand Tactics, for the Use of Officers of the Militia and Volunteers* (New York: J. Wiley & Son, 1869)—Mahan was professor of engineering and military science at West Point from 1830 to 1871. His textbook was an invaluable guide for company-grade officers as well as regimental commanders;

Mahan, *Descriptive Geometry, as Applied to the Drawing of Fortification and Stereotomy. For the Use of the Cadets of the U.S. Military Academy*i (New York: J. Wiley, 1864)—a textbook focusing on the value of field fortifications, especially the use of trenches in defensive positions;

George B. McClellan, *The Complete Report on the Organization and Campaigns of the Army of the Potomac* (N.p., 1864?);

Irvin McDowell, *Statement of Major Gen. Irvin McDowell, in Review of the Evidence before the Court of Inquiry, Instituted at His Request in Special Orders, no. 353,* *Headquarters of the Army* (Washington: L. Towers, 1863);

Judith White McGuire, *Diary of a Southern Refugee During the War* (New York: E. J. Hale & Son, 1867)—the reminiscences of a Virginia resident from May 1861 to May 1865;

James M. McKim, *The Freedmen of South Carolina* (Philadelphia: W. P. Hazard, 1862)—a study of the newly freed African Americans in the Port Royal Sound area;

Charles C. Nott, *Sketches of the War: A Series of Letters to the North Moore Street School of New York* (New York: C. T. Evans, 1863)—excellent narrative of the first battles in the West by an Iowa cavalry officer;

James B. Rogers, *War Pictures. Experiences and Observations of a Chaplain in the U.S. Army, in the War of the Southern Rebellion* (Chicago: Church & Goodman, 1863)—excellent account of the Battle of Shiloh and Corinth;

Fitzgerald Ross, *A Visit to the Cities and Camps of the Confederate States* (Edinburgh and London: W. Blackwood and Sons, 1865)—insightful observations of the Southern war effort written by a Scotsman who traveled throughout the South from 1863–1864;

William Tecumseh Sherman, *General Sherman's Official Account of His Great March through Georgia and the Carolinas* (New York: Bunce & Huntington, 1865)—includes Sherman's evidence before a congressional committee on the conduct of the war. In addition he defends his actions against Secretary of War Edwin Stanton and Gen. Henry Halleck;

Alexander H. Stephens, *A Constitutional View of the Late War Between the States; Its Causes, Character, Conduct and Results,* 2 volumes (Philadelphia: National Publishing, 1868–1870)—one of the first histories of the war to appear in print, written by the former vice president of the Confederacy;

Edwin W. Stone, *Rhode Island in the Rebellion* (Providence: G. H. Whitney, 1864)—one of the best and first memoirs about life as a Civil War soldier;

George Alfred Townsend, *Campaigns of a Non-Combatant* (New York: Blelock, 1866)—a journalistic account of the war, rich in information about the life of the soldier.

Ulysses S. Grant (at left, above) enjoying a cigar on Lookout Mountain, Tennessee, after it fell to Union forces in 1863

COMMUNICATIONS

by RICHARD LAYMAN

CONTENTS

Sidebars and tables are listed in italics.

1850

- The first U.S. clipper ship, the *Oriental,* arrives in London from Hong Kong carrying a sixteen-hundred-ton cargo.

- American Express is formed by a merger of Wells and Company, Livingston, Fargo and Company, and Butterfield Wasson and Company.

27 Apr. The S.S. *Atlantic,* owned by the U.S. Mail Steamship Company, leaves New York on its maiden voyage to England. Its return voyage sets a record time of ten days and sixteen hours.

1 July The first overland mail delivery west of the Missouri River is made—from Independence, Missouri, to Salt Lake City, Utah.

1851

3 Mar. The Postal Act of 1851 is passed, effective 1 July. It standardizes postal rates (three cents per half ounce for distances under three thousand miles) and declares stamp counterfeiting a felony, among other stipulations.

1 Apr. Hiram Sibley incorporates the New York and Mississippi Valley Printing and Telegraph Company (which eventually becomes Western Union).

18 Sept. The *New York Daily Times* begins publishing. It will shorten its name to *The New York Times* in 1857.

1852

- Wells, Fargo and Company starts up express service in California. Within the decade the company enjoys a virtual monopoly and runs 108 stations.

- The *Washington Evening Star,* a two-page penny newspaper, is published; by the end of the year it has been bought by William Wallack, who expands it to a four-page paper.

20 Feb. The first train from the East arrives in Chicago.

20 Aug. The SS *Atlantic,* a Lake Erie steamer, sinks off Point Albino, New York, with $50,000 worth of valuables entrusted to American Express for delivery.

1853

- The clipper ship *Northern Light* makes a record-setting seventy-six-day, six-hour voyage from San Francisco to Boston.

- Andrew Carnegie goes to work for Thomas A. Scott as a telegraph operator on the Pennsylvania Railroad.

5 Mar. The American Telegraph Convention meets in Washington, D.C., to discuss coordination of message flow between various companies.

1855

- Congress authorizes funding for a telegraph line from the Mississippi River to the West Coast.

- The eight-year-old *Chicago Tribune* is purchased by Joseph Medill.

- *Frank Leslie's Illustrated Newspaper* is published in New York.

- Inventor David Hughes patents a teleprinter.

- A railroad across the Isthmus of Panama is completed.

3 Mar. The Postal Act of 1855 is passed, effective 1 January 1856, requiring that all letters be prepaid with postage stamps or stamped envelopes.

1856

- Western Union is formed by Ezra Corness and Hiram Sibley from a group of telegraph companies; Sibley is named president.

- The New York and Mississippi Valley Telegraph Company reorganizes as Western Union.

1857

- New York to San Francisco freight rates that had been as high as $60 per ton since the Gold Rush of 1848 drop to $10 per ton.

- Horace Greeley's *New York Tribune* declares that northerners are superior to southerners because they have a better system of labor.

3 Mar. Congress grants a subsidy of $70,000 to Cyrus Fields to lay transatlantic cable.

1858

- Francis S. Street and Shubael Smith form Street and Smith Publications to publish *New York Weekly*.

- Cornelius Vanderbilt begins a transatlantic shipping line.

16 Aug. Queen Victoria and President Buchanan exchange the first transatlantic telegraph messages. A few weeks later, the cable parts.

9 Oct. Overland Mail Company's first stage between San Francisco and Saint Louis completes its run, a journey of twenty-three days and four hours.

1859

- The *Rocky Mountain News* is first published.

- The nation's five largest telegraph companies form a pool association, the North American Telegraph Association, to divvy up the U.S. market.

1860

- Hiram Sibley wins government subsidies to build a transcontinental telegraph line.

3 Apr. The first Pony Express rider leaves Saint Joseph, Missouri, for Sacramento, California.

1861

- Western Union completes the first transcontinental telegraph line, linking at Fort Bridger, Utah.

- Ansell N. Kellogg of the *Baraboc* (Wisconsin) *Republic* founds the first news syndicate, offering "readyprint" to other papers.

Mar.	Jefferson Davis appoints John H. Reagan postmaster general for the Confederate States of America.
1 June	Delivery of U.S. Mail is suspended in the Confederate states.
24 Oct.	The first coast-to-coast telegraph reaches President Abraham Lincoln in Washington, D.C.

1862

4 Feb.	The organizational meeting of the Press Association of the Confederate States of America is held in Augusta, Georgia.
25 Feb.	U.S. Secretary of War Edwin M. Stanton orders that war correspondents for newspapers must submit copy to provost marshals before transmitting it by telegraph to their papers.
30 June	U.S. postmaster Montgomery Blair reports that there are 19,973 U.S. Post Office employees.
Aug.	The postal privileges of the *New York Daily News* are suspended for eighteen months because of the paper's open hostility to the war effort.

1863

3 Mar.	The Postal Act of 1863 establishes lower postal rates and divides mail into three classes.

1864

•	Railway mail service begins.
May	U.S. General John A. Dix suppresses the *New York World* and the *Journal of Commerce* after they publish a fabricated story about a presidential proclamation ordering the draft of four hundred thousand men.

1865

15 Nov.	U.S. Postmaster William Dennison reports that 241 mail routes have been reestablished in the South and that 3,234 post offices have been restored to the federal system; there were 8,902 southern post offices before the Civil War.

1866

- With funding from the Vanderbilt family, Western Union absorbs United States Telegraph and American Telegraph, effectively giving it a monopoly.

- The *San Francisco Examiner* begins publication.

•	Western Union takes over two smaller rivals, gaining control of 75,000 miles of telegraph lines.
27 July	The transatlantic telegraph cable is successfully reconnected.

1867

•	The Pacific Mail Steamship Company begins regular service between San Francicso and Hong Kong.
26 Oct.	The transcontinental telegraph is completed.

1868

•	American Express and the Merchants Union Express merge to become American Express. It will begin offering money orders in 1882 and traveler's checks in 1891.
•	The *San Francisco Chronicle* is first published as a full-coverage newspaper.
•	A patent is issued to Christopher Sholes, Carlos G. Glidden, and Samuel W. Soule for the first typewriter.
•	The *Atlanta Constitution* begins publication.
•	The *Louisville Courier-Journal*, edited by Henry Watterson, is formed by the merger of two local newspapers.

1869

10 May	The first transcontinental railroad is completed when the Union Pacific and Central Pacific link tracks at Promontory Point, Utah.

1871

•	The Hoe web press, which prints both sides of a paper at once from a continuous sheet of paper, is introduced for sale. Developed from a technology patented in 1863, it prints eighteen thousand newspapers an hour.

1872

4 Mar.	The *Boston Daily Globe* begins publication as the tenth, and largest, newspaper in the city.
2 Apr.	Western Electric is established to sell telegraphic equipment and develop the telephone.

1873

•	Remington and Sons Fire Arms Company buys the patent for the typewriter for $12,000 and begins manufacturing machines that sell for $125.

1875

- Thomas Edison completes work on his wax stencil duplicating machine.

- Richard Hoe invents a high-speed newspaper folder.

2 June   The first successful experiment that leads to the development of the telephone is completed by Alexander Graham Bell and his assistant, Thomas A. Watson.

25 Dec.   The *Chicago Daily News* begins publication.

1876

- Alexander Graham Bell patents his telephonic device. He forms the Bell Association the following year, opening service from Boston to New York and New Brunswick.

- Thomas Edison begins building an industrial research laboratory in Menlo Park, New Jersey, where he will invent and perfect the telephone transmitter, the phonograph, and the incandescent lamp within the next three years.

10 Mar.   Alexander Graham Bell demonstrates voice transmission over a telephone wire. A patent was issued to him for the device one week earlier.

8 Nov.   Charles A. Dana's *New York Sun* sells a record 220,000 papers with its coverage of the Hayes-Tilden presidential election.

1877

- The Bell Telephone Association is organized in New York. By the end of the year the association leases one thousand telephones a month.

- Northwestern Bell Telephone Company is organized in Lyons, Iowa.

May   The first Bell telephones are sold; by August nearly eight hundred telephone sets are in operation.

17 May   The first telephone switchboard goes into service in Boston.

6 Dec.   The *Washington Post* begins publication.

OVERVIEW

The Wireless Age. At the time of the Civil War, the primary means of communication for most Americans was through personal contact. There were less than one-fifth as many people in the United States as there are today, and only one-fourth of them lived in cities. Most of the population led isolated lives in which contact was restricted to family and close friends. In the middle of the nineteenth century people got their information about the world outside their experience through face-to-face contact, correspondence, and newspapers. There was no radio or television; the telephone was available by the end of Reconstruction, but only to a small, privileged group. The telegraph offered something approaching instant communication, but its use was restricted to areas where lines had been constructed, and practical concerns, including cost and the awkwardness of the system, caused telegraphic messages to be brief.

Snail Mail. Letters were costly to mail and slow to be delivered. Delivery of mail to people's doors was introduced in Northern cities during the Civil War, but outside cities it was still some thirty-five years off, at best. In 1850, there were 18,417 post offices, and they issued 1.5 million ordinary postage stamps: about one stamp for every fifteen people in the nation; by 1878 there were 38,345 post offices and they issued 170 million stamps, more than three per person. In 1851 a first-class letter could be sent up to three thousand miles for three cents, or five cents if postage was to be collected on delivery. In 1878, the rate was two cents per half ounce or a penny for a postcard in the United States. But those were days when a man's tie cost a dime and pennies counted.

The Penny Paper. Newspapers were read daily in only about 10 percent of American families, and people in the country had limited access to newspapers and magazines. Some small towns had newspapers, but they tended to be published weekly and focus on local news. City newspapers, with their more comprehensive coverage of national events, were only available in rural areas by mail. Nearly 80 percent of the Negro population and more than 10 percent of the white population was illiterate in 1870, and these people had little knowledge of the world outside their daily routines.

All the News That Fits. News had a different meaning in the mid nineteenth century. Even those with access to a daily newspaper were hardly well informed by today's standards. Only about three-fourths of the reports in a daily newspaper of 1860 were of events that had occurred in the past week, and 8 percent of the news coverage was of stories over a month old. The look and the contents of daily papers were also different from today. Papers lacked photographs. During the Civil War magazines and newspapers began to publish line drawings of maps and images of people, but the technology to publish photographs was not yet generally available. Opinions far outweighed news reports in newspapers, because they were easier to come by. News editors shared information, and free postal service was extended to newspaper publishers for the purpose of sending copies of their papers to one another as a means of facilitating coverage of distant events: Chicago news editors reprinted New York reports because, like their readers, the editors knew only what they read in the paper about events outside their city. In 1850 there were 254 daily newspapers in the United States with a combined circulation of 758,000. By 1880 the number of dailies had increased to 971, with a combined circulation of 3.566 million.

Coded Communication. The growth of the telegraph had a direct influence on news reporting. Telegraph was the electronic transmission of messages in a coding system that could be decoded by a receiving machine operator hundreds or even thousands of miles away. With the telegraph, a news story could be communicated almost immediately to stations in other parts of the country. There were three problems: first, telegraph signals passed through cable, so wire had to be laid from station to station, a costly and labor-intensive process; second, telegraph was an expensive way to communicate, and although newspapers paid only one-third to one-half as much as individual users, they also sent more messages —the normal rate for ten words or fewer from San Francisco to New York was $7.45 in 1850 and $2.00 in 1876; third, news stories had to be communicated in abbreviated form by operators who were likely to be indifferent to content, so stories had to be elaborated by copywriters at the receiving end and accuracy was often sacrificed.

Between 1866 and 1877 the number of telegraph offices in the United States tripled to seventy-five hundred. The amount of wire laid increased from 76,000 miles to 194,000 miles, and the number of messages sent increased from 5,879 to 21,159.

Narrow Circles. People's concerns were narrower; their lives were more focused; and their storehouse of information was smaller a century and a half ago. The effects of these differences were profound. Without the distractions of impersonal communication, such as radio, television, and a surplus of newsprint, people spent more time engaging one another. Family life was certainly harder without the conveniences of modern life, but there were also fewer diversions from the responsibilities of the household. In this sense, travel and communication are closely related. In the country, travel was on horseback or in a horse-drawn carriage during this era. A ten-mile journey to a town center for news and conversation about current events might take four unpleasant hours round-trip. City life was concentrated in small areas because of the difficulty of getting around the city. The result was that people had close contact with their neighbors and little knowledge of the area outside their direct experience. It was, indeed, a simpler time, but it was also a time of intense curiosity that could only be satisfied by more efficient methods of communicating.

TOPICS IN THE NEWS

NEWSPAPERS

The State of the Industry. In 1850 about 10 percent of the adult population in the United States subscribed to one of the 254 daily newspapers, which usually cost a penny per issue, though in New York a paper cost three cents by the time of the Civil War. Newspapers could be distributed by mail without charge in the county of publication until 1856, and in cities newsboys hawked papers on street corners. The rural population was poorly served, especially before the Civil War. Before the war most news was local because reports from distant locations were hard to gather. Papers were filled with opinion, and much, if not most, of the space in the paper was devoted to prose other than reportage. The average paper was six columns wide and eight pages or fewer. There were few illustrations, though different sizes and fonts of type introduced some variety to the newspaper page. As many as three pages of an eight-page paper were typically devoted to classified advertising, and local merchants took advantage of newspaper advertising space with increasing frequency. As circulation of newspapers grew, especially in large cities, publishers were faced with limits on the capacity of their presses. The introduction of Richard Hoe's revolving press in the late 1840s alleviated the problem. By the time of the Civil War, James Gordon Bennett's *New York Herald* was able to print 20,000 newspapers per hour using a Hoe press. On the Sunday after the fall of Fort Sumter in 1861 Bennett printed 135,000 papers, the most ever produced in a single run. The fast web-perfecting press, which printed both sides of a paper at the same time from a continuous roll of paper, was patented in 1863 and became a standard piece of equipment after the Civil War.

Telegraphic Reporting. In the decade before the Civil War the telegraph had already begun to transform the daily newspaper. The Associated Press, formed in 1848 by a group of New York newspaper editors to share news sources, had spread to other cities, and journalism became more uniform from city to city as many newspapers printed the same reporter's account of an event. The most successful papers responded to reader interest in national news by sending out their own news correspondents. By 1860 there were twenty-three Washington correspondents assigned to the U.S. Senate and fifty-one correspondents in the House of Representatives. As the telegraph became a central part of a reporter's work, it affected the content of reports. Opinion was less common in telegraphed reports because the cost was so expensive that only the facts could be transmitted. Objectivity became a practical matter.

Politics of the News. On the pressing issues of the time, however, editors spoke their minds. Papers were typically associated with political positions, and the editors vigorously used their clout to promote their parties' causes. Abolitionist papers such as Horace Greeley's weekly *New York Tribune* (which had a circulation of two hundred thousand copies and was distributed in the West) and Joseph Medill's *Chicago Tribune* were important voices in both supporting Abraham Lincoln's election to the presidency and promoting the war effort. The urgency of events during the Civil War increased readers' reliance on daily newspapers. At the outset of the war,

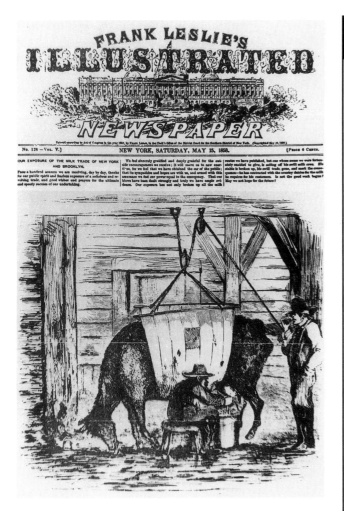

Front page of the most successful illustrated newspaper of the 1850s

In 1850 all writing was done with pencil or pen and ink. Offices employed scribes to keep records, and the only practical way to make a copy of a document was to rewrite it longhand. For individuals, this practice was rarely a hardship. For business, state and federal governments, and the courts, copy work was tedious and time-consuming.

As early as 1829 there were working models of awkward typing machines developed by inventors in the printing business, but they were more significant as curiosities than as working tools. The modern typewriter was not introduced until 1867, when Christopher Latham Sholes, a printer, Carlos Glidden, a lawyer, and Samuel Soule, a draftsman and engineer, introduced a refinement of a machine that Sholes had been using in his print shop to print page numbers. Their typewriter, which featured a keyboard with the familiar "qwerty" arrangement of letters used today, was patented in 1868.

In 1873 the Remington Arms Company, seeking to replace revenues lost from the sale of guns after the war ended, bought the typewriter patent for $12,000, and began producing what were called kitchen-table typewriters—that is, machines small enough to set on a kitchen table—in 1876. Despite being displayed at the Centennial Exposition of 1876, the new machine failed to capture the attention of potential buyers. Only about four thousand typewriters were sold in the first four years, including one unit to Mark Twain in 1874. It was not until the turn of the century that the typewriter had its enormous impact on the American workplace.

Source: Richard N. Curent, *The Typewriter and the Men Who Made It* (Urbana: University of Illinois Press, 1954).

Gen. George McClellan called a press conference, at which he made editors promise in writing not to publish information of military value to the enemy in return for his promise to provide them reports on matters of public interest. In February 1862 Secretary of War Edwin Stanton issued an order requiring journalists to submit their reports to provost marshals for censorship on matters related to military actions.

Confederate Newspapers. When the Civil War began, eight hundred newspapers, of which about eight were dailies, were published in the eleven Confederate states. Most Southern papers had a small circulation and were printed on hand presses. When the war began, a consortium of editors formed the Press Association of the Confederate States of America to report the war, and most Southern battle reports came from the PA, as it was called. The chaos of the war played havoc with the newspapers. By 1863 many Southern newspapers were no more than a single sheet because of paper shortages. Publication was irregular, and extras printed on one side only were common. By the war's end papers were printed on whatever material was available, including wallpaper. By 1865 only twenty Southern newspapers survived.

Postwar Developments. In the decade after the war the Northern press flourished, and the foundations of national reporting were firmly laid. The number of newspapers in the United States doubled during that time, and the quality of the best newspapers, which is to say, for the most part, those published in large cities, increased accordingly as journalistic standards were established. The breadth of reportage was a particularly notable improvement. An increase in telegraph cable allowed easier access to remote news sources, and the development of railroads allowed the most prosperous papers to send correspondents to distant locations for on-the-spot coverage. By the end of Reconstruction, the circulation of daily newspapers was more than 3.5 million.

Telegraph office on Main Street, Salt Lake City, where the first transcontinental telegraph line was
joined on 24 October 1861

Source:

Michael Emery and Edwin Emery, *The Press and America: An Interpretive History of the Mass Media,* seventh edition (Englewood Cliffs, N.J.: Prentice-Hall, 1992).

THE TELEGRAPH

Morse Code. Samuel F. B. Morse demonstrated a simple but stunning invention in 1837. It was a machine that could send a clicking signal across a wire. Using his code that related clicking patterns to letters of the alphabet, Morse could transmit messages wherever he could string his telegraph cable. The new technology was promising enough to encourage Congress to foot the bill for a test line between Baltimore and Washington in 1843, and within a year the experiment had proved successful. The challenge was to cover the country with telegraph cable.

Messages in Minutes. Before the telegraph, the only way people could communicate with others in distant places was to send them letters or to travel to meet them. The telegraph allowed a person to transmit a message over hundreds and, eventually, thousands of miles in the space of perhaps an hour. By the 1850s there were telegraph stations in major eastern and midwestern cities. Operators there sent and received messages, decoded them, and passed them to runners who hand-delivered the telegrams. The cost varied depending on the location of the station, but it was normally calculated at twenty-five cents per hundred miles for ten words or less in the early 1850s.

Connects with Cable. The problem with the telegraph was that communication was limited to stations linked by a cable. The investment cost was huge, and stringing the cable took time. It cost between $100 and $200 a mile to construct the lines, and workers had to overcome the difficulties posed by rough terrain. Nonetheless, in October 1861 the first transcontinental telegraph cable was completed, and in 1866 a cable was successfully laid across the floor of the Atlantic, linking North America and England. By 1866 more than one hundred thousand miles of telegraph cable linked cities and towns all over the United States, and the telegraph industry employed thousands of workers.

Telegraphic Journalism. Among the most significant effects of the telegraph was its importance to newspapers. Timely national news coverage was made possible as newspaper editors from various regions of the country were able to share stories promptly. Before the telegraph, editors mailed their papers to one another and allowed stories to be reprinted liberally. The postal service was slow. The telegraph was quick, but it was also costly and the charge was by the word. Newspapers paid discounted rates, but they had so much to communicate that charges were still steep. So newsmen invented a form of abbreviated communication called telegraphic reporting to keep the words to a minimum. Sometimes they ran words together to trick the system; other times they left out non-essential words. Newspaper rewriters at the receiving end deciphered the reports and restored them to journalistic prose.

S. O. S. Western Union emerged after the war as the dominant company in the field. A merger in 1866 with the United States Telegraph Company and the American Telegraph Company gave Western Union a monopoly. The merger created a company with more than $40 million in capital. But the industry was soon threatened by a new advance in technology. In 1876 Alexander Graham Bell patented the first practical telephone, and within a decade telephone lines had been constructed, allowing people in large cities instant, direct access to one another.

Source:

Robert Luther Thompson, *Wiring a Continent: The History of the Telegraph Industry in the United States, 1832-1866* (Princeton: Princeton University Press, 1947).

In the 1850s mail delivery to the West was problematic. The most efficient route was the ocean route from New York down the Eastern seaboard, into the Caribbean Sea to Panama, overland to the Pacific, and up the Western seaboard to San Francisco. U.S. postmaster Aaron Brown, who took office in 1857, decided there had to be a better way. He stipulated two overland routes from east to west (later replaced by a single route) and awarded a contract to the private Overland Mail Company to deliver mail by stagecoach. The trip from Saint Louis to San Francisco took twenty-five days; the coaches carried between five hundred and six hundred pounds of mail plus as many as four passengers, and horses had to be changed every ten or fifteen miles. Overland Mail operated successfully until the Civil War.

In 1860 a private carrier who also traveled the same route as the Overland Mail Company decided to introduce an express service. Early in 1860 entrepreneur William H. Russell advertised for "young, skinny, wiry fellows not over 18. Must be expert riders willing to risk death daily. Orphans preferred." Ninety riders answered the ad and agreed to Russell's requirement that they swear not to cuss, fight, or mistreat their horses. Russell provided them with a team of five hundred well-bred mounts and challenged his riders to complete a 1,966-mile route in ten and one-half days. Riders carrying an average of about 350 letters raced between about 120 relay stations normally set at ten-or-fifteen mile intervals, where they got fresh horses. They were allowed two minutes in station to change horses and pick up whatever sustenance they required. Each rider covered seventy-five to one hundred miles a day before he was relieved. The service was called the Pony Express. It operated for nineteen months, charging five dollars a half ounce at first and later two dollars to deliver mail in half the time of conventional postal service.

The Pony Express was legendary, and its riders were heroes. Among the most colorful riders was Cowboy Bob Haslam, who was chosen to ride the most dangerous stretch of the trail on the day President Lincoln's first inaugural speech was being carried to Sacramento, where, it was hoped, the president's words would help influence the debate raging in the California state legislature about whether to secede from the Union. Haslam was attacked by a Paiute Indian attack party riding horses they had stolen from other Pony Express riders. He emptied his pistol at them while racing toward his destination. They shot arrows at him, wounding him in the arm. When he arrived at the next relay station, he refused to give up to a substitute rider and continued on, completing his 120-mile portion of the route in eight hours and ten minutes.

The completion of the transcontinental telegraph cable in 1861 meant the end of the Pony Express. It had been a costly venture. William Russell estimated that he had lost a half a million dollars, but he provided a wealth of stories about his fearless, colorful riders.

Source: Peter T. Rohrbach and Lowell S. Newman, *American Issue: The U.S. Postage Stamp, 1842-1869* (Washington, D.C.: Smithsonian Institution Press, 1984.

THE UNITED STATES POSTAL SERVICE

Adhesive Stamps and Three-Cent Letters. Mail delivery was not a service taken lightly in the mid nineteenth century. There were few mechanical devices to assist in mail handling, and the postal system was in an early stage of development. Local postmasters did much of the work as they saw fit, including canceling stamps so they could not be reused. Until the early 1850s, this process was done by the postmaster in writing or with a hand stamp he designed himself. A key development in the history of mail delivery was the introduction in 1842 of the adhesive postage stamp and envelopes with printed postage, which allowed people to affix stamps themselves or use postpaid envelopes. When postal workers were freed from some of the fee-collection duties, they could spend more of their time sorting mail for distribution. Even so, until 1855 letters could still be sent with stamps affixed or with postage due on delivery. The Postal Act of 1851 introduced some uniformity into the administration of the U.S. Post Office. It stipulated a uniform postage rate: for letters under one-half ounce going up to three thousand miles, three cents for prepaid postage and five cents for postage due on delivery. For distances over three thousand miles, the rate doubled.

City Service. For people living in cities, correspondence within the city limits was easy to manage. Private carriers competed with the U.S. Postal Service, and rates varied depending on the carrier, distance, and size of the letter or package. To send a letter, a person took it to the post office, and a carrier took the letter to the post office closest to the recipient. There was no guaranteed free delivery of mail in cities until 1863. Before then, recipients paid a premium to a private messenger service for delivery or, more commonly, picked up their mail at their local post office. Sometimes the mail was delivered by the sender to the post office for pickup by the recipient; in

Rural news delivery during the Civil War (photograph by Mathew Brady)

some cases the local postmaster had to advertise in the local newspaper that mail was being held for specified recipients.

Rural Service. Mail service between cities or to rural areas was a more complicated matter because travel was difficult: roads were primitive, and the only motorized transportation was by train or steamship. By 1850 mail was being carried by rail when the routes allowed and by steamboat and stagecoach to places not served by trains. But service was slow and unpredictable, especially in the West; the first intercontinental railroad line was not completed until 1869. Railroad tracks were heavily concentrated in the Northeast and Midwest, making delivery in the South and West a difficult chore until the end of the century. Overland postal routes were often served on a biweekly basis at best, and that service was to central distribution centers, where mail was sorted and sent out to local stations. Delivery of a letter from the East to a rural western destination could easily take weeks or even months. In rural areas delivery took longer, especially if the recipient was not near a railroad route, and access to a post office was likely to require a time-consuming journey for people living on farms.

War Mail. The Civil War paralyzed the mail service. Some eighty-five hundred post offices in the South separated themselves from the U.S. Post Office, and on 1 June 1861 the federal government forbade delivery of mail to the South, though by mutual agreement between the federal and confederate governments, prisoners of war were able to send letters, which were gathered, ex-

changed between the sides, and distributed by the prisoners' postal service. The Confederacy established its own postal service and issued its own stamps, but the newly established government had difficulty finding printing plants to print the new issues, and, as the war progressed, inflation caused the postal rates to quadruple from their initial level, which was the same as in the North. Paper shortages added to the problem, as envelopes became scarce. People used any wrapping materials they could find to cover letters, including wallpaper. In most cases, the system simply failed, and people resorted to personal messengers—acquaintances traveling toward the destination of the letter—or private carriers, such as American Express, to carry their correspondence. By the end of the war more than fifty-five hundred post offices in the South had closed.

The System Flourishes. The Postal Act of 1863 designated classes of mail—first class for letters; second class for periodical publications; third class for the rest—and authorized free delivery of mail in the cities. That year New York City and Philadelphia employed about 120 mail carriers each to meet the new delivery obligation, and by 1864 there was free delivery of mail in sixty-six cities, requiring the services of 685 mailmen. Rural free delivery was still thirty-three years off. With free delivery in the cities, the postal system flourished. Attempts were made to improve efficiency of distance mail at the same time. Postal workers were assigned to railroad mail routes to sort mail while it was in transit to speed up distribution. Postal rates dropped to two cents

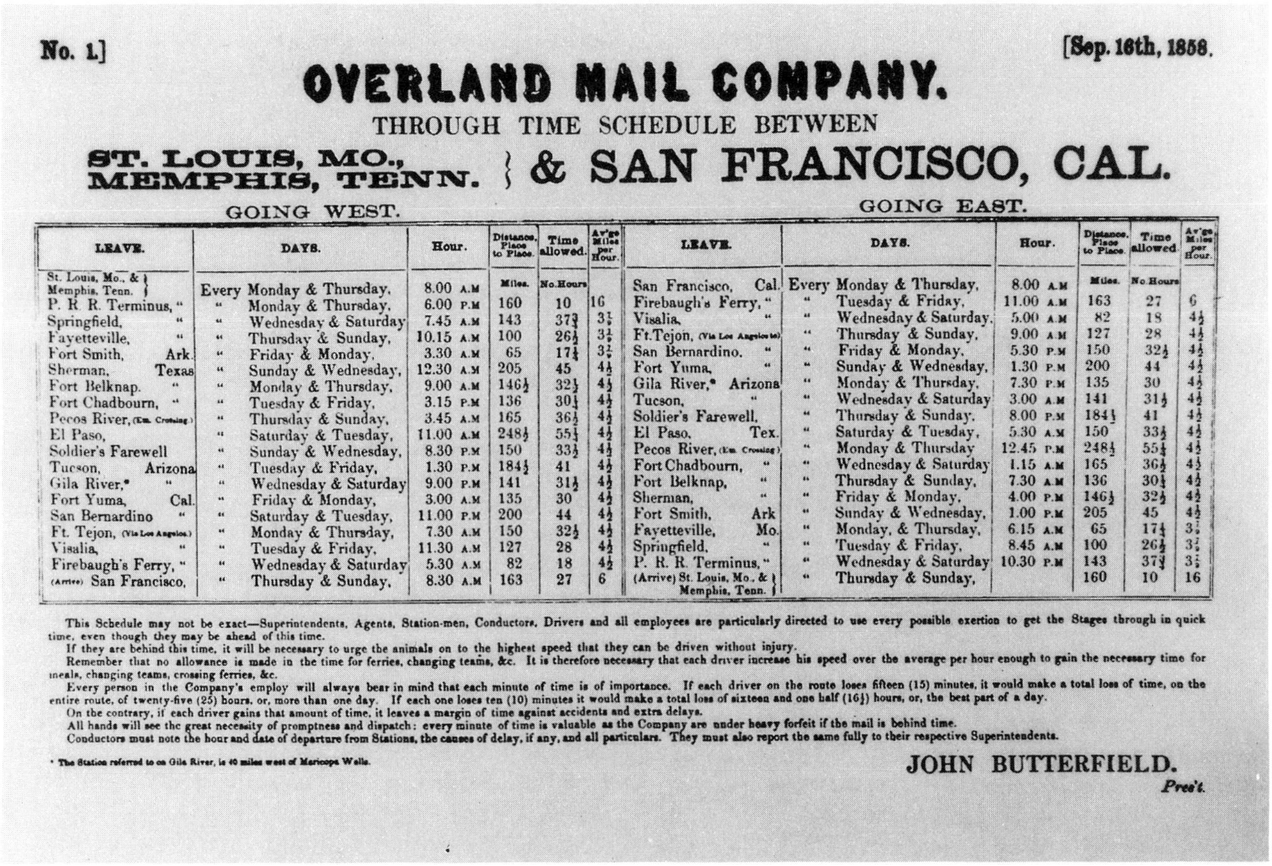

No. 1] [Sep. 16th, 1858.

OVERLAND MAIL COMPANY.

THROUGH TIME SCHEDULE BETWEEN

ST. LOUIS, MO., MEMPHIS, TENN. } & SAN FRANCISCO, CAL.

GOING WEST.

LEAVE.	DAYS.	Hour.	Distance, Place to Place.	Time allowed.	Av'ge Miles per Hour.
St. Louis, Mo., & Memphis, Tenn. }	Every Monday & Thursday,	8.00 A.M	Miles.	No. Hours	
P. R. R. Terminus, "	" Monday & Thursday,	6.00 P.M	160	10	16
Springfield, "	" Wednesday & Saturday	7.45 A.M	143	37¾	3¾
Fayetteville, "	" Thursday & Sunday,	10.15 A.M	100	26½	3¾
Fort Smith, Ark.	" Friday & Monday,	3.30 A.M	65	17¼	3¾
Sherman, Texas	" Sunday & Wednesday,	12.30 A.M	205	45	4½
Fort Belknap. "	" Monday & Thursday,	9.00 A.M	146½	32½	4½
Fort Chadbourn, "	" Tuesday & Friday,	3.15 P.M	136	30¼	4½
Pecos River, (Em. Crossing.)	" Thursday & Sunday,	3.45 A.M	165	36½	4½
El Paso,	" Saturday & Tuesday,	11.00 A.M	248½	55¼	4½
Soldier's Farewell	" Sunday & Wednesday,	8.30 P.M	150	33½	4½
Tucson, Arizona	" Tuesday & Friday,	1.30 P.M	184½	41	4½
Gila River,* "	" Wednesday & Saturday	9.00 P.M	141	31½	4½
Fort Yuma, Cal.	" Friday & Monday,	3.00 A.M	135	30	4½
San Bernardino "	" Saturday & Tuesday,	11.00 P.M	200	44	4½
Ft. Tejon, (Via Los Angelos.)	" Monday & Thursday,	7.30 A.M	150	32½	4½
Visalia, "	" Tuesday & Friday,	11.30 A.M	127	28	4½
Firebaugh's Ferry, "	" Wednesday & Saturday	5.30 A.M	82	18	4½
(Arrive) San Francisco,	" Thursday & Sunday,	8.30 A.M	163	27	6

GOING EAST.

LEAVE.	DAYS.	Hour.	Distance, Place to Place.	Time allowed.	Av'ge Miles per Hour.
San Francisco, Cal.	Every Monday & Thursday,	8.00 A.M	Miles.	No. Hours	
Firebaugh's Ferry, "	" Tuesday & Friday,	11.00 A.M	163	27	6
Visalia, "	" Wednesday & Saturday,	5.00 A.M	82	18	4½
Ft. Tejon, (Via Los Angelos)	" Thursday & Sunday,	9.00 A.M	127	28	4½
San Bernardino, "	" Friday & Monday,	5.30 P.M	150	32½	4½
Fort Yuma, "	" Sunday & Wednesday,	1.30 P.M	200	44	4½
Gila River,* Arizona	" Monday & Thursday,	7.30 P.M	135	30	4½
Tucson, "	" Wednesday & Saturday	3.00 A.M	141	31½	4½
Soldier's Farewell,	" Thursday & Sunday,	8.00 P.M	184½	41	4½
El Paso, Tex.	" Saturday & Tuesday,	5.30 A.M	150	33½	4½
Pecos River, (Em. Crossing)	" Monday & Thursday	12.45 P.M	248½	55¼	4½
Fort Chadbourn, "	" Wednesday & Saturday	1.15 A.M	165	36½	4½
Fort Belknap, "	" Thursday & Sunday,	7.30 A.M	136	30¼	4½
Sherman, "	" Friday & Monday,	4.00 P.M	146½	32½	4½
Fort Smith, Ark	" Sunday & Wednesday,	1.00 P.M	205	45	4½
Fayetteville, Mo.	" Monday, & Thursday,	6.15 A.M	65	17¼	3¾
Springfield, "	" Tuesday & Friday,	8.45 A.M	100	26½	3¾
P. R. R. Terminus, "	" Wednesday & Saturday	10.30 P.M	143	37¾	3¾
(Arrive) St. Louis, Mo., & Memphis, Tenn. }	" Thursday & Sunday,		160	10	16

This Schedule may not be exact—Superintendents, Agents, Station-men, Conductors, Drivers and all employees are particularly directed to use every possible exertion to get the Stages through in quick time, even though they may be ahead of this time.

If they are behind this time, it will be necessary to urge the animals on to the highest speed that they can be driven without injury.

Remember that no allowance is made in the time for ferries, changing teams, &c. It is therefore necessary that each driver increase his speed over the average per hour enough to gain the necessary time for meals, changing teams, crossing ferries, &c.

Every person in the Company's employ will always bear in mind that each minute of time is of importance. If each driver on the route loses fifteen (15) minutes, it would make a total loss of time, on the entire route, of twenty-five (25) hours, or, more than one day. If each one loses ten (10) minutes it would make a total loss of sixteen and one half (16½) hours, or, the best part of a day.

On the contrary, if each driver gains that amount of time, it leaves a margin of time against accidents and extra delays.

All hands will see the great necessity of promptness and dispatch: every minute of time is valuable as the Company are under heavy forfeit if the mail is behind time.

Conductors must note the hour and date of departure from Stations, the causes of delay, if any, and all particulars. They must also report the same fully to their respective Superintendents.

* The Station referred to on Gila River, is 40 miles west of Maricopa Wells.

JOHN BUTTERFIELD.
Pres't.

Timetable for postal delivery by the Overland Mail Company for fall 1858

for a half-ounce letter. By the end of Reconstruction, the postal system handled some three billion pieces of mail annually.

Source:

Peter T. Rohrbach and Lowell S. Newman, *American Issue: The U.S. Postage Stamp, 1842-1869* (Washington, D.C.: Smithsonian Institution Press, 1984).

FRANK LESLIE (HENRY CARTER)

1821-1880
PUBLISHER

Wood Engraver. The publisher of illustrated journalism known as Frank Leslie was born Henry Carter in Ipswich, Suffolk, England, in 1821, the son of a successful glove manufacturer. In school, the boy showed himself to be a talented artist, and he learned to put his skill to use as an engraver by the time he was a teenager. In 1842, when he was twenty-one, he took charge of the engraving department of the *Illustrated London News,* a successful paper that pioneered the use of illustrations in a newspaper. Engravings, which were typically done in steel at the time, had been restricted to journals because the illustrations took so long to render. Carter worked effectively in wood, a faster medium, so he was able to meet the deadlines demanded by newspapers.

Efficiency. At the time, there were not more than twenty wood engravers in the United States, where Carter sought his fortune in 1848. Within a year he was working professionally under the nameFrank Leslie. When the popular singer Jenny Lind came to America in 1850 for a tour promoted by P. T. Barnum, Leslie engraved the programs and formed a friendship with the boss. Two years later Barnum was a partner in a venture to introduce an American version of the *Illustrated London News,* using a technique devised by Leslie to produce woodcuts quickly. He divided large woodcuts into pieces and parceled out the work to different engravers; their work was then integrated by a master engraver. In this way Leslie could produce in a day or two work that would take five times as long under the old system.

American Success. Within five years the paper was called *Frank Leslie's Illustrated Newspaper,* and it was a huge success. The weekly paper was sixteen pages and sold for either ten cents a copy or four dollars per year. News stories were illustrated within a couple of weeks of their occurrence, normally, and in addition to news there were features on music, the stage, fine arts, sports, and literature, including serial fiction. No other publisher could match Leslie's speed of production, and so he captured a market of both barely literate readers, who appreciated having the news presented in pictures, and more sophisticated subscribers, who appreciated his coverage of the arts and sports. By the end of 1858 circulation was about 140,000 and Leslie was a major periodical publisher. He energetically pursued the illustrated market. In 1853 he had started *Frank Leslie's Lady's Gazette of Fashion and Fancy Needlework;* in 1855 he started *Frank Leslie's New York Journal of Romance;* and over the next two decades he launched new publications, usually bearing his name, at the rate of well more than one a year.

Competition. By the time of the Civil War, Leslie had a serious competitor in the field of magazine illustration—*Harper's.* Between them, *Leslie's Illustrated News* (which then cost six cents a copy) and *Harper's* brought readers the most vivid pictorial reports of war ever published. Leslie employed as many as twelve correspondents and eighty artists, and he published approximately three thousand war pictures. He offered to publish war drawings by both Union and Confederate soldiers. But *Harper's* did a better job and by the war's end had become the most popular illustrated weekly.

Marriage. By 1865 Leslie's empire had grown large enough that he could not give much attention to a single publication. The Leslie Publishing House employed seventy engravers and published a half a million copies a week of its various publications. Leslie himself took a salary of $60,000 a year (at a time when skilled workers made about three dollars a day), and he had a distracting love interest, the wife of a business associate, whom he married in 1874. After his marriage, Leslie spent lavishly, despite the effects of the economic depression, and in 1879 his company went into a partial receivership. He died on 10 January 1880, having developed a quick-growing tumor in his throat. Mrs. Frank Leslie, his widow, took over control of Leslie Publications, and it prospered under her direction.

Source:
George Everett, "Frank Leslie," in *Dictionary of Literary Biography, Volume 43: American Newspaper Journalists, 1690-1872* (Detroit: Bruccoli Clark Layman/Gale, 1985), pp. 290-303.

HIRAM SIBLEY

1807-1888
TELEGRAPH ENTREPRENEUR

Background. Hiram Sibley, the man who more than any other single figure knit together a national telegraph network and monopoly, spent his youth and early business career working in a series of mechanical and manufacturing ventures in western Massachusetts and upstate New York. He was born in North Adams, Massachusetts, and attended village school there before working in a shoemaking shop. As a young man he moved to the Genesee Valley region of New York and found work as a machinist in a cotton factory until he started up a machine shop of his own. He also operated a wool carding business in the region. By the time he moved to Rochester in 1838 he had amassed a solid fortune, which he deployed in banking and real estate. It was a career that placed him squarely in the context of the early New England Industrial Revolution at its western fringes. Sibley did not engage in the telegraph business until he was forty-two years old.

Initial Venture. He first became intrigued with the telegraph in the 1840s, when Royal Earl House, the inventor of the House printing telegraph, fell into financial difficulties and approached Sibley for help. Sensing the technology's potential, Sibley in 1849 joined several partners to form the New York State Printing Telegraph Company, bidding for western New York territory. But the initial foray foundered when it went up against the well-equipped and tightly managed New York, Albany and Buffalo Telegraph Company. As he struggled to keep the venture going, Sibley became convinced that the telegraph industry would have to be centralized somehow—its confused tangle of competing companies and overlapping lines ungnarled—if it were to achieve maximum efficiency and realize its full potential. This conviction shaped Sibley's future telegraph investments and management. It also put him in on a course of alternating collision and cooperation with other, equally ambitious and consolidation-minded telegraph entrepreneurs.

Western Union. In 1850, after only a year in the business, Sibley spelled out his vision for his partners, proposing to turn west and broaden the company's scope of activity by building a company that would bring all of the telegraph lines west of Buffalo under its control. Buying up the House patents and raising $100,000 in capital, he organized the New York and Mississippi Valley Printing Telegraph Company in April 1851 to build a line west from Buffalo and woo the smaller western companies into strategic alliances. Progress was initially slow, but after recapitalizing and reorganizing the company in 1854 Sibley scored a major coup when he persuaded managers of the Cleveland and Toledo, the Michigan Southern, and the Northern Indiana railroads to build and equip telegraph lines to Detroit and Chicago on the company's behalf in exchange for stock in the New York and Mississippi Valley and free use of the telegraph for railroad business. In short order he also acquired control over a rival company, the Lake Erie Telegraph, widening his territory. In 1856 Sibley again reorganized and renamed the company, choosing a label that clearly identified what was now not only vaunting ambition but growing reach: he called it Western Union.

Strategic Alliance. By 1857, as he modernized equipment, linked up his acquisitions and systemized operations, Sibley had basically accomplished his first goal. The Western Union Telegraph Company controlled a vast western territory, extending from the northern Atlantic to the burgeoning cities of the Midwest. His main competitor had also emerged by this point: the American Telegraph Company, which had developed an eastern network as comprehensive as Sibley's western version. In 1859 he approached the American, proposing a strategic alliance. Samuel Morse and other original telegraph developers temporarily blocked the move. But eventually Sibley was able to broker a far-reaching agreement, the "Treaty of Six Nations" (referring to the six major companies participating), which pooled telegraph traffic and allocated geographical territories to each participant. Sibley claimed Ohio, Indiana, Michigan, most of Wisconsin, part of western New York, and slices of Pennsylvania and Virginia for Western Union. The companies formalized the treaty by forming the North American Telegraph Association. Diplomacy did not end competition, however, and Western Union continued to contest the American for territory and traffic.

Transcontinental Expansion. At this point Sibley again turned west. Unable to convince Western Union's board of directors to build a transcontinental line, he took on the project independently, securing an annual federal subsidy in 1860 of $40,000 for ten years to open California to telegraphic communication. To handle construction, Sibley sent a lieutenant to California to organize the small companies there into the California State Telegraph Company, which in turn set up the Overland Telegraph Company and began building from Carson City to Salt Lake City. Meanwhile, Sibley tackled the eastern end, organizing the Pacific Telegraph Company to build from Omaha to Salt Lake City. Financial improprieties marred the completion of the project, both companies engaging freely in stock watering and wildly inflating the costs of construction as they sold the line to Western Union. But in addition to making Sibley and his associates millions of dubious dollars, it made Western Union in geographic terms the largest network and private business in the world. Sibley retired in 1865 and devoted the remainder of his career to railroad and western land investments and a seed-and-nursery business in Rochester.

Source:
Robert L. Thompson, *Wiring a Continent: the History of the Telegraph Industry in the United States* (Princeton: Princeton University Press, 1947).

HENRY WELLS

1805-1878
FOUNDER, AMERICAN EXPRESS;
ORGANIZING PARTNER,
WELLS FARGO AND CO.

Stuttering Teacher. Born in Vermont, where his father was a Congregationalist preacher, Henry Wells was a big, self-educated man who dressed sharply and spoke with a stutter. One of his first jobs was as a teacher at a school for students with speech defects, but, as his own problem did not improve, he lost the confidence of his charges and sought his fortune in the field of transportation. He took a job as a ticket agent facilitating the movement of freight and passengers for shippers on Lake Erie. Then, in 1839, he came to the attention of William Harnden, an entrepreneur who had just begun offering Harnden's Package Express, a delivery service from Boston to Manhattan that moved valuables requiring special handling more quickly (between those cities) than the U.S. Mail. Harnden's business flourished. When he extended his service to Albany, he hired Wells to manage the new station.

Express Career. Wells saw a grand future for express delivery, and he had ambitious ideas about expanding Hernden's service, first to Buffalo and then throughout New York. When he failed to convince the boss, Wells quit in 1841 and sold his friend George Pomeroy on the idea of initiating an express service between Buffalo and Albany. He and Pomeroy alternated trips carrying a valise of packages on a train and stagecoach between the two cities, a treacherous trip that took three days and four nights. After three trips, Pomeroy quit, and Wells, with the help of an investor, bought him out. Within eighteen months a rail link was completed between Albany and Buffalo, and Wells and Company became a thriving business, aided significantly by a failed grocer turned express agent named William George Fargo. When Hernden died in 1845 at the age of thirty-two, Wells bought his express business and moved his offices to New York. He sold a portion of his routes in 1846 to Fargo, who expanded his business as aggressively as Wells, and by the end of the 1840s Wells and Fargo controlled the express freight business in the state of New York, which had increased a hundredfold during the decade.

American Express. The lucrative New York express attracted competitors, the most serious of whom was entrepreneur John Butterfield, partner in the firm of Butterfield, Wasson and Company. Butterfield negotiated freight contracts on the same terms as Wells, and then a price war began. Soon, both companies were losing money, and the principals decided to merge their companies. In 1850 Butterfield engineered a merger of Wells and Company, Livingston, Fargo and Company, and his own company. The new organization, called American Express, was instituted for ten years to serve as an umbrella corporation for the three merging companies, which continued to operate more or less autonomously. It was an uneasy alliance controlled initially by Butterfield, the most powerful of the partners, who sought to consolidate his authority. Wells was elected president, but it was a hollow office. Wells showed minimal interest in the company and went into semiretirement at the age of forty-five, intending to enjoy his riches. But the ongoing power struggles between Butterfield and Fargo required Wells to act as mediator. As Butterfield and Fargo exhausted their energies contending with one another, Wells served as president of a very prosperous company.

Wells Fargo. In 1852 Wells and Fargo proposed that American Express initiate a delivery service to the West. Butterfield objected, so Wells and Fargo decided to form their own company to serve Western routes. They called their new business Wells Fargo, and Wells paid particular attention to developing this service, which he could run without the annoyance of the boardroom politics that plagued American Express. Seeing the opportunity of expanding overland express service westward, Butterfield developed his own express service to the West called the Overland Mail Company, an adventuresome coach service from Saint Louis to San Francisco that both made history and lost money, despite a government contract to deliver the U.S. Mail.

Business Fortunes. The Civil War was a boon time for American Express, which delivered messages behind the lines, where other delivery services feared to go. By 1862 American Express had 890 offices and employed over fifteen hundred workers. It served ten states with some ninety-two hundred miles of delivery routes run each day. Every year during the Civil War American Express paid stock dividends of at least 20 percent, $115 per share, and in 1866 the directors declared an 80 percent stock dividend. After the war competition stiffened, and Fargo became the dominant voice among the directors as American Express began to suffer substantial losses. When American Express merged with the competing Merchants Union Express despite Wells's protest, he was forced out of the presidency of the company and replaced by Fargo, though he remained on the board until his death. Meanwhile, Wells Fargo prospered, but Henry Wells did not. He made a series of bad investments after the war that prevented him from realizing his dream of building a college in Aurora, New York. The school was completed after his death with funding from Wells's friend, E. B. Morgan, and named Wells College. Henry Wells died in 1878 while traveling in Scotland.

Sources:

Peter Z. Grossman, *American Express, The Unofficial History of the People Who Built the Great Financial Empire* (New York: Crown, 1987);

Alden Hatch, *American Express: A Century of Service* (Garden City, N.Y.: Doubleday, 1950).

PUBLICATIONS

E. B. Grant, *Report on the Western Union Telegraphy Company* (New York: Sun Job Printing, 1869)—an early company history of the most successful American telegraph company;

Frederic Hudson, *Journalism in the United States, from 1690–1872* (New York: Harper, 1873) —a survey of the development of American journalism.

Alexander Jones, *Historical Sketch of the Electric Telegraph, Including Its Rise and Progress in the United States* (New York: Putnam, 1852)—an early report on the importance of telegraphy in the United States;

George B. Prescott, *History, Theory, and Practice of the Electric Telegraph* (Boston: Ticknor & Fields, 1860)—a survey of long-distance messaging throughout the world;

Robert Sabine, *The History and Progress of the Electric Telegraph* (New York, 1869)—a progress report, with historical background, on development of the modern telegraph;

T. P. Shaffner, *The Telegraphic Manual* (New York: Pudney & Russell, 1859)—a history and description of the semaphoric, electric, and magnetic telegraphs and their use throughout the world, from antiquity to the 1850s;

Isaiah Thomas, *The History of Printing in America*, second edition, 2 volumes (Boston: American Antiquarian Society, 1874)—first published in 1810, this collecton of materials related to the printing industry that the author thought ought to be preserved for posterity is the most significant early source of printing history;

Lawrence Turnbull, *The Electro-Magnetic Telegraph* (Philadelphia: Hart, 1853)—a historical account of the development of the telegraph that attempts to assess its impact as of 1850 and to predict its uses.

BJUYT .KIOP M LKJHGFDSA:QWERTYUIOP:._9BV864328W RT
HA

HARTFORD, DEC. 9.

DEAR BROTHER:

I AM TRYING T TO GET THE HANG OF THIS NEW F
FANGLED WRITING MACHINE, BUT AM NOT MAKING
A SHINING SUCCESS OF IT. HOWEVER THIS IS THE
FIRST ATTEMPT I EVER HAVE MADE, & YET I PER-
CEIVETHAT I SHALL SOON & EASILY ACQUIRE A FINE
FACILITY IN ITS USE. I SAW THE THING IN BOS-
TON THE OTHER DAY & WAS GREATLY TAKEN WI:TH
IT. SUSIE HAS STRUCK THE KEYS ONCE OR TWICE,
& NO DOUBT HAS PRINTED SOME LETTERS WHICH DO
NOT BELONG WHERE SHE PUT THEM.
THE HAVING BEEN A COMPOSITOR IS LIKELY TO BE
A GREAT HELP TO ME,SINCE O NE CHIEFLY NEEDS
SWIFTNESS IN BANGING THE KEYS.THE MACHINE COSTS
125 DOLLARS.THE MACHINE HAS SEVERAL VIRTUES
I BELIEVE IT WILL PRINT FASTER.THAN I CAN WRITE.
ONE MAY LEAN BACK IN HIS CHAIR & WORK IT. IT
PILES AN AWFUL STACK OF WORDS ON ONE PAGE.
IT DONT MUSS THINGS OR SCATTER INK BLOTS AROUND.
OF COURSE IT SAVES PAPER.

SUSIE IS GONE,
NOW, & I FANCY I SHALL MAKE BETTER PROGRESS:
WORKING THIS TYPE-WRITER REMINDS ME OF OLD
ROBERT BUCHANAN, WHO, YOU REMEMBER, USED TO
SET UP ARTICLES AT THE CASE WITHOUT PREVIOUS-
LY PUTTING THEM IN THE FORM OF MANUSCRIPT;I
WAS.LOST IN ADMIRATION OF SUCH MARVELOUS
INTELLECTUAL CAPACITY.

LOVE TO MOLLIE.
YOUR-BROTHER,
SAM.

Samuel Langhorne Clemens's letter to his brother, written in 1874 on his
new typewriter

EDUCATION

by BRIAN KELLY

CONTENTS

Sidebars and tables are listed in italics.

1850

- The New York state legislature passes acts mandating local school taxes, thus clearing the way for universal public education. Some oppose these measures as an infringement on property rights.

- Genesee College (later Syracuse University) is founded as a coeducational institution in upstate New York.

- Educational reformers in Ohio suffer a setback when advocates of local control abolish the office of State Superintendent of Schools, which had been established only three years earlier.

4 Jan.   James McCune Smith, a prominent New York African American educator, writes a letter to William Lloyd Garrison's *Liberator* expressing his resolve to "improve the colored schools in this city—believing them to be better only than no schools at all."

1851

- Francis Wayland, president of Brown University, allows undergraduates to choose courses, replaces semester-length courses with more-flexible study schedules, and creates programs in agriculture, applied sciences, law, and pedagogy.

- Legislation is passed in Massachusetts permitting towns to raise taxes in order to support public libraries. This law follows similar legislation enacted by the city of Boston and the state of New Hampshire (1849). Maine and Vermont follow suit a few years later.

1852

- Massachusetts passes the first compulsory-attendance law, requiring children between eight and fourteen to attend school at least twelve weeks per year (six weeks continuous).

- Catharine Beecher founds the American Womens' Education Association to train female factory workers as teachers for schools in the West.

- Avery College, an all-black institution, opens in Pittsburgh, Pennsylvania.

- The First Plenary Council of the Catholic Church, meeting in Baltimore, argues against separation of religious instruction from other forms of instruction and urges parents to give their children a Christian education "based on religious principles, accompanied by religious practices, and always subordinate to religious influence." The Catholic school system evolves out of this and later meetings in 1866 and 1884.

- Henry P. Tappan assumes the presidency of the University of Michigan.

1853

- The Southern Commercial Convention at Memphis recommends sectional independence from northern schools. In the following year, members appoint a committee at Charleston to encourage publication of southern textbooks.

- Antioch College opens in Yellow Springs, Ohio, as a coeducational institution, following Oberlin, the nation's first coed college (1838), and New York Central College (1849).

- The office of State Superintendent of Schools is reestablished in Ohio.

1854

- Rhode Island establishes a state normal school at Providence.

- The state of New York establishes the office of State Superintendent of Public Instruction. Supervision of public schools begins to shift from district to state authorities.

- Ashman Institute (later Lincoln University) is founded in Pennsylvania as a black college. It is the oldest college in the United States having as its original purpose the higher education of black students.

- Astor Library opens in Lafayette Place, New York City, with a gift from sponsor John Jacob Astor of $400,000 and one hundred thousand books, making it the largest library in North America. (It becomes the basis of the New York Public Library in 1895.)

- Wilberforce College, an all-black school, opens in Wilberforce, Ohio.

26 Dec. The American Association for the Advancement of Education calls upon the federal government to establish a separate department to oversee public education.

1855

- The "rate bill" system for funding schools is abolished by law in New York. Within four years similar acts are implemented in Ohio, Rhode Island, Michigan, and New Jersey.

- The first kindergarten in the United States is founded by Mrs. Carl Schurz in Watertown, Wisconsin. The students are the children of German-speaking immigrants.

- Massachusetts adopts a law barring religious sects from receiving state education funds. Catholics perceive this as an attack on the rights of immigrant children.

- The Southern Commercial Convention at New Orleans urges southerners not to patronize seminaries and colleges in the North and encourages the production of southern textbooks that offer prizes for authors.

- In his 1855 Annual Report to the Saint Louis Board of Public Schools, President Isaiah Forbes notes the "unexampled success of our school system, and the great popularity of the schools."

17 Mar. The Massachusetts state legislature passes a bill outlawing racial or religious discrimination in admitting students to public schools, culminating a fifteen-year campaign by black Bostonians and their abolitionist allies. Passage of the act encourages blacks to press for an end to segregation elsewhere.

Dec.   City officials in Sacramento, California, veto appropriations for black schools because they are "particularly obnoxious to those of our citizens who have immigrated from Southern States."

1856

- The Savannah Convention appoints a group of southern professors to prepare schoolbooks with a "southern orientation."

- Francis Wayland is replaced as president of Brown University after faculty members clamor for his dismissal.

- The Massachusetts State Industrial School for Girls, known as the Lancaster School, opens, and the first group of girls referred by the Boston courts is admitted.

1857

- Chicago officials abolish ward-by-ward school districting and place the city's schools under the direction of one board of education.

- A report of the New York Society for the Promotion of Education Among Colored Children finds white children attending schools in "splendid, almost palatial edifices" while black youth are "pent up in filthy neighborhoods, in old and dilapidated buildings."

1858

- John G. Fee, son of a slaveholder and a Quaker mother, founds a biracial college at Berea, Kentucky. The hostility of local whites forces the college to shut its doors until after the Civil War.

- New York Central College, founded in 1849 by the American Baptist Free Mission Society, declares bankruptcy. The school had been a center of controversy from its founding because of its biracial, coeducational policy.

26 Aug. The National Teachers' Association is established at Philadelphia to "promote the educational welfare of our country by concentrating the power and wisdom of numerous minds. . . ."

1859

- Elizabeth Palmer Peabody charters the first English-speaking kindergarten in the nation. It opens the next year in Boston as a private institution.

- Elmira College in New York becomes the first female college to award bachelor of arts degrees to women.

- In his role as chancellor of the University of Wisconsin and a member of the State Board of Regents, Henry Barnard organizes teacher-training institutes throughout the state. By the end of the year there are twenty such institutes operating under Barnard's supervision.

- Horace Mann dies at the age of sixty-three.

Mar.   In a declaration of his long-standing support for the campaign for school integration, Frederick Douglass writes that "The point we must aim for is to obtain admission for our children into the nearest school house, and the best school house in our respective neighborhoods."

1860

- The University of Iowa, founded in 1856, becomes coeducational.

- The abolitionist Gerrit Smith buys New York Central College, but closes the school again after a year.

14 Mar.   Citizens of Beverly, Massachusetts, vote at a town meeting to abolish the public high school. Under pressure from the courts and the efforts of educational reformers, the school is reestablished within a year. By this time there are some three hundred high schools in the nation, over one hundred of them in Massachusetts. There are also six thousand private "academies" in America.

Oct.   Episcopalian bishop Leonidas Polk lays the cornerstone for the University of the South at Sewanee, Tennessee, hoping thereby to train a ministry for the Episcopal Church and insulate southern collegians from the influence of abolitionism.

1861

- Susan B. Anthony urges an end to discrimination against blacks in the North. "Let us open to the colored man all our schools, from the common District to the College...."

15 Sept.   Rev. L. C. Lockwood founds a Sunday school for freed slaves behind Union army lines at Fortress Monroe, Virginia. Two days later the first school for freed men and women is opened by the American Missionary Association under the direction of Mary S. Peake, a northern freed black.

1862

- John Swett becomes the California State Superintendent of Schools. By the end of the 1860s California provides "a model of state commitment to public education."

- Superintendent of Schools William H. Wells publishes his *Graded Course of Instruction for the Public Schools of Chicago* in an effort to institute a uniform citywide course of graded instruction.

Mar.   A contingent of teachers and superintendents organized by the freedmen's aid societies sails from New York to Port Royal, South Carolina, to begin educating freed slaves.

2 July The Morrill Land Grant College Act is passed, setting aside millions of acres of federal land for states to "teach such branches of learning as are related to agriculture and the mechanic arts . . . in order to promote the liberal and practical education of the industrial classes. . . ."

11 Nov. Gen. Ulysses S. Grant appoints Col. John Eaton to oversee the Freedmen's Bureau in Arkansas. Eaton proceeds to establish a "school system" in the Department of the West.

1863

• Andrew D. White, a prominent antislavery Republican and the future president of Cornell University, is appointed chairman of the New York state legislature's Education Committee. His efforts to abolish segregation in schools are unsuccessful.

• Under its new state constitution, West Virginia becomes the first southern state to establish public schools for blacks.

5 Aug. Abraham Lincoln writes Gen. Nathaniel Banks in New Orleans, urging that "some provisions should be made for the education of the young blacks."

1864

22 Mar. General Order Number 38, issued by Gen. Nathaniel Banks, establishes "one or more common schools in each and every school district," as defined by parish provost marshals in Louisiana. The decree also authorizes the purchase of land and books for schools, recruitment of teachers, and the establishment of boards of education in each district.

May The Rhode Island state legislature's Education Committee recommends abolition of segregation in public schools. The bill fails due to opposition of Newport senators.

1865

• In remarks before the National Teachers' Association, President Richard Edwards of Illinois Normal University tells educators that the extension of public education to the defeated South will be the "chief unifying process on which we can rely for a permanent peace."

• Ballard Normal School is founded in Macon, Georgia, to train black schoolteachers.

• Vassar Female College is established in Poughkeepsie, New York.

Sept. With prominent abolitionist Thomas Wentworth Higginson as a member of its school board, Newport, Rhode Island, abolishes segregation in its public schools. Within a year the legislature votes to prohibit segregated schools throughout the state.

1866

• The National Teachers' Association grants equal membership status to women.

1867

- Beach Institute in Savannah and Storr's Normal School at Atlanta are established in an effort to train black teachers.

- Atlanta University is founded by Edmund Asa Ware under the direction of the American Missionary Association.

- The city of Boston opens the first public school for the deaf in the nation.

Feb. The Augusta Institute is founded in Augusta, Georgia, to train black teachers and ministers, but fails after a short period.

14 Mar. Henry Barnard is appointed the first U.S. Commissioner of Education.

1868

- Thaddeus Stevens, eulogized as the "father of Pennsylvania's public schools," dies.

- The Connecticut state legislature abolishes segregation in public schools.

1869

- In his inaugural remarks at Harvard University, President Charles William Eliot complains that "It is very hard to find competent professors for the University. Very few Americans of eminent ability are attracted to this profession. The pay has been too low, and there has been no gradual rise out of drudgery, such as may reasonably be expected in other learned callings."

1870

- Clark University is founded in Atlanta, Georgia, under the direction of the Northern Methodist Society.

- The state of Mississippi establishes all-black Alcorn University in an attempt to head off black demands for admission to the state university.

1871

- Yale University president Theodore Dwight Woolsey, whose career at Yale began in 1823, resigns. His successor, Noah Porter, warns in his inaugural remarks that "college and university education are not merely agitated by reforms; they are rather convulsed by a revolution—so unsettled are the minds of many who control public opinion, so sharp is the criticism of real or imagined defects in the old methods and studies, and so determined is the demand for sweeping and fundamental changes."

- The Augusta Institute (later Morehouse College) reopens under the direction of the American Baptist Home Mission Society.

1872

- Speaking at the National Educators' Association's national convention, E. E. White charges that classification and grading in the public schools is producing "lock step" mechanical education aimed at average students, handicapping bright students as well as slow learners.

- Several black students are admitted to the University of Arkansas. Classes for them are conducted in the president's office after regular hours.

1873

- South Carolina College in Orangeburg opens its doors to blacks as students and faculty. "Mixed" schools with separate classrooms follow in Columbia and Charleston.

- Henry E. Haynes becomes the first black student at the University of South Carolina when he enrolls in medical school; a majority of white students and white faculty withdraw. In response the state legislature employs northern teachers, abolishes tuition charges, and establishes preparatory courses for underprepared students in a successful attempt to lure back white students.

- The first public-school kindergarten opens in Saint Louis, Missouri. There are forty-two kindergartens in existence in the United States, with seventy-three teachers and over twelve hundred pupils.

- Boston University is founded as a coeducational institution.

1874

- The New York state legislature passes a compulsory attendance law.

- S. H. Hill of Florence, Massachusetts, contributes funds to open a charity kindergarten there.

- Samuel King, the first superintendent of schools for Portland, Oregon, develops uniform curricula and tests children at year's end to determine whether they have been "thoroughly drilled in the work assigned." In seven of the twenty-one classrooms tested, none of the children pass. Only in six classrooms are more than half the children promoted. King publishes the names and test scores of children in local newspapers.

- William T. Harris and Duane Doty publish *The Theory of Education in the United States of America*.

1875

- The Boston School Committee is reduced from 116 members elected by district to twenty-four elected at large. Critics charge that the change is designed to weaken local, working-class, and ethnic influence on schools.

20 Apr. Col. Francis W. Parker, a student of European educational reform and formerly an educator in New Hampshire and Ohio, is appointed superintendent of schools for Quincy, Massachusetts. One of his many innovations is the establishment of a teachers' training school for female high-school graduates.

1876

- Dr. Felix Adler establishes the Ethical Culture Society, a movement devoted to the belief that man must develop morally, aesthetically, and logically if he is to be truly educated.

1877

- Samuel King is forced to resign as the school superintendent in Portland, Oregon, by parents and teachers angered by his publication of student test scores.

OVERVIEW

The State of Education. By 1850 American educational reformers, led by Horace Mann, had succeeded in convincing many leading citizens of the merits of establishing a system of publicly supported "common schools." Inspired by newly developed European models of public education, the common-schools crusade had been initiated in the 1830s and won its first enthusiastic supporters in the larger, established towns of New England. From the beginning these schools were conceived not only as centers for learning, but as important vehicles for projecting the moral values considered essential to the American social order. Mann himself had stressed the importance of "moral education" in canvassing support for the common schools, and in the hands of New England descendants of the Puritans, this morality came to be closely identified with Protestantism and with the values of industriousness, frugality, and personal responsibility. Although by midcentury the common-school crusade had begun to win adherents beyond New England, American public education remained fairly disorganized, more notable for its remarkable variation than its homogeneity. In the still sparsely settled regions of the West, for instance, the availability of schooling could vary widely from one settlement to the next. In the South "public education" in the sense familiar to the North barely existed: the meager public funds spent on education went to subsidize "pauper schools" for indigent whites or private academies that were attended mainly by the sons and (occasionally) daughters of wealthy planters. Even in New England, conditions could vary widely between urban and rural schools. The primary challenge facing advocates of public education, then, was to forge an organized system of public education out of the disparate initiatives that had begun to show success across the country.

Contested Aims. From the beginning of the common-schools campaign, the task facing educational reformers was complicated by the fact that no clear consensus existed about the role or even necessity of public education in national life. Among the more privileged classes, whose own children already enjoyed access to private schooling, the very idea of taxing the citizenry in order to finance the education of working-class and poor children seemed, besides being wasteful, an infringement upon property rights. One of the crucial problems faced by reformers lay in convincing the more well-to-do that public education would benefit society as a whole. Mann, Henry Barnard, and others stressed the value of "moral instruction" for ensuring social stability and reinforcing the existing social order. Between 1840 and 1870, with the prodding of reformers, public financing evolved from a laissez-faire approach, where almost no tax money went toward education, to the "rate-bill" system, under which parents paid according to the number of children they had enrolled in the public schools, to a flat-rate system more closely resembling the one we are familiar with today. Common-school promoters faced a challenge at the other end of society as well: labor reformers also favored the establishment of public schools, though often for different reasons than those advanced by Mann and his followers. They resented the stigma associated with sending their children to "charity schools" and looked on public education as a means of reversing the growing inequality perceived by them as the main threat to American society. In many ways the most formidable task faced by educational reformers lay in attempting to reconcile these divergent expectations. These tensions would continue to manifest themselves in different forms throughout the period from 1850 to 1877, but by midcentury the reformers had managed to build a fairly solid consensus among diverse constituencies in favor of public education.

Moral Instruction. The massive transformation of American society during the middle of the nineteenth century swept aside much of the ambivalence toward educational reform. Reflecting developments in western Europe, the cause of public education in the United States found a new resonance precisely at the time that industrialization began to alter the face of society. By 1850 the revolutionary-era republic of small farmers and independent artisans was increasingly giving way (in the Northeast, at least) to an unprecedented concentration of wealth and the rise of a large class of factory operatives and other wageworkers. Although most Americans continued to live in rural areas, in 1850 nearly one of five people lived in cities. By 1880 that proportion would double to 40 percent. From only six cities of one hundred thousand or more in 1850, there would be nineteen in

1880, including one (New York) with over a million inhabitants. In the wake of rapid industrialization came growing social stratification, with large numbers in the factory towns and cities seemingly locked into a cycle of poverty and resorting increasingly to strikes and other means to press their grievances. Equally alarming for many established New Englanders was the dilution of the citizen population with immigrant stock. Famine in Ireland and social upheavals in central Europe brought hundreds of thousands of newcomers to America; by 1849 Horace Mann reported that more than half of Boston's 10,162 public-school students were the children of immigrants. City administrators complained that the influx was "countervailing the Puritan leaven of our people, and reducing the scale of public morality and public intelligence." With fears of cultural disintegration and social upheaval never far from their minds, many who had been unconvinced of the merits of public education before 1850 now supported the reform project and its prescription of "moral instruction" as an antidote for the restlessness taking hold of the lower classes and as a bulwark of national identity in the face of large-scale immigration.

Centralization. The transformation of public education from a diverse and uncoordinated mixture of local experiments into a coherent system required organization. From 1850 onward, reformers spent much of their time developing ideas that would bring some uniformity to the emerging national system. At the local level, this involved the introduction of an administrative structure inside the schools that challenged the tradition of direct community control of education. Previously, individual teachers had exercised a great degree of control over the content of their courses, and conditions varied greatly from one schoolroom to the next; in the 1850s a uniform course of study was introduced, along with new officials—school principals and city, county, and state superintendents—to oversee instruction. The growing importance of the school principal during this period indicated the bureaucratic trend. Cincinnati school board members noted in their report for 1858 that although principals "till the last two years" were "only teachers of the highest classes of their respective schools," their new supervisory responsibilities made it necessary to assign them "small recitation rooms . . . where they keep records, examine classes, and transact the general business of the school." In the Northeast the principals' new role was reflected in architecture: one of the notable innovations in school construction after 1850 was the principal's office itself. Overseeing the principals was another layer of city and county district officials, who themselves answered to state superintendents. Establishing an office of state superintendent of schools in 1854, New York reported that overburdened town and city superintendents had made over twenty-two thousand visits to the state's schools in the previous year. By the early 1860s, the trend had begun to take hold even in the Far West, with California appointing its own state superintendent in 1862. Centralization reached its zenith in 1867, when prominent educational reformer Henry Barnard was appointed the first U.S. Commissioner of Education.

Professionalization. Along with their attempt to bring organizational coherence to public education, reformers embarked on an ambitious program of teacher training. One of the most pressing problems faced by school districts across the country was the high turnover and subsequent lack of experience among teachers. Pennsylvania authorities found in 1856 that of some six thousand teachers in the state, nearly two-thirds had been teaching for under three years; other states reported similar figures. The employment of more women, a trend accelerated by the drain of young men during the Civil War, meant that teachers frequently joined the workforce for only a few short years before marriage. Nearly 80 percent of teachers in southeastern Michigan in 1860 were between seventeen and twenty-four years of age, and in one Wisconsin county more than one-quarter of teachers were under eighteen. Low wages partially explained this instability: rural teachers earned less than common laborers throughout this period, and urban teachers could expect only slightly better conditions. In any case reformers were determined to train a corps of educators, and several initiatives begun during this period left a permanent imprint on the American teaching profession. One of the major functions of early superintendents was to introduce a uniform course of study in school systems under their direction. City Superintendent William H. Wells's *Graded Course of Instruction for the Public Schools of Chicago,* published in 1862, was adopted as a teachers' manual by many cities and set an example that would be emulated for years afterward.

Normal Schools. The rise of normal schools represented another significant development. The first state-supported teachers' training school had been opened in Lexington, Massachusetts, in 1839, but by midcentury only a half-dozen other states had followed suit. As late as 1860 there were only twelve state normal schools in the country, but Edward Sheldon's pioneering efforts in opening the Oswego Normal School in New York a year later proved to be a turning point in establishing the normal schools as a permanent fixture in American education. Within twenty-five years of the school's founding, Oswego graduates had taught in forty-six states of the Union and at least six foreign countries. The Oswego school became the model, and most states and many cities began establishing their own normal schools. By 1871 U.S. Commissioner of Education Henry Barnard reported that fifty-one publicly funded normal schools existed in twenty-three states, training over six thousand future teachers annually.

Attendance and Access. One telling illustration of the trend toward greater uniformity and organization in education was the change in official policy on school attendance. Not surprisingly, few children outside of the major New England towns attended school with any kind of regularity before midcentury. In many areas, schooling was considered the responsibility—and prerogative—of individual parents. In agricultural areas children's labor often played a critical role in helping families secure a livelihood, and formal schooling was subordinated to the seasonal rhythms of planting and harvesting. In these areas children might attend school as little as three months during the year. The average duration of a child's common-school experience in 1858 was eight years. Even by the end of this period in 1877, high school was still a luxury that many young people and their families could not afford. Extending mandatory school attendance across different regions and intensifying the academic experience of those enrolled in public schools became obvious priorities for reformers determined to create a uniform system of education. Beginning in the Northeast in 1852, a series of laws were passed that made attendance compulsory for school-age children. Massachusetts, characteristically taking the lead in this movement, required children between eight and fourteen to attend school at least twelve weeks per year, with at least six of them continuous. Many school systems set up special "truant schools" to compel attendance, and by 1860 some one hundred "reform schools" existed across the United States for those considered especially troublesome. Interestingly, however, these measures did not necessarily translate into a higher proportion of children attending ordinary public schools. While the length of the school year was extended from 150 days to 192, the percentage of children in school actually declined in Massachusetts between 1840 and 1880. In part, this was due to the uneven enforcement of existing laws and the large influx of immigrants who did not register their children. But the most difficult obstacle to universal attendance seems to have been the increasing trend toward child labor in industry. Children made up over half of the workforce at the Rhode Island's Hope Factory, one observer noted in 1853, working fifteen or sixteen hours a day. Important as they were in laying a foundation for public education, the accomplishments of educational reformers during this period would have to await more fundamental changes in public attitudes toward child labor before they could guarantee equal access to education.

African Americans. While educational reformers worked to extend the influence of public schooling, the fruits of their efforts seem to have eluded at least one important segment of the population: African Americans. The southern states, ever conscious of the threat of insurrection, had barred even rudimentary education for slaves and increasingly, from the 1830s onward, passed further restrictions preventing even freed blacks from attending school. Outside the South, conditions were somewhat better, though far from ideal. While in most northern and western states blacks had won the right to attend public schools by midcentury, almost every school they attended was segregated and inferior to those available to white children. African American delegates to an 1847 convention in Troy, New York, complained that the instruction of black youth was "shamefully limited" throughout the North. Three years later, a convention of fugitive slaves gathering in Albany urged black northerners not to send their children to any school "which the malignant and murderous prejudice of white people has gotten up exclusively for colored people." Education was "too costly," they declared, "if it is acquired at the expense of such self-degradation." In one school system after another, blacks petitioned for integrated and equal facilities for their children. The turning point in the fight against school segregation came in 1855 in Boston. Blacks elsewhere in New England had won the right to send their children to integrated schools, but in Boston school officials resisted such efforts until Benjamin Roberts, the father of a young black girl who had been rejected from four different primary schools, filed a lawsuit alleging discrimination. Roberts was supported in his efforts by the Massachusetts Anti-Slavery Society and the prominent abolitionist Charles Sumner, who argued the girl's case before the court. The end of legal segregation in Boston cleared the way for similar victories elsewhere across the country.

Higher Education. Though they served a far smaller proportion of the public than elementary schools, the nation's colleges and universities were also affected by the powerful forces transforming American society at midcentury. During the colonial period and well into the first half of the nineteenth century, colleges understood their primary mission to be the preparation of young men for careers as ministers or public leaders. These priorities were reflected in the curriculum, where a strong emphasis on classical learning and the study of Greek and Latin was evident, and in the very sponsorship of these institutions: of 1812 colleges still surviving today that were extant at the outbreak of the Civil War, 104 of them were affiliated with various religious denominations. The demand for technological and scientific knowledge, complemented by a popular backlash against the "aristocratic" pretensions of higher education, led many in and out of the academy to press for reform. College trustees feared that unless their institutions adapted to changes in society, increasing numbers of prospective students would opt for careers in business and industry, forgoing higher education completely. Rensselaer Polytechnic Institute had been founded in 1824, offering degrees in engineering and the natural sciences, and its success was emulated with the appearance of Brooklyn Polytechnic Institute (1854), Cooper Union in New York City (1859), and the Massachusetts Institute of Technology (1865). Even traditional institutions such as Yale, Harvard, and Dartmouth, which had earlier resisted the calls for reform, had by 1860 installed programs in the applied sciences. "Practical" education won its permanence in national life, however, with passage of the Morrill Land Grant Act in 1862, which laid aside federal lands for the support of state-run schools "where the leading object shall be . . . to teach such branches of learning as are related to agriculture and the mechanic arts." The democratization of higher education was evident in at least one other area: women's increasing access to college training. The female seminaries and teacher-training institutes had somewhat cautiously opened the door to higher education for women, and Oberlin College's inauguration of a coeducational policy in 1838 marked an important advance, but it was not until the 1850s that coeducation gathered momentum. Genesee College (later Syracuse University) was founded as a coeducational institution in 1850, followed by Antioch in 1853 and the University of Iowa seven years later. In 1859 Elmira College in New York became the first women's college to award a baccalaureate degree to women. Although college education remained out of reach for the vast majority of Americans during this period, the practical needs of a rapidly industrializing society and the spirit of reform had decisively altered the mission of higher education and laid the foundations for broader access in the future.

A System of Public Education. "By 1870," a chronicler of the common-schools movement observed, "the pendulum had swung from no system to nothing but system." Another observer, this one a European visitor, was similarly struck by the "system of free schools" he found in America. "In place of a few casual schools dotted about town and country," a historian of American education has remarked more recently, there arose in the second half of the nineteenth century "true education systems." Rather than the laissez-faire approach which had been established in the early years of the American republic, new circumstances between 1850 and 1877 seemed to demand that the state play a more direct role in overseeing the education of its young. Reformers saw a need to maintain social equilibrium in the face of growing inequalities of wealth and to preserve a common sense of America's national identity during a period of massive foreign immigration.

TOPICS IN THE NEWS

BEYOND THE ONE-ROOM SCHOOLHOUSE

Schools. Before midcentury, most communities that devoted resources to public education would have felt a sense of accomplishment if they had managed to maintain a single, one-room building whose sole function was to serve as a school. In some areas of the country, schoolrooms consisted of little more than the corner of a church or a town hall, though in many rural communities, and especially in larger towns and cities, the "one-room schoolhouse" had emerged as the standard model for common-school instruction. Inside the schoolhouse, teachers faced the daunting task of trying to conduct classes that would benefit children at all levels, from toddlers of only five or six years old to young adults of fourteen and fifteen. With educational standards still only beginning to take shape by 1850, no two classrooms were exactly alike. Many students attended school irregularly, enrolling as family or work pressures dictated. Some were illiterate or barely able to read, while others had become proficient enough to serve as teacher's assistants, or even to become teachers themselves. This system survived long past midcentury in more sparsely settled rural areas, but increasingly, beginning in the larger urban areas in New England and New York, the "one-room schoolhouse" became unmanageable and—from the perspective of educational reformers—inefficient, and a new type of school began to emerge.

Growing Pains. On one level the emergence of a school system based on age groups was a testament to the growing success of common schooling. In the early 1830s educators in Boston were still building schools with the aim of teaching three hundred students of various ages in a single classroom. In nearby Providence, Rhode Island, school-board authorities thought it proper, when they built a new grammar school in 1840, to take the model of the one-room schoolhouse and simply expand it. Each floor of the newly designed building consisted of a large, single classroom with room for 228 students, and instruction for the entire student body was the responsibility of a single "master teacher" aided by several assistants. The problems associated with this arrangement are not hard to imagine: teachers expressed frustration at their inability to manage such a large and diverse group, and more-advanced students who had al-

A typical one-room rural schoolhouse, built about 1875 in Genesee Falls, New York

ready acquired reading and writing skills felt their own progress was being held back by having to sit through classes aimed at beginners. Educational reformers felt that the ungraded system had outlived its usefulness and needed to be adapted to complement the expansion of public education they had in mind. In their search for a solution, leading educators were attracted by the Ger-

The interior of a one-room schoolhouse, as depicted by Winslow Homer in his 1871 painting *The Country School* (City Art Museum of Saint Louis)

man system of graded schools, whose strength, Horace Mann wrote, "consists of the proper classification of the scholars."

Birth of the Graded School. The most important advance in applying the German model in the United States came in the late 1840s, when Boston educator John D. Philbrick convinced the school board there to build a new "model" school embodying the latest wisdom regarding classification. With Philbrick as its first principal, the Quincy School opened to great fanfare in 1848 and revolutionized American schooling in a way few other developments have. In place of the large halls intended to seat hundreds of students, the Quincy School consisted of smaller rooms, each built to seat fifty-six students and a single teacher. Its architecture embodied all of the most innovative ideas about educational reform: later dubbed the "egg-crate school," the building consisted of four floors and a total of twelve classrooms. The fourth floor of the school contained an assembly hall capable of seating the entire student body, and in line with the reformers' penchant for professionalization, the structure also contained a separate principal's office. Its most important innovation, however, as remarked upon by many contemporary observers, was the provision of separate, individual desks and chairs for each pupil.

Graded Texts. Throughout the 1850s, the graded school pioneered by Philbrick became the model in larger towns and cities across the country. "For the next fifty years," one educational historian has noted, it became the standard for schools systems everywhere. "More than any other single influence it stimulated the introduction of the graded classroom form of schooling." The advent of the graded school was one indication of the growing complexity of common-school education, and in its wake other important developments followed.

These schools required a graded course of study, and school textbooks during this period began to reflect the classification taking place inside the schools. The nationally renowned *McGuffey's Readers,* which by this time had become the most popular classroom texts in America, underwent major revisions in 1857 and again in 1879 to reflect the new trend toward grading of materials. The new system also translated into an increase in textbook sales: in the fifteen years before midcentury, seven million *McGuffey's Readers* had been sold; over the next two decades sales increased to forty million.

Codification. Frequently the task of designing an appropriate curriculum fell to city superintendents such as William H. Wells. As Chicago superintendent of schools between 1856 and 1864, Wells published *Graded Course of Instruction for the Public Schools of Chicago* in 1862, and the book was adopted as a standard guide by many school systems across the country. In it he attempted to establish uniform guidelines to be followed at different levels:

> Children began with the alphabet at the age of five, learned to count to 100 and do simple addition in the next grade, and proceeded in the next years to learn about the mysteries of Roman numerals, the hanging gardens of Babylon, the Crusades, and the Trojan War.

By the end of this period, the era of the one-room schoolhouse was coming to an end, and the graded school model had won the admiration of educators throughout the United States. In rural areas, particularly in the South and the West, practical implementation of the new ideas associated with classification would be delayed by a lack of financial resources or, in some cases, a lack of enthusiasm on the part of public officials. Nevertheless the graded school we are familiar with today was here to stay.

Sources:

Frederick M. Binder, *The Age of the Common School, 1830–1865* (New York: John Wiley & Sons, 1974);

Ellwood P. Cubberley, *Public Education in the United States: A Study and Interpretation of American Educational History* (Boston: Houghton Mifflin, 1934);

Carl F. Kaestle, *Pillars of the Republic: Common Schools and American Society, 1780–1860* (New York: Hill & Wang, 1983);

Michael B. Katz, "From Voluntarism to Bureaucracy in American Education," in *Education in American History: Readings on the Social Issues,* edited by Katz (New York: Praeger, 1973);

Joel Spring, *The American School: 1642–1985* (New York: Longman, 1986).

COMMON SCHOOLS AND THE INDUSTRIAL ORDER

Rapid Change. The triumph of the common-schools movement in America, and of the idea of public-supported education in general, occurred against a backdrop of dramatic social transformation and growing uncertainty about the future. Well into the nineteenth century, most Americans conceived of their society as a relatively homogenous nation of small producers and independent farmers, a self-image that seemed to harmonize with the ideals fought for in the Revolution. By midcentury, however, the first stirrings of industrialization had begun to render that image obsolete. There were still, to be sure, tremendous opportunities for many Americans who wanted to set out on their own in farming or the various skilled crafts. For some, moreover, the rise of industry seemed to portend a future of unbounded national wealth and greatness. But for others, the fruits of the advancing industrial revolution seemed elusive; more and more, independent craftsmen in the cities and towns saw their livelihoods undermined by the availability of cheap manufactured goods, and many found themselves as wage laborers in the factories sprouting up around the Northeast. Many began to look upon the changes under way as a threat to the way of life they had known in an earlier era and worried that the social stratification prevalent in Europe was gaining a foothold on this side of the Atlantic, where it would undermine the equality that many Americans had come to consider their birthright. In the years leading up to 1850, these fears had translated into a new volatility in popular politics; the advent of universal white male suffrage in the 1820s and 1830s had led to the formation of parties committed to redressing the grievances of laborers and the poor, and many at the top of American society began to express their own concerns that the new cleavages in society might lead to social unrest.

The Great Equalizer. It was in this atmosphere of growing unease at all levels of American society that educational reformers such as Horace Mann and Henry Barnard solicited support for their vision of educational reform, and it was perhaps inevitable that their appeal would tailor itself to the looming concerns of the age. In his *Twelfth Annual Report* to the Massachusetts Board of

TEACHER TRAINING

"Normal Schools beget an *esprit du corps,* and kindle a glowing enthusiasm among their pupils. They tend to exalt the business of teaching. They show it up in its nobler instead of its meaner colors. By infusing an element of philosophy into the very work of instruction, they dignify every step of it. Under this influence the work of primary instruction becomes the worthiest of the whole task, because, considered with respect to the child's wants, it is the most important. It takes profounder insight into the child's nature to lay aright the foundations of his culture in the primary school, than to help him at any other stage of his progress, because the primary teacher must see the end from the very beginning. His plans for the future must embrace the child's entire career. No partial view of the field is sufficient. This the Normal School brings into view and insists upon. Admit this truth and you at once exalt the work of elementary instruction into a dignified science, into something worth the study of any mind. Make the excellence of teaching to depend upon *what* you teach. . . ."

Source: Richard Edwards, "Normal Schools in the United States," National Teachers' Association, *Lectures and Proceedings* (1865): 277–282.

Education, written in 1848, Mann explicitly referred to common-school education as a balm for the growing division between rich and poor. He warned of the "danger of . . . those hideous evils which are always engendered between Capital and Labor, when all the Capital is in the hands of one class and all the Labor is thrown upon another. . . . Now surely," he wrote, "nothing but Universal Education can counter-work this tendency toward the domination of capital and servility of labor." The spread of education through all classes, Mann argued, "would do more than all things else to obliterate factitious distinctions in society," by "disarm[ing] the poor of their hostility towards the rich." Mann's prescription of the common school as a solution for social conflict relied on two important elements. First, he was convinced that by mixing children from every level of society in "common schools," the tendency toward social strife would be undermined by mutual exposure and "would provide society with a common set of political and moral values." Wrote another reformer, "The Common School is common, not as inferior, not as the school for poor men's children, but as the light and air are common." Mann also believed that public education would act as a bulwark of equality in a changing America by providing the tools with which even the children of the poor might rise to the top. "Education," he wrote in a now-famous passage of his *Twelfth*

Annual Report, "is the great equalizer of the conditions of men—the balance-wheel of the social machinery."

Popular Appeal. Mann's formula of public education seems, in retrospect, to have been a perfect example of the right idea arriving at precisely the right time. The "chief contribution" of the reformers, one observer has written, was to make their appeal "relevant to the aspirations and anxieties of the age." Events in Rhode Island during the years leading up to 1850 illustrated how the common-school program succeeded in building a diverse constituency of supporters. Protests against property qualifications on the right to vote in that state had led, in 1842, to a civil uprising known as Dorr's War. Eventually, conservatives were able to quash the rebellion, but fears of a repetition led them to enact a series of reforms, including the establishment of a system of state-supported common schools. In 1843 Rhode Island legislators appointed moderate reformer Henry Barnard to oversee the work. Within seven years the state had constructed " one of the best systems of public instruction in the world," as described by Horace Mann. This talent for straddling popular demand for free education and the conservatives' requirement for social stability was essential to the success of educational reform during this period. Although reformers shared the conventional attitudes of many conservatives—that poverty was a result of moral weakness and individual failing rather than injustice or a flawed social order—they genuinely believed universal education would provide a solution to the social ills that beset American society. Barnard had appealed to Rhode Island legislators in terms designed to allay their fears and at the same time rouse their sense of public obligation. It was "the responsibility of civilized men," he told them, "to decide for the urban poor how best to raise them from barbarism."

Harmony and Efficiency. The degree to which the common-schools crusade was adapted to fit the changing needs of an industrializing America is evident not only in the manner in which Mann and others solicited support for their ideas, but in day-to-day classroom instruction as well. The common-school classroom presented educators with an ideal opportunity for training young people in the habits required in an increasingly complex industrial society. Punctuality, obedience to authority, personal thrift, moral restraint—the inculcation of these qualities became the common objective of moral instruction. "The first requirement of the school is Order," Saint Louis superintendent William T. Harris wrote in 1871. In modern industrial society, he pointed out, "conformity to the time of the train, to the starting of work in the manufactory," and to other "activities of the city" required strict precision and regularity. "The pupil must have his lessons ready at the appointed time, must rise at the tap of the bell, move to the line, return; in short, go through all the evolutions with equal precision." By preparing students for participation in modern society, reformers pointed out, public education would result in in-

creased productivity and economic growth, benefiting all of society. Access to a well-rounded education, George Emerson and Alonzo Potter wrote in their *School and Schoolmaster* (1873), "multiplies the ways in which [workers] can be employed with profit to themselves, and with advantage to the community." The triumph of common schooling in the years after 1850 was a product, therefore, of major forces in American life as the nation moved away from a simpler, agrarian past and toward greater complexity and stratification. Though education reformers conceived their project neither as a counterweight to growing inequality, as labor reformers had, nor merely as the guarantor of social stability desired by industry, their ability to offer something of value to diverse constituencies was key to their success.

Sources:

Merle E. Curti, *The Social Ideas of American Educators* (New York: Scribners, 1935);

Michael B. Katz, *Class, Bureaucracy and Schools: The Illusion of Educational Change in America* (New York: Praeger, 1971);

Henry J. Perkinson, *The Imperfect Panacea: American Faith in Education, 1865–1965* (New York: Random House, 1968);

David B. Tyack, *The One Best System: A History of American Urban Education* (Cambridge, Mass.: Harvard University Press, 1974).

THE FEMINIZATION OF TEACHING

Expanding System. Alongside the expansion of public education rose the demand for an expanded teacher corps that could be trusted with the increasingly critical task of overseeing proper moral instruction. This demand, together with women's own aspirations for an alternative to the narrow opportunities available to them and the rise of an intermediary, bureaucratic layer of administrators, opened the door to large-scale employment of women in the classroom. Prior to 1850, popular acceptance of the notion handed down from the revolutionary period—that women were especially suited for the role of raising and training a republican citizenry—had meant that teaching was one of very few professions open to women. Even before midcentury, women made up a significant proportion of the teaching corps, though in most places men still predominated. Between 1840 and about 1860, however, the trend was reversed. Almost every school district in the country reported a shift in the direction of employment of women. In Massachusetts the percentage of male teachers in the public schools fell from 60 in 1840 to just 14 in 1860. In Connecticut, where women made up 56 percent of the teaching corps in 1846, they represented over 71 percent a decade later. In New Jersey the state superintendent reported in 1862 that it was "somewhat remarkable that the number of female teachers has been gradually increasing from year to year, until it now exceeds the number of male teachers. Ten years ago," he reported, "the number of male teachers was more than double that of female teachers; now the whole number of males is 1104 and the whole number of females is 1108." Similar

A new female teacher meeting her students (illustration from an 1873 issue of
Harper's Weekly)

trends were reported throughout the country, exacerbated in later years by the Civil War and its drain upon local male populations: from 80 percent of the Indiana teaching workforce in 1859, men comprised just over 50 percent by the war's end in 1865. Similarly, New York reported a loss of 1,119 male teachers between 1862 and 1863 alone.

Public Role. No single factor can explain this dramatic shift in the teaching workforce; rather, several developments seem to have converged to propel women into the classroom in large numbers. From the revolutionary era American women had been bequeathed, for better or worse, definite ideas about their appropriate role in a republican society. While proscribing open, public involvement in politics, republican notions of womanhood placed a premium on women's role, as mothers, in "shaping the character of their sons as future republicans." Just before midcentury, one leading educator expressed his faith that American women would "never seek distinction in our public assemblies for public discussion, or in our halls of legislation" but hoped at the same time that they would continue to "distinguish themselves" in "their appropriate work of educating the young" and "forming the opening mind to all that is good and great." Limited though this conception was, it did have an effect on women's access to education. Women could not be expected to raise an intelligent and well-informed citizenry unless they themselves had access to knowledge. As the common-schools movement gathered momentum toward midcentury, its emphasis on moral instruction seemed to provide a bridge between women's role as the guardians of republicanism in the home and their suitability as teachers outside the home. Teaching

in the common schools was viewed as a natural extension of their domestic roles into the public sphere; its ambiguity suited both traditionalists who might otherwise have shown little interest in extending public opportunities for women and those women frustrated with the limited horizons and lack of independence offered them under existing arrangements.

A Woman's Place. To some enthusiastic supporters of the common schools' emphasis on moral instruction, the shift toward a female-dominated profession seemed appropriate and even necessary. Women, they argued, were not only the equals of men as teachers but were actually better suited for the mid-nineteenth-century classroom. In language typical of the reformers, Henry Barnard expressed approval of the trend in an 1857 editorial in his *Journal of Education:*

> Our experience in New England has already shown, not only the capacity of women, but their superiority to the male sex, in the whole work of domestic and primary instruction. . . . Their more gentle and refined manners, purer morals, stronger instinctive love for the society of children, and greater tact in their management—their talent for conversational teaching, and quickness in apprehending the difficulties which embarrass the young mind, and their power . . . of governing the most wild and reckless dispositions. . . .

Interestingly, the reformers' enthusiasm for women as classroom teachers did not extend to their employment as principals or administrators. In the increasingly elaborate division of labor that was developing in step with professionalization, women occupied the bottom rungs of the education workforce hierarchy: "The emerging pattern in nineteenth-century education," one study concluded, "was for men to manage and women to teach." Female teachers were assigned primarily to teaching children in the lower grades, and female principals and superintendents were practically nonexistent. It was frequently the case that female teachers, who had attended normal schools, had undergone more formal training than administrators. This points to another, less obvious reason for the shift toward a predominantly female teaching corps: the expansion of the common schools was made possible, in part, by the easy availability of a low-paid female workforce. The abandonment of the teaching profession by men after 1840 had to do, in part, with their access to greater opportunities elsewhere. Women's options during the same period were far more restricted: "There is not the same variety of tempting employment for females as for men, they can be supported cheaper . . . ," a contemporary advocate of the feminization of teaching observed. "How much more satisfying was the classroom and a chance for a modest income," a historian reasoned more recently, "than a life as an unwelcome dependent in the home of a relative." The lack of alternative employment meant that women teachers were paid less than men doing the same work: where rural male teachers earned an average of $4.25 per week in 1850, females averaged just $2.89; low salaries in the countryside were offset by the practice of "boarding round" with students' families. The differential between male and female teachers in the cities was far worse and remained fairly constant through the mid 1860s. Whereas the salary of male urban teachers in 1864, over $20 per week, paid them nearly three times as much as common laborers and almost double the amount earned by skilled artisans, their female counterparts brought

home a pittance of $7.67, making them the least compensated of all.

A Breach in Restrictions. One consequence of the meager financial incentives was high turnover among teachers. Women who entered the profession in order to gain some level of independence often found marriage a more attractive option after several years in teaching. Nevertheless, the importance of women's employment as teachers in opening a breach in the restrictions on their role in nineteenth-century America cannot be gauged through measuring changes in their financial status alone. Access to paid work outside the home afforded women an unprecedented opportunity for independence, and their enrollment in normal schools and teacher-training institutes paved the way for large-scale entry of women into higher education, a development that could not have been contemplated by an earlier generation.

Sources:

Anne Firor Scott, "The Ever-Widening Circle: The Diffusion of Feminist Values from the Troy Female Seminary, 1882–1892," in *The Social History of American Education*, edited by B. Edward McClellan and William J. Reese (Urbana: University of Illinois Press, 1987);

Joel Spring, *The American School, 1642–1985* (New York: Longman, 1986).

A HOUSE DIVIDED: NORTH VS. SOUTH

Southern Exceptionalism. The overall trend in American education by 1850 was toward greater uniformity across state and regional boundaries and less disparity between rural and urban school systems: gradually, a standard system of education was beginning to emerge across the country that shared many essential features. But in one important respect, schooling in midcentury America was moving in the opposite direction, toward greater divergence. The developing confrontation between different social systems in the free-labor North and the slave South manifested itself in sharply diverging outlooks on schooling. The structure of southern society had produced a very different regional system of education than that advocated by northern educational reformers, making many leading southerners not only indifferent but actually hostile to the democratic vision of public education emanating from the Northeast. At precisely the same time that the reform current was gaining prominence in the North, mounting attacks on slavery were pushing the South to adopt a defensive posture regarding its own institutions, fencing the region off from even the most modest reform ideas. By 1850 two very different systems of education had developed in the United States whose geographical boundaries corresponded closely to the battle lines that would emerge during the Civil War.

An Aristocratic System. On one level the South's educational achievements were impressive. By 1850 the South had more private academies than New England. Virginia on the eve of the Civil War had "more colleges,

GUARDIANS OF MORAL VIRTUE

The large-scale entry of women into the teaching profession both challenged and reinforced stereotypes about women's "place" in American society, as exhibited in this excerpt from an article in the June 1857 *American Journal of Education:*

Our experience in New England has already shown, not only the capacity of women, but their superiority to the male sex, in the whole work of domestic and primary instruction, not only as principal teachers of infant and the lowest class of elementary schools, but as assistants in schools of every grade in which girls are taught, and as principal teachers, with special assistants in certain studies, in country schools generally. Their more gentle and refined manners, purer morals, stronger instinctive love for the society of children, and greater tact in their management—their talent for conversational teaching, and quickness in apprehending the difficulties which embarrass a young mind, and their power, when properly developed and sustained by an enlightened public sentiment, of governing the most wild and reckless dispositions. . . .

Education reformer Horace Mann, advocate of public education for children of all social classes

education. The southern states were, in the words of one historian, "virtual wastelands of common schooling," where the aristocratic pretensions of the planter class erected a formidable barrier to educational reform. The aversion of propertied interests to any form of tax-supported schooling, which reformers had only gradually succeeded in overcoming in the North, was even more pronounced among southern planters. Schooling of any kind was, of course, unavailable to slaves before the war and off-limits to free blacks since the 1830s. Non-slaveholding whites did not fare much better: unwilling to subject themselves to the humiliation of attending pauper or charity schools, many of them opted to forgo formal education completely. Census figures for 1850 illustrate the effects: among southern whites twenty years of age or older, over 20 percent were illiterate, while the comparable figure for the Middle Atlantic states was 3 percent and for New England less than one-half of 1 percent. Attendance figures tell a similar story: at the outset of the Civil War, school-age southerners attended school on the average of only 10.6 days per year, while northerners spent anywhere from 50 to 63.5 days of the year in class.

A Matter of Principle. Agitation over the issue of slavery after 1850 accelerated the drift toward a distinct regional education system and raised southern opposition to educational reform to a matter of principle. Increasingly, leading southerners feared that the northern-based common-schools movement was fraught with peril to their sacred institutions, and throughout the 1850s the call for southern cultural independence gathered momentum. Southern conventions called for purging the region of northern textbooks, which they suspected to be tainted with abolitionism. "The primers have slurs and innuendoes aimed at slavery . . . the histories almost ignore the South . . . the classical works have marginal notes denouncing the institution (of slavery), and the moral philosophies teem with free-soil doctrines," one piqued southern editor complained. During the Civil War itself, new textbooks appeared that reflected the Confederacy's approval of slavery: math texts, for example, included "many problems involving 'servants' or 'slaves,' " such as one that asked: "If 5 white men can do as much work as 7 negroes, how many days of 10 hours each will be required for 25 negroes to do a piece of work which 30 white men can do in 10 days of 9 hours each?" Southern nationalists launched a powerful campaign aimed at discouraging leading southern families from sending their children to college in the North, and many state college systems were established explicitly for the purpose of repatriating southern collegians and shielding them from "Yankee" influence. The most important of these, the University of the South, was founded at Sewanee, Tennessee, in 1860 as an institution where the sons of southern planters could drink "pure and invigorating draughts from unpolluted fountains." The prominent role of education in the new southern na-

more college graduates, and expended more money on higher education than Massachusetts," and a higher proportion of white Virginians than Northerners attended college during the 1850s. The southern states had, in fact, taken the lead in establishing state institutions of higher learning and could boast, too, of being home to seven of the nation's eight military academies, including the Virginia Military Academy in Richmond (1839), The Citadel at Charleston, and the Arsenal Academy at Columbia (both created by an act of the South Carolina legislature in 1842). Until the final decade before the Civil War, moreover, many young men from the leading families of the South were educated in the North's most prestigious institutions: Gov. Henry A. Wise of Virginia had been educated at Washington College, Pennsylvania; the articulate South Carolinian John C. Calhoun was a Yale graduate; Confederate politician Robert Toombs studied at Union College; and Confederate president Jefferson Davis and Gen. Robert E. Lee were both products of West Point.

"Wastelands." The antebellum South's impressive record in higher education contrasts sharply with the region's failure to provide more than a small minority of its white population with access to even rudimentary public

Residence hall at The Citadel, a military academy in Charleston, South Carolina

tionalism was highlighted in remarks made by Virginia governor Wise to a trainload of medical students returning from Philadelphia after John Brown's raid:

Let us employ our own teachers, [applause], especially that they may teach our own doctrines. Let us dress in the wool raised on our own pastures. Let us eat the flour from our own mills, and if we can't get that, why let us go back to our old accustomed corn bread. [Loud applause.]

Traitors. Hand-in-hand with the drift toward separatism there developed a more strict policing of the sectional loyalties of educators in the South. In 1849 Dr. Howard Malcolm of Georgetown College in Kentucky was forced to resign after speaking out in favor of emancipation. During the 1856 presidential campaign, professor Benjamin Sherwood Hendrick was ejected from his position at the University of North Carolina after expressing his support for the candidacy of Republican candidate John C. Frémont. Hendrick's colleague Henry Harrisse wrote a scathing denunciation of the affair, arguing that although defenders of slavery "may eliminate all the suspicious men from your institutions of learning" and "establish any number of new colleges which will relieve you of sending your sons to free institutions," their efforts would be in vain. So long as "people study, and read, and think among you," he wrote, "the absurdity of your system will be discovered and there will always be found some courageous intelligence to protest against your . . . tyranny." Not surprisingly, Harrisse himself was forced to leave the university a short while later.

"A War of Education." The precarious condition of intellectual freedom in southern society and the southern leaders' hostility to reform currents only reaffirmed for northern educational reformers the superiority of the common schools and their importance as bulwarks of democracy. They unanimously condemned the lack of provision for public education in the South and viewed the developing confrontation through the prism of education: the free-labor North was superior to the slave South, in their eyes, precisely because it provided for uni-

LET US LEARN

In this excerpt taken from "Life on the Sea Islands" in *Atlantic Monthly* (May 1864), African American teacher Charlotte Forten describes the former slaves' desire for education:

The tiniest children are delighted to get a book in their hands. Many of them already know their letters. The parents are eager to have them learn. They sometimes said to me—

"Do, Miss, let de chil'en learn eberyting dey can. *We* nebber hab no chance to learn nuttin', but we wants de chil'en to learn."

They are willing to make many sacrifices that their children may attend school. One old woman, who had a large family of children and grandchildren, came regularly to school in the winter, and took her seat among the little ones. She was at least sixty years old. Another woman—who had one of the best faces I ever saw—came daily, and brought her baby in her arms. It happened to be one of the best babies in the world, a perfect little "model of deportment," and allowed its mother to pursue her studies without interruption.

versal education; conversely, nowhere was the South's inferiority more apparent than in its neglect of education. Indeed, the underlying basis of the Civil War was, in reformer Francis Wayland's view, a result of "the fact of a diffused and universal education in the North and a very limited education in the South." Six months after Robert E. Lee's surrender at Appomattox Courthouse in Virginia, Wayland declared in a speech before the National Teachers' Association that the Civil War "had been a war of education and patriotism against ignorance and barbarism." And not the least important element in northern plans for reconstructing the South were their plans for extending the common-schools ideal throughout the conquered territory.

Sources:

Horace Mann Bond, *The Education of the Negro in the American Social Order* (New York: Prentice-Hall, 1934);

Clement Eaton, *The Freedom-of-Thought Struggle in the Old South*, revised edition (New York: Harper & Row, 1964).

IMMIGRATION

Newcomers. Two related developments brought a new sense of urgency to the work of reformers during the years between 1840 and 1860. First, a trend in the migration of Americans from rural areas to the cities of the Northeast (a product of industrialization) was already well under way by midcentury, leading to increased public concern over the growing concentrations of poor people in urban areas. These concerns were compounded after the mid 1840s, however, by the influx of hundreds of thousands of new immigrants into cities such as Boston, New York, Philadelphia, and Chicago. Of the two main sources of immigration during this period, Ireland and Germany, the Irish made up the vast majority of newcomers. Successive failures of the potato crop in Ireland had reduced its population by half between 1845 and 1855: up to two million died of hunger and another two million immigrated, many of them to the port cities of North America. The most striking feature of this wave of immigration was the sheer poverty of its participants: "no other contemporaneous migration," historian Oscar Handlin wrote in *Boston's Immigrants* (1959), "partook so fully of . . . poverty-stricken helplessness." According to one contemporary observer, many of the new immigrants had "left Ireland with barely the passage money" and "landed . . . without a single penny." Under the impact of this new influx, the population of Boston grew by a third between 1840 and 1850, and the result was increased strain on public and private institutions and panic on the part of descendants of the Puritans that their society would be overwhelmed by an "alien" culture.

A New Challenge. In every major northern city, the sudden influx of immigrants forced an additional burden upon common-school reformers: the success of their project would be judged not only by its ability to defuse the tensions arising out of industrialization, but by its effectiveness in sustaining America's cultural identity in

Cartoon in the 1 October 1859 issue of *Harper's Weekly*, expressing the fear of immigrant influence in the schools. The figure in the center is a stereotypical Irishman.

the face of massive immigration. The problem of visible, urban poverty and social conflict, one historian has pointed out, "took on a much more troubling character as it came to be associated with religious and cultural differences." Against a backdrop of increasingly strident anti-immigrant prejudice, Horace Mann and others endeavored, from the late 1840s onward, to point out the utility of common schools as vehicles for assimilating the immigrant and welding a national identity out of the increasingly diverse populace.

Secular Education. Mann had anticipated one of the potential flashpoints for conflict that would arise after 1850—sectarian conflict over religious instruction in the classroom—and, in the process, had established an important precedent by winning support for "religiously neutral" schooling well in advance of the peak in immigration. In his *Twelfth Annual Report* (1848) Mann pointed out that more than half of all children enrolled in Boston's primary schools were from immigrant families. The vast majority of these were Irish and Catholic, Mann noted, reinforcing his view that the schools must observe a careful neutrality in religious matters. Otherwise, he argued, these youngsters would be lost to public education and the job of assimilating them made much more difficult, if not altogether impossible. His policy faced hostility from two sources: evangelical Protestants feared that the advent of secularism in the schools would lead to moral and social collapse. Spokesmen for the Catholic Church objected that the formal purge of Protestantism from the schools was not sufficient: in their eyes the schools remained bastions of anti-Catholicism, and, as an example, they pointed out the standard use of the Protestant King James Version of the Bible in the classroom. While large numbers of Irish immigrant chil-

Frontispiece and title page for an 1854 edition of a reader for the children of
German immigrants

dren attended public schools in Boston, New York, and Philadelphia throughout this period, their religious leaders operated Sunday schools to compensate for the lack of Catholic instruction and were busy constructing an autonomous system of parochial, or religious, schools.

Accommodation. Determined to bring immigrant children into the public schools, educational reformers displayed a flexible sensitivity toward Catholic fears of religious domination. In the industrial mill city of Lowell, Massachusetts, for example, educators had reached an agreement with church leaders whereby the town funded two Catholic schools. "The public School Committee would examine and hire teachers, and the books used would be those prescribed for other schools, but the teachers would be Catholic and the books would contain no facts not accepted by the church and no remarks reflecting upon Catholicism." This system was in effect until 1852 but collapsed under the weight of growing anti-immigrant sentiment. Still, Mann's associate John Green wrote from Lowell that the experiment had been a success: "the Irish may be found in every school in the city in considerable numbers. . . . " By 1856 Catholic schools had been discontinued in nearby Lawrence, and public officials there noted that 2,279 of their students had been received into the public schools.

Compulsory Attendance. The effectiveness of the public schools as vehicles for assimilation was greatly hampered, reformers believed, by the high absentee rates among immigrant children. It was during this period, therefore, that the first compulsory-school-attendance laws began to be passed by state and local legislatures. Prior to the 1850s, lawmakers shied away from any measure that might be viewed as interfering with individual parents' prerogatives with respect to child rearing. But any remaining qualms were overwhelmed by the flood of immigration at midcentury and the sense of an impending social crisis. Barnas Sears, secretary of the Massachusetts State Board of Education, expressed his concern in 1851 that "The non-attendance of a part of those children for whose benefit the Public Schools are especially intended, particularly the children of foreigners in our large cities and manufacturing towns, is assuming a fearful importance; and it will not be safe long to delay such measures as may be necessary to avert the impending danger." A year later Sears secured a partial solution to the attendance problem: the state passed the first compulsory-attendance laws in the nation, and a corps of truant officers was dispatched through the major cities to keep school-age children off the streets.

Bilingual Education. While the religious question constituted an important obstacle in efforts to assimilate the Irish, another difficult problem arose in relation to immigrants from Germany and elsewhere: how to overcome the language barrier. In Boston no special language provisions had to be made for immigrant children during this period, but elsewhere—in New York, Chicago, and San Fran-

A kindergarten class in West Newton, Massachusetts, 1864

cisco—reformers launched the first efforts at bilingual education in what they considered a necessary concession to bring the children of immigrants into the public schools. Before San Francisco schools began offering classes in French and German, the superintendent there recalled in 1877, "hundreds of children of foreign parents were attending private schools in order that they might receive instruction in the language of their 'Fatherland.' Now they are found under the care of American teachers, and are being molded in the true form of American citizenship." In Chicago school officials began holding classes in German in an effort to draw students away from the "private schools . . . to be found in every nook and corner of the city," hoping thereby that "the children of all nationalities" would be "assembled in the public schools, and thereby be radically Americanized." By the end of this period, eight states in the Union permitted some form of bilingual education, establishing an important precedent for the next wave of immigration toward the end of the century.

Sources:

Charles Leslie Glenn Jr., *The Myth of the Common School* (Amherst: University of Massachusetts Press, 1988);

Oscar Handlin, *Boston's Immigrants: A Study in Acculturation* (New York: Atheneum, 1959);

David K. Schultz, *The Culture Factory: Boston Public Schools, 1789–1860* (New York: Oxford University Press, 1973).

KINDERGARTEN, HIGH SCHOOL, AND THE LAND GRANT COLLEGE

New Horizons. By 1860 common-school advocates had put their most crucial battles behind them; the publicly supported common school had become an established institution in most parts of the country, and the initiatives that continued to draw their attention were concerned mainly with intensifying the experience of schooling: extending the annual term, keeping children in school until a later age, and regularizing attendance. But as elementary-school education came to be seen as standard across the country, educators and civic leaders began efforts to extend the common-schools ideal to younger and older Americans. It was during this period that the kindergarten and the public high school made their first appearance in American society.

The Kindergarten Movement. Like so many features of the common-school model, the kindergarten had been founded in Germany, and German immigrants to the United States played an important role in early efforts to launch it here. True to his goal of creating a "children's garden," educator Friedrich Froebel had founded the kindergarten movement on the belief that young children acquired knowledge not through being directed from above or learning by rote but "in a natural way through playing games and manipulating objects." The "fundamental principles of education, instruction, and teaching," he wrote, "should be passive and protective, not directive and interfering." The first kindergarten in America was organized by Mrs. Carl Schurz in Watertown, Wisconsin, and by 1855 a handful of similar facilities had appeared across the country, most of them still affiliated with German American private academies. The idea, however, had already begun to attract the attention of Americans. After an encounter with Schurz and a pilgrimage to Germany, Horace Mann's sister-in-law Elizabeth Palmer Peabody became the leading advocate of kindergarten education and opened a school in Boston in 1860. "A kindergarten," she wrote, is "children in society—a commonwealth or republic of children. . . ." The movement continued for some time to be exclusive, with access limited mainly to children of the affluent, but various articles in American journals, including one in Henry Barnard's influential *Journal of Education,* gave the experiment a wider audience. In 1873 Saint Louis became the first city to include a kindergarten as part of its public school system. In his appeal to the local school board for funding, Superintendent William T. Harris emphasized a new usefulness for the kindergarten as an instrument of social reform. Troubled by the same concerns that dominated discussion of public education generally—the problem of poverty and its threat to social stability, mass immigration and its challenge to national

Chicago High School, 1857

The Des Peres kindergarten in Saint Louis. Friedrich Froebel was the founder of the kindergarten movement.

identity—Harris favored early education as a means of saving the urban poor from "all manner of corruption and immorality."

High Schools. The development of high-school education followed a very different path. The 1850 census reported that there were some 6,085 private academies then in existence across the United States, most of them unregulated and with curricula that varied enormously. These were privately controlled tuition schools catering mainly to the sons of middle-class families. Sometimes referred to as "people's colleges," they represented the highest stage of education that most of their pupils would attend; only a minority would go on to seek college degrees. The decline of the private academies after 1855 was a measure not of the failure of secondary education but of its growing popularity. Beginning, characteristically enough, in the industrial Northeast, middle-class city dwellers began to demand tax-supported schools that would perform the same function as the academies, and the subsequent rise of publicly funded high schools made it impossible for private academies to compete. The new development was not without its critics, however. In a period when, for various reasons, many younger children were unable to attend even elementary school on a regular basis, high-school education was seen by many as a luxury that did not merit public support and even, by some, as a subsidy for children of the wealthy. Throughout the 1860s and 1870s, Saint Louis citizens battled over high-school funding, with opponents terming the curriculum overly "aristocratic." "What do we want of a High School to teach rich men's children?," asked critics of the idea in Norwich, Connecticut. In Beverly, Massachusetts, working-class residents, emboldened by their participation in a shoe strike, voted to close down their high school at a town meeting in March 1860. Although the modern high school had its origins during this period, and in the academy movement that

preceded it, considerable obstacles had to be overcome before it would be accepted as a necessary part of growing up in America. It was not until well into the twentieth century that a majority of young Americans would attend high school.

Land Grant Colleges. Prior to 1860 twenty-one public universities had been established in twenty states across the United States. Most had benefited from state funding; those in the western states had been made possible by federal land grants. But passage of the Morrill Land Grant Act in 1862 paved the way for a much more extensive system of public higher education. Originally introduced in Congress in 1857, the bill had been vetoed by Democratic president James Buchanan as a violation of states' rights and a dan-

DEVELOPING YOUNG MINDS

"There is a kind of thing done in Kindergarten, which retains the best characteristics of childish play, and yet assumes the serious form of occupation. . . . Everybody conversant with children knows how easily they will "make believe," as they call it, . . . out of any materials whatever; and are most amused, when the materials to be transformed by their personifying and symbolizing fancy are few, for so much do children enjoy the exercise of imagination, that they find it more amusing to have simple forms, which they can "make believe"—first to be one thing, and then another—than to have elaborately carved columns, and such like materials, for building. There is nothing in life more charming to a spectator, than to see this shaping fancy of children, making everything of nothing, and scorning the bounds of probability, and even of possibility."

Source: Elizabeth P. Peabody, *Guide to the Kindergarten and Intermediate Class* (New York: E. Steiger, 1877), pp. 43–47, 52–53.

gerous precedent for federal aid to education. The final version of the act provided each loyal state in the Union with thirty thousand acres of public land (or its equivalent in funding) for each senator and representative serving in Congress. The schools to be established on the land were to emphasize agriculture, home economics, engineering, and mechanical arts. Although sectarian institutions and private colleges opposed the bill, the Morrill Act passed both houses of Congress and spurred the growth of large state universities in the Midwest and West. While some land-grant colleges were associated with public universities already in existence, such as Michigan State (1855) and Iowa State (1858), others became the basis of a new state system of higher education, such as Purdue University in Indiana (1865). Throughout the remainder of this period the land-grant colleges remained fairly modest institutions, frequently consisting of a "single professorship in agriculture or perhaps a summer course," but like so many innovations during this period, they played an important role in laying the foundations for the fully developed system of public universities and vocational schools that would emerge later.

Sources:

Susan E. Blow, "Kindergarten Education," in *Education in the United States,* edited by Nicholas M. Butler (New York: Arno, 1969);

Carl F. Kaestle, *Education and Social Change in Nineteenth Century Massachusetts* (New York: Columbia University Press, 1980);

Michael B. Katz, *The Irony of Early School Reform: Educational Innovation in Mid-Nineteenth Century Massachusetts* (Cambridge: Harvard University Press, 1968);

Marvin Lazerson, "Urban Schools and Reform: Kindergartens in Massachusetts, 1870–1915," in *Education in American History,* edited by Michael B. Katz (New York: Praeger, 1973);

Selwyn K. Troen, *The Public and the Schools: Shaping the St. Louis System, 1838–1920* (Columbia: University of Missouri Press, 1975).

LIBRARIES

The Lyceum Movement. Although the nation's public libraries first opened their doors during the 1850s, their origins go back at least two decades earlier, to the Lyceum Movement founded by Connecticut educator Josiah Holbrook. Inspired in part by the democratic impulse of the American Revolution, lyceums were intended as a "federation of adult educational organizations" whose members would "hold weekly . . . meetings, for reading, conversation, illustrating the sciences, or other exercises designed for mutual benefit." By 1835 there were over three thousand lyceums spread throughout the country and gradually began to accumulate book collections and build up archives filled with documents of local historical interest. In many areas the lyceums functioned as informal schools, compensating for the "failure of traditional institutions to respond to popular educational needs." Women, in particular, became avid participants in the affairs of local lyceums, and the institution played an important role in breaking down educational barriers against them. Factory girls from Lowell, Massachusetts, were said to have "saved their pennies" to attend lyceum courses, but for the most part it was the middle classes that made up the audiences for lyceum lectures and courses. Public lectures typically featured discussions on literature or science, but toward midcentury the lyceums became an important venue for representatives of the various reform currents: woman's rights advocates, abolitionists, and education reformers were frequent visitors to the lyceum podium.

The Free Public Library. Early attempts at establishing public libraries often consisted of no more than a call by individuals to open the lyceum collections to the general public. Expressing an egalitarian optimism typical of American intellectuals before midcentury, Francis Wayland urged members of the Providence Athenaeum in 1838 to make available to the average citizen of Providence, Rhode Island, "all the reading which shall be necessary to prepare him for any situation for which his cultural endowments have rendered him capable." In the view of reformers, libraries would serve as the "arsenals of a democratic culture" by developing an intelligent and informed citizenry. Significantly, they viewed the public library campaign as an important extension of the common-schools movement. Boston's tireless advocate George Ticknor considered the public library "the crowning glory of the public schools system," recommending the issue of "special library tickets for school children in order to create the reading habit early in life." By 1850 this impulse had moved considerably beyond the call to open private collections. In Boston, Ticknor and former governor Edward Everett, both allies of Horace Mann, had managed to win public funding for a city library, and their achievement was reinforced by similar successes elsewhere. New Hampshire legislators voted in 1849 to permit public funding for libraries "open to the free use of every inhabitant of the town or city . . . for the general diffusion of intelligence among all classes of the community," making it the first state in the Union to do so. The state of Massachusetts followed with similar legislation in 1851, to be joined by Maine (1854), Rhode Island (1867), and Connecticut (1869). By the mid 1870s most major towns in New England had established public libraries, and their popularity was noted by U.S. commissioner of education William T. Harris, who recognized the library as "one of the most efficient auxiliaries of the public schools." Melvil Dewey, for whom the Dewey decimal system would later be named, founded the American Library Association in 1876.

Struggle. Outside of New England, the success of the public library campaign was more modest. The largest collections in the United States remained in private hands. The John Jacob Astor Library in New York City, with 100,000 volumes the largest collection in the United States at the time, opened its doors in 1854 but only to a limited, private readership; within twenty years it had added another 135,000 volumes to its collection. Harvard University, with 72,000 books, was closed to the public as well. The Library of Congress at Washington, by comparison, contained a modest 50,000 volumes dur-

Melvil Dewey, founder of the American Library Association

ing this period, and the largest of the public libraries, at Philadelphia, just 60,000. In this situation, social welfare agencies very often attempted to fill the void. In New York, for example, after efforts to establish a free public library there failed in 1858, the YWCA established its own library and attempted to make its collection available to working women. One of its librarians described the atmosphere "by the librarians desk in the evening, when the women and girls from the shops and factories are free. . . . And . . . the jostling crowd presses in, embarrassed and awkward, half awed by the very beauty and refinement of the place, and abashed at the sight of so many books." Though it would not be until 1895 that New York would establish a free public library of its own (based, in part, on the Astor collection), by 1877 the notion that Americans from every background should have ready access to quality reading materials, a corollary of the common-schools ideal, had become fixed in the popular mind as one of the distinguishing features of life in America.

Sources:

Sidney H. Ditzion, *Arsenals of a Democratic Culture: A Social History of the American Public Library Movement in New England and the Middle States from 1850 to 1900* (Chicago: American Library Association, 1947);

David B. Tyack, *George Ticknor and the Boston Brahmins* (Cambridge, Mass.: Harvard University Press, 1967).

POSTWAR SOUTH

A New Field. The North's victory in the Civil War opened up a vast new field for the application of educational reform. Laws prohibiting the education of slaves had been inscribed into the legal apparatus in every southern state for more than three decades, and the rejection of educational reform had left a large population of white Southerners with little experience of formal schooling; in fact, many of them were illiterate. In his address before the National Teachers' Association in 1865, Illinois Normal (later Illinois State) University president Richard Edwards summoned educators to "finish what the soldier had so well begun." In the view of like-minded northern educators, the extension of the common-schools ideal to the conquered South was an essential element in the democratic reconstruction of the region. Public education, Edwards declared, would be "the chief unifying process on which we can rely for a permanent peace." His thoughts were echoed by the northern missionary societies set up during the war to oversee the education and "uplift" of freed slaves: The American Missionary Association (AMA) newsletter declared, "The war with bullet and bayonet is over at the South; the invasion of light and love is not."

An Army of Teachers. Reform of the South's education system did not wait until the end of the war, however. As early as June 1861, the AMA was anticipating that the war would create "one of the grandest fields of missionary labor that the world ever furnished" and began laying plans to educate approximately seven hundred freed slaves who had sought refuge behind Union army lines in Virginia. At Fortress Monroe, Rev. L. C. Lockwood and Mary S. Peake, a northern freed black, founded the first school for freed slaves in September of that year. Northern "schoolmarms" sponsored by the missionary societies followed close behind the Union army, establishing makeshift schools in the areas wrested from Confederate control. Gradually, the advance of the northern armies forced upon the national government the necessity of formulating a policy in regard to freedmen's education. On the South Carolina sea islands much of the relief and educational effort remained in private hands, but in the Union-controlled area around New Orleans, the federal government played a more direct role, establishing school districts and appointing superintendents to oversee the work. The project of educational reform received a tremendous boost with the formation of the Freedmen's Bureau by an act of Congress in March 1865. Its director, Gen. O. O. Howard, considered education a vital instrument in remaking southern society in the image of the free-labor North, and within four years some 150,000 pupils would be attending Bureau-affiliated schools. By the end of the 1860s some 1,500 women and men had gone South to teach in the black schools. The vast majority were women from a New England background; a third hailed from Massachusetts alone, and nearly all had received some training in normal schools, female seminaries, or colleges.

Freedmen. The southward march of northern schoolmarms would have been far less effective if it had not corresponded with a universal hunger for education on the part of emancipated slaves. Harriet Beecher

Stowe's remark in 1879 that freedmen had "cried for the spelling book as bread, and pleaded for teachers as a necessity of life" is almost universally borne out by the comments of teachers, military officials, and former slaves themselves. Union brigadier general Rufus Saxton, under whose jurisdiction some two thousand freed slaves attended schools along the eastern coast of South Carolina, Florida, and Georgia in the early stages of the war, observed that "they all manifested an intense desire to learn.... During harvesting and planting it is a common sight to see groups of children going to school after having completed their tasks in the field." Schools were opened in the least likely places: the Old Bryan Slave Mart in Savannah served as a schoolhouse; in Atlanta the AMA conducted classes in an old railroad boxcar. Booker T. Washington described the scene among blacks after emancipation as "a whole race trying to go to school." "Few were too young, and none too old, to make the attempt to learn," he recalled, and throughout the South freedmen and northern reformers established night and weekend schools to extend the rudiments of formal education to working adults.

Black Institutions. African American men and women were not merely passive observers in this movement; in many cases their own, independent efforts had laid the groundwork for the campaign undertaken by northern missionaries. People only recently freed from slavery devoted a substantial amount of money to their schools. In Georgia the state superintendent of schools reported in 1867 that blacks themselves contributed some $3,500 per month to support the schools, compared to just $2,000 from the Freedmen's Bureau itself and $5,000 from the northern missionary societies. At New Orleans in 1866, when the Freedmen's Bureau announced cost-saving measures which included closing their schools, former slaves "could not consent to have their children sent away from study" and petitioned bureau officials "to levy an added tax upon their community to replenish the school fund." In some areas Northerners found that an informal school system had been established by slaves well in advance of the Union victory, sometimes going back even to the prewar period, and that blacks were not always anxious to hand over control of these institutions. John V. Alford, superintendent of schools for the Freedmen's Bureau after September 1865, reported on the system of "native schools" that he found in his travels across the South. At Goldsboro, North Carolina, Alford had found that one such school, run by "two colored young men, who but a little time before commenced to learn themselves, had gathered 150 pupils, all quite orderly and hard at study." He estimated that there were at least five hundred schools of this kind operating throughout the South. In Savannah, Georgia, freed blacks established the Savannah Educational Association and built a system of public schools well before the arrival of AMA teachers, and the ultimately successful attempt of Northerners to take control of the Savan-

Laura M. Towne, sent by a missionary society to teach former slaves on the South Carolina Sea Islands, with some of her pupils in 1866

nah system caused bitterness between blacks and their erstwhile allies: "blacks desire assistance without control," an astute AMA official observed. "They have a natural ... pride in keeping their educational institutions in their own hands."

The Common School. Given the vast cultural differences between northern teachers and their pupils, and the powerful impetus given to black institution building by emancipation, some tension between teachers and their new constituency was inevitable. Some of this derived from the paternalist ethos at the center of missionary efforts: the idea that they were the agents of civilization sent to bring enlightenment to a "backward" race. In more than a few cases, the racial prejudice of individual teachers and officials struck freed blacks as reminiscent of their treatment at the hands of their former masters. But the more general problem was the incongruity of the northern middle-class values with the former slaves' condition: if industry, thrift, sobriety, and deference were no guarantee of personal success in the North, they were even less useful as guides in a society that still contained vast inequalities and had not begun to eradicate the stigma of race. "The tenet of individualism was worthless, rarely if ever rewarded by the master class and potentially threatening to group solidarity," writes histo-

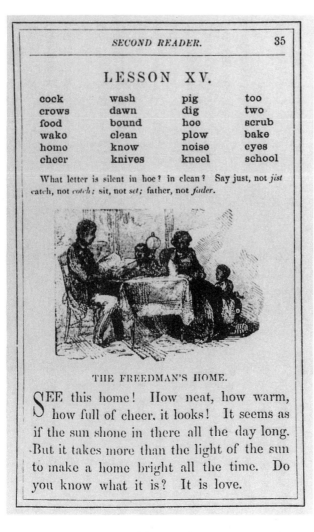

Page from a reader published for the Freedmen's Bureau

With the beginning of the Civil War in April 1861, Southern schools could no longer depend on receiving textbooks from the North. For educators and school administrators in the Confederacy, this development presented them with a unique opportunity to compile schoolbooks that reflected Southern attitudes and values. Typical arithmetic assignments included problems involving "servants" or "slaves," as: "If 5 white men can do as much work as 7 negroes, how many days of 10 hours each will be required for 25 negroes to do a piece of work which 30 white men can do in 10 days of 9 hours each?" M. B. Moore's *The First Dixie Reader* (1864) contained comparisons between the life of the black slave laborer in the South and the white wage laborer in the North. The slaves were supposedly so well fed that "many poor white people would be glad of what they [the slaves] leave for the hogs." As for "Old Aunt Ann": "When she was young she did good work, but now she cannot work much. But she is not like a poor white woman. Aunt Ann knows that her young Miss, as she calls her, will take care of her as long as she lives. Many poor white folks would be glad to live in her house and eat what Miss Kate sends her out for her dinner."

rian Jacqueline Jones. "The slaves' religion was one of joy and collective hope, not self-denial and personal guilt." Occasionally individual teachers resigned in frustration and packed their bags to return northward, but others adapted admirably and won the respect of freed men and women in the process. For some, the experience was the beginning of a lifelong commitment to racial equality. For others, whose commitment to freedmen's education had grown out of a long-standing commitment to abolition, the postwar South presented a new arena for advancing their ideas: Lydia Maria Child, for example, designed *The Freedmen's Book* (1865) for use in the southern schools, a textbook that "sought to develop a sense of racial pride through brief biographies of black figures from Benjamin Banneker to Toussaint L'Ouverture."

Terror. Although Northerners had experienced some modest success in their attempts to "soften and allay [white] antipathy against colored schools" by extending their work to include the instruction of indigent white children, efforts to defuse white Southerners' hostility toward freedmen's education fell far short of success. Even among those whites who might have been favora-

bly disposed toward public education, the stigma of sending their children to black schools left all-embracing reform stillborn. Generally speaking, the white South was violently opposed to freedmen's education and had only been reconciled to it by northern military occupation. Planters feared that education would "ruin" blacks as willing, obedient laborers and were outraged at the presence of northern schoolteachers, whom they imagined (sometimes, but not always, correctly) to be filling the heads of their pupils with dangerous notions of racial equality. Within two years of Robert E. Lee's surrender at Appomattox, whites were organizing underground resistance to the Reconstruction governments through organizations such as the Ku Klux Klan, and freedmen's schools became one of the principal targets of those who, through force and intimidation, hoped to restore the state of affairs that had existed prior to the war. In Mississippi, for example, where "many of the school buildings in use had been constructed by Negroes themselves," the Klan engaged in a virtual "crusade against public schools," a campaign in which "even some white schools suffered." Many schools were "burned or torn down in large numbers, and an even greater number of teachers of both races . . . were called upon by bands of disguised nocturnal visitors. Some received warning to stop teaching, others were whipped or driven away or both, and a few were killed." In Winston County not a single freedmen's school was left standing by 1871, while in Monroe County twenty-six were closed and school superintendent A. P. Hughes was whipped by the Klan.

Abandonment. The most devastating blow to black education in the South came with the withdrawal of federal troops from the region in 1877 and the overthrow of the Reconstruction governments. Over the next decades, black primary-school enrollment, which had reached levels approximating those found among white northerners at the height of Reconstruction, would decline considerably, and the Supreme Court's enshrining of the doctrine of "separate but equal" would seal the retreat from equal access to public education until the middle of the next century.

Sources:
Eric Foner, *Reconstruction: America's Unfinished Revolution, 1863–1877* (New York: Harper & Row, 1988);

Jacqueline Jones, *Soldiers of Light and Love: Northern Teachers and Georgia Blacks, 1865–1873* (Athens: University of Georgia Press, 1980);

Leon F. Litwack, *Been in the Storm So Long: The Aftermath of Slavery* (New York: Knopf, 1979);

James McPherson, *The Struggle for Equality: Abolitionists and the Negro in the Civil War and Reconstruction* (Princeton: Princeton University Press, 1964);

Allen W. Trelease, *White Terror: The Ku Klux Klan Conspiracy and Southern Reconstruction* (Baton Rouge: Louisiana State University Press, 1971).

HEADLINE MAKERS

HENRY BARNARD

1811-1900
COMMON-SCHOOLS PIONEER

Background. With the possible exception of Horace Mann, no nineteenth-century figure had such a profound and lasting impact on American education as Henry Barnard. Born in Hartford, Connecticut, on 24 January 1811, Barnard graduated from Yale College in 1835 and spent two years touring Europe, surveying the latest developments in education and studying firsthand the Pestalozzian methods then winning adherents among leading educational reformers. (Johann Heinrich Pestalozzi was an early-nineteenth-century educator who emphasized observation, experimentation, and reasoning.) Forsaking a promising career in law, Barnard committed himself, over the next forty years, to maintaining the common-schools ideal in American national life. Barnard brought energy, commitment, and creativity to his role in establishing public education systems in Connecticut and Rhode Island before midcentury, providing educators outside the Northeast with models that would be widely emulated. His unwavering commitment to teacher training did much to make the normal school a permanent feature of the educational landscape, and in his one-man crusade to perfect "the art of teaching" Barnard played an important role in disseminating the most advanced ideas in educational theory among teachers throughout the United States. The professionalization of teaching and even the evolution of a "system" of common schools, which constituted the most important developments in education during this period, were largely the work of Barnard.

Public Schools. Upon his return to the United States in 1837, Barnard was elected to the Connecticut legislature. There he sponsored legislation, modeled on a measure recently adopted in Massachusetts, creating a State Board of Commissioners for Common Schools. Barnard served as its first secretary, charged with the difficult task of reinvigorating a state school system that had declined "from probably the best schools of any State at the end of the colonial period" to a "very inferior position" by the late 1830s. Less than half of Connecticut's children were attending school, and even among those, many were opting for private schools over the second-rate schools maintained by the state. Undaunted, Barnard embarked on an energetic campaign aimed at winning public support for an overhaul of the schools, visiting and inspecting classrooms and addressing audiences of parents and educators throughout the state. Prefiguring the importance he attached to professionalization throughout his career, Barnard told the state legislature in 1838 that the day of "school-keeping" had passed; it was "idle to expect good schools until we have good teachers," and he urged "appropriate training in classes and seminaries established for that specific purpose." That same year Barnard founded the *Connecticut Common School Journal* and organized the nation's first teacher-training institute, a six-week seminar designed to standardize teaching methods across the state. He emphasized the need for well-maintained school libraries and attempted to upgrade the physical condition of the schools through his writings on schoolhouse construction. Despite his rendering a service to Connecticut "scarcely less important than that of Horace Mann in Massachusetts," Barnard found himself temporarily out of a job when elections in 1842 returned a governor hostile to the common schools and the Board of Commissioners was abolished.

Rhode Island. By this time, however, Barnard had acquired a reputation as one of the foremost educators in the nation, and during a cross-country tour following his dismissal he solidified that image, addressing the legislatures in ten states, visiting school districts, and collecting materials for a projected history of American education. When he arrived back in Connecticut in June 1843, an invitation from Rhode Island governor James Fenner to "test the practicability of his own plans of educational reform" awaited Barnard. As with Connecticut, schools in Rhode Island were at the time in a pitiful condition: outside of Providence, schools were in session only three months of the year, and Dorr's Rebellion a year earlier had given a new potency to wrangles over public education. Employed initially to examine and report on the state of the schools, in 1845 Barnard was appointed state commissioner of public schools and charged with "revolutioniz[ing] the public sentiment of the State." Over the next five years he hosted some eleven hundred public hearings on education throughout the state and distributed some sixteen thousand educational pamphlets. In 1845 he founded the Rhode Island Institute of Instruction for teacher training. One of his most interesting innovations in Rhode Island was the traveling model school, which came to be known as "Baker's Circus." Aboard a covered wagon filled with "boxes of minerals, insects, and flowers," eccentric schoolteacher W. S. Baker and a dozen of his star pupils traversed the state. "Wherever an audience could be assembled," Barnard's biographer recalled, "Baker brought out his bell, set up his blackboard, and held a school session." Despite his unorthodox methods, Barnard established a normal school at Providence, Rhode Island, and state legislators credited him with having installed a viable public-school system.

Connecticut. Barnard returned to oversee Connecticut schools in 1851. After an important four-year stint shoring up the foundations of public education in the state, he launched his first volume of the *American Journal of Education* in 1855 and for the rest of his life would be identified with popularizing educational theory through print. His contemporary cothinker William T. Harris described the thirty-one volumes of the *American Journal of Education* as "an educational course of reading of 24,000 pages and 12 million words," which "gave to American educators, who had so long been isolated and who had been slowly evolving a thoroughly native school system out of the English inheritance, a needed conception of historical development in

other countries." Building on his success with statewide journals in Connecticut and Rhode Island, Barnard's *American Journal of Education* quickly established itself as the standard handbook for American educators, mixing biographies of leading educators with reports from training institutes around the country and providing a forum for discussion of the latest thinking on classroom pedagogy. In addition, Barnard was the author of at least seventy-five separate titles covering a range of education-related subjects, from schoolhouse architecture to public education in Europe and teacher training in the United States.

University Administrator. Barnard's national stature had attracted the attention of college administrators, and in 1858 he accepted an offer from the University of Wisconsin to serve as its chancellor. His association with the state of Wisconsin dated from 1846, when he had addressed the state legislature on the subject of public education. Five years later he had organized teachers' institutes in twenty counties throughout the state. After an illness lasting almost a year, he was inaugurated chancellor on 27 July 1859. He served the university for two years, training some fifteen hundred teachers and pleading the cause of educational reform before some twelve thousand citizens in public lectures before resigning to devote himself full-time to editing the *American Journal of Education*. For the next six years he held no public office but decided again, in 1866, to try his hand as a college administrator. He was inaugurated president of St. John's College, in Annapolis, Maryland, in January 1866 but resigned just over a year later to become the United States' first commissioner of education.

"A Dismal Experience." Barnard's entire career in public life had been devoted to educational reform, and his assignment as education commissioner seemed a natural outgrowth of his lifelong interests. Barnard was assigned to "collect statistics and facts showing the condition and progress of education in the several states and territories, and to diffuse such information respecting the organization and management of schools . . . and methods of teaching, as shall aid the people of the United States in the establishment and maintenance of efficient school systems and otherwise promote the cause of education throughout the country." He went about his task with characteristic enthusiasm, producing an 881-page annual report for 1868 which Harris hailed as "the chief monument of Dr. Barnard's career." Despite his diligence, however, Barnard's career once again fell victim to political maneuvering. The party factionalism of the post–Civil War period took its toll on educational reform: Barnard's clerk at the Education Department was a Democratic Party informer, who testified that his boss spent too much time away from the office on frivolous matters, and on 20 June 1868 the entire department was abolished. Barnard stayed on for almost two years at a reduced salary, but finally resigned on 15 March 1870, declaring "All my experiences with wild beasts and stolid asses in an experience of 30 years did not lead me to expect what I am now receiving." The sole entry in his diary from his years at the capital read: "Washington—a dismal experience." Although he would remain involved in educational reform, particularly through the *Journal of Education,* Barnard would never again return to the public spotlight. He died on 5 July 1900 in the same house he was born in at Hartford, Connecticut.

Sources:

Merle E. Curti, *The Social Ideas of American Educators* (Paterson, N.J.: Littlefield, Adams, 1965);

Robert B. Downs, *Henry Barnard* (Boston: Twayne, 1977);

Edith N. MacMullen, *In the Cause of True Education: Henry Barnard and Nineteenth-Century School Reform* (New Haven: Yale University Press, 1991).

WILLIAM T. HARRIS

1835-1909
EDUCATIONAL PHILOSOPHER, ADMINISTRATOR

Early Years. Without slighting the accomplishments of educational giants such as Henry Barnard or Horace Mann, historian Lawrence Cremin has described William Torrey Harris as "the commanding figure of his pedagogical era." Born in Killingly, Connecticut, on 10 September 1835, Harris came of age after the foundations for public education had already been laid by Mann, Barnard, and others, and his public life straddled two critical periods: the formative years around midcentury, when the public school system was beginning to take definite shape in urban areas throughout the country, and the period following the Civil War, when the strains of industrialization, urbanization, and immigration threatened to bring the system tumbling down. His own philosophy thus embodied both the optimistic faith of the reformers who had preceded him and the growing conservatism of those alarmed by new potential for social instability and unrest. He was born into a well-to-do farming family and attended the district school for several years before finishing his elementary education in Providence, Rhode Island. Following this, he was enrolled in one academy after another before attending Yale College in 1854. His restlessness and dissatisfaction with the curriculum at Yale led him to leave after only two and one-half years, and shortly thereafter he began his career as an educator in Saint Louis.

Saint Louis Public Schools. Harris began teaching in the Saint Louis public school system in 1857 and was married a year later to Sarah T. Bugbee. By all accounts, he did well in his capacity as teacher and won the respect of his colleagues. Within several years he was made principal of the Clay School, became assistant superintendent of the city's public schools in 1866, and two years later was elevated to the office of superintendent. Under his energetic direction, the Saint Louis public-school system became an object of national acclaim, and his name became a household word among reformers. With its large German and working-class population, the city provided a vast laboratory for broad implementation of Harris's educational philosophy, and his thirteen *Annual Reports* were regarded by contemporaries as a mine of practical guidance and information. Unlike many reformers Harris viewed the Pestalozzian fad with some skepticism. "It is false psychology which says we derive all our knowledge from sense-perception," he complained, positing instead a uniform curriculum, built around his concept of the "five windows of the soul." It was through the study of grammar, art and literature, mathematics, geography, and history that students would find the key to the common storehouse of culture, Harris maintained, a body of knowledge that would serve them in any endeavor. His opposition to "sense-learning" did not prevent Harris from adopting other reforms, however, when they fit with his overall philosophy. It was under his direction, after all, that Saint Louis became the first public school system in the country to operate kindergartens.

The Hegelian Influence. Harris's management of the Saint Louis public schools and his later career as United States Commissioner of Education were intimately bound up with his philosophical ideas. Shortly after his arrival in Saint Louis, Harris made the acquaintance of Henry C. Brokmeyer and a small circle of German émigrés influenced by the ideas of the German philosopher Georg Wilhelm Friedrich Hegel, a relationship that would deeply influence Harris's outlook for the rest of his life. Harris became the most prominent exponent of Hegel's idealist philosophy in the United States, and the influence of the so-called Saint Louis Movement would in turn reflect his educational ideas. According to Hegel the elevation of the state as an arbiter of the shortcomings of individuals "justified the existing order and authorities by declaring that whatever is, is an inevitable stage in the unfolding of objective reason or the world spirit, and is therefore right."

Conservatism. Harris's version of Hegelian theory was a philosophy ready-made for preserving the status quo against the chaos and confusion of the mid nineteenth century: social unrest, in the view of Harris, was not symptomatic of social injustice, or of defects in the social order, but of a people who had not been sufficiently reconciled to obedience and self-discipline. "All the evils which we suffer politically," he told a convention of the National Education Association in 1874, "may be traced to the existence of an immense mass of ignorant, illiterate, or semi-educated people who assist in governing the country while they possess no insight into the true nature of the issues which they attempt to decide." Where his contemporaries had struggled to reconcile their reformist optimism with the need for social stability, Harris's conservative course was implicit in his outlook. He emphasized the school as a means for instilling "punctuality," "regularity," "attention," and "silence," traits which would "preserve and save our civil order." He also viewed the kindergarten as the means by which a "divine sense of shame" could develop among children who might otherwise be lost to "all manner of corruption and immorality."

Commissioner of Education. In keeping with his philosophical interests, Harris had founded the *Journal of Speculative Philosophy* in 1867, and when in 1880 he resigned his position in Saint Louis, he moved to Concord, Massachusetts, where he devoted himself full-time to aiding the establishment of the Concord School of Philosophy. After nine years with little success in this endeavor, Harris accepted an appointment as U.S. Commissioner of Education, a position he held from 12 September 1889 until 30 June 1906. During this period he wrote hundreds of articles in magazines and journals and exerted an influence upon American schooling that was unmatched among his contemporaries. He continued to attempt to develop a philosophical basis for educational practice and to advocate a leading role for industrialists and corporations in formulating educational policy. Harris voluntarily resigned his position in 1906 and died in Providence three years later.

Sources:

Neil Gerard McCluskey, *Public Schools and Moral Education: The Influence of Horace Mann, William Torrey Harris, and John Dewey* (Greenwood, Conn.: Greenwood Press, 1975);

John Stacey Roberts, *William T. Harris: A Critical Study of His Educational and Religious Philosophical Views* (Washington, D.C.: National Educational Association, 1924);

Selwyn Troen, *The Public and the Schools: Shaping the St. Louis System, 1838–1920* (Saint Louis: University of Missouri Press, 1975).

ELIZABETH PALMER PEABODY

1804-1894
KINDERGARTEN PIONEER

Background. Looking back over the course of Elizabeth Palmer Peabody's life, every important development in her early years seems to have prepared her for a life in educational reform and a role as America's foremost advocate of kindergarten education. Her mother, Elizabeth Palmer, was an "independent, well educated" woman who managed a boardinghouse for students in Atkinson, New Hampshire, and went by the name of the "Walking Dictionary" because her extensive reading enabled her to answer all questions put to her by the boarders. Palmer married Nathaniel Peabody, a teacher at the academy, in November 1802 and moved to Andover, Massachusetts, where they administered the North Andover Free School. In 1804 they moved again, to Billerica, Massachusetts, where Elizabeth Palmer Peabody was born on 16 May. There Elizabeth's mother established a boarding school for girls but abandoned it after two years and moved again to Cambridge and finally to Salem, where Peabody spent the remainder of her childhood. In Salem, Elizabeth's mother established a school for children and pioneered an innovative approach to early childhood education that would make a lasting impression on her daughter. "It seems to me," she remarked some years later, "that the self-activity of the mind was cultivated by my mother's method in her school. Not so much was poured in—more was brought out." Peabody followed in her mother's footsteps in one other important way: education was at the center of her life from an early age. Elizabeth's father instructed her in Latin, and she eventually learned ten other languages; by 1820, at the age of sixteen, she had established her own school in Lancaster, Massachusetts.

The Unitarian Legacy. Peabody's life as a reformer was shaped very profoundly by the reform impulse that animated Boston's social and intellectual elite from the 1830s through the third quarter of the nineteenth century. She was raised, as Peabody herself put it, "in the bosom of Unitarianism," at a time when deep philosophical and religious differences within the Unitarian Church itself were generating a lively intellectual ferment and spilling over into animated discussions about the need for reform in American society. (Unitarianism stressed individual freedom of belief, the free use of reason in religion, a united world community, and liberal social action.) Some Unitarians charged that their doctrine was becoming a "religion of the commercial classes," and as a result the church's tradition of tolerance increasingly gave way to attempts to stop reform, to "set limits on free thought and inquiry."

Channing and Alcott. Peabody came of age just as this schism reached its peak, and as a young adult she straddled both sides of the debate, maintaining relationships with individuals who were at the center of the controversy. Probably the single individual who exerted the greatest influence upon Peabody was William Ellery Channing. Peabody first came into contact with the great Unitarian leader when she moved to Brookline in 1825 and opened a girls' school there. A year later she convinced Channing to allow her to publish a collection of his sermons and eased into a role as his unpaid personal secretary. Interestingly, given her later devotion to children's education, one of the many things that impressed Peabody about Channing was his manner with children. "He treats children with the greatest consideration," she wrote in 1825, "and evidently enjoys their conversation, and studies it to see what it indicates of the yet unfallen nature. He will never tire, I see, of the observation of children of which I am so fond. . . ." A half-century later, when she introduced Friedrich Froebel's kindergarten idea to New England mothers, she recalled that "this is nothing new; more than fifty years ago Dr. Channing taught us to live with our children and to look upon them as capable of the life of Christ." In 1834 Peabody became an assistant to educator Amos Bronson Alcott at the private Temple School in Boston, an experience that left its mark on Peabody's developing ideas about childhood education. Peabody quickly became disillusioned with Alcott's introspective classroom methods, objecting to his insistence that young children keep detailed journals and bemoaning the lack of physical stimulation.

Importing the Kindergarten. Her lifelong association with schooling and close acquaintance with some of the foremost educational reformers (including Horace Mann, with whom she was romantically involved before he married her sister Mary) made Peabody receptive to the early childhood education concepts being imported by German immigrants after midcentury. In 1859 Peabody met Carl and Margarethe

Schurz and was impressed with their young daughter Agathe, who had attended the kindergarten opened several years earlier by her mother in Watertown, Wisconsin. "That little girl of yours is a miracle, so childlike and unconscious, and yet so wise and able, attracting and ruling the children, who seem nothing short of entranced," she reportedly told Margarethe Schurz. "No miracle, but only brought up in a kindergarten," Schurz replied, "a garden whose plants are human." After acquainting herself with the ideas of Froebel, founder of the kindergarten movement, Peabody opened her own kindergarten—the first English-speaking one in the country—in Boston in 1860. She directed the school until 1867, when she traveled to Germany in order to study Froebel's work firsthand, and, after her return fifteen months later, devoted the next twenty-five years of her life to this revolutionary approach to childhood education. Between 1873 and 1875 she published the magazine *Kindergarten Messenger*.

Boston Reform. In addition to her tireless work on behalf of the kindergarten movement, Peabody was associated in the post–Civil War period with the causes of freedmen's education and Indian rights, and she continued her involvement with Boston's intellectual reform milieu. By the end of the 1870s she had earned a reputation as the "grandmother of Boston reform," and in *The Bostonians* (1886), novelist Henry James reportedly based his character "Miss Birdseye" on a rather unflattering portrait of Peabody. She lived long enough not only to see the kindergarten grow from being a marginal experiment among immigrants and the well-to-do to a permanent feature in America's urban public schools, but even to hear many of her ideas attacked by a new generation of educators as old-fashioned and outdated. Peabody died in 1894 in Jamaica Plains, Long Island, New York.

Sources:

Bruce A. Ronda, ed., *Letters of Elizabeth Peabody, American Renaissance Woman* (Middletown, Conn.: Wesleyan University Press, 1984);

Louis H. Tharp, *The Peabody Sisters of Salem* (Boston: Little, Brown, 1950).

GEORGE PEABODY

1795-1869
MERCHANT, FINANCIER, PHILANTHROPIST

Early Years. George Peabody was born on 18 February 1795 in South Danvers (now Peabody), Massachusetts. His parents being of modest means, Peabody attended the local village school for only four years before taking up an apprenticeship with a local grocer at age eleven. Several years later he became a clerk in his brother David's dry-goods store in nearby Newburyport until the business was destroyed in a fire in 1811. In May 1812 Peabody moved to Georgetown, outside of Washington, D.C., where he was made a partner in Elisha Riggs's substantial dry-goods business. The company was relocated to Baltimore in 1815, and when, in 1829, Riggs retired, Peabody became the senior partner in the firm. In his efforts to expand his business, Peabody made several trips to London, which was at this time still the world's financial capital. In 1837 he settled permanently in London, becoming something of a celebrity and serving as an unofficial American ambassador. Through his role as a financier, Peabody also succeeded in becoming extremely wealthy and began a remarkable career as one of the most noted philanthropists of the nineteenth century. The objects of his gift-giving varied: he outfitted the ship used by Sir John Franklin in his Arctic explorations (1845–1847); when Congress was not forthcoming with support, he gave a large sum to finance the American exhibit at the 1851 International Exposition in London; and he donated $2.5 million to the City of London to aid in building sanitary dwellings for workers and their families.

London. During his years in London, Peabody maintained a special affection for the land in which he had been born. His ostentatious Fourth of July parties were attended by English nobility and by many of the country's most prominent business and political leaders. In 1835 Peabody secured an $8 million loan to rescue the state of Maryland, then on the verge of bankruptcy. When, in the late 1830s and early 1840s, American credit suffered a series of setbacks on the international market, Peabody intervened personally with contacts in London to help restore confidence in American enterprise. He also made substantial gifts to his hometown of Danvers, financing the construction of a public library there along with other public projects, and to the city of Baltimore, where he established the Peabody Institute with a $1.5 million gift. The Peabody Museum of Natural History, at Yale University, and Harvard's Peabody Museum of Archaeology and Ethnology both had their origins in large donations from him.

Affection for the South. Perhaps out of regret at having been deprived of an education as a youngster, Peabody seems to have been an early and enthusiastic supporter of the common-schools crusade. In 1852 he remarked that he was full of hope for the United States so long as "we plant the New England institution of the common schools liberally among the immigrants who are filling up the valley of the Mississippi." His stay in Baltimore some years earlier and his travels throughout the South had developed in Peabody a strong bond of sympathy with the South, and his financial dealings had put him in touch with prominent businessmen throughout the region. Though firm in his conviction that southerners had erred in seceding from the Union, Peabody was greatly distressed over the outbreak of the Civil War and expressed his regret that tensions had spilled over into military carnage. At the close of the war, he was one of the individuals most clearly calling for sectional reconciliation. "Never during the war or since have I permitted the contest to interfere with the warm friendships which I had formed for a very large number of the people of the South," he told a Baltimore audience at the war's end, "and now, after the lapse of these eventful years, I am more deeply, more earnestly, more painfully convinced than ever, of our need of mutual forbearance and conciliation, of Christian charity and forgiveness, of united effort to bind up the fresh and broken wounds of the nation."

Southern Education. Education was to be the centerpiece of Peabody's formula for reconciliation. In February 1867 he established the Peabody Education Fund and began appointing well-known educators and public figures from both the North and South as trustees, including, most prominently, Brown University president Barnas Sears. When, in 1869, he augmented his original endowment with additional funds (bringing the total donation to $3.5 million), Peabody told trustees, "This I give to the suffering South for the good of the whole country." Under Sears's direction, the fund developed a strategy aimed at rooting public education in the region. With limited funds and a vast field of work in which to operate, Sears established clear guidelines that directed the trustees and shaped the future of southern education: the bulk of the fund's resources would be devoted to substantial towns and cities, where large numbers of students could take advantage of the schools, rather than sparsely settled rural areas; faced with a severe shortage of trained teachers, the establishment of teacher-training institutes and normal schools would be made a priority; finally, Sears made it clear that their intention was to spur the development of a comprehensive school system, not to fund it entirely. He devoted considerable effort to involving local communities and state government in funding and administering the new schools.

Mixed Schooling. In the charged atmosphere of Reconstruction, when many southern whites remained bitter over the manifold results of the war, educators inevitably had to confront the dilemma of sharp racial antagonism. Specifically, they were faced with a choice between organizing an integrated or a segregated system of public education. Although integrated schools had been successfully established in a few areas—most notably New Orleans—many whites refused outright to send their children to school alongside blacks. Former slaves and their descendants harbored a different perspective. While they did not necessarily desire to attend school with whites either, and in some cases valued the autonomy that separate schools offered, they resented the stigma of inferiority that segregationists endeavored to maintain, and generally spoke out in favor of integrated schools. This set them at odds with the trustees of the Peabody Fund, who employed their considerable prestige and influence—besides money—to undermine efforts at integration. Sears in particular railed against the "futile attempt to force 'mixed schools,'" and warned that "any authoritative interference with the schools of these States would be disastrous to the dearest interests of education."

Separate but Equal. Although his death in London in 1869 removed him from the controversy before it reached its zenith, Peabody himself apparently acquiesced in Sears's judgment, and the fund as a whole came in for severe criticism. The abolitionist William Lloyd Garrison called Peabody "conservative by structure, taste, and affinity," while others complained that Sears had "imbibed the Southern prejudice against the Negro." Sears's controversial proposal to devote less per capita funding to black schools than the fund expended upon white schools, which he justified with the claim that "it costs less to maintain schools for the colored children than for the white," further raised the ire of fund critics. With some justification they claimed that northern philanthropy was being used to restore the racial order that the Civil War had aimed to topple.

Source:
J. L. Curry, *A Brief Sketch of George Peabody, and a History of the Peabody Fund through Thirty Years* (New York: Negro Universities Press, 1969).

MARY SMITH PEAKE

1823-1862

AFRICAN AMERICAN EDUCATOR

Beginnings. Mary S. Peake, born Mary Kelsey in Norfolk, Virginia, in 1823, was the daughter of an Englishman and a light-skinned, free black woman. At the age of six she was sent to Alexandria to live with her aunt, Mary Paine, in a house owned by abolitionist sympathizer Rollins Fowle. There she attended a "select colored school," studying dressmaking along with reading, writing, and arithmetic, until growing sectional tensions and fear of slave unrest prompted local lawmakers to close all colored schools in the city. Peake was deeply religious, and upon her return to Norfolk at the age of sixteen she joined the First Baptist Church, then under the direction of antislavery pastor Rev. James A. Mitchell. In 1847 at the age of twenty-four, Peake moved to Hampton, Virginia, supporting herself by making clothes and clandestinely teaching black children and adults. In 1851 she married Thomas Peake, a former slave, and they lived together until Confederate troops burned the black section of town while retreating from a Union army attack in 1861.

Fortress Monroe. Almost immediately upon their seizure of Fortress Monroe, Virginia, Union army commanders found themselves hard-pressed to cope with the steady stream of "contraband" slaves from neighboring plantations who flocked to their lines expecting liberation. The American Missionary Association had been preparing for just such a contingency, and within days of the military victory it dispatched Rev. Lewis C. Lockwood to instruct the freedmen. Lockwood opened the first Sabbath school in early September, and when he mentioned to students his desire to open a full-time freedmen's school, they suggested he contact Mary Peake, who was apparently well known in the area. Peake began classes on 17 September 1861 with "only about half a dozen" pupils, but within several days attendance had grown to between fifty and sixty students. When adults expressed an interest in schooling, Peake organized night classes for their benefit and continued as the primary teacher at Fortress Monroe until she contacted tuberculosis several months later. Shortly after Christmas 1861 Peake was forced to give up her teaching role and was confined to her bed until she died six weeks later, on 22 February 1862.

"Uplifting the Race." Although her personal role in freedmen's education was thus preempted, the very ground upon which Mary Peake taught at Fortress Monroe would later become home to the renowned Hampton Institute, and her own commitment to the education of her people would be emulated by other African Americans. In 1861, for example, Charlotte Forten, a freed black from a prominent Philadelphia abolitionist family, arrived in Beaufort, South Carolina, and spent the next two years teaching freedmen and women on Saint Helena Island. Forten's classes aimed not only to provide children and adults with the elements of a rudimentary education but to instill among them a sense of racial pride. "Talked to the children a little while to-day about the noble Toussaint [L'Ouverture]," she noted in her diary. "They listened very attentively. It is well that they should know what one of their color could do for his race. I long to inspire them with courage and ambition, and high purpose." The self-sacrifice and commitment of Mary Peake, Charlotte Forten, and hundreds of others went a long way toward overturning the traditional, racist assumptions that many white Americans shared about black racial inferiority. "Some say we have not the same faculties and feelings with white folks," one of Peake's students would protest, in remarks glowing with deep faith in the regenerative power of education. "What would the best soil produce without cultivation? We want to get wisdom. That is all we need. Let us get that, and we are made for time and eternity."

Sources:

Charlotte L. Forten and Lewis C. Lockwood, *Two Black Teachers During the Civil War* (New York: Arno, 1969);

Leon F. Litwack, *Been in the Storm So Long: The Aftermath of Slavery* (New York: Random House, 1979).

EDWARD AUSTIN SHELDON

1823-1897
NORMAL-SCHOOL EDUCATOR

Youth. Born in Perry Center, New York, on 4 October 1823, Edward Sheldon worked on his father's farm as a young boy. He attended the private Perry Center Academy and enrolled in 1844 at Hamilton College. When he was overcome with an attack of pleurisy, Sheldon was forced to withdraw from college in 1847 without having received his degree. He worked several months with the noted horticulturists Charles and Andrew Jackson Downing at Newburgh, New York. Sheldon then tried his hand briefly at the nursery business, but after disappointment with that venture and with his attempt to find employment in New York City, Sheldon returned to the upstate in 1848. His concern for the plight of the poor led him to establish in November of that year the Orphan and Free School Association in Oswego. He attempted, unsuccessfully, to convince local leaders of the importance of making the city's schools free to the public, but his frustrations in this effort, and with growing public apathy over the "Ragged School," as the school under his direction was known, led him to resign in 1849 and open a private coeducational school. After a short tenure Sheldon won an appointment as superintendent of the Syracuse public schools. As superintendent he established school libraries and implemented advanced approaches to classification and gradation. His proposal for free common schools finally won the approval of Oswego city officials in 1853. For almost thirty years afterward, Sheldon was a central figure in education at local and state levels and became widely known as the leading national advocate of Pestalozzian methods in the classroom.

Pestalozzian Schooling. One of the important influences on Sheldon and his generation of American educators was the "new education movement" inspired by Swiss reformer Johann Heinrich Pestalozzi. The methods pioneered by Pestalozzi provided a sharp challenge to the rote learning and formalism that had characterized American schooling throughout the colonial period and into the early nineteenth century. At his European schools Pestalozzi advanced the theory that observation and impression, rather than memorization, should serve as the basis for instruction. Pestalozzi, in turn, influenced another educational reformer, Friedrich Froebel, who codified his ideas into a kindergarten curriculum based on "object teaching." After viewing a display of teaching materials during a visit to Toronto, Sheldon, too, became an ardent advocate of Pestalozzian methods, seeking to extend them to more-mature students and attempting to disseminate their importance to a generation of common-school teachers.

The Oswego Normal School. The crowning achievement of Sheldon's life was his establishment of the Oswego Primary Teachers' Training School in 1861. His work at Syracuse had won him a position as president of the state teachers' association in 1860, and in the same year he became editor of the *New York Teacher*, the counterpart to Henry Barnard's Connecticut and Rhode Island teachers' journals and Calvin Wiley's in North Carolina. Sheldon was appointed principal at Oswego after its first year of operation and held that position until his death in August 1897. The school won financial support from the state of New York in 1863, and its name was changed in 1866 to the Oswego State Normal and Training School. Under Sheldon's leadership the school became "the most important center of Pestalozzianism in objective instruction in the United States," the "Mecca of American education," according to one account. The school played such a prominent role in disseminating Pestalozzi's ideas throughout the United States, in fact, that the development became known as the "Oswego movement." The school "not only provided principles of teaching, but a methodology that could be taught to prospective teachers, who, by their diligent application, could become skillful in selecting lesson materials and arranging them." Eleven books and other learning materials based on Pestalozzi's concepts were published at Oswego. Students flocked to Oswego from every region of the United States, and its graduates supplied the backbone of the common-schools crusade. By 1865 hardly a corner of the country could be found, including the defeated South, where Oswego graduates had not left their mark.

Sources:

Ellwood P. Cubberley, *Public Education in the United States* (New York: Houghton Mifflin, 1962);

Newton Edwards and Herman G. Richey, *The School in the American Social Order: The Dynamics of American Education* (Boston: Houghton Mifflin, 1947).

CALVIN HENDERSON WILEY

1819-1887

SOUTHERN EDUCATIONAL REFORMER

Early Life. The life of Calvin Henderson Wiley, the most prominent antebellum Southern educational reformer, in many ways parallels that of his Northern counterpart, Henry Barnard. Born on a North Carolina farm to Scotch-Irish Presbyterian parents in 1819, Wiley prepared for college in one of David Caldwell's "log-college" academies and later studied law at the University of North Carolina.

Graduating in 1840, Wiley practiced law for several years and gained prominence as editor of the *Oxford Mercury.* Politically associated with the Whig Party in a state increasingly loyal to the Democrats, he was elected to the state legislature in 1850 and sponsored a bill creating an office of state superintendent of schools, a position that he himself was elected to three years later. He served as state superintendent until the position was abolished in 1866 and was almost single-handedly responsible for creating the best public school system in the South. "The history of education" in North Carolina throughout this period, as one study of his life has put it, "is almost the biography of Wiley."

Obstacles to Reform. The fact that North Carolina was still without a superintendent of schools as late as 1850 revealed much about the state of public education in the South. In some ways the impediments to common-school reform in the region paralleled those found in the North: resistance to public taxation had been nearly as fierce in Rhode Island and Connecticut as it was below the Mason-Dixon line; the stigma attached to "pauper schools" turned poor white Southerners away just as it had Northern workers and their children; and the severe shortage of trained teachers, which the proliferation of normal schools and teacher training institutes had only recently begun to alter in the North, remained an important obstacle in both the South and the West. North Carolina enjoyed several important advantages over its southern neighbors. The state had been the recipient of over $1.5 million in federal aid in 1839, a grant that helped spur the passage of limited school legislation. By 1846 every county in North Carolina had taken strides toward establishing tax-supported schools. Additionally, public figures influenced by the educational revival under way in the North, including Trinity College founder Braxton Craven and University of North Carolina president David Caldwell, had urged the establishment of normal schools to overcome the state's "educational backwardness."

A Beacon for Change. From 1850 onward Wiley brought a new energy to the project of educational reform, traversing the state in the same manner as Barnard had done a decade earlier in Rhode Island, speaking before teachers, legislators, businessmen, and parents. He established a state-supported normal college in 1850, founded the State Teachers' Association, and established the *North Carolina Journal of Education*, both in 1856. By 1858 North Carolina was widely recognized as having the best school system of any of the slaveholding states: its teachers were better paid than their counterparts elsewhere in the South; its students attended school for a longer annual term (an average of four months per year) and in better-maintained buildings than their peers in neighboring states. By 1860 some 160,000 North Carolinians were enrolled in four thousand primary schools. Not surprisingly, Wiley's success made the state a beacon for educational reformers throughout the South. "Virginia, South Carolina and Georgia sought to copy" his example, and "Wiley was invited to appear before the legislature of Georgia for the purpose of aiding that State in improving its school system."

The Civil War. Wiley's career as state superintendent coincided, of course, with a sharp rise in sectional hostility between the North and the South leading, in 1861, to the outbreak of the Civil War. Inevitably, the rise of Southern nationalism influenced Wiley's conception of the role of public schooling. Though acutely familiar with some of the more-reactionary features of Southern society, and impressed by the progress of educational reform in the North, Wiley was sympathetic to the increasingly strident expressions of Southern separatism during the 1850s. Echoing calls for "homegrown" education, Wiley warned in 1856 that educators would have an important role to play in the event of an outbreak of military hostilities. "Surely," he wrote, "if the awful crisis that many dread should come, the South cannot . . . af-ford to spare any effort to unite the people . . . for co-operative, enlightened and manly action in the day of trial." To his credit Wiley never left his post as superintendent during the difficult years of the conflict and resisted the efforts of Confederate officials to divert educational funds for war needs. The survival of North Carolina's schools was largely the result of Wiley's unflagging efforts, and when, at the war's end in 1865, he was removed from his office, Wiley could report with satisfaction that "the common schools lived and discharged their useful mission through all the gloom and trials of the conflict, and when the last gun was fired . . . the doors were still kept open, and they numbered their pupils by the scores of thousands." Wiley died in 1887.

Sources:

Ellwood P. Cubberley, *Public Education in the United States* (New York: Houghton Mifflin, 1962);

E. W. Knight, *Public Education in the South* (Boston: Ginn, 1922).

PUBLICATIONS

Francis Adams, *The Free School System of the United States* (London: Chapman & Hall, 1875)—broad survey of the achievements of the American common-school crusade by a British admirer. Adams emphasizes the relation between the common-schools movement and the evolving American democracy;

Henry Barnard, *Normal Schools, and Other Institutions, Agencies, and Means Designed for the Professional Education of Teachers* (Hartford: Case, Tifany, 1851)—because of the teacher-training institutes pioneered by Barnard, more permanent, professional normal schools had become part of the educational landscape by midcentury. This book represents an early attempt to spread the institution beyond the Northeast;

Barnard, *Object Teaching, and Oral Lessons on Social Science and Common Things* (New York: F. C. Brownell, 1860)—an attempt to apply the concept of object teaching in the upper-level classroom. It includes practical advice for object instruction in science and geography;

Barnard, *Pestalozzi and Pestalozzianism* (New York: F. C. Brownell, 1859)—a critical appraisal of Pestalozzi's methods and an attempt to disseminate his system among American educators;

Barnard, ed., *Memoirs of Teachers, Educators and Benefactors of Education, Literature, and Science*, volume 1 (New York: F. C. Brownell, 1859)—Barnard's attempt to generalize the experience of midcentury educators across the United States; part of the comprehensive effort to bring uniformity to the public-school system;

George S. Boutwell, *Thoughts on Educational Topics and Institutions* (Boston: Phillips, Sampson, 1859)—a collection of lectures by Massachusetts congressman Boutwell that address a range of contemporary issues, including female education, public financing for high schools, and normal-school training;

J. T. Clark, *Essay on Common School Education in New Jersey* (Trenton, N.J., 1865)—a summary of the New Jersey experience with common schools by the state's superintendent of schools;

George Barrell Emerson, *Education in Massachusetts: Early Legislation and History* (Boston: J. Wilson & Son, 1869)—a comprehensive survey of developments in education from colonial times through midcentury by a prominent Boston educator;

William T. Harris, ed., *A Statement of the Theory of Education in the United States of America as Approved by Many Leading Educators* (Washington, D.C.: U.S. Government Printing Office, 1874)—a manifesto for public schooling signed by seventy-seven college presidents and city and state superintendents. The contributors emphasize the relation of common schools to industrial society;

Horace Mann, *Life and Works* (Boston: Lee & Shepard, 1865–1868)—collected writings of the towering figure of the American common-schools movement, covering a range of topics from pedagogy to schoolhouse construction and classification of pupils;

Elizabeth P. Peabody, *Guide to the Kindergarten and Intermediate Class* (New York: E. Steiger, 1877)—Peabody's attempt to popularize the approach to early childhood education pioneered by Friedrich Froebel. The book complemented Peabody's efforts to bring the kindergarten out of the German immigrant community and into mainstream public education;

Peabody, *Record of Mr. Alcott's School, Exemplifying the Principles and Methods of Moral Culture* (Boston: Roberts Brothers, 1874)—a classic summary of the content of moral education as understood by one of the most prominent Boston reformers of the century;

Edward A. Sheldon, *A Manual of Elementary Instruction* (New York: Scribners, 1862)—an early attempt by the leading American advocate of Pestalozzian methods to bring "object teaching" into the classroom;

Sheldon, *Teachers' Manual of Instruction in Reading* (New York: Scribner, Armstrong, 1875)—one of the most influential teachers' manuals of the period. It combines innovations in grading, classification, and teaching methods to offer a systematic approach to classroom reading instruction;

William Harvey Wells, *Graded Course of Instruction for the Public Schools of Chicago; with Accompanying Directions to Teachers,* revised edition (Chicago: Dean & Ottaway, 1866)—one of the most popular of a series of books motivated by the call for a comprehensive approach to classification and grading. Written by the Chicago superintendent of schools and adopted widely in school systems throughout the Midwest, it outlines specific class lectures and prescribes proper teaching methods;

Calvin H. Wiley, *The North-Carolina Reader* (Philadelphia: Lippincott, Grambo, 1851)—probably the most advanced curriculum developed in any of the Southern states prior to the Civil War. Wiley was the region's leading educational reformer.

CHAPTER SEVEN

GOVERNMENT AND POLITICS

by THOMAS J. BROWN

CONTENTS

Sidebars and tables are listed in italics.

1850

5–6 Feb. Sen. Henry Clay's major speech in favor of compromise on the slavery issue.

4 Mar. Sen. John C. Calhoun's last address, in opposition to compromise on slavery.

7 Mar. Sen. Daniel Webster's speech in support of compromise.

10 June The Nashville Convention adopts a resolution calling for the extension of the Missouri Compromise line to the Pacific Ocean.

9 July Millard Fillmore becomes president upon the death of Zachary Taylor.

Sept. Several compromise measures on slavery are passed in Congress. These bills include the admittance of California to the Union as a free state; allowing the residents of Utah and New Mexico to decide whether they want slavery; the enforcement of a stricter fugitive slave law; and banning the slave trade in the District of Columbia.

11 Nov. The second Nashville Convention attracts a small gathering of Southern radicals who denounce compromise.

14 Dec. The Georgia Platform is announced.

1851

24 Dec. A fire at the Library of Congress in Washington, D.C., destroys two-thirds of its collection.

1852

20 Mar. Publication of Harriet Beecher Stowe's *Uncle Tom's Cabin* in book form.

1 June The Democratic Party nominates Franklin Pierce for president over rivals Stephen A. Douglas and Lewis Cass.

16 June The Whigs nominate Gen. Winfield Scott for president over rivals Millard Fillmore and Daniel Webster.

2 Nov. Pierce defeats Scott and Free Soil candidate John P. Hale to become president.

1853

4 Mar. The inauguration of Pierce.

30 Dec. U.S. emissary James Gadsden signs a treaty with Mexico to purchase almost thirty thousand square miles in what is now southern Arizona and New Mexico; the acquisition is intended to facilitate construction of a southern railroad line to the Pacific coast.

1854

23 Jan. Stephen A. Douglas's Senate Committee on Territories designs a bill that voids the Missouri Compromise in the Kansas and Nebraska Territories and makes the status of slavery in those areas be decided by settlers.

28 Feb. A coalition of Whigs, Democrats, and Free Soilers meet in Ripon, Wisconsin, suggesting the name "Republican" for a new party pledged to bar slavery from the territories.

31 Mar.	Commodore Matthew C. Perry signs the Treaty of Kanagawa, opening Japanese ports to American trade.
26 Apr.	Eli Thayer organizes the Massachusetts Emigrant Aid Society to promote antislavery settlement of Kansas.
30 May	The Kansas-Nebraska bill is signed into law by President Franklin Pierce.
18 Oct.	The Ostend Manifesto declares the intent of the United States to acquire Cuba from Spain, by force if necessary.
	Congressional elections result in the loss of sixty-six Northern Democratic seats in the House of Representatives.

1855

30 Mar.	Missouri "border ruffians" and other proslavery settlers elect a proslavery legislature in Kansas.
Oct.	American adventurer William Walker declares himself dictator of Nicaragua.
23 Oct.	A free state constitutional convention meets in Topeka, Kansas, repudiating the territorial legislature and drafting a constitution prohibiting slavery.

1856

15 Jan.	A free state governor and legislature are elected in Kansas, which now has two governments.
22 Feb.	The Know Nothing Party nominates Millard Fillmore for president.
21 May	The antislavery town of Lawrence, Kansas, is sacked by border ruffians, touching off a civil war in the territory.
22 May	Rep. Preston S. Brooks of South Carolina assaults Sen. Charles Sumner of Massachusetts after Sumner's speech "The Crime Against Kansas."
2 June	The Democrats nominate James Buchanan for president.
17 June	The Republicans nominate John C. Frémont for president.
11 Sept.	John Geary is appointed territorial governor of Kansas and suppresses the civil war.
4 Aug.	Townsend Harris is appointed consul general to Japan.
4 Nov.	James Buchanan is elected president.

1857

12 Jan.	The proslavery legislature meets in Lecompton, Kansas.
4 Mar.	James Buchanan is inaugurated as president.
6 Mar.	The Supreme Court announces its decision in the Dred Scott case.
1 May	William Walker surrenders his self-appointed position as dictator of Nicaragua.
26 May	Robert J. Walker becomes territorial governor of Kansas.

24 Aug.	The failure of the New York branch of Ohio Life Insurance and Trust Company triggers a financial panic.
5 Oct.	Territorial elections in Kansas produce an antislavery legislature.
19 Oct.	A proslavery convention meets in Lecompton, Kansas, to draft a state constitution that would not require a public vote on slavery.
25 Nov.	William Walker leads a second expedition to Central America; his mission is thwarted by the U.S. Navy.
9 Dec.	Stephen A. Douglas announces his opposition to the Lecompton constitution of Kansas.
17 Dec.	Kansas governor Robert J. Walker resigns in protest over President James Buchanan's support for the Lecompton constitution.

1858

2 Feb.	Buchanan recommends that Congress admit Kansas as a slave state under the Lecompton constitution.
4 May	Congress passes the English Bill, providing for a popular vote on the Lecompton constitution; land grants and early admission to the Union are offered as incentives for ratification.
16 June	Abraham Lincoln, nominated for the Senate by Illinois Republicans, delivers his "House Divided" speech.
2 Aug.	Kansas voters overwhelmingly reject the Lecompton constitution.
21 Aug.	The first of seven Lincoln-Douglas debates is held in Ottawa, Illinois.
15 Oct.	The last Lincoln-Douglas debate is held in Alton, Illinois.
Oct.–Nov.	Congressional elections occur in which anti-Lecompton Democrats hold the balance of power between administration supporters and Republicans.

1859

May	A Southern commercial convention held in Vicksburg, Mississippi, calls for a legalization of the Atlantic slave trade.
	The antislavery Wyandotte constitution is ratified in Kansas.
16–18 Oct.	John Brown's raid on Harpers Ferry, Virginia.
2 Dec.	John Brown is executed for treason and attempting to incite a slave insurrection.

1860

2 Feb.	Jefferson Davis calls on the Senate to pass slave codes for the territories.
23 Apr.	The Democratic National Convention meets in Charleston, S.C.; delegates from eight Southern states withdraw when Stephen A. Douglas supporters block a demand for a territorial slave code.
9 May	The Constitutional Union Party nominates John Bell of Tennessee for president.

16 May	The Republican National Convention meets in Chicago and nominates Abraham Lincoln for president.
18 June	Reassembled Democratic convention nominates Stephen A. Douglas for president.
28 June	Southern Democrats who withdrew from the Charleston convention nominate John C. Breckinridge of Kentucky for president.
12 Sept.	William Walker is executed in Honduras after launching another filibustering expedition.
6 Nov.	Abraham Lincoln is elected president.
13 Nov.	South Carolina authorizes elections for a convention to consider secession.
18 Dec.	Sen. John J. Crittenden proposes recognizing slavery south of the Missouri Compromise line and maintaining the institution where it already exists in the Union; he is opposed by Republicans.
20 Dec.	South Carolina declares secession from the Union.

1861

Jan.	Kansas is admitted to the Union.
9 Jan.-1 Feb.	The remaining states of the Lower South secede.
4 Feb.	A Confederate constitutional convention meets in Montgomery, Alabama.
4 Feb.	A Peace Convention meets in Washington, D.C., chaired by former president John Tyler.
9 Feb.	Jefferson Davis is elected president of the Confederate States of America.
4 Mar.	Abraham Lincoln is inaugurated as president of the United States.
6 Apr.	Lincoln notifies South Carolina authorities of his intent to supply provisions to the garrison at Fort Sumter.
12 Apr.	Confederate batteries open fire on Fort Sumter.
15 Apr.	Lincoln calls for seventy-five thousand volunteers to suppress the insurrection.
17 Apr.– 20 May	Virginia, Arkansas, Tennessee, and North Carolina secede from the Union.

1862

16 Apr.	The Confederacy enacts conscription.
22 Sept.	President Abraham Lincoln issues a preliminary Emancipation Proclamation.
1 Dec.	Lincoln submits to Congress a plan for compensated emancipation; the initiative wins little support.

1863

1 Jan.	The Emancipation Proclamation is declared in effect.
25 Feb.	Congress creates a national banking system.

3 Mar.	Congress passes the Conscription Act.
13–16 July	Antidraft riots occur in New York City.
8 Dec.	President Abraham Lincoln announces amnesty for Southerners who take a loyalty oath. He also agrees to recognize a Southern state's government if 10 percent of the 1860 voters in a specific state take the oath and emancipate their slaves.

1864

7 June	The Republican National Convention meets and renominates Abraham Lincoln for president.
4 July	Lincoln vetoes the Wade-Davis bill, which conditions readmission to the Union on loyalty oaths by 50 percent of a state's 1860 voters.
5 Aug.	The Wade-Davis Manifesto denounces Lincoln.
29 Aug.	The Democratic National Convention meets and nominates Gen. George B. McClellan for president.
8 Nov.	Abraham Lincoln wins reelection as president of the United States of America.
29 Nov.	Col. John M. Chivington's seven hundred Colorado Volunteers massacre Cheyenne Indians along Sand Creek, Colorado. Chivington orders his men to "kill and scalp all, big and little," because "nits make lice." Ninety-eight Indian women and children are among the dead. Gen. Nelson A. Miles calls this event the "foulest and most unjustifiable crime in the annals of America."

1865

3 Feb.	Lincoln and Secretary of State William Seward meet Confederate peace commissioners at Hampton Roads, Virginia.
4 Mar.	Lincoln is inaugurated for a second term.
20 Mar.	The Confederate Congress authorizes the arming of slaves.
9 Apr.	Robert E. Lee surrenders his army at Appomattox Courthouse, Virginia.
14 Apr.	Lincoln is assassinated at Ford's Theater by John Wilkes Booth; Andrew Johnson becomes president.
29 May	Johnson announces his plan for readmitting Southern states into the Union.
6 Dec.	Johnson reports to Congress that the Union is restored.

1866

9 Apr.	A civil rights act is passed over Johnson's veto.
13 June	Congress approves the Fourteenth Amendment to the Constitution.
20 June	The Congressional Joint Committee of Fifteen recommends against readmission of Southern states per Johnson's plan.
16 July	Freedmen's Bureau bill passes over Johnson's veto.

30 July	A race riot occurs in New Orleans.
28 Aug.	President Andrew Johnson embarks on the "swing around the circle" speaking tour.
21 Dec.	Captain William J. Fetterman and eighty soldiers are killed by an estimated two thousand Cheyenne and Lakota warriors under Crazy Horse on the Bozeman Trail outside of Fort Phil Kearny, Wyoming.

1867

2 Mar.	The Military Reconstruction Act passes over Johnson's veto. Congress also passes the Command of the Army Act and Tenure of Office Act, restricting Johnson's control of the army and the cabinet.
May	The Ku Klux Klan adopts a constitution; former Confederate general Nathan Bedford Forrest is the first Grand Wizard.
12 Aug.	President Andrew Johnson suspends Secretary of War Edwin Stanton.

1868

21 Feb.	Johnson dismisses Secretary of War Stanton.
24 Feb.	The House of Representatives impeaches President Johnson.
30 Mar.	The impeachment trial of Johnson begins.
16 May	President Andrew Johnson is acquitted of violating the Tenure of Office Act.
22–25 June	Alabama, Arkansas, Florida, Georgia, Louisiana, North Carolina, and South Carolina are readmitted to the Union by Congress.
3 Nov.	Ulysses S. Grant is elected president.
6 Nov.	Red Cloud and other Lakota tribal leaders sign a treaty with U.S. government officials at Fort Laramie, Wyoming, establishing a reservation in nearly all of present South Dakota west of the Missouri River. This area includes the sacred Black Hills.
27 Nov.	Lt. Col. George A. Custer and eight hundred cavalrymen massacre Black Kettle's band of Cheyenne Indians along the Washita River, Oklahoma.

1869

Sept.	The Georgia legislature expels black members, and the state is returned to military rule.

1870

30 Mar.	The Fifteenth Amendment is declared to be in effect.
31 May	Congress passes the Enforcement Act to protect black voters.

1871

4 Mar. President Ulysses S. Grant appoints George William Curtis to head the first Civil Service Commission.

20 Apr. Congress passes the Ku Klux Klan Act to enforce the Fourteenth Amendment.

8 July *The New York Times* launches an exposé of the Tweed Ring that culminates in the conviction of William Marcy Tweed and other corrupt officials in New York City.

1872

1 May The Liberal Republican Party nominates Horace Greeley for president.

9 July The Democratic National Convention also nominates Greeley for president.

5 Nov. Ulysses S. Grant is reelected president.

1873

12 Feb. The Coinage Act makes gold the sole monetary standard, eliminating the silver dollar.

27 Feb. The House of Representatives censures Oakes Ames of Massachusetts and James Brooks of New York in the Crédit Mobilier scandal.

3 Mar. The "Salary Grab" Act doubles the president's salary to $50,000 per year and increases Congressional pay from $5,000 to $7,500 per year.

1874

20 Jan. Public pressure induces the repeal of the "Salary Grab" Act.

Summer Gold is discovered in the Black Hills of South Dakota.

1875

14 Jan. The Specie Resumption Act limits greenbacks in circulation to $300 million, and provides for a return to specie payments by 1879.

1 Mar. Congress passes the Civil Rights Act; key provisions are held unconstitutional in the *Civil Rights* cases of 1883.

9 Dec. President Grant's private secretary Orville H. Babcock is indicted for participation in the Whiskey Ring, which defrauded the federal government of tax revenues.

1876

2 Mar. Secretary of War William W. Belknap resigns after his impeachment for receiving bribes in relation to trade in the Indian territory.

25 June Lt. Col. George A. Custer and 262 troopers of the Seventh Cavalry are wiped out along the Little Bighorn River, Montana, by approximately two thousand Cheyenne and Lakota warriors led by Crazy Horse, Gall, and Lame White Man.

1877

7 Nov.	The presidential election results in a dispute between Republican nominee Rutherford B. Hayes and Democratic nominee Samuel Tilden over returns from four states.
29 Jan.	Congress appoints the Electoral Commission to settle the disputed returns in the presidential race.
Feb.	The Electoral Commission supports the claims of Rutherford B. Hayes.
Mar. 4	Rutherford B. Hayes is inaugurated president.
Apr.	The last remaining federal troops in the South are withdrawn from South Carolina and Louisiana.

OVERVIEW

National Epic. The events of 1850–1877 form the central drama in the history of American politics, a sequence of riveting episodes enacted by a cast of colorful characters and featuring astonishing twists of plot with profound implications. Although the major events of course connect to earlier and later developments, the narrative coherence of the period is remarkable. The set piece that opens the era, the Compromise of 1850, was perceived even by contemporaries as a grand conclusion to previous phases of American history. The debate marked a transition between the era of Henry Clay, John C. Calhoun, and Daniel Webster, who had played leading roles in politics since the War of 1812, and a generation of newcomers that included Stephen A. Douglas, Jefferson Davis, William Henry Seward, and Salmon P. Chase. The primary issue at hand—the status of slavery in the federal territories wrested from Mexico—was one that Congress had memorably faced in organizing the territories won in the American Revolution and the territories obtained in the Louisiana Purchase. From this starting point, the story of the sectional conflict can be seen as a succession of famous scenes: the resistance to the Fugitive Slave Law; the Kansas-Nebraska Act, the Dred Scott decision, the Lincoln-Douglas debates; secession; the crisis at Fort Sumter; the decision to issue the Emancipation Proclamation; Radical Reconstruction and the impeachment of Andrew Johnson; and the disputed presidential election of 1877.

Narrative Hinges. Looking at the sectional conflict as a story helpfully points toward analysis of its parts, beginning with an overall division of the era into the coming of the Civil War, the war itself, and Reconstruction. Within each of these components, the turning points and dramatic peaks suggest important questions. How did the Republican Party come to power? Why did the lower South secede on the election of a Republican president? How did the Union disavowal of any interference with slavery turn into a commitment to emancipation? Why did Reconstruction not do more to establish equal rights? These questions trace crucial structures of American government, such as the Democratic-Republican party system or the Fourteenth Amendment of the Constitution, back into circumstances that might have developed in very different ways and that contemporaries could not have predicted. For example, shortly after Congress approved the Thirteenth Amendment abolishing slavery, Lincoln observed that neither North nor South "anticipated that the *cause* of the conflict might cease with, or even before, the conflict itself should cease. Each looked for an easier triumph, and a result less fundamental and astounding." The analysis of such political contingencies in the Civil War and Reconstruction era has produced some of the greatest works of American historical scholarship.

Political Culture. As an alternative to detailed examination that breaks into segments the years from 1850 to 1877, it is useful to consider the period in its entirety and to consider some of the features that distinguished American political culture at the height of the sectional conflict from the patterns of the preceding Jacksonian era or the following Gilded Age. In some ways the similarities are more striking than the differences. Most important, throughout all three periods the dominant characteristic of American politics was active participation by a high percentage of the electorate, organized by mass political parties to which voters were consistently loyal. The Whig and Democratic parties, which had coalesced in every state except South Carolina by the end of the 1830s, were the first institutions of their sort in the world. Unlike Hamiltonian Federalists and Jeffersonian Republicans, the Whigs and Democrats identified political parties not merely as temporarily necessary evils in a republic but as valuable instruments for generating alternative approaches to public problems, mobilizing candidates and voters, and containing conflict. Party alignments changed decisively during the Civil War and Reconstruction era, but for the most part the Republican and Democratic parties aimed to serve the same functions as their predecessors, and with some important exceptions voter turnout and loyalty remained high throughout the period. The casting of ballots by approximately 80 percent of the electorate in ordinary elections, the tendency of most voters to support the entire ticket of the same party throughout their lives, and the strong partisan affiliation of almost every newspaper typified nineteenth-century American politics.

New Expectations. The unchanged aspects of politics masked ways in which Americans made new demands on government during 1850–1877, or revised their traditional demands, and disillusionment often resulted from finding current institutions unequal to the challenges. At the beginning of the period, for example, the influx of immigrants and capital into the United States presented the Whig and Democratic parties with a fundamentally different social and economic framework from the context in which the parties had established their identities. As was common during the nineteenth century, voters' expectations of policies to address these developments centered primarily on state and local government. Immigration, for example, intensified the focus on government responsibility for civic education, on the regulation of cultural customs like the drinking of alcohol, and on the incorporation of newcomers into the political community. The feeling that the parties did not offer alternatives on these issues—that Whigs and Democrats were both simply pursuing the support of immigrant voters—caused many xenophobic Americans to renounce the major political parties. The vehicle for their protest, the Know Nothing movement, was perceived by nativists as a revolt against the machinations of political managers. Similarly, new economic conditions transformed the familiar responsibility of the government to promote growth through policies on matters like banking, the tariff, and the chartering of corporations. The new relationship between politics and money created by rapid, self-sustaining economic expansion helped make the administrations of James Buchanan and Ulysses S. Grant among the most corrupt in American history, although no more venal than many state and local governments in the era of Boss Tweed. Critics increasingly sensed a gap between outsiders like themselves and powerful insiders who benefited from awards of contracts for public construction projects, municipal investment in enterprise, or federal land grants to support railroad expansion.

Expectations about Slavery. One of the central social and economic institutions in antebellum America, slavery was profoundly affected by changing circumstances and produced the most spectacular example of increased voter distrust of politics. One of the traditional responsibilities of government in the South had been to protect the institution of slavery. Southern Whigs and Democrats competed during the Jacksonian era to demonstrate their ability to safeguard slavery in controversies over the Gag Rule in Congress and the annexation of Texas. During the 1850s, however, slavery faced more serious threats than ever before. The drain of slaves from the upper South into the cotton belt and the sugar district had made Delaware only nominally a slave state and was rapidly undermining the institution in Maryland, Kentucky, and Missouri. It was not difficult to foresee similar developments in Virginia, Tennessee, and North Carolina. At the same time, the realignment of politics had produced in the much more rapidly growing Northern states a Republican Party united by opposition to the extension of slavery into the federal territories. For decades

slaveholders had dominated the federal government and effectively defended the institution against attacks by men as capable and committed as John Quincy Adams. The Southerners most experienced in Washington, including future Confederate president Jefferson Davis and future Confederate vice president Alexander Stephens, anticipated no greater difficulty in checking the Republican Party. Most slaveholders disagreed, however, fearful that their representatives could not protect them from a Northern majority that might form alliances with Southern critics of slavery like Cassius Clay of Kentucky and Hinton Rowan Helper of North Carolina. Seeing their only safety outside of the Union, they led the movement for secession. Later, many slaveholders would similarly look upon themselves as powerless outsiders when the exigencies of war impelled the Confederate government to assume new roles.

Alienation of Intellectuals. Like nativists and slaveholders, intellectuals largely became disillusioned with politics in the third quarter of the nineteenth century and reversed what had been a remarkable record of immersion in public affairs. Partisan politics had long attracted the energies of creative minds who found philosophical resonance in the reform agenda and organic nationalism promoted by Whigs or the more conservative view of human nature expressed by Democrats. George Caleb Bingham's series of paintings about the electoral process vividly expressed the fascination with political rituals as a form of American popular culture, a sentiment reflected in Walt Whitman's observation that "I know nothing grander, better exercise, better digestion, more positive proof of the past, the triumphant result of faith in human-kind, than a well-contested American national election." Nor were intellectuals merely observers of the political scene. Nathaniel Hawthorne wrote a campaign biography for his Bowdoin College classmate Franklin Pierce; William Dean Howells performed the same service for Abraham Lincoln. Both were rewarded with diplomatic posts. Hawthorne had previously held a patronage appointment in a customhouse, as had Herman Melville and George Bancroft. Bookish men like Charles Sumner and Edward Everett devoted themselves to political careers and pursued their artistic aspirations in oratory; the speeches of Daniel Webster made him not only one of the leading statesmen but also one of the major literary figures of the Jacksonian era. The crisis over slavery intensified intellectual participation in politics, mobilizing the Transcendentalist circle around Ralph Waldo Emerson and Henry David Thoreau that had mostly remained aloof from partisan affairs. But after the Civil War, intellectuals increasingly denounced politics as corrupted by corporate wealth, immigrant voters, and unprincipled bosses. Their estrangement was best expressed by Henry Adams, whose satiric novel *Democracy* (1879) articulated his deepening sense that politics offered no place for him as it had for his great-grandfather

John Adams, grandfather John Quincy Adams, and father Charles Francis Adams.

Women in Political Culture. While party politics no longer satisfied some of the key participants of the Jacksonian era, women generally abandoned the formidable critique of American political culture that they had developed in the first half of the nineteenth century. Denied the vote and ineligible for office, women had often disdained politics as a sordid struggle for self-interest and a debasing excitation of popular passions. They sought instead to influence public affairs through their roles as wives, mothers, schoolteachers, or lobbyists, and also through voluntary benevolent organizations that performed public functions like the distribution of charity. Thoughtful and public-minded women like Catharine Beecher and Louisa McCord argued strenuously that woman suffrage would undermine their special authority in society, and such important leaders as Emma Willard, Dorothea Dix, Lydia Maria Child, Elizabeth Palmer Peabody, Sarah Josepha Hale, and Harriet Beecher Stowe either agreed with Beecher and McCord or regarded the franchise as relatively unimportant. The woman's rights conference organized by Elizabeth Cady Stanton and Lucretia Mott in Seneca Falls, New York, in 1848 signaled the growing support for a strategy of entering into traditionally male-dominated political processes rather than competing with them. The rights-based approach to gender politics appealed overwhelmingly to women coming of age after midcentury who often did not share the religious premises of their predecessors. One commentator declared in 1852 that "moral suasion is moral balderdash." The roles of women in the Civil War and the expansion of government in Reconstruction added to women's determination to participate equally in politics. The passing of the older critique might be observed, for example, in Julia Ward Howe's decision after the war to join the ranks of the suffragists that she had previously spurned.

African American Participation. The strategies pursued by African Americans mirrored the embrace of politics by women. Like women, blacks before the Civil War developed a stimulating alternative to the political system that denied them basic rights. The African American alternative was emigration, a repudiation of American government and its unkept promises, and a reformulation of racist colonization policies that had sought to exclude blacks from the country. The idea of emigration won support from many leading African Americans during the antebellum period, including Martin Delany, William Wells Brown, and Henry Highland Garnet. Brown declared that "to emigrate to Hayti, and to develop the resources of the Island, and to build up a powerful and influential government there, which shall demonstrate the genius and capabilities of the Negro, is as good an Anti-Slavery work as can be done in the Northern States of this Union." The movement failed, however, not merely because the initial attempts to implement it met with frustrations but because the opponents of emigration won the debate within the African American community. John Rock summarized the majority view that "This being our country, we have made up our minds to remain in it, and to try to make it worth living in." When Reconstruction revolutionized the political situation of blacks, they would be firm supporters of government institutions as instruments for achieving justice.

Labor. Although the two-party system managed to encompass challenges based on gender and race, the politics of the hardening class structure in industrialized regions of America proved to be more diffuse. The large, highly diverse group of wage-earning workers pursued their various interests through many different political strategies. Participation in electoral politics was an important approach, either through one of the major parties or through one of the labor political organizations that carried forward the legacy of the workingmen's parties of the Jacksonian era. But another means to contest the division of power in society, direct action at the workplace, became increasingly important in the postwar era, culminating in the railroad general strike of 1877. The intensifying violence of postwar strikes, the radical example of the Paris Commune, and the growing international attention to socialist philosophies caused observers to anticipate at the end of the period that labor would be at the center of any impending upheaval in American political culture.

TOPICS IN THE NEWS

COMPROMISE OF 1850

Wilmot Proviso. The crisis over the status of slavery in the territory acquired from Mexico grew out of the struggle for partisan advantage. A breach in the Democratic Party opened when James K. Polk defeated former president Martin Van Buren for the presidential nomination in 1844, and the split deepened over the next two years. When Polk guided the United States into a war with Mexico, planning to annex territory extending to the Pacific Ocean, the Van Burenites moved to exact their revenge. Representative David Wilmot of Pennsylvania proposed to add a clause, or proviso, to military appropriations for the war stipulating that slavery would not be permitted in any territory obtained from Mexico. Wilmot's proposal imitated restrictions by which slavery had been barred from the Northwest Territory in 1787 and from the Louisiana Purchase Territory north of the 36° 30' latitude in the Missouri Compromise of 1820. Congressional response to the Wilmot Proviso confirmed the Van Burenites' calculations that the gambit would be received enthusiastically by Democrats and Whigs in the North. Bipartisan support enabled the proviso to pass in the House of Representatives, where the more populous Northern states enjoyed a commanding majority, but it was stymied in the Senate, where free and slave states were evenly divided.

Alternative Proposals. As the Mexican War ended with the cession of more than six hundred thousand square miles of land to the United States, Democratic and Whig leaders adjusted to the polarizing impact of the Wilmot Proviso by developing strategies for the 1848 presidential campaign that promised to restore the intersectional alliances on which the parties were based. The Democrats, led by Sen. Lewis Cass of Michigan, promoted a policy of "popular sovereignty" under which the residents in any territory would decide whether or not to permit slavery; this approach would effectively remove the issue of slavery in the federal territories from national politics and make the question a local matter. The Whigs nominated war hero Zachary Taylor, who remained non-committal about slavery in the territories but who appealed to both sections because he was a Louisiana slave owner with influential Northern advisers. Meanwhile, two other approaches to the question con-

Senator Henry Clay of Kentucky, whose "omnibus bill" linked settlement of the territorial problem with several other slavery problems and provoked heated debate in Congress; photograph by Mathew Brady, 1849

tinued to attack the intersectional pattern of politics. Martin Van Buren made the Wilmot Proviso the cornerstone of his campaign for the presidency on the Free Soil ticket. His strong showing divided Democratic voters and contributed to the victory of Taylor. Meanwhile, John C. Calhoun tried unsuccessfully to form a Southern coalition around the policy that slavery must be permitted throughout the federal territories. Perhaps more surprising was the collapse of the solution suggested by the Missouri Compromise, extension of the 36° 30' line to the Pacific Ocean. The North's rejection of this option

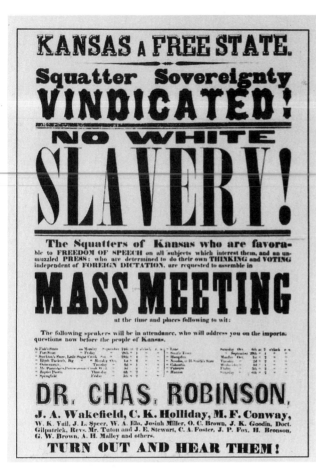

KANSAS A FREE STATE.

Squatter Sovereignty
VINDICATED!
NO WHITE
SLAVERY!

The Squatters of Kansas who are favorable to FREEDOM OF SPEECH on all subjects which interest them, and an unmuzzled PRESS; who are determined to do their own THINKING and VOTING independent of FOREIGN DICTATION, are requested to assemble in

MASS MEETING

at the time and places following to wit:

The following speakers will be in attendance, who will address you on the important questions now before the people of Kansas.

DR. CHAS. ROBINSON,

J. A. Wakefield, C. K. Holliday, M. F. Conway,
W. K. Vail, J. L. Speer, W. A. Ela, Josiah Miller, O. C. Brown, J. K. Goodin, Doct. Gilpatrick, Revs. Mr. Tuton and J. E. Stewart, C. A. Foster, J. P. Fox, H. Bronson, G. W. Brown, A. H. Malley and others.

TURN OUT AND HEAR THEM!

Poster circulated by the Free-Soil Party in Lawrence, Kansas, in autumn 1855

reflected an increasing tendency to treat the issue as a matter of principle that should not be compromised.

The Omnibus Bill. The situation in the Mexican cession assumed a new urgency when the California Gold Rush of 1849 produced a large population on the Pacific Coast that required the prompt organization of a government. Sen. Henry Clay of Kentucky, who had played a lead role in defusing the Missouri controversy during 1819–1821 and the Nullification controversy in 1833, took the legislative initiative by seeking to combine the settlement of the territorial problem with several other slavery issues. Clay proposed to admit California to the union as a free state, which was clearly the preference of the majority of inhabitants; to organize territorial governments for Utah and New Mexico without restrictions on slavery; to draw the Texas–New Mexico border in a way that made the slave state of Texas smaller than it might have been; to provide for the federal government to assume the debt contracted by Texas before annexation; to pass a new law governing the retrieval of fugitive slaves; to prohibit public slave auctions in the District of Columbia; and to forswear congressional interference with the legality of slavery in the District of Columbia or with the interstate slave trade. Because President Taylor favored the admission of California as a free state but op-

posed the provisions for the organization of New Mexico and Utah, Clay put the linked proposals together into one piece of legislation known as the "omnibus bill."

The Great Debate. The congressional deliberations on the omnibus bill were among the most dramatic in American history. Clay, brandishing a fragment of George Washington's coffin, led off by calling for each section to make concessions to preserve the Union. John C. Calhoun, who would be dead within a month, watched in enfeebled silence while a colleague read the South Carolinian's speech opposing the compromise and calling for a restructuring of the federal government to protect Southern interests. Daniel Webster answered by supporting the compromise in his "Seventh of March address," for which he was pilloried by his antislavery constituents in Massachusetts. The eloquent curtain calls of this triumvirate were matched by the rising generation. William Henry Seward of New York memorably appealed to a "higher law" than the Constitution to justify his opposition to a compromise that recognized slavery; Salmon P. Chase of Ohio took a similar position. Jefferson Davis of Mississippi in turn opposed the compromise on the ground that Congress had no authority to interfere with slavery.

Breakthrough. Although Clay had initially planned to present each proposal separately and had only adopted the omnibus strategy to counter the threat of a veto by Taylor, the compromise remained a single bill after the president died on 9 July 1850 of acute gastroenteritis caused by overindulgence in raw vegetables, cherries, and iced milk at Fourth of July ceremonies in Washington. The measure failed to pass in the omnibus format: most Northerners would not vote for the fugitive slave bill or for legislation that recognized the possibility of slavery in the territories, while most Southerners continued to oppose the admission of California as a free state and the reduction in the size of Texas. After the collapse of the omnibus, Clay left Washington for a vacation in Newport, Rhode Island, and Democrat Stephen A. Douglas of Illinois took charge of the measure. Douglas had already been working behind the scenes to cement intersectional harmony by sponsoring the first grant of federal land to promote railroad construction, for a line stretching from Chicago, Illinois, to Mobile, Alabama. The advance of other land grants similarly defused sectional tensions, and financier William Wilson Corcoran effectively promoted the compromise measures by interesting members of Congress in the Texas bonds that would stabilize in value once assumed by the United States government. When Douglas broke up the omnibus into a series of bills in September, all of Clay's original proposals passed in a modified form. But different measures depended on the votes of different coalitions. Northerners from both parties and Whigs from the border states secured the admission of California, the abolition of the slave trade in Washington, and the adjustment of the Texas border. Southerners and Northern Democrats passed the Fugitive Slave Law and organized Utah and New Mexico without restrictions on slavery. The "compromise" had won no real concessions from either side, but supporters nonetheless hoped that it would achieve a final resolution of slavery disputes in national politics.

Northern Reactions. The limits of acquiescence in the compromise measures became apparent more immediately in the North. The Fugitive Slave Law had not been a primary focus of the congressional debates:

THE GEORGIA PLATFORM, 1850

To the end that the position of this State may be clearly apprehended by her Confederates of the South and of the North, and that she may be blameless of all future consequences—

Be it resolved by the people of Georgia in Convention assembled, First. That we hold the American Union secondary in importance only to the rights and principles it was designed to perpetuate. That past associations, present fruition, and future prospects, will bind us to it so long as it continues to the be the safe-guard of those rights and principles. . . .

Third. That in this spirit the State of Georgia as maturely considered the action of Congress . . . and whilst she does not wholly approve, will abide by it as a permanent adjustment of this sectional controversy.

Fourth. That the State of Georgia, in the judgment of this Convention, will and ought to resist, even (as a last resort) to a disruption of every tie which binds her to the Union, any future Act of Congress abolishing Slavery in the District of Columbia, without the consent and petition of the slaveholders thereof, or any Act abolishing Slavery in places within the slave-holding States, purchased by the United States for the erection of forts, magazines, arsenals, dock-yards, navy-yards, and other like purposes; or in any Act suppressing the slave-trade between slave-holding States; or in any refusal to admit as a State any Territory applying because of the existence of Slavery therein; or in any Act prohibiting the introduction of slaves into the Territories of Utah and New Mexico; or in any Act repealing or materially modifying the laws now in force for the recovery of fugitive slaves.

Fifth. That it is the deliberate opinion of this Convention, that upon the faithful execution of the Fugitive Slave Bill by the proper authorities, depends the preservation of our much loved Union.

the issue necessitating action had been the admission of California; the main collision of principle had been over the status of slavery in the territories; and the stickiest negotiating point had been the adjustment of the Texas border. But the new mechanisms for retrieving runaway slaves soon inflamed the North and sparked several highly publicized episodes of resistance. The Fugitive Slave Law also impelled Harriet Beecher Stowe to write one of the most politically important novels of American history, *Uncle Tom's Cabin.* Published as a book in the spring of 1852 after appearing in installments in an antislavery newspaper, Stowe's exploration of slavery and evangelical Christianity sold three hundred thousand copies within a year. By the end of that time, however, it seemed that the compromise might be taking hold. The federal government under Millard Fillmore had demonstrated its willingness to commit the resources necessary to subdue local resistance to the Fugitive Slave Law. Controversy also declined because the number of African Americans returned to the South fell by two-thirds in the second year under the law, in part because so many blacks had resettled in Canada. The Free Soil Party, which had received about 10 percent of the vote in the presidential election of 1848, received only about half as much in 1852.

Southern Reactions. The Southern response to the Compromise of 1850 was outwardly less volatile but in the end more dangerous to the Union than the Northern reactions. The immediate result of the compromise was to take the wind out of the sails of advocates of secession. The Nashville Convention, held in June 1850, which had agreed to meet after the compromise to decide policy, could muster only a handful of radicals in November 1850. Unionist candidates won the races for governor in Georgia and Mississippi, and supporters of the Compromise won fourteen of the nineteen congressional seats from Georgia, Mississippi, and Alabama. Even in South Carolina, by far the most aggressively disunionist state, voters overwhelmingly rejected an appeal for secession in a statewide referendum. Unionism in the lower South after the Compromise seemed stronger. Several states embraced the "Georgia Platform" of 1850, which threatened resistance and even secession if Congress enacted additional antislavery measures. Moreover, the Compromise left leading Whigs from the lower South estranged from their party. Northern Whigs like William Henry Seward had not only led the protest against permitting slavery in the Mexican cession but had seemed to control Whig president Zachary Taylor. Repairing the intersectional bonds of party politics would be crucial to cementing loyalty to the Union.

Sources:

William W. Freehling, *The Road to Disunion* (New York: Oxford University Press, 1990);

Holman Hamilton, *Prologue to Conflict: The Crisis and Compromise of 1850* (Lexington: University of Kentucky Press, 1964).

DISINTEGRATION OF THE SECOND PARTY SYSTEM

Parties and the Sectional Conflict. It is easy to oversimplify the coming of the Civil War as a series of steadily intensifying collisions over slavery issues. Focusing solely on the episodes of confrontation loses sight of the fact that American politics provided a mechanism for resolving conflicts—including bitter conflicts over slavery issues—for many years. The crisis of the 1850s was more explosive not because the country faced more-intractable issues than it had before but because the Whig-Democratic party system collapsed early in the decade. Disagreements over slavery were only a part of the reason for this development. The social and economic transformation of the country had by the 1850s eroded the underpinnings of the Whig-Democratic rivalry in a way that left American politics ready to be reorganized along sectional lines.

Fading National Issues. The acquiescence in the Compromise of 1850, unenthusiastic though it was in many cases, symbolized the predicament of the national parties. Whigs and Democrats had commanded remarkable voter loyalty because they competed vigorously on important issues. The Compromise of 1850 was one such issue. In the North, Whigs had generally opposed the compromise and Democrats had supported it; in the upper South, Whigs had supported the compromise and Democrats had opposed it. Competition along these lines continued for some time, especially over the implementation of the Fugitive Slave Law, but by 1852 the national platforms of both parties endorsed the compromise as a final solution of the sectional conflict. Nor did any other national issues replace the compromise as a focus of competition. Territorial expansion, which had been an important source of contention during the 1840s, was controlled largely by the executive branch, and the Whigs did not favor such initiatives. When Charles Sumner of Massachusetts arrived in the Senate in 1851, Thomas Hart Benton told him that he "had come to the Senate too late. All the great issues and all the great men were gone."

Local Economic Issues. The neutralization of national issues was not necessarily fatal to the Whig-Democratic party system, which owed its vitality primarily to competition over the economic problems that were most pressing to voters. But the changing structure of the economy made the traditional arguments of the parties increasingly irrelevant. Although specifics varied from state to state, the Whig Party in general owed much of its identity to policies intended to stimulate economic growth despite the limited availability of investment capital. This premise, formulated in the economic recession that followed the Panic of 1819, was expressed in specific policies on tariffs, banking, corporate charters, and subsidies to entrepreneurs. The Whig logic became less compelling in the boom times that followed the California gold rush and the diversion of European in-

Millard Fillmore, the last Whig president

vestments to America in the wake of the continental uprisings of 1848. For example, the availability of specie to back paper notes issued by banks mooted longstanding debates that had taken place in almost every state over the appropriate reserve requirements. Meanwhile, the Democrats reversed their traditional hostility to the chartering of new banks. Similarly, the tariff issue lost much of its resonance in a mature economy, as the traditional Whig support for high duties no longer appealed to textile manufacturers who wanted protection from new domestic rivals as well as foreign firms. The most important economic issue of the early 1850s—the promotion of railroad construction—did not replace the old litmus tests of party loyalty. The universal enthusiasm for new railroads translated into competition between different localities or regions rather than between the two parties.

State Constitutional Issues. Some forms of party conflict disappeared as a result of the state constitutions adopted between 1848 and 1852 in New Hampshire, Maryland, Virginia, Ohio, Indiana, Michigan, Wisconsin, Kentucky, and Louisiana. Whigs and Democrats had long battled in most states over whether to hold these constitutional conventions and over specific issues that were now resolved permanently. For example, the growing tendency of constitutions to restrict or ban government investment in improvement projects eliminated a steady source of partisan disagreement, as did the commonplace adoption of Democratic preference for free incorporation laws rather than the attachment of special

ANXIETIES OF KNOW NOTHINGS

In a letter to Justice John McLean of the U.S. Supreme Court dated 11 January 1855, Detroit judge Ross Wilkins expressed hope that *"secret jesuitism* in America might be triumphantly met by a *secret American movement"*:

> You know that for the last quarter of a century political traders and gamesters have so manufactured public opinion, & so directed party organization, that our Union has been endangered, & bad men elevated to place & power, contrary to the true sentiment of the People. And there seemed to be no hope for us. Both parties courted what was called the foreign vote; & the highest aspirants of the Senate, to ensure success, strove which could pay more homage to a foreign Prince, whose ecclesiastical subjects, constituted so large a portion of this imperium in imperio. The Papal Power at Rome, apprised fully of this state of things, gave direction to her vassal priesthood, to use their supposed power for the propaganda files, and hence the attack on our school systems in Cincinnati, New York, Baltimore, and Detroit. I give thanks to God, that they commenced the warfare at the time they did, and that their plan was discerned and defeated.

Source: Michael F. Holt, *The Political Crisis of the 1850s* (New York: John Wiley & Sons, 1978), p. 164.

privileges to corporate charters issued by legislatures. Other popular provisions weakened party machinery without regard to the specifics of any issue. By providing for direct popular election of judges, sheriffs, and other local officials, the state constitutions reduced the opportunities available to cement party loyalty through the distribution of patronage. Legislative sessions commonly became biennial, rather than annual, which slashed the capacity of the political system to enact laws and the ability of the parties to generate allegiances.

Nativism. As the defining economic and political questions of the Jacksonian era lost their urgency, the massive immigration into the United States during the late 1840s and early 1850s became the focus of party rivalry. The Democrats had traditionally welcomed immigrants into the party while the Whigs had appealed more to old-stock Americans troubled by infusions of Germans and, especially, Catholics. The politics of nativism played out on many different subjects, of which the consumption of alcohol was the most conspicuous. The Maine Law of 1851 provided a national model for a prohibition measure that differed significantly from previous campaigns to promote temperance on a voluntary basis. The changed demographics presented Whigs with a choice between intensifying their previous nativist leanings or competing with Democrats for newly arrived voters. In the 1852 presidential election, the Whigs decided for the first time to appeal to Catholic immigrants. The strategy partly reflected a calculation that Irish and German immigrants were undeniably an immense voting

group while nativists were difficult to count and unite; for example, prohibition did not enjoy the support of every old-stock voter troubled by the new populations. The leading promoter of the new policy, William Henry Seward, had long called on Whigs to abandon their nativist leanings and as governor of New York had supported public funding for parochial schools. Although informed both by a pragmatic assessment of the electorate and by considerations of principle, Seward's reform of the party destroyed one of the last features that distinguished Whigs from Democrats.

Whig Collapse. The election of 1852 showed that the Whigs were on the brink of extinction as a major party. Although Democratic candidate Franklin Pierce was young, inexperienced, and not widely known, he lost only four states in the presidential race to Whig nominee Winfield Scott, a hero of the Mexican War. The Democrats also won two-to-one majorities in both houses of Congress. This lopsided result was not primarily the result of the slavery controversy, although the sharp decline in Whig votes in the lower South reflected a continued estrangement from the party after the Compromise of 1850. More striking was the inability of the Whigs to win new votes in the North or even to hold formerly reliable supporters. The appeal to immigrants made few Whig converts and alienated the sizable anti-Catholic wing of the party. Beyond this particular grievance, the convergence of the parties generally left voters disillusioned and uninterested. One Cincinnati Whig reported that "General Apathy is the strongest candidate out here." Voter turnout was low by the standards of the mid nineteenth century. A Democrat in Connecticut remarked that "the Whigs here seem disposed to let the election go pretty much by default."

Fragmentation. Contemporaries recognized that the breakdown of the Whig Party left American politics ripe for reorganization. Not only were the Whigs moribund, but the Democrats lost the party identity that came from uniting against a common opposition. Almost immediately after the election of Pierce, factional struggles over the distribution of patronage broke out with extraordinary bitterness. Democratic leaders eager to avenge grudges dating back to the Free Soil schism of 1848 took advantage of the situation to thwart the weak president's hope to unite his party. The potential for realignment was best expressed by Millard Fillmore, the last Whig president, shortly before the first meeting of the Congress elected in 1852. "What new combinations will grow out of this it is difficult to foresee," Fillmore wrote to a friend, "as national parties can only be formed by the action of the general government. Parties are broken up by local causes and that centrifugal force which throws individuals and masses beyond the attraction of the central power; but new parties of a national character can only be gathered from these fragmentary nebula of dissolving systems by the magnet of some great national and centripetal force at Washington." Fillmore asked: "Will

Members of the Kansas Free State battery in Topeka in 1856, during the conflicts between
Southerners and antislavery settlers

any question present such a magnet at the ensuing session of Congress?" In fact, the session would generate precisely the force that he anticipated.

Sources:

Michael Holt, *The Political Crisis of the 1850s* (New York: John Wiley & Sons, 1978);

David M. Potter, *The Impending Crisis, 1848–1861* (New York: Harper & Row, 1976).

FORGING A REPUBLICAN MAJORITY

Filling a Void. The decline of the Whigs eliminated an important bond of Unionism but did not necessarily mean that politics would become polarized along sectional lines. To the contrary, in the immediate aftermath of the 1852 election it seemed that the major response to voters' dissatisfaction would take the form of initiatives unrelated to sectional disputes. In much of the country, the future evidently lay with prohibitionist and nativist movements. Coalitions enacted adaptations of the Maine Law throughout New England and in New York, Delaware, and much of the Midwest from 1852 to 1855. These efforts fed into broader nativist impulses that received a new organization when two secret fraternal organizations, the Order of United Americans and the Order of the Star Spangled Banner, merged in 1852 to form the Know Nothing Party. The Know Nothings did not seek to restrict immigration but tried to limit newcomers' influence in politics by calling for a waiting period of twenty-one years before an immigrant could be naturalized and by proposing that officeholding should be limited to native-born Americans. The anti-Catholic movement also came to focus on disputes over public funding of parochial schools and the legal control of church property. Passions intensified when Vatican emissary Gaetano Bedini arrived in July 1853 to address property ownership questions on behalf of Pope Pius IX. One observer declared that "He is here to find the best way to rivet Italian chains upon us which will bind us as slaves to the throne of the most fierce tyranny the world knows."

Kansas-Nebraska Act. A different basis for the organization of politics emerged from the first session of the Thirty-third Congress, which assembled in December 1853. Stephen A. Douglas, who had watched with chagrin as the inept Franklin Pierce tried to lead the Democratic Party, moved to assert his leadership with a legislative program for western development. Douglas had long been interested in chartering a transcontinental railroad line from Chicago to the Pacific, which required the organization for settlement of additional territory that had been obtained in the Louisiana Purchase. His bid to open the so-called Nebraska Territory faced strenuous opposition from Missouri senator David Rice Atchison of Missouri, a state in which the slave population was rapidly declining as labor flowed to the richer lands of the South. Atchison staked his political career on preserving slavery in Missouri, aware that the erosion of the institution would accelerate if the state were surrounded not only by free states on the east and north but also by new territory to the west that the Missouri Compromise required to be free. Douglas sought to accommodate Atchison and his Southern allies in January 1854

Campaign poster for Lincoln's 1860 presidential campaign

by ignoring the restriction on slavery north of the 36° 30' line. When Atchison's faction called for more-explicit concessions, Douglas revised his proposal to establish two territories, Kansas and Nebraska, and to declare the Missouri Compromise superseded by the principle of popular sovereignty that the Compromise of 1850 applied to the New Mexico and Utah territories. Douglas saw little practical significance to this formulation, for he correctly predicted that settlers in the new territories would mostly come from free states and would not favor the establishment of slavery. He nevertheless anticipated that what he called "a hell of a storm" would result in the North from jettisoning of the hallowed Missouri Compromise, and he prepared for the furor by committing Pierce to make the Kansas-Nebraska bill a test of loyalty to the Democratic Party.

Reactions. Douglas's expectations of an outcry were fulfilled many times over. On the day after the Illinois senator introduced his revised proposal, a small Free Soil contingent in Congress led by Sens. Salmon P. Chase and Charles Sumner and Rep. Joshua Giddings of Ohio published an "Appeal to the Independent Democrats" arguing that Douglas had acted as the pawn of slavery interests in order to advance his ambition to become president. Throughout the North, coalitions of anti-Nebraska Democrats, Whigs, and Free Soilers met to express opposition to the repeal of the Missouri Compromise. The extension of slavery into the territories mobilized many moderates who had accepted the Fugitive Slave Law as the unfortunate price of Unionism,

including Abraham Lincoln. The influence of the anti-Nebraska meetings was counteracted in Washington by the marshaling of patronage and other party resources to maintain Democratic discipline in support of the bill. While Northern Democrats were forced to choose between party and section, Whigs divided almost completely along sectional lines on the bill. When Congress passed the measure in May 1854, anti-Nebraska leaders intensified the organizational efforts that produced a Republican Party limited entirely to the Northern states. The potential appeal of the party was demonstrated by the congressional elections of 1854. The contingent of Northern Democrats in the House of Representatives fell from 93 to 23. Where the Democrats had won control of all but two free-state legislatures in 1852, they lost all but two in 1854. The Democratic ascendancy in the North was shattered; within the party, moreover, the Southern wing now became dominant.

Slave Power. The principal development in Northern politics between 1854 and 1856 was a struggle between nativists and Republicans to succeed the Whigs as the major party rival to the Democrats. The competitors in some ways made similar appeals. Just as the Know Nothings argued that the Pope secretly manipulated immigrants to subvert American liberties, the Republicans maintained that a conspiracy of powerful slaveholders was covertly working through the Democratic Party to subvert American liberties. The Republican argument was not based on racial egalitarianism but on a conviction that slavery was an impediment to modernization

Abraham Lincoln's "House Divided" speech, delivered on 16 June 1858, upon his acceptance as the Illinois Republican nominee for the U.S. Senate, was one of the strongest statements of the argument that a secret Democratic conspiracy was expanding and entrenching slavery. The workmen to whom he refers are Stephen A. Douglas, Franklin Pierce, Roger B. Taney, and James Buchanan.

A house divided against itself cannot stand.

I believe this government cannot endure, permanently half *slave* and half *free*.

I do not expect the Union to be *dissolved*—I do not expect the house to *fall*—but I *do* expect it will cease to be divided.

It will become *all* one thing or *all* the other.

Either the *opponents* of slavery, will arrest the further spread of it, and place it where the public mind shall rest in the belief that it is in course of ultimate extinction; or its *advocates* will push it forward, till it shall become alike lawful in *all* the States, *old* as well as *new*—*North* as well as *South*.

Have we no *tendency* to the latter condition?

Let anyone who doubts, carefully contemplate that now almost complete legal combination—piece of *machinery* so to speak—compounded of the Nebraska doctrine, and the Dred Scott decision. . . .

When we see a lot of framed timbers, different portions of which we know have been gotten out at different times and places and by different workmen—Stephen, Franklin, Roger and James, for instance—and when we see these timbers joined together, and see they exactly make the frame of a house or a mill . . . we find it impossible to not *believe* that Stephen and Franklin and Roger and James all understood one another from the beginning, and all worked upon a common *plan* or *draft* drawn up before the first lick was struck.

It should not be overlooked that, by the Nebraska bill, the people of a *State* as well as *Territory*, were to be left "*perfectly free subject only to the Constitution.*"

Why mention a *State?* They were legislating for *territories*, and not *for* or *about* States. Certainly the people of a State *are* and *ought to be* subject to the Constitution of the United States; but why is mention of this *lugged* into this merely *territorial* law? Why are the people of a *territory* and the people of a *state* therein lumped together, and their relation to the Constitution therein treated as being *precisely* the same?. . .

In what *cases* the power of the *states* is so restrained by the U.S. Constitution, is left an *open* question, precisely as the same question, as to the restraint on the power of the *territories* was left open in the Nebraska act. Put *that* and *that* together, and we have another nice little niche, which we may, ere long, see filled with another Supreme Court decision, declaring that the Constitution of the United States does not permit a *state* to exclude slavery from its limits?. . .

We shall *lie down* pleasantly dreaming that the people of *Missouri* are on the verge of making their State *free*; and we shall *awake* to the *reality*, instead, that the *Supreme Court* has made *Illinois* a *slave* State.

and that Southern efforts to preserve the institution were infringing upon the political rights of whites. Thus, Republicans emphasized the suppression of free speech in the South, where only a few courageous individuals like Cassius Clay of Kentucky braved physical attacks to criticize slavery as incompatible with economic development and social progress in such matters as the education of whites. As settlers moved into the newly opened Kansas territory, Republicans publicized the ways in which "border ruffians" from Missouri perverted democratic processes and relied on violence to set up a proslavery government. The clash between the Southerners and antislavery settlers led to the establishment of two separate legislatures in Kansas and eventually to the outbreak of civil war in the territory. The Republican critique of "slave power" found its most dramatic focus when Rep. Preston S. Brooks of South Carolina brutally assaulted Charles Sumner in the Senate chamber in May 1856 after the Bostonian made derogatory remarks about Brooks's relative, Sen. Andrew Pickens Butler, in a speech titled "The Crime Against Kansas." Sumner did not return to the Senate for three years, his vacant seat serving Republicans as a constant reminder of the fate of civil liberties in a government dominated by slaveholders.

The Dred Scott Decision. The twin issues of "Bleeding Kansas" and "Bleeding Sumner" propelled the Republicans to a strong showing in the 1856 presidential election. Their nominee, John C. Frémont, easily outdistanced Know Nothing candidate Millard Fillmore, whose party served mostly to provide an alternative to Democrats in the upper South, and posed a formidable challenge to Democratic winner James Buchanan. Two days after Buchanan's inauguration in March 1857, the Supreme Court announced its ruling in *Dred Scott* v. *Sandford* that Congress did not have constitutional authority to prohibit slavery from the Louisiana Purchase Territory and that African Americans—whether slave or free—could not be citizens of the United States. The decision about the invalidity of the Missouri Compromise bar on slavery struck directly at the Republican Party, which was united by a common desire to restore the ban. Here again, Republicans argued, was the hand of the slave power, now seeking to remove a vital issue from democratic processes by ruling for the first time in

Harpers Ferry, Virginia. The engine house at left was the site where John Brown was captured by Marines under the command of Lt. Col. Robert E. Lee.

more than a half century that an act of Congress was unconstitutional.

The Lecompton Controversy. The conflict over slavery in the Kansas Territory came to a climax in 1857 as settlers prepared to request admission into the Union. Federal judgment on the validity of any proposed constitution was complicated by the fact that proslavery and antislavery elements remained separate political communities, although violence had largely been suppressed. Antislavery Kansans did not participate in the drafting of a proslavery constitution in Lecompton, which did not allow for a popular vote on whether to permit settlers to keep their slaves. President Buchanan caved in to pressure from Southern leaders in Washington and supported the admission of Kansas under the Lecompton constitution. This decision proved catastrophic to the Democratic Party, the last intersectional political institution in the country. Stephen A. Douglas broke with Buchanan to lead efforts in Congress to block the admission of Kansas. The eventual resolution finally provided Kansas voters with an opportunity to reject the constitution, although it offered the state a large grant of federal land if the state adopted the proslavery charter and stipulated that additional population would be required to apply for admission as a free state. The antislavery majority in Kansas overwhelmingly spurned the bribe in an August 1858 referendum and rejected the Lecompton constitution. Kansas would enter the Union as a free state. More important than that outcome, however, was the fierce resentment of Douglas harbored by Southern political leaders as a result of the most prominent Northern Democrat's part in the struggle.

Lincoln-Douglas Debates. The Lecompton controversy defined the national stakes in Douglas's campaign for reelection in 1858. Douglas maintained that his policy of popular sovereignty had been vindicated. He had proven that he was not a pawn of slave power; he had helped to preserve the integrity of democratic processes in Kansas; and, although he professed to indifference whether Kansas voters in fact adopted or rejected slavery, his tacit premise that popular sovereignty would produce free states had been confirmed. Some Republicans, including influential *New York Tribune* editor Horace Greeley, consequently called on the party to endorse Douglas for reelection as the most effective counterbalance to the slave power. Taking the lead in opposition to this strategy was Abraham Lincoln, a lawyer who had served one term in Congress during the Mexican War and who had narrowly lost a race for the Senate in 1856. Public campaigns for Senate seats were rare because state legislatures elected senators, but Lincoln arranged for the Illinois Republican Party to nominate him for the Senate in June 1858 so that he could present himself as the nominee during the election of state legislators. This shrewd maneuver attracted national attention to the seven formal debates between Lincoln and Douglas. Upon accepting the nomination Lincoln delivered the "House Divided" speech that echoed the charges of a slave power conspiracy, claiming that Douglas was in league with Presidents Pierce and Buchanan and Supreme Court justice Roger B. Taney to subvert liberty in the North. As the debates progressed, however, he refined this theme to emphasize "the difference between the men who think slavery a wrong and those who do not think it wrong." Republicans thought that slavery was wrong and sought to contain it; hiding behind the policy of popular sovereignty, Douglas had "the high distinction of never having said slavery is either right or wrong '

Republican Ascendancy. Douglas narrowly defeat:d Lincoln in the Senate campaign, but the Republican political momentum was vividly illustrated when the new House of Representatives attempted to elect a Speaker. The roll call included 113 Republicans and 101 Democrats; former Whigs elected from the upper South under the banner of the American Party could tip the balance in either direction. The Republicans nominated John Sherman of Ohio, a moderate former Whig. Sherman, however, was one of sixty-eight Republican congressmen who had signed an advertisement for *The Impending Crisis of the South,* an 1857 book in which white North Carolinian Hinton Rowan Helper had attacked slavery as "the root of all the shame, poverty, ignorance, tyranny and imbecility of the South." Like some Northern Republicans, Helper did not disguise his racism. But he extended the Republican appeal in calling on the three-fourths of Southerners who did not own slaves to topple "this entire system of oligarchical despotism." Southern Democrats denounced Sherman for endorsing the work of Helper, whom they branded "a traitor" and an "insurrectionary," and they carried with them enough border-state Americans to deadlock the House of Representatives for forty-four ballots continuing over two months. Eventually Sherman withdrew and the Republicans elected another candidate. But the speakership contest not only demonstrated the growing Republican majority in the North; the tempest over *Impending Crisis of the South* revealed Southern fears that Republican voices were emerging in the South as well.

Sources:

Eric Foner, *Free Soil, Free Labor, Free Men: The Ideology of the Republican Party before the Civil War* (New York: Oxford University Press, 1970);

William E. Gienapp, *The Origins of the Republican Party, 1852–1856* (New York: Oxford University Press, 1987).

Lincoln's inauguration, 4 March 1861

of a slave-based empire extending through Central America. William Walker, a sometime physician, lawyer, and journalist, illustrated the restlessness that found an outlet in filibustering. Winning control of Nicaragua, Walker became a hero to Southerners by reinstituting slavery. He was soon overthrown, mainly because he clashed with Cornelius Vanderbilt's interests in the development of interocean transportation, but when the federal government charged him with violation of neutrality laws a New Orleans jury refused to convict him. Walker's downfall, like the failure of other expansionist initiatives, caused some supporters of slavery to conclude that a grander hemispheric destiny might await the South outside the United States.

John Brown's Raid. Their desire for expansion frustrated, slaveholders soon found cause to ask whether they were safe within the Union. John Brown had contributed to the fray in Kansas, where he massacred five randomly chosen slaveholders in May 1856 in retaliation for the sack of the antislavery headquarters at Lawrence. Over the next three years he developed a plan to invade the South and lead an uprising of slaves. On 16 October 1859, he led a squad of eighteen men in an attack on the virtually undefended federal arsenal at Harpers Ferry, Virginia. The quixotic, mismanaged foray failed to mobilize a single slave, and a company of U.S. marines commanded by Col. Robert E. Lee easily captured Brown within thirty-six hours of his arrival at Harpers Ferry. Republican leaders like Abraham Lincoln, brushing aside Southern attempts to link Brown to the party, dis-

A HOUSE DIVIDING

Southern Expansionism. The Kansas-Nebraska controversy not only initiated a political realignment in the North but wrecked any chance to fulfill the primary ambition of the Pierce administration and many of its Southern supporters, the acquisition of Cuba. After initially looking benignly on "filibustering" expeditions through which Americans sought to foment revolution in Cuba, the beleaguered Pierce adopted a new policy in May 1854 threatening to prosecute violations of American neutrality laws. The administration then authorized a futile effort to buy the island, but when the minister to Spain, Pierre Soulé, and two other American diplomats issued the "Ostend Manifesto" declaring that the United States would be "justified in wresting it from Spain," the president forced Soulé to resign. Meanwhile, other expeditions held out to Southerners the tantalizing prospect

The firing on Fort Sumter in Charleston, 12 April 1861

missed the incident as an isolated, hapless venture by a man of questionable sanity. But even a poorly conducted investigation revealed evidence that Brown had been backed by a group of influential abolitionists called "the Secret Six," including ministers Theodore Parker and Thomas Wentworth Higginson and humanitarian Samuel Gridley Howe. Perhaps even more galling to Southerners, Brown cultivated an image as a biblical martyr that captured the imagination of New England intellectuals. Ralph Waldo Emerson declared that Brown would "make the gallows as glorious as the cross." William Dean Howells, soon to write a campaign biography for Lincoln, observed that "Brown has become an idea, a thousand times purer and better and loftier than the Republican idea."

Democratic Schism. The election returns of 1858–1859 indicated that, barring a mistake, the Republican candidate would be in an excellent position to win the presidential election in 1860. That outcome was virtually assured by the final breakdown of the alliance between Southern Democrats and followers of Stephen A. Douglas that had been ruptured in the Lecompton controversy. Southerners eager to embarrass Douglas seized on the difficulty of reconciling his policy of popular sovereignty with the *Dred Scott* decision. In his debates with Lincoln, Douglas had maintained that even if the Constitution prohibited Congress from barring slavery in the federal territories, settlers could still exercise choice in the matter because they might decide not to enact the laws needed to enforce a system of slavery. This position became known as the Freeport Doctrine, after the Illinois town at which Douglas stated his position. Led by Sen. Jefferson Davis of Mississippi, Southerners attacked the Freeport Doctrine by arguing that settlers in the territories should not be able to circumvent constitutional protection for slavery and that Congress should

therefore enact a federal slave code for the territories. At the Democratic National Convention in Charleston, South Carolina, in April 1860, Douglas supporters refused the demand to include a federal slave code in the party platform. Fifty delegates from the Deep South thereupon bolted the convention pursuant to a strategy organized by William Lowndes Yancey of Alabama. After the convention deadlocked on the nomination of Douglas, the party collapsed. Douglas's supporters subsequently reassembled to nominate him for the presidency while anti-Douglas Southerners convened to nominate John C. Breckinridge of Kentucky.

The Election of Lincoln. William Henry Seward of New York was the best-known Republican in the country and the leading contender for the Republican nomination when the convention met in Chicago in May 1860. Salmon P. Chase of Ohio, a leader in the organization of the party since the Kansas-Nebraska controversy, was also a strong candidate. The nomination eventually went, however, to Abraham Lincoln, who had little national experience but had established himself as the leading Republican in the potentially pivotal state of Illinois. Apart from his western background and his fine showing in the race against Douglas, Lincoln's chief qualification for the campaign was that he did not have anywhere near as many enemies as Seward and Chase had made in their more-active careers. Both were considered more radical than Lincoln on slavery issues, which in Chase's case was an accurate reputation. Seward was also despised by anti-Catholic voters whom Republicans quietly sought to attract while continuing to build their strong support among Protestant immigrants from Germany. Following the nominations, the most remarkable feature of the political contest was the campaign of Douglas, who declared himself the only national candidate in the race. Lincoln did not appear on ballots in the South, and Breckinridge was not a contender in the North. John Bell of Tennessee, running on the Constitutional Union ticket, was nominally a national candidate but in fact appealed almost solely to planters who had formerly supported the Whigs. Not implausibly regarding his candidacy as the last hope of the Union, Douglas conducted an exhausting speaking tour throughout the North, South, and West. His efforts were in vain, however; he won only 12 percent of the popular vote in the slaveholding states. Meanwhile, although Lincoln's popular plurality represented only 39 percent of the national vote, he would have had a clear majority of electoral votes even if his opponents' totals were combined.

Secession of the Lower South. South Carolina radicals, recalling that the attempt to coordinate action among Southern states had forestalled any prospect for disunion during the controversy over the Compromise of 1850, moved swiftly to secede from the Union without awaiting a program of cooperation. Immediately after the November election the South Carolina legislature called for a convention to consider secession. On 20 De-

Henry Timrod noted in the subtitle of his "Ethnogenesis" that it was written during the first meeting of the Confederate Congress in Montgomery, Alabama. The poem expresses lyrically some of the economic, proslavery, and imperialist strands of the secessionist movement.

Hath not the morning dawned with added light?

And shall not evening call another star

Out of the infinite regions of the night,

To mark this day in Heaven? At last we are

A nation among nations; and the world

Shall soon behold in many a distant port

    Another flag unfurled!

    . . . . . .

But let our fears—if fears we have—be still,

And turn us to the future! Could we climb

Some mighty Alp, and view the coming time,

The rapturous sight would fill

    Our eyes with happy tears!

Nor only for the glories which the years

Shall bring us; not for lands from sea to sea,

And wealth, and power, and peace, though these shall be;

But for the distant peoples we shall bless,

And the hushed murmurs of a world's distress;

For to give labor to the poor,

    The whole sad planet o'er,

And save from want and crime the humblest door,

Is one among the many ends for which

    God makes us great and rich!

The hour perchance is not yet wholly ripe

When all shall own it, but the type

Whereby we shall be known in every land

Is that vast gulf which lips our Southern strand,

And through the cold, untempered ocean pours

Its genial streams, that far off Arctic shores

May sometimes catch upon the softened breeze

Strange tropic warmth and hints of summer seas.

cember the convention by a vote of 169–0 adopted an ordinance declaring that all connections between South Carolina and the United States were dissolved. Mississippi, Florida, Alabama, Georgia, Louisiana, and Texas soon followed suit, as the South Carolinians had hoped. The arrangements by which the voting public expressed its opinions on secession varied from state to state. Espe-

cially in Georgia, Louisiana, and Alabama, however, a significant minority expressed reservations about the decision. To the opponents of secession, it was not at all clear that the newly elected Lincoln administration would be able to pose a serious threat to slavery or even hold together the Republican coalition of former Whigs and former Democrats. But immediate state-by-state secession had effectively undercut the best tactic of Southern moderates, a call for cooperative action among slaveholding states that would result in a delay during which cooler heads might prevail. Cooperation was no longer a synonym for Unionist delay; it now meant participation in the Confederate States of America, which held a constitutional convention in Montgomery, Alabama, and elected Jefferson Davis to the presidency.

Failure of Compromise. The states of the upper South, which did not secede upon the election of Lincoln, led efforts to find a compromise solution to the situation. The most important proposal came from John Crittenden of Kentucky, who occupied the Senate seat once held by Henry Clay. The so-called Crittenden Compromise called for a constitutional amendment protecting slavery in the states where it already existed, a constitutional amendment prohibiting slavery in any federal territories north of 36° 30' latitude, and constitutional protection for slavery south of 36° 30' latitude. This proposal and other initiatives failed partly because, unlike the situation at the time of the Missouri Compromise, the Nullification crisis, and the Compromise of 1850, secession was not a legislative issue. Congress could not pass a law that would bring the Southern states back into the Union, as it had passed compromise laws in the previous crises. More fundamentally, however, compromise did not work because neither side supported it strongly. Lincoln endorsed a constitutional amendment protecting slavery in the states where it already existed, but the Republicans would not accept slavery in any part of the federal territory—particularly if that federal territory might come to include eventual acquisition of Cuba or the Central American areas that expansionists coveted.

Crisis at Fort Sumter. As secession progressed, Southern states closed federal courts, prepared to replace the United States mails, and asserted sovereignty over military bases throughout the South. James Buchanan, who remained in office until 4 March 1861, did little to stop this process beyond declaring secession illegal. When Lincoln came to office, he learned that there were two major federal military outposts left in the South: Fort Pickens near Pensacola, Florida, and Fort Sumter in the harbor of Charleston, South Carolina. The besieged garrison at Fort Sumter was quickly running out of food, which forced Lincoln to decide whether to surrender the federal presence in the cradle of secession or to try to reinforce or at least bring supplies to the soldiers. Secretary of State William Henry Seward urged Lincoln to retreat from Fort Sumter and to make a symbolic stand by reinforcing Fort Pickens. He warned that an outbreak of hostilities at Fort Sumter would drive the states of the upper South into the Confederacy and dramatically increase the chances for a lasting division. Seward argued that the seven states of the lower South could eventually be coaxed back into the Union; if combined with some or all of the other eight slaveholding states, they would have the resources to sustain themselves independently and perhaps even to resist an attempt to restore the Union by force.

Decision. Establishing that he, not the better-known and more experienced Seward, would be the head of the administration, Lincoln decided to send supplies to the garrison at Fort Sumter. Upon receiving notice of this intention before the belated arrival of the delivery ships, which also carried reinforcements, Jefferson Davis ordered the Confederate commander in Charleston to bombard Fort Sumter. Opening fire on 12 April 1861, the Confederate forces destroyed the fortress in a day and forced the federal garrison to surrender. The Confederate flag replaced the United States flag at the military installation on 14 April. The next day, Lincoln called for seventy-five thousand volunteers to suppress the rebellion. As Seward had predicted, this announcement sparked a powerful secession movement in the upper South. Virginia, Tennessee, North Carolina, and Arkansas soon left the Union. These states dramatically strengthened the Confederacy by sharply increasing the white population available to fight, the supply of food and livestock, and the capacity for industrial production.

Sources:

Daniel W. Crofts, *Reluctant Confederates: Upper South Unionists in the Secession Crisis* (Chapel Hill: University of North Carolina Press, 1989);

David Potter, *The Impending Crisis, 1848–1861* (New York: Harper & Row, 1976).

POLITICS IN THE WARTIME NORTH

Persistence of Partisanship. The outbreak of war prompted a strong bipartisan expression of Unionism. After a highly publicized visit to the White House, Stephen A. Douglas declared from his home in Chicago that "There can be no neutrals in this war, only patriots—or traitors." But Lincoln entered office determined to govern as a Republican president, not as the head of a coalition. He did not invite any active Democrats to join his cabinet, although he carefully balanced the group between former Whigs and former Democrats. Patronage remained the glue of partisanship, and Lincoln proved to be a master at accommodating different factions. On the other hand, military appointments—also an important form of patronage—called for special bipartisan handling, and Lincoln was careful to recognize the applications of qualified Democratic commanders. Although party lines thus remained important, the Republicans enjoyed an overwhelming political advantage at the outset

A NEW BIRTH OF FREEDOM

President Abraham Lincoln did not often deliver speeches rallying support for the Union war effort. The leading spokesman for the North was Whig statesman Edward Everett of Massachusetts, whose efforts to summarize the federal cause for the benefit of American audiences and foreign readers led to his invitation to deliver the main address on 19 November 1863, at the dedication of a cemetery at the Gettysburg battlefield. After Everett's oration, Lincoln offered some dedicatory remarks:

Four score and seven years ago our fathers brought forth on this continent, a new nation, conceived in Liberty, and dedicated to the proposition that all men are created equal.

Now we are engaged in a great civil war, testing whether that nation, or any nation so conceived and so dedicated, can long endure. We are met on a great battle-field of that war. We have come to dedicate a portion of that field, as a final resting place for those who here gave their lives that this nation might live. It is altogether fitting and proper that we should do this.

But in a larger sense, we can not dedicate—we can not consecrate—we can not hallow—this ground. The brave men, living and dead, who struggled here, have consecrated it, far above our poor power to add or detract. The world will little note, nor long remember what we say here, but it can never forget what they did here. It is for us the living, rather, to be dedicated here to the unfinished work which they who fought here have thus far so nobly advanced. It is rather for us to be here dedicated to the great task remaining before us—that from these honored dead we take increased devotion to that cause for which they gave the last full measure of devotion—that we here highly resolve that these dead shall not have died in vain—that this nation, under God, shall have a new birth of freedom—and that government of the people, by the people, for the people, shall not perish from the earth.

of the war because the Democratic Party had become concentrated in the South in the years since the Kansas-Nebraska crisis. The Republican advantage increased when Douglas, the most powerful Northern Democrat, died suddenly in June 1861. In the Thirty-seventh Congress that symbolically mustered on 4 July 1861, the Republicans were able to pass many of the legislative proposals with which they had rounded out the party platform in recent years. Chief among these were the Homestead Act, which provided free land to settlers on the public domain, and the Morrill Act, which provided land grants to states to endow colleges. Both of these measures had been passed by the last Republican Congress but vetoed by President Buchanan. The absence of Southern Democrats also made it possible for the first

The first reading of the Emancipation Proclamation before the cabinet; painting by Francis B. Carpenter (Library of Congress)

time to charter a transcontinental railroad, as there was now no protest to the adoption of a northern route.

Border States. In addition to his military responsibilities as commander in chief, Lincoln's primary political concern at the outset of the war was to prevent the remaining slaveholding states from leaving the Union. Delaware quickly aligned itself on the federal side, but secession movements were strong in Maryland, Missouri, and Kentucky, which stood to add another 45 percent to the white population of the Confederacy, almost 40 percent to its livestock supply, and 80 percent to its manufacturing capacity. The administration acted forcefully to forestall disunion in nearby Maryland, arresting legislators who favored the calling of a secession convention and holding them in prison until the state was stabilized. In contrast, Lincoln adopted a more restrained approach to his native state of Kentucky, whose declaration of neutrality he showed a willingness to respect. Meanwhile, the situation in Missouri was utterly chaotic, and early fighting in the fiercely divided state provided the context for a crucial decision by Lincoln. Shortly after assuming command of Union forces in the Western theater, John C. Frémont issued a proclamation freeing the slaves and confiscating the property of Confederate supporters in Missouri. This order went well beyond a recent congressional enactment providing for forfeiture of property, including slaves, that were used directly to support the rebel army, and it went well beyond the military policy developed by Gen. Benjamin Butler to regard runaway slaves as "contrabands of war" and disclaim any duty to return them to Southern masters. Lincoln, who had repeatedly insisted that the federal purpose was solely to preserve the Union, and not to end slavery, countermanded Frémont's order. He wrote to a friend that emancipation "must be settled according to laws made by law-makers, and not by military proclamations," and he warned that Frémont's policy risked the secession of Kentucky. "To lose Kentucky is nearly the same as to lose the whole game," he reasoned. Unionists did establish control of the Kentucky government, partly in reaction to a Confederate invasion of the supposedly neutral state in September. But Lincoln's decision cut sharply into his support among antislavery Northerners.

Transformation of the War. The failure of George B. McClellan's much-anticipated Peninsula invasion in the Seven Days' battles of 25 June–2 July 1862 prompted a fundamental rethinking of the Union war effort. The retreat from Richmond left no end to the war in sight and clearly called for a revamped Union strategy. The response took several different forms. A second Confiscation Act, passed in July 1862, declared forfeit the property of rebels and provided that slaves "shall be deemed captives of war and shall be forever free." In the same month Congress passed legislation authorizing the president to order state militia into federal service for up to nine months; this legislation mostly served to stimulate states to recruit volunteers to meet federal requisitions of troops, but in Ohio, Wisconsin, Indiana, and Pennsylvania a draft was put into effect to satisfy the quotas. Resistance to the draft in turn led the administration to extend across the country its suspension of the writ of habeas corpus and to provide military judicial proceedings for "all persons discouraging volunteer enlistments, resisting militia drafts, or guilty of any disloyal practice affording aid and comfort to the rebels." The beginnings of conscription, which would be expanded one year later, were

"Emancipated Negroes Celebrating the Emancipation Proclamation of President Lincoln"; illustration from *Le Monde Illustré*, 21 March 1863

one of several important ways in which the rejuvenated Union war effort undermined the powers of states. Another significant federal incursion was the National Banking Act passed by Congress in February 1863. The creation of a system of federally chartered banks, aided by taxes that drove out of existence the banknotes of state-chartered banks, helped to fund the Federal army and established the financial framework of the nation until the introduction of the Federal Reserve system in the twentieth century.

Emancipation. The most important rethinking of the war after the Seven Days' battles was Lincoln's decision to issue a proclamation emancipating the slaves. In early May 1862 he had rescinded an emancipation decree issued by Union commander David Hunter for South Carolina, Georgia, and Florida. By July, however, the president felt that emancipation was a military necessity. Seward persuaded him to withhold the announcement until it could follow a Union victory, which turned out to mean waiting until McClellan's army turned back Lee's invasion of the North at the battle of Antietam on 17 September 1862. Five days later, Lincoln warned that slaves in the Confederacy would be "forever free" if the rebellion did not end by 1 January 1863. Because military necessity provided justification for the decree, it did not affect slaves in the loyal border states or in areas of the South under federal control. Accordingly, the *Times* of London taunted that "where he has no power Mr. Lincoln will set the negroes free; where he retains power he will consider them as slaves." But Lincoln remained scrupulous about the constitutional basis for emancipation.

Ultimately he would make sponsorship of a constitutional amendment resolving the issue the main political priority of his administration.

Radical Criticism. The Emancipation Proclamation did not erase the distrust of Lincoln that radicals had developed. Part of the friction resulted from conflicting ambitions. Unlike Seward, Chase never surrendered his ambition to be president, and he sought to undermine the administration even while serving it as secretary of the treasury. But important policy matters were also at stake. For example, Lincoln retained what radicals considered a hopelessly outdated and appalling interest in the idea of colonizing the former slave population. As the war turned in favor of the North, plans for reconstruction of conquered states like Louisiana became an increasingly important area of contention between the administration and its radical critics. In December 1863 Lincoln proposed to grant pardon and amnesty to rebels who swore allegiance to the United States and accepted emancipation; he would consider recognition of a state government formed by declared loyalists equal to at least 10 percent of the voting population in 1860. Radicals responded with a bill sponsored by Sen. Benjamin Wade of Ohio and Rep. Henry Winter Davis of Maryland requiring promises of loyalty from 50 percent rather than 10 percent of the prewar voters and disfranchising former Confederates. When Lincoln vetoed the law in July 1864, Wade and Davis published a manifesto condemning him for violating "the rights of humanity, and the principles of Republican government." Although Lincoln had outmaneuvered Chase to win nomination for reelection, the 1856 Republican presidential candidate, John C. Frémont, led a third-party bid to unseat Lincoln.

Conservative Criticism. Even more worrisome to Lincoln were his critics from the other side of the political spectrum. Emancipation, conscription, and the suspension of habeas corpus became powerful issues for Democrats, who made modest gains in the congressional elections of 1862. As the war slowed to a grinding, deadly stalemate in the spring of 1864, critics argued that Lincoln stood in the way of a negotiated settlement. They called on him to agree to an armistice and to enter into negotiations with Southern representatives, but he realized that if the North stopped fighting temporarily it might be unable to resume the war. Critics also argued that emancipation clouded the prospects for peaceful reunion, but Lincoln adamantly refused to retreat from the position that emancipation was both a strategic necessity and a sacred moral commitment. "I should be damned in time & in eternity for so doing," he declared. At the same time, he concluded as the Democrats prepared to hold their national convention in late August 1864 that "it seems exceedingly probable that this Administration will not be re-elected. Then it will be my duty to so cooperate with the President elect, as to save the Union between the election and the inauguration; as he will have secured his election on such ground that he can not possibly save it afterwards."

Reelection. Lincoln's pessimism notwithstanding, he moved adroitly to strengthen his chances for reelection. A reshuffling of patronage at the New York customhouse improved his position in that key state, and after a lengthy negotiation he forced the resignation of Postmaster General Montgomery Blair, one of the most conservative members of the Cabinet, in exchange for Frémont's withdrawal from the race. The commander in chief also paid special attention to balloting by soldiers, who overwhelmingly voted Republican. In addition to these measures, Lincoln benefited from Democratic divisions that the national convention made evident. The Peace wing of the party, led by Clement Vallandigham of Ohio, pushed through a platform more critical of the war than nominee Gen. George B. McClellan could present to the men he had once commanded in the Union army or sustain before the country. Most important, Lincoln benefited from the smashing Union military victories in September 1864 at Atlanta, Mobile Bay, and Cedar Creek. With Union triumph now in sight, he easily won reelection in November 1864. His return to office ensured ultimate federal success, for the reins of power remained in the hands of a president who would persist until the rebellion had been suppressed.

Sources:

David Herbert Donald, *Lincoln* (New York: Simon & Schuster, 1995);

Philip Shaw Paludan, *The Presidency of Abraham Lincoln* (Lawrence: University Press of Kansas, 1994).

POLITICS IN THE WARTIME SOUTH

Constitution. The Confederate Constitution differed in several significant ways from its model, the United States Constitution. Most notably, the charter of government reflected a determination to prevent state sovereignty from giving way to consolidation of powers in the central government. Attempting to avoid the means by which centralization had increased since 1788, the Confederate Constitution omitted clauses authorizing Congress to levy taxes and make expenditures to promote the general welfare of the people. Appropriations for internal improvements were limited to projects in navigable waterways and were required to recoup government outlays. State legislatures could impeach some officers of the general government, and although the constitution authorized a Supreme Court none was created by Congress, leaving state courts to dominate the interpretation of the constitution. The amendment process enabled only three states to call a constitutional convention, as compared to the three-fourths of all states required by the United States Constitution, and did not provide for Congress to propose amendments to the states. The Confederate drafters also adjusted the branches of government. Cabinet officers were permitted to sit in Congress, and the president, who was to serve for one six-year term, was provided with line-item veto power. Finally, the constitution acknowledged the centrality of slavery to the new nation. The document candidly used the word *slave*, which had been carefully left out of the United States Constitution. One much-debated clause barred the international slave trade, reflecting the interests of slave-exporting states of the upper South. Other clauses revisited recent controversies over slavery by providing a slave code for any Confederate territories and prohibiting Congress from passing any laws "denying or impairing the right of property in negro slaves."

Nationalism. The creation of the Confederate States of America involved not only the design of political institutions but the development of a politically charged culture. Confederate nationalism was promoted in schools, in churches, and in popular songs and literature. In this stimulation of a collective identity, Southerners recognized themselves as participants in a nation-building process. Popular music of the era included several Southern adaptations of "The Marseillaise," which the French Revolution had made the universal anthem of nationalism. Similarly, Secretary of State Robert Toombs compared the Confederacy to the unification of Italy, observing that Southerners had responded to "reasons no less grave and valid than those which actuated the people of Sicily and Naples." The most important model for Confederate nationalism was naturally the most familiar. Notwithstanding their modifications of the inherited structures of government, Southerners left no doubt that they regarded the Confederacy as the authentic heir to the legacy of the American Revolution. The Confederate seal featured an image of George Washington. Jefferson

Jefferson Davis being sworn in as president of the Confederacy, Montgomery, Alabama, 18 February 1861

Davis, inaugurated on Washington's birthday in front of a statue of the Founding Father, devoted much of his inaugural address to the parallels between 1776 and 1861.

Mobilization. As in the Union, military frustration prompted the Confederate government to depart from its original plans for waging the war. The Peninsula invasion threatening Richmond in the spring of 1862 led to a dramatic expansion of central government powers. The Confederate Congress enacted the first conscription law in American history in April 1862, requiring able white males between the ages of eighteen and thirty-five to serve in the military for three years. The Congress also authorized President Davis to declare martial law and suspend the writ of habeas corpus in areas under attack, although the legislature guarded these powers by extending them to Davis only for several limited periods that totaled sixteen months over the course of the war. One year later, the Confederacy resorted to taxation to finance its bid for independence. The measure particularly

antagonized Southerners because Congress provided for a "tax in kind," consisting of 10 percent of a farm family's nonsubsistence agricultural produce, to compensate for the rapidly deteriorating value of Confederate currency. The three thousand agents of the Confederate government required to collect the tax served as vivid reminders that the Southern quest for national independence could not easily be reconciled with the desire to limit the powers of the central government.

Class Tensions. In addition to clashing with the principle of state sovereignty, Confederate nationalism deepened Southern divisions about democracy within the states. Secession had been led by the slaveholding class that comprised about one-fourth of white families and especially by the planters, customarily defined as owners of twenty or more slaves, who comprised about 10 percent of white Southerners. Several Confederate policies fueled the resentment of yeomen (landowning farmers who had few or no slaves) who felt that privileged South-

THE CORNERSTONE OF THE CONFEDERACY

Confederate president Jefferson Davis avoided celebrations of slavery for fear of antagonizing world opinion, but Vice President Alexander H. Stevens did not hesitate to proclaim the peculiar institution "the cornerstone" of Southern nationalism: . . . Not to be tedious in enumerating the numerous changes for the better, allow me to allude to one other—though last, not least: the new Constitution has put at rest *forever* all the agitating questions relation to our peculiar institutions—African slavery as it exists among us—the proper *status* of the negro in our form of civilization. *This was the immediate cause of the late rupture and present revolution.* Jefferson, in his forecast, had anticipated this, as the 'rock upon which the old Union would split.' He was right. What was conjecture with him, is now a realized fact. But whether he fully comprehended the great truth upon which that rock *stood* and *stands*, may be doubted. *The prevailing ideas entertained by him and most of the leading statesmen at the time of the formation of the old Constitution were, that the enslavement of the African was in violation of the laws of nature; that it was wrong in principle, socially, morally and politically.* It was an evil they knew not well how to deal with; but the general opinion of the men of that day was, that, somehow or other, in the order of Providence, the institution would be evanescent and pass away.

Our new Government is founded upon exactly the opposite ideas; its foundations are laid, its cornerstone rests, upon the great truth that the negro is not equal to the white man; that slavery, subordination to the superior race, is his natural and moral condition. This, our new Government, is the first, in the history of the world, based upon this great physical, philosophical, and moral truth."

Source: Alexander H. Stephens, "Slavery the Cornerstone of the Confederacy" (1861).

---

erners did not share fairly in the burdens and sacrifices of the struggle. The "tax-in-kind" despised by yeomen farmers, for example, did not extend to wealth held in slaves. Most notoriously, when Congress raised the upper age limit of the conscription law from thirty-five to forty-five in September 1862, subjecting more household heads to the draft, it exempted one white male for every plantation with twenty or more slaves. Defended as necessary to maintain order on plantations, the law became a focal point for the observation that the conflict was "a rich man's war and a poor man's fight." To be sure, the same refrain echoed through the North, where one of the most violent riots in American history exploded in New York City in July 1863 upon implementation of a draft that exempted anyone who could afford to pay a $300 commutation fee. But in the South the reinforcement of class hierarchy was not merely a social and economic fact but an ideological principle. In several states secessionist leaders sought to use the fresh start of the Confederacy to redress what they perceived as the recent democratic excesses of the United States. The paradoxical relationship between this conservative impulse and the imperatives of war was best illustrated in Virginia, where the legislature was simultaneously presented in November 1861 with measures calling on soldiers to reenlist and eliminating their right to vote if they were not property owners.

Opposition to the War. Pockets of Southern resistance to secession existed from the outset of the war. A referendum held by residents in western Virginia in October 1861 approved the detachment of their counties from the Old Dominion, and the new state of West Virginia entered the Union in June 1863. East Tennessee was a bastion of Unionist sentiment that Confederate authorities vigorously but unsuccessfully sought to suppress. As the war lengthened and class divisions deepened, other antiwar centers developed in Arkansas, northern Alabama and Georgia, and especially in western North Carolina. After the battles of Vicksburg and Gettysburg, editor William W. Holden of the Raleigh *North Carolina Standard* became the leading Southern spokesman for the view that the costs of the Confederate war effort were too much for the implausible prospects of success. Holden proposed that North Carolina open its own peace negotiations with the federal government, and in 1864 he ran for governor on a peace platform. Although he was defeated in the summer election, his assessment gained additional supporters after the string of Confederate disasters that began with the fall of Atlanta. But the Southerners who reconsidered their commitment did not include Jefferson Davis. As Abraham Lincoln had not wavered in his promise of emancipation or his resolution to continue the war until the Union was restored, Davis refused to contemplate any sort of peace that did not include recognition of Southern independence. As a result, hopes for political negotiations to end the war remained futile.

Factionalism. Like many emerging nations, the Confederacy was eager to present to the world an appearance of unity rather than acknowledging internal political divisions. Political parties accordingly were not organized, consistent with a longstanding notion that true patriotism did not admit of partisanship. In practice, however, the absence of parties contributed significantly to the bitter factionalism that characterized Confederate politics. In the North, Lincoln was able to use the party system to rally supporters and deflect critics. Republicans disagreed, often strenuously, but in the end they usually came together to retain control of the government against a Democratic challenge. Davis in contrast could not count on other political leaders to advance their self-interest by coming to his defense, and he could not easily draw policy lines that separated friends and foes of the administration. In the absence of the framework that the two-party system provided for identifying and discussing issues, political conflict in the Confederacy most often centered on Davis himself. The resulting personal bitterness pervading public life only reinforced Davis's tendency to immerse himself in the details of administration rather than drawing upon the abilities of other Confederate leaders.

Sources:

Paul D. Escott, *After Secession: Jefferson Davis and the Failure of Confederate Nationalism* (Baton Rouge: Louisiana State University Press, 1978);

Emory M. Thomas, *The Confederate Nation, 1861–1865* (New York: Harper & Row, 1979).

RECONSTRUCTION

Alternatives. The main tendencies of Reconstruction might be appreciated by comparing the process to scenarios that some observers predicted, or recommended, but that did not in fact take place after the war. For example, while many Northerners argued that justice demanded severe punishment for the leaders of an insurrection that had cost over six hundred thousand lives and millions of dollars, little retribution took place. The federal government did not systematically confiscate planters' lands. Jefferson Davis spent two years waiting in federal prison for a trial that was dismissed shortly after it began, but commandant Henry Wirz of the notorious Andersonville prison was the only Confederate executed for his role in the war. Similarly, some Confederates suggested that the rebellion might be sustained as a guerrilla movement in the hills and mountains of the South, while others fled to Mexico and Brazil. Most returned home, however, and tried to rebuild their lives. Although the armed resistance of the Ku Klux Klan and other white Southern groups would be an important part of Reconstruction, there was no coordinated campaign to wear down federal authority by force. The campaign of violence to subordinate blacks also differed markedly from the race war that many white Southerners regarded as the likely outcome of emancipation. The fact that these scenarios did not come to pass suggests the strength of the desire for a peaceful reconciliation and the limits of the upheaval that took place in Reconstruction. Yet it should also be noted that in other parts of the world the end of slavery during the nineteenth century had led to the establishment of separate political castes. The progress of former slaves not only to freedom but to full rights of citizenship, however imperfectly enforced, was an extraordinary revolution.

Presidential Reconstruction. Because the Civil War ended while Congress was not in session, and not sched-

FORTY ACRES AND A MULE

In January 1865 Gen. William T. Sherman ordered the setting aside of land abandoned by planters in the lowcountry of South Carolina for distribution to former slaves. Each family would receive a homestead of forty acres, and Sherman indicated that the army could lend them the use of mules. This promise, likely the basis for the phrase "forty acres and a mule" associated with Reconstruction, was rescinded by President Andrew Johnson in September 1865. When Gen. Oliver O. Howard, head of the Freedmen's Bureau, informed freedmen of the policy reversal, they presented a formal response:

General, we want Homesteads, we were promised Homesteads by the government. If it does not carry out the promises its agents made to us, if the government having concluded to befriend its late enemies and to neglect to observe the principles of common faith between its self and us its allies in the war you said was over, now takes away from them all right to the soil they stand upon save such as they can get by again working for *your* late and their *all time* enemies . . . we are left in a more unpleasant condition than our former. . . . You will see this is not the condition of really freemen.

Source: Eric Foner, *Reconstruction: America's Unfinished Revolution, 1863–1877* (New York: Harper & Row, 1988), p. 160.

uled to return to Washington for almost eight months, President Andrew Johnson was in a strong position to define Reconstruction policy during the crucial period after he took office upon the assassination of Abraham Lincoln. The former tailor's apprentice from Tennessee had achieved his national political reputation as a spokesman for Southern yeomen and as a firm Unionist, and observers expected his policies to be guided by his oft-quoted declaration that "treason must be made odious, and traitors must be punished and impoverished." To the contrary, however, he did little to interfere with the political structure of the states that had seceded. He did not use federal patronage, one of his most important resources, to broaden Southern political leadership. He appointed provisional governors in each state who were committed to the Union but not to genuine reform. Even his boldest choice, North Carolina governor William W. Holden, had "unqualified opposition to what is called negro suffrage." More generally, Johnson extended amnesty to almost all participants in the rebellion. His other plans similarly sought little change. He overruled policies providing for at least limited redistribution of land to former slaves, and he did not attempt to interfere with the adoption of the "Black Codes" by which Southern whites sought to limit the meaning of emancipation. Requiring Southern states only to nullify their ordinances of secession, ratify the Thirteenth Amendment, and re-

Freedmen in Jacksonville, Florida, in the mid 1870s

pudiate the state debts incurred in the rebellion, he notified Congress shortly after it assembled in December 1865 that Reconstruction was finished.

Congress and the President. Johnson's Reconstruction policy did not satisfy the Republican majority in Congress, including moderates as well as those committed to a radical restructuring of Southern society. In the eyes of many Northerners, the folly of the President's approach was most clearly illustrated when the Georgia legislature elected Alexander H. Stephens, the former vice president of the Confederacy, to represent the state in the Senate. Congress denied the seating of the Southern delegations and set up a Joint Committee on Reconstruction to formulate a more meaningful political expression of the outcome of the war. This process resulted in passage of the Civil Rights Act of 1866 and reorganization of the Freedmen's Bureau, the federal agency chartered at the end of the war to facilitate the transition from slavery to freedom for African Americans. When Johnson unexpectedly vetoed these bills, Congress overrode his objections. The first time in American history that Congress had passed significant legislation after a presidential veto, this confrontation marked the outbreak of open hostilities between Johnson and the Republicans in Congress. Johnson attacked Republicans, especially the radical members, in a highly publicized speaking tour and urged Southern states not to ratify the proposed Fourteenth Amendment. Congress responded by reducing the size of the Supreme Court to prevent Johnson from filling vacancies and by passing a Tenure of Office Act that required the president to seek congressional approval before he appointed or removed cabinet members. When Johnson tested the restriction by firing Secretary of War Edwin Stanton, a supporter of the congressional radicals, the House of Representatives impeached him in the spring of 1868.

Although the vote acquitting the president showed that he had come within a single vote of removal from office, several Republican moderates had expressed a willingness to block the impeachment process because they were wary of a triumph for the radical wing of the party and because they were satisfied by reassurances that he would no longer try to undermine Republican policy.

Radical Reconstruction. The extension of the Freedmen's Bureau and passage of the Civil Rights Act of 1866 were preludes to adoption of the principal framework for congressional policy, the Military Reconstruction Act of 2 March 1867. This legislation divided the former Confederacy into five military districts until each state held a constitutional convention. To obtain readmission to the Union, the states were required to provide for black male suffrage and to ratify the Fourteenth Amendment. One important guide to the ideas underlying this Reconstruction program was the emphasis on the guarantee of suffrage and the absence of any provision for redistribution of land. In part the failure of land redistribution reflected the sanctity of property rights in American thought, but the Republican priorities also expressed a judgment about the relative importance of political and economic power. Representative James M. Ashley of Ohio declared that "if I were a black man, with the chains just stricken from my limbs . . . and you should offer me the ballot, or a cabin and forty acres of cotton land, I would take the ballot." Republicans called for the elimination of legal barriers that prevented African Americans from participating in public life on an equal footing with whites, and the Fourteenth Amendment provided for a strengthening of the federal government to enforce this political equality and to provide equal opportunity for economic advancement. The radicalism of conservative Republicans did not envision a society divided into sharply defined, antagonistic classes by the ownership of property.

Southern Political Leadership. The Republican governments that emerged in the South during Reconstruction drew on several different bases of support. By far the most important was the enfranchised freedmen. African Americans comprised a majority of the population in South Carolina, Mississippi, and Louisiana; almost half of the population in Alabama, Georgia, and Florida; approximately 40 percent of the population in Virginia and North Carolina; and about one-quarter of the population in Arkansas and Texas. African Americans not only provided the core of votes for the Republican Party but also some of its most important leaders, including Hiram R. Revels and Blanche K. Bruce of Mississippi, both of whom served in the United States Senate; Robert B. Elliott and Robert Smalls of South Carolina, who served in the House of Representatives; and P. B. S. Pinchback, who became governor of Louisiana. Reconstruction could not be sustained without white support as well, which the Democratic opponents of reform divided into two groups. The more frequently excoriated were settlers

Illustration from an 1871 issue of *Frank Leslie's Illustrated News* of Klansmen preparing to murder a freedman

from the North, derided as "carpetbaggers" because they supposedly brought with them no more than the contents of a small suitcase made from old carpet and sought to make their fortune by corruptly exploiting the South. In fact, transplanted Northerners varied widely in background and motives and included such thoughtful newcomers as Albion Tourgée, who drew on his experiences in North Carolina in his novel *A Fool's Errand* (1879). The bulk of white supporters were native Southerners, whom Democrats preferred to pretend did not exist but acknowledged when necessary as "scalawags," a term for low-grade livestock. These Republicans were particularly concentrated in the hill country that in many states had long fought political domination by the plantation districts. Other scalawags were planters or entrepreneurs, particularly former Whigs who felt more at home in the Republican than in the Democratic Party. Democratic hatred for scalawags is well illustrated by the postwar career of Gen. James Longstreet, one of the leading commanders in the Confederate army. To most Southerners his military record could not overcome his lapse into Republicanism, and he became the highest-ranking figure not to be honored by a monument when he died.

Republican Achievement. For the constitutional conventions required by Congress and the Republican leaders that came into power under the new governments, the chief priority was the establishment of public school systems. Their efforts in this direction established a principle of state responsibility for education that promised to transform the South. More controversial were attempts to make the new public schools racially integrated, a point of overlap between the emphasis on education and the attention of Republican legislatures to civil rights issues. Reconstruction governments enacted a variety of antidiscrimination laws governing access to railroads, theaters, and other public accommodations, but many of these would remain unenforced from the outset, and almost all would be displaced with the hardening of segregation at the end of the century. Republicans in the South also sought strenuously to promote economic development, especially through aid to railroad construction. The rail lines running through the region multiplied rapidly, but as in the Midwest, the dream of general prosperity through public investment in transportation usually proved an illusion. The promotion of railroads in the end undercut Republican governments because many associated them with the taxes necessary to pay unsuccessful bonds, the corruption that accompanied railroad construction everywhere in the country, and the loss of independence felt by hill-country farmers as they became enmeshed in wider commercial markets.

Sources:

Eric Anderson and Alfred A. Moss Jr., eds., *The Facts of Reconstruction: Essays in Honor of John Hope Franklin* (Baton Rouge: Louisiana State University Press, 1991);

Michael Les Benedict, *A Compromise of Principle: Congressional Republicans and Reconstruction, 1863–1869* (New York: Norton, 1974);

Eric Foner, *Reconstruction: America's Unfinished Revolution, 1863–1877* (New York: Harper & Row, 1988).

TOWARD AN INDUSTRIAL POLITY

The Grant Administration. The campaign slogan of Ulysses S. Grant in 1868, "Let Us Have Peace," expressed a waning of support for additional federal initiatives to reconstruct the South. Grant's margin of victory over Democratic candidate Horatio Seymour was remarkably narrow considering the national admiration for the victorious Union commander, and Seymour may well have carried a majority of the white voters in the country. Most of the Southern states had been readmitted to the Union in June, when the Fourteenth Amendment was declared in effect. One of the most powerful Radical Republicans, Rep. Thaddeus Stevens of Pennsylvania, died later in the summer; as he had requested, he was buried in a racially integrated cemetery "to illustrate in my death the principles which I advocated through a long life, Equality of Man before his Creator." Before Grant's inauguration took place Congress submitted to the states the last of the Reconstruction amendments to the Constitution, the Fifteenth Amendment prohibiting states from discriminating on the basis of race in voting laws. Vigilant federal attention to the South was not over. To the contrary, violent attempts to thwart Reconstruction prompted Congress to enact far-reaching Enforcement Acts in 1870 and 1871. But the impulse to translate the meaning of the Civil War into law was considerably weaker than it had been a few years earlier. This development was acutely recognized by advocates of woman suffrage, who were bitterly disappointed that the Fifteenth Amendment, like the Fourteenth, failed to bar discrimination on the basis of sex.

Organizing Capital. The politics of the sectional conflict gradually gave way to the politics of large-scale economic development. The federal government from 1862 to 1872 gave railroads millions of dollars in aid and more than one hundred million acres of land to advance construction, concentrating on the transcontinental routes mapped during the war. Mining companies also benefited from the donation of millions of acres of valuable land through legislation such as the National Mineral Act of 1866. If the principle underlying these grants did not differ from previous attempts by state governments to stimulate economic growth, the interests of corporations like the Pennsylvania Railroad and the Union Pacific Railroad defied the traditional geographic boundaries of politics. The potential of these firms to blur even the national boundaries of politics was illustrated by one of the major scandals of the era, the revelation that the Crédit Mobilier firm, contracted to build the transcontinental railroad, had paid inflated prices and given free shares to government officials, including the vice president and the speaker of the House of Representatives.

Organizing Labor. Workers responded to the political influence of pooled capital by exploring political strategies to defend their interests. These interests, of course, varied widely in an economy that still included many independent artisans as well as unskilled operatives in mechanized factories. But workers increasingly found common ground, increasing the number of national labor unions from three in 1865 to twenty-one by the early 1870s. The transition from the politics of sectional conflict to the politics of the Gilded Age could best be observed in Massachusetts, a hotbed of the antislavery movement and the most industrialized state in the country. When the state legislature denied a petition by the shoemakers' union, the Knights of Saint Crispin, to form cooperatives that would provide more profits to workers, a coalition of unions formed a labor reform party. In its first statewide election the new organization elected twenty-three members of the legislature. The party helped to create the first Bureau of Labor Statistics in the country, and Massachusetts congressman George F. Hoar suggested that the federal government should establish a similar commission to collect and publish information about wages, hours, and working conditions. In the ensuing debate, Henry Wilson of Massachusetts summarized the feelings of many longtime Republicans when he shuddered that he "never heard the term 'laboring class' here without the same sort of sensation which I used to have on hearing the word 'slave.'" He exhorted the Senate never to acknowledge the existence of "classes in this land of equality." Wilson's comments reflected the logic of antebellum Northern politics that labor was either slave labor or free labor and the reluctance of his

Ulysses S. Grant, the Republican president whose administration was rocked by scandal during the final years of Reconstruction

generation to accept the idea that wage laborers might have only an artificial freedom.

Machine Politics. With the waning of the sense of crisis that shaped public life from the 1850s, American politics came to focus more narrowly than ever before on the scramble for government-created wealth. Unlike the patronage battles between Federalists and Jeffersonian Republicans or between Whigs and Jacksonian Democrats, the Gilded Age contests between Republicans and Democrats seemed to be devoid of ideas. The emergence of Simon Cameron as the most powerful figure in Pennsylvania politics symbolized the transition. He had been thoroughly overshadowed in Abraham Lincoln's cabinet by William Henry Seward and Salmon P. Chase, who shared Cameron's talents for political infighting, but also articulated visions of the future of the nation. Forced to resign from the War Department on grounds of mismanagement, Cameron resurfaced after the war as the representative of the Pennsylvania Railroad and patron of political machines in Philadelphia and Pittsburgh. These interests propelled him into the United States Senate, where he served with other powerful political bosses like Roscoe Conkling of New York, John A. Logan of Illinois, Zachariah Chandler of Michigan, and Oliver P. Morton of Indiana. Their bases of support reflected trends that disturbed many observers. Cameron and other bosses relied on the large corporations growing out of the expansion of the economy, who received the federal largesse in land grants and lobbied state governments on daily decisions that affected business. Critics also deplored the urban political machines—most notoriously the "Tweed Ring" in New York City—which built upon the political power of immigrants as a voting bloc. A parallel on a national level was the Republican strategy to mobilize Union veterans by seeking pensions and "waving the bloody shirt" to taint Democrats with Southern secessionism.

Republican Schism. The transformation of politics after the war was dramatized by the rupture of the Republican Party in the election of 1872. The divisions in the party had largely crystallized two years earlier in a struggle over one of the main priorities of the Grant administration, the annexation of Santo Domingo (now the Dominican Republic). Charles Sumner, chairman of the Senate Foreign Relations Committee, successfully led the opposition to the treaty, primarily because he saw the expansionist measure as a threat to Haiti, the only republic in the western hemisphere governed by African Americans. He was joined not only by Democrats eager to thwart the Grant administration but also by Republicans like Lyman Trumbull and Carl Schurz. These reformers wanted the administration to focus on the challenge to government presented by corporate interests and urban machines; their central priority was the enactment of civil service legislation, which had been first introduced in Congress in 1865. Grant in turn strengthened his ties to the so-called Stalwart wing of the party headed by Conkling and Morton. Despairing of winning the Republican Party back from Grant and his allies, the reformers organized a separate Liberal Republican campaign in the presidential election of 1872. They eventually chose as their nominee Horace Greeley, longtime editor of the *New York Tribune.* The subsequent campaign departed sharply from the established pattern of politics, particularly after the Democrats decided to back Greeley as well. It was odd for Greeley or Charles Francis Adams, leaders of the antislavery movement, to oppose the Republican Party that they had helped to found while men less motivated by principle, such as Conkling and Morton, represented the call to sustain racial progress in the South. The incongruity reflected the shift away from the issues that had long dominated politics. In this transition, the reform constituency of the Liberal Republican movement would increasingly find no comfortable base in national politics.

Politics of Depression. The long-term deflationary period touched off by the Panic of 1873 created a new political environment. Massive joblessness caused relations between capital and labor to loom larger on the national agenda. The leading labor issues of the immediate postwar era, the eight-hour day and formation of cooperative enterprises among workers, gave way in the most severe phases of the depression to a demand for public relief. Bitter labor disputes in the mining and railroad industries during 1874–1877 pointed toward the question that would soon emerge at the forefront of labor matters: the role of government in strikes pitting employers against employees. The tendency of government to side with capital was foreshadowed by the 1875 strike in the anthracite coal fields of Pennsylvania, in which Gov. John Hartranft intervened to help crush the Workingmen's Benevolent Association. After the strike, testimony by operatives of the Pinkerton Detective Agency who had infiltrated the "Molly Maguires" (a secret labor organization) led to the conviction and execution of twenty miners for alleged acts of violence during the conflict. Similarly, when striking railroad workers stopped traffic on trunk lines through much of the country in the summer of 1877, several governors mobilized militia units, and when they failed, President Rutherford B. Hayes called out U.S. Army troops to crush the general strike. The confrontations added to ranks of workers concluding that their best political strategy might be socialism. As one leading financial editor warned at the end of the strike, "the Communist is here."

Politics of Inflation. The impact of the depression was no less convulsive in agriculture. Farmers hit hard by the worldwide decline in prices began to experiment with independent political parties calling for regulation of railroads and, increasingly, expansion of the money supply. The inflation resulting from circulation of more money in the economy would aid farmers and other debtors because they would be making repayments with money that cost less than at the time their obligations were contracted. In the years between the end of the Civil War and the Panic of 1873, debates over monetary policy had centered on the fate of paper money or "greenbacks" issued by the federal government to finance the Union war effort. When the depression hit, Congress passed the Inflation Bill of 1874, which would have issued more greenbacks in an attempt to boost the economy, but President Grant refused to sign the legislation. A year later he approved Sen. John Sherman's Specie Resumption Act, which called for the government to redeem all circulating paper money in gold by 1879. With the close of the greenback era, farmers and other advocates of inflation—strongly encouraged by silver mining interests—shifted to a demand for coinage of silver, which had been eliminated by the Coinage Act of 1873 and reintroduced in only a limited form by the Specie Resumption Act of 1875. In finance, as in other areas, the definition of issues in the Civil War and Reconstruction era had given way to a new formulation that would preoccupy American politics for the remainder of the nineteenth century.

Compromise of 1877. Voters in 1874 responded to the depression by turning against the party in power. In the House of Representatives, a Republican majority of 110 seats became a Democratic majority of 60 seats. The elections marked the end of Republican dominance and the beginning of a period of remarkably close competition between the two national parties, which translated into an era of legislative deadlock. The presidential election of 1876 illustrated the precarious balance. Demo-cratic candidate Samuel Tilden won a majority of the popular vote but failed by one vote to achieve an electoral majority. Results were disputed in South Carolina, Louisiana, and Florida, where violence and intimidation kept African American supporters of Republican candidate Rutherford B. Hayes from voting; the eligibility of one of the three electors from Oregon was also challenged. Congress referred the controversy to a special electoral commission composed of five representatives, five senators, and five Supreme Court justices; the eight Republicans and seven Democrats voted on straight party lines to award the disputed electoral ballots and the presidency to Hayes. Behind the scenes, meanwhile, Hayes made commitments through his key political advisers to withdraw

THE INDIAN WARS

Between 1850 and 1877 a series of Indian wars plagued the western frontier and added to the woes of the U.S. government. In the 1860s federal authorities implemented a reservation policy. Aside from its claim to humanitarianism, this policy also saved money: it cost less to house and feed Indians on reserved plots of land than it did to fight them. Many tribes were not willing to comply. During the Civil War, the Navajo of the Southwest tried to expel whites from their tribal lands. Between 1862 and 1871 the Apache leaders Mangas Coloradas and Cochise came close to reclaiming most of Arizona. In the Northwest the Modoc and Nez Percé of Oregon rose up in 1872 and 1877, respectively. However, the most famous Indian wars occurred on the Great Plains. In the 1860s the Lakota and Cheyenne attempted to bar white encroachment on their lands in the Dakota Territory, Wyoming, and Montana. Little Crow met defeat in 1863, but Red Cloud managed to wrest some concessions from the federal government in 1868, including the Powder River country as "unceded Indian territory" on which no whites might trespass without Indian consent. With the completion of the Union Pacific Railroad, thousands of settlers streamed into the area. When gold was discovered in the Black Hills in 1874, the Lakota and other tribes began sporadic attacks on the interlopers. On 25 June 1876 the best-known battle of the Indian wars occurred at the Greasy Grass, or Little Bighorn, River, Montana, where a detachment of the Seventh Cavalry under George A. Custer was annihilated. After this defeat, the U.S. Army methodically hunted down the various Indian bands and crushed all resistance in the West by 1890.

Source: Dee Brown, *Bury My Heart at Wounded Knee: An Indian History of the American West* (New York: Holt, Rinehart & Winston, 1970).

the federal troops still posted in the South and to accept the violence-tainted elections that had returned Democrats to power in the governments of the three Southern states. This agreement completed the "redemption" of the South, as the reestablishment of conservative government was called, that had taken place in Virginia and Tennessee in 1869, North Carolina in 1870, Georgia in 1871, Texas in 1873, and Alabama and Arkansas in 1874. Although the national Republican Party sporadically contemplated renewed federal en-

forcement of black voting rights in the South until 1890, the Com promise of 1877 effectively signaled the end of Reconstruction.

Sources:

Morton Keller, *Affairs of State: Public Life in Late Nineteenth Century America* (Cambridge, Mass.: Harvard University Press, 1977);

David Montgomery, *Beyond Equality: Labor and the Radical Republicans, 1862–1872* (New York: Knopf, 1967).

HEADLINE MAKERS

MARTIN ROBINSON DELANY

1812-1885
AFRICAN AMERICAN NATIONALIST

Early Years. Born 6 May 1812 in Charles Town, Virginia, later the capital of West Virginia, Martin Robinson Delany was a third-generation American. All of his grandparents had been imported from Africa as slaves; his father's father was a Mandingo prince and his mother's father was the chieftain of a Golah village. Delany's father remained enslaved but his mother was free, which meant that Delany was born free. Nevertheless, after a Northern traveler taught Delany and his siblings to read, white harassment induced his mother to move the family to Chambersburg, Pennsylvania, where they were soon joined by Delany's father after he was able to purchase his freedom.

Reform Leader. At the age of nineteen Delany moved to Pittsburgh to study divinity and later medicine. He made the city his home for the next quarter of a century, participating in literary and temperance societies as well as the antislavery movement and the call for equal rights for blacks in the North. After briefly publishing his own newspaper, *The Mystery,* Delany joined the staff of Frederick Douglass's newspaper, *North Star,* in 1848. He traveled widely through the Midwest to promote the newspaper, deliver lectures, and report on racial conditions. In November 1850 he enrolled in Harvard Medical School, but because of protest by his fellow students the faculty dismissed him after one term. He returned to

Pittsburgh and became active in resistance to the Fugitive Slave Act, but his own experiences and the course of the nation left him doubtful that the United States would ever recognize African Americans as equal citizens.

Emigration. With the publication of *The Condition, Elevation, Emigration and Destiny of the Colored People of the United States, Politically Considered* (1852), Delany became one of the leading proponents of African American emigration from the United States. "We are a nation within a nation," Delany declared. "We must go from our oppressors." After organizing a National Emigration Convention that met throughout the 1850s, he explored potential homelands in Central America and Africa. Between voyages he joined the approximately five thousand blacks who left the United States for Canada after passage of the Fugitive Slave Act. He kept in touch with the antislavery movement in the United States, however, and helped John Brown's efforts to recruit blacks in Canada for a projected invasion of the South. Delany also advocated emigration in two important publications: *Blake; or the Huts of America* (1859), a novel about a slave rebellion, and *Official Report of the Niger Valley Exploring Party* (1861).

Army Officer. The African American debate over emigration, which assumed a new urgency while the federal government disavowed interference with slavery and refused to enlist black volunteers, quickly subsided after the issuance of the Emancipation Proclamation. Delany became a recruiter for the Fifty-fourth Massachusetts Regiment, which had among its ranks his son Toussaint. (All of his children were named for heroic figures of African descent.) Delany continued his recruiting work for several other regiments; commissioned as a major, the highest-ranking African American in the U.S. Army, he ended the war recruiting former slaves in South Carolina. He remained in the state to serve in the Freedmen's Bureau, helping to develop the educational, judicial, and contractual framework for the transition from slavery to free labor.

Reconstruction. Delany returned to civilian life in the summer of 1868, his eligibility for political office in Radical Reconstruction announced by the admiring *Life and Services of Martin R. Delany* (1868), written by woman journalist Frances Rollins Whipper under the pseudonym Frank A. Rollin. After serving on the Republican State Executive Committee, however, Delany entered into a coalition with Democrats seeking to "redeem" the state. In 1874 he ran for lieutenant governor on the conservative ticket of the Honest Government League, and two years later he supported the victorious gubernatorial candidacy of former Confederate general Wade Hampton. During the campaign Delany was attacked by a mob of African Americans outraged by his political stance. He soon began to focus again on plans for expatriation, aiding a company that transported emigrants to Liberia. His *Principia of Ethnology: The Origin of Races and Color* (1879) drew on biblical interpretation and anthropology to detail the cultural achievements of African peoples and present a final expression of the racial pride that prompted Frederick Douglass to remark, "*I* thank God for making me a man, but Delany thanks him for making him a *black* man." Delany died on 24 January 1885.

Sources:

Dorothy Sterling, *The Making of an Afro-American: Martin Robinson Delany, 1815–1882* (Garden City, N.Y.: Doubleday, 1971);

Eric J. Sundquist, *To Wake the Nations: Race in the Making of American Literature* (Cambridge: Belknap Press of Harvard University Press, 1993).

DOROTHEA DIX

1802-1887
CONSERVATIVE REFORMER

Unitarian Influence. Dorothea Dix carried to fulfillment the ideas about social order and personal harmony advanced by Unitarianism, which an evangelical critic dubbed "the Boston religion" because it was the faith of the elites in that city but enjoyed little following anywhere else. Dix was born 4 April 1802 in Hampden, Maine. She lived at times with the family of the most famous spokesman of the Unitarian faith, minister William Ellery Channing. Although Dix received little formal education, she recognized that teaching offered the readiest outlet for advancing her ideals. Her stern methods antagonized her pupils, however, and her plans to make her mark in education crumbled.

Asylum Lobbyist. In the 1840s Dix shifted her ideas from the schoolroom to a different institutional context, the insane asylum. Like Dix's classes, asylums providing the so-called moral treatment essentially offered a program of education that emphasized the importance of industriousness and emotional tranquillity. Dix became famous as a lobbyist traveling from state to state advocating the establishment of new mental hospitals. In her early campaigns she attracted attention and developed credibility by preparing reports on the condition of the insane in each state. As her reputation spread she was able to rely on individual appeals to state legislators and cooperation with other supporters of asylum construction, including boosters of town development and physicians specializing in the treatment of mental illnesses. By 1850 her efforts had been instrumental in the founding of new mental hospitals in New Jersey, Pennsylvania, Kentucky, Illinois, Tennessee, North Carolina, Alabama, and Mississippi in the seven years since her first crusade in her home state of Massachusetts had ended in the expansion of the Worcester State Asylum.

Land Politics. Dix's most important legislative initiative was a petition to Congress to appropriate ten million acres of public lands to endow state mental hospitals. Introduced in 1848, "Miss Dix's bill," as politicians and journalists usually called the measure, made Dix a fixture in Washington until 1854. She professed to complete disgust with party politics, and among other goals her proposal would insulate public asylums from the political complications of relying entirely on legislative appropriations. At the same time, the bill grew out of a Whig tradition of looking to federal land sales to fund improvement projects, and Dix's strongest supporters were Whigs. She became especially friendly with President Millard Fillmore and through him exercised key decision-making authority in the establishment of the Government Hospital for the Insane (later Saint Elizabeths Hospital). Contrary to her nonpartisan stance, the bill eventually advanced into the national spotlight because of its Whig origins. As bitter infighting broke out in the Democratic Party during debates on the Kansas-Nebraska bill, Southern Democrats relaxed their resistance to Dix's measure in order to set up a veto by Franklin Pierce that for a brief but crucial period helped to rally the party. The tactic illustrated the ways in which the Democratic and Whig parties defined themselves through opposition to each other.

Civil War. During the sectional conflict Dix illustrated the situation of conservative Whigs whose party had dissolved. She supported her friend Fillmore on the Know Nothing ticket in 1856 and her friend John Bell on the Constitutional Union ticket in 1860. When the war came, her political savvy and humanitarian reputation earned her an appointment as Superintendent of Women Nurses for the Union army, a position of greater authority in the federal government than any woman had ever held. She hoped that she would be able to replicate the success of Florence Nightingale five years earlier in not merely providing aid to sick and wounded soldiers but also in providing a political symbol that helped to unify a divided nation. But Dix's war was instead a disastrous series of feuds with the United States Sanitary Commission, the Army medical bureau, and the younger generation of women eager to contribute to the war effort as nurses. The shattering of her reputation revealed the ways in which American values changed during the war, underlining particularly the determination of women to manifest the organizational discipline fostered by the war rather than applauding the self-reliance that Dix sought to exemplify. When she returned to the politics of insane asylums after the war she found that similar growth of bureaucratic management had undermined much of her influence. She died in 1887 after living for years in guest suites of mental hospitals that she had helped to found.

Source:

Thomas J. Brown, *Dorothea Dix: New England Reformer* (Cambridge, Mass.: Harvard University Press, forthcoming, 1998).

WENDELL PHILLIPS

1811-1884
ORATOR

Beacon Hill. Bostonians looking back on the life of Wendell Phillips observed that he was born on Beacon Street and died on Common Street. He epitomized the exclusive social circle that his cousin Oliver Wendell Holmes dubbed "the Brahmins," an allusion to the caste system of India. The Phillips family tree led directly back to one of the Puritan ministers who arrived on the *Arbella* with John Winthrop; Wendell Phillips's father served as a mayor of Boston and was buried in a grave between Samuel Adams and James Otis upon his sudden death after a year in office. Phillips's closest boyhood friends were future historian John Lothrop Motley and Thomas Appleton, son of the visionary manufacturer whose textile mills at Lowell generated fortunes for the Boston elite. Phillips was the only student in his Harvard College class for whom a private carriage called on every Saturday morning.

Abolitionist. After preparing briefly for a career in law Phillips was introduced to the antislavery movement by his future wife, Anne Greene, who had moved upon the death of her parents into the household of her cousin Maria Weston Chapman, one of the central figures in Boston abolitionism. Phillips made his debut for the cause at a meeting in Faneuil Hall after the murder of abolitionist editor Elijah Lovejoy in Alton, Illinois, in November 1837. Stirred to respond when the attorney general of Massachusetts defended the mob that attacked Lovejoy as a legitimate successor to the mobs led by Samuel Adams, Phillips demonstrated his quiet, mesmerizing speaking style and his passion for preserving the integrity of Boston that had been "consecrated by the prayers of Puritans and the blood of patriots."

Radical Vanguard. Phillips soon became chief lieutenant of abolitionist leader William Lloyd Garrison, delivering addresses for the cause and developing its theoretical premises. He joined Garrison in spurning any participation in politics, which he considered incompatible with the promotion of moral principles. Although Phillips sometimes shared goals with antislavery politicians, his rigid insistence on complete conformity with every implication of abolitionism led him into conflicts with men as sympathetic to his cause as Horace Mann and Charles Sumner. When the Republican Party nominated Abraham Lincoln for president, Phillips branded him "the Slave-Hound of Illinois" because in proposing the gradual abolition of slavery in the District of Columbia while in Congress, Lincoln had included temporary arrangements for the retrieval of fugitive slaves. Particularly outraged by the pursuit of runaways into Boston, Phillips joined Garrison in adopting the motto "No Union with Slavery" and calling for Massachusetts to break all ties with the Southern states.

Politics. Notwithstanding Phillips's policy of disunion, he declared support for the war after the bombardment of Fort Sumter. Contrary to the declared federal intent to avoid interference with slavery, he welcomed every opportunity that the war provided to strike at the institution. He also came to take a more active role in politics, including strong support for a radical challenge to the reelection of Lincoln. Political involvement helped undermine Phillips's relationship with Garrison, who had entered the fray on Lincoln's side. When the war ended, Garrison moved to dissolve the American Anti-Slavery Society on the ground that it had fulfilled its purpose. Phillips engineered the defeat of the proposal and upon Garrison's retirement assumed the presidency of the organization, for which he adopted the new motto "No Reconstruction without Negro Suffrage." His efforts over the next five years were rewarded by the ratification of the Fifteenth Amendment in March 1870.

New Directions. Phillips concentrated in the 1870s on labor reform as the emerging issue of the future. After declining for decades to seek office as an antislavery politician despite advantages that gave him excellent prospects for success, he accepted the nomination for governor of Massachusetts on the Labor Reform ticket in 1870. He called for legislation to limit working hours and also distinguished his campaign through his defense of Chinese immigrants that employers sought to exploit and laborers sought to exclude. In the years following this unsuccessful candidacy his program for labor shifted to support for expansion of the money supply through circulation of paper currency. These views on regulation and finance were even more unpopular within Phillips's social class than his abolitionism had been. He also spoke in support of many other political causes during the 1870s, including the enforcement of civil rights in the South, woman suffrage, and temperance, as well as delivering many addresses on casual topics. From the end of the war until his retirement in 1880 he was the most popular lecturer in the country, the last of the great orators of New England. He died on 2 February 1884.

Sources:

Irving H. Bartlett, *Wendell Phillips: Brahmin Radical* (Boston: Beacon, 1961);

James Brewer Stewart, *Wendell Phillips, Liberty's Hero* (Baton Rouge: Louisiana State University Press, 1986).

ROBERT BARNWELL RHETT

1800-1876
SECESSIONIST

Lowcountry Aristocrat. Robert Barnwell Rhett was born Robert Barnwell Smith on 21 December 1800 in Beaufort, South Carolina, part of a small but significantly distinctive economic and social region of the South. Unlike the rest of the Lower South, which cultivated a hardy short-staple cotton, tidewater South Carolina offered conditions favorable to long-staple cotton, which commanded higher and more stable prices. Nearby was the rice-growing district, which similarly provided the economic base for a particularly aristocratic planter culture. Although Smith's family connections were distinguished, his own branch did not prosper, and with his brothers he changed his surname in 1837 to honor an illustrious ancestor, William Rhett. Shortly beforehand, he had established the foundation for his own wealth through the careful purchase of a plantation. By the 1850s he personified the ideal of the South Carolina planter, with almost two hundred slaves on two plantations, a town house in Charleston, and extensive debts to the Bank of South Carolina.

Beyond Calhoun. The long controversy over the tariff of 1828 was for Rhett as for many South Carolinians the crucial phase of political maturation. Elected to the state legislature in 1826, he soon earned a reputation for his strident attacks on the protective tariff. He reluctantly deferred to John C. Calhoun's strategy of nullification of the tariff as a peaceful, constitutional method of resistance, and after winning election to Congress in 1837, he advanced in political influence by supporting Calhoun's efforts to control the Democratic Party, win the presidency, and adjust government policy to satisfy the concerns of the South. When Calhoun's bid for the Democratic nomination faltered in 1844, Rhett reverted to his earlier approach by leading the so-called Bluffton movement, which called for unilateral state action to block the Whig tariff of 1842. He remained in the House of Representatives for another five years, and uniquely among South Carolina politicians he managed to maintain considerable independence from Calhoun, although they agreed on key matters like opposition to the Wilmot Proviso. After Calhoun's death in 1850, the state legislature elected Rhett to replace him in the United States Senate.

Disunion. Rhett took the lead in calling for the South to repudiate the Compromise of 1850. From the time of the Nashville Convention in June 1850 he made disunion his basic goal. His initial efforts met with disappointment, for secessionists were defeated in the South Carolina elections for a state convention. When the assembly contented itself in 1852 with simply affirming the right of secession, Rhett resigned his Senate seat and abandoned politics rather than share in what he branded "submission." He took over the editorship of the Charleston newspaper *Mercury* and agitated through its columns for disunion. For much of the rest of the decade the prospects for a separate Southern nation continued to seem dim. Even in the radical hotbed of South Carolina, the strategy of working through the national Democratic Party found a powerful exponent in James L. Orr. Similarly in Virginia, which also produced several prominent "fire-eaters," the presidential aspirations of Sen. Robert M. T. Hunter and Gov. Henry Wise served as a strong moderating influence in politics.

Triumph. Coordinating his efforts with like-minded leaders in other states, most notably William Lowndes Yancey of Alabama, Rhett sought to undermine confidence in the Democratic Party to which he still belonged. The Lecompton controversy between Stephen A. Douglas and Southern Democrats provided a valuable opportunity, on which Yancey capitalized by masterminding a schism in the 1860 national convention when the party refused to endorse a congressional slave code for the territories. Although a delegate to the Richmond convention that nominated John C. Breckinridge, Rhett continued to hope for a Republican victory to touch off secession. Upon the election of Lincoln he led the call for the immediate secession of South Carolina, eager to avoid the delays and loss of momentum that had occurred in 1850–1851 as a result of attempts to arrange cooperative action by several states. Enactment of the ordinance of secession on 20 December 1860 realized the dream that he had long held, and on behalf of the convention he prepared the "Address to the Slaveholding States" inviting others to join the lead of South Carolina.

Disappointment. From the outset Rhett was one of many fire-eaters who exercised little influence in the Confederate government he had worked to create. Recognized as an impulsive agitator rather than a constructive statesman, he not only failed in his hope to be the first president of the Confederacy but was passed over in the selection of other officials. *Mercury*, edited since 1857 by his son Robert Barnwell Rhett Jr., early became a critic of Jefferson Davis, first charging that he was too slow to take the military offensive and later emphasizing that the centralizing measures of the Confederate government infringed on the rights of states. Beaufort was overrun by the Union army early in the war, and when Rhett ran for the Confederate Congress in 1863 from the district that he had long represented in the United States Congress, the beleaguered electorate turned against him. In the final days of the war he made his last stand as an opponent of Davis's desperate willingness to free and arm the slaves. He outlived the shattering of his world and died in 1876, still hoping that the South would someday be "separate and free."

Source:
Laura A. White, *Robert Barnwell Rhett: Father of Secession* (New York & London: Century, 1931).

SITTING BULL

1831-1890

LAKOTA TRIBAL LEADER

Returns-Again. Some of the myths about Sitting Bull describe him as a white man in disguise, a West Point graduate, and a Freemason; the facts of his life, however, need no embellishment. He was born in 1831 near the Grand River, in what is now South Dakota. His father, Returns-Again, was a mystic and warrior of the Hunkpapa clan of the Sioux, or Lakota, tribe. (The name Sioux came from the Ojibway term *nadouessioux* used to describe the Lakota people; it means "snake" or "enemy.") Initially, Returns-Again called his son "Slow," because he was deliberate in his actions. One night, after a long day of hunting, Returns-Again and three other warriors heard strange sounds as they sat near the campfire. The noise came nearer and the four men saw that it emanated from a lone buffalo bull. As a mystic, Returns-Again could communicate with animals, and he soon realized that the buffalo was repeating a name: *Ta-tan-ka I-yo-ta-ke*, or Sitting Bull.

Young Warrior. Slow grew up like any other Lakota boy, listening to the men repeat their stories of battle and dreaming of the day in which he would meet an enemy in hand-to-hand combat. He also inherited his father's ability to communicate with the spirit world through animals and dreams. When Slow turned fourteen, his father presented him with a coup stick, a slender pole with which he could gain prestige by striking an enemy. He quickly proved himself by "counting coup" against the Crow, the traditional enemy of the Lakota. His father was so proud of him that he changed his son's name to Sitting Bull. In time, Sitting Bull would count coup more than sixty times and claim the deference of every warrior in the Hunkpapa band.

Leader. By the age of twenty-five Sitting Bull was made a leader of the Strong Hearts, an elite warrior society. He became chief of the Hunkpapas in the 1860s, at a time of severe white encroachment on tribal lands. In 1868 he refused to sign the Treaty of Laramie, which designated the entire western half of present-day South Dakota as a reservation for the Lakota, northern Cheyenne, and Arapaho. Over the next few years Sitting Bull led his warriors on sporadic raids against railroad workers and settlers along the Yellowstone River.

Greasy Grass River. In 1874 geologists accompanying an army expedition discovered traces of gold in western South Dakota. Within a year, nearly one thousand prospectors were illegally camped in the Black Hills, which the Lakota regarded as a sacred dwelling place of the spirits. When government officials offered to purchase the region, tribal leaders balked. As a result, the commissioner of Indian Affairs in November 1875 ordered all Lakota to report to the reservation. Sitting Bull and his followers ignored the order, even after the arrival of U.S. Army troops. In June 1876 Sitting Bull and the Oglala war chief Crazy Horse summoned Lakota, Cheyenne, and Arapaho bands to a large council on Rosebud Creek, Montana. After a six-hour battle on 17 June, the Native Americans temporarily halted an army column under Gen. George Crook. Eight days later, in the best-known battle of the Indian wars, they wiped out a detachment of the Seventh Cavalry under Lt. Col. George A. Custer on the Greasy Grass, or Little Bighorn River, Montana.

End. Contrary to popular belief, Sitting Bull did not lead his warriors into battle on either occasion, preferring to stay in his tepee and "make medicine" or pray. He had predicted a victory for his people, but at a heavy price. The U.S. government reacted swiftly to the "massacre" of Custer and his men. They hounded the various Indian bands until they surrendered one by one. Sitting Bull took his followers to Canada in May 1877. When U.S. peace commissioners offered him a full pardon in October, Sitting Bull retorted: "We did not give our country to you; you stole it. You come here to tell lies; when you go home, take them with you." By 1881, however, the proud Hunkpapa leader had only a few followers left, and he returned to the United States. After a brief imprisonment, he toured for a year (1885) with Buffalo Bill's Wild West Show, becoming a celebrity to the many whites who wanted to see "the Slayer of General Custer." He became good friends with the show's owner, William Cody, who paid the Hunkpapa leader fifty dollars a week and treated him with the utmost respect. Rumored to be an instigator of the Ghost Dance movement, Sitting Bull was killed in a scuffle with Indian police in South Dakota on 15 December 1890. Although there were chiefs, such as Crazy Horse, whose credentials as warriors were greater, Sitting Bull represented something more to his people. His powers to communicate with the spirits made him, in the words of a fellow tribesman, "big medicine."

Source:
Benjamin Capps, *The Great Chiefs*, revised (Alexandria, Va.: Time-Life Books, 1977).

ELIZABETH CADY STANTON

1815-1902
WOMAN'S RIGHTS LEADER

Quest for Equality. Born on 12 November 1815, in Johnstown, New York, Elizabeth Cady Stanton was from an early age determined to demonstrate that women were the equal of men and to help them secure better treatment. In her father's law office, she heard the grievances of women whose property passed into the control of their husbands on marriage and whose children were presumptively awarded to the father in divorce proceedings. She later recalled that upon the death of her only brother in 1826 she took motivation from her father's lamentation to her, "Oh, my daughter, I wish you were a boy!" Her education included studies in Greek, Latin, and mathematics as well as development of proficiency in traditionally male activities like horseback riding and chess. In 1832 she graduated from Emma Willard's Troy Female Seminary, perhaps the most influential women's educational institution in the country.

Reform Community. During the 1830s Elizabeth Cady became involved in temperance and antislavery activities in part through the connections of her cousin Gerrit Smith, a wealthy supporter of reform initiatives. In 1840 she married abolitionist Henry B. Stanton and immediately after their wedding traveled to London so her new husband could serve as a delegate to the World's Anti-Slavery Convention. Controversy broke out at the convention over the exclusion of women delegates, in the course of which she became friendly with Lucretia Mott, the distinguished Quaker reformer from Philadelphia. The two agreed to hold a convention for woman's rights in the United States, but little came of the project for the next several years. Stanton spent part of that time in Boston, where she developed close relations with Lydia Maria Child, Maria Weston Chapman, Frederick Douglass, Theodore Parker, and other reformers. She also had three children during the first five years of her marriage, with another four to follow during the 1850s.

Woman's Rights Movement. One year after her husband's health prompted a move from Boston to Seneca Falls, New York, Stanton and Mott sponsored in July 1848 the woman's rights convention that they had projected in London. Stanton drafted the Declaration of Sentiments for the convention, a pointed adaptation of the Declaration of Independence that represented the first public call for woman suffrage. Prior to the Seneca Falls convention she had lobbied in support of the married women's property act passed by the New York legislature in March 1848. Stanton promoted her cause in many ways, contributing articles to the *New York Tribune*, wearing for a time the "Bloomer" outfit developed by her cousin Elizabeth Smith Miller, and in 1851 forming a historic friendship with Susan B. Anthony. The two women were in many ways different. Stanton was cosmopolitan, gregarious, wide-ranging in her interests, and an able writer; Anthony was single-minded in her dedication to the suffrage movement, tenacious, and effective in administrative matters. Often kept at home by family duties, Stanton wrote many speeches and resolutions that Anthony presented at meetings. Stanton also made personal appearances in New York, addressing the legislature in 1854 in support of an expanded married women's property act and serving as president of the Woman's State Temperance Society, through which she advocated liberalization of divorce laws to protect wives of alcoholics.

Civil War and Reconstruction. Stanton moved from her isolated base in Seneca Falls when her husband was appointed to a position in the New York Custom House, and in May 1863 she teamed again with Anthony to form the Women's Loyal National League. The organization collected three hundred thousand signatures on a petition for a constitutional amendment to abolish slavery, and Stanton also sought to promote emancipation by endorsing the nomination of a Republican presidential candidate more radical than Abraham Lincoln in 1864. When the war ended, Stanton and Anthony moved swiftly to demand the inclusion of women in the redefinition of citizenship and voting rights under the Fourteenth and Fifteenth Amendments to the U.S. Constitution. But even strong supporters of reform agreed with Wendell Phillips that "this is the Negro's hour." Stanton and Anthony in turn launched a campaign to block the Reconstruction amendments, hoping for a reconsideration. Their resort to arguments grounded in privileges of class and ethnicity alienated many former allies. "Think of Patrick and Sambo and Hans and Ung Tung," Stanton baited, "who do not know the difference between a Monarchy and a Republic, who never read the Declaration of Independence . . . making laws for Lydia Maria Child, Lucretia Mott, or Fanny Kemble." In May 1869 the bitter dispute shattered the Equal Rights Association, which had urged enfranchisement of women as well as blacks.

Continuing the Struggle. After the breakup of the Equal Rights Association, Stanton and Anthony promptly organized the National Woman Suffrage Association, which Stanton served as president for the next twenty-one years. She continued to promote the cause of woman's rights through various lectures and publications during this period. When in 1890 the National Woman Suffrage Association merged with its more conservative rival, the American Woman Suffrage Association, Stanton headed the combined organization for two years before retiring to devote more time to writing. She spent much time during her last years absorbed in the study of religion and working on the *Woman's Bible* (1895–1898), which reinterpreted passages of scripture that were derogatory to women. In a gala at the Metropolitan Opera House in New York on the occasion of her eightieth birthday, she underscored one of the most important themes of her career by dismissing the idea that religion or nature assigned women to a "separate sphere" from the domain of men and urging women to continue the struggle to assume positions of leadership in churches, business, and politics. Stanton died in 1902.

Sources:

Ellen Carol Dubois, *Feminism and Suffrage: The Emergence of an Independent Women's Movement in America, 1848–1869* (Ithaca, N.Y.: Cornell University Press, 1978);

Elisabeth Griffith, *In Her Own Right: The Life of Elizabeth Cady Stanton* (New York: Oxford University Press, 1984).

ZEBULON VANCE

1830-1894
NORTH CAROLINA GOVERNOR

Tarheel Whig. The background of Zebulon Vance shares many features with the emergence of Abraham Lincoln and that of their mutual hero, Henry Clay. Vance's home in western North Carolina was similar to Kentucky and Illinois, and he, too, was a self-made man (a phrase coined to describe Clay) who had achieved success as a lawyer after a spotty formal education. Like Clay and Lincoln he had considerable charisma and a striking personal appearance—his photograph was selected for inclusion in an elementary geography textbook as the ideal of the Caucasian race. He also possessed an excellent sense of humor that not infrequently overstepped contemporary standards of good taste. Like Clay and Lincoln, Vance was a devout believer in the Whig Party; his chief political mentor would become William A. Graham, the state party leader who served at various times as North Carolina governor, U.S. senator, member of Millard Fillmore's cabinet, and Confederate senator. When the Whig Party disintegrated while Vance was in his early twenties, he aligned himself with the American Party rather than join the Democrats and entered Congress in 1858.

Crisis of the Union. Vance tried while in Congress to promote Unionism, adopting a moderate course in the 1859–1860 speakership struggle centered on the antislavery polemic *Impending Crisis of the South* (1857) by Hinton Rowan Helper of his state. In the presidential election of 1860 Vance supported the Constitutional Union ticket of John Bell of Tennessee and Edward Everett of Massachusetts. He vigorously and effectively opposed secession by North Carolina until Lincoln called for troops following the bombardment of Fort Sumter. Vance then urged his state to join the Confederacy, and he organized a regiment which he led with distinction in the New Bern campaign during the spring of 1862 and at Malvern Hill, Virginia, the following July. His military heroism and his attractiveness to former Whigs propelled him into the governor's chair at the age of thirty-two as a substitute for William A. Graham, who declined to run.

Confederate Governor. Vance's tenure as governor, like that of such counterparts as Joseph E. Brown of Georgia, was dominated by conflicts with the Jefferson Davis administration. Vance sought to protect the state-controlled recruitment of regiments from the centralizing process of conscription, and he blocked the Confederacy from drafting state officials. He took particular pride in his resistance to the Confederate suspension of the writ of habeas corpus, citing as the greatest achievement of his administration that no North Carolinian was denied the privilege of the writ or the right to trial by jury, and he angered Davis by his lenient treatment of army deserters. Vance's Whig antecedents and his controversies with Davis brought him into cooperation with newspaper editor William W. Holden, but the relationship shattered when, following the Confederate reverses of 1863, Holden called for North Carolina to negotiate a separate peace with the Union government. Vance crushed Holden to win reelection in 1864 and remained in office until he surrendered the following May to Union troops who had marched into North Carolina with Gen. William T. Sherman.

Return to Power. Briefly imprisoned in Washington, D.C., at the end of the war, Vance resettled in Charlotte, a city with railroad connections that promised future growth. He resumed the practice of law and sought to reenter politics, now aligning himself with the Democratic Party. The state legislature elected him to the U.S. Senate in 1870, but Congress refused to seat him. In 1876 he won a hard-fought race against Thomas Settle to "redeem" the state from Republican rule as governor. His administration emphasized traditional Whig policies that now found a home in Southern Democratic organizations, including support for public education and charitable institutions, energetic promotion of railroad projects, and protection of the interests of the holders of state bonds. The state legislature sent him to the United States Senate in 1879, and for fifteen years until his death he remained in Washington as a spokesman for Southern acceptance of defeat without bitterness or apology.

Sources:

John C. Inscoe, *Mountain Masters, Slavery, and the Sectional Crisis in Western North Carolina* (Knoxville: University of Tennessee Press, 1989);

Glenn Tucker, *Zeb Vance: Champion of Personal Freedom* (Indianapolis: Bobbs-Merrill, 1965).

PUBLICATIONS

Sidney Andrews, *The South Since the War* (Boston: Ticknor & Fields, 1866)—a tour of inspection by a representative of *Atlantic Monthly;*

Timothy Shay Arthur, *Ten Nights in a Bar-Room, and What I Saw There* (Philadelphia: J. W. Bradley, 1855)—sensational support for the temperance movement;

William G. Brownlow, *Sketch of Parson Brownlow, and His Speeches* (New York: E. D. Baker, 1862)—outlook of a Unionist from east Tennessee;

Orestes Brownson, *The American Republic: Its Constitution, Tendencies, and Destiny* (New York: O'Shea, 1866)—an analysis of American nationalism by an intellectual converted to Catholicism;

John C. Calhoun, *A Disquisition on Government, and a Discourse on the Constitution and Government of the United States* (Columbia, S.C.: A. S. Johnston, 1851)—a posthumous publication of the theoretical underpinnings to Calhoun's states' rights views;

Anna Ella Carroll, *The Great American Battle* (New York: Miller, Orton & Mulligan, 1856)—anti-Catholic arguments on behalf of the Know Nothing Party;

E. N. Elliott, *Cotton Is King and Pro-Slavery Arguments* (Augusta, Ga: Pritchard, Abbot & Loomis, 1860)—an anthology of influential essays defending slavery as not merely an unfortunate reality but as a desirable institution;

George Fitzhugh, *Cannibals All! or, Slaves without Masters* (Richmond: A. Morris, 1857)—defends slavery as an institution without regard to considerations of race, suggesting a rationale for enslavement of the white lower class;

Fitzhugh, *Sociology for the South; or, the Failure of Free Society* (Richmond: A. Morris, 1854)—argues for superiority of a slave-based social structure over relations predicated on wage labor;

Hinton Rowan Helper, *The Impending Crisis of the South: How to Meet It* (New York: Burdick Brothers, 1857)—an important attack on slavery as an impediment to Southern development and an oppression of nonslaveholding whites;

Elizabeth Keckley, *Behind the Scenes* (New York: G. W. Carleton, 1868)—the view of life inside the White House by the African American dressmaker for Mary Todd Lincoln;

Frances Anne Kemble, *Journal of a Residence on a Georgian Plantation in 1838–1839* (London: Longman, Roberts, & Green, 1863)—the famous British actress recounts her visit to an estate owned by her new husband; the journal was published for the first time during the war to influence public opinion;

Thomas Kettell, *Southern Wealth and Northern Profits* (New York: G. W. & J. A. Wood, 1860)—an argument that American tariff and commercial policies had diverted the revenues created by the slaveholding economy;

Francis Lieber, *On Civil Liberty and Self-Government*, 2 volumes (Philadelphia: Lippincott, Grambo, 1853)—a theoretical exposition by a German nationalist and political scientist who taught for years at South Carolina College;

Herman Melville, *Moby-Dick; or The Whale* (New York: Harper & Brothers, 1851)—among many other things, an allegory of the Compromise of 1850 and ominous view of the fate of "thirty *isolatoes* federated on one keel";

Charles Nordhoff, *The Cotton States in the Spring and Summer of 1875* (New York: D. Appleton, 1876)—a New York journalist supports restoration of local powers in the South;

Frederick Law Olmsted, *The Cotton Kingdom* (New York: Mason Brothers, 1861)—condensation of three books based on Olmsted's travels through the South in the 1850s, dedicated to English philosopher and economist John Stuart Mill;

James S. Pike, *The Prostrate State* (New York: D. Appleton, 1874)—racist denunciation of Reconstruction in South Carolina by a New York journalist;

Whitelaw Reid, *After the War: A Southern Tour* (Cincinnati & New York: Moore, Wilstach & Baldwin, 1866)—a report by the influential writer for the *New York Tribune;*

Alexander H. Stephens, *A Constitutional View of the Late War Between the States* (Philadelphia: National Publishing; Chicago: Zeigler, McCurdy, 1868–1870)—the vice president of the Confederacy attempts to recount the Civil War as conflict over state sovereignty;

Harriet Beecher Stowe, *Uncle Tom's Cabin; or, Life Among the Lowly* (Boston: J. P. Jewett; Cleveland: Jewett, Proctor & Worthington, 1852)—appeared previously in serial installments in *The National Era,* an antislavery newspaper.

Free blacks sorting cotton on a plantation at Edisto Island, South Carolina, during the Civil War,
when Northern managers ran businesses on the Sea Islands

LAW AND JUSTICE

by THOMAS J. BROWN

CONTENTS

Sidebars and tables are listed in italics.

1850

- Michigan and Pennsylvania switch from appointed to elected supreme courts.

- In *Brown* v. *Kendall* Chief Justice Lemuel Shaw of the Massachusetts Supreme Court sets forth the principle that liability for injuries caused in an accident will result only if the defendant failed to exercise reasonable care.

30 Aug.	Following a well-publicized trial, Harvard professor John Webster is executed in Boston for the murder of Dr. George Parkman.
18 Sept.	President Millard Fillmore signs the Fugitive Slave Act.
22 Oct.	The Chicago City Council passes a resolution nullifying the Fugitive Slave Act.
30 Oct.	Slave catchers trying to retrieve runaways William and Ellen Craft in Boston leave the city out of fear for their safety.

1851

- Chief Justice Lemuel Shaw of Massachusetts introduces the doctrine of legislative police power in *Commonwealth* v. *Alger.*

15 Feb.	The fugitive Shadrach escapes from slavecatchers in Boston.
Apr.	The fugitive Thomas Sims returns from Boston to slavery in Georgia.
2 June	Passage of the "Maine Law" provides a nationwide model for legislation prohibiting the sale of alcohol.
12 Aug.	Isaac Merrit Singer is granted a patent for his sewing machine. He soon organizes I. M. Singer and Company, leading to litigation with inventor Elias Howe.
11 Sept.	In the Christiana Massacre, Pennsylvania, a slave owner is killed and his son seriously wounded when they attempt to retrieve a runaway slave.

1852

- The state of Massachusetts establishes an insurance commission to collect data and report to the legislature.

- An Ohio statute on local governments applies as its model an 1835 English law regulating municipal corporations.

- The state of Rhode Island abolishes the death penalty.

- In *Haring* v. *New York and Erie Railroad Company* the doctrine of contributory negligence is applied to bar an award of damages in the death of a man hit by a train while sledding across a railroad track.

24 Oct.	Daniel Webster, legendary lawyer, orator, senator, and secretary of state, dies.

1853

- The state of Wisconsin abolishes the death penalty.

1854

- The law firm headed by Clarence A. Seward relocates to Wall Street from Auburn, New York; later it develops into Cravath, Swaine and Moore.

24 May   The arrest of fugitive Anthony Burns in Boston begins agitation over proceedings to return him to slavery in Virginia.

2 June   The "Rendition of Anthony Burns" occurs when the runaway is marched through the streets of Boston by state and federal troops, who return him to slavery.

1855

- The state of New York establishes a railroad commission.

1856

- Manufacturers of sewing machines form a patent pool to share new technology in the industry.

8 July   Rep. Preston S. Brooks (S.C.) is indicted for assault and battery in the 22 May caning of Sen. Charles Sumner (Mass.) in Congress. Brooks pleads guilty and is fined $300.

1857

- The New York Railroad Commission is abolished on the recommendation of the commissioners, who had been bribed by railroad executives.

- Stephen J. Field is elected to the California Supreme Court. Later, as a U.S. Supreme Court justice, Field would gain a reputation for upholding the individual's right to property.

6 Mar.   The Supreme Court announces its decision in *Dred Scott* v. *Sandford,* holding that blacks—whether free or slave—are not citizens of the United States. Furthermore, the court rules that the Missouri Compromise ban on slavery above the 36° 30' line in the Louisiana Purchase Territory is unconstitutional.

1858

- Theodore W. Dwight assumes direction of the Columbia University Law School and holds that position until his retirement in 1891.

1859

- The New York case of *Lawrence* v. *Fox* establishes the principle of third-party beneficiary contract: a person not a party to a contract may enforce it in court if the contract is intended to benefit him or her.

- The U.S. Supreme Court invalidates Wisconsin personal liberty laws in *Ableman* v. *Booth.*

26 Apr.   Congressman Daniel E. Sickles is acquitted of murder charges after killing his wife's lover, U.S. District Attorney Philip Barton Key, in Washington, D.C.

25 Oct.	The trial of abolitionist John Brown begins. He is quickly convicted of murder, treason against the state of Virginia, and criminal conspiracy to incite a slave rebellion.
2 Dec.	John Brown is hanged in Charlestown, Virginia.

1860

•	In *Lemmon* v. *The People,* the New York Court of Appeals upholds the free status of blacks brought to New York City by a Southerner merely changing ships for a direct boat to New Orleans. Antislavery Northerners expect the decision to be reversed by the U.S. Supreme Court, but the Civil War begins before the case can be heard.

1861

•	Congress passes a statute requiring an oath of future loyalty from all federal employees.
21 Feb.	The Senate rejects President James Buchanan's nomination of Jeremiah S. Black to the Supreme Court. Black had a reputation for strictly enforcing federal laws relating to the return of fugitive slaves.
30 Mar.	Massachusetts Supreme Court Chief Justice Lemuel Shaw dies.
27 Apr.	President Abraham Lincoln authorizes the suspension of the writ of habeas corpus in the area between Philadelphia and Washington, D.C.
26 May	Chief Justice Roger B. Taney issues a writ of habeas corpus in *Ex Parte Merryman.* President Lincoln refuses to execute the writ.

1862

•	The Morrill Act seeks "to punish and prevent the practice of polygamy in the territories." This federal statute is held constitutional in 1878, but it is slow to affect the practices of Mormons.
2 July	President Abraham Lincoln signs the "ironclad test oath" which demands past loyalty from all federal officials; later it is extended to federal contractors, attorneys, jurors, and applicants for passports.
8 Aug.	Secretary of War Edwin Stanton declares the writ of habeas corpus suspended throughout the country for cases of disloyalty and draft evasion.
24 Sept.	President Abraham Lincoln ratifies Edwin Stanton's order of 8 August.
26 Dec.	Thirty-eight leaders of a Sioux uprising in Minnesota are executed.

1863

•	Massachusetts creates the first State Board of Charities to regulate administration of services to the poor.
10 Mar.	The Supreme Court, in the *Prize* cases, approves by a 5–4 vote the legality of the blockade ordered by President Abraham Lincoln at the outset of war.
25 May	Peace Democrat Clement Vallandigham of Ohio is exiled to the Confederacy for a public speech criticizing the war effort and a new conscription law.

1864

•   Thomas Cooley is elected to the Michigan Supreme Court. He serves for twenty years and plays an important role in the growth of the University of Michigan Law School.

12 Oct.   U.S. Supreme Court Chief Justice Roger B. Taney dies. Taney is best known for writing the majority opinion in the *Dred Scott* case.

1865

•   The Iowa Law School opens in Des Moines as the first night school for law training.

Jan.   African American war hero Robert Smalls is ejected from a Philadelphia street-car for violating segregation laws.

31 Jan.   The Thirteenth Amendment, abolishing slavery, is approved by Congress and submitted to the states for ratification.

5 Feb.   John S. Rock of Boston becomes the first black lawyer admitted to practice before the U.S. Supreme Court.

May   Massachusetts enacts the first comprehensive law banning racial discrimination in public accommodations.

7 July   Mary Surratt and three other convicted conspirators in the assassination of President Lincoln are executed; four accomplices receive prison sentences.

Oct.   The publication of the Mississippi black code provides a model for other Southern states.

Oct.   The American Association for the Advancement of Social Science is established in Boston; its charter includes a section on jurisprudence.

18 Dec.   The Thirteenth Amendment is signed into law after being ratified by three-fourths of the states.

1866

•   The United States Constitution, stored in the Treasury Building since 1820, is moved to the Washington Orphan Asylum.

3 Apr.   In *Ex parte Milligan* the U.S. Supreme Court invalidates trials by military commissions outside combat zones.

9 Apr.   Congress passes the first Civil Rights Act over the veto of President Andrew Johnson.

8 May   Former Confederate president Jefferson Davis is indicted for treason against the United States.

16 June   The Fourteenth Amendment, establishing the citizenship of all persons born or naturalized in the United States, is submitted to the states for ratification.

16 June   Oliver Wendell Holmes Jr. graduates from Harvard Law School after service in the Union army. He would later gain renown as an associate justice of the U.S. Supreme Court.

1867

- Congress passes a national bankruptcy act for the first time since prior laws were repealed in 1841. The new law is repealed in 1878, leaving the country without a uniform bankruptcy system until 1898.

14 Jan. The Supreme Court announces its decisions in *Ex parte Garland* and *Cummings v. Missouri,* together known as the *Test Oath* cases, invalidating loyalty oaths for former Confederates.

1 Mar. Nebraska becomes the thirty-seventh state and adopts for its motto "Equality Under the Law."

May Jefferson Davis is released from Fortress Monroe, Virginia, after two years of imprisonment.

1868

27 Mar. Congress deprives the Supreme Court of jurisdiction in *Ex parte McCardle,* a case involving a Vicksburg, Mississippi, newspaper editor arrested for inciting insurrection and tried by a military tribunal. Republican leaders in Congress struck at the Court's authority by repealing the provision of the Habeas Corpus Act allowing direct appeals to the Supreme Court.

30 Mar. The impeachment trial of President Andrew Johnson begins.

16 May The Senate votes 35–19 to impeach President Andrew Johnson, falling one vote short of the two-thirds majority required to remove him from office.

25 May Congress enacts an eight-hour-workday law for federal employees.

June The Congressional Committee on Lawlessness and Violence reports that 373 freed slaves have been killed by whites in the past two years, while only ten whites have been killed by freed slaves in the same time period.

28 June The Fourteenth Amendment is proclaimed to be in effect.

3 Oct. Myra Bradwell begins publication of the *Chicago Legal News.*

3 Dec. The treason trial of Jefferson Davis begins in Richmond before federal judges Salmon P. Chase and John C. Underwood; the charges, however, are dropped after President Andrew Johnson proclaims a general pardon and amnesty for all charges of treason arising from the Civil War.

1869

Jan. The Law Department at Howard University, Washington, D.C., opens.

23 Jan. Massachusetts establishes the first state bureau of labor statistics.

26 Feb. The Fifteenth Amendment, affirming the right of citizens to vote, is submitted by Congress to the states for ratification.

12 Apr. The Supreme Court announces its decision in *Texas* v. *White,* holding that the Confederate states were at all times part of the Union.

1870

- The city of Saint Louis legalizes prostitution; this social experiment lasts until 1874.

- Michigan Supreme Court Justice Thomas Cooley writes the majority opinion in *The People* v. *Salem*, invalidating legislative authorization of local taxes to fund bonds for railroad construction.

3 Feb. The Senate rejects the nomination of Ebenezer R. Hoar to the U.S. Supreme Court. Hoar's past insistence that federal judgeships be filled with men of ability and integrity earned him the animosity of many senators, who considered these positions as opportunities for political patronage.

7 Feb. In *Hepburn* v. *Griswold* the Supreme Court invalidates greenbacks, paper currency used to finance the Civil War.

15 Feb. The Association of the Bar of the City of New York is founded; 450 attorneys join in the first year.

30 Mar. The Fifteenth Amendment is declared to be in effect.

31 May Congress passes the Enforcement Act of 1870 to secure the voting rights of citizens in the South.

Sept. Christopher Columbus Langdell is appointed dean of Harvard Law School.

Oct. Oliver Wendell Holmes Jr. becomes coeditor of the *American Law Review.*

Oct. The National Congress of Penitentiary and Reformatory Discipline advocates the implementation of a parole system for the nation's prisons.

4 Oct. President Ulysses S. Grant appoints the first solicitor general of the United States, Benjamin H. Bristow.

1871

Feb. The first graduation ceremonies are held in the Law Department of Howard University.

15 Apr. The Illinois Railroad Act authorizes a state commission to set maximum railroad rates.

20 Apr. Congress passes the Ku Klux Klan Act, outlawing conspiracies, the wearing of disguises, resisting law enforcement officers, and intimidating government officials. It also authorizes the president to suspend habeas corpus when necessary to suppress "armed combinations."

26 Apr. A sensational San Francisco criminal trial ends with the jury finding Laura Fair guilty of murdering her lover, Alexander Parker Crittenden; Fair is sentenced to death.

1 May The Supreme Court announces its decision in *Legal Tender* cases, reversing *Hepburn* v. *Griswold* and upholding the financing of the Civil War through issuance of currency not redeemable in gold or silver.

24 May The Senate ratifies the Treaty of Washington, providing for international arbitration of American claims against Britain for damages caused by English-built ships supplied to the Confederacy. A tribunal is convened in Geneva, Switzerland, to hear the cases.

1872

- A California statute authorizes school districts to establish separate schools for persons of Asian descent.

30 Sept. Laura Fair is acquitted of murder charges after an appeal produces an order for a retrial.

19 Nov. William Marcy "Boss" Tweed, leader of Tammany Hall, is convicted on 204 counts of political corruption in New York City.

1873

- Judge Albert Cardozo of the New York Supreme Court resigns to avoid impeachment for impropriety in the Erie Railroad bankruptcy proceedings. His son Benjamin, then three years old, would later become a U.S. Supreme Court justice.

- Congress enacts the Comstock Law, prohibiting the mailing of "obscene, lewd, or lascivious" books or any "article or thing designed or intended for the prevention of conception or procuring of abortion."

14 Apr. In the *Slaughterhouse* cases the Supreme Court has its first opportunity to interpret the meaning of the Fourteenth Amendment. The majority of the justices limit the Privileges or Immunities Clause of the first section of the amendment.

7 May U.S. Supreme Court Chief Justice Salmon P. Chase dies. Chase had presided over the impeachment trial of President Andrew Johnson in 1868.

1874

19 Jan. President Ulysses S. Grant appoints Morrison R. Waite of Ohio to be chief justice of the U.S. Supreme Court. Waite had served on the Geneva arbitration tribunal.

11 Mar. Wisconsin passes the "Potter Law," regulating railroads; Iowa follows suit with a similar law twelve days later.

8 May Massachusetts passes the Ten Hour Act, limiting working hours for women and children.

20 Aug. New York journalist Theodore Tilton sues minister Henry Ward Beecher for seducing Tilton's wife, Elizabeth. The jury is unable to agree whether or not Beecher initiated the affair.

1875

- The United States Constitution is moved from the Washington Orphan Asylum to cellar storage in the War and State Building, where it remains until transferred to the Library of Congress in 1921.

- Congress passes the Jurisdiction and Removal Act, permitting any claim arising under federal law to be filed in a federal court or, if filed in a state court, to be removed to federal court at the defendant's option.

- Eighteen-year-old Louis Brandeis, a future U.S. Supreme Court justice, enters Harvard Law School.

•	Eighteen-year-old Clarence Darrow enters University of Michigan Law School. Darrow would later become famous for his participation in the Scopes Trial (1925), during which he argued for the teaching of evolution in schools.
25 Jan.	Pinkerton detectives raid the home of Jesse and Frank James, killing their half brother but failing to find the outlaws. Jesse would be killed seven years later by Robert Ford, and Frank would surrender to law enforcement authorities shortly afterward.
1 Mar.	Congress passes the Civil Rights Act, barring discrimination in hotels, theaters, railroads, and other public facilities.

1876

27 Mar.	The Supreme Court announces its decision in *United States* v. *Cruikshank*, finding that the Fourteenth and Fifteenth Amendments bar violations of civil rights by the states and do not cover racially motivated crimes committed by private individuals.

1877

21 June	Ten members of the Molly Maguires, a secret labor organization, are executed for murder in Pennsylvania. They had been tried and convicted following an investigation initiated by railroad executives and conducted by undercover operatives of the Pinkerton Detective Agency.

OVERVIEW

After the Golden Age. Observers of American law during 1850–1877 frequently remarked on the passing of a heroic era of legal creativity. By 1860 nobody in the country associated with the law enjoyed the stature that had been shared by a dozen figures a generation earlier. Gone were the Olympian jurists such as John Marshall, Joseph Story, James Kent, Lemuel Shaw, John Bannister Gibson, and Thomas Ruffin. No longer did any lawyer grip the public imagination as Daniel Webster, William Wirt, and Rufus Choate once did. Few people continued to discuss the penitentiary movement that had brought Alexis de Tocqueville to the United States on a tour of inspection in 1831–1832, during which he concluded that "it is at the bar or the bench that the American aristocracy is found." The sectional convulsions over the Constitution notwithstanding, the third quarter of the nineteenth century seemed lackluster in comparison as an epoch of law. Paradoxically, however, this era saw the establishment of institutions and the development of ideas that would remain central to American law for decades to follow. The emerging principles, moreover, would prove to be central to the constitutional resolution of the crisis of the Union.

Law and the Economy. The decline in the public profile of judges and lawyers partly reflected the new role played by law in the American economy. During the first half of the nineteenth century, the law had been instrumental in the profound reordering of society from a network of local agricultural exchanges into a more varied, wide-ranging, and intensified capitalism in which industry was the most dynamic sector. This process partly took place in state legislatures, through grants of property and special privileges to entrepreneurs; and it partly took place in constitutional law, through judicial protection of property interests from legislative interference and through federal supervision of state regulations that threatened to impair the workings of the American common market. No less important than these features of public law, or the relations between government and individuals, was the transformation of private law, or the relations between individuals. Under the Anglo-American common-law tradition, the rules governing these relations were defined by judicial decisions in lawsuits, which produced an accumulation of precedents to guide the handling of similar situations. By midcentury, decisions in such cases had overhauled the laws governing the enforcement of contracts and the use of property in order to facilitate commercial exchanges and spur industrial development.

The Invention of Torts. Perhaps the most spectacular example of the relationship between common law and economic development at midcentury was the blossoming of an entirely new area of law called "torts" governing the availability of compensation for personal injuries. The very existence of the subject reflected the industrial revolution, for the injuries covered by tort law usually resulted from the acceleration of technology and especially from the expansion of railroads. Of course torts could occur in other settings as well; the watershed statement in the field—Chief Justice Lemuel Shaw's opinion for the Massachusetts Supreme Court in *Brown* v. *Kendall* (1850)—involved an accident that took place when one man hit another while using a stick to break up a fight between two dogs. But the principle set forth by Shaw in the case was of vital importance in the cases between business enterprises and individual victims, for Shaw found that liability for injuries caused in an accident would only result if the defendant was "negligent." In other words, if a railroad company exercised reasonable care, the disastrous consequences of accidents that occurred through sheer mishap would be a burden borne by victims rather than by the railroads. English courts moved to modify this principle in *Rylands* v. *Fletcher* (1868), finding that entrepreneurs engaged in an hazardous activity like dynamite blasting should be responsible for any injuries that resulted, even if the activity was conducted with reasonable care. American courts, meanwhile, moved slowly to adopt this rule of "strict liability," preferring to shift more of the costs of economic activity away from entrepreneurs by applying the rule of negligence even to hazardous activities.

Development and Distribution. American zeal for economic development certainly did not decline after midcentury; to the contrary, it continued to deepen. The impact of economic policy on the distribution of wealth in the nation increasingly became the chief focus of lawmakers, as is illustrated by changing approaches to the authority of municipalities to invest in railroads. Ruling in "the most important case that has ever been in this Court since the formation of the government," Pennsylvania Chief Justice Jeremiah S. Black in *Sharples* v. *Mayor of Philadelphia* (1853) resoundingly endorsed the state legislature's power to sanction railroad investments; similar rulings occurred in New York, Connecticut, Illinois, Ohio, Virginia, Kentucky, and Tennessee. "A railroad is a public highway for the public benefit," Black argued, because "travel and transportation are cheapened by it to a degree far exceeding all the tolls and charges" and because it provided the public with "rapidity, comfort, convenience, increase of trade, opening of markets, and other means of rewarding labor and promoting wealth." In short, the state could use its taxing power to regulate the railroads, which benefitted the general public as well as the private investors. Black's analysis contrasts sharply with the decision on the same question reached by Thomas Cooley of the Michigan Supreme Court in the 1870 case of *People* v. *Salem*, which held that "the money when raised is to benefit a private corporation; to add to its funds and improve its property; and the benefit to the public is to be secondary and incidental." Cooperation with the legislature to promote economic growth had given way to supervision of the legislature to prevent redistribution of wealth.

Judicial Power and Profile. The increasing attention to the distribution of wealth in a mature economy changed the relationship between judges and the general public. No longer did judges win fame for patriotically adapting the English common law to American circumstances or for unshackling the law from centuries-old doctrines that inhibited economic development or for defending federal authority from state usurpation. The issue of wealth distribution posed particular difficulties for judges because the same desire to attack economic privilege had also called into question the legitimacy of judge-made law in a democratic society. This challenge to judicial legitimacy was clearest on occasions when courts declared unconstitutional, and hence invalid, statutes that had been enacted by elected legislatures. The chief response of the bench to this democratic critique was to emphasize that judicial decisions reflected professional expertise. Arguments about the law increasingly took place in a more specialized, abstract, and neutral-sounding vocabulary. Judicial opinions became less comprehensible to the general public than the decisions of justices John Marshall or Joseph Story, whose writings had often been directed to the community at large. Paradoxically, therefore, judges tended to be more obscure in their renderings after midcentury even as the exercise of judicial review increasingly involved courts in political controversies.

Advocates. The changing role of the lawyer in American society in some ways paralleled that of the judge. It remained true, as Tocqueville had observed, that almost every important political issue in the country was at some point translated into a constitutional case. These con-

tests before the United States Supreme Court continued to feature a small circle of influential lawyers, which during 1850–1877 included Jeremiah S. Black, David Dudley Field, Reverdy Johnson, William Maxwell Evarts, and Charles O'Conor. But just as the language of judicial opinions had changed, so had the language of lawyers' arguments. The golden age of American oratory was ending during the 1850s, and lawyers' speeches inside and outside of the courtroom no longer formed a major part of American literature, as they had in the era of Daniel Webster. Beyond the decline of oratory, the intensifying specialization of the law meant that attorneys less often engaged broad audiences. One implication was that the passage from law to literature, which had been followed by such prominent authors as Washington Irving and William Cullen Bryant, became more difficult to navigate. The novelist Henry James, shuddering at the memory of the year he spent at Harvard Law School during the Civil War, expressed gratitude that he had "recognized the false steps, even though few enough, already taken, and consciously committed myself to my particular divergence."

The Age of Contract. Even as judges and lawyers retreated into a more secluded but strategically powerful position in American society, the intellectual frameworks of the law continued to diffuse into everyday life. Law influenced Americans not only by direct command, but also by supplying analogies and concepts for thinking about social relations. This trend might be observed in politics, where disagreements about the spread of slavery into the federal territories became a matter of constitutional principle after it had been handled in less systematic ways since the Northwest Ordinance of 1787. The most sweeping claim of legalistic thinking was the famous observation of Sir Henry Maine in his *Ancient Law* (1861) that "the movement of the progressive societies has hitherto been a movement from Status to Contract." Civilization itself, he suggested, was defined by the treatment of individuals on the basis of their voluntary agreements rather than on the basis of their classification into a group. Maine offered his generalization about world history at a particularly significant moment for the United States, at the outset of a war that would culminate in the destruction of a society based on the status of slavery. In the Reconstruction era that followed, Northerners would define the rights of freedom largely as the power to make and enforce contracts.

Marriage as Contract. The pervasiveness of contract as a model for social relations was illustrated by the continuing transformation of marriage, a process that had begun before 1850. Anglo-American common law traditionally treated the property rights of married women in the status of coverture. As summarized by James Kent as late as 1832, the basic principle of coverture was that "the husband and wife are regarded as one person, and her legal existence and authority in a degree lost or suspended, during the continuance of the matrimonial union." Beginning with Mississippi in 1839, states eroded this principle through legislation that extended to women the capacity to hold, manage, and dispose of property; seventeen states had passed married women's property acts by 1850. The reform continued to expand into new states after midcentury and to recognize in additional ways the rights of married women to make contracts and control property. For example, in 1869 Illinois passed legislation securing to married women the rights to their own earnings; one of the principal advocates of the bill was Elizabeth Packard, who had accumulated considerable earnings as the author of a sensational memoir attacking the legal structure that had enabled her husband to commit her involuntarily to a lunatic asylum. The increasing liberalization of divorce similarly reflected the reconceptualization of marriage as a contract that the parties might agree to dissolve rather than a permanent status. Other states liberalized their divorce laws after 1850; South Carolina permitted divorce for the first time during Reconstruction. Yale College president Theodore D. Woolsey's *Divorce and Divorce Legislation* (1869) signaled a backlash that would become fairly powerful by the 1880s, but this book also measured the extent to which law had displaced religion as a basic framework for understanding social relations.

Law as Theater. Legislatures and appellate courts articulated the changing rules of law, but it was the trial process that continued to grip the public imagination. Sensational cases—usually involving sex, murder, or both—had long been part of the American scene, and the expanding popular press now publicized them more widely than ever before. Often these cases illuminated social tensions. The San Francisco trial of Laura Fair in 1871 for the murder of her lover, Alexander Parker Crit-tenden, became a rallying point for woman's rights advocates outraged that the defendant's fate rested with an all-male bench and jury. The 1874 trial of New York preacher Henry Ward Beecher for seducing the wife of journalist Theodore Tilton similarly served as a crucible for analysis of gender relations and religion. At times these cases even involved innovations in legal doctrines. In 1859 Congressman Daniel Sickles, acquitted of murder charges after killing his wife's lover, became the first defendant to maintain that temporary insanity excused his crime; Laura Fair put forward a similar defense of insanity.

Continuities after 1877. The developing law of criminal insanity, which claimed central stage in American law with the trial of President James Garfield's assassin, Charles Guiteau, in 1881–1882, was one of many areas of continuity between the third and fourth quarters of the nineteenth century. The period from 1850 to 1877 is more sharply defined in law at the beginning than at the end. Key developments in the law during the Civil War and Reconstruction era—including the rise of legal formalism, the redefinition of the corporation, and the expansion of judicial review—reached full realization in the later nineteenth century. Significantly, it was the dissenting opinions in the *Slaughterhouse* cases (1873), perhaps the most important Supreme Court decision of the era, that provided a blueprint for future constitutional thought. But if the story of American law between 1850 and 1877 lacks its logical conclusion, within that narrative can be seen the main outlines of the legal culture that remained dominant in the United States until the Progressive Era of the late nineteenth and early twentieth centuries.

THE ASCENDANCY OF LEGAL FORMALISM

Law and Politics. Beginning around midcentury, a fundamental transformation in legal thinking responded to growing charges that the judicial process was merely a disguised, undemocratic form of political decision making. This criticism of American law had gained strength for several reasons. Jacksonian Democrats identified the law as a bastion of elitism that stood in the way of government by the people. The shift from appointment to election as the dominant method for choosing state judges reflected the belief that voters could adequately understand legal issues and should be able to control the bench. After 1846 every new state provided for election of at least part of the judiciary; the supreme courts of Michigan and Pennsylvania became elective bodies in 1850. Moreover, the long period of economic stagnation following the Panic of 1837 led to widespread dissatisfaction with the strategies used to foster development, including the candid formulation of economic policies by the courts. Finally, the acknowledgment of sharpening class divisions during this economic downturn prompted the beneficiaries of open-ended judicial powers to foresee that future courts might use the same policy-making flexibility to approve redistributions of wealth in favor of the disadvantaged. These pressures shaped new assertions of the old idea that the legal decision-making process was a neutral, objective activity unlike the political contest of interests and subjective values.

Formalism. The most powerful response to these challenges is known as legal formalism because it maintained that judicial decisions should be based on abstract, general rules rather than explicit policy considerations or an evaluation of fairness in individual cases. By emphasizing what it was not, formalism identified two important areas of institutional conflict for a judiciary struggling to consolidate the power that it had successfully claimed in the first half of the century. First, formalism underscored that courts were not legislatures. To the contrary, courts increasingly cast themselves in opposition to legislatures as defenders of timeless values and exercised the authority to declare statutes unconstitutional. Second, legal formalism reinforced the distinction between judge and jury. Fundamental inquiries—such as the question whether two parties had formed a legally

Massachusetts Supreme Court Chief Justice Lemuel Shaw, one of the leaders in restricting the application of the power of the state to take private property for public purposes

binding contract—came to be regarded as issues of law to be decided by a judge rather than issues of fact to be decided by a jury. The new legal reasoning may be traced through the four areas that the most influential advocate of formalism, Christopher Columbus Langdell of Harvard Law School, would identify as the major fields of civil law: property, contracts, torts, and civil procedure.

Property. The changing law of eminent domain—that is, the power of a government to take private

Dred Scott, the slave who sued for his freedom after his master took him into free territory; and Supreme Court Chief Justice Roger B. Taney, who wrote the 1857 opinion that kept Scott in bondage

property for a public purpose, provided that the property owner is compensated—most clearly illustrated the nature of formalism and the social changes underlying the shift in ideas about law. Vigorous use of eminent domain played an important role in economic development, as the national and state governments exercised the power to make possible the construction of turnpikes, canals, and, later, railroads. One especially important variation of the principle, so-called milldam acts, involved the flooding of lands that resulted from damming streams to generate power. In effect, this practice subsidized the transfer of land from agricultural to manufacturing uses. Although the milldam acts greatly benefited entrepreneurs at the expense of farmers, the courts held that the resulting expansion of the economy was a public purpose that justified the use of eminent domain powers. By midcentury, however, state courts retreated from this policy-based approach in an effort to rein in the applications of eminent domain. Chief Justice Lemuel Shaw of the Massachusetts Supreme Court, who had relied on economic considerations in extending the milldam principle from gristmills to manufacturing corporations, came to argue that the milldam acts reflected unique principles of water law and that the promotion of economic development was not a public purpose that would justify use of eminent domain powers in other contexts. The Supreme Court of Wisconsin similarly ruled in 1860 that precedent alone justified the redistribution of re-

sources to benefit mills. Although eminent domain remained essential to the construction of railroads, exercise of state power was no longer based on the stimulation of economic growth; instead, courts looked to the public's right of access to railroads as the purpose that justified the taking of private property.

Contracts. Decisions in the decades prior to midcentury had established that a contract was a "meeting of the minds" enforceable through the judicial process. As the great jurist James Kent explained in 1832, the "plain intent" of the parties was more important in interpreting the agreement than "the strict letter of the contract." Beginning with Theophilus Parsons's *Law of Contracts* (1853–1855), however, the law placed less emphasis on the subjective will of the contracting parties. Instead, Parsons maintained that a court should only bring interpretation of a contract as close to the parties' actual meaning "as the words they saw fit to employ, when properly construed, and the rules of law, will permit." This so-called objective theory aptly fit the mature economy in which contracts often involved depersonalized exchanges that depended on uniformity and predictability in the governing rules of law. The objective theory of contract made it logical to read business customs and other standard practices into a contract to give meaning to commercial transactions. Like the "meeting of the minds" principle championed by Kent, the formalist approach to contract law did not call for courts to inquire

Salmon P. Chase during his tenure as secretary of the treasury

whether a particular deal was fair, although the customs and standard practices applied by the courts offered some new protections for parties. The traditional rule of caveat emptor—"let the buyer beware"—slowly began to erode as courts concluded that sales contracts implicitly promised that goods met certain standards. For example, as goods increasingly came to be sold on the basis of samples, courts read into contracts a promise (or warranty) that all of the goods sold matched the samples. This sort of warranty reflected the goal of contract law to facilitate efficient transactions among merchants.

Torts. As in the decades before 1850, courts hesitated to require industry to pay for all of the damages that it caused to people and property. The New York Court of Appeals expressed this reluctance with unusual bluntness in *Ryan* v. *New York Central Railroad* (1866) in ruling that a railroad which had negligently caused a fire owed damages only to the homeowner adjacent to the track and not to the individuals whose homes were destroyed when the fire spread. The court concluded that "in a commercial country, each man, to some extent, runs the hazard of his neighbor's conduct, and each, by insurance against such hazards, is enabled to obtain a reasonable security against loss." More often courts adopted rules based less explicitly on policy-based allocations of the risks and costs of development. One important example was the principle of contributory negligence. Under this doctrine, an injured person who had failed to exercise

reasonable care for his safety could not recover damages, even if most of the fault for the accident was attributable to the defendant. For example, contributory negligence often prevented juries from deciding whether to award damages to a person injured while crossing railroad tracks on a clear day, even if the train was speeding and failed to signal its approach into a populated area. Although this rule obviously subsidized railroads, courts defended it as an effort to maintain neutrality in the judicial process. In "certain controversies between the weak and strong," one judge explained, juries tended to be moved by a "compassion . . . which, however honorable to them as philanthropists, is wholly inconsistent with the principles of law and justice."

Civil Procedure. Jacksonian Democrats argued that ordinary people were denied access to the courts by arcane methods for filing suits and pursuing claims. The laws were "in closed books," declared attorney David Dudley Field, "and the lawyers object to the opening of these books." The movement for simplification of procedures reached a milestone in 1848 when New York adopted the Field Code, named after its chief proponent. The Field Code and a variety of modified versions and alternative codes were adopted through much of the country over the next half century. The new states of the West proved especially receptive, and California adopted a code in 1872. These codes sought to eliminate the highly convoluted system of custom and precedent that had evolved in Anglo-American courts. The Field Code, however, was not always accessible to nonlawyers, and it became less so through this period. In 1849 it included 473 sections; by 1880 the New York codes for civil and criminal procedure included 3,356 sections. To Field and his allies the central aim of the reform was to rationalize procedure. Like traditional procedures, his code would be developed by experts, but the neutral and democratic character of the law would now be guaranteed by the order and logic of its forms.

Sources:

Lawrence M. Friedman, *A History of American Law,* second edition (New York: Simon & Schuster, 1985);

Morton J. Horwitz, *The Transformation of American Law, 1780–1860* (Cambridge, Mass.: Harvard University Press, 1977).

CORPORATIONS AND BUSINESS REGULATION

Free Incorporation. Like private law, the changing legal treatment of corporations reflected an assault on privilege and the impact of an erratic economy. Anglo-American law originally viewed the process of incorporation as a grant of authority issued by the government to private persons charged with performing specific tasks that benefited the public as well as the investors in the corporation. A good example is a corporation created to build a bridge, which would improve transportation for the community and make a regulated profit by charging tolls. The mechanism for policing corporations was the corporate charter, issued on a one-by-one basis in special legislation and subject to revocation if the corporation exceeded its carefully defined grant of authority. Beginning with the Revolution, Americans criticized this approach to incorporation as an abuse of government powers that gave undue privileges to the few people who obtained a special corporate charter. That attack intensified during the 1830s and 1840s, and beginning around mid-century, egalitarian principles led states to adopt new procedures for the creation of corporations. Entrepreneurs no longer needed to obtain a special charter but merely to comply with a standardized set of requirements. The Alabama constitution of 1867 typified the trend in providing that "corporations may be formed under general laws, but shall not be created by special act." The decline of the special charter posed a new problem in law, however, for the charter had been the principal mechanism for regulating corporations. The charter did not altogether lose this function in any state until New Jersey enacted its general incorporation law in 1889, but alternative approaches to regulation began to emerge as the principle of free incorporation became established.

Decline of Mixed Enterprise. The relaxation of traditional supervision of corporations was paralleled by a shift in the financing of large-scale enterprise. State and municipal governments—which since the 1820s had invested actively in a variety of transportation schemes that promised to repeat the success of the Erie Canal—retreated from similar ventures as one unsuccessful business after another failed to produce anything but higher taxes. By 1874 sixteen state constitutions barred the state from owning corporate stock. As government investment dried up, corporations turned to private capital markets that expanded rapidly after British businessmen invested in American outlets following the European uprisings of 1848 and the discovery of gold in California (1849). And as government oversight disappeared along with government capital, the unregulated scramble for financing ushered in an era of unscrupulous and powerful businessmen and financiers known as Robber Barons. State laws reacted belatedly to specific tricks that had cheated investors, such as "watered stock"—free stock given to promoters which induced unwary investors to purchase stock in the belief that it was backed by real corporate assets. For example, the Illinois constitution of 1870 provided that "no railroad corporation shall issue any stock or bonds, except for money, labor or property actually received." Informed observers recognized, however, that such piecemeal efforts could not substitute for new regulatory structures.

Shareholder Suits. If the corporation was no longer to be regarded as an extension of government authority, one new approach was to give the victims of corporate mismanagement new tools with which to protect themselves. This was the idea behind the type of lawsuit known today as the shareholder derivative suit. Through this device, one stockholder could bring suit on behalf of all stockholders against corporate officials whose abuses of power had cheated investors. The shareholder derivative suit was built upon the

Christopher Columbus Langdell, dean of the Harvard Law School during the 1870s

idea that the corporation was a sort of trust fund, that is, a fund that one group of people managed for the benefit of others. In the case of a corporation, the beneficiaries of the fund were the investors and, if the corporation dissolved, the people to whom it owed money. The comparison of a corporation to a trust fund sought to restore the accountability that had eroded with the waning idea of the corporation as a state-conferred privilege. As the U.S. Supreme Court declared in 1875, "the idea that the capital of a corporation is a football to be thrown into the market for the purposes of speculation . . . is a modern and wicked invention."

Police Power. The weakened tie between corporations and government caused courts to rethink not only the nature of the corporation but also the nature of government. Traditionally jurists reasoned that regulation of corporations was based on authority reserved by governments when they granted charters, and the terms of the charter defined the scope of the regulatory authority. In *Commonwealth* v. *Alger* (1851) Massachusetts justice Lemuel Shaw articulated a new view that the "police power" to regulate health, safety, and morals was an inherent attribute of government sovereignty. Shaw declared that "every holder of property, however absolute and unqualified may be his title, holds it under the implied liability that his use of it may be so regulated, that it shall not be injurious to the equal enjoyment of others having an equal right to the enjoyment of their property, nor injurious to the rights of the

PINKERTON'S NATIONAL DETECTIVE AGENCY

The son of a Scottish constable, Allan Pinkerton (1819–1884) founded the nation's first detective agency, which is still in existence. Born in Glasgow and trained as a cooper, Pinkerton became involved in labor demonstrations and fled to the United States in 1842 in order to avoid arrest. He settled in Dundee, Illinois, where, as a freelance detective, he helped apprehend a band of local counterfeiters. While in Illinois Pinkerton also became an ardent abolitionist and smuggled fugitive slaves into Canada. After becoming the first detective on the Chicago police force in 1850, he established Pinkerton's National Detective Agency, specializing in railroad security. Its emblem was an eye, and its motto was "We Never Sleep." In 1861 Pinkerton uncovered a plot to assassinate Abraham Lincoln, and he personally guarded the president-elect as he traveled to Washington, D.C., for his inauguration. When the Civil War started in April, Lincoln appointed Pinkerton chief of the Secret Service Bureau. During the course of the conflict Pinkerton, under the alias "Maj. E. J. Allen," organized espionage rings that operated behind enemy lines.

The Pinkerton Agency greatly expanded after the war, compiling the nation's most complete files on criminal activity. By this time criminals feared Pinkerton so much that they referred to him as "The Eye" (from which the term "private eye" later arose). Starting in the 1870s the agency became increasingly identified with management in labor disputes. Pinkerton men infiltrated the Molly Maguires, a secret labor organization, in 1875–1877 and attempted to break the Homestead Strike of 1892. Some of the western outlaws they encountered included Frank and Jesse James and Butch Cassidy and the Sundance Kid.

Source: James D. Horan, *The Pinkertons: The Detective Dynasty That Made History* (New York: Crown, 1967).

view, the most clear-cut situations involved the practices of governments as employers, which could reduce hours of employment without prompting complaints that regulatory legislation was interfering with private enterprise. The federal government passed the first of several eight-hour laws in 1868, and several state governments acted similarly. The regulation of work for private firms began with child labor. Every northeastern state had enacted some sort of child-labor legislation by 1851, but the precedent spread slowly to other parts of the workforce. Massachusetts limited women working in manufacturing to ten hours per day and sixty hours per week, but a parallel proposal for men failed to pass. Enforcement of labor legislation was generally weak. A New Jersey law of 1851 barred children under ten from factories, but the penalty for a violation was only a fine of $50.

Railroad Regulation. State railroad commissions were the most important regulatory agencies to emerge during the third quarter of the nineteenth century. The Massachusetts railroad commission created in 1869 brought to culmination a line of administrative development in New England that dated back to the first state railroad commission, established in Rhode Island in 1839. Provided with inspection powers to undertake "general supervision of all railroads," the Massachusetts commission filed annual reports to the legislature and notified the companies of needed repairs, unfair rates, or infractions of law. Although it gained considerable influence, especially through the work of Commissioner Charles Francis Adams Jr., the agency had no powers to fix rates or order changes in railroad practices. The so-called Granger laws adopted in the Midwest during the 1870s adopted a more aggressive regulatory stance. In Illinois, Wisconsin, and Iowa farmers and small merchants combined to pass legislation that set maximum railroad rates and authorized the state railroad commission to prosecute railroads or warehouses found to be in violation of any state law.

Sources:

Lawrence M. Friedman, *A History of American Law*, second edition (New York: Simon & Schuster, 1985);

Morton J. Horwitz, *The Transformation of American Law, 1870–1960: The Crisis of Legal Orthodoxy* (New York: Oxford University Press, 1992).

community." In essence Shaw found that state legislatures could pass laws applying the traditional maxim *sic utere tuo, ut alienum non laedas* ("use your own so as not to injure another's"), which courts had enforced when a property owner claimed to suffer from a neighbor's use of property, such as the noises or odors emanating from a factory. Legislatures and courts would wrestle with the usefulness of this reasoning as a variety of groups sought protection from different types of corporate activities.

Labor Regulations. Most legislation to protect laborers focused on the length of the working day. Workers rallied for "Eight hours for work, eight hours for rest, and eight hours for what we will!" From a legal point of

EXPANSION OF JUDICIAL REVIEW

Constitutionality of Legislation. The power of courts to invalidate unconstitutional legislation is often regarded as one of the hallmarks of the American system of government, but judges had struck down laws very rarely and in narrowly defined situations prior to 1850. Only once in American history, in *Marbury* v. *Madison* (1803), had the U.S. Supreme Court declared an act of Congress unconstitutional, and the law involved in that case was a jurisdictional technicality. State courts had not been much more exacting. The New York Court of Appeals, the highest court in the state, invalidated only three stat-

The graduating class of the Union College of Law, Chicago, in 1877

utes before 1820 and only three more in each of the next two decades. The U.S. Supreme Court under Chief Justice John Marshall (1801–1835) had ruled that various state laws violated the federal constitution, but this exercise of judicial review had focused primarily on preventing state infringements on national authority. In the period from 1850 to 1877, coordinate review emerged as an important element of federal and state governance, and federal review of state laws expanded. At times the new judicial activism sparked vehement protest, but the trend nevertheless continued and set the stage for more intense confrontations in the years ahead.

Substantive Due Process. The more assertive stance of the judiciary first became apparent in the state courts. New York courts struck down fourteen statutes in the 1840s and twenty-five in the 1850s. The dominant force behind this trend was the determination to protect property rights from adverse legislation. In *Wynehamer* v. *People* (1856), for example, the New York Court of Appeals invalidated a state law prohibiting the sale of alcohol. Judge George F. Comstock declared that "theories of public good or public necessity may be plausible or even so truthful as to command public majorities. But whether truthful or plausible merely, and by whatever numbers they are assented to, there are some absolute private rights beyond their reach, and among these the constitution places the rights of property." This protection for what Comstock called "absolute private rights" of property was an early application of the concept known as "substantive due process." In contrast to an analysis of the procedural steps required of government

in order to deprive a person of liberty or property, the doctrine of substantive due process identified fundamental rights—in *Wynehamer* v. *People*, the right to sell liquor—that courts would safeguard from any infringement, no matter what procedure the government followed. *Wynehamer* v. *People* notwithstanding, state courts rarely invalidated prohibition statutes, which most analysts regarded as examples of state police power to regulate health, safety, and morals. Nonetheless, the concept of substantive due process began to develop into one of the most important ideas in constitutional law.

The *Dred Scott* Case. A hint of the explosive potential of substantive due process appeared in *Dred Scott* v. *Sandford* (1857), one of the most notorious decision in American legal history. Dred Scott was a Missouri slave whose owner, an army surgeon, had taken him first to the free state of Illinois and subsequently to Fort Snelling in what is now Minnesota and was then part of the Louisiana Purchase Territory, in which the Missouri Compromise prohibited slavery above the 36° 30' latitude. Scott filed suit in federal court claiming that he was entitled to freedom as a result of his residence in a free state and a free territory. Chief Justice Roger B. Taney's opinion for the Supreme Court made two momentous rulings: first, the federal court did not have authority to hear the case because blacks, whether free or slave, were not citizens of the United States; and second, Dred Scott's residence in the Louisiana Purchase Territory did not entitle him to freedom because the Missouri Compromise ban on slavery was unconstitutional. The latter ruling was only the second time in which the Supreme Court found an act of

Congress unconstitutional. Unlike *Marbury* v. *Madison*, however, the statute invalidated in *Dred Scott* v. *Sandford* was a crucial piece of federal legislation. In finding that Congress did not have power to bar slavery from the Louisiana Purchase Territory, Chief Justice Taney mostly relied upon his reading of the constitutional grant of authority to regulate the federal territories. But part of the opinion invoked the protection of substantive due process for property interests in slaves. Taney wrote that "an act of Congress which deprives a citizen of the United States of his liberty or property, . . . who had committed no offence against the laws, could hardly be dignified with the name of due process of law."

Property Interests. During and after the Civil War, judicial review developed most significantly in cases involving state and local railroad investments that had turned sour. In *Gelpcke* v. *Dubuque* (1864) the U.S. Supreme Court required a city to honor the railroad bonds it had issued even though the Iowa Supreme Court had found that the bonds were issued in violation of state law. But the courts, paralleling the stricter definition of "public purpose" emerging in eminent domain cases, also helped to close the door to municipal investments in railroads. Thomas M. Cooley's opinion for the Michigan Supreme Court in *People* v. *Salem* (1870) rejected a long line of precedents approving the use of taxation powers to fund railroad construction. "To lay with one hand the power of the government on the property of the citizen, and with the other to bestow it upon favored individuals to aid private enterprises and build up private fortunes, is none the less a robbery because it is done under the forms of law and is called taxation," the U.S. Supreme Court agreed in *Loan Association* v. *Topeka* (1874). Typical was the situation of Quincy, Illinois, which approved a $500,000 bond by a vote of 1,949 to 185 one year before the 1870 Illinois constitution barred such investments. One resident declared that "an excited and howling mob, which may call itself a city railroad election, hardly amounts to the dignity of deliberation. Its acts should never be held by the courts as affording a sufficient foundation for the creation of a lien against the private property of any man." Another area of special judicial attention was the property interest in pursuing a particular trade or profession. Two related cases in the U.S. Supreme Court—*Cummings* v. *Missouri* (1866) and *Ex Parte Garland* (1867)—reviewed a loyalty oath prescribed by the Missouri Constitution that barred former Confederates from obtaining a preaching license and a loyalty oath prescribed by a federal statute that prohibited former Confederates from practicing law. The Supreme Court struck down both of the requirements, marking the first time that it had declared that part of a state constitution violated the federal constitution and only the fifth time that the Court had invalidated an act of Congress.

Popular Response. As at other points in American history, controversy often broke out over judicial invalidation of laws passed by elected representatives. Horace Greeley, editor of the *New York Tribune*, wrote that the Supreme Court decision in *Dred Scott* v. *Sandford* was "entitled to just so much moral weight as would be the judgment of a majority of those congregated in any Washington bar-room." Abraham Lincoln spoke for Republicans everywhere when he called on members of Congress to pass legislation barring slavery from the territories despite the Court's ruling that the Congress had no power to enact such a ban. *Cummings* v. *Missouri* and *Ex Parte Garland*, which had been brought by individuals wishing to limit Reconstruction in the South, similarly angered Republicans who believed that the Supreme Court was interfering with legislative responsibilities. The most forceful response was reserved for the Court's decision in *Hepburn* v. *Griswold* (1870), which threatened to overturn the financial system of the country. During the Civil War, the federal government, under Treasury Secretary Salmon P. Chase, had expanded the supply of money by issuing $450 million of paper currency (greenbacks) that was not redeemable in gold or silver. In *Hepburn* v. *Griswold* the Supreme Court ruled in an opinion by Chase, now chief justice, that the so-called greenback laws were unconstitutional. President Ulysses S. Grant immediately appointed two new justices to the Court who were known to support the constitutionality of the greenback laws, and in the *Legal Tender* cases (1871) the Court reversed the 1870 decision. A later chief justice, Charles Evans Hughes, would call *Dred Scott* v. *Sandford* and *Hepburn* v. *Griswold* two of the most grievous "self-inflicted wounds" in the history of the Supreme Court.

Challenges to Regulation. The increasing state efforts to regulate factory work and railroad rates prompted complaints that the legislatures had violated the rights of businesses. In addressing these cases, state and federal courts searched for a test that would determine whether a particular regulation was a valid exercise of the police power. In *Munn* v. *Illinois* (1877) the U.S. Supreme Court addressed the issue in ruling on the validity of laws that set maximum rates for the storage of grain. The Supreme Court found that the state legislature was authorized to set maximum rates because warehouse owners had devoted their property to a use that "affects the community at large" and therefore had to "submit to be controlled by the public for the common good." In dissent, however, Justice Stephen Field argued that the public had less interest in the use of buildings for the storage of grain than in the use of buildings for the residence of families. If a legislature could set rates for grain warehouses, it could set rents for apartments or sale prices for home. "If this be sound law . . . ," Field declared, "all property and all business in the State are held at the mercy of a majority of its legislature."

Common Law. The terms of the debate in *Munn* v. *Illinois* identified a test by which courts might measure legislation for validity. In basing its decision on the finding that the warehousing was an activity that "affects the community at large," the majority was applying the maxim of *sic utere* that courts had traditionally invoked to resolve disputes between neighboring landowners. In using common-law concepts to uphold state regulatory power, the Court was following the reasoning of Lemuel Shaw in *Commonwealth* v. *Alger*. For the next several decades, however, the most important constitutional cases would center on the converse principle: private conduct that did not violate common-law rules was protected by the Constitution from legislative interference. Most notably, because the law of contracts did not judge the fairness of a bargain or regulate agreements to redress unequal market power, the Court concluded that so-called liberty of contract barred legislatures from mandating fair bargains between railroads and shippers or regulating agreements between employers and employees to redress unequal market power. Under this version of the doctrine of substantive due process, the Supreme Court would invalidate more than 150 statutes until a revolution in constitutional law took place in the 1930s.

Sources:

Don E. Fehrenbacher, *The Dred Scott Case: Its Significance in American Law and Politics* (New York: Oxford University Press, 1978);

Harold M. Hyman and William M. Wiecek, *Equal Justice Under the Law: Constitutional Development, 1835–1875* (New York: Harper & Row, 1982).

Abraham Lincoln in 1854, while he was practicing law in Springfield, Illinois

THE LEGAL PROFESSION

Professionalism. Changes in the practice of law during the mid nineteenth century fit into a broader development of professionalism as a theme unifying different sorts of work. Just as training in law became more structured and admission to practice became more closely regulated, similar trends could be seen in other fields ranging from medicine to architecture. The overarching rise of professionalism was tied to the expansion of the economy, which provided new markets for various specialists, and also to the increasing prestige of science, which helped to explain why professionalization in medicine preceded comparable developments in law by a generation. The analogy of law to science that was so pervasive during the third quarter of the nineteenth century would later lose much of its appeal, but not until it had left a lasting imprint on the organization of the legal profession.

Langdell's Law. The vanguard of professionalism in legal education was Harvard Law School, where Christopher Columbus Langdell assumed the new position of dean in September 1870. Langdell promptly revolutionized legal education, which even in the leading schools consisted of a one-year program of lectures and independent reading not markedly different from traditional apprenticeship arrangements between practitioners and novices. Langdell lengthened the Harvard program to two years in 1871 and to three years in 1876, which remains the standard at American law schools. For the first

time he required entrants to have a college degree or to pass a formidable examination. Langdell also developed an entirely new curriculum. He divided the field of law into sets of courses progressing from the basic to the advanced, requiring students to pass examinations in order to move forward. Throughout the United States, law students are still required in their first year to take courses in subjects that Langdell identified as fundamental, including contracts, torts, property, and civil procedure.

Formalism in the Classroom. Most important, Langdell developed a new method for teaching all subjects. Students would no longer be assigned to read the same sort of treatises and commentaries that practitioners used; no longer would they listen to professors deliver lectures explaining the law. Instead, Langdell introduced the "casebook," consisting of the legal decisions that had contributed the most to the development of each field. Students probed for the principles underlying these cases in a Socratic dialogue conducted by the professor, who now became a full-time member of the university faculty rather than a part-time practitioner. Langdell published the first casebook in 1871. His approach was not an instant success—by the end of his first term only seven students remained in his class, and Boston University Law School was established in 1872 to offer a traditional education. Gradually, however, Langdell's revolution came to dominate all instruction in American law schools.

Fields of Practice. The maturation of the economy provided new opportunities for lawyers to make money. Even in large cities, few attorneys practiced in lucrative specialties in 1850; the noteworthy exception had traditionally been marine insurance. Even leaders of the bar spent much of their time on conveyances of real estate, the drafting of wills and the administration of estates, and routine debt collection. Industrialization placed a premium on different fields such as patent law, torts, and eminent domain. In the more advanced stage of economic development that characterized the years after 1850 the problems of corporate finance and management became specialties broad enough to support a much larger number of commercial lawyers. Although railroads and other corporate clients affected practice in every city of significant size, the trend was most advanced on Wall Street, New York, where leaders of the bar focused on the issuance of stocks and bonds and on the designing of increasingly complex corporate structures. The appearance of law firms that would long remain influential illustrated the entrenchment taking place in the period. The forerunner of the firm of Cravath, Swaine and Moore moved to New York in 1854. The founders of Shearman and Sterling met in the practice of David Dudley Field, who represented the famous Wall Street operators Jim Fisk and Jay Gould. As one of the most distinguished practitioners in the country, Field confirmed young John W. Sterling's sense that the era of the legal generalist was over and guided him into developing an expertise in the law of corporations.

Bar Associations. Concern over the involvement of attorneys in corrupt machinations prompted the founding of the first professional organizations. The Association of the Bar of the City of New York was organized in 1870 to combat the tainting of the law through the highly publicized battle over control of the Erie Railroad. Organizations quickly spread to other parts of the country; Chicago lawyers founded a bar association in 1874. By 1878 eight city and eight state bar associations had been founded in twelve states. In the same year, the American Bar Association was founded at the resort in Saratoga, New York, with a charge to "advance the science of jurisprudence . . . uphold the honor of the profession . . . and promote cordial intercourse among members of the American Bar." Like farmers who were at the same time organizing to bargain collectively with railroads over shipping rates, and like laborers who were organizing to bargain collectively with employers over the conditions of work, attorneys saw themselves as organizing to deal collectively with corporations in asserting professional independence, including ethical standards. As one founder put it, the early bar associations were troubled that lawyers "do simply what their employers desire." And like the organization of physicians, bar associations also sought to suppress competition, actively seeking to suppress informal training by apprenticeship

and supporting the reforms in legal education spearheaded by Langdell.

Lincoln the Lawyer. The legal practice of Abraham Lincoln reflects the changes in the profession that affected lawyers in modest towns such as Springfield, Illinois. After serving as a junior partner first to the politically connected John Todd Stuart and then to Stephen T. Logan, Lincoln opened a firm with the younger William Herndon in 1844. As the head attorney of the firm he assumed responsibility for spending about ten weeks twice each year riding with Judge David Davis and other attorneys to each courthouse in the eleven thousand square miles of the Eighth Judicial District. (He would later appoint Davis to the U.S. Supreme Court.) In each town he handled a wide variety of cases, many of which were small disputes among neighbors. In 1851 he handled his first significant case for a railroad, enforcing a stock subscription by an investor unhappy about a change in the planned route of the road. By middecade Lincoln was spending much of his time on cases involving railroads. For example, he successfully represented the powerful Illinois Central in a suit brought by a county challenging the state's authority to exempt the railroad from all local taxes. He also defended the builders of the first railroad bridge to cross the Mississippi River in a suit brought by the owners of a steamboat that crashed into a pier. Although one of the leading lawyers in Illinois, he encountered the exclusivity of nationally prominent attorneys when he became the local counsel in patent litigation over the mechanical reaper invented by Cyrus McCormick. "Why did you bring that d—d long armed Ape here," Pittsburgh attorney Edwin Stanton asked the Philadelphia lawyer who headed McCormick's legal team; "he does not know anything and can do you no good." Snubbed, Lincoln dropped out of the litigation; as president of the United States seven years later, he appointed Stanton to the position of Secretary of War.

Sources:

Maxwell Bloomfield, *American Lawyers in a Changing Society, 1776–1876* (Cambridge, Mass.: Harvard University Press, 1976);

David Herbert Donald, *Lincoln* (New York: Simon & Schuster, 1995);

Lawrence M. Friedman, *A History of American Law*, second edition (New York: Simon & Schuster, 1985);

Arthur E. Sutherland, *The Law at Harvard: A History of Ideas and Men, 1817–1967* (Cambridge, Mass.: Harvard University Press, 1967).

RESISTANCE TO THE FUGITIVE SLAVE ACT

Expanded Federal Role. The Fugitive Slave Act that formed part of the Compromise of 1850 supplemented the mechanisms established by Congress in 1793 for the retrieval of runaways. Under the 1793 law, slaveholders could seize an alleged runaway in free territory and bring the accused before a federal judge or local magistrate to prove title to the slave and obtain a certificate of rendition entitling the master to remove the slave from the free jurisdiction. The law placed most of the burden of slave catching on masters, including the burden of dealing with uncooperative Northerners, and it made rendition hearings inconvenient to arrange because few federal judges were available to participate. The 1850 Fugitive Slave Act provided for federal circuit courts to designate commissioners specifically to hear rendition proceedings, and it authorized commissioners and federal marshals to form a posse of bystanders to capture runaways. The latter provision made every adult male a potential slave catcher. In addition, the act obligated the federal government to pay all expenses associated with foiling escape attempts, and it provided that obstruction of the law was punishable by a fine of $1,000 and imprisonment for six months.

Perversion of Justice. The Fugitive Slave Act enraged Northerners not only because it represented federal intervention in support of slave catching but also because it trampled on basic guarantees of fairness. Alleged slaves were barred from testifying on their own behalf and precluded from invoking the legal process of habeas corpus, the traditional method for courts to review whether or not a person was being held in custody lawfully. The commissioners who heard rendition cases earned a fee of $10 if they found in favor of the slaveowner but only $5 if they found that the alleged slave had been misidentified. Comparing the commissioners' fees with the fine for obstruction of the law, abolitionist Anson Burlingame commented that the Fugitive Slave Act set the price of a Carolina black at $1,000 and a Yankee soul at $5. The apparent unfairness of the legislation made it difficult for the act to find support even among more moderate Northerners willing to accept some sort of federal role in the capture of runaways.

Constitutional Challenges. Resistance to the Fugitive Slave Act proceeded along several fronts. In Washington, Free Soil members of Congress called in vain for repeal of the legislation. In the Northern states, many black residents left for Canada; the black population of Ontario doubled to eleven thousand during the 1850s. Meanwhile, batteries of antislavery lawyers argued that the law was unconstitutional. They relied on several arguments. The commissioners created by the Fugitive Slave Act were not judges, they reasoned, and therefore not authorized to make final decisions in rendition hearings. They maintained that the legislation denied the rights of alleged slaves to a jury trial, to the writ of habeas corpus, and to cross-examination of their accusers. They also argued that the Constitution may have permitted the rendition of fugitive slaves but did not authorize the federal government to participate in the process. In the leading decision on the issue, however, Lemuel Shaw upheld the constitutionality of the law against a legal attack in Massachusetts led by prominent antislavery attorneys Richard Henry Dana, Samuel Sewall, and Robert Rantoul.

Forcible Resistance. When legislative appeals and litigation campaigns broke down, some Northerners resorted to direct action to rescue alleged slaves. When

IS VIRTUE CONSTITUTIONAL?

The judges and lawyers,—simply as such, I mean,—and all men of expediency, try this case by a very low and incompetent standard. They consider, not whether the Fugitive Slave Law is right, but whether it is what they call *constitutional*. Is virtue constitutional, or vice? Is equity constitutional, or iniquity? In important moral and vital questions, like this, it is just as impertinent to ask whether a law is constitutional or not, as to ask whether it is profitable or not. They persist in being the servants of the worst of men, and not the servants of humanity. The question is, not whether you or your grandfather, seventy years ago, did not enter into an agreement to serve the Devil, and that service is not accordingly now due; but whether you will not now, for once and at last, serve God,—in spite of your own past recreancy, or that of your ancestor,—by obeying that eternal and only just CONSTITUTION, which He, and not any Jefferson or Adams, has written in your being.

. . . I have lived for the last month—and I think that every man in Massachusetts capable of the sentiment of patriotism must have had a similar experience—with the sense of having suffered a vast and indefinite loss. I did not know at first what ailed me. At last it occurred to me that what I had lost was a country. I had never respected the government near to which I lived, but I had foolishly thought that I might manage to live here, minding my private affairs, and forget it. For my part, my old and worthiest pursuits have lost I cannot say how much of their attraction, and I feel that my investment in life here is worth many per cent. less since Massachusetts last deliberately sent back an innocent man, Anthony Burns, to slavery. I dwelt before, perhaps, in the illusion that my life passed somewhere only *between* heaven and hell, but now I cannot persuade myself that I do not dwell *wholly within* hell. The site of that political organization called Massachusetts is to me morally covered with volcanic scoriae and cinders, such as Milton describes in the infernal regions. If there is any hell more unprincipled than our rulers, and we, the ruled, I feel curious to see it.

Source: Henry David Thoreau, "Slavery in Massachusetts" (1854).

Georgia slave catchers arrived in Boston a few weeks after the passage of the Fugitive Slave Act to bring back the runaways William and Ellen Craft, abolitionists hid the couple while a vigilance committee harassed the agents into leaving the town. A runaway from Virginia

Guards stationed on the front steps of the Boston Court House in April 1851 to prevent attempts to rescue the runaway slave Thomas Sims

named Shadrach, seized in February 1851 in a Boston coffeehouse by slave catchers to whom he was serving coffee, was rescued from a federal courthouse by a group of African Americans who overpowered the marshals guarding the fugitive. The most violent clash took place in the Quaker community of Christiana, Pennsylvania, in September 1851, where a Maryland slaveowner was killed and his son seriously wounded in a gunfight with a group of African Americans resisting an attempt to seize three former slaves. Shortly afterward a group of black and white abolitionists broke into a police station in Syracuse, New York, rescued a captured runaway known as Jerry, and helped him cross Lake Ontario into Canada.

Federal Response. Resistance to the Fugitive Slave Act deeply disturbed President Millard Fillmore, who called a special meeting of his cabinet to discuss the rescue of Shadrach. Vigorous enforcement of the law became a central priority of the administration. One measure of this determination was the willingness to invoke the ultimate sanction against rescuers: prosecution for treason, punishable by execution. After the Christiana massacre, federal prosecutors brought treason charges against two Quakers who had refused to help recapture the runaways, along with some forty other defendants, but the court ruled that the evidence did not justify the

charges. Another measure of the administration's commitment to the Fugitive Slave Act was the expense it assumed to defeat rescue attempts. An escort of three hundred armed deputies and soldiers guarded the runaway Thomas Sims when he was removed from the Boston courthouse to the navy yard in April 1851 and put on a ship bound for the South. This show of force ended open attempts to rescue fugitives in Boston for three years, but the arrest of runaway Anthony Burns in March 1854 reopened the contest. After one federal marshal died in an abolitionist assault on a courthouse, the administration of President Franklin Pierce spent approximately $100,000 to return Burns to Virginia, refusing to allow the slaveowner to consider offers for the purchase of the fugitive's freedom.

Personal Liberty Laws. The rendition of Anthony Burns, which occurred at the same time as the passage of the Kansas-Nebraska Act, prompted increasing numbers of Northern states to adopt so-called personal liberty laws in an effort to frustrate the Fugitive Slave Act. Vermont had already led the way in 1850 with legislation that defied the federal mechanism by offering the writ of habeas corpus to detained fugitives, affirming their right to a jury trial, and requiring the state's attorney in each county to intervene on behalf of fugitives in rendition proceedings. In 1854–1855 Vermont extended its protections, and Maine, Massachusetts, Rhode Island, Connecticut, Ohio, Wisconsin, and Michigan passed laws to prevent state officials from taking part in the enforcement of the federal law. The Massachusetts personal liberty law vacated the office of any state official who authorized the rendition of a fugitive, barred any such person from holding state office, and disbarred attorneys who represented slaveholders. The Fugitive Slave Law and personal liberty laws thus presented a striking reversal in the alignment of sectionalism and constitutionalism that had become familiar in the 1830s. The Southern states now called for an extension of federal power in support of slavery; the Northern states sought to block the initiative through an exercise of state sovereignty.

Vindication of Federal Authority. The U.S. Supreme Court examined the constitutionality of the personal liberty laws in *Ableman* v. *Booth* (1859). The case arose in Wisconsin, where abolitionist Sherman Booth had helped to rescue the alleged slave Joshua Glover and send him to Canada. Writing for a unanimous court, Chief Justice Roger B. Taney held that the personal liberty laws were unconstitutional. "Although the State of Wisconsin is sovereign within its territorial limits to a certain extent," Taney wrote, "yet that sovereignty is limited and restricted by the Constitution of the United States." A few years later the Wisconsin Supreme Court conceded that the state had been in error and apologized for disturbing the proper relations between state and federal government. By that time, however, Wisconsin might have been expected to be deferential to the principle of national authority, for thousands of state citizens were serving in a federal army organized to suppress the secession of the Southern states.

Sources:

Stanley W. Campbell, *The Slave Catchers: Enforcement of the Fugitive Slave Law, 1850–1860* (Chapel Hill: University of North Carolina Press, 1970);

Paul Finkelman, *An Imperfect Union: Slavery, Federalism, and Comity* (Chapel Hill: University of North Carolina Press, 1981);

Thomas D. Morris, *Free Men All: The Personal Liberty Laws of the North, 1780–1861* (Baltimore: Johns Hopkins University Press, 1974).

WARFARE AND THE RULE OF LAW

Civil Liberties in Wartime. War and the apprehension of war have tested and sharpened American ideas about free speech and the judicial process ever since the sedition controversy of 1798–1800. During the Civil War, a conflict fought to enforce allegiance to the federal government, the problem of reconciling duties of loyalty and rights of expression was particularly acute. Not surprisingly, at times the federal government significantly restricted the liberties of its citizens, especially at moments and in places of particular peril to Union authority. For the most part, however, the federal government interfered with constitutional freedoms less aggressively in the Civil War than it would in either World War I or World War II. The political leaders of the mid

A draft riot in New York City in July 1863

nineteenth century were not necessarily more libertarian than their successors, but the government machinery available to suppress dissent was much weaker and less rationally organized.

Maryland. Some of the most forceful federal measures took place at the outset of the war, while Maryland debated disunion. The secession of the state would have compelled the abandonment of the federal capital in Washington, D.C., and the Lincoln administration moved decisively to suppress supporters of the Confederacy. In May 1861 Army officials imprisoned suspected Baltimore secessionists in Fort McHenry, including the grandson of Francis Scott Key, who had written the "Star Spangled Banner" during a British attack on the fortress during the War of 1812. When the state legislature met in Frederick four months later, the army arrested thirty-one suspected secessionist delegates and several of their supposed allies, including the mayor of Baltimore. All of these prisoners were held until Unionist sentiment stabilized and the state elected a new legislature in November. The army then released prisoners who took an oath of allegiance to the federal government; the last of the group remained in prison until December 1862.

Suspending the Writ of Habeas Corpus. The writ of habeas corpus (Latin for "you should have the body") is a document that a law enforcement individual must possess in order to bring a party before a court or judge. The "Great Writ," as it is called, is part of Anglo-American common law tradition and protects an individual from illegal imprisonment. As part of the military intervention in Maryland, President Lincoln ordered suspension of this procedure in the area between Philadelphia and Washington. John Merryman, one of the Maryland secessionists imprisoned in May 1861, challenged Lincoln's order by filing a petition in the federal circuit court in Baltimore for issuance of a writ of habeas corpus. The Supreme Court justice responsible for the circuit was Chief Justice Roger B. Taney, who granted the petition in *Ex Parte Merryman*. Although Congress was not in session, Taney reasoned that the Constitution permitted only Congress, not the president, to suspend the writ of habeas corpus. The Lincoln administration defied the order. "Are all the laws, *but one,* to go unexecuted," the president asked Congress when it assembled on 4 July, "and the government itself go to pieces, lest that one be violated?" During the next sixteen months, Lincoln extended north to Maine the military line along which the writ was suspended, and he also declared the writ suspended in Missouri and on Key West, Florida.

Conscription. The transformation of the Union war effort after the failure of the 1862 campaign in Virginia, and particularly the gradual institution of a draft, led to a more expanded suspension of the writ of habeas corpus. Secretary of War Edwin Stanton declared the writ of habeas corpus suspended throughout the country on 8 August 1862, for draft evaders and "all persons arrested for disloyal practices," especially the act of discouraging enlistment in the army. This proclamation gave federal officials sweeping powers to identify individuals as disloyal and lock them up, and within one month more than 350 Northerners were imprisoned. By the time Lincoln confirmed Stanton's order in September, however, public outcry over the arrests and the successful filling of the draft quota had caused the War Department to relax its enforcement practices. Renewed conscription efforts and suspension of the writ again went together in March 1863, when Congress ratified Lincoln's habeas corpus policy and enacted a more stringent draft. The unpopularity of the conscription act, dramatized by the New York City draft riots in July 1863, in turn prompted Lincoln to proclaim again in September that the writ was suspended throughout the North. By this time, however, such proclamations essentially served as publicity gestures to reinforce the draft rather than actual changes in the administration of justice.

Military Jurisdiction. The expanded authority of military tribunals in the Civil War raised legal issues that went beyond the suspension of the writ of habeas corpus, for the writ is only one of the many procedural guarantees of fairness recognized by the American judicial system. Trial of civilians by military courts raised the question of how far judicial processes would be displaced by army standards of justice. It should be noted that military law often provided for its own procedural safeguards, including an appellate process that in capital cases reached

up to the president. But military proceedings inevitably tended to be improvisational and could easily be perceived as merely executing the orders of a commanding officer. Careful analysis of these cases has revealed a striking disparity between the broad authority granted to military commissions and the limited circumstances un-

THE JAMES BROTHERS

In the legends of the Old West, no other outlaws are more preeminent than Frank (1844–1915) and Jesse (1847–1882) James. Popular imagination views them as latter-day Robin Hoods who stole from the rich and gave to the poor; however, the historical facts are not so flattering. The brothers were born in Clay County, Missouri, the sons of a preacher. During the Civil War they rode with Confederate guerrilla leaders William C. Quantrill and "Bloody Bill" Anderson, and participated in several atrocities. When the conflict ended in 1865, Missouri guerrillas, unlike regular Confederate soldiers, did not receive amnesty from the federal government.

Frank and Jesse James went home as outlaws, and between 1866 and 1881 they robbed banks, stagecoaches, and trains in Missouri, Kansas, Kentucky, Iowa, Mississippi, West Virginia, Texas, and Minnesota. The James gang usually consisted of former Confederate guerrillas such as the Younger brothers—Cole and Jim. They became heroes to many former Confederates living in Missouri, and eastern newspapers sensationalized their exploits. Pinkerton detectives made several unsuccessful attempts to capture the brothers, and the governor of Missouri placed a $5,000 bounty on each of their heads.

Jesse was the more violent of the two brothers, pistol-whipping and shooting his victims indiscriminately. During a December 1869 robbery at the Daviess County Savings Bank in Gallatin, Missouri, Jesse shot the cashier merely because he resembled a Union officer who had killed "Bloody Bill" Anderson during the war. The most spectacular robbery by the James gang occurred in Northfield, Minnesota, in 1876, during which it fought a twenty-minute gun battle with the townspeople. Jesse James was killed in 1882 by a former gang member. Frank James surrendered to the authorities two years later, stood trial for murder, and was acquitted. He lived the remainder of his life in a peaceful manner, giving tours of his birthplace and selling pebbles from his brother's grave.

Source: Paul Trachtman, *The Gunfighters* (New York: Time-Life Books, 1974).

Clement Vallandigham (center) and some of his fellow "Copperheads"(Confederate sympathizers who lived in the North)

der which these tribunals tried civilians. In 1863, for example, Congress recognized military contractors as a part of the army and authorized military commissions to hear and pass sentence in cases of contract default. In practice, however, most cases involved defendants directly aiding the Confederacy. Of the approximately forty-two hundred cases in which military courts tried civilians, almost half pertained to the guerrilla war in Missouri, many involving bridge burning, horse stealing, or acts of violence. Similar patterns applied throughout the border states and occupied territory of the Confederacy, which together with Washington, D.C., accounted for 95 percent of military trials of civilians.

The Court of Public Opinion. The most celebrated military trial of the war did not involve a blockade-runner or saboteur, but a leading Democratic critic of the Lincoln administration. While commanding along the Ohio River in April 1863, Gen. Ambrose Burnside issued an order threatening execution or banishment to anyone committing "express or implied" treason. Clement Vallandigham, leader of the peace wing of the Democratic Party and a candidate for governor of Ohio, tested the decree in a well-publicized antiwar address. Burnside had Vallandigham arrested at his home in Dayton and tried by a military commission in Cincinnati. On the recommendation of the commission, Burnside ordered Vallandigham imprisoned for the duration of the war. The affair prompted an outcry that military tribunals had become a tool for suppressing free speech and ensuring Republican Party domination. Lincoln re-

sponded by commuting Vallandigham's sentence to exile to the Confederacy, and on 25 May 1863 Union soldiers escorted Vallandigham across the lines under flag of truce. The candidate traveled through the Confederacy before leaving for Canada on a blockade-runner and resuming his campaign for governor of Ohio. Meanwhile, Democrats led protests throughout the North that forced Lincoln to issue his most extended wartime pronouncement on civil liberties in a letter addressed to Democratic congressman Erastus Corning. As usual Lincoln focused less on analyzing constitutional niceties than on winning popular support for his determination "to do as much as may seem to be required by the public safety."

The Supreme Court. The retreat of army officials from military trials of civilians demonstrates the restraint in this practice that was more typical than the sensational case of Clement Vallandigham. In February 1864 an army commission reviewing sentences imposed on blockade-runners concluded that military commissions could only try civilians in sites of ongoing war where martial law had been declared. This conclusion anticipated a similar ruling by the Supreme Court in 1866 in *Ex Parte Milligan,* a case reviewing the imprisonment of Indiana Democrat Lambdin P. Milligan, who had spoken against the war. In a ringing celebration of civil liberties, the Supreme Court ruled that the military could not try a civilian if the local courts remained open. The Court declared that the Constitution "is a law for rulers and people, equally in war and in peace. . . . No doctrine involving more pernicious consequences, was

Abraham Lincoln, from letter to Erastus Corning and Others, 12 June 1863:

He who dissuades one man from volunteering, or induces one soldier to desert, weakens the Union cause as much as he who kills a Union soldier in battle. Yet this dissuasion or inducement may be so conducted as to be no defined crime of which any civil court could take cognizance.... [The] provision of the Constitution that 'the privilege of the writ of habeas corpus shall not be suspended, unless when, in cases of rebellion or invasion, the public safety may require it,' is *the* provision which specially applies to our present case. This provision plainly attests the understanding of those who made the Constitution, that ordinary courts of justice are inadequate to 'cases of rebellion'—attests their purpose that, in such cases, men may be held in custody whom the courts, acting on ordinary rules, would discharge.

Society for the Diffusion of Political Knowledge, from reply to President Lincoln's Letter of 12 June 1863:

We can not acquiesce in your dogmas that arrests and imprisonment, without warrant or criminal accusation, in their nature lawless and arbitrary, opposed to the very letter of constitutional guarantees, can become in any sense rightful, by reason of a suspension of the writ of *habeas corpus*. We deny that the suspension of a single and peculiar remedy for such wrongs brings into existence new and unknown classes of offenses, or new causes for depriving men of their liberty.... [Y]our doctrine undisguisedly is, that suspension of this writ justifies arrests without warrant, without oath, and even without suspicion of treason or other crime.

ever invented by the wit of man, than that any of its provisions can be suspended during any of the great exigencies of government." In a sense the ruling had little practical effect, for the war was now over. But in another way the implications of *Ex Parte Milligan* were far-reaching, for the decision was widely interpreted in order to limit the power of Congress to work through the army or federal agencies during Reconstruction.

Sources:

Mark E. Neely Jr., *The Fate of Liberty: Abraham Lincoln and Civil Liberties* (New York: Oxford University Press, 1991);

J. G. Randall, *Constitutional Problems Under Lincoln,* revised edition (Urbana: University of Illinois Press, 1951).

WRITING CITIZENSHIP INTO THE CONSTITUTION

Search for Definition. The attempt to establish the meaning of American citizenship was central to constitutional development during the Civil War and Reconstruction era. Previous generations had not done much to clarify the concept. Neither judicial decisions nor legal commentators offered "a clear and satisfactory definition of the phrase citizen of the United States," Attorney General Edward Bates observed in the middle of the war. He sighed that "eighty years of practical enjoyment of citizenship, under the Constitution, have not sufficed to teach us either the exact meaning of the word or the constituent elements of the thing we prize so highly." The best-known analysis of American citizenship had emerged from the interpretation of Article IV, section 2 of the Constitution, which provides that "the Citizens of each State shall be entitled to all Privileges and Immunities of Citizens in the several States." Supreme Court Justice Bushrod Washington, sitting on a lower federal court in *Corfield* v. *Coryell* (1823), declared that this clause barred states from discriminating against nonresidents in matters "which are in their nature fundamental; which belong of right to the citizens of all free Governments; and which have at all times been enjoyed by the citizens of the several States which compose this Union." This statement identified three different sources of law to which Americans might look to determine the rights of citizenship: philosophical principles of natural law, the structure of republican government, and established customs. Washington thought that a list of all privileges and immunities protected by the clause would be "more tedious than difficult to enumerate," but he noted that American citizenship included the right to acquire and possess property; the right to pass through or reside in any state; the privilege of habeas corpus; and the right to maintain lawsuits. The *Corfield* v. *Coryell* definition of citizenship was not only incomplete as a catalogue of rights but significantly limited in its application, for Article IV, section 2 applies only to state-to-state relations. The guarantee of equal treatment for out-of-state residents did not set limits on a state's treatment of its own residents. Nor did the Bill of Rights protect a citizen in this situation, for the Supreme Court had ruled in *Barron* v. *Baltimore* (1835) that the Bill of Rights did not constrain state governments.

***Dred Scott* Decision.** In *Dred Scott* v. *Sandford* (1857) the Supreme Court made the definition of federal citizenship a problem of critical importance in American law and politics. Before evaluating Scott's claim to freedom, the Supreme Court asked whether Scott was a citizen within the meaning of Article III, section 2 of the Constitution, which authorizes federal courts to hear lawsuits "between Citizens of different States." Chief Justice Roger B. Taney found for the Court that African Americans—whether free or slave—could not be citizens within the meaning of the Constitution, even if state governments regarded free blacks as citizens. Taney's analysis invoked the sources of law identified by Bushrod Washington—natural law, republican theory, and custom—but his reasoning was skewed by racism. At the time the Constitution was framed, the chief justice argued, blacks "had for more than a century before been regarded as beings of an inferior order, and altogether unfit

Debate in U.S. Senate, 23 February 1865, on a proposal to place a bust of late Chief Justice Roger B. Taney in the chamber of the United States Supreme Court:

Lyman Trumbull (Illinois): I trust that the bill will be taken up; that a person who has presided over the Supreme Court of the United States for more than a quarter of a century, and has added reputation to the character of the judiciary of the United States throughout the world is not to be hooted down by an exclamation that the country is to be emancipated. Suppose he did make a wrong decision. No man is infallible. He was a great and learned and an able man. I trust the Senate will take up the bill, and not only take it up, but pass it.

Charles Sumner (Massachusetts): The Senator from Illinois says that this idea of a bust is not to be hooted down. Let me tell that Senator that the name of Taney is to be hooted down the page of history. Judgment is beginning now; and an emancipated country will fasten upon him the stigma which he deserves. The Senator says that he for twenty-five years administered justice. He administered justice wickedly, and degraded the judiciary of the country, and degraded the age.

Reverdy Johnson (Maryland): I cannot fail to express my astonishment at the course of the honorable Senator from Massachusetts, which he thinks it, I suppose, his duty to pursue. Sir, if the times in which we are living are honestly and truly recorded by the historian, I think the honorable member from Massachusetts will be very happy if he stands as pure and as high upon the historic page as the learned judge who is now no more.

The honorable member seems to suppose that the decision in the *Dred Scott* case was a decision of the Chief Justice alone. It was not so. In that decision a majority of the court concurred. Whether that decision is right or not, permit me to say to the honorable member there are men belonging to the profession at least his equals, who think it to have been right; but whether right or wrong, those who knew the moral character of the Chief Justice as well as I did would blush to say that his name is to be execrated among men. . . . [Besides] it is a matter of history. Every judge who has been at the head of that tribunal has his bust placed in that court-room. Does the honorable member wish to have it unknown in future times that there was such a Chief Justice?. . .

Sumner: . . . If a man has done evil during life he must not be complimented in marble. . . . I know that in the court-room there are busts of the other Chief Justices. Very well. So in the hall of the doges, at Venice, there are pictures of all who filled that high office in unbroken succession, with the exception of Marino Faliero, who, although as venerable from years as Taney, was deemed unworthy of a place in that line. Where his picture should have been there was a vacant space which testified always to the justice of the republic. Let such a vacant space in our court-room testify to the justice of our Republic. Let it speak in warning to all who would betray liberty.

---

to associate with the white race, either in social or political relations; and so far inferior, that they had no rights which the white man was bound to respect." In fact, the legal frameworks governing the status of free blacks varied widely in the years after African Americans fought in the Revolutionary War; in some states, blacks voted on the ratification of the Constitution. Taney's invention of a federal citizenship restricted to whites plainly reflected his fear that the United States was developing into the sort of biracial society that might already be foreseen in his home state of Maryland, where the erosion of slavery had created the largest population of free African Americans in the nation.

Black Codes. After the war the definition of federal citizenship became intertwined with the question of what freedom would mean, beyond simply the absence of slavery. Provided by President Andrew Johnson with latitude to reshape their governments, Southern states quickly tried to establish that emancipation did not confer full rights of citizenship. The so-called black codes enacted immediately after the war acknowledged that slavery was illegal and extended basic rights to blacks, but only in severely limited and closely regulated ways. The laws permitted African Americans to make contracts and own property, but they barred blacks from working as physicians or merchants and required a li-

cense for freedmen who sought to become preachers; meanwhile, elaborate labor laws sought to reinstitute the antebellum organization of plantation work. The black codes recognized the right to travel, but controlled the movements of African Americans through vagrancy laws and a pass system reminiscent of slavery. Blacks could sue and be sued, but they were barred from serving on juries and could only testify in cases that involved blacks as parties. Former slaves could now marry, but interracial marriages were strictly forbidden. Blacks were also prohibited by the codes from voting, holding office, assembling, or owning guns. Altogether the black codes essentially sought to replace slavery with a legal caste system based on race.

Civil Rights Act of 1866. The general response of Southern lawmakers to emancipation was not very difficult to predict, and the Thirteenth Amendment—which Southern states were forced to ratify as they reorganized their governments—had not only declared that slavery was abolished but had authorized Congress to enact legislation necessary to enforce emancipation. When Congress assembled in December 1865 for the first time since the end of the war, it accordingly moved swiftly to counter the black codes with a statute defining the rights of American citizenship. The Civil Rights Act of 1866 provided that all persons born in the United States (ex-

Lithograph commemorating the 1870 ratification of the Fifteenth Amendment, granting the right to vote to all males regardless of "race, color, or previous condition of servitude"

cept Indians) were citizens entitled regardless of race to "full and equal benefit of all laws and proceedings for the security of person and property." While Congress protected the basic economic power to make contracts and maintain lawsuits, it treated suffrage not as a right protected by the federal government but as a privilege extended by state governments. But although the Civil Rights Act of 1866 did not address all forms of inequality, it expressed an unprecedented approach to the role of the federal government in American life. "I admit that this species of legislation is absolutely revolutionary," declared one Republican supporter. "But are we not in the midst of a revolution?"

The Fourteenth Amendment. At the same time that Congress introduced the idea of federal citizenship in the Civil Rights Act of 1866 to respond directly to the black codes, Republican lawmakers also began working to make the concept of American citizenship a new centerpiece of the U.S. Constitution. The resulting Fourteenth Amendment, adopted in 1868, created two sets of guarantees in its crucial first section. First, it provided that "no State shall make or enforce any law which shall abridge the privileges or immunities of citizens of the United States," defining citizens to include all persons born or naturalized in the United States. Second, it provided that no state could deprive any person, whether or not a citizen, of "life, liberty or property, without due process of law; nor deny to any person within its jurisdiction the equal protection of laws." Because the Fourteenth Amendment became the core for much subsequent constitutional decision making, lawyers as well as

historians have attempted to determine exactly what its framers meant by these phrases. Their research has often been unsatisfying, however, because many of the questions that later Americans asked—for example, whether federal law now barred the establishment of "separate but equal" public schools—were not addressed fully by the framers or were subject to contradictory interpretations by different supporters of the amendment. Rather than anticipating particular court cases, Congress sought to embed in the Constitution a general principle summarizing the meaning of the Civil War. As in the Thirteenth Amendment, Congress reserved for itself a leading role in elaborating this principle through a provision authorizing legislation to enforce the Fourteenth Amendment.

Enforcing Legislation. For contemporaries, the most important area of ambiguity in the Fourteenth Amendment was probably its impact on voting rights. The Fifteenth Amendment, ratified in 1870, clarified much of the confusion by prohibiting federal or state governments from abridging suffrage "on account of race, color, or previous condition of servitude." Immediately after ratification of the Fifteenth Amendment, Congress passed the Civil Rights Act of 1870, which mostly provided penalties for state election officials or others who sought to interfere with blacks' exercise of their right to vote. The crescendo of unpunished racial violence in the South led one year later to the passage of another Civil Rights Act, known as the Ku Klux Klan Act of 1871, which aimed to enforce the civil rights recognized by the Fourteenth Amendment as well as the voting rights recognized by the Fifteenth Amendment. The Ku Klux

Drawing of Sen. Charles Sumner of Massachusetts, a champion of racial equality

Klan Act would become one of the most important laws ever passed by Congress for two reasons. First, its enforcement mechanisms not only provided federal officials with additional powers but also authorized private individuals to bring a lawsuit if they had been deprived of federal rights by someone acting "under color of state law." This provision became the basis for a considerable percentage of all litigation in federal courts and a vital process through which Americans sought to defend their constitutional rights. Second, by striking at the Ku Klux Klan, Congress unequivocally turned its attention from the discriminatory acts of state governments that had been the focus of the Civil Rights Acts of 1866 and 1870, and addressed racial injustices perpetrated by private individuals. The direct federal intervention into relations between private individuals became the center of intense dispute. For example, Sen. Lyman Trumbull of Illinois,

the sponsor of the Civil Rights Act of 1866, strenuously opposed the Civil Rights Act of 1871 because he believed that it violated the proper province of state government.

Institutional Change. Responsibility for enforcement of the new guarantees of citizenship transformed the federal legal apparatus, including attorneys for the United States government as well as the court system. The administrative duties of the attorney general had expanded considerably during the Civil War; only in 1861 had the attorney general begun to superintend the U.S. attorneys posted at the federal judicial districts around the country, who devoted most of their time to prosecuting the relatively few federal crimes such as counterfeiting or maritime infractions. Even so, in 1865 the staff of the attorney general consisted of eight persons. But the civil rights laws made attorneys for federal courts responsible for implementing a crucial aspect of national policy and for the first time required extensive cooperation between Washington officials and district attorneys. Congress recognized this new role in 1870 by creating the Department of Justice as a full-fledged unit of the federal bureaucracy. Attorney General Amos T. Akerman signaled the priority of the department by establishing its headquarters in the Freedmen's Savings Bank building. Meanwhile, the jurisdiction of the federal court system was expanding rapidly. Before the Civil War, lower federal courts primarily heard cases between citizens of different states ("diversity" cases) and cases involving either the narrow range of federal crimes or a similarly small group of civil actions, most notably admiralty proceedings, reserved for federal administration. Only Supreme Court review ensured that the states did not undermine federal constitutional law. But the civil rights laws circumvented the state court system, authorizing individuals to file their claims in federal court and authorizing defendants to "remove" civil rights cases from state to federal court (but not vice versa). In 1875 Congress extended "federal question" jurisdiction to the limits prescribed by the Constitution, authorizing federal courts to hear not only claims under the civil rights acts but all cases arising under federal law.

Judicial Retreat. The Supreme Court decision in the *Slaughterhouse* cases (1873) sharply reversed the development of federal citizenship as a potential source of rights. These cases reviewed the lawsuits brought by a group of butchers excluded from a monopoly that the Louisiana legislature had chartered to regulate the meat-processing industry in New Orleans. The butchers claimed that by depriving them of their trade, the Louisiana legislature had violated the privileges and immunities of federal citizenship guaranteed by the Fourteenth Amendment. The question was essentially whether the Fourteenth Amendment not only promised racial equality but redefined the property rights of American citizens. Justice Samuel Miller's opinion for the majority of the court concluded that the privileges-and-immunities clause did not protect the butchers. He argued that the Fourteenth Amendment did not bring into the Constitution a set of natural rights, as Bushrod Washington's opinion in *Corfield* v. *Coryell* had suggested in interpreting the privi-

leges-and-immunities clause of Article IV of the Constitution. Instead, the *Slaughterhouse* cases ruled that the privileges and immunities clause of the Fourteenth Amendment protected only a few narrow activities peculiar to the federal system, such as ensuring that all citizens enjoyed access to Washington, D.C., and to the seaports and navigable waters of the United States. As a result, the privileges-and-immunities clause essentially ceased to be a dynamic part of the Constitution. The idea that the Fourteenth Amendment recognized new categories of fundamental but unenumerated rights—vigorously argued by the dissenting justices in the *Slaughterhouse* cases—would instead come to be developed primarily through the Fourteenth Amendment guarantee of due process of law.

Civil Rights Act of 1875. Congress enacted the last civil rights law of Reconstruction in large part as a tribute to Charles Sumner of Massachusetts, the Senate champion of racial equality who died in March 1874. For the previous several years, Sumner had advocated a bill that would outlaw racial discrimination in schools, churches, hotels, theaters, railroads, and other public facilities. Congress dropped the provisions regulating churches and public schools, but the rest of the legislation nevertheless represented a remarkable expansion of federal authority over the conduct of private individuals. The expansion was too much for the Supreme Court, which invalidated the mandate for integration of public accommodations in the decisions known as the *Civil Rights* cases (1883). The Court ruled that the guarantees of the Fourteenth Amendment applied only to "state action," or discriminatory measures by state governments. When Congress returned to the issue of racial equality in public accommodations—almost a full century later—the legislation would be framed not as an enforcement of the Fourteenth Amendment but as a regulation of interstate commerce.

Sources:
Robert J. Kaczorowski, *The Politics of Judicial Interpretation: The Federal Courts, Department of Justice, and Civil Rights, 1866–1876* (Dobbs Ferry, N.Y.: Oceana, 1985);

James H. Kettner, *The Development of American Citizenship, 1808–1870* (Chapel Hill: University of North Carolina Press, 1978);

William E. Nelson, *The Fourteenth Amendment: From Political Principle to Judicial Doctrine* (Cambridge, Mass.: Harvard University Press, 1988).

AMOS T. AKERMAN

1821-1880
ATTORNEY GENERAL

Southern by Choice. Amos T. Akerman typified the Northerners who adopted the South as their home long before such cross-sectional transplants became stigmatized as "carpetbaggers." Born in Portsmouth, New Hampshire, he attended Phillips Exeter Academy and graduated from Dartmouth College in 1842. He took his first job as a teacher near Augusta, Georgia, and soon moved to Savannah as a tutor for the children of Judge John McPherson Berrien, who had been Andrew Jackson's attorney general and was now a prominent Whig politician. After preparing under Berrien for admission to the bar, Akerman practiced briefly in Peoria, Illinois, where his sister lived, before returning to Georgia, where he established himself in the combined roles of lawyer, farmer, and ultimately, owner of eleven slaves. A Whig in politics, he opposed secession as an unwise strategy but followed his adopted home into the Confederacy. For much of the war he served in the Georgia state militia, and he joined in the mobilization of these troops upon Sherman's invasion in 1864.

Politics of a Scalawag. "Some of us who had adhered to the Confederacy felt it to be our duty when we were to participate in the politics of the Union, to let Confederate ideas rule us no longer . . . ," Akerman once observed. "In the great conflict, one party had contended for nationality and liberty, the other for state rights and slavery. We thought that our surrender implied the giving up of all that had been in controversy." Akerman expressed this policy as a delegate to the constitutional convention of 1867–1868, where he supported the extension of suffrage to African Americans. He protested when the Georgia legislature expelled the blacks who had been elected to office under the state constitution. At the same time, he demonstrated the economic conservatism that

often accompanied progressive political views. He did not endorse redistribution of land to blacks, and he strenuously opposed repudiation of the state debt accumulated during the war. In short, he spoke for the group of white Southerners on whom rested much of the hope for rebuilding the region through the Republican Party. As a result President Ulysses S. Grant appointed him U.S. district attorney for Georgia in 1869.

Enforcing Civil Rights. After distinguishing himself in enforcement of the Civil Rights Act of 1866 while serving as the local representative of federal law, Akerman made the leap from district attorney to U.S. attorney general in 1870. His sudden elevation reflected his strategic importance in Washington politics. President Grant, embroiled in a feud with Sen. Charles Sumner over the senator's opposition to a proposal to annex Haiti, dismissed Sumner's ally Rockwood Hoar from his post as attorney general. By appointing Akerman to head the new Justice Department, Grant continued to favor the growth of the Republican Party in the South, courted potential allies of his Caribbean initiative, and sought to prevent the faction coalescing around Sumner from monopolizing the leadership in civil rights. Passage of the Ku Klux Klan Act in April 1871 provided Akerman with legal tools that matched his political mandate. Recently returned from a trip home that had provided firsthand reports of Southern recalcitrance and violence, he initiated systematic criminal prosecution of Klan members. U.S. attorneys in North Carolina and Mississippi obtained hundreds of indictments; convictions for federal civil rights violations jumped from thirty-two in 1870 to 128 in 1871.

Law and Order. The vigor of the Justice Department underscored the important point that the federal government could assert authority in the South without sustaining a prolonged military occupation. In South Carolina, however, Akerman recognized that the Ku Klux Klan was too powerful for his office to suppress without assistance. On his recommendation, Grant declared a "condition of lawlessness" in nine South Carolina counties in October 1871 and suspended the writ of habeas corpus. Federal troops made arrests for civil rights violations, and as many as two thousand other Klansmen fled the state. Klan violence declined significantly after the early 1870s, an accomplishment for which Akerman and his fellow Justice Department attorneys deserved much credit, even though white Southerners were resorting less frequently to violence in part because political and economic factors were establishing white domination.

Dismissal. Akerman's tenure as attorney general was as brief as it was spectacular, and the circumstances of his dismissal revealed some of the forces that undermined Reconstruction. His fixation on the civil rights crisis was not uniformly shared in Washington. Secretary of State Hamilton Fish recorded in his diary after one cabinet meeting that Akerman "tells a number of stories, one of a fellow being castrated, with terribly minute and tedious details in each case. It has got to be a bore to listen twice a week to this same thing." In addition, although Akerman was far from an economic radical he had made enemies among the powerful railroad interests whose affairs he had affected in supervising compliance with contracts that promised vast land grants. In December 1871 Grant asked for his resignation and replaced him with a former senator from Oregon who continued the prosecutions initiated by Akerman but represented the hope for Southern reform less powerfully than his predecessor. Although Grant offered the outgoing attorney general a seat on the federal bench or a diplomatic mission, Akerman returned home to Cartersville, Georgia, and practiced law until his death in 1880.

Source:
William S. McFeely, "Amos T. Akerman: The Lawyer and Racial Justice," in *Region, Race, and Reconstruction: Essays in Honor of C. Vann Woodward,* edited by J. Morgan Kousser and James M. McPherson (New York: Oxford University Press, 1982), pp. 395–415.

MYRA BRADWELL

1831-1894
ADVOCATE OF WOMAN'S RIGHTS

New England Inheritance. The early years of Myra Colby Bradwell illustrate the extension of New England influence westward during the nineteenth century. Descended on both sides from early settlers of Boston, she was born in Manchester, Vermont, and moved shortly afterward with her parents to the Genesee River valley of New York. Her parents were friendly with abolitionists in the famous "burnt-over district," so called because of the frequency and intensity of evangelical revivals. When Myra was twelve, the family moved to a township near Elgin, Illinois, where she attended the Ladies' Seminary. Like many New England women of her generation, she then taught school for several years. In 1852 she married James Bradwell, and together they conducted a successful private school while he completed his studies for admission to the bar.

Chicago. After James was admitted to the Illinois bar, he and Myra's brother opened a law firm in Chicago. In 1861 James was elected county judge of Cook County. Myra read law with her husband and had four children between 1854 and 1862. As with many women of her generation, the Civil War provided Myra Bradwell with a valuable opportunity to demonstrate her executive skills. She was active in the Northwestern Sanitary Commission and helped to organize the massive fund-raising fair held in Chicago in the last year of the war. After the war she maintained a lasting interest in the Soldiers' Aid Society, of which she was president, and continued contacts with other leaders of the Northwestern Sanitary Commission, including Mary Livermore, one of the best-known advocates of woman suffrage.

Editor and Businesswoman. In 1868 Bradwell began to publish the *Chicago Legal News,* a weekly legal newspaper. For the next twenty-five years her editorials influenced legal opinion in the Midwest. She was an early advocate of legislation regulating railroads, a proponent of temperance, prison reform, and woman's rights, and a strong supporter of the bar associations and law schools that institutionalized the development of the profession. She was effective as an entrepreneur as well as a contributor to political and social debates. As the president of *Chicago Legal News* and an affiliated printing company, she secured the most advertising business of any Illinois newspaper and also prospered in the sale of stationery and legal forms. The Bradwells purchased a mansion on Michigan Avenue and traveled extensively in Europe. Myra was a potent civic force in countless Chicago initiatives from the rebuilding after the 1871 fire through the World's Columbian Exposition of 1892.

Political Advocate. Bradwell participated actively in the woman suffrage movement. She lobbied for extension of the franchise to women in the Illinois constitution of 1870, helped to organize the American Woman Suffrage Association, and served for many years on the executive committee of the Illinois Woman Suffrage Association. While her husband served in the state legislature between 1873 and 1875, Myra Bradwell pushed through legislation that made women eligible to hold school offices, to become notaries public, and to enjoy equal guardianship of children. Bradwell exercised her greatest political influence in the movement to provide women with equal property rights. She drafted the law passed by the Illinois legislature in 1869 that recognized the right of married women to their own earnings and also led a successful campaign to protect the interest of a widow in the estate of her husband.

Bradwell* v. *Illinois. In 1869 Bradwell applied to join the Illinois bar. Although her qualifying examination reflected her superb qualifications and although Arabella Mansfield of Iowa had earlier in the year become the first American woman admitted to the practice of law, the Illinois Supreme Court refused to admit Bradwell because she was a woman. She petitioned the Supreme Court to compel Illinois to admit her in accordance with the Fourteenth Amendment, drawing on the recent promise of *Cummings* v. *Missouri* that federal law would prevent arbitrary denial of the property interest in pursuit of a profession. In *Bradwell* v. *Illinois* (1873), however, the Court ruled that the Fourteenth Amendment did not require states to admit women to the practice of law. Before the Court announced its decision, Illinois passed a new law that opened the bar to women, but Bradwell did not reapply. In 1890 the Illinois Supreme Court admitted her to the bar on the basis of her 1869 application. By that time she had served four terms as vice president of the Illinois State Bar Association, of which she was an honorary member. Bradwell was admitted to practice before the U.S. Supreme Court in 1892, ten years after her daughter graduated at the head of her class at the Union College of Law (later Northwestern University Law School). Myra Bradwell died in 1894.

Source:
Jane M. Friedman, *America's First Woman Lawyer: The Biography of Myra Bradwell* (Buffalo, N.Y.: Prometheus Books, 1993).

THOMAS MCINTYRE COOLEY

1824-1898
JURIST

Humble Beginnings. Although Thomas M. Cooley's jurisprudence became an important tool for the entrenchment of elite interests in the late nineteenth century, his own background was not privileged. The tenth of fifteen children born into a family that supported itself on a one-hundred-acre farm near Rochester, New York, Cooley would come to feel disadvantaged by his lack of social opportunities and education. He was the only one of the Cooley children to advance beyond the local common schools and attend Attica Academy. Upon graduating in 1842 he began to study law in nearby Palmyra under the direction of Democratic congressman Theron Strong. The next year he moved to Michigan, where he was admitted to the bar in 1846. He soon associated himself with the Democratic faction charging that the party had come to be dominated by a small circle of insiders—headed in Michigan by longtime U.S. senator Lewis Cass—who promoted railroads and other corporate interests as well as territorial aggrandizement in the Mexican War. Like many others who took a similar position, Cooley drew inspiration from the 1848 revolutions in Europe and from English reform leaders such as Richard Cobden, who championed free trade, popular education, and world peace. He participated actively in the Free Soil movement in Michigan in 1848. He then tried his fortunes for several years in Toledo, Ohio, where he returned to the Democratic fold and ran for the state bench in 1854. Overwhelmed by a two-to-one margin in the political tidal wave that followed the Kansas-Nebraska Act, he returned to Michigan and followed many of his former political allies into the new Republican Party.

Opportunities. Cooley's move into the Republican Party proved to be more politically rewarding than his move to Toledo. As the party forged a majority that would place his law partner in the governor's office, Cooley received some valuable appointments. In 1857 the Republican legislature selected him to compile the statutes of the state, which he performed with a speed and skill that contributed to his appointment one year later as reporter for the Michigan Supreme Court. In 1859 he became one of the first three faculty members at the new law school opened by the University of Michigan. His position as Supreme Court reporter—then a significant editorial role in the circulation of judicial opinions—and his lectures at the Michigan Law School provided opportunities to earn a reputation for his legal scholarship. In 1864 he was elected on the Republican ticket to a position as associate justice of the Michigan Supreme Court.

National Reputation. During the next twenty years, Cooley became one of the most influential figures in American law. A man of remarkable energy, he continued to teach at the University of Michigan Law School and drew upon his lectures to publish several books that long influenced legal thinking on vital topics. His *Treatise on the Constitutional Limitations which Rest Upon the Legislative Power of the States of the American Union* appeared in 1868, followed by an edition of *Blackstone's Commentaries* (1871), an edition of Joseph Story's *Commentaries on the Constitution* (1873), *Treatise on the Law of Taxation* (1876), and *Treatise on the Law of Torts* (1879). At the same time, he was a prolific author of judicial opinions that addressed problems confronting many other state courts. For example, in *People* v. *Salem* (1870) he wrote for the court in a case analyzing state legislation that permitted the town of Salem to issue municipal bonds to support construction of the Detroit and Howell Railroad. Cooley found the authorizing legislation to be an invalid exercise of state taxing power because construction of the railroad was not a public purpose. The liberal Republican movement publicized this decision widely as a heroic stand against the legislative influence of special interests, although one consequence for Cooley was that this publicity precluded any possibility that he would be named to the U.S. Supreme Court by the Liberal Republicans' nemesis, President Ulysses S. Grant.

Legal Theory. *People* v. *Salem* illustrated the Jacksonian determination to thwart economic privilege and maintain equality of opportunity that informed Cooley's influential *Constitutional Limitations.* As business enterprises increasingly came to fear government regulation more intensely than they sought government assistance, Cooley's doctrines offered a shield against legislative interference. Under "due process of law" clauses, for example, a state government could not redistribute wealth from one party to another. Lawyers and judges applying Cooley's treatise reasoned that the same notion of "substantive due process" precluded redistribution of wealth through regulation of railroad rates or working conditions just as it precluded redistribution of wealth through tax subsidies for railroads. The implications of Cooley's ideas could so easily be reversed because he understood law to be an abstract, logical set of axioms and inferences, detached from the social context of American life. In this way the academic conceptualization of law as a science during the mid nineteenth century transformed the Jacksonian critique of privilege into a bulwark of elites.

Interstate Commerce Commission. After twenty years on the Michigan Supreme Court, Cooley was defeated in 1885. He was sharply attacked as a corporate pawn because his *Treatise on the Law of Torts* and his judicial opinions supported several conventional doctrines that enabled defendants to escape liability for the personal injuries that accompanied industrialization. Even before this defeat his career had been moving in new directions. He had switched from the law faculty at Michigan to the teaching of history, which led to the publication of his *Michigan, a History of Governments* (1885). Upon leaving the court he devoted increasing amounts of his time to problems of railroad administration in which he had become immersed in 1882 as an arbitrator on the Advisory Commission of Differential Rates. Upon the creation of the Interstate Commerce Commission in 1887, President Grover Cleveland appointed Cooley the first chairman. He exercised considerable influence in molding the agency, and his reports for the agency were widely read. Cooley relied on information gathering, persuasion, and publicity to promote moral integrity in business dealings. But his contribution to the growth of the Interstate Commerce Commission was ironic, for just as Cooley's antiprivilege Jacksonianism had become a theory of constitutional protection against government regulatory power, he now played a key role in building the institutional framework through which regulatory powers would later expand. Cooley served on the commission until September 1891 and died seven years later.

Sources:

Alan R. Jones, *The Constitutional Conservatism of Thomas McIntyre Cooley: A Study in the History of Ideas* (New York: Garland, 1987);

G. Edward White, *The American Judicial Tradition: Profiles of Leading American Judges,* revised edition (New York: Oxford University Press, 1988).

DAVID DUDLEY FIELD

1805-1894

STEPHEN JOHNSON FIELD

1816-1899
BROTHERS OF BAR AND BENCH

Family of Achievers. The eight sons and two daughters of Congregationalist minister David Dudley Field and Submit Dickinson Field constituted one of the most remarkable families of the mid nineteenth century. Cyrus Field became an entrepreneur best remembered for successfully promoting the Atlantic telegraph cable; Henry Martyn Field became a popular author of travel books; Jonathan Edwards Field served several terms as president of the Massachusetts state senate; Emilia Fields was the mother of David J. Brewer, a justice of the U.S. Supreme Court. The first child in this extraordinary group, named for his father, was born in Haddam, Connecticut, in 1805; his brother Stephen followed eleven years later, shortly before the family moved from Haddam to Stockbridge, Massachusetts. Both attended Williams College, one of the academic centers of New England religious orthodoxy.

Politics and Legal Codification. David Dudley Field entered the practice of law in New York in 1828. He aspired to a political career as a Jacksonian Democrat, but his personality did not lend itself to working within a party or appealing to voters. Field would eventually join the Free Soil movement and later the Republican Party, strongly supporting Lincoln's 1860 campaign for the presidential nomination against the New Yorker William H. Seward. By that time, however, he had won fame as the foremost proponent of the codification of law. The codification movement argued that judge-made common law was not consistent with American principles and should be replaced by legislatively enacted codes of law. A code, Field maintained, was "the necessary complement of a written constitution for a free people." In 1847 the New York State Assembly appointed him to a commission to study the reform of courtroom procedures. Field took charge of the committee and produced the Field Code for procedure in civil cases, which New York adopted in 1848 and twenty-four states and territories had imitated by 1873. He also proposed a code for procedure in criminal cases in 1848, and although the New York legislature did not enact it, eleven states did in the next twenty-five years.

A Western Road. Stephen J. Field followed the professional and political lead of his brother, completing his training for the bar in the office of President Martin Van Buren's son John, known in New York politics as "the Prince." Stephen then became his brother's partner for seven years, although by the end of that period David Dudley Field was devoting much of his time to the codification movement. Stephen struck out in a different direction, joining the California Gold Rush of 1849. He soon focused not on mining but on real estate speculation, law practice, and the government offices that he helped to set up. He was elected to the California state legislature in 1850 and to the state supreme court in 1857. His climb along the rough-and-tumble western path to prominence made for one of the most colorful backgrounds in the history of the American bench. He was disbarred twice; he accepted two challenges to duels (from which his adversaries retreated); and his bodyguard shot to death a judge who seemed likely to make good on a threat to kill Field. A strong Democrat, he met the federal need for a judge with expertise in the specialized legal field of mining claims. When Congress created a federal judicial circuit in California and added a seat on the Supreme Court in 1863, Lincoln appointed Field to the positions.

Reconstruction. During his first few years on the Supreme Court, one of the advocates whom Justice Stephen Field often saw in the most important political cases was his brother. Reverting to his Democratic allegiances when the Republican Congress began to take energetic measures to transform the South, David Dudley Field joined a distinguished legal team that attacked the constitutionality of Radical Reconstruction. Other lawyers contributing to this effort included former attorney general Reverdy Johnson; former postmaster general Montgomery Blair; and Jeremiah S. Black, who had served as chief justice of Pennsylvania, U.S. attorney general, and secretary of state. Field appeared in several major Reconstruction cases. In *Ex Parte Milligan* (1866) his group successfully argued that the Constitution prohibited trials by military commissions in areas outside of an active war zone. In *Cummings* v. *Missouri* (1867) they secured invalidation of a provision in the Missouri constitution that barred former Confederates from public life. *Ex Parte McCardle* (1869) was a broad attack on the Reconstruction Act of 1867 based on the denial of a writ of habeas corpus for a Mississippi advocate of resistance to Reconstruction. After the Supreme Court heard argu-

ments but before it announced a decision, Congress forestalled the case by requiring all pending and future appeals from denial of the writ of habeas corpus to work their way through the lower federal courts before reaching the Supreme Court. Field made another major constitutional argument in *United States* v. *Cruikshank* (1876), representing one of three white Louisianans convicted under the Civil Rights Enforcement Act of 1870 after the Colfax Massacre of 13 April 1873, in which more than one hundred blacks were killed. The Supreme Court overturned the conviction, concluding that murder was a matter for state authorities—even if it was mass murder with racial and political motives. In *United States* v. *Reese* (1876) the Supreme Court found for another of Field's clients on similar grounds, invalidating two sections of the 1871 Ku Klux Klan Act in a decision which foreshadowed the conclusion that the civil rights laws could only regulate state action, not private conduct.

Wall Street Wars. Field was the central attorney in another of the great legal dramas of the mid nineteenth century, the financial battles between his clients Jay Gould and Jim Fisk and rival railroad promoter Cornelius Vanderbilt. This flurry of business made Field one of the most highly paid lawyers in the country during the late 1860s and early 1870s, earning about $75,000 per year. The cases also put him at the center of controversy within the New York legal community over professional ethics, a struggle for identity that led to the 1870 formation of the Bar Association of the City of New York. Field blocked repeated efforts within the Bar Association to censure or expel him, defending his own conduct and pointing out that almost every prominent lawyer in New York had at some point represented Fisk, Gould, or their financial adversaries. He did not enhance his ethical stature within the bar by serving as chief counsel to William Marcy "Boss" Tweed in the criminal and civil cases that lasted from 1872 to 1876, culminating in conviction of Tweed on more than two hundred counts of graft and corruption. After these cases David Dudley Field represented one of the key prosecution witnesses whom he had vigorously cross-examined in the Tweed cases, Gov. Samuel Tilden of New York, in the proceedings organized to resolve the 1876 presidential election.

Constitutional Orthodoxy. The judicial opinions of Stephen J. Field similarly helped to define the constitutional meaning of liberty and property. In *Cummings* v. *Missouri* (1866) and *Ex Parte Garland* (1867) his opinions for the slim majorities invalidated the use of loyalty oaths to bar former Confederates from the practice of a profession, declaring that the right to pursue a trade was a vital property interest. He broadened this point in his famous dissent in the *Slaughterhouse* cases (1873), arguing for protection of New Orleans butchers from legislation that would eliminate their business by creating a meat-processing monopoly. In *Munn* v. *Illinois* (1877) Justice Field denounced legislative price setting as a deprivation of property. As his dissenting opinions became constitutional orthodoxy, the judiciary increasingly claimed, in Field's words, "a negative power, the power of resistance." Judicial exercise of this power would set the tone for American constitutional law in the late nineteenth and early twentieth centuries. Stephen J. Field died in 1899, five years after the death of his brother David.

Sources:

Daun van Ee, *David Dudley Field and the Reconstruction of the Law* (New York: Garland, 1986);

Paul Kens, *Justice Stephen Field: Shaping Liberty from the Gold Rush to the Gilded Age* (Lawrence: University Press of Kansas, 1997);

Carl B. Swisher, *Stephen J. Field: Craftsman of the Law* (Washington, D.C.: Brookings Institution, 1930).

JOHN MERCER LANGSTON

1829-1897
AFRICAN AMERICAN ADVOCATE

Opportunities and Constraints. John Mercer Langston spent his life challenging racial boundaries and contributing to their breakdown. His father was a plantation owner who scandalized his neighbors in Louisa County, Virginia, by living openly with a former slave whom he had freed, Lucy Langston, whose mother was Native American and whose father was African American. Both of Langston's parents died when he was five, leaving him a substantial inheritance and directing that he be raised in the free state of Ohio. There he attended the public schools of Chillicothe. One of his teachers was George B. Vashon, who in 1844 became the first black graduate of Oberlin College, then the most progressive academic institution in the country. Langston also attended Oberlin, taking his bachelor's degree in 1849 and a master's degree in 1852. When he ventured outside the college, however, he encountered the aggressive racism that was common in Ohio. He was denied accommodations in a Columbus hotel, was forced to flee from an antiabolitionist mob in Cincinnati, and when he chose law for his profession was denied admission to law school. After preparing privately with a judge, he might have been denied admission to the bar had not a visual inspection satisfied the Ohio Supreme Court that Langston had more white than black blood.

Practice and Politics. Routine criminal matters accounted for much of Langston's early practice. The most sensational of these cases came in 1863 when he successfully defended an Oberlin student of African American and Native American ancestry, the future sculptor Edmonia Lewis, against charges that she had poisoned a white classmate. As an attorney, moreover, Langston ex-panded the involvement in politics that he had begun at Oberlin. Coauthor of the Declaration of Sentiments for the State Convention of Colored Citizens of Ohio in 1849, he later headed the Ohio State Anti-Slavery Society. His leadership in Ohio brought him onto the wider stages of the American Anti-Slavery Society and the Colored National Convention in Rochester, New York, in July 1853. Two years later he ran on the Liberty Party ticket for the position of town clerk in Brownhelm, Ohio, and became the first black to win elective office in the United States. Moving back to Oberlin a few years later, he was elected town clerk and won additional positions on the city council and the board of education.

Reconstructing Law. In addition to aiding the Union effort in the Civil War by helping to recruit three black infantry regiments, Langston also assumed a prominent role in working to establish racial justice in the restored nation. As president of the National Equal Rights League, a lobbying organization that he helped to found in October 1864, he toured widely, delivering speeches about the need to provide blacks in the North as well as the South with citizenship and voting rights. After the war he traveled throughout the South as general inspector of schools for the Freedmen's Bureau, working with local officials and delivering public addresses promoting education and encouraging active support for the Republican Party.

Reconstructing the Legal Profession. Langston's legal, educational, and political achievements led in October 1868 to an invitation to organize a law school at Howard University, which Congress had chartered in March 1867 to train black teachers and ministers. Langston's program opened in Washington, D.C., in January 1869. In addition to Langston, the early faculty consisted of an abolitionist congressman from Ohio, the chief clerk of the Freedmen's Bureau, and a federal judge. The school offered students a traditional preparation that qualified them for admission to the District of Columbia bar, although aspects of the program underscored its unique origins. Sen. Charles Sumner delivered the commencement address to the first graduating class in February 1871. A year later the graduates included Charlotte E. Ray, the first woman to earn a diploma at an American law school and the first woman to practice before the U.S. Supreme Court. Langston continued to head the Howard University Law School until 1875 (for the last two years he also served as acting president of the university.) His tenure as the Law School dean was marked by the challenges of dealing with economic depression, intensified by the failure of the Freedmen's Savings and Trust Company, for which Langston served on the board of directors. Langston's egotistical personality doubtless contributed significantly to the tensions, but he nevertheless helped to hold the school together through an extremely difficult period. As a result, Howard Law School survived to institutionalize black representation in the legal profession and to become in the twentieth century one of the most important training grounds for the leaders of the civil rights movement.

Back into Politics. After the Howard University board of trustees passed over Langston when choosing a successor to outgoing president O. O. Howard—in a vote that according to Langston divided the trustees along racial lines—he returned to public speaking and politics. President Rutherford B. Hayes rewarded him with appointments as minister to Haiti and chargé d'affaires to Santo Domingo. In 1888 Langston ran for election to the U.S. House of Representatives from the 4th Congressional District of Virginia. After an investigation demonstrated that his opponent's plurality resulted from voting fraud, the House seated Langston in September 1890. This incident illustrated one of the most pressing debates at that time, whether or not Congress would provide additional means to enforce the Fifteenth Amendment ban on racial discrimination in voting. Langston vigorously favored stronger federal protection. Congress nevertheless defeated the major initiative for this purpose, the so-called Force Bill introduced in 1890 by Sen. Henry Cabot Lodge of Massachusetts. Langston served only one year in the House of Representatives; he died in 1897.

Sources:

Maxwell Bloomfield, *American Lawyers in a Changing Society, 1776–1876* (Cambridge, Mass.: Harvard University Press, 1976);

John Mercer Langston, *From the Virginia Plantation to the National Capitol: Or, the First and Only Negro Representative in Congress from the Old Dominion* (Hartford, Conn.: American, 1894).

PUBLICATIONS

Horace Binney, *The Privilege of the Writ of Habeas Corpus under the Constitution* (Philadelphia: C. Sherman & Son, 1862–1865)—a defense of Lincoln administration policy that became the central publication in an extended debate among lawyers;

Joel P. Bishop, *Commentaries on the Law of Marriage and Divorce* (Boston: Little, Brown, 1852)—an analysis of contemporary morals as well as laws;

Thomas R. R. Cobb, *An Inquiry into the Law of Negro Slavery in the United States of America* (Philadelphia: T. & J. W. Johnson, 1858)—a treatise by one of the future drafters of the Confederate Constitution;

Thomas Cooley, *A Treatise on the Constitutional Limitations which Rest upon the Legislative Power of the States of the American Union* (Boston: Little, Brown, 1868)—a highly influential work contributing to more exacting judicial review in defense of economic liberty;

Cooley, *A Treatise on the Law of Taxation, Including the Law of Local Assessments* (Chicago: Callaghan, 1876)—defines the public purpose necessary to sustain taxation and in requiring equal and uniform, rather than progressive, taxation;

John Forrest Dillon, *The Law of Municipal Corporations* (New York: J. Cockcroft, 1872)—the eminent commentator, and later judge, establishes enduring principles of local government law;

Sidney George Fisher, *The Trial of the Constitution* (Philadelphia: J. B. Lippincott, 1862)—maintained that the Constitution provided Congress and the President with the powers necessary to sustain the Civil War;

Henry W. Halleck, *Elements of International Law and Laws of War* (Philadelphia: J. B. Lippincott, 1866)—reflects the Union military commander's recognition of the importance of the subject to the conduct of war;

Francis Hilliard, *The Law of Torts or Private Wrongs* (Boston: Little, Brown, 1859)—this first systematic treatise on torts marks the maturity of the subject;

Hilliard, *The Law of Taxation* (Boston: Little, Brown, 1875)—one of several treatises prompted by local tax initiatives during the middle decades of the century;

John Codman Hurd, *The Law of Freedom and Bondage in the United States* (Boston: Little, Brown, 1858–1862)—a Bostonian defends the legitimacy of slavery;

John A. Jameson, *A Treatise on Constitutional Conventions; Their History, Powers, and Modes of Proceeding* (Chicago: Callaghan, 1867)—a general survey prompted by the Illinois constitutional convention of 1862;

Christopher Columbus Langdell, *A Selection of Cases on the Law of Contracts* (Boston: Little, Brown, 1871)—the first casebook designed for use in law schools;

John A. Marshall, *American Bastile* (Philadelphia: T. W. Hartley, 1869)—a widely selling partisan denunciation of Lincoln administration policy on civil liberties;

John Belton O'Neall, *Biographical Sketches of the Bench and Bar of South Carolina* (Charleston: S. G. Courtenay, 1859)—one of the best sets of profiles of contemporary lawyers;

Joel Parker, *Personal Liberty Laws and Slavery in the Territories* (Boston: Wright & Potter, 1861)—an analysis by a conservative Harvard Law School professor;

Theophilus Parsons, *The Law of Contracts* (Boston: Little, Brown, 1853–1855)—a critique of the prevailing theory of contract; one of the best-selling treatises of the era;

Isaac Redfield, *The Law of Railways* (Boston: Little, Brown, 1858)—railroads had by this point changed American life so profoundly as to become a distinct field of legal practice;

Theodore Sedgwick, *A Treatise on the Rules Which Govern the Interpretation and Application of Statutory and Constitutional Law* (New York: J. S. Voorhies, 1857)—a guide to reading legal enactments;

George Sharswood, *A Compend of Lectures on the Aims and Duties of the Profession of the Law* (Philadelphia:

T. & J. W. Johnson, 1854)—statement of principles that would be adopted by early bar associations;

Thomas Shearman and Amasa Redfield, *A Treatise on the Law of Negligence* (New York: Baker, Voorhis, 1869)—an update on the developing field of torts;

John N. Taylor, *A Treatise on the American Law of Landlord and Tenant* (Boston: Little, Brown, 1866)—reflects the increasingly typical living arrangements in American cities;

Emory Washburn, *A Treatise on the American Law of Real Property*, 2 volumes (Boston: Little, Brown, 1860–1862)—a survey of law relating to land ownership;

Francis Wharton, *Commentary on the Law of Agency and Agents* (Philadelphia: Kay & Brother, 1876)—establishes the principal-agent relationship as a concept distinct from the law of employer-employee relations;

Wharton, *A Suggestion As to Causation* (Cambridge, Mass.: Riverside Press, 1874)—an attempt to allocate liability for injuries with multiple causes through a principle of moral causation;

William Whiting, *The War Powers of the President, and the Legislative Powers of Congress in Relation to Rebellion, Treason and Slavery* (Boston: J. L. Shorey, 1862)—the solicitor of the War Department defends the Lincoln administration's approach to the Constitution;

Theodore Dwight Woolsey, *Divorce and Divorce Legislation* (New York: Scribner, 1869)—Yale president and law professor denounces the laws facilitating divorce;

Woolsey, *Introduction to the Study of International Law* (Boston: J. Munroe, 1860)—the most current authority at the outbreak of the Civil War.

LIFESTYLES, SOCIAL TRENDS, AND FASHION

by SILVANA SIDDALI

CONTENTS

Sidebars and tables are listed in italics.

1850

- The population of the thirty-one states in the United States is just under 23.3 million.

- The Female Medical College is founded in Philadelphia by a group of Quakers. Eight women enroll in the first class. The college remains a women's institution until 1969, when it becomes coeducational.

- Vermont passes a personal-liberty law declaring that fugitive slaves who escape to that state do not have to be turned over to federal authorities for return to their masters. By 1858 similar laws have been passed in Connecticut, Rhode Island, Massachusetts, Michigan, Maine, Kansas, and Wisconsin.

- More than eighteen thousand homeless people are living in the cellars of buildings in New York City. By 1856 the construction of tenement apartment houses has helped to ease this problem.

23–24 Oct. Delegates from nine states meet in Worcester, Massachusetts, for the first national women's rights convention. Among the participants are Susan B. Anthony, Sojourner Truth, and Lucretia Mott. The delegates call for the right to vote and equal rights "without distinction of sex or color."

1851

- Maine passes a law prohibiting the sale of intoxicating beverages.

- The first North American chapters of the Young Men's Christian Association, founded in Great Britain in 1844, are established in Boston and Montreal.

- In New York six thousand seamstresses establish the Shirt Sewers Cooperative Union and pledge to share their profits.

12 Aug. Isaac Merrit Singer is awarded a patent for his continuous-stitching sewing machine, the first such machine that is practical for home use.

1852

- New York City and Boston start passenger horsecar lines. Unlike earlier horse-drawn omnibuses, horsecars run on train tracks.

- After she is denied the right to speak at a temperance rally because she is a woman, Susan B. Anthony founds the Women's New York State Temperance Society.

- The popular magazine *Godey's Lady's Book* begins publishing brief reports about working women under the heading "Employment for Women."

Oct. Rev. Thomas Gallaudet founds a church for deaf mutes in New York City.

1853

- Antoinette Blackwell becomes the first ordained female minister in the United States when she is installed as pastor of the Congregational Church in South Butler, New York.

- American restaurants begin hiring "waitresses" to serve food, formerly a job only for male waiters.

Feb.	In Washington, D.C., Paulina Wright Davis publishes the first issue of *Una*, a woman's suffrage magazine edited by Caroline H. Dall.
May	Texan Gail Borden, who has been experimenting with methods for preserving milk and other perishable foods, applies for a patent on his sweetened condensed milk. The patent is finally issued on 19 August 1856.

1854

•	Amanda M. Way, a Quaker minister, founds the Woman's Temperance Army in Indiana to shut down local saloons.
•	Timothy Shay Arthur's *Ten Nights in a Barroom and What I Saw There* is published in New York City. This influential temperance tract becomes a bestseller, second in sales only to Harriet Beecher Stowe's powerful antislavery novel *Uncle Tom's Cabin* (1852).
2 June	Fugitive slave Anthony Burns is taken from a Boston jail to begin the trip to Richmond, Virginia, where he is returned to his master. In protest Bostonians who oppose slavery drape their houses in black. Because of the furor surrounding the case thousands of policemen and federal troops guard the streets of the city, costing the federal government some $100,000.
31 Oct.	The *Nebraska Palladium* reports that there are 128 female postmasters in the United States. The women receive the same pay as their male counterparts.

1855

•	Sarah Josepha Hale launches a campaign to eliminate the word *female* from the name of Vassar Female College and then from all other references to women in public life. This goal becomes one of the objectives of women's rights activists.
4 July	A law prohibiting the sale of alcoholic beverages goes into effect in New York State. By the end of this year twelve states have passed similar laws. The New York law, however, is declared unconstitutional in March 1856.

1856

•	After disaffected followers assassinate Jesse Strang, self-proclaimed king of a Mormon colony on Beaver Island in Lake Michigan, other Michigan residents break up the colony and force the twenty-five hundred Mormons to leave their state.
•	A California slave, Bridget (Biddy) Mason, sues her Mormon owners for her freedom. She wins her case and moves to Los Angeles, where she purchases a homestead and eventually makes a fortune in real-estate transactions.

1857

•	Massachusetts requires its citizens to pass a literacy test in order to vote.
18 Nov.	A national temperance convention is held in Chicago.

1858

- A passenger horsecar service begins operation in Philadelphia.

- The first overland mail service connects the Atlantic and Pacific coasts.

- H. C. Wright publishes *The Unwelcomed Child; or, the Crime of an Undesigned and Undesired Maternity,* a pamphlet in which he advocates birth control.

1859

- Women in the Kansas Territory are allowed to vote in school elections.

- The first hotel passenger elevator is installed at the Fifth Avenue Hotel in New York City.

- The American Medical Association declares that abortion should be outlawed. By 1880 forty states and territories have passed laws against abortion.

- George M. Pullman's first sleeping car goes into service on a U.S. railroad.

1860

- According to the U.S. Census the population of the United States is nearly 31.5 million, including about 448,000 freed blacks and nearly 4 million slaves.

- New York revises its Married Women's Property Law, which allows women to own property and to keep their wages. The new law permits women to enter into contracts and bring suit in court, as well as giving them equal rights in child-custody cases.

22 Feb.–
10 Apr. During a major shoemakers' strike in Lynn, Massachusetts, some eight hundred women join their male colleagues, carrying signs declaring that "American Ladies Will Not Be Slaves."

24 Nov. A grand ball honoring the Prince of Wales is given at the Academy of Music in New York City. It is long considered the greatest social event ever to take place in the United States.

1861

- Antonio (Tony) Pastor opens his first theater on Broadway in New York City, attracting whole families by offering women dress patterns and kitchenware. Pastor becomes known as "The Father of Vaudeville."

- Red "Garibaldi shirts," modeled after the Italian revolutionary's uniform, become popular with American women.

12 Apr. Confederate troops fire on Fort Sumter in Charleston harbor, beginning the Civil War.

5 Aug. Congress imposes a federal income tax to help fund the Civil War.

1862

- Congress establishes the Department of Agriculture.

•   Elizabeth Keckly, a dressmaker and former slave, helps to found the Contra-band Relief Association to assist free blacks and runaway slaves in Washington, D.C.

1863

•   Congress institutes free mail delivery in U.S. cities.

•   Elizabeth Cady Stanton and Susan B. Anthony found the National Women's Loyal League to support emancipation and the war effort.

•   Ebenezer Butterick begins selling to home sewers paper patterns for boy's and men's clothing. In 1867 he begins making patterns for women's clothes and marketing them in his own magazines.

1 Jan.   President Abraham Lincoln issues the Emancipation Proclamation, freeing all slaves in Confederate territory not held by Union troops.

3 Oct.   President Abraham Lincoln declares Thanksgiving Day a national holiday.

1864

•   "In God We Trust" appears for the first time on a U.S. coin, a two-cent piece.

30 June   Congress passed an Internal Revenue Act, which raises taxes on items such as tobacco and increases income-tax rates.

1865

•   Ellen Curtis Demorest begins selling paper patterns women's clothing, marketing them in her own magazine, *Mme. Demorest's Mirror of Fashion.*

•   John Batterson Stetson opens a hat factory in Philadelphia and begins manufacturing the popular western-style hat that now bears his name.

9 Apr.   Gen. Robert E. Lee surrenders to Gen. Ulysses S. Grant in Appomattox, Virginia, marking the end of the Civil War.

24 Dec.   The Ku Klux Klan is founded by Confederate army veterans in Pulaski, Tennessee.

1866

10 Apr.   Philanthropist Henry Bergh founds the American Society for Prevention of Cruelty to Animals.

1867

•   Already popular in Europe, cigarettes begin to appear in the United States, introduced with the aim of making smoking more appealing to women.

•   Oliver H. Kelley founds the National Grange of the Patrons of Husbandry as a social and educational organization for farmers. During the 1870s the group becomes involved in the political fight to end the exploitation of farmers by railroads and middlemen.

• The Illinois Soldiers' Orphans' Home, the first home for orphans of Civil War veterans, is founded in Bloomington, Illinois.

1868

• Susan B. Anthony founds a newspaper, *The Revolution*, to advance the campaign for woman's suffrage.

1869

• Arabella Mansfield is admitted to the Iowa bar, becoming the first woman lawyer in America since Mistress Margaret Brent served as attorney for Lord Proprietor Cecilius Calvert of Maryland during the 1640s.

• Susan B. Anthony and Elizabeth Cady Stanton found the National Woman Suffrage Association. Stanton serves as president until 1890.

• Lucy Stone founds the American Woman Suffrage Association.

• Wyoming Territory grants women the vote.

• Henry J. Heinz and L. C. Noble establish a food-packing plant in Sharpsburg, Pennsylvania. Their first product is grated horseradish.

1870

• According to the U.S. Census the population of the United States is nearly 39.9 million. It also reaveals that one in eight children is working.

• The Utah Territory grants the vote to women.

25 Feb.   Sen. Hiram R. Revels, a Republican from Mississippi, becomes the first African American to serve in the U.S. Congress.

1871

8–11 Oct.   The Great Chicago Fire destroys most of the city, killing 250 people and leaving some 98,500 homeless.

1872

• In Rochester, New York, Susan B. Anthony leads a group of sixteen women who register to vote in the presidential election.

22 Feb.   The Prohibition Party holds its first national nominating convention in Columbus, Ohio.

1873

• Congress passes the Comstock Law prohibiting the sending of "obscene materials," including birth control information, through the U.S. Mail.

1874

- The Woman's Christian Temperance Union (WCTU) is established in Cleveland, Ohio, with Annie Wittenmyer as its first president.

21 Aug. A civil-court jury finds popular preacher Rev. Henry Ward Beecher not guilty in a suit brought by Theodore Tilton, who has accused Beecher of entering into an adulterous affair.

1875

- Henry Bergh founds the Society for the Prevention of Cruelty to Children.

1876

- Americans celebrate the centennial of the Declaration of Independence.

- Juliet Corson founds the New York Cooking School, the first cooking school in the United States.

1877

15 June Henry O. Flipper becomes the first African American to graduate from the U.S. Military Academy at West Point.

OVERVIEW

The American Spirit at Midcentury. Throughout the first half of the nineteenth century, Americans were among the most optimistic people on earth. Economic growth and territorial expansion all contributed to a sense of apparently boundless opportunity. Dedicated to individualism, Americans sometimes struck European visitors as being materialistic to the point of greed and optimistic to the point of arrogance. At the same time many Americans were devoted to a largely unrealistic cultural and social ideal that included strict attention to morality and the work ethic and the exaltation of home life. As the growing middle class became more attached to convenient, cheaply produced consumer goods, they also became more worried about declining morals and social problems. Although their religious zeal had abated somewhat, the reform movements that had arisen from evangelical religious revivals of 1830s and 1840s—including temperance, women's rights, and abolitionism—continued to influence American life at midcentury.

Conflicting Loyalties. Americans were still more alike than different. The majority of them still lived on farms (53 percent in 1870). Most of them spoke English as their first (and only) language, worshiped in Protestant churches, and revered the precepts passed down to them by their forebears of the Revolutionary War generation. Though they still found these principles worth fighting for, Americans did not always agree on how to interpret them. In the decade before the Civil War the debate between North and South over the expansion of slavery into new territories forced a growing awareness that the country was heading toward some sort of division. Most Americans hoped that these sectional differences could somehow be ironed out, and later they prayed that the country would survive the gathering storm.

The Civil War. The tragedy of the Civil War overshadowed every aspect of daily life. In addition to the split between North and South the war also brought to light, and worsened, internal divisions in both regions. Union sympathizers in eastern Tennessee and western Virginia deplored the secession of their states, while in some nothern cities draft riots revealed the reluctance of some potential soldiers, particularly new immigrants, to risk their lives while wealthier men purchased exemptions.

Reform Movements. The war accelerated social changes already underway in some areas of American life. The wave of reformism that had swept across the country in the 1830s and 1840s had left behind hundreds of organizations dedicated to the betterment (and perhaps eventual perfection) of the American people. Temperance, abolitionism, and a nascent women's rights movement were joined by a host of more-eccentric crusades. The war and the Reconstruction era that followed it offered some women new career opportunities in teaching and nursing, and women who had been active abolitionists went on to reinvigorate the women's rights movement. By the end of the war, however, the idealistic spirit of reform and Americans' optimistic sense of their national destiny had given way to weary resignation. No longer dedicated to individualism and the dream of perfecting human society, people began to look toward larger institutional solutions.

Industrialization. The Industrial Revolution had already been well underway in the United States, particularly in the North, for twenty years before the Civil War. Before the Industrial Revolution, American customs and daily life changed only slowly over the years. Since most people lived on farms, they ate what they could grow, wore clothes they could sew at home, and oriented their daily life around seasonal rhythms. Their houses were built along the same lines as those of their grandfathers, and they kept to their old customs even when they moved to new locations. The new technologies of the nineteenth century brought labor-saving inventions such as sewing machines and cast-iron cooking stoves, improved transportation via railroads and steamboats, and better methods of preserving foods. A machine that could do the work of ten men ensured that consumer goods could be produced quickly and cheaply. The abundance of inexpensive goods such as printed cloth, dishes, cookware, farm implements, and furniture raised the standard of living considerably for free white Americans. As the Industrial Revolution advanced, technology began to transform every aspect of life in antebellum America. Mobilization for the war effort promoted some aspects of industrialization.

Urbanization and Standardization. Millions of immigrants from Europe found work in American factories, contributing to the creation of a class of urban wage-earners, including women and children. Though some women welcomed the new opportunity to earn money and some parents were happy to find a way in which their children could contribute to the family's income, factory work was arduous, poorly paid, and dangerous. Many social critics called this "wage slavery" one of the great evils of modernization. The war also hastened standardization. For example, standardization of printed money and the institution of an income tax had a profound effect on the way Americans perceived their relationship to their government. Such vast increases in the interference of the federal government in private lives contributed—along with urbanization—to a decreased sense of individualism among Americans.

Household Economy. A city-dwelling, working-class family needed between $500 and $600 per year for food, rent, clothing, and fuel. Since the average unskilled laborer rarely earned more than $300 to $450 per year, it became necessary for women and children to contribute to the family's income. Working-class women often worked in the sewing trades or as domestic servants. Many also took in work at home, such as doing laundry, plaiting straw for hats and fans, or stitching fabric uppers for shoes. Farm families all had to work hard. Farming was a seasonal activity, and they usually had to put their cash into seeds and supplies, or borrow ahead against the next year's crop. It cost between $500 and $750 to start a 150-acre farm. Throughout the nineteenth century most Americans had little cash, and farmers, domestic help, and laborers alike all worked long hours, typically six days per week and ten hours per day. During the Civil War, the Union blockade of southern ports resulted in severe shortages and massive inflation throughout the South. A Richmond family that had spent $6.65 a week for groceries in 1861 was paying $68.25 two years later. Food shortages, partly caused by speculation and inflation, eventually caused bread riots in several southern cities. In the twenty years following the war, farm acres devoted to food production tripled as settlers flocked to western territories. Technological innovations such as harvesters and reapers also contributed to increased food production. Improved transportation not only got farm products to cities faster but also expanded the farmers' markets, making it possible for most Americans to enjoy a healthier, more varied diet. As factories that had stepped up production to serve the war effort turned to making consumer goods, prices came down, allowing wage-earners to enhance their quality of their home life.

"Victorian" Americans. Americans of the mid nineteenth century were enamored of all things British and especially adored Queen Victoria. American women followed her lead in fashions. Although wealthy American ladies also copied the beautiful Empress Eugénie of France, who popularized hoop skirts, Parisian fashions had little practical influence in the United States. American ladies pored over French fashion plates and sometimes adapted these styles to suit American taste, but Queen Victoria's taste for plaid and the deep mourning she began to wear after the death in 1861 of her beloved husband, Prince Albert, were far more influential than French fashions in the United States.

European Influences. English and French political events, and especially European attitudes toward the Civil War, made front-page news on a daily basis in every American newspaper. In addition to influencing American literature, theater, music, fine arts, and fashion, European tastes also shaped Americans' ideas about home furnishings, fine cuisine, and etiquette. European immigrants also contributed to the changing panorama of American daily life, bringing with them traditional foods and customs.

Manners and Social Life. From the 1840s through the end of the century an immense assortment of etiquette manuals appeared in the United States. The authors of these books borrowed heavily from European publications, but they also frequently alluded to differences between Americans and Europeans. One of the most frequently praised American characteristics was a "frankness and easiness of manners," which American etiquette writers considered the basis for all good breeding. At the same time strict rules of behavior were being applied by the emerging middle class. Calling cards, visits of ceremony, proper comportment toward ladies, and correct dinner-table behavior were all discussed with intense interest and in the most minute detail. Throughout American society, and especially in the South, women were treated with singular politeness and respect. At the same time, however, American men were given to some deplorable habits, including widespread tobacco chewing and spitting. The universality of this custom excited scorn, criticism, and contempt among European travelers in the United States. During the Civil War society matrons in the North and the South threw huge public balls to raise money for their causes. Some observers commented on the almost inappropriate level of "frantic gaiety" at these wartime social events. Even the harshest critics, however, acknowledged that although American society was not free from class distinctions, public behavior—at least among white persons—was scrupulously egalitarian.

TOPICS IN THE NEWS

CLASS AND COMMUNITY

Class Distinctions. One of the first qualities European visitors to antebellum America noticed was the natives' fierce belief in democracy and equality. Another was that most Americans were constantly on the move: the English writer Harriet Martineau commented that asking the average American about the state of his well-being was likely to produce the answer "moving, Sir." It is true that, by comparison to Europe, America was a relatively egalitarian society: there were no aristocratic titles, and the idea of the "self-made man" was a cherished one. Everyone, it was widely held, could achieve prosperity with the application of sufficient effort and "Yankee shrewdness." The American public was enchanted with Horatio Alger's rags-to-riches stories, which were published throughout the period. But the truth is a bit more complex. By the eve of the Civil War inequalities in wealth had become pronounced in American society, and by the end of Reconstruction, class differences were firmly entrenched. Class distinctions varied widely from region to region, and even from state to state; in addition, the differences between urban and rural life contributed to the way in which people experienced their relative levels of wealth. It can, however, be said that most white Americans saw themselves as the equals of even the wealthiest, at least at the ballot box and under the law. Further, most believed fervently in the possibility of upward mobility, and many of them acted on the belief by pulling up stakes and moving west or to a nearby town. Thus, upward mobility translated roughly into geographic mobility.

Sectional Differences. From colonial times, northerners had become used to a diversified economic life based on independent farming, manufacturing, artisan crafts, and shipping. After the Industrial Revolution began, large cities drew both natives and immigrants, who formed a cheap source of labor. In the West, the gold rush and the pioneer movement brought a rough equality: few gold miners became rich, and most of the farmers who made the westward trek had to work hard to eke out

Belle Grove in Louisiana, a planter's house in the Greek revival style often built on large southern plantations, and slave quarters on a Georgia plantation

THE AGE OF SHODDY

An editorial in the 6 October 1863 issue of the *New York Herald* denounced unscrupulous northern manufacturers and financiers who made immense fortunes during the war, often at the expense of the war effort. These men included such notable businessmen as railroad magnates Jay Gould and Jim Fisk, and meatpacker Philip Armour. The term *shoddy* is the name for the poor-quality, reused wool that was used to make uniforms for soldiers. These uniforms (as well as poorly made boots, blankets, and other supplies) did not hold up well in the field, and the term came to refer to any inferior product with pretensions of being better than it really is:

The world has seen its iron age, its silver age, its golden age and its brazen age. This is the age of shoddy. The new brown stone palaces on Fifth Avenue, the new equipages [carriages] at the Park, the new diamonds which dazzle unaccustomed eyes, the new silks and satins which rustle over loudly, as if to demand attention, the new people who live in the palaces and ride in the carriages and wear the diamonds and silks—all are shoddy. From devil's dust they sprang, and unto devil's dust they shall return. They live in shoddy houses. They ride in shoddy carriages, drawn by shoddy horses, and driven by shoddy coachmen who wear shoddy liveries. They lie upon shoddy beds which have just come from the upholsterers and still smell of shoddy varnish. They wear shoddy clothes purchased from shoddy merchants who have erected mammoth stores, which appear to be marble, but are really shoddy. They set or follow the shoddy fashions, and fondly imagine themselves *à la mode de Paris* when they are only *à la mode de* shoddy. Their professions and occupations are pure shoddy. They are shoddy brokers in Wall Street or shoddy manufacturers of shoddy goods, or shoddy contractors for shoddy articles for a shoddy government. Six days in the week they are shoddy business men. On the seventh they are shoddy Christians. . . .

Source: *New York Herald*, 6 October 1863.

a meager living. The South had the most stratified society, consisting of wealthy white plantation owners, poor white farmers, and black slaves. Deference on the part of the lower-class whites toward those of the upper class combined paradoxically with a stubborn individualism, as well as a perennial hope of joining the wealthy class by obtaining slaves.

Urban Poverty. By 1860 there were more than five million immigrants, crowded into unimaginably dirty and dangerous slums, in the big northeastern cities. Even the most hopeful reformer could hardly conceive of a social program that could cope with the massive influx of poor, unskilled workers who flooded into the port cities of Boston and New York, willing to take almost any job at almost any wage. Housing shortages made overcrowd-

ing a serious problem; three or four families would share a tenement apartment in some of the worst slums, such as Boston's notorious Half Moon District, where more than a hundred people used one filthy outhouse. An observer in the early 1850s claimed that "There has never been so deplorable an exhibition of mendicancy in our streets as may be witnessed daily at this time . . . hundreds of destitute men and scores of women . . . little girls are to be found in front of the city saloons at all hours of the day, going through their graceless performances." While there was little chance of any of these families acquiring great fortunes, such as those of the Astors or the Vanderbilts, over the next few generations many of them did improve their lot in life.

From Artisan to Skilled Laborer. Experiencing a significant decline during this period was the artisan class—shoemakers, carpenters, bricklayers, blacksmiths. Once the head of a thriving workshop, the master oversaw the work of journeymen and apprentices. This little group formed a kind of "family," in which the master craftsman bore the moral as well as professional responsibility for the workers under his supervision. But with the advent of the Industrial Revolution, as well as the increased demand of a growing market, it became necessary to divide tasks into ever smaller components. This process was particularly evident in the shoemaking industry. In the past, master craftsmen fitted, cut, stitched, and finished one pair of shoes at a time. After the advent of the factory system, workers could be trained to perform smaller portions of the original task, such as stitching the same seam on hundreds of pairs of similar shoes. The workshops gave way to larger concerns, and smaller groups who lived, prayed, and drank whiskey with their master dissolved into larger groups of workers, answerable to the factory manager. Although this process took several generations to complete, the status of formerly skilled artisans declined after the Civil War.

Protests. Antebellum workers did protest unfair working conditions and mounted strikes. Such demonstrations were usually aimed at improving specific conditions. Factory owners and workers alike had faith in the Jacksonian-era "self-made man" and held fast to Victorian ideas of self-reliance. They believed that everyone had to pull himself up by his bootstraps, and that industry, energy, and "Yankee shrewdness" would result in a successful life. By 1860 one-fourth of all native New Englanders had moved to different states. Naturally, this philosophy applied mainly to native-born white Americans, not to immigrant workers and certainly not to slaves.

The Emerging Middle Class. Most antebellum Americans considered themselves to be of the "middling" classes. This meant that they were part of the largest group in the nation—people who were self-sufficient, making their own living on farms or in workshops. Most middling Americans, then, were skilled artisans or independent farmers. The average American, during this period, still lived on an independent, self-sufficient farm and was relatively cash-poor. But the era of the Civil War saw a significant change; a new class was emerging. Now husbands left the home in the morning to go to work; wives stayed home to take care of the housework and children; and a new fluidity of spending money made it possible (and even important) to acquire the symbols of comfort and wealth. Perhaps the single most important status symbol was the parlor piano, which naturally included piano lessons for the daughter of the house. The increasing growth of markets, the availability of cheap consumer goods (however poorly produced), and the gradual increase in spending money allowed the growth of the new middle class. This class would not become firmly entrenched until after Reconstruction in the late 1870s. Meanwhile, the increased industrialization of the wartime economy helped shape the future of the American family.

Merchants and Manufacturers. Perhaps the most upwardly mobile group in northern society were those men who recognized the possibilities of making a profit in the newer manufacturing processes. Although extensive mechanization did not set in until after the Civil War, the new way of breaking up processes allowed greater control, increased speed, and far more productivity. Naturally, these changes took their toll on workers. At the same time, in the years before the Civil War, bankruptcies destroyed many of these budding fortunes. Still, most entrepreneurs simply picked up and moved on, or else began a new business, many of which failed again. Other professionals who tended to earn at least a comfortable income, if not extreme wealth, were attorneys, bank and corporate officers, and physicians.

The Very Rich. In 1860, 5 percent of American families owned half the nation's wealth. Among southern planters and northern industrialists, the disparity in wealth was particularly pronounced. In addition it is among the very wealthiest Americans that we find the greatest refutation of the "self-made man" myth. The very rich inherited their wealth, and married within their own social circles. Family connections counted for a great deal in mid-nineteenth-century courtships, and vast fortunes were often enhanced and increased through prudent marriages. This was an exclusive club indeed; Horatio Alger's congenial myths notwithstanding, very few poor men ever entered this exalted company. The great American fortunes, furthermore, were roughly comparable to the great European ones; lavish country estates, great houses on New York City's Fifth Avenue, and immense plantations all testified to the enormous wealth of America's richest families. In comparing the wealthiest individuals in the United States and England, one historian has found that although American wealth originated in business, and English wealth was largely derived from landed estates, the respective fortunes were about equal. John Jacob Astor's immense fortune could be compared favorably with that of the Duke of Bedford,

SOUTHERN SLAVE-OWNING FAMILIES IN 1850		
No. of Families	No. of Slaves	Percent
1,733	100 or more	.49
6,196	50-99	1.7
29,733	20-49	8.5
54,595	10-19	15.7
80,765	5-9	23.3
105,683	2-4	30.4
68,820	1	19.8

6,120,825 southern whites (75 percent of the population) owned no slaves.

Source: U.S. Department of Commerce, Bureau of the Census, *Historical Statistics of the United States, Colonial Times to 1970* (Washington, D.C.: U.S. Government Printing Office, 1976).

or Nathan Mayer Rothschild of France, generally regarded as the richest man in Europe.

Southern Planters. The wealthiest class in the antebellum South were those families owning more than one hundred slaves. Fewer than one-half of 1 percent of southern families belonged to this elite group. Some of the richest families lived deceptively simple lives. The fabled white plantation houses were rare. Most of them had sunk all their capital into slaves and next year's crop and could not afford to build fancy homes or furnish them with European imports. Still, sharp class distinctions were respected. Independent yeoman farmers deferred to their social betters and hoped one day to join them. The one sure way of moving upward in the southern social scale was to purchase slaves. Even successful professionals did not feel that they had "arrived" in southern society until they owned slaves. All whites enjoyed political equality and democracy before the law. Still, the poorest southern whites, the "clay eaters" who were not given the same respect as their betters, suffered the most during the Civil War.

The Civil War. During the Civil War, however, some underlying class tensions broke through—visible in the South as well as in the North. The protest of "a poor man's blood for a rich man's war" was heard on both fronts. When the U.S. government enacted a draft in 1863, many poor laborers took to the streets in protest. They were outraged by the commutation clause, which provided that a drafted man could pay $300 for a substitute. Naturally, poorer men could not buy their way out of military service. Although fewer southerners "bought" substitutes, the Confederate government did make allowances for white men on plantations with more than twenty slaves. Since most Union and Confederate soldiers were from the independent farmer class, they felt that such provisions were unfair and clearly favored the wealthy.

The Ruined South. After the devastation of the Civil War, some of the extremes of wealth along with slavery disappeared. But the old distinctions died hard. The military titles of "major" and "colonel" remained in usage to honor former officers who served during the conflict. Perhaps most poignantly, black people remained on the bottom of the social ladder. After the enactment of the Black Codes and the rigorous enforcement of segregation laws, their status seemed irremediably fixed in southern society.

Sources:

Paul Faler, *Mechanics and Manufacturers in the Early Industrial Revolution: Lynn, Massachusetts, 1780–1860* (Albany: State University of New York Press, 1981);

Mathew Josephson, *The Robber Barons: The Great American Capitalists, 1861–1901* (New York: Harcourt, Brace, 1934);

Edward Pessen, *Riches, Class and Power before the Civil War* (Lexington, Mass.: D. C. Heath, 1973);

Christine Stansell, *City of Women: Sex and Class in New York, 1789-1860* (New York: Knopf, 1986);

Stephan Thernstrom, *Poverty and Progress: Social Mobility in a Nineteenth-Century City,* revised edition (Cambridge, Mass.: Harvard University Press, 1991).

ETHNIC IDENTITIES

Five Million Newcomers. In the forty years before the Civil War five million newcomers reached America's shores. Most came from northwestern Europe and the British Isles, fleeing famine, wars, revolutions, and religious persecution. News of the discovery of gold in California in 1848 brought thousands of immigrants from China as well. The greatest period of immigration to the United States occurred between 1847 and 1857, when 3.3 million people arrived. Between 1865 and 1875 another 3.5 million landed in American seaports. In all nearly ten million newcomers arrived in the United States during the 1850s, 1860s, and 1870s. The two largest groups were the Irish and the Germans, who composed nearly three-quarters of all immigrants residing in the United States in 1860. About 60 percent of all immigrants were men. The disparity between males and females was perhaps greatest among Chinese immigrants, of which men outnumbered women 16 to 1 in 1860. The ratio was about 1.5 to 1 among northern European immigrants. European men more often came with their families or brought them over within a year. About two-thirds of all immigrants were between the ages of fifteen and thirty-nine. The majority were farmers or unskilled laborers, and many were illiterate.

Why They Came. Perhaps the most significant reasons for leaving Europe were poverty and overcrowding. Most of those who eventually decided to come to America were in fact part of a much larger movement. Europe was in the midst of one of the greatest periods of migration in world history. While European population growth during the nineteenth century was less than that of the United States, the population of Europe had doubled between 1750 and 1850, and the lack of available land forced young people to leave farms in search of work in the cities. Most of the immigrants who crossed the Atlantic had first made the difficult move from the family farm to a nearby city. From there they had gone to a seaport where they sought cheap transatlantic passage. Work and food were scarce, and some people faced other problems as well. A small percentage were revolutionaries escaping imprisonment for their political activities or members of radical religious groups fleeing persecution.

Inducements. Immigrants were drawn to the United States by tales of ample work and high pay. The dream of farming one's own land lured millions of Germans, Scandinavians, and Irish. After the late 1840s increased transatlantic shipping and trade lowered the price of passage, making the crossing affordable to many poor Europeans. American entrepreneurs, boosters, and railroad builders actively encouraged immigration. Many western states, such as Wisconsin, advertised heavily in European newspapers, touting rich farmlands and the many opportunities for employment. Many newcomers sent relatives at home "American letters" that included glowing descriptions of new freedoms and high wages. One young Irishman wrote home to his sister that it would give him "great pleasure to think that you Come here, for I think you would do verry well in this Country."

How They Came. Most European immigrants could afford only the cheapest passage, in steerage on cargo ships. Steerage, the lowest deck on the vessel, often lacked bathing facilities or adequate numbers of toilets. With hundreds of passengers crowded together, sickness was often rampant; nearly seventeen thousand Irish immigrants died of an infectious disease they called "ship fever." Chinese immigrants crossed the Pacific under similar conditions.

What They Found. Most newcomers landed in seaport cities such as Boston or New York. Although many Germans, French Canadians, and Scandinavians moved westward to settle on their own farms within a generation, most other immigrants stayed in urban areas. Many lacked the funds to buy land and start a farm, and large numbers of them had no experience as farmers. Their arrival had a profound impact on American city life. By 1860 the population of New York City was 25 percent foreign-born. Boston had a significant Irish population, and Germans gravitated to neighborhoods in Philadelphia. In such urban areas hucksters and swindlers often cheated immigrants of their hard-earned savings. Many immigrants were crowded into some of the worst urban slums, such as the notorious Half Moon District in Boston or the Lower East Side in New York City.

The Irish Exodus. In the mid 1840s the Catholic poor of Ireland, who were already paying high farm rentals to Protestant, usually absentee landlords, suffered an appalling disaster. A blight, or fungus, caused their potato

Irish emigrants in County Kerry crowding aboard a mail coach to travel to a port where they can book passage on a ship to the United States

crops, the main part of their daily diet, to rot in the fields. By the early 1850s about two million people, one fourth of the population of Ireland, had died of starvation. Ireland's starving poor flocked to American seaport cities such as New York and Boston. Typically, the oldest son or daughter left Ireland for the "Land of Plenty" first, paying for passage in steerage with money scraped together by the rest of the family. Once in America they hoped to earn enough money to pay the fares of their siblings and parents.

Discrimination. Perhaps the greatest obstacle the Irish faced was the severe anti-Catholic sentiment that was rampant throughout the United States. Many Protestants, including potential employers of the new immigrants, believed that the Irish owed their first allegiance to the Pope rather than the American government. Furthermore, many considered the Irish to be overly fond of intoxicating drink and prone to violence. These stereotypical views made it difficult for Irish immigrants to find work. Throughout the second half of the nineteenth century, shops and factories frequently sported signs proclaiming "No Irish Need Apply." Relegated to backbreaking labor, the men often toiled in mines or worked at building canals and railroads. The women went into domestic service as kitchen maids and laundresses.

Self-Help. During the 1840s the Ancient Order of Hibernians, a secret society imported from Ireland, looked out for the welfare of the Irish laborer. By the 1850s and 1860s Irish immigrants had become influential in the Democratic Party, making use of corrupt but highly efficient urban party machines such as Tammany Hall in New York City. In return for promises of politi-

cal support, machine politicians supplied cash for emergency expenses or helped immigrants find jobs. Through the influence of urban machines, Irishmen became policemen in many cities.

The Irish in the Civil War. Irish regiments served on both sides of the War Between the States. In the Confederate army eight southern states had Irish units, including the elite Emerald Guards. The Union army had forty regiments composed entirely of Irish volunteers, including the famous "fighting Irish" of the Emerald Brigade. Not all Irish immigrants supported the war effort, however. In July 1863 one of the worst riots in U.S. history exploded in New York City just a week after Irish soldiers fought in the Battle of Gettysburg. For more than a week rampaging mobs surged through New York City, protesting the newly enacted draft law. Much of the Irish population of New York was outraged by the "commutation clause" of this law, which allowed wealthy northerners who had been drafted to pay $300 to avoid conscription—a price few Irish laborers could afford. They were also angry over the Emancipation Proclamation, which President Abraham Lincoln had issued on 1 January 1863, because they feared that freed blacks would take jobs away from Irish laborers. Hundreds of people were killed, including many free black workers. Millions of dollars worth of property was damaged or destroyed, including an orphanage for black children and houses of prostitution known to cater to black sailors.

The Germans. In 1848 a small group of idealistic German revolutionaries called the "Forty-Eighters" fled to the United States after the failure of their attempt to create a unified, democratic Germany. (The various Ger-

NORTHERN EUROPEAN IMMIGRATION TO THE UNITED STATES, 1830-1880

Decade	Germany	Ireland	England Scotland Wales	Scandi-navia	Italy	Austria-Hungary	Russia Baltic States	Asia	Totals
1831-40	152,454	207,654	75,810	2,264	2,253	—	277	55	599,180
1841-50	434,626	780,719	267,044	13,122	1,970	—	551	141	1,713,392
1851-60	951,657	914,119	423,929	24,680	9,231	—	457	41,538	2,639,752
1861-70	827,468	435,697	607,076	126,392	11,725	7,800	2,515	64,759	2,379,583
1871-80	718,182	436,871	548,043	242,934	55,795	72,969	39,287	124,160	2,936,351

Source: U.S. Census data.

man states did not become a single nation until 1871.) Other Germans came to the United States seeking religious freedom, among them Jews, Mennonites, and the Amish. Most Germans, however, immigrated to America for more-practical reasons. The revolutions and economic disruptions of early-nineteenth-century Europe affected the German countryside as they did the rest of the continent, resulting in high rents, overcrowding, and a scarcity of jobs. Though the infestation on the continent was less severe, potato crops in Germany and the Netherlands were afflicted with the same potato blight that devastated the economy of Ireland.

Distribution. German immigrants typically reached the United States with savings and some experience in farming. They kept to themselves, particularly the religious sects who practiced their simple ways of life in the heartland of Pennsylvania and in the Midwest. Between 1815 and 1865 about three thousand members of the Amish sect settled in Pennsylvania. They were soon followed by similar groups, which settled in Indiana and Ohio. Following the dictates of Swiss religious leader Jacob Amman, the Amish fled religious persecution, mainly because of their deeply rooted opposition to infant baptism. Some Germans settled in Wisconsin and began dairy farming. About 1.3 million settled west of the Ohio River, in or near cities such as Cincinnati, Saint Louis, and Milwaukee. By 1854 the Germans were the single largest group of immigrants arriving in the United States. Wherever they went, they took their own culture and customs, including the Christmas tree and kindergartens.

Acceptance. Because they seemed to fit more easily into established American communities, Germans commanded more respect than other immigrant groups. Many were highly skilled artisans and craftsmen, who had come to the United States because they had been displaced by the Industrial Revolution. While many native-born Americans perceived German immigrants favorably as industrious, self-reliant, and thrifty, these newcomers were sometimes criticized, especially for

their custom of celebrating Sunday not merely as a day of rest but of amusement. Native-born Americans who were accustomed to celebrating the Sabbath in a reserved and pious manner were often shocked by the German customs of eating, drinking beer, playing cards, listening to band music, singing traditional songs, and even dancing on Sunday.

The Chinese. After the discovery of gold in 1848 in California, more than forty thousand Chinese men flocked to the West Coast, hoping to earn enough money to return to their native land and establish themselves in wealth and comfort. (The Chinese characters for San Francisco roughly translate as "Gold Mountain.") Most of these immigrants came from Toishan, a depressed agricultural region about 150 miles northwest of Hong Kong. Unable to survive as farmers, many people from this region had gone to live in the seaport cities of Hong Kong and Canton, where they engaged in commercial activities that brought them into contact with European and American merchant ships. About 90 percent of Chi-

Chinese and American miners in California

nese immigrants were male. The majority of women who did make the journey were prostitutes, although many of them were probably forced into this way of life after their arrival in the United States. Two-thirds of all Chinese immigrants settled in California, mostly in San Francisco, and nearly all remained in the western states. For most their initial dreams of prosperity were quickly disappointed, and they found employment only as manual laborers, building railroads or working in mines. In part because they competed with other working-class men for jobs and in part because of racism, the Chinese encountered a great deal of hostility in the United States. Beliefs that the Chinese were an inferior, immoral race, prone to prostitution, gambling, and drug abuse, became widespread, particular on the West Coast. A movement to ban Chinese immigration to the United States arose in California in the 1870s and resulted in the Chinese Exclusion Act of 1882, which refused admittance to any individuals except "white persons and persons of African descent."

Sources:

Leonard Dinnerstein and David M. Reimers, *Ethnic Americans: A History of Immigration and Assimilation* (New York: Dodd, Mead, 1975);

Richard A. Easterlin, David Ward, William S. Bernard, and Reed Ueda, *Immigration* (Cambridge, Mass.: Harvard University Press, 1982);

Oscar Handlin, *Boston's Immigrants: A Study in Acculturation*, revised and enlarged edition (Cambridge, Mass.: Harvard University Press, 1959).

Wedding gowns of the early 1850s, for brides who chose to be married in the newly popular large church weddings (illustration from an 1850 issue of *Godey's Lady's Book*)

FAMILY LIFE: COURTSHIP AND MARRIAGE

Changing Morality. In the eighteenth century some 10 percent of American brides arrived at the altar already pregnant with their first child, a level unequaled until the late twentieth century. In rural New England during the 1780s and 1790s as many as one-third of all young women were pregnant at the time they were married. Most people felt that so long as the couple married, there was little shame in premarital pregnancies. During the first quarter of the nineteenth century, however, this attitude underwent a significant change. By 1840 there were fewer than one in five premarital pregnancies in most New England towns, and by 1860 the rate had dropped to one in twenty. With the rise of the sentimental domestic ideal, which held American womanhood as an example of purity, Americans now set much stricter moral and sexual codes.

Courtship. The typical courtship began in church or at a family celebration. While in the past parents often chose their children's spouses with an eye to increasing the family's wealth or landholdings, by the mid nineteenth century most young people, and many parents, believed that men and women should marry for love. This romantic idea of love based on mutual attraction was reinforced by sentimental poetry and short stories in magazines such as the *Ladies' Repository* and *Godey's Lady's Book*. Permission from parents was still important, but young people often followed their own inclinations, even in the South, where parents still exercised greater control over their children's lives. Most young people frowned on flirtations. The notion that someone would "make up to" a person of the opposite sex without serious intentions of marriage was considered "fast," not to say disreputable. Although this rule applied to both men and women, criticism of the female flirt was sharper.

Engagement and Marriage. Long engagements were common; it was not considered proper for a young couple to marry until the man could support his wife in a decent home and until the bride had collected her bridal clothes and established her trousseau, which included such important items as bedding, linens, curtains, and kitchenware. Engagements could be broken off for several reasons, usually misunderstandings, jealousies, or the discovery that one's partner was not compatible. Before 1860 the typical couple was married at the bride's home in the presence of immediate family members and a few close friends. During the 1860s and 1870s middle-class weddings became more elaborate. The bride's family often sent engraved invitations to a wide range of relatives and acquaintances. Church weddings became more common because the typical family parlor could not hold all the guests, and weddings were often followed by lavish receptions. Many middle-class brides who could afford

DR. BRONSON'S
FEMALE PILLS

Have never yet failed, when the directions have been strictly followed, in removing difficulties arising from Obstruction, or Stoppage of Nature, or in restoring the system to perfect health when suffering from Spinal Affections, Prolapsus Uteri, the Whites, or other weakness of the uterine organs. Also, in all cases of Debility, or Nervous Frostration, Hysterics, Palpitations, &c., &c., which are the forerunners of more serious diseases. ☞ These Pills are perfectly harmless on the constitution, and may be taken by the most delicate female without causing distress ; at the same time they act like a charm by strengthening, invigorating, and restoring the system to a healthy condition, and by bringing on the monthly period with regularity, no matter from what cause the obstructions may arise. They should, however, NOT be taken during the first three or four months of pregnancy, though safe at any other time, as miscarriage would be the result in most cases. Sold in boxes containing 60 Pills. Price One Dollar. Post paid to any address, and sent secure from observation.

———— ·•◆•· ————

SPECIAL NOTICE.

In obstinate and old standing cases of Obstructions that have failed to find the desired relief by the use of the above Pills,

DR. BRONSON'S INFALLIBLE PILL NO. 2

are recommended, being four degrees stronger than the Female Pill No. 1, and are expressly prepared for such cases. They can never fail, and are safe, sure, prompt, and healthy. No female who values health and happiness with married life should be without these Pills. Price $5 per box, with full and explicit directions for use. Sent post paid, and free from observation, by mail.

THOS. F. CHAPMAN,
SOLE IMPORTER,
831 BROADWAY, NEW YORK.

Advertisement for one of many medicines used in the 1860s by women hoping to end early-stage pregnancies

to do so wore flowing white gowns and veils, a style that originated with wealthy women in the 1830s. American brides and grooms married somewhat later than their European counterparts. By 1860 most Americans were in their early to mid twenties when they married, with the average age somewhat lower in the South. Slave women married in their late teens and began their childbearing years around the age of nineteen.

Divorce. Although divorce statistics are incomplete, it had become easier to obtain a divorce by the middle of the nineteenth century. By that time most states had passed laws that allowed a couple to obtain a divorce in a court of law, instead of having to petition the state legislature as in the past. Beginning in 1839 some states began passing laws that allowed married women to keep their own property and earnings, making it easier for a woman to support herself after her marriage was dissolved. During the nineteenth century the divorce rate in the United States grew more rapidly than in European countries, but the number of divorces was small in comparison to statistics for the United States in the twentieth century.

Contraception. The nationwide birth rate in the United States declined from seven or eight children per family around 1800 to five or six by the Civil War. (Average family size was somewhat higher among southerners, both black and white.) Although these statistics suggest that Americans were deliberately limiting the size of their families, there is little information available on the methods they employed. The topic was considered taboo, even obscene. Contraception was rarely discussed in diaries or letters, and Americans who wanted to practice birth control found it difficult to learn about the options available to them. The few books and pamphlets that were available became even harder to obtain after the passage of the Comstock Law in 1873. The primary target of this law, which made it illegal to send obscene materials through the U.S. mail, was publications discussing methods of birth control. Presumably, Americans practiced the same contraceptive methods that were prevalent in Europe, including male withdrawal, the rhythm method, abstinence, or various crude and ineffective barrier methods (early versions of condoms and diaphragms). Most women also knew that intensive breastfeeding would often inhibit conception.

Abortion. Abortion was also used as a birth-control method. Around 1840 the abortion rate began to increase dramatically, not only among poor unmarried women, but also among the more affluent married women. Many Americans believed that prior to "quickening," the first sign of movement or life in an unborn fetus, the removal of an "obstruction" or "stoppage" was not an abortion. In fact, such early-term abortions were legal in nearly all states, and some states had no laws against abortion at any stage of a woman's pregnancy. Beginning in the mid 1850s there was a nationwide movement to make abortions illegal; these laws were directed mainly at abortionists and motivated largely on the high incidence of deaths from botched instrumental abortions. Between 1860 and 1880 at least forty states and territories passed new abortion laws, most banning abortion at any stage. Many people continued to believe that ending a pregnancy before quickening was not an abortion. Rural women usually resorted to home remedies, including herbal infusions and douches, while young women in cities and towns were more likely to risk their lives by resorting to abortionists.

Childbirth. Beginning around 1820, more and more upper-class and middle-class women, particularly in urban areas, were attended by male physicians during childbirth. Yet midwives continued to deliver most babies. (Even in 1910 midwives attended the births of nearly half the babies born nationwide.) Most babies were born at home. Hospital births occurred only in cases of extreme emergency. A few upper-class women were beginning to try new birthing methods, including the use of drugs such as ether and morphine to make labor easier. Puerperal fever, an infection caused by inadequate sanitation measures during childbirth, took the lives of many women. The death rate from this disease dropped gradually after the 1880s.

Sources:

Nancy Cott, *The Bonds of Womanhood: "Woman's Sphere" in New England, 1780–1834* (New Haven: Yale University Press, 1977);

Carl N. Degler, *At Odds: Woman and the Family in America from the Revolution to the Present* (New York: Oxford University Press, 1980);

Daniel E. Sutherland, *The Expansion of Everyday Life, 1860–1876* (New York: Harper & Row, 1989).

FAMILY LIFE: NEW ROLES FOR WIVES AND CHILDREN

The "Ideal" Family. One of the most popular songs of mid-nineteenth-century America was the sentimental ballad "Home, Sweet Home," written by American expatriate John Howard Payne in 1823. It was sung in soldiers' camps on both sides of the Civil War, as well as in parlors for the rest of the century. Like their European counterparts, Americans envisioned an ideal family life in which a strong, authoritative father figure was the main breadwinner and a loving mother ran the household and provided its moral center. This "angel of the house" tried to create a refuge from a corrupt modern world, a quiet, clean, and comfortable place of repose for the weary father at the end of his working day.

New Roles for Women. Most Americans still lived and worked on independent farms, where the mother and children played a crucial role in earning the family's liv—ing. For farm women the new domestic ideal had little relationship to reality. In towns and cities, however, the Industrial Revolution was transforming the way business was conducted, which in turn changed the father's relationship to the family. While once a merchant or craftsman typically worked in a shop in or connected to his home, by the mid nineteenth century he was more likely to be spending his days away from home, working in a mill, an office, or a shop. As a result women gained more authority over their children and a larger role in running the household. While the father had once exercised control over the way children were raised, once he was absent from the household for most of the day, women began making the important child-rearing decisions, meting out punishments and controlling their offsprings' daily lives. At the same time, however, the woman became divorced from the outside world, in part because of the widespread belief that, as the moral center of the family, she needed to be protected from its temptations and evils. Gradually, nineteenth-century women were relegated to life in a small domestic circle. Women carried on their daily activities in their homes and neighborhoods and did not often venture into business or politics. Nevertheless, after about 1820 there was a steadily growing trend toward considering women's and men's roles as roughly equal, though separate and distinct. The changes in a woman's role were the result not only of shifting work patterns, but also of lower fertility rates, new attitudes toward children, the greater availability of consumer goods, and high mobility, which eroded community ties. This shift had just begun in the middle of the nineteenth century and did not become entrenched until the end of the century. Yet most American families—whether rich or poor, free or slave, native-born or immigrant—attempted to approach the new domestic ideal in some fashion.

Children. Traditionally children had been considered important contributors to the family economy and were later expected to support their parents in old age. As American society began to change, children became more of an expense than a source of income. Although children could help out around the house and farm or in a home-based business, once fathers began working away from the home, they did not bring their children into the workplace unless compelled by economic necessity. Many parents realized that to succeed in an industrial society their children needed more education than children of earlier generations. (Poor children, immigrants, and slaves, of course, either did not attend school or left it to work at an early age.) A few years in a high school or an academy cost much more than a grammar-school education. As raising children became more expensive, families began to limit the number of their offspring, and as children stayed in school longer and no longer contributed to the family income, Americans developed a new attitude toward childhood itself. While earlier children

MEMOIR OF A FEMALE SLAVE

In her *Incidents in the Life of a Slave Girl* (1861), Harriet Jacobs, an escaped slave, described her former master's sexual advances:

During the first years of my service in Dr. Flint's family, I was accustomed to share some indulgences with the children of my mistress. Though this seemed to me no more than right, I was grateful for it, and tried to merit the kindness by the faithful discharge of my duties. But now I entered on my fifteenth year a sad epoch in the life of a slave girl. My master began to whisper foul words in my ear. Young as I was, I could not remain ignorant of their import. I tried to treat them with indifference or contempt. My master's age, my extreme youth, and the fear that his conduct would be reported to my grandmother, made me bear this treatment for many months. He was a crafty man, and resorted to many means to accomplish his purposes. Sometimes he had stormy, terrific ways, that made his victims tremble; sometimes he assumed a gentleness that he thought must surely subdue. . . . He tried his utmost to corrupt the pure principles my grandmother had instilled. He peopled my young mind with unclean images, such as only a vile monster could think of. I turned from him with disgust and hatred. But he was my master. . . . He told me I was his property; that I must be subject to his will in all things. . . . The mistress, who ought to protect the helpless victim, has no other feelings towards her but those of jealousy and rage.

Source: Harriet A. Jacobs, *Incidents in the Life of a Slave Girl*, edited by Lydia Maria Child (Boston: Privately printed, 1861).

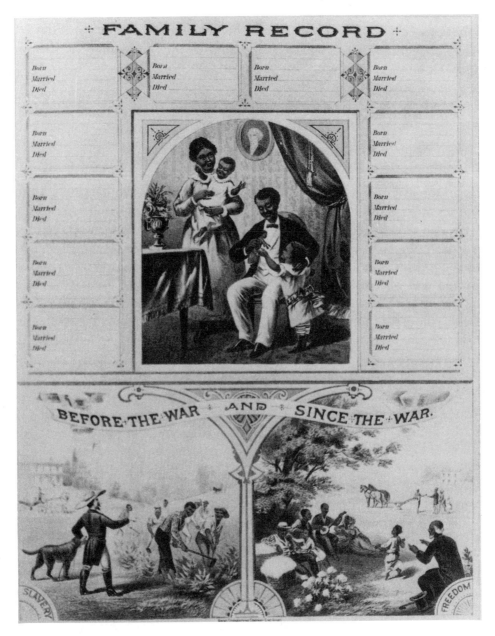

An illustrated form sold to freed blacks who wanted to record their family history

had been viewed as simply small adults, Americans began to think of childhood and adolescence as important and distinct life phases that should be protected and cherished. Childhood was viewed as a time of irresponsible enjoyment. Since mothers had fewer children to worry about, they could lavish more time and attention on each son and daughter, and the age at which a child took on adult responsibilities grew later. Advice books for young mothers stressed the woman's nurturing and emotional qualities. Mothers were advised to correct their children with gentle admonitions, not by applying physical punishment. In fact, many European visitors to the United States were appalled by the undisciplined, rude behavior of American "brats."

Household Structure. Another important change that took place during the first half of the nineteenth

century was in the size and extent of households. Before the 1820s and 1830s American households included many non-family members. For example, a master craftsman was responsible for the apprentices working under him. They lived in his house, where he supervised not only their work but their moral and religious education. Servants, farm help, live-in distant relatives, and long-term visitors were also considered part of the family unit. As the nineteenth century progressed, however, the American family became smaller and much more private. Now the ideal was the nuclear family: the biological parents and their own children. This change took place in the Northeast first and did not reach the South until later in the century.

Antebellum Southern Plantation Life. In upper-class plantation families the father had primary authority over

A polygamous Mormon family in Utah, 1870

a large extended household that included not only family members but also various servants and slaves. He exerted greater control over his wife and children, including grown children, than in other parts of the country. One of the most complex relationships was the one between plantation mistresses and slaves. Because there were often close physical and emotional ties between the white family and domestic slaves, plantation life held a particular danger for black women. Some owners and owners' sons expected them to be sexually available. Resistance was usually not possible because there were no laws to prevent these men from resorting to violence to get their way. This situation enraged and frustrated the planters' wives, who had to acquiesce and often visited their anger and revenge on the slave women.

Slave Families. American slaves could not legally marry, nor could they exercise any control over the destinies of their children. Frequently separated by sale, slave families had to make painful compromises and adjustments. One historian has calculated that during his or her lifetime the average American slave experienced the loss by sale of eleven family members. Most slaves, however, attempted to create and maintain the traditional family structure. In 1851 a slave owner advertised for a runaway slave, stating that he was most likely "lurking in the neighborhood of E. D. Walker's at Moore's Creek, who owns most of his relatives, or Nathan Bonham's who owns his mother; or perhaps, near Fletcher Bell's, at Long Creek, who owns his father."

Slave Marriages. Though such unions had no legal standing, slaves did marry, and many marriages lasted twenty years or more. Slave marriages could be ended by the sale of a spouse. Ministers who officiated at slave weddings pronounced the couple husband and wife until "death or *distance* do you part." Some slave marriages took place between men and women who lived on different plantations and had different owners. In such cases, a husband who wanted to visit his wife had to obtain a written pass from his owner and often had to walk for many miles to see her.

Kinship Networks. Slave families could rarely attain the privacy so prized among nineteenth-century Americans. Gang labor, communal eating, and inadequate living accommodations that forced many people to live together in a single small cabin all tended to break down privacy and individuality. Yet historians have found that most black families, whether enslaved or free, lived in two-parent households. In 1850 approximately 64 percent of all slaves lived in two-parent families, and 25 percent were in single-parent families. Around their fragile nuclear families slaves built extensive kinship networks that did not depend on blood ties. Older people, whether related or not, watched their friends' children and cared for them when parents were working or when one or both parents were sold away. Younger slaves addressed these older slaves using the honorific titles *aunt* and *uncle*.

Free Black Families. After emancipation freed slaves attempted to shape their family life according to the nineteenth-century ideal. For the first few years after the end of the Civil War, there was a significant drop in the labor performed outside the home by black women, who tried to create a home life similar to that of other American families. In the South two-parent families were the norm, while in other parts of the country there were more female-headed black households. This difference has been attributed in part to the high mortality rate among black males, which made black women widows at an earlier age than their white counterparts and in part to the disruptive influence of the urban environment on individuals reared in rural surroundings.

Immigrant and Working-Class Households. Nearly all Americans lived in some kind of family unit. About 85 percent of all American households followed the traditional pattern of two parents and their children. Another 10 or 12 percent included distant relatives or unrelated people, and only 1 to 3 percent of Americans lived alone. Unlike the middle-class American family, the working-class or immigrant family needed financial contributions from every family member. Women often did laundry and sewing for more-affluent families. Nearly one third of all working-class families took boarders into their already crowded households. In most immigrant families, attitudes toward children followed the older tradition of expecting children to contribute financially to the family and later to care for elderly parents. Immigrant children usually left school and went to work at an earlier age than native-born white children. Child labor was not recognized as a major social problem until later in the century, but in 1870 nearly 13 percent of all American children were working. Among the poorest Americans, family structures broke down completely. Their children took to streets, where they picked pockets or stole from fruit and vegetable sellers. Daughters left home to find work and often fell into prostitution. Alcoholism and spousal or child abuse were rampant, prompting many middle-class women to join the temperance crusade.

Alternative Families. Several religious groups experimented with alternative family arrangements. The United Society of Believers in Christ's Second Coming, or Shakers, believed in complete celibacy. They established their first American community at Watervliet, New York, near Albany in 1776 and had eighteen communities in the United States by 1826. They lived communally with men and women, often living in unconnected halves of the same building, and became well-known for their simple but well-made furniture and handicrafts. By 1860 Shakerism had gone into decline, but some communities lasted into the twentieth century. Almost from the time the Church of Jesus Christ of Latter-Day Saints, or Mormons, was founded by Joseph Smith in 1830, its members were attacked and persecuted for their unconventional beliefs. In 1847 they settled in Utah hoping to practice their religion in peace. During the 1850s, however, they became the subject of a nationwide rash of scandalous newspaper stories, after their leader, Brigham Young, made public their doctrine of "plural marriage," or polygamy, which allowed men to have more than one wife. Fewer than one-fifth of the Mormons actually practiced polygamy, and in two-thirds of those cases the husband had two wives. The Mormons' polygamy brought them into conflict with the federal government during the 1850s and stood in the way of Utah statehood. Their leader formally renounced plural marriage in 1890, and Utah became a state six years later.

Sources:

Robert H. Bremner, ed., *Children and Youth in America: A Documentary History*, 3 volumes (Cambridge, Mass.: Harvard University Press, 1970–1974);

Nancy Cott, *The Bonds of Womanhood: "Woman's Sphere" in New England, 1780–1834* (New Haven: Yale University Press, 1977);

A housewife using one of the Singer sewing machines

Carl N. Degler, *At Odds: Woman and the Family in America from the Revolution to the Present* (New York: Oxford University Press, 1980);

Joseph M. Hawes, *Children in Urban Society: Juvenile Delinquency in Nineteenth-Century America* (New York: Oxford University Press, 1971);

Daniel E. Sutherland, *The Expansion of Everyday Life, 1860–1876* (New York: Harper & Row, 1989).

FASHION

New Technologies. The most significant changes in the way Americans dressed during the middle decades of the nineteenth century came about because of improvements in technology. Though various types of sewing machines had been invented during the 1830s and 1840s, the first practical, workable machine for the home sewer was invented by Isaac Merrit Singer in 1850. By the middle of that decade sewing machines were selling at the rate of one hundred thousand per year. In 1871 manufacturers made seven times that number. While a woman might have spent days sewing a man's shirt by hand, she could make one in an afternoon with her sewing machine. New technologies also changed textile production, making it possible for manufacturers to mass-produce printed cottons that were both cheap and pretty. Aniline dyes, invented in the 1850s, permitted silks and wools to be dyed in astonishingly bright, sharp colors such as fuchsia, magenta, and violet. A fashionable Civil War–era theater or dinner party was often a colorful sight. With these fabrics and her new sewing machine the average middle-class housewife could make dresses that would have been too expensive and too time-consuming for her to tackle in the past. Sewing machines also permitted greater ornamentation of clothing. As women's fashions became more elaborate in the 1860s, sewing-machine manufacturers produced attachments such as binders, tuckers, rufflers, shirrers, puffers, braiders, quilters, hemstitchers, and embroiders that allowed the middle-class woman to copy these styles at home. Some commentators, mostly men, noted that the sewing machine did not seem to be such a labor-saving device after all. Commercial printed-paper patterns also helped middle-class women dress like their upper-class counterparts. Fashion designer Madame Demorest—who despite her French-sounding name was Ellen Curtis Demorest, the American-born wife of New York publisher William Demorest—began marketing paper patterns for her versions of Paris fashions in her own magazine, Mme. Demorest's Mirror of Fashion, in 1865. Ebenezer Butterick, who started manufacturing patterns for boys' and men's clothing in 1863, began making patterns for women's clothes in 1867 and also marketed them in his own magazines.

The Seamstress. Some clothing could be bought ready-made, but most clothing was made expressly for the wearer. Wealthy women in cities such as New York or Philadelphia had their clothes custom-made by exclusive dressmakers who copied designs from magazines

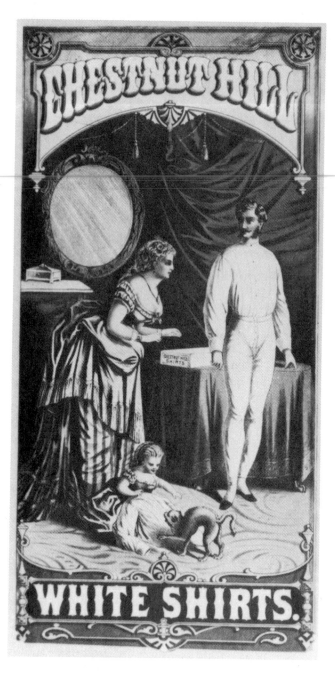

Advertisement for a ready-made man's shirt, 1874

such as *Godey's Lady's Book* and *Peterson's*. These magazines pirated French fashion plates in their monthly issues. Studies of photographs from this period show, however, that American women did not wear line-for-line copies of these styles. Their gowns were usually three or even four years out of date. Middle-class women usually had a seamstress come in to cut and fit clothing which they would later finish themselves. Sometimes, the seamstress would stay with the family in a separate "sewing room," producing dresses, shirts, and clothing for the children. Respectable women still did a great deal of fine hand sewing in public or at gatherings with friends. On southern plantations the mistresses were responsible for all the clothing worn by family and

Fashions of the 1850s–1870s: (top left) a woman wearing an elaborate silk taffeta dress in a style popular during the late 1850s; (top right) a Union soldier with women wearing hoop skirts and wide-sleeved coats that may have been copied from the January 1862 issue of *Peterson's Magazine;* (bottom left) a toddler boy in a plaid dress, 1860s; and (bottom right) women wearing the slimmer skirts with bustles that replaced hoop skirts in the 1870s

The "Turkish trouser" suit popularized by feminist Amelia Bloomer in 1851

by gearing up production and developing a system of standard sizing. After the war they applied this new technology to manufacturing civilian clothing for men.

Women's Clothing. In the 1850s middle-class and upper-class women wore voluminous full-skirted cotton or silk dresses for day. All women wore several petticoats. By mid-decade they had begun wearing crinoline petticoats, originally made of stiffened horsehair, to hold the skirt away from the body. About 1858 hoop petticoats, with large circles of flexible watch-spring steel sewn into them, began to serve a similar purpose. A woman who wore one of these garments had to learn not to sit on one of the hoops because if she did so, her skirt would fly up in front, exposing her ankle-length pantalets. During the second half of the century these drawers gradually became shorter. These full-skirted fashions with narrow waists were popularized by the beautiful Empress Eugénie of France. Corsets, which had been worn since colonial days, became more heavily boned to give a woman the neat, small-waisted look she desired. Critics pointed out that women who wore tight corsets were injuring their health. The worst excesses in such "tight lacing," however, did not occur until the 1880s and 1890s. During the Civil War women wore closely fitted bodices and dropped shoulders, with full skirts pleated into a corseted waist. After the war skirts became relatively flat in front with a full train in back. By the early 1870s the hoop skirt had disappeared and was replaced with a bustle made of wire or crinoline to create fullness at the back of the skirt. Full skirts, especially with hoops, were impractical, and sometimes dangerous, for farm work. Rural women and poor women wore less-elaborate clothing made of simpler, less expensive fabrics, including homespun cloth. Like more-affluent women, farm women wore several petticoats, but their skirts were not as full because they seldom wore hoops or crinolines. Instead of the feather-and-ribbon-trimmed hats favored by city women, rural women, particularly in the West and the South, often wore simple sun bonnets.

Dress Reform. Often linked to the women's rights movement, dress reformers, and some doctors, charged that the heavy skirts and tight bodices were unhealthy and unsanitary. In 1851 abolitionist and social reformer Amelia Bloomer became one of the first American women to wear a "Turkish trouser" suit, loose trousers, worn under a fitted tunic. Because it "exposed" a lady's legs, this garment, which quickly became known as the "bloomer costume," caused a scandal. While some people praised it as a practical garment for overland travel, a woman who wore "bloomers" was more often than not criticized by other women and ridiculed by men. The fact that variations of this style were worn by many Mormon women during their cross-country trek to Utah and by women in the Oneida colony in upstate New York did not help to spread this new style. Both groups were heavily criticized during the 1850s for their advocacy of mar-

workers alike. One of their most important chores was to cut out the cloth, which they would then give to slaves to sew. Most women also did charity sewing in addition to making clothes for their families (at least the family's underwear and shirts). People of all ages and social classes wore cotton underwear, which they washed as often as they could afford.

Men's Clothing. Men working on the farm wore simple calico shirts, often flowered or checked, trousers, waistcoats, coats with full sleeves, and a straw or felt hat. In public a man always wore a white or black neck cloth, or "stock." For town he wore a checked or black coat, and a black waistcoat. Black wool, summer or winter, was the respectable businessman's uniform. The most favored headgear for men in the city was the tall, narrow "stovepipe hat" like the one often seen in photographs of President Abraham Lincoln. In the South a broad-brimmed felt or straw hat was more popular than the stovepipe. By the 1870s the skirted frock coat favored by gentlemen for dress occasions had mainly been replaced by the shorter sack coat. Before the Civil War only work clothes for slaves and sailors were mass-produced in the United States. During the Civil War, however, manufacturers met the demand for hundreds of thousands of uniforms riages involving more than two partners. Most women kept on wearing their corsets and petticoats.

Children's Clothing. As childhood increasingly became recognized as a separate and important phase of life, children were no longer dressed as miniature adults, but with some effort toward comfort and freedom of movement. Babies and toddlers of both sexes wore short hair and low-necked dresses. As in the past, small boys wore skirts at least until they were out of diapers. After they reached the age of five or six, boys began to wear short pants and tunics. Between the ages of ten and twelve a boy received his first pair of long pants, which was an unmistakable sign of maturity and approaching manhood.

Slave Clothing. What slaves wore depended a great deal on their owners. Some gave their slaves their own cast-off clothing, while on other plantations slaves wore nothing better than rags. Usually domestic slaves were better dressed than field workers. Their outfits consisted of simple cotton clothing. Few had real shoes, wearing instead "slops" or "slaps" on their feet. These shoes were crude sandals with one leather strap across the instep, manufactured in Lynn, Massachusetts.

Sources:

Daniel J. Boorstin, *The Americans: The Democratic Experience* (New York: Random House, 1973);

Priscilla Harris Dalrymple, *American Victorian Costume in Early Photographs* (New York: Dover, 1991);

J. C. Furnas, *The Americans: A Social History of the United States, 1587-1914* (New York: Putnam, 1969);

Lee Hall, *Common Threads: A Parade of American Clothing* (Boston: Little, Brown, 1992);

Estelle Ansley Worrell, *American Costume, 1840-1920* (Harrisburg, Pa.: Stackpole, 1979).

FOOD AND DRINK

Typical Diet. The American diet at midcentury was based on two common staples: corn and salt pork. (Fresh pork was available only at slaughtering time.) One European traveler, tired of being served these ubiquitous foods, complained about "the eternal pork, which makes its appearance on every American table, high and low, rich and poor." Subsistence farmers, who grew their own food with a little left over to sell to others, often enjoyed more-varied diets than those who were farming market crops such as cotton and tobacco. Yet even those farmers who were free to grow the foods they wanted to eat were limited to what grew best in their regions. For example, New Englanders supplemented their diets by fishing for the plentiful cod. southerners grew sweet potatoes. Another important consideration was what the farmer could most effectively preserve to last the families through the winter. Corn was less susceptible to blight than wheat, and cornmeal kept well and could be used in a variety of dishes. Milk, which spoiled quickly in hot weather, was made into butter and cheese, which kept better. Leafy vegetables spoiled easily, so farmers were more likely to grow vegetables such as beans, which were easier to preserve, or beets, apples, carrots, pumpkins, potatoes, and turnips, which could be stored for long periods of time in root cellars. Orchard fruits such as apples were often grown for cider and brandy. Because foods such as fresh fruit and leafy vegetables were available mainly in the summer, American nutrition suffered from seasonal imbalances. By the 1850s, however, improved transportation and preservation techniques began to bring a greater variety of fresh vegetables and fruits to the American table. Even allowing for wide regional variations, Americans (especially farmers) had one thing in common; they all ate heavy, rich, and plentiful meals, especially at noontime. This meal, commonly called dinner, was the most important meal of the day throughout the nineteenth century and was considered by many to be an important time for gathering the family together for prayer and companionship.

Consumption and Calories. One historian has estimated that the average American farmer in the mid nineteenth century consumed about four thousand calories daily. This astounding food intake is about twice modern consumption and probably three times that of the average nineteenth-century laborer or farmer in Europe. Americans' caloric excesses were largely the result of their fondness for fried foods, especially those prepared in bacon grease. Of course, there were significant regional variations in the kinds and quantities of food that Americans consumed. People who lived in the Northeast and the mid-Atlantic states had access to the cheese, butter, and salted beef produced on dairy farms. Proximity to seaport cities also made seafood, as well as imported fruits and other out-of-season delicacies, available at least to the wealthier classes. Contrary to popular belief, most Americans did have fairly well-balanced diets. Backyard vegetable gardens ensured that even lower-middle-class city dwellers had access to fresh vegetables in season. Some of the vegetables that were available included artichokes, peas, many kinds of beans, tomatoes, turnips, potatoes, parsnips, lettuces, cabbages, radishes, carrots, spinach, and cauliflower. As Catharine Beecher, sister of novelist Harriet Beecher Stowe, wrote in her treatise on domestic economy, "As regards the department of Vegetables, their number and variety in America are so great that a table might almost be furnished by these alone."

Improved Preservation. One of the most important changes in the American diet during the early nineteenth century was the increased availability of foods that had once been available only during the growing season. Self-sealing glass jars for home canning of fruits and vegetables became available in the 1850s, with Mason Jars, introduced in 1858, quickly becoming the most popular preserving jar in America. Cookbooks and housekeeping manuals advised every housewife to enrich her family's diet with canned or preserved goods in winter. Yet until the home pressure cooker became available in the early twentieth century, the housewife could pre-

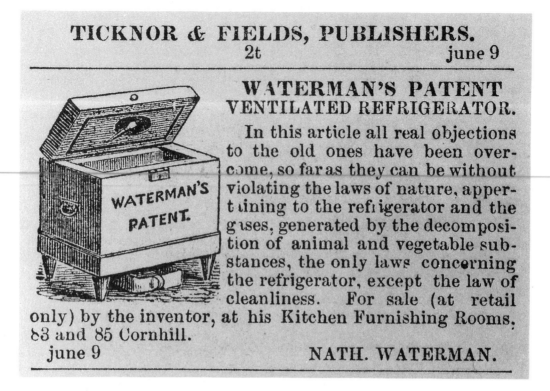

Advertisement for an icebox in an 1855 issue of *Ballou's Pictorial Drawing-Room Companion*

serve only acidic vegetables such as tomatoes, or fruits and vegetables that could be preserved with sugar or in brine. Even in those cases food sometimes spoiled because the seals on canning jars were less reliable than they became in the twentieth century. Peppers, corn, cucumbers, and onions could be preserved in brine as pickles, chutneys, and relishes. While fruits could be turned into jams and jellies, the high cost of sugar throughout the nineteenth century limited the quantities that many housewives could make. As in the past, meats and fish were preserved for the winter mainly by salting or smoking them.

Tin Cans. With the perfection of the tin-can food processing in the first quarter of the nineteenth century and the expansion of railroad lines, a wide variety of commercially preserved foods, including meats, vegetables, and fruits, were becoming available across the nation. By 1860 commercial canners were producing nearly five million cans of food a year. Within a decade that number rose to twelve million. The Swift and Armour meatpacking companies made their fortunes supplying canned meat to soldiers in the Union army, and after the war they shipped their products nationwide. In 1856 Gail Borden patented his formula for preserving milk by adding sugar and heating it in a vacuum. During the Civil War his plants distributed large quantities of this sweetened condensed milk to the Union army, creating a national market for the product after the war. Cheese, however, remained the most common dairy product in the American diet.

Ice Boxes. Beginning in the 1840s Americans also began to make use of ice from ponds and lakes to preserve their foods. Farmers earned extra income in the winter by chopping blocks of ice from local ponds and storing it underground for use during the summer. Although many household manuals of the 1860s declared that an ice box was an indispensable convenience, only city and town dwellers owned them. Made of wood and lined with tin or zinc, an ice box kept food fresh in a compartment cooled by a block of ice. Beginning in the mid 1850s people in towns and cities, particularly in the North, had ice delivered to their homes at the cost of around two dollars a month for fifteen pounds of ice per day.

Mealtime in the City. As people moved from farm to city, many "old-fashioned" Americans began to notice around 1870 that the proper noon-time dinner was beginning to give way to a quickly prepared "lunch." Fathers working in town could not rush home for dinner in the middle of the day and ate at oyster bars or restaurants instead. For city and town dwellers, supper became the only meal where all the family members saw one another.

Regional Variety. Despite the increased availability of foods from other regions, tastes in food varied from region to region. The traditional southern fare of corn and pork was supplemented with local varieties of vegetables, such as okra, sweet potatoes, and greens. Rice was popular only in rice-growing areas; it did not become a dietary staple in the rest of the country until late in the nineteenth century. Chicken was a favorite meat for special

BUYING GROCERIES

In 1851 the *New York Tribune* reported the prices for items on a typical weekly grocery list for an average family of five living in Philadelphia:

Butcher's meat, at 2 lbs. per day, 10 cents per pound, for a total of $1.40

A barrel of flour, 62 cents (Purchased once in two months)

2 lbs. of butter, 63 cents

1.2 bushels of potatoes, 50 cents

4 lbs. sugar, 32 cents

Coffee and tea, 25 cents

milk, 2 cents per day

salt, pepper, vinegar, starch, soap, soda, yeast, cheese and eggs: 40 cents

occasions everywhere, but only northerners and south-westerners ate much lamb. While southerners liked sweet potatoes, northerners preferred white, or "Irish" potatoes, and while New Englanders ate cod, often preserved for winter by salting, southerners enjoyed fried catfish served with hush puppies (fried cornmeal batter). Seafood was an important part of the diet in all coastal areas, especially in Louisiana, where the city of New Orleans became renowned for its culinary arts. The richest families in the South served lavish meals and imported delicacies. Slaves subsisted on dishes made with cornmeal and less desirable cuts of pork. Because agricultural journals of the period told plantation owners that slaves who ate a more varied diet were healthier and lived longer, many slave owners allowed slaves to grow their own greens and other vegetables on small plots of ground near the slave cabins after their regular work was finished. A slave's main meal might consist of hogs' feet, chitterlings ("chitlins," or fried hog intestines), greens, and some sort of corn dish such as hoecake, corn pone, or hominy grits.

Immigrant Fare. Immigrants brought their own traditional foods and recipes, some of which eventually made their way into the American diet. The Germans brought seasoned ham served with potatoes and cabbage. Midwestern German immigrants introduced what was first called "German fried" potatoes, which became known as "home fries." The Irish introduced corned beef and cabbage, which became a popular meal in Boston and other parts of New England. Cajuns, French Canadian immigrants from Acadia (Nova Scotia), created spicy cuisine in Louisiana. By the end of the Civil War "French fried" potatoes had been introduced, but probably not by French immigrants. This food became immensely popular in many urban centers, because it was so easily and quickly prepared by street vendors and at public events.

What Americans Drank. The drinking habits Americans formed during the first half of the nineteenth century changed little during middle decades of the century. After the temperance crusades of the 1830s, alcohol consumption fell considerably, from four gallons per capita per year in the 1820s to one and a half gallons in the 1840s. Temperance crusaders, many of whom were women, encouraged everyone to drink water instead of whiskey or rum. As a result, the distinctively American custom of drinking a glass of water with meals was established around the middle of the century. During the Civil War, however, drinking increased among soldiers on both sides even though both the Union and Confederate armies' regulations strictly forbade liquor sales to enlisted men and punished offenders with prison sentences. Only officers were allowed to possess whiskey, but other soldiers found many ways to circumvent this unpopular regulation and had little trouble obtaining alcohol. Alcohol consumption varied greatly among ethnic groups. For Irish and German immigrants alcohol was an important ingredient in family celebrations. On the whole, however, alcohol consumption continued to decline until the end of the nineteenth century.

Coffee and Tea. Coffee was the favorite morning beverage for almost all Americans. In the summer lemonade and other fruit drinks were popular, iced if one could afford it. Historians are uncertain about exactly when American ladies began to drink tea in the afternoon, but the practice was already well established in both urban and rural areas by the mid 1840s. Women's diaries from the 1850s through the 1870s include frequent references to afternoon tea parties or sharing a pot of tea and baked treats with a single female visitor.

Sources:

Daniel J. Boorstin, *The Americans: The Democratic Experience* (New York: Random House, 1973);

Susan Strasser, *Never Done: A History of American Housework* (New York: Pantheon, 1982);

Daniel E. Sutherland, *The Expansion of Everyday Life: 1860–1876* (New York: Harper & Row, 1989).

FROM SLAVERY TO FREEDOM

Southern Slave Ownership. During the decade before the Civil War three-quarters of southern whites did not own slaves, and 72 percent of those who did owned fewer than ten. In fact, half of the slave owners in the South had fewer than five. More than half of the nearly four million slaves in the South lived on plantations with more than twenty slaves. Approximately one-fourth lived among fifty or more slaves.

Slaves' Work. The slaves' experiences varied greatly according to where they lived, the sort of labor they were expected to perform, and the kind of masters they had. Slaves in South Carolina, Georgia, Louisiana, and Mississippi often lived on big plantations where blacks vastly outnumbered whites. These slaves were part of large work gangs that tended large-scale cash crops such as

Freedmen in a Union army camp

cotton, tobacco, sugar, and rice. In the Upper South and the slave-holding border states such as Kentucky and Missouri, however, many slaves worked side-by-side with their owners, who grew a diverse assortment of smaller crops. These slaves had more-varied routines, including tasks such as digging irrigation ditches, hoeing and harvesting crops, feeding livestock, shoeing horses, repairing farm implements, and carpentry. On these smaller farms the master usually supervised his bondsmen's work closely, while on a large plantation work gangs were usually under the direct supervision of a black slave driver, who was more likely than the master of a small farm to give slaves some control over the speed with which they worked. By the beginning of the Civil War, about half a million slaves lived in cities and towns, some as domestic servants, others temporarily hired from their masters, by businessmen such as merchants, factory owners, shipyards, sawmills, or lumberyards.

Treatment. Some masters developed an indulgent, patriarchal attitude toward "their people" and rarely resorted to harsh punishments. These planters usually attempted to keep slave families together and seldom sold slaves except in times of economic hardship or perhaps to settle a bequest. Other slaves experienced many hardships, such as long work hours, poor food, inadequate housing, clothing that was inadequate to protect them from winter cold or summer sun, and brutal treatment at the hands of irrational or incompetent overseers. Although it is difficult to generalize about the experience of

American slaves before the Civil War, it is safe to say that most agricultural slaves worked fifteen to sixteen hours a day during the peak seasons (about 290 days a year), were sold at least twice, and were rarely able to maintain lifelong family ties.

A Typical Plantation Day. On large plantations slave families lived in slave villages of small cabins. They were awakened an hour before sunrise by a bell or a horn. After a frugal breakfast of corn cakes and perhaps some salt pork, the slave driver led them to the fields. Men worked alongside women, some of them pregnant or nursing. Elderly slaves and those too weak for field work stayed home and tended the gardens, watched babies, spun yarn and wove cloth, or did kitchen work. Small children carried water to the field workers and took them their midday meal, prepared by one of the kitchen slaves. After resting briefly, the field hands worked until dark. Domestic workers, who did all the indoor work, including cooking, cleaning, child care, and personal services for the planter's family, generally remained on duty longer than field hands and had to be prepared to work at unpredictable hours.

Discipline. On large plantations overseers were usually responsible for managing crops and livestock, keeping records, supervising and disciplining slaves, and meeting crop quotas. They were also in charge of the slave drivers and meted out punishments that could range from fairly mild reproofs to brutal discipline, including whippings and brandings. Before his escape to

Members of the Ku Klux Klan in Alabama, 1868

of the invading Union army were considered "contraband property," and some were actually returned to their owners. In March 1862, however, the U.S. Congress enacted an article of war forbidding the army to return escaped slaves to their masters, and the following July it passed the second Confiscation Act, stating that slaves who crossed into Union-held territory "shall be forever free." This law not only made escape attractive, it cleared the way for former slaves to join the Union army. Some blacks celebrated emancipation several times, as they gained their freedom after a Union advance, lost it each time Confederate troops retook the territory, and regained it with each fresh Union victory. With most able-bodied white men away from home fighting for the Confederacy, escaping was much less dangerous for a slave than it had been in the days before secession. There was little an overseer or plantation mistress could do to hold slaves when blue-coated soldiers appeared in the district.

Steps toward Emancipation. Freedom came in stages. On 1 January 1863 President Abraham Lincoln issued the Emancipation Proclamation, declaring that all slaves in areas held by the Confederacy on that day were "forever free." The proclamation exempted Confederate territory in Union hands and the slave-holding states that had remained in the Union: Delaware, Maryland, Missouri, Kentucky, and—after it became a state in 1863—West Virginia. Some states had abolished slavery by the end of the war in April 1865, but in others emancipation did not come until the following December, with the ratification of the Thirteenth Amendment, which declared: "Neither slavery nor involuntary servitude . . . shall exist within the United States, or any place subject to their jurisdiction."

Wartime Options. By late 1863 the trickle of runaway slaves, or "contrabands," had swelled to a flood. Many of these people worked for the Union army as guides, laborers, or spies, and some became soldiers. For most black men, escaping from slavery meant leaving their wives and children behind, but a few women did run away as well, and some cooked and washed clothes for Union soldiers. Many Union officers reported that they had acquired hundreds of fugitive camp followers. If slaves found escape too difficult as the war came closer to home, they often took intermediate steps. Some slaves simply refused to work; others slowed the pace of their labors or destroyed livestock or implements. Still others negotiated with their mistresses to determine how much work they would do and how quickly they would perform it. Fears of insurrection gripped many southern white women whose husbands, sons, and fathers had left them behind to supervise plantations alone.

Black Soldiers. For many male slaves the surest way to ensure their freedom was enlistment in the Union army. After the second Confiscation Act was passed in July 1862, black regiments were formed in occupied New Orleans and on the Sea Islands of Georgia and South Caro-

freedom, the prominent abolitionist Frederick Douglass experienced severe beatings after he was leased to a master who was determined to break Douglass's spirit. Even pregnant women were not exempt from beatings; the overseer would force her to lie face down with her belly in a hole in the ground while he beat her. Some slaves were forced to wear shackles or head irons (a kind of cage fastened to the face). Another punishment was hanging a slave by the thumbs for hours. Of course, the worst punishment was to be sold away from one's family, usually to a harsher owner.

The Promise of Freedom. News of the Civil War spread by an informal but highly effective underground news network that had long existed throughout the South.Mary Chesnut, who lived on a plantation in South Carolina, commented in her diary that it was impossible to tell how much slaves knew because they remained impassive in the presence of their owners. During the first year of the war slaves who fled to the camps lina, but full-scale enlistment of blacks did not begin until after President Lincoln issued the Emancipation Proclamation the following January. By the end of the war nearly 179,000 black men had served in the U.S. Army; more than half came from Confederate states.

Postwar Reunions. After the war ended, the first task for many newly freed slaves was the search for loved ones who had been sold away. Because of the well-established underground communication network, a surprising number of freed slaves were able to locate family members. Others were less fortunate. There are heartbreaking stories of black people who had been forced by circumstance to remarry after losing a spouse through sale and then met the first husband or wife again after the war.

Transition to Free Labor. After gaining their freedom some former slaves attempted to scrape together a meager living by hunting small game, working as day laborers, or practicing a craft. Some plantation owners tried to help their former slaves, but the destruction of southern agriculture during the war, followed by extremely poor harvests in 1866 and 1867 and a severe economic depression in 1873, made life difficult for everyone. Many planters tried to reestablish the old gang-labor system for tending and harvesting their crops. They often created working conditions remarkably similar to those that existed under slavery. Most freedmen were unwilling to work under these dehumanizing conditions and dreamed of owning their own small farms. The era of gang-labor agriculture had come to an end, and planters had to find a new way to produce the South's largest cash crop, cotton, with a labor force that refused to work under the old system.

The Freedmen's Bureau. In March 1865, just before the end of the war, Congress established the Freedmen's Bureau for a term of one year, giving it the responsibility of providing relief, education, and employment for former slaves. The following year its life was extended for another three years. The Freedmen's Bureau and the occupying federal army helped freed people to work out labor contracts with plantation owners that were at least marginally fair, usually promising a year's labor in return for a share of the planter's crop. The bureau and the army also counteracted the so-called Black Codes enacted by southern states immediately after the end of the war. Varying from state to state, these laws mandated racial segregation of public places and a ban on interracial marriages, as well as declaring blacks ineligible to serve on juries or to testify against whites in court. They also instituted strict curfews and vagrancy laws aimed at blacks who had not signed work contracts with white planters. In some cases a black arrested for vagrancy could be compelled to work for anyone who payed his fine. During the existence of the Freedmen's Bureau and the military occupation of the South enforcement of these laws was suspended, and some were repealed. After federal troops started pulling out of the southern states in 1872, however, laws similar to the old Black Codes were reinstated.

A BLACK SOLDIER'S LETTER HOME

John Boston, who escaped slavery in Maryland and joined a New York regiment of the Union army, wrote the following words to his wife from Virginia on 12 January 1862:

My Dear Wife

it is with grate joy I take this time to let you know Whare I am i am now in Safety in the 14th Regiment of Brooklyn this Day i can Adress you thank god as a free man I had a little truble in giting away But as the lord led the Children of Isrel to the land of Canon So he led me to a land Whare fredom Will rain in spite Of earth and hell Dear you must make your Self content i am free from al the Slavers lash and as you have chose the Wise plan Of Serving the lord i hope you Will pray Much and i Will try by the help of god to Serv him With all my hart . . . i trust the time Will Come When We Shall meet again and if we dont met on earth We Will Meet in heven Whare Jesas raines . . . Write my Dear Soon as you C Your Affectionate Husban Kiss Daniel For me

John Boston

Forty Acres and a Mule. Rumors that the federal government had promised each freedman "forty acres and a mule" circulated throughout the South after the Civil War, fueling blacks' dreams of owning their own small farms. There were a few small-scale attempts at land redistribution, but all were largely unsuccessful. The first occurred in January 1865 when Gen. William T. Sherman set aside some of the confiscated land on the Sea Islands of South Carolina to be divided into forty-acre farms for former slaves. In August of the same year, however, President Andrew Johnson ordered the land returned to its original owners, following a policy he had established in a 29 May 1865 proclamation promising restoration of property rights to any former Confederate who pledged his loyalty to the Union and promised to support emancipation. This proclamation also hampered the carrying out of a provision in the Freedmen's Bureau Act of March 1865, which specified that each freedman or white southerner who had been loyal to the Union could lease forty acres of confiscated land with the option of buying it after three years. The Southern Homestead Act, which Congress passed in 1866, designated some 44 million acres of public land in five southern states to be divided into farms for freedmen and loyal whites. Much of this land had poor soil. Even freedmen who got land under these two laws fared poorly. Many lacked the finances to provide for their families until the first harvest and to pay for necessary livestock and farm equipment. By 1869 only four thousand black families had received land under the Southern Homestead Act, and many later lost their farms.

Sharecropping. After their hopes of land ownership faded, many blacks entered into farm tenancy agreements with white plantation owners. Once they realized

Women using an early washing machine, 1869

that black people were no longer willing to work on plantations under the gang-labor system, many landowners divided their property into smaller plots, which they leased to tenant farmers in exchange for a share of the crop grown on that land, usually half. This system allowed plantation owners to continue producing important cash crops such as cotton while satisfying, in a limited way, the freedmen's desire for independence. The practical realities of the sharecropping system, however, all favored the planter. Sharecroppers were forced to buy tools, seed, and other farmer supplies on credit from local merchants who were often the planters themselves and charged inflated prices. By the time they harvested their crops, sharecroppers were usually deeply in debt, and crop failures could drive them into bankruptcy. If a dispute arose between a planter and his tenant, the laws generally favored the landowner.

The Ku Klux Klan. During the Reconstruction period the Ku Klux Klan sparked terror among freed blacks throughout the South. Founded by six young Confederate veterans in Tennessee in December 1865, the Klan had spread to all former Confederate states by 1868 and had become a terrorist organization dedicated to reasserting white supremacy and preventing newly enfranchised blacks from voting. One freedman in Alabama reported that in 1869 his home was invaded by Klansmen, who beat him, raped a young girl who was visiting his wife, and wounded a neighbor "because we voted the radical [Republican] ticket." The Klan used its vigilante tactics to support the Democratic Party in its efforts to turn out Republican-dominated state governments throughout the South. Anyone connected with the hated Republican Party or who attempted to help former slaves could be targeted for beatings or even murder. Most of the victims of violence, however, were black people, especially those who had become active in the Republican Party or had become local political leaders.

Sources:

Ira Berlin, Barbara J. Fields, Steven F. Miller, Joseph P. Reidy, and Leslie S. Rowland, *Slaves No More: Three Essays on Emancipation and the Civil War* (Cambridge: Cambridge University Press, 1992);

Robert William Fogel, *Without Consent or Contract: The Rise and Fall of American Slavery* (New York: Norton, 1989);

Eric Foner, *Reconstruction: America's Unfinished Revolution, 1865–1877* (New York: Harper & Row, 1988);

Eugene D. Genovese, *Roll, Jordan, Roll: The World the Slaves Made* (New York: Random House, 1974);

Kenneth M. Stampp, *The Peculiar Institution: Slavery in the Ante-Bellum South* (New York: Knopf, 1956).

HOUSEWORK

Laundry Day. The average American farm wife's week began with "Blue Monday," the traditional laundry day in most regions. She began her day by hauling many buckets of water from the outdoor pump or well into the kitchen. Next, she had to start a fire in the stove and boil the water in large pots. It took about fifty gallons of water (weighing four hundred pounds) for one load. Sheets and underwear had to be "cooked" and scrubbed with rough lye-based soaps until they came clean. Then came

A typical kitchen of the 1850s and 1860s, as depicted in an 1854 lithograph by Lilly Martin Spencer, and a plan for a well-organized "modern" kitchen in Catharine Beecher and Harriet Beecher Stowe's widely read housekeeping manual, *The American Woman's Home* (1869)

rinsing, bluing (adding a faint blue dye to the rinse water to make the linens look whiter), starching, wringing water out of the heavy wet laundry, and finally spreading linens on the grass so that the sun could bleach them or hanging them on the clothesline with the rest of the wet laundry. Repeating this process several times until all the wash was done, a woman typically spent all day at this backbreaking task. Nothing was ever wasted; women poured their used laundry water on their rose-bushes or vegetable patches. The first washing machines, which became available after the Civil War, provided some help with scrubbing, but the housewife had to turn a hand crank to work the agitator instead.

Ironing. Tuesday brought another difficult chore: ironing. The heavy cast irons (some of them filled with live coals) had to be heated in the stove. A woman had to be very careful pressing shirts, ruffled dresses, and table-cloths lest she burn holes into them.

Indoor and Outdoor Chores. Early before sunrise, every day of the week, the wife was the first to rise in order to start breakfast, which consisted of freshly baked biscuits, fried eggs and bacon, sliced meats, and cooked oatmeal or grits. As the day progressed, she had to feed the chickens, rabbits, and geese; she had to remember to clean out coops and hutches, milk the cows, gather eggs, and tend her vegetable garden. She also had to churn butter and do a great deal of baking—most nineteenth-century Americans distrusted "store-bought" bread. The next chore was to prepare an enormous midday meal for all the workers and family; then washing the dishes, which meant hauling more water from outside and heating it. Then, perhaps with the help of her

daughters, the woman began to clean the house, making beds, shaking out rugs, and scrubbing floors. Besides tending livestock, and depending upon the time of year, she also had to schedule canning, preserving, sewing, "doing" for a sick neighbor or an elderly relative, and completing whatever seasonal tasks lay in store. This would include helping with the butchering, salting or smoking meats, cutting out shirts for the menfolk, and helping with the harvests or the cornhusking. Meanwhile, she also had to watch over her numerous children and try to teach them their tasks. In the evening she cooked another meal (the "supper"), did the dishes again, and then sat down to do a little sewing, while her children read aloud what they had learned in school that day. Long before nine in the evening, she put out her lamps and fell exhausted into bed. Sunday was a day of rest for most, but women still had to do the cooking and dishes for Sunday dinner. This life was backbreaking—day after day of long, hard labor for women. But neighborly women also helped each other out; if someone was sick, people attended each other's needs. No woman ever made a quilt by herself, and friends found ways to make work light by sharing conversation, advice, and even songs over needlework.

Sources:

Jack Larkin, *The Reshaping of Everyday Life: 1790–1840* (New York: Harper & Row, 1988);

Susan Strasser, *Never Done: A History of American Housework* (New York: Pantheon, 1982);

Daniel E. Sutherland, *The Expansion of Everyday Life: 1860–1876* (New York: Harper & Row, 1989).

HOUSING

American Homes. The American landscape changed considerably during the middle decades of the nineteenth century. Until about 1840 many farmers lived in small wood-frame houses. On the western frontier and in the southern backcountry the most common family home was a one-room log cabin with floors of dirt or split logs, an open hearth, and a primitive wooden chimney. Housing styles varied by region, often according to the builder's ethnic origin or the demands of the climate. These small, crowded houses were typically dirty, untidy, and hard to heat. There were larger, two-story houses, usually built along the symmetrical lines of classical Greek architecture, but such homes were rare and belonged only to the wealthiest Americans. By 1840 smaller dwellings were being built in this Greek Revival style as well, and by the 1850s glass windows had become common even in rural areas, making houses brighter and easier to clean and heat. At the same time there appeared a host of new styles in architecture. The new pattern books featured such designs as Gothic Revival cottages and Italianate villas. Many middle-class families could now afford to build a two-story wood-frame house. The floor plans of these new houses were designed to emphasize family relationships, to enhance Americans' growing sense of a need for privacy, and to meet the mother's needs. Kitchens, servants' quarters, and backstairs were all hidden from view, reflecting a growing attention to propriety and respectability. Modern kitchens came equipped with coal-burning cast-iron stoves, which were safer to use than the open fireplaces in older kitchens. Other downstairs rooms—such as parlors, dining rooms, music rooms, or libraries—had a specific purpose and function and were furnished accordingly. By the 1860s middle-class householders could buy machine-made furniture and carpets that were less expensive than similar handmade furnishings. Consequently they could afford to be concerned with "taste." While most earlier middle-class homes were furnished with hodgepodges of practical but often unmatched objects, matching "suites" of furniture became popular in the 1860s. At the beginning of the century the parents' bed was often located in

Gas chandeliers in the New York City mansion built by A. T. Stewart in 1869

A Michigan farmhouse in the 1870s

the best room of the house, where the family also ate and entertained guests. The children usually slept together in a single room, often an unheated loft. By 1850 families who could afford to do so set aside a private bedroom for the parents and each child. The upstairs of the typical middle-class house was private space for sleeping, bathing, and dressing. Sometimes the mother had her own upstairs room for sitting or sewing, or she used the master bedroom as her private sanctuary, where she also dispensed comfort, discipline, and advice to her children.

Town Houses and City Apartments. In towns and cities wood-frame two- or three-story houses were common until the 1840s, when uniform, brick row houses began to change the look of city streets. Although these houses were often criticized for their lack of individuality, they were more fireproof than wooden buildings, as well as cooler in summer and warmer in winter. The back of the typical middle-class row house looked out on a small garden, where a housewife could grow flowers and vegetables and where the family had its own private outhouse, or "privy." At the same time, steeply rising land prices put home ownership out of reach for many city dwellers. Most people who lived in cities had to rent their dwellings. Advertisements in New York newspapers indicate that an attractive house in a good neighborhood cost about twenty or thirty dollars a month. The poorest city dwellers often lived in large barracks-style apartment houses. The word *tenement* was applied to buildings constructed specifically to house multiple families, not large dwellings built for single families and later subdivided into apartments. Some were quite airy

and comfortable and up to five stories high. As more and more immigrants settled in American cities, however, many of these building became overcrowded and unsanitary, and the word *tenement* became more or less synonymous with slum housing.

The Mansions of the Wealthy. The most luxurious new urban buildings were the mansions of the wealthy, constructed along fine avenues according to European designs. These houses were furnished in eclectic "revival" styles such as the highly ornamented, carved, and gilded rococo style or the more somber Gothic style influenced by medieval architecture. Only the most prosperous Americans could afford such amenities as imported carpets from Brussels or France, glittering chandeliers, velvet curtains, and mirrors or paintings in gilded frames. One of the first and finest homes in New York City was the marble mansion of department-store owner A. T. Stewart at Fifth Avenue and Thirty-fourth Street, which was completed in 1869. All the rooms had elaborate bronze, porcelain, and etched-glass chandeliers fueled by gas, the latest technological advance in lighting.

Water and Sanitation. Farmers' water came from a well or cistern and was usually hauled into the house in buckets by housewives. Although sixty-eight cities had established public waterworks by the beginning of the Civil War, most city dwellers had no indoor running water. Town dwellers drew their water from hydrants in the street unless they had their own wells or cisterns. All water for bathing, laundry, cleaning, or cooking had to be heated on the kitchen stoves. Even the 10 percent of New York City residents who had running water in their homes had to heat the water themselves. Hot running water did not become generally available in American homes until the 1930s. Until the widespread availability of indoor plumbing, most Americans considered a daily bath expensive and time-consuming. Bathing too frequently was also considered unhealthy. Taking a bath meant dragging water inside from the well or hydrant, heating it on the kitchen stove, filling a tub, and then emptying the tub. Still, nineteenth-century Americans were probably not as dirty as popular myth has painted them. Most people took full sponge baths daily, pouring water—which was ice cold in the winter—from a pitcher into a basin. Nearly every etiquette book advised readers to use soap and water on a daily basis, decrying such contradictions as "silk stockings on dirty feet." Before the 1870s neither men nor women washed their hair more than once a month, preferring instead to oil it on a daily basis and comb it flat. Only with the popularization of fuller hairstyles in the later decades of the nineteenth century did women begin to wash their hair more frequently. Middle-class Americans brushed their teeth every day and tried to keep their hands and fingernails clean. Indoor toilets were in use in populated areas of the United States by the 1860s but would not come into general use until the 1880s. In addition to flush toilets similar to those used in the twentieth century, some people had indoor "dry-earth" commodes that buried waste in dirt instead of flushing it away with water. Yet in Boston in 1860, for example, there were only five thousand flushing toilets for 178,000 residents. Most people still used outhouses and had chamberpots in their bedrooms for use at night and by people too ill to make the trip to the outhouse. Middle-class families usually had their own privies, but poor city dwellers often had to share overflowing outhouses with dozens, perhaps even hundreds, of neighbors.

Heat and Light. While they were no longer the only source of heat and light, fireplaces still graced new homes built during the mid nineteenth century. By the 1860s most middle-class houses in the North were also heated by coal-burning cast-iron stoves. By the end of the Civil War hot-air central heating could be found in the mansions of affluent Americans. Because wood and coal were both expensive, hardly anyone heated their bedrooms, unless they were wealthy. Families congregated in the kitchen, which was usually the warmest room in the house. Candles made from beeswax or animal fats such as tallow, and lamps that burned a variety of oils, continued to provide light in some homes, but kerosene, invented in 1854, became the lamp fuel of choice. The discovery of gasoline in Pennsylvania in 1859 made kerosene plentiful and cheap, and by 1870 it was used in more American homes than any other lamp fuel.

Sources:
Jack Larkin, *The Reshaping of Everyday Life: 1790–1840* (New York: Harper & Row, 1988);

Daniel E. Sutherland, *The Expansion of Everyday Life: 1860–1876* (New York: Harper & Row, 1989).

THE WOMAN'S MOVEMENT

Pure Womanhood. The restructuring of economic life in nineteenth-century America led to a rethinking of the roles that had traditionally been assigned to men and women. On family farms the two sexes worked side by side, but in the cities men brought in the family income while women raised the children and ran the household. The gradual expansion of the urban middle class produced a change in the way women were perceived: they came to be regarded as morally superior, but intellectually inferior, to men; they were seen as the standard-bearers of all that was pure and refined, their lives dedicated to creating a moral atmosphere in the home and maintaining a benevolent influence on their children. Women were not, therefore, to be contaminated by the corrupting influences of politics. Some historians have called this attitude the "cult of true womanhood."

Trends and Transformations. During the first quarter of the nineteenth century evangelical religious revivals inspired Americans to believe in the possibility of perfecting themselves and their society. This spirit of perfectionism brought about a wave of reform movements throughout the first half of the nineteenth century. Women such as the Grimké sisters, Harriet Beecher Stowe, and Lucretia Mott were active in the abolitionist and temperance crusades from the 1820s to the 1840s, in the process acquiring fund-raising, organizing, and publicity skills. When some of these women, such as Susan B. Anthony, found themselves shut out of abolitionist conventions during the 1840s, they decided to focus on women's rights.

A BRITISH OFFICER OBSERVES SOUTHERN WOMEN

It has often been remarked to me that, when this war is over, the independence of the country will be due, in a great measure, to the women; for they declare that had the women been desponding they could never have gone through with it; but, on the contrary, the women have invariably set an example to the men of patience, devotion, and determination. Naturally proud, and with an innate contempt for the Yankees, the southern women have been rendered furious and desperate by the proceedings of [Union generals] Butler, Milroy, Turchin, &c. They are all prepared to undergo any hardships and misfortunes rather than submit to the rule of such people; and they use every argument which woman can employ to infuse the same spirit into their male relations.

Source: Arthur Fremantle, *Three Months in the Confederate States* (London: J. Bradburn, 1864).

Delegates at an 1859 woman's rights convention, as depicted in the 11 July 1859 issue of *Harper's Weekly*

Politics and Benevolence. There were two overlapping but distinct movements toward women's rights. The first flowed from the general reform impulse: temperance workers realized that alcoholism created serious problems for women when husbands spent their earnings on drink or came home drunk and beat their wives and children; and hospital, prison, and asylum reformers were often motivated by the sufferings of female inmates. Women interested in these issues worked as individuals and in unofficial groups, rather than attempting to address the problems politically. The second branch of the women's rights movement focused on political and legal issues, such as getting women the vote, passing legislation to give married women a share in control of family property, increasing opportunities in education, and allowing women to work outside the home. Susan B. Anthony, perhaps the women's rights movement's most able organizer, spoke eloquently before many state legislatures on the subject of married women's property rights. Lucy Stone kept her maiden name after her marriage and gave rise to imitators called "Lucy Stoners." Amelia Jenks Bloomer attempted to popularize a more comfortable costume for women, consisting of baggy trousers worn under a knee-length tunic; although the outfit was actually designed by Elizabeth Smith Miller, the pants came to be known as "bloomers" and were decried in insulting verses and comments by men and women alike.

The Civil War. The outbreak of war brought women to a new level of participation in national affairs. The war brought violence and privation directly into the homes of many American women, especially in the South. Although they could not vote, both northern and southern women took a keen interest in political issues such as se-

cession and emancipation. Many southern women caught the war spirit, some openly expressing bloodthirsty sentiments. Women supported the war effort by becoming nurses, sewing uniforms, writing encouraging letters to soldiers, and taking over the civilian jobs the soldiers had left behind. An attempt to blend support for the Union cause with the women's rights and abolition movements was the Women's Loyal League, founded by Susan B. Anthony and Elizabeth Cady Stanton in 1863. After the war northern women made important strides in entering professions such as teaching and nursing, while many southern women, left destitute and widowed by the war, had to engage in small businesses such as dairy-and-egg farming. Women made little headway, however, in gaining legal and political rights. While the Fifteenth Amendment to the Constitution, ratified in 1870, gave the vote to male former slaves, women would not receive the right to vote until the Nineteenth Amendment was adopted in 1920.

Volunteers. In addition to learning new tasks and facing new challenges at home, some women participated directly in the war: it is estimated that around four hundred women donned male uniforms and joined the fighting, and there are highly romanticized accounts of women spying for both sides. But most found more socially acceptable ways to participate. In 1861 Dr. Elizabeth Blackwell founded the Women's Central Relief Association, which raised funds for supplies for Union soldiers and recruited and trained female nurses. Later that year a group of influential New Yorkers formed the United States Sanitary Commission, which oversaw all relief efforts and briefly took over the selection and training of nurses. At the same time, Dorothea Dix was commissioned superintendent of women nurses for the Union army, partly in recognition of her work in hospital and insane-asylum reform. Clara Barton, who would later found the American branch of the International Red Cross, gave first aid and supplied candles, medicines, and food to northern soldiers; they would long remember her as the "Angel of the Battlefield."

Nursing. Women nurses did not have an easy lot. Being members of the upper classes who were accustomed to deferential treatment and clean, well-appointed homes, many found the transition to rough field hospitals trying. They had to accustom themselves to shocking and distressing sights, assist at amputations, and watch their patients die. Further, although the nurses were admired by the soldiers on both sides, they received a marked lack of respect from the male doctors.

Feminization of Professions. At least partly as a result of the Civil War, American women came to dominate two professions. Nursing emerged from the war as a mainly female occupation. Women had been moving into teaching since colonial days; by 1860, 25 percent of all teachers were women (the percentage was somewhat higher in the North than in the South). During the Civil War, with the men away fighting, women constituted the majority of teachers on both sides. Twenty years later, two-thirds of all teachers in the primary grades would be women.

Temperance, Again. With the end of slavery, many women reformers who had been active in the abolitionist movement turned to other causes, including—once again—temperance. Women protested drunkenness by kneeling in prayer on the sidewalks in front of saloons; some entered these dens of iniquity and smashed bottles of liquor. On 18 November 1874, 135 female activists met at the Second Presbyterian Church in Cleveland, Ohio, and founded the Woman's Christian Temperance Union. Quickly becoming the largest women's organization in the history of the United States, the WCTU attracted far more adherents than the woman's rights movement had ever been able to rally. Later in the decade the organization formally disavowed the cause of woman suffrage.

Sources:

Barbara I. Berg, *The Remembered Gate: Origins of American Feminism—The Woman and the City, 1800–1860* ((New York: Oxford University Press, 1978);

Carl N. Degler, *At Odds: Women and the Family in America from the Revolution to the Present* (New York: Oxford University Press, 1980);

Ellen Carol DuBois, *Feminism and Suffrage: The Emergence of an Independent Women's Movement in America, 1848–1869* (Ithaca, N.Y.: Cornell University Press, 1978).

MARY TODD LINCOLN

1818-1882
FIRST LADY

Kentucky Childhood. Mary Todd was born into a prominent Lexington, Kentucky, family on 13 December 1818. Although her family owned three female slaves, her father, Robert, a staunch Whig, disapproved of slavery. When Todd was six years old her mother died; shortly thereafter her father married Betsey Humphreys, with whom he would have eight more children. Todd was an intelligent, self-willed child who often came into conflict with her stepmother, and she later recalled her childhood as lonely and unhappy. Since Betsey insisted on sending Todd away to the Shelby Female Academy, the difficult relationship with her stepmother may have resulted in Todd's excellent education; but her father had always believed that a solid education would make women more desirable as marriage partners. Later, Todd attended Mme. Mentelle's academy, where she learned to speak fluent French.

Springfield Belle. In the summer of 1837 Todd traveled to Springfield, Illinois, to visit her sister Elizabeth Edwards, who had married the son of a former Illinois governor. Todd may have met Abraham Lincoln at this time; in any case, she certainly knew him when she returned two years later to live with the Edwardses. Todd became the belle of Springfield society, and she attracted many suitors. A friend described her as having "clear blue eyes, long lashes, light brown hair with a glint of bronze and a lovely complexion." Todd always considered herself too plump, but some of her youthful admirers thought her figure beautiful. She was a brilliant conversationalist, with a sparkling wit and a talent for mimicry; she was also highly sensitive to criticism. When William H. Herndon, Lincoln's law partner, compared her waltzing to the "gliding of a snake" she conceived a dislike for him that would last for the rest of her life. Perhaps as a result of this animosity, Herndon would depict Mary in an ungracious and highly critical way in the 1889 biography of Lincoln that he coauthored with Jesse W. Weik; this portrayal has contributed to the negative myths surrounding her.

Courtship and Marriage. In late 1839 Todd's friendship with Lincoln became romantic. Because of Todd's temper and Lincoln's awkwardness, the courtship did not go smoothly. Although the story of the "bride deserted at the altar" is almost certainly false, there was a break in their engagement around January 1841. As a result, Lincoln became deeply depressed. Toward the end of 1842 a series of satiric letters about a political rival of Lincoln's, the state auditor James Shields, published in a local newspaper, brought Todd and Lincoln back together. Lincoln wrote some of these letters under a female synonym, and Todd contributed one or two. (Shields challenged Lincoln to a duel, but the two agreed to part without exchanging shots.) On 4 November 1842 Lincoln and Todd were married; they had arranged the wedding hastily, giving some of their relatives barely a week's notice. Four sons were born to the couple while Lincoln was expanding his law practice: Robert Todd on 1 August 1843, Edward Baker on 10 March 1846, William Wallace ("Willie") on 21 December 1850, and Thomas ("Tad") on 4 April 1853. Ony Robert would survive to adulthood. The unhappiness of the Lincolns' marriage has probably been exaggerated. Mary later recalled the years in Springfield as the happiest of her life, and one of her sisters commented that Mary and Abraham "knew each other perfectly. They did not lead an unhappy life at all. She was devoted to him and his children and he was certainly all to her a husband could have been."

White House Hostess. After Abraham Lincoln won the presidential election in 1860, the family moved into the White House. At this time Mary began to acquire a reputation as a spendthrift. With great taste and skill, but no sense of economy, she chose wallpaper, carpets, furnishings, china, and lace curtains for the White House. Everything, she declared, had become shabby, and the president's residence ought to reflect his high office. In less than a year she overspent the administration's budget of $20,000 for redecoration, which was supposed to last until 1864. At the same time she built a striking wardrobe, ordering sixteen dresses in the first year from her seamstress, Elizabeth Keckley.

Civil War. Mary was in a difficult position during the Civil War, with four brothers and three half-brothers serving in the Confederate forces. Charges that she was disloyal to the Union, however, were untrue. She was deeply committed to her husband's cause and party, and although she was not an abolitionist, she was firmly against the extension of slavery. She frequently visited military hospitals, bringing wounded soldiers fruit and other comforts. People who met her at society affairs were forced to reconsider their prejudices against this "frontier" lady: they found her to be kind, gracious, charming, and a lively conversationalist. When her son Willie died on 20 February 1862, however, Mary grieved to such an extent that some historians have said that she became permanently disabled. For the rest of her life she would exhibit irrational outbursts of temper and jealousy. Her husband's assassination on 14 April 1865 left her barely able to function.

After the War. After recovering from the shock of the assassination Mary moved to Chicago, where she learned that Herndon had been publicly claiming that her husband had never loved her but had mourned an early sweetheart, Ann Rutledge, all his life. The public humiliation, together with her other grief, caused Mary to suffer a further emotional breakdown. Although she had an adequate income, she became convinced that she was financially ruined; nevertheless, she continued to spend extravagantly. During the late 1860s, partly to escape public criticism of an attempt to sell her clothes and jewels under an assumed name, she left for Germany; later she moved to England, where she placed her youngest son in school. She eventually returned to Chicago. In 1870 Congress voted to give her an annual pension. During the following years her son Robert became worried that his mother would spend all of her money and become a financial burden to him, and in 1875 he sought to have her declared insane. Although the court could find nothing more serious than extravagant shopping and a belief in her own poverty, she was placed in a private sanatorium in Batavia, Illinois. After four months—with the assistance of Myra Bradwell, the first woman to practice law in the United States—she was released in the care of her sister, Mrs. Edwards. A second trial found her competent, and she returned to Europe for a few years. There she indulged her passion for spiritualism, with which she had become fascinated during the late 1850s. During her final years she was ill, partially blind, and crippled by a back injury. She died on 16 July 1882 and was buried beside her husband in Springfield.

Source:
Jean H. Baker, *Mary Todd Lincoln: A Biography* (New York: Norton, 1987).

SOJOURNER TRUTH

CIRCA 1797-1883
ABOLITIONIST, REFORMER

Early Life in Slavery. Isabella Bomefree was born around 1797 on the estate of a Dutch patroon in Ulster County, New York, where her parents were slaves. Her first language was Dutch, and she would speak with an accent all her life. One of the formative events of her early childhood was witnessing her parents' grief over the loss of children who had been sold away. When she was nine Isabella herself was sold, and she was sold several more times in her early life. She worked from 1810 to 1827 in the household of John J. Dumont of New Paltz, New York. There she married a fellow slave named Thomas, with whom she had at least five children: two daughters and a son were sold away from her. When Dumont demanded that she serve another year after New York declared slavery illegal, Bomefree escaped. That year she also became a Christian; her religious commitments, combined with a deep knowledge of the Bible, would influence her profoundly throughout her life. Isaac and Maria Van Wagener took her in, and she adopted their last name. With the help of Quaker friends she successfully sued her former owner for the return of her son Peter, who had been sold illegally to an Alabama planter.

Freedom and Faith. Around 1829 Isabella Van Wagener moved to New York City with her two youngest children, Peter and Sophia. She joined the Methodist Church and adopted the evangelistic, "perfectionist" religious beliefs that inspired her own mystical faith. Throughout her life she would hear voices and see visions. In New York she met Elijah Pierson, a wealthy and erratic social reformer whose primary work was with prostitutes, and joined Pierson and his wife in preaching in the streets. In the 1830s Van Wagener moved to a commune in Ossining, New York, remaining there for five years. She eventually returned to New York City, where she lived quietly and attended the African Zion Church, until 1843, when an inner voice told her to change her name to Sojourner Truth. She became an itinerant minister, traveling around the Connecticut River valley to preach, sing, pray, and evangelize at camp meetings, in churches, or wherever she could find shelter and an audience. Her message was that God was loving and perfect, and that human beings had nothing to fear from him. She said often that "God is from everlasting to everlasting" and that "Truth burns up error." She believed that God was present everywhere and that all beings lived in him as "fishes in the sea." In the winter of 1843 Sojourner Truth moved to the Northampton Industrial Association, another utopian community, where she lived until 1846. There she met important members of the abolitionist movement, including Frederick Douglass and George Benson, brother-in-law of the antislavery leader William Lloyd Garrison. As a result of this experience, abolitionism and women's rights became important to Sojourner Truth and were always expressed in her preaching. She never compromised on the importance of these causes, disagreeing with abolitionists such as Douglass, who maintained that equality for women ought to be subordinated to the elimination of slavery.

Autobiography and Speeches. In 1850 Truth published her autobiography, ghostwritten by Olive Gilbert. She supported herself by selling *The Narrative of Sojourner Truth* at women's rights meetings for twenty-five cents a copy. Truth's "Ar'n't I a Woman?" speech at the Akron Women's Rights Convention in 1850 has gone down in history as one of the most significant expressions of the combined abolitionist and women's rights movement. When Truth rose to speak she was severely heckled; undaunted, she pointed out that as a female slave she had experienced the profound grief of having her own children sold away and had had to work like a man all her life; she then asked, "And ar'n't I a woman?" She left the stage to tumultuous applause. At a women's rights convention in Indiana she responded to charges that she was a man posing as a woman by baring her breast to her accusers.

Civil War and Freedpeoples' Rights. In the mid 1850s Truth moved with her daughters to Battle Creek, Michigan, a center of religious and antislavery reform movements. There she joined a commune called Harmonia. During the Civil War she met President Abraham Lincoln and worked on freed slaves' relief projects such as the Freedmen's Hospital and the Freedmen's Village at Arlington Heights, Virginia. One of her grandsons served in the celebrated black regiment, the Fifty-fourth Massachusetts Volunteers. In an article that appeared in *The Atlantic Monthly* during the war the antislavery writer Harriet Beecher Stowe immortalized Truth as the "Libyan Sybil"; the name would be associated with Truth for the rest of her life. After the war Truth worked tirelessly to assist former slaves; in 1870 she sent a petition to Congress, signed by hundreds of supporters, pleading for the allocation of government lands in the West to former slaves. Although Congress took no action on the petition, her outspoken support of western migration inspired thousands of former slaves to establish homesteads in Kansas. She traveled throughout Kansas and Missouri, exhorting the former slaves to "Be clean! for cleanliness is godliness." She also continued to speak to white audiences in the Northeast, preaching her message of a loving God and advocating temperance, woman suffrage, and equal rights for blacks.

Final Years. In the mid 1870s Truth's autobiography was revised and republished. She continued to travel and speak on social reform issues such as temperance as long as she was able, and she received hundreds of visitors in Battle Creek until her death on 26 November 1883. Her funeral was said to have been the largest ever held in Battle Creek.

Sources:

Olive Gilbert, *Narrative of Sojourner Truth* (Boston, 1850);

Nell Irvin Painter, *Sojourner Truth: A Life, a Symbol* (New York: Norton, 1996).

VICTORIA WOODHULL

1838-1927
FEMINIST, REFORMER

Vicky and Tennessee. Victoria Claflin was born on 23 September 1838 into a large and impoverished family in Homer, Ohio. By the time she and her sister, Tennessee Celeste, were in their early teens, their family was staging medicine shows at which one of the brothers sold cancer "treatments" and the parents hawked an "elixir of life" with a picture of the attractive Tennessee on the bottle. The two girls entered spiritualistic trances in which they offered comfort to the bereaved and the ill.

Marriage and Social Reform. When she was fifteen Victoria married a physician, Canning Woodhull, with whom she had two children. Leaving her husband, Victoria worked briefly as an actress in California, then returned to Ohio and teamed up with Tennessee to perform feats of spiritualism and mesmerism. The sisters were dogged by accusations of fraud, prostitution, and moral turpitude. When one of Tennessee's cancer "patients" died, they had to flee Ottawa, Illinois, to avoid an indictment for manslaughter. In 1865 Victoria met an attractive Civil War veteran, Col.James Harvey Blood; prompted by Victoria's "inner voice," both parties quickly decided to divorce their spouses, although Victoria would always retain Woodhull's last name. She claimed to have married Colonel Blood, but no record of the marriage exists. By this time Victoria and Tennessee were becoming famous for their exploits. They cut their curly hair short, appeared in men's clothing, and continued to support their parents, their siblings, and Victoria's children through spiritualistic feats. Americans were shocked, titillated, and endlessly fascinated by the beautiful and daring sisters.

Demosthenes, Finance, and Politics. In 1868, Victoria claimed, the spirit of the ancient Greek orator Demosthenes appeared to her in one of her trances and told her to go to New York City. There she and Tennessee gained an appointment with the ailing and recently widowed railroad promoter Cornelius Vanderbilt. The "Commodore," who had long been a devotee of mysticism, was charmed by the sisters' beauty and liveliness and soon became a silent partner in their surprising new career. Setting themselves up as stockbrokers on Wall Street, the sisters soon became known as the "Queens of Finance." The brokerage firm of Woodhull, Claflin and Company quickly prospered, no doubt supported by insider tips—as well as capital—supplied by Vanderbilt. Also in 1868 Victoria met the eccentric Stephen Pearl Andrews, a disciple of various European radical social reformers and a proponent of a philosophy he called "pantarchy." According to pantarchy, marriage was unnatural and should be replaced by "free love." Andrews advocated equal rights for women and the communal ownership of property. He and Victoria wrote a treatise on free love and shared property, *Origin, Tendencies and Principles of Government,* which was published in 1871. Around this time Victoria decided to run for president of the United States. On 14 May 1870, partly to publicize her candidacy, she and Tennessee brought out the first issue of *Woodhull and Claflin's Weekly,* edited by Andrews and Blood. The journal quickly gained a reputation for muckraking and for propounding outrageous beliefs. It was in its pages that Karl Marx and Friedrich Engels's *Communist Manifesto* (1848) was first published in America. The magazine also advocated legalized prostitution, short skirts, and free love. The *Weekly* lasted for about six years.

Women's Rights and Scandals. Congressman Benjamin F. Butler, a former Civil War general, helped draft Woodhull's first important speech, an 1871 appearance before the United States House Judiciary Committee in which she argued that the Thirteenth and Fourteenth Amendments to the Constitution, which granted black men the right to vote, also enfranchised women. Leaders of the National Woman Suffrage Association were present in the galleries, and her modest, attractive demeanor charmed even the most rigid moralists among them. Her revolutionary words, however, were at variance with her manner. She declaimed boldly that "we mean treason; we mean secession . . . we are plotting revolution . . . we will overthrow this bogus Republic and plant a government of righteousness in its stead." Woodhull's attempt to become the leader of the National Woman Suffrage Association was defeated by Susan B. Anthony. Undaunted, Woodhull ran for president in 1872 under the auspices of the Equal Rights Party. But on 2 November 1872, a few days before the election, the *Weekly* ran a story claiming that the preacher and reformer Henry Ward Beecher had carried on an affair with one of his parishioners, the beautiful wife of Woodhull and Claflin's friend Theodore Tilton, and another story alleging that a stockbroker, Luther C. Challis, had seduced two young girls. Woodhull and Claflin were arrested on obscenity charges, and Woodhull received no votes in the election. The sisters were later acquitted.

England and High Society. Vanderbilt died in 1877, leaving the sisters without his support. They left for England, where they caused their usual sensation. An enamored English fan, John Biddulph Martin, to the dismay of his wealthy banking family, asked Woodhull to marry him; they were finally wed in 1883. Two years later Claflin married Francis Cook, a wealthy aristocrat. The sisters became noted for charity work and in their later years were finally accepted into English society. In July 1892 Woodhull launched a new periodical, the *Humanitarian,* which she coedited with her daughter, Zula Maud. Both sisters traveled back to America on several occasions, raising excitement with each visit. Tennessee died in 1923; Victoria on 10 June 1927.

Sources:
M. M. Marberry, *Vicky: A Biography of Victoria C. Woodhull* (New York: Funk & Wagnalls, 1967);

Emanie Sachs, *"The Terrible Siren": Victoria Woodhull, 1838–1927* (New York: Harper, 1928).

PUBLICATIONS

Timothy Shay Arthur, *Ten Nights in a Bar-Room and What I Saw There* (Philadelphia: J. W. Bradley, 1854)—an influential, best-selling temperance tract;

Casimir Bohn, *Bohn's Manual of Etiquette in Washington and Other Cities in the Union* (Washington, D.C.: Casimir Bohn, 1857)—manners for the new urban middle class;

Lydia Maria Child, *A Brief History of the Condition of Women, in Various Ages and Nations,* 2 volumes (New York: C. S. Francis / Boston: J. H. Francis, 1854)—revised edition of Child's *The History and Condition of Women* (1835), which was highly praised by nineteenth-century feminists as an important compendium of information on the "woman question";

Child, *The Duty of Disobedience to the Fugitive Slave Act* (Boston: American Anti-slavery Society, 1860)—an abolitionist tract by Child, who had been well known for her stand on human rights ever since the publication of her novel *Hobomok* (1824), about the marriage of a white woman and a Native American man;

David Christy, *Cotton is King, or the Economical Relations of Slavery* (Cincinnati, Ohio: Moore, Wilstach & Keys, 1855)—a defense of the antebellum plantation system that introduced the phrase "King Cotton";

Juliet Corson, *The Cooking Manual of Practical Directions for Economical Every-Day Cooking* (New York: Dodd, Mead, 1877)—cookbook by the founder of the New York Cooking School, the first such institution in the United States;

George Fitzhugh, *Cannibals All! or, Slaves Without Masters* (Richmond, Va.: A. Morris, 1857)—a southerner's defense of slavery;

Horace Greeley, *Hints Toward Reforms* (New York: Harper, 1850)—essays on subjects such as temperance, land reform, and education by the editor of the *New York Tribune;*

Sarah Josepha Hale, *The Ladies' New Book of Cookery: a Practical System for Private Families in Town and Country* (New York: Long, 1852)—cookbook by the author of "Mary Had a Little Lamb" and the leader of the successful campaign for a national Thanksgiving Day;

Hale, *Manners; or, Happy Homes and Good Society All the Year Round* (Boston: Tilton, 1868)—a popular etiquette book by Hale, who was the editor of *Godey's Lady's Book;*

Hale, ed., *Women's Record* (New York: Harper, 1853)—Hale's attempt to compile "a comprehensive and accurate record of what women have accomplished," proving "that WOMAN is God's appointed agent of *morality*";

Harriet A. Jacobs, *Incidents in the Life of a Slave Girl,* edited by Lydia Maria Child (Boston: Privately printed, 1861)—an influential memoir by a slave who escaped to freedom;

Mrs. Manners, *At Home and Abroad; or, How to Behave* (New York: Evans & Brittan, 1853)—a popular etiquette book;

Frederick Law Olmsted, *The Cotton Kingdom* (New York: Mason, 1861)—observations based on a well-known landscape architect's travels throughout the South in the early 1850s, including his denunciation of slavery;

Whitelaw Reid, *After the War: A Southern Tour, May 1, 1865 to May 1, 1866* (New York: Moore, Wilstach & Baldwin, 1866)—firsthand observations by a reporter who had covered the war for the *Cincinnati Gazette;*

Henry M. Robert, *Pocket Manual of Rules of Order for Deliberative Assemblies* (Chicago: Griggs, 1876)—procedures for running business meetings, now known as *Robert's Rules of Order* and widely used worldwide;

Victoria Woodhull, *The Origins, Tendencies and Principles of Government* (New York: Woodhull, Claflin, 1871)—a book that expresses Woodhull's views on free love, 1871.

H. C. Wright, *The Unwelcomed Child; or, the Crime of an Undesigned and Undesired Maternity* (Boston: Marsh, 1858)—birth control advice from an advocate of planned parenthood.

RELIGION

by MARY ELIZABETH BROWN

CONTENTS

Sidebars and tables are listed in italics.

1850

- Three German pastors sent to America by a German Lutheran society organize the Wisconsin Evangelical Lutheran Synod.

- The Free Methodist Church expands to Canada.

- The U.S. government organizes the Utah Territory, putting itself on a collision course with the Mormons, who had organized the autonomous state of Deseret in 1849.

- The New School (Presbyterian) General Assembly repudiates the proposition that slavery is divinely sanctioned.

1851

- The first Young Men's Christian Association (YMCA) in the United States opens in Boston.

- Spiritualists briefly organize a communal society at Mountain Cove, Virginia.

- Isaac Hecker, a convert from Methodism to Catholicism and a member of the Congregation of the Most Holy Redeemer (Redemptorists), returns to the United States from his priestly training in Rome.

13 Apr.   Sabato Morais is elected rabbi of the congregation of Mikveh Israel, the Sephardic synagogue in Philadelphia, and goes on to become a founder of Conservative Judaism.

3 Aug.   Irish-American Francis P. Kenrick succeeds Samuel Eccleston, S.S., as Roman Catholic archbishop of Baltimore.

1852

- Episcopalian bishop George Washington Doane of New Jersey is tried and acquitted of possible financial wrongdoing in the management of two schools he had founded.

- Louis Kossuth tours the United States promoting Hungarian independence and denouncing Catholics for siding with the Hapsburgs.

- The Universalists establish Tufts College in Medford, Massachusetts.

- The Society of Jesus founds Loyola College in Baltimore.

- The First Plenary Council of Baltimore meets and recommends the establishing of parochial schools.

28 Mar.   John Nepomucene Neumann becomes Roman Catholic bishop of Philadelphia.

13 Aug.   Gustaf Palmquist and followers organize the first Swedish Baptist church in the United States.

18 Nov.   Rose-Philippine Duchesne, a missionary who worked among the Potowatomi Indians in Sugar Creek, Kansas, dies at her religious community, Sacred Heart, in Saint Charles, Missouri.

1853

- Charles Loring Brace organizes the Children's Aid Society.

- Joseph Michael Bäumler (or Bimeler) dies. He had founded Zoar, Ohio, as a community for German Separatists from Württemberg, Bavaria, and Baden in 1817.

- Episcopalian William Augustus Muhlenberg, pastor of the Church of the Holy Communion in New York City, sends his "Memorial" to the House of Bishops, outlining ways the church could be a force for Christian unity in the United States. Specifically, he suggests ordaining men willing to carry out Christ's Great Commission (to preach the gospel to all nations), regardless of how well they conform to Episcopalian tenets.

- The American Unitarian Association rejects Transcendentalism and affirms the divine origin and authority of Christ.

30 June Alessandro Gavazzi, an Italian former priest lecturing in New York City, falsely accuses Archbishop Gaetano Bedini, visiting the United States as a papal representative, of being the "Butcher of Bologna," responsible for executing Italian republican leaders who were actually killed by Austrian troops.

24 Nov. Jean-Baptiste Lamy is consecrated Bishop of Santa Fe in the New Mexico Territory.

1854

- Members of the religious community of Bethel, Missouri, under the leadership of the charismatic Wilhelm Keil, build covered wagons and cross the Great Plains and Rocky Mountains to establish a second community at Aurora, Oregon.

8 Dec. Pope Pius IX announces the doctrine of the Immaculate Conception, that is, that the mother of Jesus did not share in the sin that had caused Adam and Eve to be expelled from the Garden of Eden and that had been transmitted to all their human descendants.

1855

- Matthias Brinser organizes the United Zion Church, a branch of the United Brethren in Christ, in Lancaster County, Pennsylvania.

- The Cape Fear Conference of Free Will Baptists is organized in North Carolina.

- Ellen Gould Harmon White, the "Adventist Prophetess," moves to Battle Creek, Michigan.

- David Einhorn, later to become a prominent Reform rabbi, arrives in the United States.

- The nativist, anti-Catholic American Party sweeps the California state elections, which leads to the state's halting its practice of distributing tax receipts to private denominational schools. Spurred by nativists in its legislature, New York State passes a law requiring lay trusteeship of religious property. Nativists also win elections in Connecticut, Maryland, New Hampshire, and Rhode Island.

6 Aug. Nativist rioting in Louisville, Kentucky, kills more than twenty people.

1856

- Ebenezer and George Draper, majority stock owners in the Christian community of Hopedale near Milford, Massachusetts, liquidate their shares.
- The first YMCA in New York City opens.
- Dwight Moody has a conversion experience and moves to Chicago.

1857

- The African Methodist Episcopal Church acquires Wilberforce University in Ohio.
- The American Party nominates Millard Fillmore, then on a European tour which includes an audience with Pope Pius IX, as its presidential candidate.

1858

- New School Presbyterians divide over slavery.
- James Lloyd Breck establishes Seabury Divinity School in Faribault, Minnesota, for the training of Episcopal ministers untainted by the Tractarian, or Oxford, Movement (an attempt to convert Episcopalians to Catholicism).

8 Apr.   The Christian Reformed Church is formed in Zeeland, Michigan, by Dutch immigrants.

1859

- The Association of Reformed Presbyterian Churches drops "of the South" from its title when its northern counterpart joins the United Presbyterian Church.
- The Board of Delegates of American Israelites is formed to help explain Judaism to Gentiles and to counter acts of anti-Semitism.
- Temple Sinai opens in Chicago. It is the third Reform temple to open in the United States, following Temple Har Sinai (Baltimore, 1842) and Emmanuel (New York, 1845).

Sept.   *Atlantic Monthly* publishes Oliver Wendell Holmes Sr.'s "The Deacon's Masterpiece, or, The Wonderful 'One-Hoss Shay': A Logical Story," a mock-allegorical poem about the Puritan theological system then dying out in New England.

1860

- Isaac Hecker opens the Church of Saint Paul the Apostle in New York City, the mother church of the Paulist Fathers.
- Baptists form the Southern Theological Seminary in Greenville, South Carolina.
- The Amana Society is incorporated in Iowa. Its formal name is the Community of True Inspiration, a pietistic sect founded by the German Michael Krausner.
- The American College, a residence for U.S. Catholic clergy studying in Rome, is established.

- The Society of Jesus founds the present-day University of San Francisco, California.

- Emmegahbowh, an Ojibway, becomes the first of his tribe ordained to Episcopal orders.

1861

- The Advent Christian or Seventh-Day Adventist Church is founded in Battle Creek, Michigan.

- Geneva College in upstate New York changes its name to Hobart College to honor the late High Episcopalian bishop of New York, John Henry Hobart.

- The General Conference Mennonite Church is organized.

- Southern Lutherans form their own synod.

5 Jan.   John Nepomucene Neumann dies.

10 May   Theodore Parker, minister of the Twenty-Eighth Congregational Society in Boston and a leading Unitarian and social reformer, dies.

1862

- The Swedenborgian Church is incorporated in Illinois.

- Dwight Moody retires from business to involve himself in religion, mostly through YMCA organizational work and fund-raising.

- The Protestant Episcopal Church of the Confederate States of America is organized.

- Henry W. Bellows of All Souls Unitarian Church in New York City organizes the United States Sanitary Commission to provide for the medical care of Union soldiers.

May   The General Assembly of the Old School Presbyterians affirms its loyalty to the Union, precipitating the creation of a separate General Assembly for Southern Old School Presbyterianism.

Nov.   George H. Stuart, a Philadelphia banker, organizes the United States Christian Commission to provide moral and charitable services for Union soldiers.

1863

- Congress passes a law against polygamy, aimed at the Mormons.

- Roman Catholic archbishop John B. Purcell of Cincinnati calls for the emancipation of all slaves.

1864

- The New Apostolic Church is organized.

- In a letter to Jefferson Davis, Pope Pius IX addresses him as "Your Excellency," giving rise to the rumor that the Vatican officially recognizes the Confederacy.

- The Pennsylvania Ministerium withdraws from the Lutheran General Synod to protest the inclusion of the Franckean Synod, which had been formed in western New York in 1837 and influenced by the revivalist Charles G. Finney.

- The Christian Union, a denomination of independently organized churches, is formed.

- A Mormon named Granville Hedrich acts on a vision telling him to return to Independence, Missouri, and claim Mormon property there.

- Pope Pius IX issues an encyclical titled *Quanta Cura* and its accompanying document, the *Syllabus of Errors*. In these two documents he outlines the reasons in Catholic doctrine for opposing modern philosophical developments and condemns specific trends in scientific research and political thought.

Spring   Roman Catholic Patrick Lynch of Charleston, South Carolina, becomes the official Confederate commissioner to Rome.

31 July   Martin John Spalding succeeds Francis P. Kenrick as Roman Catholic archbishop of Baltimore.

1865

- Isaac Hecker begins publication of the first popular Catholic monthly magazine in the country, *Catholic World*.

- German-speaking Baptists organize the North American Baptist Conference.

- The National Unitarian Conference formulates a statement of beliefs on the importance of submission to Jesus Christ's leadership.

- Roman Catholic archbishop Peter Kenrick of Saint Louis denies the sacraments to members of the Fenian Brotherhood, a group dedicated to the establishment of Irish independence through war if necessary.

Dec.   Bishop Patrick Lynch returns to the Diocese of Charleston, South Carolina, after obtaining a pardon for his Confederate activities during the Civil War.

1866

- The Evangelical Church-Union of the West combines German migrants' Lutheran and Evangelical synods.

- The Colored Primitive Baptist Church is organized.

- The Northern Methodist Church organizes a separate black conference, headed by a black bishop, as part of the general denominational structure.

- Henry W. Bellows becomes the president of an American committee to lobby the federal government to participate in the International Red Cross movement.

- The Southern Methodist Church releases its black members to form their own organization.

4 Oct.   Opening of the Second Plenary Council of the Roman Catholic hierarchy of the United States.

1867

- Mormons in Missouri repurchase the temple lot first bought by their sect in 1831.

- Unitarian Francis Ellingwood Abbot forms the Free Religious Association in response to the National Unitarian Conference statement on the importance of Christ's leadership.

- Mary Prout organizes the Independent Order of Saint Luke in Maryland, an African American women's society providing medical and death benefits.

- Isaac Leeser and Orthodox rabbis form Maimonides College in Philadelphia as a Jewish institute of higher education.

- Samuel Chapman Armstrong approaches the American Missionary Association for financial aid, which he uses to create Hampton Normal and Industrial Institute in Virginia.

1868

- The Seventh-Day Adventists organize their General Conference.

16 Aug. James Gibbons is appointed vicar apostolic of North Carolina.

1869

- The Universalists establish a divinity school at Tufts College.

- Elder James R. Howell of New York, a member of the African Methodist Episcopal Church, Zion, organizes the Reformed Zion Union Apostolic Church in Boydton, Virginia.

- Rabbi Samuel Hirsch chairs a rabbinical meeting in Philadelphia that produces a Reformed understanding of the Jewish Diaspora.

- Northern Presbyterian New and Old Schools merge, as Southern Presbyterian New and Old Schools had done during the Civil War.

- Phillips Brooks becomes pastor of Trinity Episcopal Church in Boston, a position he holds for twenty-five years.

11 Oct. Sister Irene Fitzgibbon of the New York Sisters of Charity sets a cradle outside the door of her new institution on West Twelfth Street in New York City, the future New York Foundling Hospital.

1870

- Black Southern Methodists form the Colored Methodist Episcopal Church.

- Dwight Moody asks Ira D. Sankey to become the organist and song leader for his religious meetings.

- Southern Methodists permit lay delegates to attend conferences.

- The first modern ecclesiastical historian, Philip Schaff, accepts a teaching position at Union Theological Seminary in New York City.

12 July   Eight people are killed in New York City when some five hundred Irish Catholics attack a parade of Protestant Irish ("Orangemen") celebrating the anniversary of the 1680 Battle of the Boyne.

5 Dec.   The Grant administration announces a new "Peace Policy" for native tribes. Concerned that competing evangelization efforts from various Christian denominations would complicate pacification, the federal government begins to assign reservations to denominations.

1871

- Herbert Cardinal Vaughan of England founds the Society of Saint Joseph of the Sacred Heart, popularly known as the Mill Hill Fathers, to evangelize among former slaves in the United States.

1872

- Old Order, or Wisler, Mennonites, form under the leadership of Jacob Wisler, in opposition to what they perceive as disturbing innovations in the faith.
- Finnish Lutherans organize the Solomon Korteniemi Lutheran Society.
- While visiting England, Dwight Moody substitutes at a London pulpit, and leads his first revival.
- Edgar P. Wadhams, a convert to Catholicism, becomes the bishop of Ogdensburg, New York.

30 July   James Gibbons becomes Catholic bishop of Richmond, Virginia.

1873

- Cornelius Vanderbilt donates $500,000 to organize a Methodist university and seminary in Nashville, Tennessee, which adopts his name.
- New York State makes Memorial Day a legal holiday.
- George David Cummins, assistant bishop of Kentucky, forms the Reformed Episcopal Church in an attempt to evade the growing interest in preserving and elaborating the rituals of Episcopalianism.
- Maimonides College closes.
- Patrick Healy, S.J., a mulatto, becomes president of present-day Georgetown University.
- Helena P. Blavatsky migrates from czarist Russia to the United States, where she becomes a leading Spiritualist.

8 July   Isaac Mayer Wise founds the Union of American Hebrew Congregations to coordinate Reform Jewish life.

2 Dec.   The Reformed Episcopal Church is organized in reaction to the ritualism and Catholicism of the Tractarian Movement.

1874

- The Seventh-Day Adventists send their first missionary to Europe.

- Southern Presbyterians organize an autonomous Colored Presbyterian Church.

- In response to a potential schism, the General Convention of the Episcopal Church reduces ritualism and increases the field of acceptable beliefs.

- Solomon Schindler, a leading secular reformer, becomes the rabbi of Temple Israel in Boston.

1875

- Jean-Baptiste Lamy is elevated to the status of archbishop.

- James F. Wood becomes the archbishop of Philadelphia.

15 Mar. John McCluskey becomes the first U.S. citizen to be named a cardinal of the Roman Catholic Church.

12 June James Augustine Healy, Patrick's brother, becomes Catholic bishop of Portland, Maine, and remains in that position until his death in 1900.

3 Oct. Isaac Mayer Wise founds Hebrew Union College in Cincinnati.

1876

- Felix Adler leaves Reform Judaism to found the New York Society for Ethical Culture.

17 Apr. Orestes Brownson, a leading Catholic writer, dies. Later, his remains are moved to the Chapel of the Sacred Heart on the grounds of the University of Notre Dame in South Bend, Indiana.

1877

- Archbishop James F. Wood opposes the Molly Maguires, a secret group of Irish American coal miners who use violent means to counter the growing power of mine owners.

- The Southern Theological Seminary moves from Greenville, South Carolina, to Louisville, Kentucky.

9 May The United Christian Church splits off from the United Brethren in Christ in Campbelltown, Pennsylvania.

3 Oct. James Gibbons succeeds James Roosevelt Bayley as Roman Catholic archbishop of Baltimore.

OVERVIEW

Common Bonds and Individualism. Americans in the mid nineteenth century had a profound sense of religious freedom. According to the First Amendment to the Constitution, Congress could make "no law respecting an establishment of religion, or prohibiting the free exercise thereof." At the level of organized religion, this provision meant that each faith had to operate its churches without government assistance. At the personal level, the First Amendment left individuals free to follow their consciences. Even after they joined religious groups, Americans retained their sense of personal control. Individuals or groups were free to reform existing faiths or to create new ones. Many people listened to their religious leaders but arranged their lives in accord with their own personal interpretations.

Branches of Protestantism. Between 1850 and 1877 Protestantism was the single largest religious sect in the United States. Protestants did not consider themselves one huge group; they were acutely aware of many differences that had divided them in the three centuries since the Reformation. One of the most important differences was polity, or how religion was organized. The most traditional group was the Episcopalians, who had a national body which appointed bishops, who in turn appointed priests to parishes in their dioceses. The Methodists also had bishops, although they did not have priests and parishes. The most radical were the Baptists and Congregationalists. Their congregations, or local groups of believers, were the basic unit of organization; there was no group that oversaw the beliefs and practices of the many individual congregations. The Presbyterians had a system similar to the Episcopalians in that it was a pyramid, but built from the bottom up. Individual congregations were organized into local synods, which in turn formed the General Assemblies. As new groups, such as the Disciples of Christ, appeared in the mid nineteenth century, they tended to start with congregations linked by common belief, and then added some sort of structure above the congregational level either to maintain orthodox beliefs or to help congregations work together in the mission field or in extending charity.

Christology. Protestants were also conscious of differences of opinion among themselves as to who Christ was and what he represented. Almost every group considered Jesus to be the son of God, and therefore God himself, a part of the Trinity of Father, Son, and Holy Ghost. The one exception was the Unitarians, who claimed that the most reasonable belief was that God was a single being and that Jesus was simply a perfect man. Nearly every group of Protestants had historically considered the Crucifixion to be the act of salvation. This idea that Christ died for sinful humanity was called the doctrine of the atonement. There were, though, competing theories as to how Christ saved humanity. The Unitarians, for example, did not consider Christ's death as having a special saving value, because it was not the death of God. Instead, they claimed that Christ's most important action was his teaching; he provided the moral laws by which human beings should live. Other Protestants focused not on death or teachings, but on Christ's life because he manifested God's love for human beings.

Predestination. Mid-nineteenth-century American Protestants were also aware of differences among themselves on the issue of how individuals came to be saved from eternal damnation. The theory of predestination held that God had chosen the people who were going to heaven even before they had a chance to live their lives. Congregationalists, Presbyterians, and some Baptists had a history of believing in double predestination, in which case God chose, before human history began, whether each individual human being was going to heaven or to hell. (It was reasonable to think that an all-knowing, all-powerful God would have this all arranged beforehand.) Accordingly, it was possible to know from the general tenor of a person's life whether God had chosen him or her. People who seemed to enjoy God's favor on earth would not suffer a sudden reversal of fortune after death. However, it was not true that everyone who prospered on earth was undoubtedly headed for heaven; a more certain sign was a conversion or an awareness of one's own sinfulness and of God's salvation despite that sinfulness. In the meantime, one lived a good life simply out of respect to the all-powerful God who had laid down the moral law. Episcopalians, Methodists, and some Baptists were universalists, who claimed that God intended all humanity, not a chosen few, to be saved. People, though, had to respond to God's call for salvation. They had to believe what the New Testament stated, that salvation came through Christ alone. They had to act as though they believed, trying to lead good lives and to make themselves in some small measure worthy of the promise of eternal life. This idea that one's own behavior was necessary to salvation helped fuel mid-nineteenth-century interest in personal moral reforms.

The Millennium. One of the theological questions that most interested Protestants was that of the millennium, or the end of the world. For all Christians, the world's end was coordinated with the Second Coming, or the return to earth, of Jesus Christ. According to Matt. 24:36: "As for the exact day or hour, no one knows it, but the Father only." This Gospel verse was interpreted to mean that God would set in motion the chain of events leading to the world's end; there would be a cataclysmic event that would sweep away sinners and unbelievers, and then Jesus would return to rule over the few who remained, known as the "saved." Small congregations arose during this period that stressed believers' personal experiences and their relationship with the divine. These congregations tended to see historical events as the working out of a history predicted long ago in Scripture. They also tended to follow a leader—such as the Seventh-Day Adventist Ellen Gould Harmon White—who interpreted Scripture and who sometimes claimed to receive personal revelations.

Liberal Evangelicals. Other groups believed that sin would be defeated first, after which Christ would return. Accordingly, Christians were supposed to reform the world and make it a fitting place for Christ to come and reign as king. Believers poured their energy into spreading the Gospel and into passing laws that reflected their understanding of how God wanted the world to run, which they developed by consulting Scripture. These Protestants were liberal because they believed God intended the world and whole human family to be saved; they were evangelical because they believed that the Gospel outlined how to carry out divine will and that part of making the world ready for the Second Coming was converting it to Christianity.

Philosophic Inquiries. Both Gentiles and Jews continued the philosophical trends of the Enlightenment, an eighteenth-century intellectual movement. One hallmark of the Enlightenment was subjecting received wisdom to common sense and scientific method of study and rejecting traditional beliefs as unreasonable. The result was a tendency to disregard those elements of Christianity which could not be proved, such as the divinity of Christ, and to emphasize those parts that were reinforced by reason, such as monotheism and the importance of morality.

Spiritualism. Another trend also tested the boundaries of American Protestantism. Throughout most of recorded history, humans have divided reality into the physical or supernatural, which did not have boundaries of time, space or physicality. All Christians shared the belief that each soul was incarnated into just one person and that the soul had a life after the death of the body. The relation between the living and the dead was a matter of debate. Catholicism taught that the living could pray that the dead would go to heaven and become saints and that the saints could intercede with God to produce miracles. Protestants believed that each soul's fate was determined by the time of death, although different groups had their own teachings as to how. In the mid nineteenth century some people believed that they could communicate with the supernatural. Educated and prominent persons such as Sir Arthur Conan Doyle, the author of the Sherlock Holmes mysteries, and First Lady Mary Todd Lincoln were among the most famous practitioners of spiritualism.

Denominationalism. American religions in general, and Protestantism in particular, were divided into various denominations, separate religious entities, each with its own history, order of worship, organization, and clerical training. The name, such as Presbyterianism or Episcopalianism, usually described some unique feature at the time of the denomination's inception, but this was not always true by the middle of the nineteenth century. Congregationalists, for example, were not the only denomination that had different communities of worshipers; it shared this trait with the Baptists. Northern and Southern Christians agreed with other denominations in the same region more than they did with those of the same denomination in another geographic area.

Diversity through Expansion. The frontier also influenced American religious history. The purchase of the Louisiana Territory (1803) and lands obtained from Mexico (1848) added many Native American faiths as well as French and Spanish Catholics to the religious population of the United States. The frontier encouraged easterners to move west, where they had more freedom to develop according to their own inclinations. John Humphrey Noyes, who founded the Oneida community in upstate New York, and the Mormon Brigham Young of Utah were just two examples of religious leaders who sought out isolated areas so that their groups could live out their convictions without interference.

Diversity through Migration. Immigrants profoundly affected the religious landscape of the country during this era. Although German Jews were not being so actively persecuted as they were in earlier or later centuries, their chances for social and economic advancement were still greater in the United States. By the 1870s efforts in Germany to create a unified nation-state included an anti-Catholic cultural movement which, in turn, encouraged Catholic migration. By and large, though, new arrivals in America were actually economic migrants, people who had been displaced by the transition from agricultural to industrial economies at home and who preferred to ply their old trades in a new setting. One group came because of an economic and ecological disaster. Although Irish Catholics had been discriminated against at home, it was not until a blight destroyed successive years of potato crops that they migrated in large numbers.

The Lutheran Experience. When they migrated, people did not simply transplant their religions from the old home to the new. The Lutherans serve as an example of the complexities that could develop. During the nineteenth century the German Lutheran farmers and artisans who had settled in the countryside and rural towns of the Middle Atlantic area were joined by Lutherans from Denmark, Finland, Norway, and Sweden. As the numbers of Lutherans grew, congregations joined together in local synods which were formed into a General Synod, the better to found new congregations, to protect doctrinal standards, and to provide for an educated ministry. Unity in a synod, though, meant all the Lutherans together had to decide what stand to take on doctrinal questions. A confrontation began brewing in 1850, when some Lutherans began to protest that the denomination was becoming too American; it was using English, instead of German; it was incorporating doctrines from outside historical, or confessional, Lutheranism; and it was dropping traditional Lutheran practices and adopting those of other Protestant neighbors.

The Lutheran Spirit. Other Lutherans, though, led by Samuel Simon Schmucker, a professor of theology at the Lutheran Seminary in Gettysburg, Pennsylvania, thought the changes made for a purer and more authentic Lutheranism, free of historical entanglements with Catholicism. In 1855 an anonymous forty-two-page pamphlet called *Definite Synodical Platform* forced Lutherans to start taking sides. It recommended that the next General Synod meeting reject specific Lutheran teachings as leftovers from Catholicism and replace them with teachings developed in America. By 1857 the Lutheran Church had two national synods, the American-leaning General Synod and the Melanchthon Synod (named for Philipp Melanchthon, a sixteenth-century Lutheran theologian and author of one of Lutheranism's basic documents, the *Augsburg Confession*). Thereafter, synods multiplied, and when the Civil War broke out, Southern Lutherans organized their own synod, not out of doctrinal considerations but simply to reflect the fact that they were now in a different country. After the war, they did not reunite with the Northern branch but maintained a separate United Synod of the South.

Divisiveness. Meanwhile, the Northern synods continued to divide. One particular group, the upstate New York Franckean Synod, borrowed heavily from non-Lutheran evangelical liberals. When the General Synod admitted the Franckean Synod in 1864, other synods left and three years later formed a new General Council. Still more splits followed as more Lutherans immigrated to the United States and had to choose between joining other Lutherans or preserving the original ethnic context of their faith. In 1866 some immigrants served notice that ethnic context was more important than doctrinal purity; Lutheran and other German Protestants combined to form the Evangelical Church-Union of the West. Non-German Lutherans also preserved their ethnic background. As early as 1872 Finnish immigrants had their own Solomon Korteniemi Lutheran Society.

Faith and Slavery. The rise of a proslavery argument in the United States coincided with a shift in the view of many churches. Before the 1830s some Protestant ministers declared slavery to be immoral. By the 1850s, however, most members of the clergy had changed their outlook, arguing that slavery was not only compatible with Christianity but also necessary for the proper exercise of the Christian faith. Clergymen maintained that slavery provided an opportunity to display Christian responsibility toward one's inferiors and helped African Americans develop the virtues of humility and self-control. Meanwhile, Southerners increasingly criticized Northern antislavery evangelicals for condemning the allegedly superior social hierarchy of the South. After the Thirteenth Amendment to the Constitution made slavery unconstitutional in 1865, the question was whether the denominations could adjust their theology again and begin to consider the ethics of race relations.

The Next Challenge. Communist theoreticians Karl Marx and Friedrich Engels saw in the American Civil War proof of their theory that history progressed on the paths hacked out by economic change and class struggle. In the Civil War the rising middle class of the Union defeated the historic aristocracy of the slaveholding South. Marx and Engels expected that soon thereafter the middle class would be challenged by a rising proletariat determined to halt capitalist exploitation of the working class. During the war troops had to be used to quell riots in which the working class protested being drafted for what seemed "a rich man's war and a poor man's fight." Although they rejected the antireligious stance of Marx and Engels, American clergymen clearly saw that the relation between classes was a major question of the day, one that challenged the theological resources of many denominations. As heavy industrialization of the United States progressed, religious leaders began to question the assumptions of classical economic theory. Clerics viewed unrestricted business competition as an arrogant denial of Christian ethics and the unfair treatment of workers as a violation of basic Protestant virtue. Nevertheless, these concerns would not receive true expression until the Social Gospel movement of the last decades of the nineteenth century.

TOPICS IN THE NEWS

BEGINNINGS OF REFORM JUDAISM

A People Set Apart. One of the most important concepts in Judaism is that the Jews consider themselves to be the chosen people. Even though they had no country in the mid nineteenth century, the Jews still thought of themselves as a nation, a distinct group held together by God's covenant with them. In Europe anti-Semitism set Jews apart from the people among whom they lived. Until the early nineteenth century, most European governments restricted Jews to living in certain sections of cities called ghettos. Some laws limited the number of Jews who could marry in a given year, thus preventing Jewish population growth. Other statutes, meanwhile, prohibited Jews from receiving an education or from entering professional careers. Whether by their own choice or by the prejudices of others, Jews were a distinct group.

Early American Judaism. Before 1850 the majority of the Jews who came to the United States were Sephardim, Jews whose ancestors had lived in Spain and Portugal and who had been expelled in 1492 after the Christian rulers Ferdinand and Isabella seized the area from the Moorish Empire. Sephardic Jews settled in seaport communities such as Savannah, Charleston, Philadelphia, New York, and Newport. Since there were so few of them, the Sephardim did not have the community support they needed to keep every Jewish law. They had no rabbis and no one to sell them kosher, or ritually fit, food. Therefore, they were pragmatic reformers. They went without the traditional head coverings that every Jewish male was supposed to wear. Each congregation appointed a hazan, or leader from among the laity, who led the devout in prayer and sometimes preached. Early American Jews generally did not speak or read Hebrew fluently, just well enough to pronounce the prayers correctly. For some parts of synagogue worship, they used Ladino, a language based on Spanish that their ancestors had used; mostly, they used English.

The German Migration. During the early nineteenth century, the American Sephardim were joined by the first Ashkenazim, Jews from the German principalities and the Austro-Hungarian empire, and were called German Jews. German migration soon led to the creation of new synagogues because Sephardic and Ashkenazic Jews differed in rituals and forms of worship. German Jews also reacted to differences between American and Jewish culture in various ways. For example, the American workweek ran from Monday to Saturday, while Jews observed Saturday as a Sabbath on which work was forbidden. Other cultural conflicts existed as well. Jews belonged to the middle class economically, but not socially, and their religious practices seemed to be one reason. Middle-class, mostly Protestant, Americans attended church on Sunday morning in family units. There they did everything together: stand, sit, sing, and recite prayers. They used a language they all understood and listened to a sermon intended to edify and uplift them. Synagogue practice seemed unaesthetically chaotic by comparison. Services were held Friday night while Gentiles finished their work or indulged in recreation. Only the men had to attend, and if the women did come, they had to sit upstairs in a curtained-off balcony. Each man prayed at his own pace from his own prayer book, rather than reciting prayers aloud in common. They used books of Hebrew prayers, and while they could pronounce the Hebrew letters, they did not necessarily know what the words meant. If there was a sermon, it would be based on the Talmud, which was not a widely shared piece of Jewish literature but a biblical commentary put together over hundreds of years that only rabbis truly had time to study. German Jews divided into congregations, depending on how much change the congregation members wanted. However, all changes were animated by the same sort of pragmatism that had earlier inspired the Sephardim.

The First Rabbis. With the German Jewish migration came the first trained and ordained rabbis to work in the United States. They had begun their rabbinical careers in Europe and had worked with reform-minded congregations there. Leo Merzbacher migrated in 1841 and was soon followed by Max Lilienthal (1846), Isaac Mayer Wise (1846), David Einhorn (1855), and Samuel Adler (1857). When they came to the United States, they found congregations that had altered Jewish tradition because they lacked the means or opportunity to practice those traditions in middle-class American society. The newly arrived rabbis quickly implemented reforms.

From Nation to Religion. The Jewish reformers were animated by an idea which found its expression in an

The first building of Hebrew Union College in Cincinnati, Ohio, 1875

and out of step with the nineteenth century, they were unnecessary if the real purpose of Judaism was to bring monotheism and a right understanding of the importance of an ethical life into the world. Isaac Mayer Wise, considered a moderate reformer, judged each custom in the light of Jewish history. Therefore, he kept the idea of a Saturday Sabbath, despite the inconvenience, because it was of scriptural origin. However, he dispensed with the bar mitzvah, a ceremony in which a thirteen-year-old boy formally assumed his responsibilities in Jewish worship, because it was not found in Scripture. Sabato Morais, who in 1851 became rabbi of Congregation Mikveh Israel in Philadelphia, thought that Jewish tradition was as appropriate to a religion as it was to a nation, and his position led him to be one of the forebears of Conservative Judaism. Isaac Leeser, who had led services at Mikveh Israel before Morais's arrival, preserved Orthodox Judaism and rejected the idea that Halakah or Jewish law was amenable to the kinds of changes, especially the deletions, that Einhorn, Wise, and sometimes even Morais advocated. Nevertheless, the development of Conservative, Orthodox, and Reform branches of Judaism did not represent such serious deviations in teaching that one party considered the others to be false.

Life in American Jewish Households. Exactly how Jews lived depended on how much of Jewish law they wished to observe, whether they lived in a community that could support their desired level of observance, and on their age and sex. In general, all Jews lived within a series of cycles. Everyday observance of Jewish law included prayers for the adult men and keeping kosher or observing dietary laws, as the women prepared the food and the family ate it. Weekly rounds included Friday night or Saturday morning visits to the synagogue for Conservative and Orthodox Jews and Sunday services for families of Reform Jews, and the women's preparation of the Sabbath meal. For Orthodox women who had access to a mikvah, or ritual bath, there was a monthly round of washings that coincided with their menstrual cycle. One interesting development in Judaism was the evolution of the annual cycle of holidays as the Jewish calendar meshed with the secular American one. The Jewish New Year started in the American autumn, with a holiday called Rosh Hashanah. It was followed by the Day of Atonement, or Yom Kippur, on which Jews fasted and prayed that God's mercy might outweigh their failures to keep the covenant. These were the High Holy Days of the Jewish calendar. Sukkoth, a harvest festival, came about a month after; usually occurring in December, Hanukkah had historically been a minor celebration. As Christmas became a more important holiday, and a more secular one, Hanukkah grew to match it. Passover had always been an important celebration, with its element of renewal. In Europe, where Jewish income was quite limited, that renewal was expressed by thorough housecleaning and by preparing and consuming foods that were specifically for Passover, using tableware especially

1869 meeting held in Philadelphia and chaired by Rabbi Samuel Hirsch. The meeting promulgated a fundamental reinterpretation of a central event in Jewish history. In 70 A.D. the Romans leveled the Jewish capital of Jerusalem, leaving only the Western Wall of the Temple standing, and scattered the Jewish population. Jews interpreted this event, as they had interpreted the period of slavery in Egypt and the Babylonian captivity, as punishment for straying from the covenant. Reform Jews added that it also facilitated the covenant. If the Jews were God's chosen people, then they could spread that revelation among the people with whom they lived. Rather than look for the restoration of Israel, Jews, therefore, should transform their concept of themselves as a nation into a concept of themselves as a religion. Aside from emphasizing the theological concept of monotheism, Judaism advanced the importance of living a good, ethical, moral, and righteous life that honored God, served humanity, and secured one's salvation. Reform Judaism asked its followers to give up the desire espoused in a Passover ritual, "Next year in Jerusalem!" Rather than wait for the Messiah to restore Jerusalem, Jews were to be the Messiah who brought truth to the world.

Branches of Judaism. The understanding of Judaism as a religion stimulated a spectrum of responses. David Einhorn, considered a radical in his day, dispensed with many Jewish customs. Not only were they inconvenient reserved for that occasion. In the United States renewal was expressed not only by housecleaning but by purchasing new clothes as well.

Community Life. In Europe anti-Semitic legislation and poverty conspired to keep the Jewish community compact. In that situation the *kehillah,* or community, provided for several services considered necessary to Judaism: it arranged for the care of the orphaned or sick, collected money for the poor, and made sure there were people competent to slaughter meat according to kosher ritual or to perform *bris,* the circumcision ceremony which brought an infant male into the covenant. In the United States capitalism and freedom of religion created a different situation. Individuals who had special skills that served the community marketed those skills. The ritual slaughterer of the ghetto became the kosher butcher with a shop. Other people found work as cantors, singing at services, or as *mohels,* performing the bris ceremony. In addition, wealthy Jews many times came together to build institutions such as orphanages and hospitals. In Philadelphia Jews borrowed from a Protestant institution to develop Sunday Schools, where poor Jews could come on their weekly day off from work to learn to read.

Organizing Reform. Although the Jewish population worked together to provide social services, the different branches of Judaism had their own institutions for education. The Orthodox rabbi Isaac Leeser was one of the most prominent Hebrew educational reformers. He began editing the weekly newspaper, *Occident,* in 1843. Between 1867 and 1873 he and a committee of Orthodox rabbis operated Maimonides College in Philadelphia. Among the Reform Jews, Isaac Mayer Wise was the leader. Beginning in 1855, conferences of Reform rabbis met in order to obtain agreement on teaching methods. In 1873 Wise organized the Union of American Hebrew Congregations, an organization through which Jews could determine which teachings and practices could be left to individual congregations to approve and which should be kept uniform. Wise hoped to keep all Jewish synagogues and temples in one organization. In 1875 he became the first president of the new Hebrew Union College of Cincinnati, which not only provided an institution of higher education for Jewish males but also provided specialized preparation for Reform rabbis.

Challenges to Judaism. While the branching out of Judaism into Conservative, Orthodox, and Reform was amiable, some Jews regarded it uneasily. Reform Judaism, which measured all traditions by nineteenth-century standards, seemed to be leaning too close to Unitarianism. In 1874 Solomon Schindler became the rabbi of Temple Israel in Boston and from that position moved so far into the circles of city reformers that he eventually resigned his post in favor of a career in secular reform. In 1876 Felix Adler left Reform Judaism to found the New York Society for Ethical Culture. The most common reason a person ceased to practice Judaism was marriage

Poor Jewish children with Talmud Yelodim, a Cincinnati community activist, circa 1870

to a Gentile. Ironically, at the same time that Jews feared Reformers were causing Judaism to lose its distinctive character, there were incidents of anti-Semitism indicating that Gentile Americans still considered the Jews as a people set apart. In December 1862 Gen. Ulysses S. Grant issued General Order No. 11, which ordered the evacuation of all Jews living in conquered Tennessee, an act meant to punish them for trading with the enemy. In 1877 Joseph Seligman, who had migrated from Germany in 1837 and had made a fortune in the clothing business and investment banking, was turned away from a resort hotel at Saratoga Springs, New York, because he was Jewish. In Europe such anti-Semitism led to Zionism, the idea that if Jews were indeed a separate national group, then they should have their own nation-state in the land of Israel.

Sources:

Hasia R. Diner, *A Time for Gathering: The Second Migration, 1820–1880,* volume II of *The Jewish People in America,* edited by Henry L. Feingold (Baltimore: Johns Hopkins University Press, 1992);

Arthur Hertzberg, *The Jews in America, Four Centuries of an Uneasy Encounter: A History* (New York: Simon & Schuster, 1989);

Israel Knox, *Rabbi in America: The Story of Isaac M. Wise* (Boston: Little, Brown, 1957);

Jacob Rader Marcus, *The American Jews, 1585–1990: A History* (Brooklyn, N.Y.: Carlson, 1995).

CHANGING FACES OF AMERICAN CATHOLICISM

International Institution. Like Judaism, Catholicism played a vital role in the international movements of people and ideas during the middle decades of the nineteenth century. Prior to 1850 Catholicism in the United States drew much of its population from a few sources. There was a small community of descendants of colonists, English Catholics relocated to Maryland, whose descendants spread out across that state and into Kentucky. To this was added the sparse population of the former French Mississippi colonies, transferred to the United States via the Louisiana Purchase (1803), and the equally small numbers of Spanish-speaking Catholics brought in when Mexico ceded territory to the United States in 1848.

Converts. American Catholicism expanded partly through a small stream of converts. Some were prominent at the time of their conversion. A particularly important group was the converts from the Protestant Episcopal Church, a denomination with roots in the Church of England. During the 1840s an upheaval affected the Church of England; it was known as the Oxford Movement, because it was centered in that university, and also called the Tractarian Movement, because its leaders wrote tracts or pamphlets that explained their evolving theology. A key event of the Oxford Movement came in 1845, when one of its leaders, John Henry Newman, converted from the Church of England to Roman Catholicism; he later became a famous writer and cardinal. American Episcopalianism had its own Oxford Movement® In 1851 Levi Silliman Ives, then Episcopal bishop of North Carolina, converted to Catholicism. In 1872 James Roosevelt Bayley, another convert from Episcopalianism, reached one of the highest positions in Catholicism when he succeeded the scion of a Maryland Catholic family, Martin Spalding, as the archbishop of Baltimore, then one of the most important dioceses in the United States.

Immigration. The real growth in Catholicism, though, came through migration. While some immigrants were displaced from their former homes by the forces of industrialism, one important group came as the result of a disaster. Famine in Ireland sent approximately one million Irish to America in ten years. (The United States had a reasonably accurate count of people arriving at its seaports but not of those arriving at Canadian seaports and walking across the border.) These immigrants were not uniformly devout or observant Catholics because the English had suppressed their religion so that it could not be used as a basis of resistance to imperial rule. In the United States, however, they could practice their religion freely and develop a distinct Irish-American Catholic identity.

Universalism and Localism. Theologically, *catholic* meant that God's reign extended throughout the world. (It was similar to what Protestants meant by universal.) Historically, the word *catholic* was also a way of conveying the idea that the unity of faith outweighed local differences. From the viewpoint of Catholic leaders, there was no problem in sending clergy from one country to minister to another. While other denominations sent American-born missionaries to convert the Indians, Catholic missionaries in this country were primarily Italian Jesuits. Some American Catholics claimed that theirs was a special expression of the worldwide faith because it was formed under conditions of separation of church and state and in a situation in which clergy were scarce. It was also culturally distinct from the way in which the incoming migrants practiced the same faith. To American Catholics' claims of uniqueness were added the immigrants' own claims that they, too, faced special situations which required them to preserve their faith in its distinctive forms, with the assistance of clergy who spoke their own language. The Vatican continued to stress the unity of faith over the diversity of its expression, while at the same time acknowledging the basic differences between American and European Catholicism.

Religious Institutes. One group with firsthand experience of the differences among Catholics were the members of religious institutes. These institutes were communities of men and women who came together to perfect their own spiritual lives. They all took vows of poverty, chastity, and obedience, and some took additional vows to promote a particular way of life or mission, like the Benedictines, who were devoted to continuous residence in one monastery. The institutes either held land or property in common or undertook some kind of missionary work. Immigrants and their institutions, formed under European circumstances, had to adjust to American conditions. An example was the Christian Brothers, an organization composed of men who did not become priests but who dedicated their lives to teaching. In Europe they taught poor boys, but because of the rigid class system common at the time, many boys who came under their care generally moved no further up than the working class. The greater socioeconomic mobility of the United States led the Christian Brothers to maintain their commitment to teaching the poor, but to switch from purely vocational training to teaching the liberal arts to prepare young men for higher education.

Establishing the Hierarchy. Religious institutes were special bodies within the Catholic community. Most Catholics were under the care of secular clergy, so called because they lived in the world and did not belong to religious communities but were responsible to bishops, the ordinary authority in the diocese. The papacy designated the geographical borders of new dioceses and appointed the bishops. In most countries, the bishops established parishes and appointed pastors. The United States was considered mission territory and thus fell under a different set of rules where parishes and pastors were concerned. What American Catholics commonly called parishes were in canon law known as missions, which could be established by the bishop as needed. What Catholics called pastors were in canon law rectors (which is why their houses were called rectories), who could be transferred according to need, as determined by the bishop. The gap between the canon law that governed most of the settled Catholic world and the exceptions that were made for American mission territory provoked problems. American bishops claimed that the exceptions, which gave those bishops extraordinary power, were needed in the special circumstances of the growing United States; they had to be able to erect or suppress missions and to transfer clergy in order to meet changing needs. The clergy, though, realized that regularly applied canon law would give them greater powers and protections. A further complication came because some bishops sent their most promising clergy for training at the Urban College of the Propagation of the Faith in Rome. Well versed in canon law and having made the acquaintance of some powerful people at the Vatican, Roman-trained clergy frequently challenged episcopal authority in the United States. The situation was not resolved until 1908, when the United States ceased to be mission territory and thus fell under regular canon law.

Institutions. Parishes were the most important institutions in Catholicism, for it was at parish churches that Catholics went to worship. However, they were not the only institutions in the faith. Catholics were supposed to be charitable, to look after the needy. The inexpensive labor provided by charitable religious orders and the funds sent by European Catholics via agencies such as the Austrian Leopoldsverein and the French Society for the Propagation of the Faith made charity possible. During the nineteenth century Catholics began to build systems of charitable care. There were foundling asylums for abandoned babies, orphanages for children who could feed and care for themselves but who were too young to work, detention centers for juveniles, rest homes for the aged, and hospitals for the sick. This charitable network was incomplete and loosely organized, and bishops called for institutions to deal with the most pressing needs, rather than focusing on long-range goals. Religious orders founded institutions in accordance with their historical missions or with the most obvious needs. Each institution was staffed, managed, and funded differently, a system which meant that some flourished while others floundered. The various agencies, though, laid the foundation for later systemization.

Devotionalism. Catholic piety was illustrated in many ways, including participation at Sunday mass and reception of the sacraments, as well as activities individuals pursued according to what they felt they needed for full spiritual lives. In the last category went prayers and countless devotions, such as pilgrimages to shrines or the wearing of medals or scapulars (a long band of cloth worn over the shoulders) to acknowledge the protection of a heavenly patron. Tradition linked devotion with particular places; for example, nineteenth-century American Catholics called the area around Jerusalem the Holy Land and venerated the places associated with Christ's birth, ministry, and death although it was too expensive for them to visit those sites. Catholics around the world also developed a sense of holy times. The holy hour was a sixty-minute period of meditation and prayer that generally took place before the Host, or reserved communion bread. A novena set aside nine days (hence the name) during which Catholics would recite special prayers to a patron saint or to Jesus or Mary. Variations on the novena were the triduum, three days of special prayer (with roots in the most important three-day period, from Good Friday to Easter Sunday), the thirteen Tuesdays

Bishop Patrick Lynch of Charleston, South Carolina

devoted to Saint Anthony of Padua before his 13 June feast day (Saint Anthony had been buried on a Tuesday), First Friday devotion to the Sacred Heart of Jesus, and First Saturday devotion to Mary and the rosary. Catholics also turned their energies to holy actions, such as saying the rosary or participating in the Corpus Christi procession. These new devotions represented a departure from colonial American Catholicism with its emphasis on quiet, inward meditation and reflection and living of a good life. While some historians have linked the new devotions with the arrival of immigrants, others maintain that Catholics altogether were actually making a transition to a distinctly nineteenth-century piety.

Civil War. When the crisis over slavery led to war, American Catholics generally supported their local government. Bishop John Fitzpatrick of Boston and Archbishop John Hughes of New York traveled to Europe to present the Union stance and to stave off foreign intervention. Bishop Patrick Lynch of Charleston, South Carolina, undertook the same task for the Confederacy. When federal conscription of soldiers met with riotous opposition among urban, ethnic, working-class Catholics, the priests of Boston contacted local government and parish leaders to avert a crisis, and the archbishop of New York addressed rioters in the name of law and order. With their tradition of charity, Catholics were especially important in ministering to the sick. Catholic sisters accounted for one-tenth of all nurses serving with both armies. Parishes near the theatre of war were frequently requisitioned for hospitals.

A Sister of Mercy with the medical staff at Douglas Military Hospital, Washington, D.C., during the Civil War

Reconstruction. American Catholic bishops had developed a system whereby each maintained diocesan independence but all could work together for specific goals. When there was only one archdiocese and a few dioceses, the archbishop and bishops met in what was called a provincial council; after the Vatican created more archdioceses, the archbishops and bishops convened in plenary councils. The American hierarchy held its second plenary council in 1866, immediately after the Civil War. The meeting resulted in several policy statements. The bishops, recognizing that they had a unique opportunity to attract newly freed slaves to the faith, called for evangelization. Few answered the call; many American bishops lacked financial and personnel resources for such a program, and many more let their prejudices hinder their ministry. Similarly, the bishops issued a call for the building of parochial schools in order to educate young Catholics while protecting them from anti-Catholic prejudice in public and other private institutions. However, again the bishops lacked the means for a concerted effort, and some of them, such as John Fitzpatrick of Boston, questioned the wisdom of building a separate school system. Therefore, the hierarchy made recommendations rather than requirements.

Vatican I. Catholicism was going through a reconstruction of its own in the late 1860s, which culminated in Pope Pius IX's call for an ecumenical council of Catholic bishops from all over the world. In this case, the papacy had established an agenda of issues for the bishops to discuss, the most significant of which was the doctrine of papal infallibility. Popes were considered to be incapable of making mistakes when, in their official capacity, they issued rulings on the teachings of Catholic faith and morals. Some American bishops, including Peter Kenrick, archbishop of Saint Louis, were not convinced of the legitimacy of papal infallibility; Kenrick thought that it was the bishops, acting together with the papacy, who were infallible. Nevertheless, the council voted in favor of pronouncing the new doctrine in December 1869. (The one time a pope has actually used this power occurred in 1950, when Pope Pius XII declared that every Catholic must believe that Mary was assumed bodily into heaven without undergoing the usual decay in the grave, a doctrine known as the Assumption.) After the 1870s one of the most important issues facing American Catholics was what was called "Romanization," the degree to which Catholics subordinated various national and ethnic traditions to a concept of the universal church as envisioned by papal authorities.

Sources:

Jay P. Dolan, *The American Catholic Experience: A History from Colonial Times to the Present* (Garden City, N.Y.: Doubleday, 1985);

Mary Ewens, O.P., *The Role of the Nun in Nineteenth-Century America: Variations on the International Theme* (New York: Arno, 1978);

James Hennesey, S.J., *American Catholics: A History of the Roman Catholic Community in the United States* (New York & Oxford: Oxford University Press, 1981);

Ann Taves, *The Household of Faith: Roman Catholic Devotions in Mid-Nineteenth-Century America* (Notre Dame, Ind.: University of Notre Dame Press, 1986).

DIFFERENCES BETWEEN CATHOLICS AND PROTESTANTS

Dimensions. Nativism, or a policy favoring native inhabitants as opposed to immigrants, gained prominence in the period 1850–1877. Many immigrants to the United States at this time were poor German and Irish Catholics who settled in urban centers. Besides the ethnic and class distinctions between native-born Protestants and newly arrived Catholics the religious differences were also important. In fact, the debate between nativists and newcomers illustrated the tremendous diversity of the American religious experience and had a practical effect on the course of American Catholicism.

Catholic Citizenry. Americans often saw the United States as the opposite of Catholic Europe. In the United States, people were self-governing. They had a certain amount of education and could generally manage their own affairs, and they could elect state and federal officials to direct those projects which benefited the whole community. Americans believed that in Europe people were not self-governing and that church leaders preached that all authority came from above, that God chose some people to be religious rulers and some to be secular rulers and placed the rest in positions where they had only to be obedient to such divinely constituted authority to be considered good, moral persons. Such notions affected American attitudes toward immigrants. Americans worried that newcomers were not adequately prepared for self-government and that they would seek to import their traditional rulers to the United States. Moreover, Americans feared that immigrants had been so accustomed to traditional authority that once they came to a place of relative freedom they would become licentious and rebellious.

The Pope. American Catholic leaders such as Orestes Brownson, Isaac Hecker, Francis P. Kenrick, Martin John Spalding, and John Hughes all argued that papal rule was a historical development which showed God's providential plan. As a citizen of Italy, Pope Pius IX was subject to Italian law, which could cut into religious freedom and the exercise of the papal office. Only as ruler of independent territory could the Pope have the political freedom to fulfill spiritual duties. In no sense was the Pope a political leader for American Catholics, and in no way was historical development of papal secular rule a model for every single country's political situation. Thus, American Catholics could be loyal to the United States government and obedient to the Pope also.

Property Rights. In the period 1850–1877 the federal government had no laws regarding how a religious body could hold property; this issue was in state hands. By the 1850s the states had disestablished religion depriving all churches of government support, and, without consulting each other, had passed similar laws permitting religious bodies to hold property. Like any other not-for-profit enterprise, religious groups incorporated and set up boards of trustees. Although this was done entirely to conform with secular law, it had a spiritual dimension. It was a symbol of American religious freedom that the people, through their trustees, owned their religious property. Because Catholicism's canon law made bishops responsible for their dioceses and pastors responsible for their parishes, these people could not be excluded from boards of trustees. Clergymen, animated either by a sense of responsibility under canon law, or as some charged, by a desire for power, insisted on holding property. Also, few lay trustee corporations had the necessary financial stability. Yet the integration of Catholic needs into the overall system of religious property ownership was relatively simple. Two models prevailed. Some states used a type of trusteeship called corporation sole, in which the bishop was the only trustee for all the diocesan property in the state. Upon entering office, the bishop made out a will naming the successor bishop as inheritor of the trusteeship, to avoid problems of probate. In other states each piece of diocesan property was separately incorporated and each parish had to have a board of trustees. The bishop, his episcopal assistant, and the pastor were always ex officio members of the board; there were also two lay men of the pastor's choosing.

Temperance. A crusade to curb excessive drinking started in the antebellum period, shedding light on the differences between Catholicism and Protestantism. Poor productivity in the workplace and a decrease in morals, as well as religious concerns, caused this movement. Those who searched the Scriptures for advice on contemporary living focused on a verse which appears in Matt. 26:29, Mark 14:25, and Luke 22:18, in which Jesus shares the cup of wine with his disciples at the Last Supper, saying "I tell you I will not drink this fruit of the vine from now until the day when I drink it new with you

THE LARGEST DENOMINATIONS, 1860	
Denomination	**Congregations**
Baptist	12,150
Congregational	2,234
Disciple of Christ	2,100
Dutch Reformed	440
Episcopal	2,145
German Reformed	676
Lutheran	2,128
Methodist	19,883
Presbyterian	6,406
Roman Catholic	2,550
Society of Friends (Quakers)	726
Unitarian	264
Universalist	664

Source: Edwin Scott Gaustad, *Historical Atlas of Religion in America,* revised edition (New York: Harper & Row, 1976), p. 43.

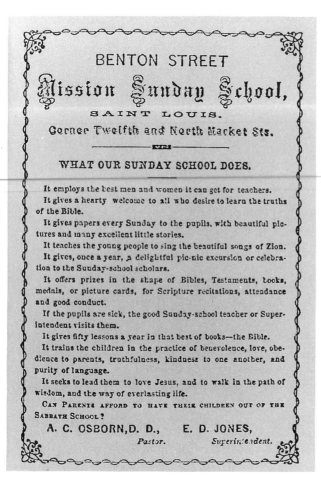

An advertisement for the Benton Street Mission Sunday School in Saint Louis, Missouri, 1860s

in my Father's reign." Some Protestants took this so literally that they substituted unfermented grape juice for wine at communion and generally abstained from all alcoholic drinks in anticipation of the Second Coming. For the Methodists, who sought to cultivate personal perfection, alcohol was like smoking or dancing, a forbidden activity. Catholics, meanwhile, distinguished between the mere use and sinful abuse of alcohol, and as a result many Protestants thought they had drinking problems. The abuse of alcohol led to parallel organizations for Catholics and non-Catholics. The non-Catholics had their Washington Society, in which men who formerly drank took a pledge to abstain from further alcohol consumption. Catholics had Father Theobald Matthew, an Irish priest who sponsored such groups as the Pennsylvania Catholic Total Abstinence Society. In general, though, Catholics lagged behind non-Catholics in their support for government action to control drinking. In 1846 towns in New York began to withhold licenses for the sale of liquor. Five years later Maine passed the first statewide prohibition law, and as Catholic immigrants poured into the country, other states followed suit. In 1852 Vermont, Rhode Island, and the Minnesota territorial legislature prohibited liquor sales; Michigan followed suit in 1853 and Connecticut in 1854.

Sabbath Observance. Protestant and Catholic conflict over the Sabbath was obscured by conflict within Protestantism. Traditionally, Protestants had observed Sunday as the Sabbath in honor of their belief that Jesus had risen from the dead on the Sunday after the Crucifixion. During the 1830s one group argued that what God really intended was for believers to follow Scripture strictly, which would mean moving the Sabbath back to Saturday; this group became known as Seventh-Day Adventists. (They took the name "Adventists" because they expected Christ's imminent return.) Among more-mainstream Protestants, the oldest American denominations, such as the Congregationalists and Presbyterians, centered their Sunday Sabbath observance on churchgoing and preaching. Even those who were not full members of the church were expected to come and sit in a pew on Sunday morning. Protestants tried to make the pews comfortable by enclosing them in structures like modern jury boxes to shield the attendees' feet from drafts and by putting plush cushions on the seats. For some, there was also an afternoon service. Work was forbidden, and, given the amount of time people were expected to be in church, it was logistically difficult. Liberal Protestants, who argued that one could receive godly instruction in manifold ways, modified this order of worship. They had no objection to attending church, but they included more activities, prayers (Congregationalists had one at the beginning and one at the end of the sermon), music played on instruments (some Congregationalists limited themselves to the voices of the attendees), and rituals. Lutheran services had their share of prayers and sermons, but they also had rituals carried over from Europe, especially singing in four-part harmony accompanied by organ music. After the service, the family might go out to a beer garden, where even the children and their mother imbibed a little and where the singing continued, albeit with more-secular songs. The main point of contention for nativists was not that the Catholics had even more ritual and even more music, but that Catholics did not explicitly prohibit all work on the Sabbath. Catholics responded that, indeed, they did not, and they turned this Protestant criticism to their advantage, claiming that God did not intend that workers sacrifice opportunities to earn a living. As long as they attended mass (which could be held as early as 5:30 A.M.) on Sunday, they could go to work.

The Sexual Order. The ability of an adult to choose or forego marriage was another difference between Protestants and Catholics. For Protestants, it seemed evident that God intended people to live in families, with specific roles for women as wives and mothers. Celibacy not only seemed contrary to the will of God, it seemed futile in the face of human sexual attraction. The early nineteenth century also saw an outpouring of sensational novels such as Rebecca Reed's *Six Months in a Convent* (1835) and Maria Monk's *Awful Disclosures of the Hotel Dieu Nunnery in Montreal* (1836). In these books innocent young women entered convents under the impression that there they would seek the will of God. What they supposedly found was a kind of brothel in which the sisters were reserved for the pleasure of the ostensibly celibate clergy. Any children born of these unions were quickly baptized, to ensure salvation of their souls, and then just as quickly murdered and buried in the basement, so that their bodies would not betray the secret of convent sexual activity. The stories were exaggerated, but many nativists sincerely believed that convents contravened the natural order of things. When they achieved political power, they attempted to do something about it.

Convent Inspection Laws. Politicians supported by the nativist American Party swept the Massachusetts state legislature elections in the fall of 1854. The nativist-dominated legislature convened in January 1855. The next month one town petitioned it to look into charges that young women were being held in convents against their will, perhaps for nefarious purposes. By March a convent inspection committee was touring the state, showing up at Catholic institutions and examining the premises, looking into closets to see if any reluctant nuns were being hidden away until the inspectors left. The activities of the committee provoked even non-Catholics, who sometimes sent daughters to convent-run schools for a portion of their education. The committee hurt its own cause by its behavior during its leisure hours on its inspection tour; the bills it submitted to the state legislature for reimbursement included many incurred at bars and saloons and one charged by a woman with a record of prostitution. By late 1855 the committee was in disgrace, as was the party that supported them. In fact, most of the American Party candidates failed at state reelection attempts in the fall of 1855.

Homes or Orphanages? The care of children was a contentious issue for Catholics and Protestants. States organized orphanages and foundling asylums, but both Catholics and Protestants objected to these—Catholics because they feared Protestant teaching dominated and Protestants because they feared there was not enough of their teaching, and that the children would be better educated and have more successful lives if they were raised in conventional family settings in small towns or on farms. To this end, private agencies such as the New York Children's Aid Society accepted children who were orphaned or whose poor parents relinquished control over them and placed the children for adoption in western communities. Catholics regarded this practice as child stealing. Because there were not enough Catholic families to adopt orphaned children, and because some children were not orphans but could not be cared for at home, Catholics erected orphanages to tend to their young under the auspices of nuns and priests.

Abolition. Pope Gregory XVI condemned the international slave trade in 1839, but the papacy never voiced concerns over domestic slave traffic or slavery itself in America. Without guidance from their leaders, Ameri-

An 1871 *Harper's Weekly* cartoon by Thomas Nast depicting Catholic bishops as alligators attempting to dominate the American way of life

can Catholics emulated the surrounding society. It is also noteworthy that people active in the antislavery movement mixed with those active in the nativist movement, and such association with nativism was enough to condemn antislavery in American Catholic minds. The result was that Catholics, who kept abreast of Protestants in reforms such as temperance, were among the most conservative when it came to the issues that divided the country before and during the Civil War.

Labor Reform. Nor were Catholics in the forefront of the discussion of the proper ethical treatment of wage laborers that began in the late 1860s. The bulk of Catholics were working-class people, but they did not consider themselves bound to that socioeconomic station. Like Protestants, some of them moved into the ranks of entrepreneurs and professionals, and so there could be no one Catholic teaching on economic life that suited all members. Catholic leaders also questioned the techniques of the labor movement. The Molly Maguires in the Pennsylvania coal region in the 1870s and the workers who started the Baltimore and Ohio Railroad strike in 1877 used violent tactics. They thought that their employers controlled the political and court systems and could not be hurt through economic tactics such as boycotts. In addition, when employers brought in substitute workers, or scabs, workers had to fight to protect their jobs. Whatever their justification, Catholic bishops saw laborers as fomenting violence against acceptably constituted authority. Furthermore, unions such as the Knights of Labor required members to take oaths of secrecy, promising not to reveal organizational confidences. While they initially took very cautious stands on these issues, American bishops were motivated to try to understand why the labor movement acted as it did and to see if these actions could be seen as acceptable to Catholic moral teaching. By the late 1870s the Catholic Church became a source of thoughtful analysis on the class and labor issues of the day.

Sources:

Ray Allen Billington, *The Protestant Crusade, 1800-1860: A Study of the Origins of American Nativism* (New York: Macmillan, 1938);

Patrick Carey, *People, Priests, and Prelates: Ecclesiastical Democracy and the Tensions of Trusteeism* (Notre Dame, Ind.: University of Notre Dame Press, 1987);

Norman H. Clark, *Deliver Us from Evil: An Interpretation of American Prohibition* (New York & London: Norton, 1976).

NORTH AND SOUTH

Heading Toward Disunion. Prior to the Civil War, no American faith took a stand on the question of what, if anything, justified secession from the Union. When the war started in 1861, some denominations escaped its divisiveness by virtue of their structure. The Disciples of Christ, for example, were organized around individual congregations with no central authority; thus different congregations could take individual stands without creating denominational dissent. For other faiths, the process was more wrenching.

Presbyterianism. The Presbyterians had begun dividing as early as 1800. Old School Presbyterians, who emphasized a trained clergy called by elders to specific congregations and gathered into synods for discussion of doctrinal matters, predominated in the South. The New School, which permitted a less educated ministry and a more congregational polity, predominated in New England and the Northwest frontier. Both Old and New Schools had General Assemblies, at which delegates from congregations and synods discussed and set doctrine for the denomination. When pressed to rule on the morality of slavery, the Old School General Assembly in 1845 pointed out that slavery was found in the Bible, and was not categorically condemned there. By 1849 it had developed a more complex position. Although slavery was found in the Bible, in the United States it was the secular authorities whose laws defined and regulated slavery, and thus the General Assembly would take no stand on it. The next year, the New School General Assembly ruled in the opposite way, saying that even though slavery could be found described in Scripture, this historical account was not meant as divine sanction. In 1857 the New School Presbyterians divided over slavery, creating Southern and Northern New Schools. In 1860 the Old School General Assembly met after the November elections had raised Abraham Lincoln to the presidency and after South Carolina had begun the process of secession. In conformity with its position of respecting established civil authority, some assemblymen professed loyalty to the Union, which created a split between Northern and Southern Old School Presbyterians.

Methodism. The Methodists also felt the divisive effects of slavery. John Wesley, the founder of Methodism, had discouraged slaveholding, but American missionaries, eager for converts, did not enforce this as an absolute requirement for membership in good standing. However, two other characteristics of Methodism guaranteed that, sooner or later, slavery would be an issue. First, Methodism emphasized the individual's efforts to be a truly good Christian and to abstain from sinful activities. Second, Methodism had bishops that met in annual General Conferences and discussed doctrines that were later binding on the whole denomination, so there had to be some kind of general agreement or a schism. The schisms started with the formation of the Wesleyan Methodist Church in Michigan in 1841 and the Methodist Wesleyan Connection in New York in 1842. ("Wesleyan" was a way of claiming that these Methodists held more closely to John Wesley's teachings than did other Methodists.) Then, in 1844, the Methodist General Conference voted that one of its own members, Bishop James O. Andrew, would have to cease acting in his episcopal capacity so long as he held slaves. Southern delegates made it clear this was unacceptable to them. At first, the overriding concern was to maintain the Christian values of peace and amity, if not unity and opposition to slavery. The General Conference agreed on a Plan of Separation for the two geographic wings of Methodism. In May 1845 delegates from Southern Methodist congregations met at Louisville, Kentucky, to establish their own General Conference. Northern Methodists were unable to maintain their equanimity. Those who took abolition seriously were upset that the Southern Methodists had been allowed to leave and that more had not been made of the sinfulness of slaveholding. There was also controversy over how to divide up the Methodists' book-publishing enterprise. The result was that in 1848 the Northern Methodists voted to consider the 1844 Plan of Separation null and void. However, it was too late. The Methodist Episcopal Church, South, was already a reality.

Baptists. When the Methodists gathered to vote on Bishop Andrew's slaveholding, the Baptists were also considering their stance on slavery. The Baptists had no central authority, such as the Methodist General Conference, that set standards for all members of the faith. They did, however, have a Board of Foreign Missions and a Board of Home Missions. In 1844 the Home Mission Board rejected James E. Reeves as a missionary on the grounds that he was a slaveholder. The Alabama Baptist Convention then requested the Foreign Mission Board to state its policy regarding the appointment of slaveholders, and the board replied that it, too, would not appoint them. The Southern Baptists' reaction turned the slavery issue from a congregational to a denominational matter. Delegates from nine southern states met at a convention held in Augusta, Georgia, on 8 May 1845. They made recommendations for incorporating an organization to provide leadership for all Southern Baptists. On 27 December Georgia granted a corporate charter to the Southern Baptist Convention. The charter contained a provision that a meeting of delegates be held every three years starting the next year, and, accordingly, delegates met in Richmond in 1846.

Julia Ward Howe, whose "Battle Hymn of the Republic" inspired Northern soldiers and citizens alike, 1861

Faith and Warfare. When the Civil War broke out in 1861, the quarrel over slavery receded temporarily into the background. War itself was a terrible thing, and, for some, such as the historic peace churches of the Amish, Mennonites, Moravians, and Quakers, bearing arms for the government was forbidden. Many Christians viewed war as divine judgment and punishment for national sins. War also contained within itself one way to expiate those sins and to return to the proper ways, through obedience to divinely sanctioned authority as expressed by military service. For Northerners, Congregationalist minister Edward Beecher formulated the doctrine of "organic sin," explaining that sin was more than personal failing; it was systemic, it could be found in a nation and its institutions, and, in the case of slavery, it could now be eradicated. All denominations accepted the importance of obedience to civil authorities, and none seemed to have used the start of the war to question the precise nature of that loyalty. For those in Union states, the authorities included the federal government, while for those in the Confederacy, the authorities included its government. In her "Battle Hymn of the Republic" Julia Ward Howe put forth a different thesis: rather than simply obeying authority, soldiers were fighting for a grand moral cause. She was not the only one who thought so. Gen. O. O. Howard, who was in charge of the Freedmen's Bureau starting in 1865, saw his wartime assignment as an opportunity to do the truly divine work of emancipation, evangelization, and education. One interesting shift that took place as the war went on was a tendency to measure goodness not by the previous standards of religious orthodoxy, but by new standards of commitment to a national cause. A case in point was the relation between Gen. William S. Rosecrans and his chief of staff, James Abram Garfield, later president of the United States. Rosecrans was a Catholic who carried a rosary in his pocket, while Garfield was a member of the Disciples of Christ and had taught in a denominational college prior to entering the army. Regardless of their religious convictions, both men developed a deep abiding respect for each other, based as it was on common service to their nation.

Moral Support for Soldiers. Common themes cut across denominational and geographic lines to reach most of the soldiers caught up in the war. First, most denominations preached the importance of divine provi-

The Great Seal of the Confederacy. The Latin motto beneath the image of George Washington means "With God as Our Defender."

dence. God was a personal God, that is, a God with compassion and sympathy to individual trials and efforts. God had a plan for every human being, and thus every soldier could rest assured that what happened in the course of battle was God's will. There were no tragic, unnecessary, or accidental deaths; each death fulfilled some purpose as God had planned it. Second, deaths in wartime seemed very close to martyrdom. Julia Ward Howe even equated battlefield deaths with the Crucifixion: "As He died to make men holy / Let us die to make men free." Third, the soldiers' sacrifices would not be without reward. Even though some denominations still believed in double predestination and in the necessity of conversion in order to achieve a heavenly reward, no one made much of these doctrines to the soldiers. Union and Confederate soldiers themselves spoke of death as "going home," to something comforting rather than to judgment with its potential for damnation.

Nationalism. The Union and the Confederacy used a common religious vocabulary to assert their claims of national identity. "Both read the same Bible, and pray to the same God; and each invokes His aid against the other," Lincoln observed. One Confederate tract quoted John Winthrop, the Puritan founder of Massachusetts, in explaining that the South was "like a city set upon a hill," pursuing a God-given mission in the history of the world. The Confederate Constitution expressly mentioned God, and President Jefferson Davis declared days of fasting and prayer on nine occasions during the war. Clergymen took the lead in a campaign to reform the cornerstone of the southern biblical commonwealth, the institution of slavery, especially by calling for legal recognition of slave marriages. One preacher warned that "God will not be mocked by us. If we take His word to defend slavery, we must submit the institution to His

government." Northerners similarly emphasized the religious basis of the federal government. Lincoln proclaimed the first national Thanksgiving holiday in 1863, and the motto "In God We Trust" began to appear on coins. But in his second inaugural address in 1865, the president emphasized that "The Almighty has His own purposes." Rather than celebrating a Northern crusade to end slavery, he described the war as a grim atonement and declared: "If God wills that it continue, until all the wealth piled by the bond-man's two hundred and fifty years of unrequited toil shall be sunk, and until every drop of blood drawn with the lash, shall be paid by another drawn with the sword, as was said three thousand years ago, so still it must be said, 'the judgments of the Lord, are true and righteous altogether.' "

Chaplain Service. The Union and Confederacy both sought to provide religious services for their military forces. Each had rules authorizing one denominationally certified chaplain per regiment. The Union had African American chaplains for its black troops. Although they had been competitive before the war, each trying to win as many souls as possible and to support its claims for being the true church, the denominations were relatively cooperative during the conflict. Even Catholic bishops, who had to answer to canon laws requiring the Catholic laity to hear mass, not just to attend some religious service on Sunday, refused to press for special privileges and urged Catholic soldiers to work with the chaplains in their regiments. Many regiments were organized locally, had soldiers who were of the same faith, and thus were able to provide a chaplain acceptable for all of them. Between 1862 and 1863 John Ireland (later the archbishop of Saint Paul, Minnesota) was a chaplain for a largely Irish American Catholic regiment from Minnesota. For him, it was an experience of camaraderie strengthened and deepened by facing dangers and fighting for a common cause. He retained the friendships he made in the Army all his life.

Institutional Support. Denominations supplied more than chaplains. They also became the foundations for whole new organizations devoted to meeting the needs of soldiers. The more heavily populated North, which had far more resources and a well-established government structure, formed two important organizations. Founded in the summer of 1861, the United States Sanitary Commission had close ties to Unitarianism. Its president was Henry Whitney Bellows, pastor of All Souls Church in New York City, who argued that Protestantism had overemphasized the "self-directing, self-asserting, self-developing, self-culturing faculties." He saw the coordination of civilians' volunteer efforts as an opportunity to create an institution that would instill national discipline. The United States Christian Commission was inspired by Vincent Colyer, a New Yorker associated with the Young Men's Christian Association, but was managed by a wealthy and devout Philadelphia banker, George H. Stuart. Starting in November 1861 it raised money and collected reading materials and entrusted both to chaplains. The chaplains and their assistants then went among the troops, holding services, distributing books, instructing those who showed an interest in catechism, and visiting the sick. Relations between the two charitable organizations were not friendly. The Sanitary Commission regarded the Christian Commission as a proselytizing campaign that distracted from the Union effort rather than contributing to it. The evangelical Christian Commission complained that its liberal rival lacked genuine religious motivation and particularly criticized the Sanitary Commission for paying its agents.

Postwar Organization. One organization that predated the conflict became important in the postwar era. In 1846 the American Missionary Association (AMA) had been created in Albany, New York, by Congregationalists who wanted their missionary endeavors to more fully reflect their abolitionist principles. The AMA was both a home mission society, sending Congregationalists to the frontier and the Upper South, and a foreign missionary society, dispatching members to the Caribbean. During the 1850s it was also active in assisting fugitive slaves. Thus, it was in a good position to expand its work to former slaves after the Civil War. In its mission to former slaves, the AMA shifted its focus away from traditional missionary work. Former slaves, after all, already had their own Christian religious traditions; what they did not have was a tradition of educational opportunities. The AMA sent men and women, black and white, south to teach school, where they encountered suspicion and even hostility from many white citizens.

Sources:

Drew Gilpin Faust, *The Creation of Confederate Nationalism: Ideology and Identity in the Civil War South* (Baton Rouge: Louisiana State University Press, 1988);

C. C. Goen, *Broken Churches, Broken Nation: Denominational Schism and the Coming of the American Civil War* (Macon, Ga.: Mercer University Press, 1985);

Reid Mitchell, *The Vacant Chair: The Northern Soldier Leaves Home* (New York & Oxford: Oxford University Press, 1993);

Anne C. Rose, *Victorian America and the Civil War* (Cambridge: Cambridge University Press, 1992).

RECONSTRUCTION

Continuity. A few faiths had organizational systems that were not torn apart before the Civil War and therefore did not suffer a difficult period of reunion. Jews, for example, had a congregational polity in which each synagogue or temple usually shared the morality of its location. Catholicism had a different polity but the same outcome. Its unity, centered in Rome and not on American nationalism, survived the war. The Protestant Episcopal Church had an organizational structure which seemed to put it at risk because it was led by a national body of bishops. When the Civil War began, it followed the division between the two nations. However, right after the war ended, the reunited Protestant Episcopal Church met, receiving delegates from the former Con-

A circuit-riding Methodist minister making his rounds (illustration from *Harper's Weekly*, 12 October 1867)

federate States of America without problem. Thereafter, the Episcopalians did not divide over sectional issues, but over the degree of ritualism to be permitted in their denomination.

The Impossible Return. The Methodists found reunification impossible. Instead of reuniting with the Methodist Episcopal Church, South, the Northern Methodists tried to colonize the South, bringing in northern ministers as pastors for southern (especially black) congregations. In June 1865 Missouri Methodists responded with the Palmyra Manifesto, calling for the Southern Methodists to take action to preserve the denomination. In 1866 Southern Methodist bishops met at New Orleans, rejected the possibility of reunion with others of the same faith, and laid out plans for a complete denominational structure. In 1873 "Commodore" Cornelius Vanderbilt, a New Yorker married to a Southerner, gave $500,000 to Southern Methodists for the establishment of a denominational college and seminary (now Vanderbilt University in Nashville, Tennessee). By this time only one link with Northern Methodism remained. Beginning in 1848 the Southern Methodists had sent a "fraternal delegate" to attend annual meetings of the Northern Methodists; they continued to do so even as the denominations developed separate structures. In 1872 this became a reciprocal arrangement, with the Northern Methodists sending their own fraternal delegate to the Southerners' annual meetings.

Presbyterians. In other denominations, forces combined with Reconstruction to shape church structure. The Presbyterians, for example, were still struggling with a split caused by differences over slavery, and in 1865 they remained divided into four groups: Southern and Northern Old and New Schools. During the Civil War, Southern Presbyterians had concluded that unity over slavery was more important than differences over polity and education, and they united. Similarly the Northern New and Old Schools merged in 1869, but the Northern and Southern Presbyterians remained separate.

Baptists. The Baptists had their own doctrinal differences. Prior to the Civil War, Hard Shell Baptists had refused to join with other Baptists in national organizations for the purposes of sending missionaries to places where the Gospel was not yet preached. During the 1850s, the Southern Baptists were more or less held together by the Southern Baptist Convention and by shared support of slavery, but they were divided by a controversy known as Landmarkism. The basic issue was common to every Christian denomination. Biblical scholars generally agreed that early Christians intended that there should be only one Christian church. While the Mormons claimed that this one true church stemmed from the new revelation given to Joseph Smith, most Christian denominations tried to trace their particular faith back in an unbroken line to apostolic times. This was particularly difficult for the Baptists, since there was a long period during which infant baptism, rather than the Baptists' use of baptism as a sacrament of adult commitment to faith, prevailed. But Southern Baptist leader James R. Graves insisted it could be done, and in 1851 he got a Baptist meeting at Bolivar, Tennessee, to adopt the Cotton Grove Resolution, proclaiming the Baptist denomination to be the one true faith and refusing to accept any other church as an equal. The movement got the name of Landmarkism from an 1854 pamphlet titled *An Old Landmark Re-Set,* written by one of Graves's colleagues, James M. Pendleton. Proclaiming Baptism to be the one true faith made it impossible to continue cooperation with other denominations in the matter of foreign missions and difficult even to work with denominations that shared the Baptist name but not this particular doctrine. Moreover, there was some doubt about Graves's and Pendleton's historical accuracy. (The evidence against the Landmark theory of Baptist origins was not published until the 1890s.) Another conflict besetting the Baptists was ethnic, as exhibited by the creation of the North American Baptist Conference by German Baptists in 1865.

African American Evangelization. In theory, American faiths had a new field for evangelization among the four million blacks whose legal status had been changed from that of property to that of persons in 1865. Roman Catholic bishops urged evangelization among African Americans in their 1866 plenary council. The Congregationalists went further, using the AMA to provide chari-

---

"O! LET MY PEOPLE GO"

The Lord by Moses to Pharoah said: O let my people go!
If not, I'll smite your firstborn dead, Then let my people go!

Chorus: O! go down, Moses, Away down to Egypt's land,
And tell King Pharoah, To let my people go!

No more shall they in bondage toil, O let my people go!
Let them come out with Egypt's spoil, O let my people go!

Haste, Moses, 'till the sea you've crossed, O let my people go!
Pharoah shall in the deep be lost, O let my people go!

The sea before you shall divide, O let my people go!
You'll cross dry-shod to the other side, O let my people go!

Fear not King Pharoah or his host, O let my people go!
They all shall in the sea be lost, O let my people go!

They'll sink like lead to rise no more, O let my people go!
And you'll hear a shout on the other shore, O let my people go!

The fiery cloud shall lead the way, O let my people go!
A light by night, a shade by day, O let my people go!

Jordan shall stand up like a wall, O let my people go!
And the walls of Jericho shall fall, O let my people go!

Your foes shall not before you stand, O let my people go!
And you'll possess fair Canaan's land, O let my people go!

O let us all from bondage flee, O let my people go!
And let us all in Christ be free, O let my people go!

This world's a wilderness of woe, O let my people go!
O let us all to glory go, O let my people go!

Source: Dena J. Epstein, *Sinful Tunes and Spirituals: Black Folk Music to the Civil War* (Urbana: University of Illinois Press, 1977), pp. 367–370.

---

table and spiritual aid to African Americans. Nevertheless, membership in these and other denominations did not increase, as was seen with AMA work among free people at Port Royal, South Carolina. A coalition of reformers under AMA auspices developed an ambitious program to assimilate former slaves into American society economically, politically, and spiritually. The reformers turned out to have conflicting approaches. Some thought they were assimilating freed people to a self-sufficient agricultural economy, which would ultimately lead to black ownership of land. Others thought they were assimilating blacks to the emerging capitalist economy, in which the blacks worked for wages and then used their wages to play the role of consumers. A more serious

A prayer meeting at an African American church (illustration from *Harper's Weekly*, 2 February 1867)

mance that they unsuccessfully tried to make her marry elsewhere.

The Irony of Separatism. Racism, combined with some sincere efforts to shield blacks from prejudice and discrimination, produced a situation in which the greater the distance between blacks and whites in religious organizations, the more space there was for blacks to exercise religious self-government. For example, in 1866, as part of their effort to expand to the South, Northern Methodists organized a separate black conference, headed by a black bishop. Southern Methodists countered the Northern challenge and thus took responsibility for southern black faith. They exercised it by releasing all black members of the Methodist Episcopal Church, South, to form their own denomination. The result was the 1870 creation of the Colored Methodist Episcopal Church. Similarly, a Colored Cumberland Presbyterian Church was organized in 1869, and a Colored Presbyterian Church was organized by the Southern Presbyterians in 1874. Like the black Presbyterian organizations, black Baptist institutions were shaped not only by racism but by doctrinal differences within the faith. In 1866 the Colored Primitive Baptists organized, as did the North Carolina state convention of regular black Baptists, the first in the nation.

African American Religious Traditions. There was another reason that denominations made little headway among former slaves, which was that even during the years of slavery African Americans had developed their own religious organizations. Many slaveholders could not bring themselves to deny their slaves' humanity so thoroughly as to deny them religion. They tried to regulate that religion, gathering slaves for owner-approved sermons on scriptural injunctions regarding obedience to masters, but, again, a sense of what religion was led them to leave their slaves some freedom to conduct their own funerals and prayer services. In these settings, African Americans combined various elements to create their own religious culture. That culture was characterized by some practices brought over from Africa, although none of those practices were preserved in their original setting. Instead, a combination of familiarity with Scripture, some common elements of Christianity, and African heritage shaped a particular understanding of religion. One important element of that understanding was the correlation between slavery and racism. Both were sins, that is, violations of God's will. Scripture promised that God's will would prevail, which meant that, by some means, slavery and racism would end. Scripture also promised that God would punish sinners, so that those afflicted by slavery and racism could depend on divine power to eventually mete out a deserved fate to everyone. Thus, while the churches were not necessarily advocates of active opposition to slavery and racism, they were advocates of faith in biblical promises and in watchful waiting for opportunities to cooperate with divine will.

problem was that neither faction of reformers reached common ground with the freed people they were trying to help. Former slaves wanted to own land, and they took advantage of the education offered, but they tried to distance themselves from too much white involvement in their community and they did not join the Congregationalists. The project came to an end when it became clear that the federal government was not going to redistribute land to freed blacks.

Racism. Race, politics, economics, and religion all had a hand in the outcome of the Port Royal experiment. The experiences of Sara G. Stanley, an AMA missionary teacher, showed the primacy of race. Stanley was born a free black in North Carolina. She graduated from Oberlin College with a teacher's certificate and taught in Ohio from 1857 until 1864, when she volunteered for AMA service. She and the other blacks with whom she taught had many unpleasant experiences with white men and women who came south to teach and convert blacks but who did not accept their black colleagues as their equals. They also made the black teachers' lives harder, assigning them to isolated rural schools with inadequate supplies and equipment. In Stanley's case, the hard work and lack of support may have contributed to a breakdown in her physical health. In 1865 she left the mission field for a two-year rest. She returned in 1867 but ran into more racism when she became engaged to a colleague, a white Civil War veteran named Charles Woodward. She was at the time living in a house for AMA teachers, and when she expressed her desire to be married at this home, her colleagues were so opposed to the interracial ro-

African American Denominations. Two entirely black denominations existed at the beginning of Reconstruction—the African Methodist Episcopal Church (founded in 1816) and the African Methodist Episcopal Church, Zion (1821). Between 1864 and 1868, the two denominations discussed cooperation in the mission field, but they were unable to reach a plan of union. Unity might have been more in accord with Christian ideals or with the goal of efficient, economic evangelization, but competition among the various black Methodists, Baptists, and Presbyterians had the advantage of bringing more people into contact with the church more quickly. The Protestant ministry became the profession in which black men could rise the fastest and farthest, and it became a starting point from which they could reach out toward political leadership. For example, in 1870 Richard Henry Boyd, son of a slave mother and white father, converted to the Baptist faith and entered its ministry. He made a career for himself as superintendent of its Sunday schools and later became leader of the American National Baptist Convention. Few denominations permitted the ordination of women, but the black church provided limited opportunities for female leadership in church-affiliated self-help and philanthropic organizations.

Lack of Theological Support. Both before and after Reconstruction, great events in American history were accompanied by theological reflection. The era of 1865–1877, however, did not produce such insight. Few people struggled with the morality of Reconstruction the way many had struggled with the morality of slavery. As it turned out, the theologians' attention was elsewhere, on the rise of corporate capitalism and the challenge of Darwin. Racism remained unstudied, just when religious people most needed to understand the nature and extent of this sin.

Sources:

C. Eric Lincoln, *Race, Religion and the Continuing American Dilemma* (New York: Hill & Wang, 1984);

Albert J. Raboteau, *Slave Religion: The "Invisible Institution" in the Antebellum South* (New York & Oxford: Oxford University Press, 1978);

Willie Lee Rose, *Rehearsal for Reconstruction: The Port Royal Experiment* (Indianapolis, Ind.: Bobbs-Merrill, 1964).

SCIENCE, SOCIETY, AND FAITH

Challenges to Faith. Historians have long argued about the relation between war and change. The Civil War obviously made some changes in American politics, economic life, and technology. However, it may well have retarded intellectual life, particularly religious thinkers' engagement with new issues. Charles Darwin began to publish his work on the eve of the Civil War; American religious leaders did not begin to discuss Darwinism much until after the war was over. Similarly, in the 1840s Karl Marx and Friedrich Engels were already offering an analysis of the impact of industrial capitalism on society. A Christian response to the economy was not part of mainstream American religious thought until the 1870s. In some ways, this lag proved injurious to the ability of various religions to hold the loyalty of some believers.

Darwin. While American pioneers were heading westward, Darwin was exploring another frontier. From 1831 to 1836 he was a naturalist aboard the H.M.S. *Beagle*. His observations of the differences between animals on South Sea islands and similar animals elsewhere led him to the theory propounded in *On the Origin of Species* (1859), that animals were subjected to an evolutionary process that led to the survival of animals more suitably adapted to their environment and to the extinction of other species. In *The Descent of Man* (1871), Darwin extended evolutionary theories to humanity. Darwin's scientific investigations challenged religion in several ways. Most obviously, a long, slow evolution in which some species survived and others perished, with human beings as part of this chain of events, contradicted the account of creation in Genesis. More generally, Darwin presented a new way of looking at nature, different from the traditional manner religious people were used to seeing it.

Faith and Science. Darwin's notion that species changed in response to environmental stimuli led to a fundamental reconceptualization of science. Previously, the model scientist had been the seventeenth-century naturalist Carolus Linnaeus, who had established a system for classifying all life according to genus and species. A scientist's job, when confronted with a new thing, was to establish what it was. The idea that there were no such fixed categories, that living things, at least, evolved and changed, threatened the traditional way of understanding science. In this case, even though there were at the time perfectly respectable scientists who adhered to the previous goals of identification and classification, the changing definition of science won out. Second, there were holes in Darwin's logic. Nineteenth-century scientists had gathered little fossil evidence of how animals evolved. Third, religious leaders argued that the ability to explain evolution was not the same as the ability to explain God and creation. Darwin confided to his notebooks that his examination of the physical world was leading him further from belief in God. For theologians, he was looking in the wrong place for his evidence.

Darwin and Genesis. By the early twentieth century, it was common to equate religious opposition to Darwin with fundamentalists who believed the literal truth of Scripture. In the nineteenth century, the subject was much more complex. First, the fundamentalists did not get their name only because they adhered to the literal truth of Scripture regarding creation. The inerrancy or truth of the Scriptures was only one of their concerns; they also disputed emerging Protestant doctrine concerning the Virgin Birth of Christ, the importance of the Crucifixion in atoning for human sinfulness, the Resurrection of the body, and the historical impact of Jesus' miracles. Second, there was no separate party of fundamentalists in the mid nineteenth century. Both lower criticism (examination of the text) and higher criticism (putting the text in literary or historical context) of Scripture dated from the early nineteenth century, but outside of a few specialists, most people took Scripture literally. Third, despite this pervasive literalism, most denominations found it easy enough to adjust to a new account of creation. Denominations that traced their roots back to early Christianity contained within their histories periods in which Scripture was not taken entirely literally; a particular passage could be interpreted in many ways. Thus, all these denominations emphasized other elements of Genesis, such as the underlying moral of the basic unity of all humanity.

Darwin and Design. Darwin pointed out the basic disorder of the universe and rejected the argument that the world was so intricately, cleverly, and beautifully made that it had to have been designed by an intelligent, purposeful creator. Species competed for survival, and the prize went to the biggest, strongest, and toughest—not the nicest or most moral. Some theologians pointed out that faith was not faith if it required scientific proof and that religion did not need the argument by design as proof of the existence of God.

Marketplace Morality. The debate over Darwin coincided with public interest in another issue. After the Civil War the economy grew more complex and troubling. Jobs required less skill, with machines doing the work that people used to do. Employers tried to save money by lowering wages, and even when they understood how to make conditions safer (by adding fire escapes to factories, for example), they often did not do anything that might cut into profits. More basically, employers treated their employees as if they were components in the manufacturing process; hiring them for as little as they could when they needed workers and then just dismissing them when the job was finished, leaving people without steady incomes.

Social Darwinism. In England pioneer social thinker Herbert Spencer was attempting to apply Darwin's thought, developed by observing the animal world, to the economic world. American preachers such as Henry Ward Beecher preached an economic survival of the fittest. Those with the traits needed to survive economically—punctuality, thrift, sobriety, chastity and industriousness—would rise to the top. Those with counterproductive traits—the shiftless, drunken, licentious, and lazy—would fall by the wayside.

The Effect on Entrepreneurs. Before the Civil War, religion was part of the entrepreneurial persona. Successful entrepreneurs were supposed to interpret their success as a sign of divine goodness poured out in some way on all people. They were supposed to do their part to merit their good fortune by upright behavior and support of ecclesiastical institutions. They were supposed to be

Lewis Tappan, circa 1866, a New York silk merchant who devoted part of his fortune to founding the American and Foreign Anti-Slavery Society

the means of spreading divine favor even further by using their wealth for charitable purposes, as did Arthur and Lewis Tappan with various evangelical and abolitionist projects. So close was the connection between business and religion that when revivals occurred in major cities in 1857–1858, the phenomenon was seen as a "businessman's revival." Some Reconstruction-era captains of industry adopted aspects of this persona: Andrew Carnegie, John D. Rockefeller, and J. P. Morgan all supported various good works, including churches. However, by the late 1860s and early 1870s churchgoing business leaders were hearing another message from their ministers, turning the traditional teaching on its head. One did not receive God's bounty and then try to merit it by good behavior. One exercised the proper virtues, and because one made these efforts, one would grow wealthy. People who remained poor obviously were not making the necessary effort.

A Reason for Unbelief. Neither theology nor popular preaching stayed in this state for long. Within twenty years theologians began using the Scripture to argue for the importance of social justice. The important issue here was that during the late 1860s and throughout the 1870s Social Darwinism undercut one development of the nineteenth century, the belief that God was good as human beings understood that term, full of compassion toward the unfortunate. For some God was not quite what the Scriptures described, and he did not create the world

IS THE BIBLE TRUE?

On 22 January 1866, agnostic Robert G. Ingersoll wrote his friend Richard J. Oglesby. Even in making fun of Scripture, he showed a great deal of familiarity with it, as well as with the personalities and peculiarities of Midwest politics.

I deplore the spread of knowledge—Science I abhor. Art is an abomination, because they deny the word of God. And therefore allow me to say in conclusion that I am rejoiced to learn that you are in favor of the good old times, when Moses was God's clerk and geologist, when Joshua was his General and Astronomer. When the Earth was flat. When the sky was a solid vault. When the stars moved in grooves and were boosted by Angels. When the sons of God came down and cohabited with the daughters of men. When children were born who grew to be Eight hundred feet high & refused to be weaned and absolutely swallowed their mothers. When Methusalem lived about a thousand years without having been a candidate for any office. When Noah was secretary of the Navy. When God himself came down and cut out and made Adam & Eve breeches & petticoats hoop skirt and clawhammer coat. When jackasses made set speeches to angels that they met in the road. When people went to Heaven in an Omnibus office [with] horses to match and dropped their ponchos to wondering crowds. When Ezekiel made sweet cake of cow dung. And that intrepid mariner Mr. Jonah finding himself in the belly of a whale—did not *blubber*. And although in the midst of the great and mysterious deep— without compass, tracts, bibles, playing cards, or tobbacco. With nothing but fish *balls* to eat—The subject of a scaly trick—without knowing what country he was near—only knowing that he was in *Finland*—still had the presence of mind to thrust an oar out of the whale[']s alimentary canal and pull himself triumphantly ashore.

Source: Mark A. Plummer, *Robert G. Ingersoll: Peoria's Pagan Politician* (Macomb: Western Illinois University, 1984), pp. 29–30.

in a simple and straightforward way. But a God that was not good was no God at all for the nineteenth century. For author and historian (and descendant of presidents) Henry Adams, Harvard president Charles Eliot Norton, and Ethical Culture founder (and son of a Reformed Jewish rabbi) Felix Adler, the logical conclusion was neither acceptance nor denial of the existence of God.

Sources:

Henry F. May, *Protestant Churches and Industrial America* (New York: Octagon Books, 1963);

James Turner, *Without God, Without Creed: The Origins of Unbelief in America* (Baltimore: Johns Hopkins University Press, 1985).

WOMEN

Feminization of Faith. During the mid nineteenth-century, women made up the majority of those attending church in every state and denomination, regardless of their formal affiliation. Women provided substantial financial support, either by giving of their own money or by forming groups that raised funds. In many denomina-

tions they gave of their labor as well. Finally, women provided the model for all the faithful. They supposedly felt or intuited their faith, rather than coming to it from study and intellectual effort, which in turn made it easier for them to empathize with people and to help them with their troubles.

Female Virtues. The Civil War changed many things, but not the gendered view of religion. In comparison to men, women were considered more religious, receptive to emotional experience, and pure. Women did not sully themselves in the competitive, even cutthroat, world of business. They were also more virtuous. Women were supposed to be passionless, not particularly interested in sex. Historical perspective, however, makes it easier to see that these traits were not innate, but were constructed by circumstances and social norms.

Middle-Class Standards. The ideal of femininity was widely publicized but not always observed. For example, Harriet Jacobs, who took the pen name Linda Brent, countered the prevailing ethos of the day. In 1861 she produced a memoir, *Incidents in the Life of a Slave Girl*, which described the anguish felt by women whose churches taught them the importance of chastity but whose lives made the ideal impossible to attain. Jacobs recalled that when she became an adolescent, her owner began to harass her sexually. To evade him, she fostered a liaison with another slaveowner, by whom she had two children. Her strategy did not work; in fact, her owner became more abusive. She then hid in the garret of the house of her free grandmother for seven years, until she could escape north. Meanwhile, the slaveowner with whom she was carrying on an affair purchased her two children (who belonged to her master) and freed them. Despite her partner's willingness to help her family become free, Jacobs still felt ashamed for having had intercourse outside of marriage and having resorted to using sex as a means to other ends.

The Power of Ideas. Middle-class women had more opportunities to live up to the ideals of religious womanhood. The promulgation of those ideals changed their lives and gave some impetus to women's liberal education, preparing females to take their place in the larger world. Even if most of them were going to be wives and mothers, they had to be well educated to influence their husbands for the good and to supervise their own children's education. Thus, concepts of greater female religiosity shaped the curriculum offerings in female seminaries. People associated seminaries with religious training (the word comes from a Latin term for "seedbed"), thus conveying the idea that at this school knowledge was not just transferred from teacher to pupil but the students grew, morally and intellectually. Catharine Beecher started from the same premises of feminine faithfulness but drew different conclusions for women's education. She reasoned that if women were naturally different from men, they needed different education. As housekeepers they needed manuals that taught them how to make their

INCIDENTS

IN THE

LIFE OF A SLAVE GIRL.

WRITTEN BY HERSELF.

———

"Northerners know nothing at all about Slavery. They think it is perpetual bondage only. They have no conception of the depth of *degradation* involved in that word, SLAVERY; if they had, they would never cease their efforts until so horrible a system was overthrown."

A WOMAN OF NORTH CAROLINA.

"Rise up, ye women that are at ease! Hear my voice, ye careless daughters! Give ear unto my speech."

ISAIAH xxxii. 9.

———

EDITED BY L. MARIA CHILD.

———

BOSTON:
PUBLISHED FOR THE AUTHOR.
1861.

Title page of the first edition of Harriet Jacobs's memoirs

households fit places for religious families, and Beecher authored one of the first such manuals. If women were naturally the first teachers of little children, then they ought to be trained for teaching; they could practice on their own children, and, if they never married, they would have a profession with which to support themselves.

Homemakers. The changing concept of religious womanhood also altered households; it even changed the furnishings. During this era some families had reed organs for their homes so that they could sing hymns. Women filled their homes with religious symbols. Bibles did not go on bookshelves but on special stands so that in between readings they could still remind family members of God's word. Protestant women introduced crosses into their homes, decorated with seasonal flowers. Catholic women traditionally kept statues of saints or images of Christ and Mary in their homes. Jewish households also accommodated nineteenth-century concepts of women's greater faithfulness, as women traditionally took a role in the Sabbath and Passover celebrations.

Most Protestant denominations retained the idea that the man of the household ought to lead the prayers, but they increasingly replaced family prayers with activities for mothers and children alone. Mothers read Bible stories to their children, catechizing gently as they read.

Outside the Home. The idea that women were naturally religious and too pure for the sordid world also functioned to expand their role to places outside the home. One of these places was Sunday school. The first American Sunday schools were modeled on English traditions, in which poor children who worked six days of the week came to Sunday school to try to catch up on their education. As more Americans gained access to public schools, Sunday school in the United States became specifically religious. By the middle of the nineteenth century each denomination had its own Sunday schools, but the legacy of earlier unity could be seen in the similar format across denominational lines. Older adolescents and young people, mostly females, taught Sunday school. Some churches had special classrooms for the purpose. Teachers told Bible stories and taught catechism to those too young to read; older children were

A prie-dieu, or prayer bench for a woman, fitted with a raised shelf on which the kneeling worshiper could rest her elbows or a prayer book (illustration from an 1872 issue of *Godey's Lady's Book*)

Women's Central Relief Association headquarters, New York City, circa 1861

supposed to read on their own. The importance of God's words in Scripture made teachers emphasize rote memorization, which was encouraged by awarding prizes for recitation. Teaching in such a setting was a common rite of passage for many young women.

The Overland Trail. Married women were responsible for maintaining Christian households wherever they went. One experience of religious housekeeping that was unique to the nineteenth century was maintaining the family's faith while crossing the continent in a covered wagon. The main issue was travel on the Sabbath. This counted as work and a violation of one of the Ten Commandments. On the other hand, the journey could take up to six months with or without a weekly day of rest. Also, there was no guarantee that each Saturday evening would find the wagon train near enough water and grass for the animals for a one-day stop. Some wagon trains did stop on Sunday, but not to observe the Sabbath; rather, both people and animals traveled better with a

regularly scheduled day of rest. Even then these wagon trains did not cease all work on the Sabbath. When the column halted the women had to cook, launder, and clean out the wagons. The sacrifice of the Sabbath was a burden added to all the physical hardships of the journey.

Careers in Religion. The first American Protestant woman to go abroad to spread her faith was Ann Hasseltine Judson in 1912. Thereafter, a small but steady stream of American women went to the Middle East, the Orient, and Hawaii. They had experiences they never would have had at home. They not only learned but used other languages, becoming so competent that they could teach and translate in their adopted tongue. They taught women and children, visited people in their homes, provided medical care, and dealt with practices that not only conflicted with their own denominational teachings but seemed contrary to wider moral standards as well, such as binding the feet of Chinese girls. They converted few people, which did not discourage them, since most believed that God, not their own efforts, would bring about conversion in good time. Unfortunately, they were very much unappreciated at the time. Married women were not recognized as missionaries at all; in fact, it was Ann Judson's husband, Adoniram, who bore the title "missionary." Unmarried women were paid only a third of what men were paid.

Home Missions. During the Civil War another field began to open for women. Their religious organizations were structures through which they could provide assistance to men at war. They could raise funds for the sick, make or collect clothing and medical equipment, and consign their donations to a nurse going to the theater of war. After the war, former slaves needed assistance, and the women who went south to teach and to work among former slaves faced some of the same problems as foreign missionaries. Although the women knew much about charitable work and teaching, the missionary associations appointed men to supervise. The agencies also sometimes used the idea of sacrifice to browbeat the missionaries into making do with tight budgets and a monotonous, if adequate, diet. Also, the whole missionary experiment lasted only a dozen years, until the federal government abandoned Reconstruction. In those twelve years scores of young women went south to teach, to distribute donated clothing, and to assist former slaves in living free lives. After Reconstruction the agencies went on to mission fields elsewhere in the United States, such as Indian reservations in the West and new urban ghettos.

Religious Women. For Catholics, joining a community of religious women was an honorable alternative to marriage. In Europe there were two kinds of communities of religious women. The older type were nuns, who took solemn perpetual vows of poverty, chastity, and obedience and lived in cloistered communities, meaning people rarely visited and few inmates went out for any purpose. The women devoted themselves to achieving spiritual perfection through prayer. They supported themselves by investing the dowries they had brought with them when they entered the convent, by donations, and sometimes by work done on their lands. The second groups were sisters who took the same vows but took them in a simpler format, because in addition to their desire for a religious life, they were committed to some charitable activity. They could leave their cloisters to teach, nurse, and tend the poor and needy. In the United States, the difference between the two groups blurred. There were few wealthy Catholics to make big donations, few women able to present dowries, and much work to be done. Even historically cloistered nuns were asked to teach. Because religious women were less independent in the United States, bishops and priests tried to direct women's community life to meet the diocesan and parish needs. Thus, the religious women had to decide how much to live up to the historical commitments of their respective communities and how much to concede to the bishops and clergy with whom they worked.

Opportunities in Convents. Despite the difference in power between men and women in Catholicism, religious women had opportunities. The need for teachers, nurses, social-service workers, and administrators meant the women had to further their education. The fact that these were predominantly female professions also meant that nuns occupied the highest ranks, becoming superiors of communities and administrators of hospitals, schools, orphanages and asylums. Sister Blandina Segale was just one example of the world that opened up to women when they entered the convent. Born in Genoa, Italy, in 1850, she migrated to the United States with her family as a young girl and joined the Sisters of Charity in Cincinnati when she was seventeen. She spent twenty-seven years *At the End of the Santa Fe Trail*, as she titled her memoirs (1932), founding schools and working in communities without many other civic institutions. When she finished this work, she began a second career among Italian immigrants then moving to Cincinnati in large numbers. She and her blood sister, Justina Segale, also a Cincinnati Sister of Charity, founded a settlement house, Casa Maria, to tend to the needs of immigrant children and their families.

Other Choices. Mid-nineteenth-century Catholicism tended to have either/or choices for women: one could enter the convent or could marry and bear children. Women who did not do either found little support in

A MEETING OF MINISTERS

This is Harriet Beecher Stowe's account of a meeting between the African American preacher Sojourner Truth and several clergymen, including Mrs. Stowe's father, the Reverend Dr. Lyman Beecher.

"Sojourner, this is Dr. Beecher. He is a very celebrated preacher."

"*Is* he?" she said, offering her hand in a condescending manner, and looking down on his white head. "Ye dear lamb, I'm glad to see ye! De Lord bless ye! I loves preachers. I'm a kind o' preacher myself."

"You are?" said Dr. Beecher. "Do you preach from the Bible?"

"No, honey, can't preach from de Bible — can't read a letter."

"Why, Sojourner, what do you preach from, then?"

Her answer was given with a solemn power of voice, peculiar to herself, that hushed every one in the room.

"When I preaches, I has jest one text to preach from, an' I always preaches from this one. *My* text is 'When I Found Jesus!'"

"Well, you couldn't have a better one," said one of the ministers.

Source: Harriet Beecher Stowe, "Sojourner Truth: The Libyan Sibyl," *Atlantic Monthly*, 11 (April 1863): 473–478.

their communities. Mary Anne Sadlier, who wrote fiction for the American Catholic middle class, dealt with these issues in her novels. In fact, the plots and characters of her books all point to the same conclusion. Catholic women realized that they had to fit into divine plans; if married, their duty was to stay quietly at home, raise children, provide emotional support for their husbands, and accept that this was God's way of securing human happiness. According to Catholics only Protestant women went gadding about seeking to overturn divine order with their cries for reform, especially woman's rights.

Faith and Feminism. Some faiths had doctrines that encouraged women to take a larger role in the world outside the home and structures that provided ways for them to do so. The best example was the Society of Friends, or Quakers. The Quakers believed that Christ dwelled within the individual Christian, providing an Inner Light that guided one's conscience. Since the Inner Light was the same in every Quaker, anyone could take a public role in life. Moreover, since the Inner Light guided everyone's conscience, anyone could be involved in the great moral questions of the day, such as slavery and woman's rights. However, some Quakers measured the Inner Light and individual inspiration against the Scriptures, and thus limited women's public activity. For the reformer Elizabeth Cady Stanton, institutionalized religion undermined women. Only men could be ministers, and these men interpreted the Scriptures in ways that discriminated against women. For a woman of Stanton's leanings, religion was a hindrance, not a help, to furthering female interests, a sentiment which continued into the 1880s and 1890s.

Sources:

Margaret Hope Bacon, *Mothers of Feminism: The Story of Quaker Women in America* (San Francisco: Harper & Row, 1986);

Anne M. Boylan, *Sunday School: The Formation of an American Institution, 1790–1880* (New Haven: Yale University Press, 1988);

Ann Douglas, *The Feminization of American Culture* (New York: Knopf, 1978);

Jacqueline Jones, *Soldiers of Light and Love: Northern Teachers and Georgia Blacks, 1865–1873* (Athens: University of Georgia Press, 1992);

Colleen McDannell, *The Christian Home in Victorian America, 1840–1900* (Bloomington: Indiana University Press, 1986);

Katheryn Kish Sklar, *Catharine Beecher: A Study in American Domesticity* (New Haven: Yale University Press, 1973).

HENRY WARD BEECHER

1813-1887
PREACHER

Difficult Childhood. Henry Ward Beecher overcame several obstacles in his early life to become one of the best-known preachers in American history. He did miserably in school and he stuttered, an inauspicious sign in someone whose father wanted him to join the ministry. (His father was the famous conservative Congregationalist minister Lyman Beecher.) Nevertheless, after receiving a bachelor's degree from Amherst College, he received a divinity degree from his father's Lane Theological Seminary in Cincinnati. He then obtained a license to preach from the Cincinnati presbytery in 1837, where he developed such a popular preaching style that he soon attracted offers from prestigious churches.

Permanent Home. Brooklyn was gaining a reputation as a "city of churches." People purchased lots, erected brownstones, and created the institutions that supported middle-class nuclear family life. Two of these people were Henry C. Bowen and John T. Howard, Republican and Democratic newspaper publishers, respectively. They helped to organize Plymouth Church and hired Beecher, hoping he would preserve the Orthodox Congregational traditions of their youth and attract many new church members. Beecher took up his duties on 10 October 1847 and, for a while, exceeded everyone's expectations. On Sunday mornings Manhattanites boarded ferries to Brooklyn, and at Plymouth Church they entered a theatrical setting, with three thousand ground-floor and balcony seats arranged in a semicircle. The focal point was not a pulpit but an easy chair located on a stage. The congregation joined in the rousing hymns, accompanied by an organ, enjoyed the flowers that decorated the church, and watched as Beecher addressed his audience informally from his easy chair or strode about

the stage. The content of Beecher's preaching was even more novel.

New Assurance of Salvation. Beecher agreed with his Calvinist forebears that God had given Scripture and social institutions to teach sinners the right way and to control them. However, not everyone still needed to be burdened by such constraints. By living a virtuous life one acquired good work habits which in turn gave him material success. Beecher told his parishioners that they should work to be persons of culture and refinement, sensitive to the gentle guidance God offered them through the beauties of nature and through the opportunities that wealth brought their way. They should strive to be good not out of a sense of duty toward God but because they were so full of love that they would not willingly do wrong.

Scandal. On 21 June 1874 Theodore Tilton published a letter accusing Beecher of seducing Tilton's wife, Elizabeth. Tilton's divorce suit against his wife, and a Congregationalist investigation into Beecher's activities, disclosed that Beecher's popularity with his flock obscured the harsher judgments of close associates. Bowen had asked Beecher to write for the newspapers he published, but the minister was so late with his essays that the publisher hired Tilton to be his editor and ghostwriter. Tilton's career had taken off from there, and soon he was on the lecture circuit, which gave Beecher the opportunity to visit his helper's wife. The case against Beecher looked bad. However, Mrs. Beecher took her husband's side, and Elizabeth Tilton took the blame for the affair. The court awarded Tilton a divorce from his wife without requiring him to pay her alimony, and the Congregationalist investigation ended with a vote that Beecher was innocent of the charges against him.

Current Events. Beecher kept perfectly in step with historical trends. Like many people in nonslave states, he opposed the Fugitive Slave Act of 1850. When Kansas became open for settlement, he advised those opposing slavery to claim it for freedom, by force if necessary. He opposed immediate abolition, but once the Civil War started, he urged President Abraham Lincoln to emancipate the slaves. He was one of the first to advocate lenient Reconstruction measures and a quick return to state government in the South. Beecher supported black voting rights but not social equality, and women's voting rights but not the radicalism of Elizabeth Cady Stanton and Susan B. Anthony. The work of Charles Darwin intrigued the preacher, and he applied the British scientist's theories to economics. Beecher continued to preach almost to the end of his life, appearing on his platform for the last time on 27 February 1887; nine days later he died of a cerebral hemorrhage.

Sources:

William G. McLoughlin, *The Meaning of Henry Ward Beecher: An Essay on the Shifting Values of Mid-Victorian America, 1840–1870* (New York: Knopf, 1970);

Altina L. Waller, *Reverend Beecher and Mrs. Tilton: Sex and Class in Victorian America* (Amherst: University of Massachusetts Press, 1982).

ANTOINETTE LOUISA BROWN BLACKWELL

1825-1921
ORDAINED MINISTER

Precocious Youth. Antoinette Louisa Brown began making headlines at an early age. Born on 20 May 1825 in Henrietta, New York, she was only eight years old when she asked to become a full member of the local Congregational church. The minister had never had a request from so young a person. However, after the minister had asked her a few questions, the congregation unanimously accepted her as a member. By the time she became a young adult, Brown was even more ambitious, wanting to become an ordained minister and pastor of her own congregation.

Early Career. Brown earned enough money to go to Oberlin College and finished a two-year undergraduate program and three years of theology (the latter without a degree, because the college would not recognize a female theologian). While there, she made new friends, including Lucy Stone, who was preparing for a career as a public speaker specializing in abolition and woman's rights. She also learned to convince others that Scriptures supported rather than condemned female church leadership. One professor assigned the Oberlin women to write an essay on 1 Cor. 14:34: "Women should keep silent in [church]. They may not speak." Brown searched the Scriptures in their original languages. She concluded that the apostle Paul's admonition need not be the rule in every case. There was in the Scriptures no universal prohibition against women in public ministry. Social convention, not God, prevented women from doing more. When members of the Orthodox Congregational Church of South Butler in upstate New York heard her speak, they were so impressed that they asked her to be-

come their minister. On 15 September 1853 Brown became the first woman ordained according to the rituals of any Christian denomination in the modern world.

Shaken Faith. As a minister, Brown was called upon to face situations which challenged her faith. When the infant of an unwed mother in South Butler died of croup, Brown was faced with viewing the death as a form of divine punishment for the sin of illegitimacy. As another boy lay dying, Brown did not know if she should warn the youngster of the impending terrors of hell and urge him to search his heart for signs of salvation that might not be there after all. Brown began to doubt that divine omnipotence extended to consigning individuals to hell and began to make allowance for divine compassion and for the human response to God's grace. Burdened by the conflict between what she was supposed to preach and what she was coming to believe, she resigned her pulpit in 1854 and never held a similar position. Meanwhile, Brown had been introduced to Samuel Charles Blackwell by their mutual friend Stone. They were married at her family's farm by her father (in his capacity as justice of the peace) on 24 January 1856. Between 1856 and 1869 the couple had seven children, five of whom lived to adulthood. While managing her household, Blackwell focused on her writing career.

New Challenges. Charles Darwin's work on evolution interested Blackwell as a theologian, and in 1869 she published a collection of essays, *Studies in General Science,* in which she examined how recent scientific discoveries and hypotheses affected believers. Evolutionary science also interested her as a woman. The work of botanists and biologists supported the theory that a living being's physical makeup determined its fate, and Blackwell became intrigued by the physical differences between men and women. In 1873 a Harvard physician, Edward Hammond Clarke, published a book on this subject titled *Sex in Education, or a Fair Chance for Girls.* In it, he argued that nature had formed girls for wifehood and motherhood. To be fair to them, girls should not be educated alongside boys, lest academic pressure damage them for future childbearing. For Blackwell it was like her youth, except that science replaced Scripture in supplying the authority for confining women to the household. Blackwell produced a series of essays in response, collected into a book titled *The Sexes Throughout Nature,* published in 1875. She pointed out that her generation's experience refuted the notion that coeducation endangered women's childbearing potential. She also argued that even if science did prove women were different from men, it did not establish that they were inferior. In fact, some of the traits nature endowed women with, such as maternal instinct, were badly needed in society.

Later Years. As her daughters grew up, Blackwell had more freedom to travel. Although she had never been in the forefront of the suffrage movement, Blackwell became a link between one era of feminism and another. She also became a link in another chain that was more valuable to her personally, that of American religious history. In 1908 Oberlin awarded her an honorary doctorate in divinity and finally enrolled her on the list of graduates of the class of 1850, recognizing the degree she had earned. She wrote two more books and in November 1920 cast her ballot in the first presidential election that allowed female voters. Blackwell died one year later in Elizabeth, New Jersey.

Source:

Elizabeth Cazden, *Antoinette Brown Blackwell: A Biography* (Old Westbury, N.Y.: Feminist Press, 1983).

HORACE BUSHNELL

1802-1876
LIBERAL PROTESTANT THEOLOGIAN

Puritan Romantic. Horace Bushnell is considered the father of American religious liberalism, and he brought to his work a particular New England Puritan heritage. Born in Bantam, Connecticut, on 14 April 1802, he grew up in the nearby farm town of Preston. Wearing his family's homespun clothing, he entered Yale University in 1823. He graduated in 1827, taught, worked briefly in journalism, then returned to New Haven to study law. During an 1831 revival he changed his career and entered Yale Divinity School. He was ordained for service at the North Congregational Church in Hartford on 22 May 1833, and that September he married Mary Apthorp.

Philosopher. Bushnell's beliefs were at variance with both his Puritan ancestors and Transcendentalist contemporaries. For Puritans, there was a kind of one-to-one correspondence between words and things. Everything, even an idea or a concept, had some precise word to describe it. Puritan sermons, which struck outsiders as long and involved, did indeed sound that way because in such exactitude and attention to detail lay the clear meaning of Scripture. Transcendentalists did not believe it was necessary to have a preacher to explain Scripture, or even to have Scripture explain God. Individuals could, through contemplation of nature, transcend creation to find the Creator. Bushnell disagreed and maintained that before people tried to reach God, he tried to reach them, using every means of communication at divine disposal. Since God is infinite and humans are finite, any symbols of communication human beings could understand would necessarily be imprecise, and thus the one-to-one correspondence the Puritans saw between a word and an idea just did not exist. However, every communication from God was rich, in the sense that people could return to it again and again to draw new meaning from it. Also, there were a great many examples of divine communication, so that if people did not pick up the divine message in one way, they might in another.

Theologian. This emphasis on communication altered the understanding of traditional Christian teaching. Bushnell drew no sharp distinction between the natural world and the world beyond. God communicated through nature, the way a schoolteacher brings in models to demonstrate abstract principles. Bushnell argued that communication was paramount and denied that the Trinity was God simultaneously as one being and three beings (Father, Son, and Holy Ghost). For Bushnell the Trinity meant humans understood God under three different expressions of divine nature, but multiple experiences of God did not mean multiple gods. The Crucifixion could also be understood in the same manner. Puritans thought that in original sin humans committed a crime against God for which they, being limited, finite beings, could not atone. As a human being, Jesus Christ could offer to atone for human sinfulness, but, as God, Christ's self-sacrifice actually had enough merit to outweigh the sin. Bushnell kept the idea of Christ as divine and added the idea of divine effort to communicate with humans. God's love was most fully expressed in Christ's humanity and self-sacrifice.

Teacher. Such theological formulations gave rise to a new understanding of how an individual came to be religious, and specifically, Christian. Predestination became illogical; rather than God selecting those to be saved and those to be damned, if all creation was one thing, then all souls had the same hopes for salvation or perdition. Conversion experiences became equally illogical. If all creation was of one piece, then each individual gradually grew into an awareness of God and of divine plans for one's life. Early family experiences and education replaced traumatic conversions. Bringing children up in the faith, rather than exposing them to religious teachings and expecting them to draw conclusions, made fundamental changes in church organization and family life. Such changes especially affected the position of women. With books such as *Women's Suffrage: The Reform Against Nature* (1869), Bushnell opposed woman suffrage because he thought of politics as a kind of necessary evil. Women had the higher task of raising children, and Bushnell maintained that, if properly nurtured, children would never know a time when they were not Christian. Throughout their lives, then, they would act according to Christ's teachings of love. That, he thought, would bring real reform to the world.

Illness. In 1855 Bushnell started to become seriously ill, and he went to Cuba that winter and California the next year, hoping the change in climate would improve his condition. (He suffered from a kind of tuberculosis that could not be diagnosed or treated at the time.) Unfortunately, his health deteriorated even more. He resigned from the pastorate of the North Church in 1859, and then entered upon what he called his "ministry-at-large," the writing of books. Among his books were

Christian Nurture (1847), *God in Christ* (1849), *Christ in Theology* (1851), *Nature and the Supernatural* (1858), and *Vicarious Sacrifice* (1866). Bushnell died at Hartford on 17 February 1876.

Sources:

Robert Lansing Edwards, *Of Singular Genius, Of Singular Grace: A Biography of Horace Bushnell* (Cleveland: Pilgrim Press, 1991);

David Wayne Haddorff, *Dependence and Freedom: The Moral Thought of Horace Bushnell* (Lanham, Md.: University of America Press, 1994);

David Lester Smith, *Symbolism and Growth: The Religious Thought of Horace Bushnell* (Chico, Cal.: Scholars Press, 1981).

JOHN JOSEPH HUGHES

1797-1864
ROMAN CATHOLIC ARCHBISHOP OF NEW YORK

Immigrant Success Story. When John Joseph Hughes was born in Ireland, his parents were farmers and linen weavers with sufficient income to send their children to school. When the Napoleonic blockades wiped out the linen export trade, Hughes's parents apprenticed him to a gardener. Hughes moved to the United States in 1817 and obtained a job gardening at Mount Saint Mary's Seminary. There he made the acquaintance of the head of the institution, John DuBois, and thus got himself into the school. Ordained a priest on 15 October 1826, he served in Philadelphia until 7 January 1838, when he was appointed coadjutor, auxiliary bishop with the right of succession, to DuBois, at that time the bishop of New York. In 1841 he help found Saint John's College, later Fordham University. By then DuBois was elderly and ailing, and Hughes became the main force in New York Catholicism, although he did not become bishop in his own right until 20 December 1842, after DuBois's death.

Building a Diocese. New York had many Catholics, but most of them were struggling immigrants crowded together in run-down houses in the lower part of the city; even Saint Patrick's Cathedral was on a block in a working-class neighborhood, between Mott and Mulberry Streets. To Hughes's mind, his flock was putting personal interest ahead of religious loyalty, and spending more money and effort on individual parishes than on diocesan progress. Hughes began by limiting the power of lay trustees, men who served as leaders and financial officers for their parishes. He further improved the diocese's financial standing by undertaking various tours through Europe, soliciting donations from the wealthy Catholics there. He also invited several religious institutes to send priests and nuns to New York, where they taught, tended the sick, ministered to the poor, and helped to build up

Catholic charitable institutions in the diocese. (In his search for workers for the young diocese, he was aided by his sister Ellen, later mother general of the Sisters of Charity of Mount Saint Vincent.) The diocese grew, and the Vatican had to reorganize it to accommodate its increasing population and complexity. The Vatican erected new dioceses and redrew New York's boundaries to include only Manhattan, Staten Island, the Bronx, and nine counties north of present-day New York City. On 3 April 1850 Hughes became the first archbishop of New York.

Combating Nativism. Hughes defended Catholicism on the debating platform and in the press. In the 1850s nativists attacked Catholic institutions throughout the United States, which led to riots between Catholics and nativists, with deaths on both sides. Hughes informed New York's mayor that he could control the Catholics if the mayor could do the same for the non-Catholics in the city. Their efforts worked, and New York did not have the same kind of violent rioting that other cities saw. Another step Hughes took to protect his flock was the creation of a modern school system. When Hughes came to the city, it did not have a school system run by public officials. Property owners paid taxes, but the money was then divided upon among the different city churches and philanthropies, with the idea that they would use the funds to educate poor children. The city changed the system when one of the agencies misused its funds. City officials then began giving all the tax money to one philanthropy, called the Public School Society. The way the society ran its schools was not uncommon at the time. At some point during the day, the children listened to a reading from the King James Bible, that is, the English translation used by most American Protestants. Hughes wanted to use an English version called the Douai translation, approved by the Catholic Church. The Public School Society refused to alter its practices and had the support of city politicians. Hughes campaigned for change. On 29 October 1841, just before city elections, he held a meeting which produced a slate of candidates who would, if elected, change the system for distributing tax money for education by giving some of it to Catholics. Hughes's candidates lost, but his effort did lead to reform. Instead of giving money to philanthropists to educate the poor, the city started a public school system. That system, however, had neither King James nor Douai Bibles, and Hughes urged his pastors to build parochial schools.

Creating Unity. When Hughes became a bishop, the Young Ireland movement was attempting to use political means to elevate Ireland from its colonial status. Hughes did not think the political leaders would accomplish much, and he was right; the movement failed. It was replaced by the Fenian movement, which advocated liberating Ireland from England by force of arms. Hughes disapproved of such violent challenges to authority and condemned Fenianism. Just as he distanced himself from

Irish issues, he also tried to distance Catholic New Yorkers from the ethnic and national concerns of other countries. Nevertheless, Hughes realized that some Catholics needed clergy who spoke their own language, and he tolerated the German, French, and Italian parishes in his archdiocese. His attempts to unite his flock around a common Catholicism drew sharp criticisms from some contemporaries who charged that he was power hungry.

Fostering Patriotism. Hughes was not an abolitionist because he saw abolition as an unnecessarily radical change in the social structure. When the Civil War started, Hughes focused on the threat states' rights posed to federal authority. He flew the American flag from his cathedral, and on 21 October 1861 he met with Abraham Lincoln and his cabinet. Shortly thereafter, he left for Europe as Lincoln's unofficial personal representative, defending the Union to heads of state there. On 13 July 1863 a riot broke out in New York in an attempt to halt the process of drafting men into the army. Many of the rioters were working-class Irish Catholics. Asked by city officials to make a calming speech, Hughes made an appearance on the balcony of his Madison Avenue home. He was so sick that he could not be heard as he tried to address the people below. He died of Bright's disease on 3 January 1864. In 1883 his remains were buried beneath the main altar of the new Saint Patrick's Cathedral on Fifth Avenue and Fiftieth Street, for which he had laid the cornerstone in 1858.

Sources:

John R. G. Hassard, *Life of the Most Reverend John Hughes, D.D., First Archbishop of New York, with Extracts from His Private Correspondence* (New York: Appleton, 1866);

Richard Shaw, *Dagger John: The Unquiet Life and Times of Archbishop John Hughes of New York* (New York: Paulist Press, 1977).

ROBERT GREEN INGERSOLL

1833-1899

AGNOSTIC

A Question of Faith. The most famous critic of religion during the Reconstruction period was the son of an Orthodox cleric. Robert Ingersoll was born on 11 August 1833 in Dresden, New York, where his father, Congregational minister John Ingersoll, was serving a church. His mother, Mary Livingston Ingersoll, died when Robert was two years old. The Reverend Mr. Ingersoll remarried, and when his second wife died, married a third time. During Robert's youth, the family moved frequently as his father sought a secure pastoral position. The moves took them from Ohio to Wisconsin to Illinois. Such frequent moves could have disrupted the Ingersoll children's education, but their father taught them at home. By the time he turned eighteen, Ingersoll was a teacher himself, working in Waverly, Tennessee. In 1854 he and his elder brother, Ebon, began reading law at the office of a local lawyer and Democratic politician. In 1860 Ingersoll secured his reputation as a public speaker by substituting for the main orator at an Independence Day celebration with only a few hours' notice and preparation time.

Military Service. Ingersoll's wartime experiences led him to question authority. When the Civil War broke out, he organized a volunteer cavalry regiment, of which he became a colonel. He saw action at Shiloh, Tennessee, and Corinth, Mississippi, before he was captured on 18 December 1862, by Confederate cavalry commanded by Nathan Bedford Forrest. Ingersoll received a parole and made his way back to Union lines, where he was assigned the command of prisoners of war awaiting exchange. When no exchanges were arranged, Ingersoll resigned his commission and returned to Illinois to practice law with his brother. His abiding memory of the Civil War was what he considered to be incompetent military leadership that refused to fight for the real purposes of the war, emancipation and the disempowering of the South. He began to question all authority and soon developed a reputation as an agnostic, or one who believes that humans can know nothing positive about the existence of God.

Politics. Back in civilian life, the Ingersoll brothers performed a political service for the Republicans. The Ingersolls had been Union Democrats and were unmoved by the Copperhead movement in Illinois. On 25 March 1864 Illinois Republican congressman Owen Lovejoy died. His district was reconfigured, and Ebon Ingersoll ran successfully for the vacancy as a Republican, partly because of his brother's abilities as a stump speaker. Together the Ingersolls helped bring the Union Democrats into the Republican fold and strengthen the Grand Old Party in Illinois. Ingersoll, who had been the chief speaker at services memorializing Stephen Douglas in 1861, performed the same function at services for Abraham Lincoln in 1865.

Reconstruction. Ingersoll achieved his only political office in this period; his friend Richard J. Oglesby, governor of Illinois, appointed him attorney general of the state, a position he held from 28 February 1867 to 11 January 1869. In March 1868 he allowed the Chicago Grant Club to place his name in nomination as governor of Illinois. Historians have thought that rumors of his agnosticism led to his defeat, but actually his lack of a firm political base in Illinois seems to have been the cause. He nevertheless remained interested in politics and delivered his most famous speech in 1876. That summer, he supported Maine senator James G. Blaine in the running for the Republican candidate for president. Although Blaine lost the nomination to Rutherford B. Hayes, the sobriquet Ingersoll bestowed on him on that occasion stuck, and Blaine became known as "the Plumed Knight."

Tradition of Agnosticism. Ingersoll went public with his private religious opinions in 1872 when asked to give the principal address at an annual observance of the birth of Thomas Paine, author of the anti-Bible tract *The Age of Reason* (1794–1796). The speech, titled "The Gods," did more than honor Paine; it emulated him. Like Paine, Ingersoll pointed out that Scripture showed a supposedly all-perfect divine being behaving in an ill-tempered and self-centered manner. Ingersoll, however, went beyond Paine in pointing out that all the world's religions had the same tendency to picture their divine beings as if they were badly behaved humans. His lecture started with a statement that writings concerning the gods really reflected humanity's concerns: "An honest God is the noblest work of man."

Speaking Career. Ingersoll emulated Paine in another way. He identified with those whose religious beliefs brought them persecution. On 3 May 1874 he spoke before the Free Religious Society in Chicago on the topic of "Heretics and Heresies," praising individualists who thought for themselves and condemning the institutions, especially churches, who tried to censure such people. Nevertheless, Ingersoll remained a popular figure. Once, while on a long train trip, he sat next to Lew Wallace, and the two men struck up a conversation about religion. Wallace was so fascinated by Ingersoll's witty criticisms of the miracles and wonders to which believers gave credence that he resolved to investigate biblical history for himself, and the result was the famous novel *Ben-Hur* (1880). Ingersoll died at Dobbs Ferry, New York, on 21 July 1899. In accordance with his wishes, his remains were cremated without religious ceremony.

Sources:

David D. Anderson, *Robert Ingersoll* (New York: Twayne, 1972);

Mark A. Plummer, *Robert G. Ingersoll: Peoria's Pagan Politician* (Macomb, Ill.: Western Illinois University Press, 1984).

JOHN HUMPHREY NOYES

1811-1886
FOUNDER OF THE ONEIDA COMMUNITY

Perfectionism. John Humphrey Noyes was born in Brattleboro, Vermont, on 3 September 1811. He had a conversion experience in 1831, after which he changed his career plans from law to the ministry. He studied theology, first at Andover Theological Seminary and then at Yale Divinity School. In February 1834 he underwent a second conversion experience that he believed set him apart forever. As he later explained, all people were born to sin; some, however, could have a converting experience. A chosen few had a second, more thorough converting experience after which it became possible for them to follow Christ's command in Matt. 5:48: "Be you perfect, even as my Father in heaven is perfect." In the terms of the day, Noyes became a "perfectionist," or someone who claimed to have attained sinlessness.

Bible Communism. Noyes converted a few friends and family members to perfectionism. On 28 June 1838 he married a perfectionist, Harriet Holton. By working with this small group, then living in Putney, Vermont, Noyes developed his ideas of how perfect people ought to live. Perfectionists were biblical people, accepting revelation as found in Christian Scriptures, although, being perfect, they did not need to go to church or observe any rules designed to bring them closer to God. Perfectionists were communists, in the sense of having an economic system in which all worked for the common good and all were entitled to common support. They were also communal rather than familial people. Adults could share sex with each other, not just with one spouse, and children were considered offspring of the whole community. When the attorney general of Vermont heard that the perfectionists were practicing "complex marriage," as Noyes called it, he tried to prosecute the religious leader for adultery. In 1848 Noyes and nearly one hundred perfectionists moved to Oneida, New York. There they could practice Bible communism and develop a perfect society as a "bridgehead" over which Christ would return to earth.

Prosperity. Several forces contributed to Oneida's development. Oneida was so far from major population centers that during the Civil War government officials neglected to register its men for the draft. The community also stuck firmly to its priorities. The members experimented with several ways of making a living and operated small factories turning out traveling bags, animal traps, canned fruit and vegetables, and tin-plated spoons. Instead of using their profits on consumer goods, Oneidans simplified their lives. They reduced housekeeping and cooking to a minimum and encouraged women to cut their hair and to wear trousers and short dresses instead of elaborate hairstyles and cumbersome stylish clothes. Thus, the Oneidans had more money left for expenses deemed important to the community, and they also had the time to read, study, and improve their minds. By 1875 approximately three hundred people lived in the community.

Complex Marriage. Outsiders feared that complex marriage would lead to sexual license. In some ways Oneida was very conventional: none of its records mentions homosexuality, and some individuals were expelled for molesting children or harassing women. Noyes regarded sex as he regarded all human activities, as something that should be subordinated to individual and community perfectionist efforts. Young adults received sex education. Men were especially taught to control themselves to avoid causing pregnancy and to make sex equally pleasurable for women. Men asked women to be their partners through a third party. (In this manner Oneidan men found it easier to take a possible "no" for an answer.) The third-party method had the side effect of bringing one other person into each liaison, giving

Noyes or other leaders opportunities to evaluate couples and terminate relationships considered harmful to the community.

Breakup. Changing times threatened the Oneidan community. In the early years the community was so poor that it discouraged people from having children. In 1869, when Oneida was on firmer financial ground, Noyes embarked on a program of stirpiculture, encouraging the most nearly perfect among the community to become parents. Problems developed when parents insisted on keeping their children to themselves rather than raising them communally. Parents also began to prepare their children to get ahead in a competitive world rather than to find their place in a communal one. Stirpiculture eroded Noyes's authority, and in 1873 a young reformer named Anthony Comstock organized the New York Society for the Suppression of Vice. It was a sign of a renewed attack on experiments in sexual relations such as complex marriage. In 1879, when he heard a rumor that he might be arrested for violating New York marriage laws, Noyes escaped to Canada and died there seven years later. During his lifetime he wrote various books on his religious beliefs, including *Male Continence* (1848) and *Scientific Propagation* (1873).

Corporation. Noyes's departure brought into the open the distance between those who wanted communal life and those who wanted family life. After Noyes's death Oneida became a corporation, with the former community members owning individual shares. In order to create the corporation, Oneida's business leaders studied the various products the community made and determined the future lay with the tin-plated spoons. In January 1881 each former Oneidan received shares of stock in Oneida, Ltd. (capitalized at $600,000), which has since become a silverware manufacturer.

Source:
Spencer Klaw, *Without Sin: The Life and Death of the Oneida Community* (New York: Penguin, 1993).

MARY BAPTIST RUSSELL

1829-1898
CATHOLIC NUN

Sister of Mercy. By doing what seemed typical for a woman of her time and place, Mary Baptist Russell lived an extraordinary life. She was born at Newry, County Down, Ireland, on 18 April 1829, baptized as Katherine. She entered the Sisters of Mercy convent at Kinsdale in November 1848. The next year she helped nurse victims of a cholera epidemic, an experience that was useful later. She received her habit on 7 July 1849, and with it the name Mary Baptist. She made her final profession of vows in August 1851, and for the next three years she taught at the convent school.

San Francisco. Meanwhile, an ocean and a continent away, Bishop Joseph S. Alemany of San Francisco was feeling the effects of Irish immigration and also of the California gold rush. Rapid population growth fueled by visions of quick wealth meant some people would fall to poverty, crime, or disease. Alemany wanted to extend Christian charity to the unfortunate, but he lacked the means to do so. Hugh Gallagher, Alemany's agent in Ireland, recruited religious communities to do some of the work, and one community that responded to his call was the Sisters of Mercy. Mary Baptist was appointed superior of the eight sisters chosen to start the mission in San Francisco, and received the title of Mother. The pioneer sisters arrived in New York City in October 1854 and reached San Francisco on 8 December. They considered the date of their arrival an auspicious sign; it was the same day as the Feast of the Immaculate Conception, a Catholic holiday honoring Mary, who was the model for the sisters' life and work and from whom they all took their first names.

Community Service. Mother Mary Baptist's experience with treating cholera soon came in handy. In 1855 there was an outbreak of the disease in San Francisco, and Mother Mary Baptist volunteered her sisters as nurses at the public hospital. The sisters worked so well that city officials signed a contract with Mother Mary Baptist whereby the sisters would staff all the public hospitals in San Francisco. The income from hospital work allowed the Sisters of Mercy to open their own institutions. In 1855 they started a House of Mercy for San Francisco's unemployed young women, and within a year the sisters were teaching in Catholic schools. Bishop Alemany wanted the nuns to take the examinations given to public schoolteachers; if they passed, then the Catholic schools of San Francisco could have a share of the tax money spent on education. Mother Mary Baptist decided not to let the sisters take the examination; even though she would lose the income from the tax money, she would have a freer hand in running her schools.

Catholic Charities. When nativists began to protest the next year, Mother Mary Baptist terminated her contract with the city. She then opened Saint Mary's Hospital, the first Catholic hospital on the Pacific coast. She went on to organize in 1861 in San Francisco the first Magdalene Asylum, an institution for prostitutes. Like most people at the time, she regarded prostitution and sex outside marriage as a sin. However, she also realized that it was more than just a moral issue; young women without skills had few job opportunities, and their most common employment, domestic service, put them in situations where men could harass them with relative impunity. The Magdalene Asylum taught women skills so that they could find other jobs. In 1872 Mother Mary Baptist founded a home for the aged and infirm.

Finances. Regular income for the sisters came from the donations of Catholics, particularly women. In 1859 Mother Mary Baptist founded the Sodality of Our Lady. Women who joined the sodality paid dues and made other charitable contributions to the Sisters of Mercy, prayed for them and their work, and organized fundraisers to attract contributions from the larger San Francisco community. Although the city did not provide regular income for the Sisters of Mercy's work among the needy, it could provide occasional bonuses. In 1868 Mother Mary Baptist and her sisters entered the city's hospitals again, this time to nurse smallpox victims at the pesthouse. As a token of gratitude, the city gave the Catholic nuns $5,000 in 1870.

Legacy. Almost as soon as she arrived, Mother Mary Baptist expanded the Sisters of Mercy beyond San Francisco and established a convent and school at Sacramento. Thanks to the work of this Catholic nun, California by the 1890s had a system of charitable care to match that of other states in the Union. Mother Mary Baptist continued her good works until her death in 1898.

Source:

M. Aurelia McArdle, *California's Pioneer Sister of Mercy: Mother Mary Baptist Russell (1829–1898)* (Fresno, Cal.: Academy Library Guild, 1954).

HENRY MCNEAL TURNER

1834-1915
AFRICAN METHODIST EPISCOPAL
BISHOP

Nothing but Freedom. Henry McNeal Turner, the best-known evangelist among former slaves, was himself born free on 1 February 1834. His father died when he was young, and Turner was raised by his mother and grandmother until 1848, when Sarah Greer Turner married Jabez Story and the family moved to Abbeville, South Carolina. There he joined the Methodist Episcopal Church, South (Methodism had only recently separated into northern and southern branches over the issue of slavery). Turner found work as a janitor in a law firm, and his employers, impressed with his desire to learn, taught him reading, arithmetic, geography, history, law, and theology. However, religion, not law, was to be his career. A white Methodist circuit rider, Robert Jones Boyd, issued him a license as an exhorter in 1851 and another as a preacher in 1853. In December 1854 he obtained a guardian, John McLauren, and court papers that permitted him to leave his hometown and served as proof of his freedom, protecting him from slave patrols who might capture him for a reward.

Preaching in Whispers. Turner became a circuit rider himself, traveling throughout the Deep South to plantations and communities of free blacks. He was in a difficult position. Many churches, such as the Methodist Episcopal Church, South, accepted slavery as God's will. Also, even though churches accepted slavery, state governments did not trust black preachers, and many states required that at least one white male be present at black religious services to monitor the sermons. It must have been a relief when in 1857 Turner discovered the African Methodist Episcopal (AME) Church while preaching in New Orleans. Yet Turner hesitated before changing his denominational affiliation because he had married Eliza Ann Peacher the previous year, and his work in the Methodist Episcopal Church, South, allowed him to support his family. In 1858 Turner presided over a revival in Atlanta, and he converted to the AME Church and moved to Baltimore. There he simultaneously served as pastor of two churches, the Waters' Chapel and the Tissue Street Mission, and studied English grammar, Latin, Greek, and Hebrew. In 1860 he became pastor of the Union Bethel Church in Baltimore, where he was ordained a deacon (1860) and then an elder (1862). He also became pastor of the Israel Church in Washington, D.C., in 1862.

Military Chaplain. Turner's first response to the Confederate attack on Fort Sumter in April 1861 reflected his ministerial profession. He was appalled by the bloodshed and did not think the Civil War would serve any good purpose. In 1862 he studied the matter and concluded that God worked in mysterious ways and was using the war for the higher purpose of human freedom. Thus he was ready for the signing of the Emancipation Proclamation in 1863. The Proclamation opened the way for blacks to join the armed forces. Turner's assistant, Thomas H. C. Hinton, turned Israel Church into a recruiting center and organized the First Regiment of the United States Colored Troops. Turner himself volunteered to be a chaplain and received his commission on 6 November 1863. Some idea of his dedication to duty may be had by learning that he contracted smallpox when he visited troops confined to the hospital. He was equally concerned for his soldiers' education, constantly soliciting donations of books, which he distributed to the troops. When a boat full of regimental supplies sank, he made sure to replace the lost spelling texts.

Political Leader. Turner's commission expired at the end of 1865, and President Andrew Johnson appointed him to a chaplaincy in the regular army, assigning him to work with the Freedmen's Bureau in Georgia. When Turner got to Georgia, he found that the unit to which he was assigned already had a chaplain and that the man in charge of Bureau operations in the state, Gen. Davis Tillson, was more sympathetic to whites than to former slaves. Turner soon resigned his army commission to organize the AME Church in the state. Part of that work involved political leadership, organizing blacks to protect their interests in the face of unrepentant Georgia Democrats. In 1866 Turner returned to Washington to make political contacts and to solicit funds for the black Georgians' Equal Rights Association. By the next year he was urging black Georgians to join the Republican Party. From December 1867 to March 1868 he was a member of the Education Committee of the Atlanta Constitutional Convention, in which position he lobbied unsuccessfully for funds for black higher education and universal public elementary education. He served two terms in the state legislature, but his career as an elected civil servant soon came to a dramatic end. He had been elected partly on the strength of an alliance between blacks and poor whites, who had united to overcome the power of the state's longtime political leaders, landowning white Democrats. Once elected, the whites wanted their black colleagues barred from the legislature, effective immediately. Turner and the other black representatives stood up, walked up the aisles among the seated white delegates to the door, and then, in biblical fashion, shook the dust from their feet. Turner's final departure from politics was more ignominious. Congressional Republicans arranged for him to be appointed postmaster of Macon, Georgia. Local whites, though, did not want him to have the job. During this time, also, Turner was caught in a local scandal: he was seen in the company of a woman who was not only a confirmed counterfeiter, but a prostitute as well.

Bishop. Turner found new work in 1872 as pastor of Saint Philip's AME Church in Savannah. In 1876 he moved from that job to a new one as head of the financially troubled church publishing department. A volume he wrote himself, *The Hymn Book of the African Methodist Episcopal Church* (1876), became a popular seller. On 14 May 1880 he was elected bishop and assigned to Georgia. In that capacity he not only worked to build up his own flock, but also labored to extend the AME faith. In addition, he traveled to Africa as a missionary, visiting Sierra Leone (1891), Liberia (1893), and South Africa (1898).

Institution Builder. Turner's election as bishop was not a foregone conclusion. He smoked, claiming he had become addicted to tobacco during his youth, when one of his chores was to keep his grandmother's pipe lit. Other Methodists took this breach of self-discipline seriously. Some also pointed out that the price of the rapid expansion of the AME in Georgia was the acceptance of many uneducated, even illiterate, ministers that compromised the status of the whole denomination. Nevertheless, Turner received the position and quickly became involved in the practical and theoretical aspects of church organization. Not only did he build up local churches, but he edited the newspaper *Voice of Missions* to develop a sense of unity in the denomination. He also wrote a book on *The Genius and Theory of Methodist Polity* in 1885.

A Black Christian Identity. Turner both reacted to and shaped an emerging black identity. His experiences before, during, and after the Civil War convinced him that the federal and state governments were determined to marginalize blacks. Some would extend that analysis to Christianity, arguing that it was really a European religion whose doctrines were useful for oppressing and exploiting the poor by promising them that accepting the status quo on earth would lead to rewards in heaven. As a clergyman, though, Christianity meant liberation for Turner; personally, it gave him a professional career. For black people generally, Christianity promised that a just God would look after the oppressed, and it encouraged blacks not to revolt, but to develop useful strategies to improve their lot. Late in his life, Turner was impressed with Elizabeth Cady Stanton's *Woman's Bible* (1895–1898) and pondered whether it might not be desirable to do a translation and commentary on Scripture from an African American point of view.

Death. By the 1880s Turner was so disappointed in the prospects for blacks in the United States that he claimed he did not want to die in a place where his race was so maligned. Invited to preside over a church meeting in Canada, he had just disembarked from a ferry that carried him from Detroit to Windsor, Ontario, when he was felled by a massive stroke at the wharf. He died on 8 May 1915, and his body was brought back to Atlanta for burial.

Source:
Stephen Ward Angell, *Bishop Henry McNeal Turner and African-American Religion in the South* (Knoxville: University of Tennessee Press, 1992).

BRIGHAM YOUNG

1801-1877
MORMON PIONEER

A Calling. Born on 1 June 1801 in Whitingham, Vermont, Brigham Young was only marginally successful as a farmer and carpenter before moving on to better opportunities. On 14 April 1832 he converted to the Church of Jesus Christ of Latter-Day Saints, or Mormons, being baptized at Mendon, New York. In the Mormon community, Young found a spiritual home and an outlet for undiscovered talents. When on 27 June 1844 a mob lynched Mormon leader Joseph Smith at a jail in Carthage, Missouri, Young was able to unite most of Smith's converts behind him as their new leader.

Exodus. Smith's efforts to develop a separate Mormon community in the midst of American society had led to near war between Mormons and Gentiles. Young reasoned that distance would give the Mormons safety, and he consulted explorers and scouts who had traveled in the West. In March 1845 he decided upon the Great Basin between the Rocky Mountains and the Sierra Nevada as the Mormons' place of refuge. The area, which the Mormons called Deseret (meaning "Land of the Honey Bee"), seemed fertile enough that they could farm and become economically self-sufficient, but was not so inviting that other settlers might disturb them. On 15 February 1846 Young and a group of pioneers left the Mormon town of Nauvoo, Illinois; they reached the Great Basin on 24 July 1847. The next year Young led a second wagon train to the new territory. After that Young himself never traveled outside Deseret, although he continued to encourage Mormon migration. By the autumn of 1848 approximately five thousand followers had arrived, and in 1849 Young established a Perpetual Emigrating Fund Company to give financial assistance to impoverished potential migrants from England and continental Europe.

Government. Mormon efforts to establish a government were shaped by the efforts of the United States to expand westward. At the same time Young was making his first trip to Deseret, the United States was at war with Mexico. In the Treaty of Guadalupe Hidalgo (1848), the Mexican government ceded land, including Deseret, to the United States. The Mormons hoped that Deseret would quickly become a state, for then they could control the local government. However, Washington politicians hoped to use the Mexican cession as an element in a great compromise over slavery and turned Deseret into the Utah Territory (1850). Many federal authorities were anti-Mormon, and official policy toward the Mormons varied, depending on the personality involved. Democratic president Franklin Pierce appointed Young his territorial governor. Pierce's successor, Democrat James Buchanan, not only refused to renew Young's appointment, but sent twenty-five hundred federal troops to install his choice for territorial governor, Alfred Cumming. Young mobilized his Nauvoo Legion to counter the U.S. Army, and during the Utah War of 1857–1858 the Mormons set grass fires, drove off livestock, and burned government supply wagons in an unsuccessful attempt to halt the advance of federal troops.

Native Tribes. The land Young chose for the Mormons was between that of two large Indian tribes, the Ute to the south and the Shoshone to the north. Mormon teachings held that Native Americans had descended from the Ten Lost Tribes of ancient Israel and thus should be treated with respect. Young also made the practical observation that it was cheaper to feed the Indians than to fight them, and the Mormons attempted to teach their new neighbors how to farm. Finally, Mormons and Native Americans had a common interest in keeping other settlers out. When in 1857 a group of one hundred settlers going from Missouri and Arkansas to California began marauding through Mormon territory, Indians and Mormons, led by John D. Lee, attacked them and killed all but eighteen children in an incident that came to be called the Mountain Meadows Massacre. However, when the Civil War began a few years later, the Indians took advantage of the reduced number of federal troops to attack stagecoaches traveling unprotected along western routes. The Mormons then assisted the federal government by protecting the stagecoaches.

Civil War. During the Civil War, Young allied the Mormons with the Union, but it was not because he opposed slavery or supported equal rights for all races. In fact, Southern Mormons had brought between seventy-five and one hundred slaves to Deseret in 1847. That same year Young forbade Mormons to ordain blacks to the priesthood. (The ban remained in effect until 1978.) Mormon support of the Union, however, was not rewarded, and in 1862 Congress passed the Morrill Anti-Bigamy Act. The law included a clause preventing religious groups advocating polygamy from holding more than a certain amount of property in the territories. Young protected his flock from the law's penalties by putting all church property in his name.

Modern Patriarch. Besides working to establish the church and community, Young did what was expected of him as a Mormon in terms of building up family life. Joseph Smith had introduced polygamy in 1843. At first Young was disturbed by this new doctrine, but he dutifully began taking more wives that same year. Over his lifetime he entered into marriage with fifty-five women. Most of these marriages seem to have been platonic relationships in which the women obtained economic security and a foothold in Mormon society, while Young enhanced his position as an example of Mormon manhood. He did, though, have to provide for all these wives and for his fifty-seven children. To that end, Young traded with goldrushers on their way to California, purchased the real estate of those who were leaving Utah Territory, and made investments in roads and other improvements.

Postwar Problems. After the Civil War, Americans resumed their westward expansion, and President Ulysses S. Grant renewed federal efforts that conflicted with Mormon interests. Young continued the task of trying to protect his flock. However, he died unexpectedly after a brief but intense illness, most likely a ruptured appendix, on 29 August 1877.

Source:
Newell G. Bringhurst, *Brigham Young and the Expanding American Frontier* (Boston: Little, Brown, 1986).

PUBLICATIONS

Felix Adler, *Creed and Deed; A Series of Discourses* (New York: Putnam, 1877)—a discussion of the basis of the Ethical Culture Movement, that morals arose from human situations, not divine commands, and are more important than right belief in evaluating a person;

Henry Ward Beecher, *The Plymouth Collection of Hymns and Tunes* (New York: A. S. Barnes, 1855)—a hymnbook for the Plymouth Congregation, a nominally Congregational church in Brooklyn, New York;

Antoinette Louisa Brown Blackwell, *The Sexes Throughout Nature* (New York: Putnam, 1875)—argues that the physical world provides no evidence for denying women an education or holding them in a subordinate role in society;

William G. Brownlow, *The Great Iron Wheel Examined; or, Its False Spokes Extracted* (Nashville, Tenn., 1856)—a Methodist defense against Baptist charges that Methodism is not the true church;

Horace Bushnell, *Christ in Theology* (Hartford, Conn.: Brown & Parsons, 1851)—advances the thesis that language used in religious discourse is, because it came from an infinite deity to finite humanity, necessarily imprecise, more given to suggestion than to exact description;

Bushnell, *Christian Nurture* (New York: Scribner, 1861)—contradicts the traditional emphasis on conversion experience with a thesis that it is possible for individuals, properly introduced to Christianity from infancy, never to know a period when they did not consider themselves Christians;

Bushnell, *Nature and the Supernatural, as Together Constituting the One System of God* (New York: Scribner, 1858)—argues for continuity between the physical world and the unseen one, meaning that God could communicate with humanity through the natural world or through other means;

Andrew Jackson Davis, *The Principles of Nature, Her Divine Revelations, and A Voice to Mankind*, eleventh edition (New York: S. S. Lyon & W. Fishbough, 1852)—Davis's first book describing his experiences in communicating with the supernatural world;

David Einhorn, *Protest Against a Conference of Rabbis in Which, On Motion of the Rev. Dr. Isaac M. Wise of Cincinnati, The Following Platform Was Accepted: "That the Talmud Is Acknowledged by All Israelites as the Legal Commentary of the Bible"* (Baltimore, 1855)—a tract detailing the controversy between Wise and Einhorn. Wise defends Jewish traditions so long as there is no modern reason to drop them while Einhorn judges all traditions by modern light, and desires to create a Judiasm based on nineteenth-century understanding of the faith;

Ralph Waldo Emerson, *Representative Men: Seven Lectures* (Boston: Phillips, Sampson, 1850)—among these essays is one on Emanuel Swedenborg, a seventeenth- and eighteenth-century Swedish bishop who became the center of a modern spiritual movement;

Charles Grandison Finney, *Memoirs of Rev. Charles G. Finney. Written by Himself* (New York: A. S. Barnes, 1876)—the autobiography of the famous and influential northern antebellum revivalist;

Octavius Brooks Frothingham, *The Religion of Humanity* (New York: D. G. Francis, 1873)—argues for basing religion on reasonable doctrinal positions and on the importance of individual work to improve the world;

James Gibbons, *The Faith of Our Fathers*, sixth revised edition (Baltimore: J. Murphy, 1877)—a popular introduction to Catholicism;

James R. Graves, *The Great Iron Wheel; or, Republicanism Backward and Christianity Reversed. In a Series of Letters Addressed to J. Soule, Senior Bishop of the Methodist Episcopal Church, South* (Nashville, Tenn.: Graves & Marks, 1855)—the editor of the *Tennessee Baptist* argues that the Baptist, not the Methodist faith is the true church;

Isaac Thomas Hecker, *Questions of the Soul* (New York: Appleton, 1855)—takes the common questions people have regarding religion (life after death, the importance of an ethical life, how to know the true faith, and so forth) and provides Catholic answers;

Charles Hodge, *What Is Darwinism? Darwinism and Its Relation to the Truths of Natural and Revealed Religion* (New York: Scribner, Armstrong, 1874)—points out that natural selection contradicts the doctrine of an omniscient, omnipotent Creator and rejects Darwinism as a Christian explanation for creation;

Levi Silliman Ives, *The Trials of a Mind in Its Progress to Catholicism; A Letter to His Old Friends* (Boston: P. Donahoe, 1854)—Ives had been an Episcopal bishop before his conversion to Catholicism, and he felt he owed an explanation to his friends and family;

Charles Porterfield Krauth, *The Conservative Reformation and Its Theology as Represented in the Augsberg Confession, and in the History and Literature of the Evangelical Lutheran Church* (Philadelphia: Lippincott, 1871)—Lutheranism has a different basis from the Reformed Protestantism prevalent in the antebellum United States. Krauth critiques Calvinism as radicalism and presents Lutheranism as best preserving early Christian doctrine;

Isaac Leeser, *Catechism for Jewish Children Designed as a Religious Manual for House and School,* third edition (Philadelphia, 1856)—an introduction to Reform Judaism;

James M. Pendleton, *An Old Landmark Re-Set* (Nashville, Tenn.: South Western Publishing House, 1855)—the *landmark* in the title refers to the birth of the Baptist denomination, which the author pushes back to the earliest Christian days, thus allowing him to claim that the Baptist Church is the true church;

Philip Schaff, *History of the Christian Church,* 4 volumes (Edinburgh: T. & T. Clark, 1869–1885)—a continuation of the author's previous work on the apostolic church, bringing the story through the Middle Ages to the Reformation;

Samuel Simon Schmucker, *The American Lutheran Church, Historically, Doctrinally and Practically Delineated, In Several Occasional Discourses* (Springfield, Ohio: Harbaugh & Butler, 1851)—an introduction to Lutheranism with an emphasis on its compatibility with assimilation to American life;

Isaac Mayer Wise, *The Cosmic God: A Fundamental Philosophy in Popular Lectures* (Cincinnati: Office of the American Israelite & Deborah, 1876)—a Reconstruction-era statement of a philosophy Wise studied in his youth, the European Romantic theology that God was not confined to the supernatural, but also spoke to the human heart through the natural world.

SCIENCE AND MEDICINE

by KIMBERLY KELLISON

CONTENTS

Sidebars and tables are listed in italics.

1850

- John E. Heath invents the agricultural binder.
- 11 Mar. The Woman's Medical College of Pennsylvania, the first medical school for women in America, is incorporated.
- 21 Aug. The Collins Line steamer SS *Atlantic* sets a new transatlantic speed record, arriving in New York after crossing from England in ten days, sixteen hours.

1851

- Dr. William P. Channing and Moses Gerish Farmer install the first electric fire alarm.
- John Gorrie receives a patent for an ice-making machine.
- The Erie Railroad opens in New York; at 483 miles, it is the longest railroad line in the world.
- 12 Aug. Isaac Merrit Singer patents a sewing machine, prompting Elias Howe, who first patented such a device in 1846, to sue him.

1852

- Alexander Bonner Latta invents the first effective steam engine.
- Elisha Graves Otis invents the passenger elevator.
- The American Pharmaceutical Association is formed in Philadelphia.

1853

- E. E. Matteson improves the sluicing process in mining.
- 3 Mar. Congress appropriates $150,000 for an army survey of possible routes for a transcontinental railroad.
- 14 July The Crystal Palace Exhibition—the first world's fair held in the United States—opens in New York City.

1854

- Walter Hunt invents the disposable paper shirt collar.
- 6 May Cyrus W. Field receives a charter and a fifty-year monopoly for his company to lay a transatlantic cable between the United States and Great Britain.

1855

- An American company completes the Panama Railroad across the Isthmus of Panama.
- John A. Roebling's Niagara Gorge suspension bridge opens.
- Congress authorizes construction of a telegraph line from the Mississippi River to the Pacific Ocean.

1856

- The Western Union Telegraph Company is established.

21 Apr. The first railroad bridge across the Mississippi River is opened, linking Rock Island, Illinois, with Davenport, Iowa.

19 Aug. Gail Borden receives a patent for a process to condense milk.

1857

- The first patent for a postmarking and stamp-canceling machine is issued.

- William Kelly receives a patent for a device to manufacture steel by channeling a current of air into molten pig iron.

12 May Elizabeth Blackwell and her sister Emily open the New York Infirmary for Women and Children.

1858

- Lyman R. Blake patents a machine that can sew shoe soles to uppers, eliminating hand sewing and making possible the production of inexpensive shoes.

- George M. Pullman invents the railroad sleeping car.

5 Aug. The first transatlantic cable, between the United States and Great Britain, is completed; after a few weeks of operation, the cable will break.

1859

- The first hotel passenger elevator in America is installed in New York City's Fifth Avenue Hotel, but many guests continue to use the stairs.

- John F. Appleby invents the harvester-binder, which binds sheaves of cut grain.

- Charles Darwin's *On the Origin of Species* is published in England.

28 Aug. Edwin L. Drake discovers oil at Titusville, Pennsylvania, marking the start of the modern petroleum industry.

1860

- Oliver F. Winchester begins production of his repeating rifle in New Haven, Connecticut.

- Dr. Abraham Jacobi of the New York Medical College becomes the first professor of children's diseases in the United States; he also establishes the first free clinic for children's diseases.

1861

- Erastus B. Alcott performs the first successful removal of a human kidney.

- The first transcontinental telegraph line is completed.

- Richard J. Gatling invents the revolving machine gun.

- The Massachusetts Institute of Technology is incorporated in Cambridge.

13 June   President Abraham Lincoln establishes the United States Sanitary Commission.

1862

- The United States Department of Agriculture is established to promote technical knowledge among farmers.

- Congress passes the Morrill Act, granting federal land for the establishment of agricultural and technical colleges.

1863

- William Bullock invents the continuous-roll printing press.

- The first orthopedic clinic in America, the New York Hospital for Ruptured and Crippled Children, opens in New York City.

3 Mar.   Congress authorizes the creation of the National Academy of Sciences.

1864

- New York City rejects Hugh B. Wilson's proposal to create an underground transit system.

- John Thompson and John Ramsey create the checkrower corn planter.

1865

- Thaddeus Lowe perfects the compression ice machine.

- At Vassar College, Maria Mitchell becomes the first female astronomy professor in the United States.

- The American Social Science Association is established.

1866

- The public is allowed to view construction of the world's first mountain-climbing railroad, the Mount Washington Cog Railroad in New Hampshire; it will be completed in 1869.

27 July   The first permanent transatlantic cable is completed.

1867

- James Cruikshank's *Primary Geography* is published; it will be widely used as a textbook for the rest of the nineteenth century.

- Christopher Latham Sholes invents the first practical typewriter.

- The first elevated railroad in the United States begins operation in New York City.

1868

- William Davis invents the refrigerator car.
- James Oliver patents the chilled-iron plow.
- *American Journal of Obstetrics* begins publication.
- George Westinghouse invents the air brake, making high-speed railroad transportation safer.

1869

- I. W. McGaffey invents the suction-type vacuum cleaner.
- Thomas Alva Edison invents the electric voting machine.
- John Wesley Hyatt Jr. and Isiah Smith Hyatt patent a process for the production of celluloid.
- The first state board of health is established in Massachusetts.
- The first history seminar is held by Charles Kendall Adams at the University of Michigan.

10 May The first transcontinental railroad in the United States is completed when the tracks of the Union Pacific, laid from east to west, and those of the Central Pacific, laid from west to east, are joined at Promontory Point, Utah.

1870

9 Feb. Congress establishes the United States Weather Bureau.

1871

- The cable car is perfected by Andrew S. Hallidie.
- In a pamphlet, *The Needs of the University*, Yale University calls for increased education in science.

1872

- Edmund D. Barbour perfects an adding machine that can print totals and subtotals.
- The American Public Health Association is founded.

1873

- The first nurses' training schools are established in New York, New Haven, and Boston.

1 Aug. The world's first cable car line begins operation in San Francisco.

27 Nov. The Hoosac Tunnel, the first major railroad tunnel in the United States, is completed in Massachusetts; construction of the tunnel marked the first practical use of nitroglycerin and the compressed air drill in the United States.

1874

- Joseph F. Glidden receives a patent for barbed wire.

- Stephen Dudley Field invents the electric streetcar.

1875

- Dr. Andrew T. Still of Kirksville, Missouri, establishes the new medical field of osteopathy.

- Horticulturalist Luther Burbank establishes a plant nursery in Santa Rosa, California, where he will produce new strains of fruits, berries, vegetables, grasses, and grains.

- The American Forestry Association is founded in Chicago.

1876

- The first meeting of the American Chemical Society is held.

- Johns Hopkins University is founded in Baltimore.

- Alexander Graham Bell patents the telephone.

10 Mar. A complete sentence is transmitted by telephone for the first time when Bell says to his assistant, "Watson, come here. I want you."

9 Oct. The first transmission of a telephone message over an outdoor wire is accomplished.

1877

- A telephone is installed in a private home for the first time.

- Thomas Alva Edison invents the phonograph.

- Astronomer Asaph Hall at the Naval Observatory in Washington, D.C., discovers two moons of Mars.

OVERVIEW

Intellectual Markets. Science, technology, and medicine went through important changes between 1850 and 1877. New findings in these fields, especially in technology, helped to give shape to a modernizing, industrializing nation; at the same time, the economic and social transformation of American society had a profound impact on science, technology, and medicine as urbanization and industrialization brought more people together to share new ideas, and organizational changes in industry created a demand for specialization and expertise. This interplay between science and social change was not limited to the United States. By the middle of the nineteenth century Americans were active participants in a competitive, capitalistic world market in which the interaction of new ideas proved to be as important as the exchange of goods for sale. Europeans remained the leaders in science, medicine, and technology, but Americans made some significant scientific contributions, especially in terms of practical inventions. During the 1850s, 1860s, and 1870s American scientists gained valuable knowledge from their European neighbors, and they gradually began to apply the lessons they learned to their own experiments and institutions.

The Professionalization of Science. Between 1850 and 1877 American science emerged as a modern profession. Before this time scientists had largely conducted their work on an individual, part-time basis. That pattern changed between the mid 1840s and mid 1870s as science became a more collective undertaking. Scientific fields became more specialized; greater emphasis was placed on scientific education; and national scientific societies were formed. The Smithsonian Institution opened in 1846 as the first national institution devoted to "the increase and diffusion of knowledge among men." Under the leadership of Princeton University scientist Joseph Henry, the Smithsonian promoted scientific research and publishing and served as a museum of natural history. A year after the Smithsonian opened, a group of prominent scientists created the American Association for the Advancement of Science to increase communication within the scientific community and to raise the standards of scientific study. Scientific societies provided an important outlet for discussion and debate: for instance, at the American Academy of Arts and Sciences in Boston and at the Boston Society of Natural History, leading American scientists debated Charles Darwin's theory of evolution in 1859 and 1860.

European Influence on American Science. The changing organization of American science was patterned on European models. Many American scientists studied abroad in the middle of the century, returning to the United States with new ideas for advancing their fields. Some foreign scientists, such as the Swiss zoologist Louis Agassiz, also immigrated to the United States. This interchange of ideas inspired a small group of leading American scientists, who called themselves "the Lazzaroni" (an Italian word referring to lower-class men or women engaged in revolt), to work for greater professionalization of the sciences. This group, which included Agassiz, Henry, and Alexander Dallas Bache, promoted not only the formation of national scientific associations but also more-rigorous standards of scientific education. The Lazzaroni emphasized the importance of scientific research in colleges and universities, a concept pioneered by German scientists. Their efforts were partially realized in 1876 when Johns Hopkins University, a research-based institution, was founded. By this time some colleges and universities were granting Ph.D. degrees in science and science courses were becoming more specialized.

Advances in Technology. Like science, American technology became more professionalized between 1850 and 1877. The formation of national technological associations and professional journals along with greater emphasis on scientific research characterized these decades. As in science, too, European trends and models proved useful, and American technologists benefited from scientific exchanges with Europeans. Some American colleges—most notably, the United States Military Academy at West Point—had emphasized science and engineering as early as the 1820s, but the mid nineteenth century witnessed an increase in engineering schools; the most influential was the Massachusetts Institute of Technology, established in 1861. While technological education increasingly emphasized the importance of scientific training, most technological innovations were still based less on scientific methods and principles than on the intuition and experience of inventors and engineers. Nevertheless, changes had been set in motion that would have a great impact on late-nineteenth- and twentieth-century technological innovation.

Changes in Medicine. Medicine, too, moved only slowly toward greater professionalization in the mid nineteenth century. The American Medical Association (AMA) was created in 1846 to raise professional standards for doctors, but the organization made little progress in influencing medical practices during its first half century. Until the 1870s standards for medical education varied widely, and few states had licensing laws for physicians. The years after the Civil War marked the beginning of state and city boards of health, the modern hospital, and professional nursing; these three phenomena were rooted in the reforms made by Florence Nightingale and the British Sanitary Commission during the Crimean War in the 1850s and by the United States Sanitary Commission and other reformers during the Civil War.

Social Sciences. Greater mobility in nineteenth-century America fostered an awareness of differences among various groups of people, and Americans turned to social science, which emerged as a new field during the middle decades of the century, to analyze and understand these distinctions. The more specialized and technical nature of course offerings in colleges and universities also promoted the study of social science, and history, political science, and economics began to stand on their own as independent disciplines. The new disciplines of sociology and anthropology were also developed during this period; they were grounded largely in the defense of slavery, the study of Native Americans, and the impact of Darwin's theory of evolution on social, economic, and religious thought.

Government Assistance. Federal, state, and local government financial support for science, medicine, and technology varied depending on the specific field and paled in comparison to levels of support in Europe. Naval and military explorations, especially surveys of the western United States, enabled scientists to make valuable studies and record many new species and phenomena. During the Civil War the federal government made funds available for land-grant colleges, which stressed agricultural and technical education, and set forth plans for a transcontinental railroad. Government support for technology, especially railroads and the telegraph, helped to facilitate modernization. In some respects, though, government remained passive—especially in medicine: state governments did not reestablish licensing requirements for physicians until the 1870s (such requirements had been in place in the eighteenth and early nineteenth centuries), and state and national governments were less active in public health than were the governments of European countries.

The Civil War. While the Civil War produced important changes in medicine, science and technology received little practical benefit from the war. Scientists were taken away from their research to fight or work with the army. The American Association for the Advancement of Science suspended its activities until the war ended, and some scientific societies were permanently dissolved. The physical and economic destruction caused by the war decimated Southern science, which had already lagged behind Northern science. While the Union army benefited from antebellum technological innovations, including efficient railroads, the telegraph, and improvements in weapons, scientists and inventors did little during the war to advance the war effort. The need for immediate production of war materials, combined with the belief that the war would not last long, helps explain why neither government nor private industry encouraged wartime technological development.

Women in the Sciences. Nineteenth-century science, medicine, and technology remained almost exclusively reserved for males. Yet at about the same time that a small group of women were becoming increasingly vocal about their right to equal participation in society, some female pioneers emerged in medicine and science. In 1849 the British-born Elizabeth Blackwell became the first female in the modern world to receive a medical degree. Her sister Emily Blackwell and her close friend and pupil Marie Zakrzewska also became physicians, despite considerable opposition from both men and women, and the three helped to establish the first women's hospitals in the United States. Women also enjoyed greater professional opportunities in nursing during and after the Civil War. Science and technology were somewhat harder fields for females to enter, although in 1865 Maria Mitchell was made professor of astronomy at the newly established Vassar College. Despite these achievements, men continued to dominate and control medicine, science, and technology in the nineteenth century, seldom treating female professionals as their equals.

CHANGES IN SPECIFIC SCIENCES, 1850–1877

The Specialization of the Sciences. By the 1850s two of every three American scientists were limiting themselves to specific fields, and many were focusing on subfields. In the six major areas—chemistry, mathematics, physics, life sciences, earth sciences, and astronomy—American scientists made notable advances, and some of them acquired worldwide reputations. Yet American science, for the most part, remained less sophisticated than European science. Unlike Europeans, American scientists tended to focus on experimentation, measurement, and description rather than theory, although important exceptions existed.

Chemistry. In the mid-nineteenth century European chemists made revolutionary discoveries, establishing the atomic theory and the periodic table of the elements and making important advances in organic chemistry. American chemists, far behind the Europeans in theory, applied the new ideas to develop new or better industrial products, such as dyes, explosives, and petroleum derivatives. The economic benefits of an alliance with industry attracted some scientists to chemistry, despite the sometimes sensational and dangerous nature of chemical experimentation: some chemists were sickened or temporarily blinded by exposure to new compounds, while others died. In 1857 the chemist Frederick Genth noted that "the gas NO [nitrous oxide] has made me sick and I fear it more than anything else." Explosions also threatened the safety of chemists and observers, as Harvard professor John W. Webster discovered when a fragment of copper embedded itself in the chair of an absent student. Although American manufacturers increasingly supplied chemists with equipment during this period, many scientists ordered their apparatus from Europe—especially from Germany. By the late 1860s American chemistry had become specialized under the categories organic, inorganic, analytical, and physical. Still, like most other sciences, chemistry remained oriented more to practice and experimentation than to theory and pure research.

Mathematics. Mathematics had been taught in American colleges longer than most other scientific disciplines, and by 1850 the majority of schools employed instructors who specialized in the field. Around this time

John McAllister, head of a Philadelphia firm that manufactured scientific instruments

mathematics began to be taught as a tool for understanding science rather than as a purely intellectual exercise. Despite this shift, most students continued to avoid mathematics courses whenever they could. The prominent mathematician and astronomer Benjamin Peirce taught mathematics classes at Harvard with drama and flair, yet so few students enrolled in math courses that the subject was made mandatory for freshmen and sophomores in 1850. One student in the 1860s spoke of the "deep-seated aversion" that students held for the subject; a Columbia College trustee lamented in 1857 the inability of juniors to understand mathematics, noting that any problem dealing with "time, space, quantity or proportion would be considered by them equally mysterious, incomprehensible, and disgusting." Mathematics requirements for college admission remained low throughout the period, with most colleges requiring a background only in arithmetic, beginning algebra, and, less frequently, geometry. Mathematics remained far less developed in the United States than in Europe between 1850 and 1877, although some notable advances were made in the 1870s. In 1870 Peirce published *Linear Asso-*

Astronomers at Burlington, Iowa, in August 1869, waiting to observe and photograph a solar eclipse

ciative Algebra, an important introduction to modern abstract algebra, and George W. Hill made key contributions in celestial mechanics. Nevertheless, mathematics did not begin to acquire a professional reputation in America until the late nineteenth century. Its slow development hindered progress in other sciences, especially physics.

Physics. By the 1850s the teaching of physics had become fairly specialized. Professors lectured on electricity, meteorology, and magnetism, and publishers printed textbooks on optics and mechanics. Yet the number of physicists, as compared to other scientists, remained small through much of the mid nineteenth century,

largely because American mathematics had not yet reached maturity. Like their counterparts in chemistry, the few American physicists who did exist tended to focus more on inventions than on theory, although Joseph Henry stood out as an important exception to the rule. Thus, physics remained largely undeveloped during the 1850s and 1860s. As in mathematics, however, changes began to appear in the 1870s. The number of physicists increased during the decade, and some important leaders emerged in the discipline. Among these was Josiah Willard Gibbs, whose "On the Equilibrium of Heterogeneous Substances," published in two installments in the *Transactions of the Connecticut Academy of Arts and Sciences* in 1876 and 1878, ranks as one of the most signifi-

GREAT ADVENTURER

Born in 1834, John Wesley Powell dedicated his life to the study of natural science. Although he attended various schools, he gained most of his knowledge of geography, geology, and ethnology through individual exertion. In the 1850s he traversed Wisconsin, Illinois, Iowa, and Missouri, collecting shells, minerals, and plants. His colleagues so admired his work that in 1859 they chose him as secretary of the Illinois Natural History Society. After the Civil War, in which he lost an arm at Shiloh, Powell received an appointment as professor of geology at Illinois Wesleyan College, Bloomington. In 1867 and 1868 he led students on geological expeditions through the Rocky Mountains. They ascended Pike's Peak (which had no trails) and Mount Lincoln, both of which are more than than fourteen thousand feet in height.

In May 1869 Powell began, under the direction of the Smithsonian Institution, his most ambitious project to that time: a geographical and geological survey of the Colorado River and the "Great Un-

known," the Grand Canyon. It took thirteen weeks for the four boats and eleven men to complete the journey. During their nine-hundred-mile odyssey they encountered rapids, whirlpools, hostile Indians, and exhaustion. Powell described his hazardous feat in *Explorations of the Colorado River of the West* (1875). In 1879 he helped establish the U.S. Geological Survey, serving as its director from 1881 to 1894.

Powell was also a pioneer in the study of Native American languages, becoming director of the Bureau of American Ethnology at the Smithsonian in 1879. He helped create an alphabet to transcribe Indian languages and organized the anthropologists who eventually produced the monumental *Handbook of American Indians* (1907–1910). Powell died in 1902.

Source: Wallace Stegner, *Beyond the Hundredth Meridian: John Wesley Powell and the Second Opening of the West* (Boston: Houghton, Mifflin, 1954).

American paleontologists trailed Europeans in emphasizing theory, focusing instead on collecting, cataloging, and describing fossil materials. A bitter feud developed in the 1870s between the paleontologists Othniel Charles Marsh and Edward Dinker Cope, who repeatedly accused one another of stealing fossil specimens and of professional ineptitude. The feud lasted into the 1890s. A letter from Cope to Marsh is typical of the exchanges that occurred during this dispute:

My dear Prof. Marsh   Philadelphia 1/30 1873

I wish you had mentioned to me about missing specimens from Kansas, Wyoming etc. When the first suspicion crossed your mind that I knew anything about them. It is far more irritating to me to be charged with dishonorable acts than to lose material, species etc.

I never knew of any losses sustained by you, or specimens taken by any one, till those were sent me that you now have. Should any such come to my hands I will return them as I did the last. . . .

On the other hand some appropriative person has stolen *Chlorastrolites Hyposaurus* jaw etc. from me.

All the specimens you obtained during August 1872 you owe to me. Had I chosen they would all have been mine. I allowed your men Chew and Smith to accompany me and at last when they turned back discouraged, I discovered a new basin of fossils, showed it to them and allowed them to camp and collect with me for a considerable time. By this I lost several fine things. . . .

Now as to a man of honor I request of you

1st. To correct all statements and innuendos you have made to others here and elsewhere, as to my ? dishonorable conduct.

2nd. To inform me at once if others make such charges to you, about me.

Hoping you will find this much on the credit side of your account I am yours for Worth

E.D. Cope

Source: Nathan Reingold, ed., *Science in Nineteenth-Century America: A Documentary History* (New York: Hill & Wang, 1964).

cant works in theoretical physics of the nineteenth century.

Life Sciences. Nineteenth-century life scientists included naturalists, zoologists, botanists, entomologists, paleontologists, conchologists, and ornithologists. Although the largest percentage of life scientists were naturalists, paleontology experienced a wave of popularity in the late 1840s and the 1850s after the Missouri paleon-

tologist Hiram Prout reported discovering a titanothere jaw fragment in the South Dakota Badlands. Joseph Leidy's *Ancient Fauna of Nebraska*, published in 1853, also attracted national and international attention to American paleontology. Fossil findings became increasingly important in the 1860s and 1870s as the debate over Darwin's theory of evolution raged in the scientific community. Botanists also made significant contributions to the life sciences. Asa Gray published *Manual of the Botany of the Northern United States* in 1848, and in the following years he catalogued plant species throughout the northern hemisphere. Life scientists were aided by new equipment such as the achromatic microscope, which eliminated the false coloring of specimens. The leading manufacturer of the microscope, Charles A. Spencer of New York, was unsurpassed in craftmanship anywhere in the world for much of the nineteenth century. Spencer's microscopes played an important part in the expansion of laboratory research, which, in turn, helped to transform the nature of American science.

Earth Sciences. The earth sciences included oceanography, geodesy, and meteorology, but in the nineteenth century geology dominated the field. The vast undeveloped lands of the western United States gave geologists ample sources for study, and for this reason the field advanced further in the theoretical area than did most other American scientific fields; by the 1840s American geology enjoyed a level of sophistication that matched that of Europe. James Dana made important theoretical contributions to the field, hypothesizing in the 1840s and 1850s on the formation of mountains. Louis Agassiz, the Swiss immigrant who came to America in 1846, had proposed in 1840 the theory of an Ice Age in which the rapid spread of glaciers had driven many species of animals to extinction. Government-sponsored geological surveys of the West by John Wesley Powell, Grove Karl Gilbert, and Clarence E. Dutton attracted worldwide scientific attention.

Astronomy. Astronomy became increasingly popular with the American public in the 1850s, 1860s, and 1870s. By the mid 1850s there were at least twenty-five permanent observatories in the country. Before 1850 most astronomers relied upon European-made equipment, but American manufacturers soon took precedence in the development of telescopes and other astronomical devices. Astronomers also began to experiment with stellar photography, although the process would not be widely used until the 1880s. The United States government offered far less financial support for astronomy than did European governments; nevertheless, Americans made significant contributions to the field and often exhibited a sense of competition with European astronomers. By 1876 Americans had discovered forty-nine asteroids—more than had been discovered by astronomers of any other country; they had also found ten comets and about two hundred binary stars. James Dana's ideas about the possibility of lunar volcanoes, Denison Olm-

Louis Agassiz and Asa Gray, who debated the merits of Darwin's theory of evolution

stead's work on the origin of meteors, and William and George Bond's studies of the physical features of planets and comets were all influential. Like other American scientists, most astronomers emphasized observation and description more than theory; but Benjamin Peirce and Sears Walker studied the orbit of Neptune, and William Ferrel developed hypotheses about the moon's effect on the tides.

Sources:

Robert V. Bruce, *The Launching of Modern American Science, 1846–1876* (New York: Knopf, 1987);

Sally G. Kohlstedt and Margaret W. Rossiter, eds., *Historical Writings on American Science: Perspectives and Prospects* (Baltimore: Johns Hopkins University Press, 1986).

DARWIN IN AMERICA

On the Origin of Species. In 1859 the British scientist Charles Darwin published *On the Origin of Species by Means of Natural Selection, or, The Preservation of Favoured Races in the Struggle for Life*, which argued that species of plants and animals, including human beings, were not changeless but evolved from other forms. Evolution occurred through survival of the fittest, in which individual organisms that were better adapted to their environment were more likely to survive long enough to reproduce and, therefore, pass on their characteristics, while less-well-adapted ones would not. While the idea of evolution was not entirely new to the scientific community, Darwin's hypothesis generated immediate controversy in Europe and the United States. The first printing of the book in Great Britain, consisting of 1,250

copies, sold out in one day; when the first American edition was published in 1860, its sales were also rapid and steady.

Impact of Darwinism in the United States. For many Americans the theory of evolution seemed to contradict biblical accounts of the creation of the world, and some religious leaders denounced Darwin's ideas as heretical. Gradually many religious men and women came to accept evolution as part of God's plan, although some steadfastly rejected such a position. Opposition to Darwinism did not come solely from a religious perspective, however. Darwin's hypothesis also provoked critical debate among American scientists.

Scientific Support for the Theory of Evolution. Darwin maintained contact with leading American scientists. He had written to his American friend Asa Gray about his theory of evolution in 1856 and 1857 but had asked Gray to keep quiet about it. After *On the Origin of Species* was published, Gray became one of the foremost defenders of Darwinism. Gray did not fully agree with all of Darwin's ideas; unlike Darwin, for example, he believed that evolution could be reconciled with religious belief. But Gray fully supported Darwin's overall hypothesis. He also championed Darwinism on the basis of freedom of scientific thought and inquiry. Joseph Henry, director of the Smithsonian Institution, promoted Darwinism as a "working hypothesis" and called for further research by botanists and zoologists to confirm or refute it.

Scientific Opposition to Darwinism. Not all American scientists accepted or supported Darwin's theory.

Charles Darwin's *On the Origin of Species by Means of Natural Selection, or, The Preservation of Favoured Races in the Struggle for Life*, published in 1859, generated fierce debate within the American scientific community. The botanist Asa Gray emerged as the most vocal defender of Darwin's theory of evolution. In 1860 he published a review of Darwin's book in the *American Journal of Science and Arts* in which he compared Darwin's ideas to those of the Swiss-born American scientist Louis Agassiz, who ardently disagreed with Darwin's theory:

> Between the doctrines of this volume and those of the other great naturalist whose name adorns the title-page of this journal [Mr. Agassiz], the widest divergence appears. It is interesting to contrast the two, and, indeed, is necessary to our purpose; for this contrast brings out most prominently, and sets in strongest light and shade, the main features of the theory of the origination of species by means of Natural Selection. . . .
>
> [The view] of Agassiz differs fundamentally from the ordinary view only in this, that it discards the idea of a common descent as the real bond of union among the individuals of a species, and also the idea of a local origin — supposing, instead, that each species originated simultaneously, generally speaking, over the whole geographical area it now occupies or has occupied, and in perhaps as many individuals as it numbered at any subsequent period.
>
> Mr. Darwin, on the other hand, holds the orthodox view of the descent of all the individuals of a species not only from a local birthplace, but from a single ancestor or pair; and that each species has extended and established itself, through natural agencies, wherever it could; so that the actual geographical distribution of any species is by no means a primordial arrangement, but a natural result. He goes farther, and this volume is a protracted argument intended to prove that the species we recognize have not been independently created, as such, but have descended, like varieties, from other species. Varieties, on this view, are incipient or possible species: species are varieties of a larger growth and a wider and earlier divergence from the parent stock; the difference is one of degree, not of kind.

Source: Asa Gray, *Darwinia: Essays and Reviews Pertaining to Darwinism* (New York: Appleton, 1876).

The geologists Edward Hitchcock and Matthew Maury publicly condemned *On the Origin of Species*, arguing that true science confirmed the biblical account of creation. The most adamant American critic of Darwinism was the Swiss-born naturalist Louis Agassiz, who believed that God had created different species at different times and places, that some species had been destroyed by natural disasters, and that God had created new and improved species in their places. Agassiz had made these claims in the first volume of his *Contributions to the Natural History of the United States* in 1857.

Pre-1860 Debates. Agassiz's ideas drew criticism even before the publication of Darwin's work. Asa Gray's studies of plant specimens led him to question the idea that God abruptly created new species; instead, he believed, species evolved from one another. In 1857 Gray challenged Agassiz's ideas in a series of debates before the American Academy of Arts and Sciences in Boston.

Scientific Debates over Darwin's Theory. In the fall of 1859 Darwin sent copies of his just-published *On the Origin of Species* to Gray, Agassiz, and the geologist James Dana. Just at that time Dana became ill, so he did not engage in the ensuing debate over Darwin's hypothesis; had he done so, he would probably have opposed the theory. With Dana out of the picture, Agassiz was the leading scientific figure to attack Darwinism. In 1860 he and the geologist William Barton Rogers engaged in a series of four debates at the Boston Society of Natural History. Agassiz faced Gray again in debates at the American Academy of Arts and Sciences; in these debates Agassiz refused to accept any aspect of Darwin's theory. He pointed to animals that had not changed significantly over a long period of time, as well as to fossils that were as diversified as modern forms of life. Rogers and Gray offered evidence of evolutionary change in species, but Agassiz was unwilling to make any concessions. His dogmatic approach did not make a favorable impression on the scientific community, since he had no real evidence to back up his argument. After the debates Agassiz mostly limited his attacks on Darwin's theory to popular journals and lectures, while Gray contributed detailed explanations of Darwinism to scholarly journals.

1860s and 1870s. The debates and publications of 1859 and 1860 showed the growing sophistication and professionalization of American science. The scientific debate over Darwinism subsided during the Civil War; after the war the American scientific community became increasingly supportive of the theory of evolution. Paleontologists discovered fossils that helped to fill in missing evolutionary links; for example, Othniel Charles Marsh found extinct birds that seemed to show a connection between birds and reptiles. By 1877 scientific support for Darwinism was so solid that Marsh opened his vice-presidential address to the American Association for the Advancement of Science by declaring: "To doubt evolution to-day is to doubt science, and science is only another name for truth."

Sources:

Robert V. Bruce, *The Launching of Modern American Science, 1846–1876* (New York: Knopf, 1987);

Edward Lurie, *Louis Agassiz: A Life in Science* (Chicago: University of Chicago Press, 1960);

Cynthia Eagle Russett, *Darwin in America: The Intellectual Response, 1865–1912* (San Francisco: Freeman, 1976).

THE ORGANIZATION OF AMERICAN MEDICINE

Changes in the Field of Medicine. Between 1850 and 1877 American medicine became more professionalized. Modern hospitals began to appear in the 1860s and 1870s, and along with them came the professionalization of nursing. The nation's physicians, however, lacked the professional cohesiveness that American scientists were beginning to find during these decades; not until the early twentieth century would a unified and independent medical profession be established in the United States. The delay occurred largely because of the lack of standardized educational and licensing requirements for doctors and because of the sharp divisions that existed within the medical community.

American Physicians. By 1850 the United States had forty-two medical schools; France, by comparison, had only three. Quantity did not signify quality, however. Many schools were established by doctors to enhance their own prestige rather than to promote a true medical education. Standards were frequently low, and the length of study was often kept to a minimum. In the 1820s, moreover, state legislatures had begun to repeal medical licensing laws that had been enacted in the eighteenth and early nineteenth centuries because many Americans viewed licensing as an abuse of privilege and an opportunity for favoritism. Lack of licensing requirements meant that American medicine in the mid nineteenth century included doctors who practiced conventional medicine and those who preferred homeopathy and other non-mainstream forms.

Attempts at Reform. In 1846 a group of physicians met in New York to establish the American Medical Association (AMA). Composed mainly of younger, less-well-established doctors, the organization's main goals were to raise and standardize educational requirements for a medical degree and to create a code of ethics that would distinguish "regular" doctors from "irregular" ones who practiced homeopathy or other "natural" forms of medicine. The AMA received little support in its first few decades: irregular practitioners, of whom there were many, viewed the organization with disdain, but established regular physicians also remained lukewarm in their support. Not until the early twentieth century did the AMA begin to exert significant influence in the medical community.

RISE OF WOMEN PHYSICIANS

In 1849 Elizabeth Blackwell became the first woman in the United States — and in the modern world — to earn a medical degree. Her sister Emily received her M.D. in 1854, and the two women lobbied for women's hospitals and greater access to professional medical education for women. In an 1864 address Elizabeth Blackwell describes the opposition she met in her quest to practice medicine and reflects on the progress women have made in the field since then:

Let us then take up the main question, and that we may realize that the practice of medicine by women is a growing influence, and cannot be overlooked, allow me to state a few facts drawn from personal experience.

In 1845 when I resolved to become a physician, six eminent physicians, in different parts of the country were written to, for advice. They all united in dissuading me, stating, "That it was an utter impossibility for a woman to obtain a medical education; that the idea though good in itself, was eccentric and utopian, utterly impracticable!" It was only by long-continued searching through all the colleges of the country, that one was at last found willing to grant admission. When I entered college in 1847, the ladies of the town pronounced the undertaking crazy, or worse, and declared they would die rather than employ a woman as a physician. In 1852, when establishing myself in New York there was the utmost difficulty in finding a boarding-house where the simple name, as physician could be placed; ladies would not reside in a house so marked, and expressed utmost astonishment that it should be allowed in a respectable establishment. I presented American and foreign testimonials of medical qualification, to one of the city Dispensaries, asking admission as assistant physician, in the department of diseases of women and children; the request was refused. I asked permission to visit in the female wards of one of the city hospitals; the application was laid on the table, not being considered worthy even of notice. There was a blank wall of social and professional antagonism, facing the woman physician, that formed a situation of singular and painful loneliness, leaving her without support, respect, or professional counsel.

... Since that time ten medical schools have received women as students, and given them the diploma of Doctor. In three states, female medical schools have been established, holding charters granted by State legislatures; the diploma conferred by them placing their graduates on exactly the same legal footing, as the ordinary physician; the corporators of these female colleges being respectable bodies of men and women, and in some instances enlisting the sanction, by subscription, of a very large number of influential citizens. From the most accurate data, which we have been able to collect, several hundred women have been graduated as physicians at these schools within the last ten years.

Source: Elizabeth and Emily Blackwell, *Address on the Medical Education of Women* (New York: Baptist & Taylor, 1864).

Bellevue Hospital, New York City, in 1879

Postwar Changes. The medical field began to move toward greater professionalization after the Civil War as doctors, like other professionals, realized that unity would help protect their economic interests. Calls for the restoration of medical licensing increased in the 1870s, and states began to reimpose such requirements. At the same time, the rise of the modern university in the United States influenced medical education: like the German schools on which they were modeled, American universities increasingly stressed professional training. Educational reformers, such as Harvard University president Charles William Eliot, led the way in establishing higher educational standards for medical students: beginning in the fall of 1871 the academic year at Harvard Medical School was extended from four months to nine, students were required to attend three rather than two years of school, and laboratory work became mandatory in certain courses. Other universities soon adopted similar changes.

Nursing. Until Florence Nightingale emerged from the Crimean War as the most celebrated woman in the world, most nurses were not professionals but rather neighbors or relatives of homebound patients. Nurses who worked in hospitals were usually untrained and were sometimes conscripted from penitentiaries or almshouses. After the Civil War the growing number of hospitals increased the need for trained, professional nurses; but even then it was social reformers, rather than doctors, who initiated the change. In New York in 1872 a group of female, mostly upper-class reformers organized a committee to regulate treatment in almshouses and hospitals. At Manhattan's Bellevue Hospital they found that patients were being kept in "unspeakable" conditions, and they noted many examples of unsanitary and

negligent practices. When reformers established training schools for nurses in New York, New Haven, and Boston in 1873, they began the establishment of nursing as a profession. They attempted to attract nurses only from the "respectable" classes so as to make hospitals more attractive to the middle class and to have an uplifting effect on the poor.

Hospitals. The rise of nursing made possible the emergence of the modern hospital. During much of the nineteenth century hospitals did not occupy a central role in medical treatment. Since medical technology existed at only a rudimentary level, patients could obtain the same treatment at home as in the hospital; therefore, although some Americans visited doctors' offices, dispensaries, or outpatient clinics, most received their medical care in their homes. Hospital patients consisted mainly

An early graduating class at the Bellevue nurses' training school

of the poor. The first American hospital survey, conducted in 1873, listed only 173 hospitals in the nation. These institutions were small, were not usually affiliated with medical schools, and did not emphasize medical research. During the Civil War conditions in hospitals began to improve. Basing their ideas on methods employed in the 1850s by the English nurse Florence Nightingale, organizations such as the United States Sanitary Commission drew attention to the need for proper medical sanitation and hygiene. Continued emphasis on hospital cleanliness and order after the war and the professionalization of nursing helped attract more Americans to hospitals in the 1860s and 1870s. Joseph Lister's invention of antiseptic surgery in 1867 also began to change the nature of hospitals, although most physicians did not adopt the practice until the late 1870s. By 1877 hospitals were improving, but not until the end of the nineteenth century would they begin to resemble the institutions of today.

Public Health. Epidemics of cholera and yellow fever, which occurred on a fairly regular basis in some cities, led in the antebellum years to the organization of citizens' sanitary associations. These groups attempted to prevent outbreaks of disease by keeping cities cleaner. Louisiana established the first state board of health in 1855, but not until the postwar years did cities and states create effective public health organizations. New York City's Metropolitan Board of Health and the Massachusetts Board of Health, established in 1866 and 1869, respectively, helped set the standards for public health agencies. In 1872 doctors and reformers founded the American Public Health Association, which advocated greater regulatory powers for public health departments. In general, however, European countries were ahead of the United States in organizing health agencies: not until the twentieth century did the federal government organize a permanent public health department.

Sources:

Susan M. Reverby, *Ordered to Care: The Dilemma of American Nursing, 1850–1945* (Cambridge: Cambridge University Press, 1987);

Charles E. Rosenberg, *The Care of Strangers: The Rise of America's Hospital System* (New York: Basic Books, 1987);

Paul Starr, *The Social Transformation of American Medicine* (New York: Basic Books, 1982).

THE SOCIAL SCIENCES

Emergence of Social Science. Between the late 1830s and the 1870s the various disciplines that make up the social sciences began to develop as a distinct field in the United States. One of the most important reasons for this development was the growing influence of science in general in America as increasing industrialization and advances in transportation and communication demanded more specialized knowledge. Colleges and universities responded to this demand by adding scientific and technical training to the literary and theological studies on which they had concentrated previously. Edu-

---

PROSLAVERY THEORY AND SOCIOLOGY

As sectional tensions escalated in the 1850s, Southerners became increasingly defensive of slavery. George Fitzhugh produced some of the most sophisticated justifications of the institution, in the process helping to establish the new field of sociology:

We hesitated for some time in selecting the title of our work. We did not like to employ the newly-coined word Sociology. We could, however, find none other in the whole range of the English language, that would even faintly convey the idea that we wished to express. We looked to the history of the term. We found that within the last half century, disease, long lurking in the system of free society, had broken out into a hundred open manifestations. Thousands of authors and schemers, such as Owen, Louis Blanc and Fourier, had arisen proposing each a different mode of treatment for the disease which all confessed to exist. Society had never been in such a state before. New exigencies in its situation had given rise to new ideas, and to a new philosophy. This new philosophy must have a name, and as none could be found ready-made to suit the occasion, the term Sociology was compounded, of hybrid birth, half Greek and half Latin, as the technical appellative of the new-born science. In Europe, the term is familiar as "household words." It grates harshly, as yet, on Southern ears, because to us it is new and superfluous — the disease of which it treats being unknown amongst us. But as our book is intended to prove that we are indebted to domestic slavery, for our happy exemption from the social afflictions that have originated this philosophy, it became necessary and appropriate that we should employ this new word in our title. The fact that, before the institution of Free Society, there was no such term, and that it is not in use in slave countries, now, shows pretty clearly that Slave Society, ancient and modern, has ever been in so happy a condition, so exempt from ailments, that no doctors have arisen to treat it of its complaints, or to propose remedies for their cure. The term, therefore, is not only appropriate to the subject and the occasion, but pregnantly suggestive of facts and arguments that sustain our theory.

Source: George Fitzhugh, *Sociology for the South; or, The Failure of Free Society* (Richmond, Va.: A. Morris, 1854).

---

cational leaders, many of whom had studied in Europe, based their reforms on European educational advances.

History. As in Europe—especially in Germany—the field of history went through important changes in the middle decades of the century. History began to be taught as a distinct discipline in the pre–Civil War years, and Jared Sparks, Thomas R. Dew, and Francis Lieber emerged as leaders in the profession. These men emphasized the importance of historical study for understanding modern thought and society; Dew's *Digest of the*

Illustrations from Josiah Nott and George R. Glidden's *Types of Mankind*

Laws, Customs, Manners, and Institutions of the Ancient and Modern Nations (1853) exemplified this trend. The German emphasis on historical method, which stressed accuracy and through data collection, influenced American historians. These historians discussed their findings in seminars, which in the 1870s and 1880s became the dominant form of teaching for graduate students in the field.

Political Science. During the 1850s, 1860s, and 1870s political science had not yet achieved the status of a separate discipline; at most universities it was taught in history departments. When political science courses were offered, they usually focused on constitutional history or analysis. Some exceptions existed, however: in the late 1840s and 1850s Yale University offered courses in political theory and international law; and at the South Carolina College, Francis Lieber taught about politics from a theoretical framework. The first separate department of political science was organized in 1880 at Columbia University; other universities did not establish political science departments until the twentieth century.

Economics. In contrast to political science, the study of economics—or "political economy," as it was then called—was fairly well developed by the mid nineteenth century. Some colleges had offered classes in commerce and trade as early as the 1750s, and by 1860 most colleges included political economy in their curricula. The first professorship of political economy was established at Harvard University in 1871, and for the remainder of the century the study of economics became increasingly specialized. The related discipline of statistics also made important progress during the mid nineteenth century. The American Statistical Association had been founded in

1839 "to secure authentic information upon every department of human pursuit and social condition." One of the association's main goals, to promote the compilation of more accurate state and federal census reports, was achieved with the 1850 census. In 1848 James D. B. DeBow of New Orleans organized the first state bureau of statistics. During the period physicians, public health workers, and insurance actuaries made many statistical surveys.

Anthropology. In the mid nineteenth century a new social science, anthropology, grew out of the older discipline of ethnology. Today ethnology, the study of human cultural systems, is a subdiscipline of anthropology, the science that examines the origins, physical characteristics, and customs of human beings, but in the mid nineteenth century the terms were often used interchangeably. The explosive issue of slavery in antebellum America promoted the study of ethnology as Southerners turned to scientific theory to try to justify the institution. Beginning in the 1830s and peaking in the 1850s, Southern writers published books and articles claiming to show that blacks were inherently inferior to whites and thus required the civilizing effects of slavery. In *Types of Mankind* (1854) Josiah Nott and George R. Gliddon theorized that blacks and whites were different species. Other Southern ethnologists, such as John Bachman and S. D. Baldwin, while supporting the notion of racial inferiority, disputed the idea that different races of human beings constituted different species. Interest in ethnology was by no means confined to the South: Northern scientists, including Samuel G. Morton and Louis Agassiz, also worked in the field. Mid-nineteenth-century ethnologists and anthropologists were also interested in Native Americans: Lewis H. Morgan's studies of the Iroquois Indians of New York, *Systems of Consanguinity* (1869) and *Ancient Society* (1877), helped to shape anthropological theory not only in America but throughout the world. The American Museum of Natural History, established in 1869, promoted the study of anthropology, and in 1876 the United States Geological Survey sponsored field studies of Native American culture and archaeology that led to the establishment of the Bureau of American Ethnology.

Sociology. Like anthropology, the discipline of sociology, which examines the roles of institutions and groups within a society, arose in America partly out of the Southern defense of slavery. Two books published in 1854 demonstrate this origin: the Mississippian Henry Hughes's *A Treatise on Sociology, Theoretical and Applied* and the Virginian George Fitzhugh's *Sociology for the South; or, The Failure of Free Society.* Both works defend slavery as the most effective means of ordering social relations. The study of moral philosophy in the early nineteenth century also contributed to the rise of sociology. In the 1830s Robert Hamilton Bishop offered a course at Miami University titled Philosophy of Social Relations, and from 1850 to 1858 William H. McGuffey, professor of moral philosophy at the University of Virginia, taught a course titled Philosophy of Social Relations, or Ethics of Society. Likewise, the subject of "social science," which first developed in the 1850s, played an important role in the formation of sociology. This subject, different from the modern-day definition of social science, focused on contemporary social issues such as immigration, race relations, poverty, crime, alcoholism, and education. Henry C. Carey published the first book on the subject, *The Principles of Social Science,* in 1858. In 1868 R. E. Thompson, a student of Carey's, offered the first independent course in social science at the University of Pennsylvania; Yale University, the University of Missouri, and Columbia University followed suit in the 1870s and 1880s. These courses tended to focus on Herbert Spencer's formulation of Social Darwinism, the idea that human societies and institutions, like organisms, evolve through a process of natural selection.

Founding of the American Social Science Association. In August 1865 the Massachusetts Board of Charities invited selected individuals throughout the nation to help establish an organization dedicated to social science. The social reformer Frank Sanborn described the organization's purpose as "the discussion of those questions relating to the Sanitary Condition of the People, the Relief, Employment, and Education of the Poor, the Prevention of Crime, the Amelioration of the Criminal Law, the Discipline of Prisons, the Remedial Treatment of the Insane, and those numerous matters of statistical and philanthropic interest which are included under the general head of 'Social Science.'" Sanborn's statement shows that the American Social Science Association (ASSA) was devoted to the older conception of social science as a means to cure contemporary social problems. As universities offered more specialized social science courses in the 1870s, a divergence became apparent between the academic view of the discipline and that of the Social Science Association. Nevertheless, the founding of the ASSA is another indication of the mid-nineteenth-century interest in the scientific study of society.

Sources:

Hamilton Cravens, "History of the Social Sciences," in *Historical Writings on American Science: Perspectives and Prospects,* edited by Sally G. Kohlstedt and Margaret W. Rossiter (Baltimore: Johns Hopkins University Press, 1986), pp. 183–207;

Thomas L. Haskell, *The Emergence of Professional Social Science: The American Social Science Association and the Nineteenth- Century Crisis of Authority* (Chicago: University of Illinois Press, 1977).

TECHNOLOGICAL CHANGE

The Spirit of Technology. In the mid nineteenth century the United States witnessed dynamic technological changes that were brought on by the growth of business and industry. European countries, linked in a competitive capitalistic market with Americans, also experienced technological advances. In 1851 the first modern world's fair, the London Crystal Palace Exhibition, was held to display new discoveries and inventions. American products, while representing a small proportion of the exhibits at the fair, made a strong impression on European visitors. Cyrus McCormick's reaper, Samuel Colt's revolver, Gail Borden's dehydrated "meat biscuit," and Charles Goodyear's vulcanized rubber were some of the most popular American attractions. So successful was the London exhibition that in 1853 the United States hosted its own world's fair in New York City to display the revolutionary pace of American technological progress to visiting Europeans as well as to the American public. Americans and Europeans alike celebrated technology, viewing it, like much else in their changing world, with optimism.

Technology and Agriculture. American innovations in agriculture had a profound impact on the lives of farmers, especially in the new agricultural lands that were opening in the West. The chilled-iron plow, patented in

The Crystal Palace at the 1853 World's Fair in New York City

John A. Roebling's Niagara Suspension Bridge, circa 1855

1868 by James Oliver, helped farmers break up the dry, hard prairie soil, while the gang plow, which had wheels, allowed the operator to ride on the machine. During the 1860s and 1870s harrows, which broke up and smoothed the soil, and grain drills, which scattered grain, were improved. By the 1870s the straddle-row cultivator had become popular; riding on the cultivator and operating the attached shovels with his feet, the farmer could cover twice as much acreage as was possible with the one-horse plow. The most important labor-saving device was the agricultural binder. The reaper, invented by Cyrus McCormick in 1834, had mechanized the cutting of wheat, but manual labor was still required to collect and bind the cut product; the binder, introduced by John E. Heath in 1850 and later improved by John F. Appleby and other inventors, mechanized these processes as well, resulting in a significant expansion in American wheat production.

Transportation. Between 1850 and 1860 railroad mileage more than tripled in the United States, and by 1860 it surpassed that of any other country in the world. In 1852 the Mississippi River was crossed by a railroad for the first time, and a year later Congress approved funds for an army expedition to select the best route for a transcontinental rail line. Sectional tensions prevented the building of the line until the 1860s, and in 1869 the first railroad extending from one coast to the other was completed when the east-to-west and west-to-east sections met at Promontory Point, Utah. Coal-burning locomotives began to replace wood-burning ones in the 1850s, and the introduction of the Pullman Luxury Car in 1858 and the Pullman Hotel Car in 1867 made train travel more appealing to Americans. Safety increased with the advent of the air brake, invented in 1868 by George Westinghouse, and the adoption of automatic signal systems to avoid accidents between trains using

the same tracks. Finally, iron and steel bridges began to replace wooden ones, further increasing safety as well as holding down costs. The first all-iron railroad bridge was built in 1845, and in 1851 the engineer John A. Roebling designed the Niagara Suspension Bridge. Construction of the Brooklyn Bridge, which accommodated both road and train traffic, began in 1869 and was completed in 1883.

Technology and the City. Technology helped foster the growth of American cities between 1850 and 1877. The first streetcar began operation in New York City in 1852; in 1873 the first cable car appeared in San Francisco; in 1864 an engineer, Hugh B. Wilson, proposed the construction of a subway in New York (the first subway system, however, would open in the 1890s in Boston). Elisha Graves Otis invented the passenger elevator in 1852; following further improvements, the elevator would become a central component of the skyscrapers that would be built in the 1880s and 1890s. Even in the 1860s and 1870s, however, engineers were using steel to build stronger and taller buildings. The Bessemer process, developed in the 1850s as a cheap and efficient means of making steel from iron, led to a large increase in steel production and helped foster this change.

Telegraph and Telephone. In 1844 Samuel F. B. Morse revolutionized American communications with the perfection of the telegraph. In the 1850s Morse and other inventors, especially Cyrus W. Field, promoted the development of a cable that would allow telegraph signals to be transmitted across the Atlantic Ocean. When the transatlantic cable was completed in August 1858, Queen Victoria cabled President James Buchanan of her hope that "the electric cable which now connects Great Britain with the United States will prove an additional link of friendship between the nations." Within a few weeks, however, the cable had lost its ability to transmit signals, and the outbreak of the Civil War delayed repairs. After 1865 new cables were laid, connecting the United States, Britain, and France; for the next fifty years ocean cables served as the quickest means of overseas communications. In 1873 Alexander Graham Bell arrived in Boston from Scotland and began looking for a way to transmit sounds through a telegraph wire. Bell and his assistant, Thomas A. Watson, conducted many experiments with pairs of telegraph instruments, and on 2 June 1875 Bell heard the vibrations of Watson's finger through the wire. Finally, on 10 March 1876 Bell communicated the first vocal message over an electric wire: "Watson, come here, I want you." By that time Bell had already received a patent for his invention: the telephone.

Electrical Innovations. In the 1860s and 1870s European and American inventors began to explore the field of electric lighting. Electric dynamos, which had been created in the 1830s and 1840s by Joseph Henry, Thomas Davenport, and Charles G. Page, provided the energy for these experiments. Before 1880 at least nineteen electric lamps had been perfected by Europeans and Ameri-

The first cable cars in San Francisco, September 1873

cans, including the arc lamp, which was used in street lighting. The most profound impact on the lighting industry, however, was made by Thomas Alva Edison, a prolific inventor who before 1877 had created an electric voting machine; the mimeograph; and the "quadraplex," by means of which four telegraph messages could be sent through a single wire. In 1876 Edison established what he called a "scientific" factory at Menlo Park, New Jersey, where, with fifteen assistants, he tried to create "a minor invention every ten days and a big thing every six months or so." In 1878 Edison would transform his factory into the Edison Electric Light Company, and in 1879 he would perfect the incandescent lightbulb.

Technology and Science. Most Americans of the mid nineteenth century viewed technology as the practical outcome of modern science. The proliferation of technological innovations during the period contributed to this perception, as did the public declarations of some American scientists. Although the president of Rensselaer Polytechnical Institute in Troy, New York, proclaimed in 1855 that "science has cast its illuminating rays on every process of Industrial Art," most technologists depended less on scientific theory than on trial-and-error experimentation and intuition. This divergence was, however, less marked in some areas than others. Developments in the field of electricity were based on scientific theories dating back to the discovery of electromagnetism and the work of such scientists as Joseph Henry and Michael Faraday. Moreover, technology became increasingly linked to science in the middle of the century as scientific education became more advanced and the number of technical schools increased. In the

1840s and 1850s Yale, Harvard, and other Ivy League institutions established "scientific schools" that stressed engineering and technology, and the Massachusetts Institute of Technology was founded in 1861. Technology, like medicine, responded to an industrializing society by becoming more scientific and more professional.

Sources:

Kendall A. Birr, "Science in American Industry," in *Science and Society in the United States,* edited by David D. VanTassel and Michael G. Hall (Homewood, Ill.: Dorsey Press, 1966), pp. 35–80;

Robert V. Bruce, *The Launching of Modern American Science, 1846–1876* (New York: Knopf, 1987);

John W. Oliver, *History of American Technology* (New York: Ronald Press, 1956).

THE UNITED STATES SANITARY COMMISSION

Beginnings. In April 1861 the Lady Managers of the New York Infirmary for Women and Children, the first hospital run for and by women, formed the Woman's Central Relief Association to train nurses and send them, as well as food and clothing, to Union army hospitals. The organization attracted a sizable group of wealthy female reformers, along with a small cadre of male leaders. Out of it emerged the Commission of Inquiry and Advice in Respect of the Sanitary Interests of the United States Forces, or the United States Sanitary Commission. The venture was modeled after the British Sanitary Commission, which had been created during the Crimean War to promote cleaner, healthier hospital conditions.

Official Recognition of the Sanitary Commission. The creation of the United States Sanitary Commission

The Agamemnon laying the transatlantic telegraph cable

attracted the interest of men and women in the medical field, and on 15 May 1861 a delegation of male physicians traveled to Washington, D.C., to secure presidential approval for their plan. The Army Medical Bureau, the official medical agency of the Union army, viewed the delegation as a threat to its powers; the head of the bureau, the surgeon general, also questioned the use of female nurses. The delegation persisted in its efforts, however, meeting with Secretary of War Simon Cameron and President Abraham Lincoln. Lincoln initially hesitated to support the commission, calling it a "fifth wheel to the coach," but on 13 June he signed a bill officially establishing the U.S. Sanitary Commission as an investigatory and advisory board.

Functions of the Sanitary Commission. Although women composed the majority of Sanitary Commission volunteers, male leaders determined the direction and ultimate goals of the organization. Henry Bellows, a Unitarian minister, was the president of the commission; Alexander Dallas Bache, professor of natural philosophy and chemistry at the University of Pennsylvania, was vice president; and the landscape architect Frederick Law Olmsted and the lawyer George Templeton Strong served as officers. The commission employed about five hundred agents, mostly men, to distribute medical supplies in army camps and hospitals and to teach sanitary procedures to soldiers; it also relied on volunteer support. By 1863 about seven thousand local affiliates existed; physicians and prominent businessmen usually served as officers of these organizations, but women made up the majority of the volunteer force. The affiliates raised money by holding bazaars and "sanitary fairs" and sent volunteer nurses and food, clothing, medicine, and other supplies to camps and hospitals. They also offered food and lodging to soldiers traveling to or from the front.

Reform in the Army. The Army Medical Bureau, which had opposed the creation of the Sanitary Commission, refused to cooperate with it, prompting the com-

mission to lobby the government for changes in the bureau. The commission especially criticized the Medical Bureau's seniority system, which kept younger, more-progressive doctors from becoming leaders. With the prodding of the Sanitary Commission, Congress in May 1862 passed a bill that eliminated the seniority system and allowed the surgeon general to appoint inspectors to reform the medical system. Lincoln appointed a new surgeon general, William Alexander Hammond. Younger and more reform minded than his predecessor, Hammond worked closely with the Sanitary Commission to produce a more efficient and hygienic army medical system.

Criticism of the Sanitary Commission. While the commission served an important philanthropic need, the motives of its leaders were not entirely humanitarian. Commissioners insisted on strict military discipline and order, sometimes to the detriment of sick or wounded soldiers. Staff surgeons who did not follow required procedures when requesting medicine, for instance, were often denied lifesaving drugs. The Sanitary Commission also prohibited volunteers from delivering supplies, medical or otherwise, to hospitalized soldiers: only hired agents could distribute provisions.

The Christian Commission. One of the most vocal critics of Sanitary Commission policies was the Christian Commission, a volunteer organization formed to provide religious and humanitarian services to Northern soldiers. Leaders of the Christian Commission were especially critical of the Sanitary Commission's insistence that only paid agents work in the hospitals and that these agents deal mainly with doctors rather than with sick or wounded soldiers. Christian Commission volunteers, by contrast, worked directly with soldiers whenever they could, in an attempt to "enhance the value of both gifts and services by kind words to the soldier as *a man*, not a

Representatives of the U.S. Sanitary Commission at
Gettysburg, Pennsylvania, July 1863

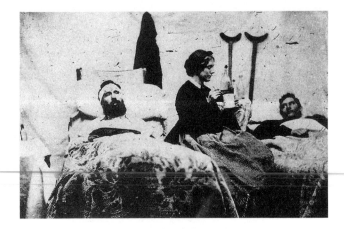

A female nurse in a Union military hospital

machine." Directors of the Sanitary Commission responded by portraying the Christian Commission as sentimental and undisciplined; board member Charles Stillé asserted that the rival organization had no use for "ideas of fitness, practical usefulness, efficiency, or of anything else essential to the success of the object in view."

Impact of the U.S. Sanitary Commission. The U.S. Sanitary Commission played a major role in mobilizing civilian support for Union war aims. It also represented the largest volunteer effort to that time in the United States. Its emphasis on discipline and efficiency reflected a greater change in American society as a whole: whereas prewar reform efforts had taken the form of individual acts of benevolence, the Sanitary Commission was a large, bureaucratic organization. Like the executives of large corporations, commission leaders based their decisions on scientific theories of management. The commission, along with the army, also helped to bring about the professionalization of nursing: in July 1862 Surgeon General Hammond ordered that at least one-third of army nurses be women, and over the course of the war more than three thousand women worked as paid army nurses; more than two thousand others served as volunteers or paid agents of the Sanitary Commission. The Sanitary Commission also stimulated awareness of the necessity for more-hygienic practices in American medicine. Postwar social reformers, many of whom had worked with the commission, pushed for improved sanitary conditions in hospitals and for the professional training of nurses. Organizations such as the American Public Health Association, established in 1872, and the American Red Cross, founded in 1881 by Clara Barton, also reflected this emphasis.

Sources:

George M. Fredrickson, *The Inner Civil War: Northern Intellectuals and the Crisis of Union* (New York: Harper & Row, 1965);

William Quentin Maxwell, *Lincoln's Fifth Wheel: The Political History of the United States Sanitary Commission* (New York: Longmans, Green, 1956);

James McPherson, *Battle Cry of Freedom: The Civil War Era* (New York: Oxford University Press, 1988).

HEADLINE MAKERS

WILLIAM ALEXANDER HAMMOND

1828-1900
NEUROLOGIST, SURGEON GENERAL OF
THE U.S. ARMY

Prewar Experience. William Alexander Hamilton was born in Annapolis, Maryland, in 1828 and received his M.D. from the University of the City of New York in 1848. He spent a year working at the Pennsylvania Hospital in Philadelphia before moving to Saco, Maine, to establish a medical practice. Within a few months he abandoned his practice and joined the army as an assistant surgeon. He held the position for a decade, serving on army posts in the Southwest, Florida, Michigan, and Kansas. He also spent some time in Europe, studying the medical organization and services of armies there. During his travels Hammond conducted botanical and physiological investigations. He published books on his findings, some of which were reprinted in England and translated into German and French. His *Experimental Researches Relative to the Nutritive Value and Physiological Effects of Albumen, Starch, and Gum, when Singly and Exclusively Used as a Food*, published in 1857, won the American Medical Association's annual prize.

The Civil War. In 1859 Hammond resigned from the army and became professor of anatomy and physiology at the University of Maryland. When the Civil War broke out he reenlisted in the army as an assistant surgeon. He helped establish army hospitals in Baltimore, Hagerstown, and Frederick, Maryland, before being transferred to West Virginia, where he became inspector of camps and hospitals under Gen. William Rosecrans. In an effort to improve medical administration in the army, the United States Sanitary Commission persuaded President Abraham Lincoln to appoint Hammond surgeon general in 1862. Hammond initiated several reforms in his new position, raising requirements for admission to the army medical corps; greatly expanding the number of general, post, and garrison hospitals; and working with the Sanitary Commission to create cleaner, less-crowded conditions in the hospitals. His efforts, as well as those of other reformers, resulted in a much lower hospital mortality rate than had been the case in previous wars. Hammond also supported plans, already in existence, for an army ambulance service and, in 1862, created an army medical museum. Despite his accomplishments Hammond's relations with Secretary of War Edwin M. Stanton were strained. As a result Hammond was court-martialed and dismissed from the army in the summer of 1864 on charges of making unauthorized purchases of medicine and other supplies. In 1878 Congress approved a bill to reopen the case, and in 1879 Hammond was exonerated on all charges.

Reentry into Civilian Life. After returning to civilian life Hammond set up practice in New York and soon became a leader in the study of neurology, which was just beginning to draw specialized attention from the medical community. In 1866 he accepted a position as lecturer on nervous and mental diseases in 1866 at the College of Physicians and Surgeons in New York; the following year he became professor of nervous and mental diseases at Bellevue Hospital Medical College. He moved to several other institutions afterward, including the University of the City of New York, before establishing a sanitarium for mental patients in Washington, D.C., in 1889. He worked at the sanitarium until he died of heart disease in 1900. During these years he devoted much attention to the therapeutic properties of animal extracts.

Contributions to Medicine. Hammond published extensively during his career. His works include *On Wakefulness: With an Introductory Chapter on the Physiology of Sleep* (1866), *Sleep and Its Derangements* (1869), and *Insanity in Its Medical Relations* (1883); his most significant work, *Treatise on Diseases of the Nervous System*, was published in 1871. Hammond also founded or cofounded several medical journals, including the *Journal of Nervous and Medical Diseases*, and published several novels and plays. By showing that at least some mental disorders were physically based illnesses that could be treated through medical means, Hammond pioneered the field of neurology in America. Had the conflict with Secretary

Stanton not occurred, Hammond might have implemented even more hospital reforms as surgeon general. While his proposals to create an army medical school and a permanent general hospital in Washington were not accepted at the time, they would be realized in later years.

Sources:

Bonnie Ellen Blustein, *Preserve Your Love for Science: Life of William A. Hammond, American Neurologist* (New York: Cambridge University Press, 1991);

William Quentin Maxwell, *Lincoln's Fifth Wheel: The Political History of the United States Sanitary Commission* (New York: Longmans, Green, 1956).

JOSEPH HENRY

1797-1878
PHYSICIST

Early Years. Joseph Henry was born in Albany, New York, in 1797. His working-class family often struggled for money, and in his early teens Henry began working as a store clerk. He also served as an apprentice to a jeweler and watchmaker, and in his extra time he acted and wrote plays for an amateur theatrical group. Reading a popular book on natural science, he became so fascinated by the subject that he committed himself to becoming a scientist. He studied assiduously, was admitted as a student at the Albany Academy, and in 1826 became professor of mathematics and natural philosophy at that institution.

Henry's Early Experiments. As a professor Henry made important advances in the study of electromagnetism. A British scientist, William Sturgeon, had invented the electromagnet in 1825, but Henry improved the device to its present-day form. Sturgeon had wrapped bare copper wire around a bar of soft iron; when a current was sent through the wire, the iron produced enough magnetic force to lift a nine-pound piece of iron or steel. By using insulated rather than bare wire Henry was able to lift heavier weights. Like Henry, the British scientist Michael Faraday experimented with electromagnetism. In 1831 Faraday discovered that the iron core of the electromagnet, when moved in and out of its surrounding copper coils, produced electricity in the wire—a phenomenon known as electromagnetic induction. It appears that Henry had discovered induction before Faraday but failed to publish his observations; he did not do so until three months after Faraday's findings appeared in the April 1832 issue of the *Annals of Philosophy*. The work of both men was important for the development of the electric-power industry in the nineteenth century.

Telegraphic Experiments. During his years at the Albany Academy, Henry also discovered that the arrangement of the wire coils of an electromagnet affected its strength and durability. Using two different coil arrangements, he created two electromagnets, which he called a quantity magnet and an intensity magnet. Using the intensity magnet, Henry transmitted signals through a wire three miles in length. He published his findings in the *American Journal of Science* in 1831. Later in the 1830s Samuel Morse improved on Henry's device by inventing the relay, which allowed the signal to be transmitted over longer distances, and the Morse Code, which made it possible for letters to be translated into electrical impulses and vice versa. Morse patented this invention in 1844 as the telegraph.

Other Inventions. Henry also invented an electric motor while at Albany Academy. He balanced an electromagnetic bar horizontally on a pivot; below each end of the bar was a vertical permanent magnet. Two wires extended from each end of the bar; when the bar was tilted in either direction the wires on that end made contact with the terminals of a battery, thereby sending current through the wires and producing magnetism in the bar. The permanent magnet on that end was arranged so that the pole nearest the bar was of the same polarity as that end of the electromagnet; since magnets of the same polarity repel each other, the bar would tilt the other way, breaking the connection with the battery on that end and establishing a connection with the battery on the other end. That end of the bar would then be repelled by the permanent magnet below it, and the electromagnet would tilt back the other way, and so on. During one experiment the oscillation continued for more than an hour. In 1832 Henry accepted a professorship in natural philosophy at the College of New Jersey in Princeton, where he not only continued to make important discoveries in electromagnetism but also conducted studies in solar physics and other branches of physics.

The Smithsonian Institution. When the Englishman John Smithson, who had never been to America, died in 1829 he bequeathed more than half a million dollars to the United States to found an institution "for the increase and diffusion of knowledge among men." Congress established the Smithsonian Institution in 1846, and Henry, the best-known scientist in America at the time, was named as its secretary, or head. Throughout his tenure Henry emphasized the necessity of original research, ensuring that the Smithsonian would be not just a natural science museum but a research institution. He introduced such innovations as the production of weather forecasts (especially storm warnings) based on reports of weather conditions obtained by telegraph. Henry remained secretary of the Smithsonian until his death in 1878. He also helped establish the American Association for the Advancement of Science in 1847 and served as president of this organization from 1868 until he died.

Sources:

Thomas Coulson, *Joseph Henry: His Life and Work* (Princeton: Princeton University Press, 1950);

Bernard Jaffe, "Joseph Henry," in his *Men of Science in America: The Role of Science in the Growth of Our Country* (New York: Simon & Schuster, 1944).

JOSIAH NOTT

1804-1873

PHYSICIAN, ETHNOLOGIST

Background. Born and raised in Columbia, South Carolina, Josiah Nott graduated from South Carolina College in 1824. He attended the College of Physicians and Surgeons in New York City for one year before moving to Philadelphia, where he received his medical degree from the University of Pennsylvania in 1827. In 1829 he returned to Columbia, where he established a private practice. Six years later he moved to Mobile, Alabama. He aided in the establishment of the Mobile Medical Society in 1841 and helped enact a law regulating the practice of medicine in Alabama. He served as professor of anatomy at the University of Louisiana in 1857–1858, then returned to Mobile to help establish the Medical College of Alabama. Nott took the position of professor of surgery at the school.

Civil War and After. When the Civil War broke out, Nott joined the Confederate army medical department as a surgeon. During the early years of the war he served as director of the Confederate General Army Hospital in Mobile; later he served in the field as medical director on the staffs of Brig. Gen. Daniel Ruggles and Gen. Braxton Bragg; finally, he returned to Mobile to fulfill other medical duties. After the war he moved to Baltimore and then to New York City, where he was a founding member of the New York Obstetrical Society. Nott returned to the South after his health began to decline, settling first in Aiken, South Carolina, and then moving back to Mobile, where he died on 31 March 1873—his sixty-ninth birthday.

Writings. Nott wrote prodigiously on many medical and scientific topics. In 1866 he published *Contributions to Bone and Nerve Surgery* as an instructional guide for new surgeons. The work describes injuries suffered by soldiers during the Civil War and offers surgical techniques to remedy them. In "A Lecture on Animal Magnetism," delivered in Mobile in 1846 and published in the *Southern Journal of Medicine and Pharmacy* the same year, he promoted hypnosis for the treatment of nervous diseases.

Yellow Fever. Nott devoted much of his medical career to the study of the causes of yellow fever. The city of Mobile was plagued by the disease, and epidemics occurred regularly. Nott lost four of his eight children to the yellow fever epidemic of 1853, although his interest in the disease had begun well before that time. Most people believed that yellow fever came from noxious vapors released by decaying vegetable and animal refuse; when they heard of yellow fever outbreaks in other cities, Mobile residents would clean waste from streets and public areas as best they could. Nott believed that the illness came not from gases but from some kind of insect or other form of animal life; he mentioned the mosquito as a possible carrier of yellow fever. The discovery that a particular type of mosquito did, indeed, transmit the virus that caused the disease would not be made until the early twentieth century; nevertheless, Nott's theory that an organism was responsible for spreading yellow fever was closer to the truth than were the beliefs of most mid-nineteenth-century physicians.

Racial Theory. In the 1840s Nott began to express publicly his ethnological ideas. His writings on the subject stemmed from his desire to justify slavery, but they also revealed a scientific interest in the subject. Like many Southerners, Northerners, and Europeans, Nott believed that the black and white races were unequal. While this theory caused little controversy among white Americans, Nott's rationale for the belief was another matter: from the moment of creation, Nott argued, blacks had existed as a separate and inferior species. Nott's claim challenged the biblical account of creation and aroused opposition in the religious community. By the late 1840s the debate over separate human races had reached a climax in American science, with Nott one of the leading figures. In 1854 Nott and the British ethnologist George R. Gliddon published *Types of Mankind,* which further elaborated the theory of multiple creations and separate human species. Nott's most important ethnological publication, the work stood as the standard scientific explanation of the origins of the races until Darwin's theories became widely accepted. In 1857 Nott and Gliddon published a sequel, *Indigenous Races,* but it did not attract the attention that their first book did.

Source:
Reginald Horsman, *Josiah Nott of Mobile: Southerner, Physician, and Racial Theorist* (Baton Rouge & London: Louisiana State University Press, 1987).

ABBY WOOLSEY

1828-1893

PIONEER IN PROFESSIONAL NURSING

Family Background. In 1828 Abby Woolsey was born into an upper-class family that included eight children, seven of them females. She and her siblings spent most of their adolescence in New York City. The Woolseys took an active role in social affairs, and Abby and her siblings engaged in many church and reform activities. Abby showed strong abolitionist sentiments in the 1840s and 1850s, especially after attending a slave auction while visiting Charleston, South Carolina, in 1859. She also supported the woman's rights and temperance movements. Her most significant contribution to reform, however, came from her work in the field of nursing.

The Civil War. During the Civil War, Abby and her sisters Georgeanna and Eliza became active members of the Woman's Central Association of Relief, organized in New York in 1861 to provide material comforts to sick and wounded soldiers. The association sent Georgeanna and Eliza to federal hospitals as nurses; Abby remained in New York, working with the organization on a full-time basis helping to coordinate the collection and distribution of clothing, bedding, and food. Some of the goods were donated, while others were purchased by the Woman's Central Association. Woolsey frequently used her own money to buy supplies, and, like other women, she often sewed clothing to be sent to the front.

New York's Presbyterian Hospital. After the war Woolsey worked with churches and other organizations to promote social reform. In 1872 the Presbyterian Hospital opened in New York City, welcoming patients "irrespective of creed, nationality, or color." The hospital's board of directors chose Jane Woolsey as "directress" of the new institution; Jane, aware of her sister's superior organizing skills, arranged for Abby to be appointed "acting clerk." Abby's position empowered her to direct hospital activities in Jane's absence, and the two women worked together to achieve an efficient and orderly hospital administration. Jane resigned the directorship in 1876 because of poor health and because of continuing objections by some male physicians to a woman occupying such a position of authority; Abby turned in her resignation at the same time.

The Beginnings of Professional Nursing. During the years Abby Woolsey worked at the Presbyterian Hospital, she was also occupied with other social-reform movements. In January 1872 she joined a group of upper-class women in founding the New York State Charities Aid Association. The stated goals of the organization reflect both a humanitarian impulse and a desire to promote social order:

> 1st. To promote an active public interest in the New York State Institutions of Public Charity with a view to the physical, mental and moral improvement of their pauper inmates; 2d. To make the present pauper system more efficient, and to bring about reforms in it as may be in accordance with the most enlightened views of Christianity, science and philanthropy.

The association appointed a visiting committee of seventy-eight "influential and benevolent citizens of New York," including Woolsey, to inspect conditions at New York City's Bellevue Hospital, which had been established as an almshouse in 1658. On its frequent visits to the hospital the committee noted that the wards were unsanitary and that the nurses were "inadequate in number, nearly all illiterate, some immoral and others intemperate."

Nursing Reform. To remedy the conditions they found at the hospital the members of the Bellevue visiting committee recommended the establishment of a nursing school. The school would be associated with the hospital, a pattern established by Florence Nightingale in England. Woolsey was chosen to draft the plan of organization for the Bellevue Training School for Nurses. Drawing heavily on Nightingale's ideas, she proposed an administration consisting of a superintendent, head nurses, and teachers; "acceptable" nursing students from the middle class should be sought out and provided with suitable living accommodations. The students should be trained not only as nurses but also as teachers, Woolsey stressed: the "graduates should feel that wherever they go, they must carry the spirit of the school with them, and that training can go on in every hospital ward where a competent head-nurse is found." The Bellevue Training School for Nurses opened its doors on 1 May 1873. Woolsey's organizational scheme, which came to be known as the Bellevue Plan, became a model for other nursing schools in the United States and Canada. Woolsey continued to work with the New York State Charities Aid Association and Bellevue Hospital throughout the 1870s and 1880s. She died in 1893.

Source:

Anne L. Austin, *The Woolsey Sisters of New York: A Family's Involvement in the Civil War and a New Profession, 1860–1900* (Philadelphia: American Philosophical Society, 1971).

MARIE ZAKRZEWSKA

1829-1902
EARLY FEMALE PHYSICIAN

Pioneering Role in Medicine. Marie Zakrzewska, an influential New England physician, played an important role in opening the field of medicine to women. After receiving her M.D. from Cleveland Medical College in 1856, Zakrzewska worked with other female physicians to establish women's hospitals in the United States. She founded the New England Hospital for Women and Children in 1862 and became a well-known physician in New England. Throughout her life she lobbied for the equal treatment of women in medicine. She was also active in the woman's rights movement and, in the antebellum years, the antislavery movement, where she became close friends with William Lloyd Garrison, Wendell Phillips, and other radical abolitionists.

Medical Studies in Germany. Of Polish ancestry but born in Berlin, Germany, in 1829, Zakrzewska was no stranger to medicine: her maternal grandmother had been a veterinary surgeon, and her mother practiced midwifery in Berlin. At fifteen Zakrzewska spent six weeks nursing her aunt and great-aunt and formed a desire to pursue medicine as a career. She enrolled at the Berlin School for Midwives in 1849 and in May 1852 was appointed chief director of the Charité Hospital, as well as the major professor of the School for Midwives. Because of her sex Zakrzewska's appointments generated intense debate and opposition among university and city officials. Continued opposition caused Zakrzewska to resign her positions in the fall of 1852.

Immigration to the United States. In March 1853 Zakrzewska and her younger sister Anna left Berlin for the United States. Zakrzewska had heard about the Pennsylvania Female Medical College, and she hoped that the climate for female doctors would be more hospitable in America than in Europe. Although their destination was Philadelphia, the sisters temporarily settled in New York City, where two more sisters and a brother soon joined them. There Marie Zakrzewska learned of Dr. Elizabeth Blackwell, the first woman to receive a medical degree in the modern world. Blackwell had graduated from the Geneva Medical College in 1849; in 1854 her sister Emily received an M.D. from the same institution. That same year the New York legislature granted the Blackwell sisters a charter to establish the New York Infirmary for Indigent Women and Children. Elizabeth Blackwell became a mentor to Zakrzewska, working with her in the dispensary and teaching her English. Blackwell also helped secure Zakrzewska's admission to Cleveland Medical College, part of Western Reserve College; the medical school had begun admitting female students in 1847.

The Importance of Hospitals. Zakrzewska completed her medical degree in 1856 and returned to New York City, where, in the spring of 1857, she helped Elizabeth Blackwell expand the New York Infirmary for Indigent Women and Children from a dispensary into a full hospital—the first hospital in the United States run and staffed entirely by women. Zakrzewska occupied several posts at the hospital, including resident physician, instructor of students, superintendent, and housekeeper. She also established a successful private practice in the city. In 1859 she accepted a position as professor of obstetrics at the New England Female Medical College in Boston, but she resigned in 1861 because she believed that the college's standards were too low and because the trustees failed to respond to her requests for the establishment of a college-based hospital.

The New England Hospital for Women and Children. A year after resigning her post at the New England Female Medical College, Zakrzewska opened a ten-bed hospital in a rented house in Boston. The purposes of the institution were to promote the training of female physicians and nurses, while offering medical care for women and children. The facility eventually grew into the New England Hospital for Women and Children. Zakrzewska oversaw the administration of the institution, and for a time she served as resident physician and head nurse. Her involvement with the New England Hospital for Women and Children lasted almost four decades. She also continued her private practice. In 1899, at seventy, Zakrzewska retired. She died in 1902.

Source:
Agnes C. Vietor, *A Woman's Quest: The Life of Marie E. Zakrzewska, M.D.* (New York: Appleton, 1924).

PUBLICATIONS

Louis Agassiz, *Contributions to the Natural History of the United States*, 4 volumes (Boston: Little, Brown / London: Thurber, 1857–1862)—Agassiz originally planned to publish ten volumes of this work but only completed four. Volume one includes "Essay on Classification," which summarizes Agassiz's views on the creation of species;

John Bachman, *Doctrine of the Unity of the Human Race Examined on the Principles of Science* (Charleston, S.C.: Canning, 1850)—claims that despite significant differences among races, all humans constitute a single species;

Elizabeth Blackwell, *The Laws of Life with Special Reference to the Physical Education of Girls* (New York: Putnam, 1852)—collection of lectures emphasizing the need for proper hygiene;

Henry C. Carey, *Principles of Social Science*, 3 volumes (Philadelphia: Lippincott / London: Trubner, 1858–1859)—examination of social issues, patterns, and policies in the United States;

James Dana, *Manual of Geology: Treating of the Principles of the Science, with Special Reference to the American Geological History, for the Use of Colleges, Academies, and Schools of Science* (New York: Ivison, Blakeman & Taylor, 1862)—geological survey of America that became a standard textbook;

Charles Darwin, *On the Origin of Species by Means of Natural Selection, or, The Preservation of Favoured Races in the Struggle for Life* (London: John Murray, 1859; New York: Appleton, 1860)—presentation of the theory of evolution through natural selection, which generated vociferous debate in Europe and America;

James D. B. DeBow, *Statistical View of the United States . . . Being a Compendium of the Seventh Census* (Washington, D.C.: Tucker, 1854)—shortened version of the 1850 United States Census report, a vastly more sophisticated undertaking than any of its predecessors; DeBow served as superintendent of the Census Bureau;

Thomas Roderick Dew, *Digest of the Laws, Customs, Manners, and Institutions of the Ancient and Modern Nations* (New York: Appleton, 1853)—traces the correlation between ancient and modern history in an effort to explain current events in light of the past;

Daniel Drake, *A Systematic Treatise, Historical, Etiological and Practical, on the Principal Diseases of the Interior Valley of North America, as They Appear in the Caucasian, African, Indian, and Eskimoux Varieties of its Population*, 2 volumes (Cincinnati: Winthrop B. Smith / Philadelphia: Lippincott, Grambo, 1850, 1854)—detailed account of the topography, climate, and cultures of the interior regions of North America;

George Fitzhugh, *Sociology for the South; or, the Failure of Free Society* (Richmond, Va.: Morris, 1854)—argues that Southern slavery was much more humane to the worker than the Northern free-market system;

Josiah Willard Gibbs, "On the Equilibrium of Heterogeneous Substances," *Transactions of the Connecticut Academy of Arts and Sciences*, 3 (1876): 108–248; 5 (1878): 343–524—work on thermodynamics that led to the establishment of the field of physical chemistry;

George R. Gliddon and Josiah Nott, *Types of Mankind; or, Ethnological Researches, Based upon the Ancient Monuments, Paintings, Sculptures, and Crania of Races, and upon their Natural, Geographical, Philosophical, and Biblical History* (Philadelphia: Lippincott, 1854)—ethnological study arguing that different human races were created at different times and in different locations;

Asa Gray, *Manual of the Botany of the Northern United States; Including Virginia, Kentucky, and All East of the Mississippi* (Boston: Munne, 1848)—description of the plant life of part of North America;

William A. Hammond, *Treatise on Diseases of the Nervous System*, second revised and corrected edition (New York: Appleton, 1872)—one of the first general texts on neurological diseases published in the United States;

Joseph Leidy, "The Ancient Fauna of Nebraska, a Description of Extinct Mammalia and Chelonia from the Mauvaises Terres of Nebraska," *Smithsonian Contributions to Knowledge*, 6 (1854): 113–164—description of fossil findings in Nebraska that helped set off a wave of interest in paleontology in the United States;

Othniel Charles Marsh, "Fossil Horses in America," *American Naturalist*, 8 (1874): 288–294—paleontological account of the discovery that prehistoric horses lived in what became the western United States;

Lewis H. Morgan, *Ancient Society; or, Researches in the Lines of Human Progress* (Chicago: Kerr, 1877)—anthropological study of Indian groups, arguing that all races of human beings share a common origin and pass through similar stages of development from savagery to barbarism to civilization;

Benjamin Peirce, "Linear Associative Algebra," *American Journal of Mathematics*, 4, no. 2 (1870): 97–229—attracted little notice when first published but later helped establish the field of modern abstract algebra.

SPORTS AND RECREATION

by
GEORGE P. ANDERSON, ANTHONY J. SCOTTI, and SILVANA SIDDALI

CONTENTS

Sidebars and tables are listed in italics.

1850

- Amateur New York baseball clubs proliferate, adopting the rules proposed by Alexander J. Cartwright in 1845 for his New York Knickerbockers.
- A Salem, Massachusetts schoolteacher invents Anagrams, a word game that will gain wide popularity.

1851

22 Aug. The U.S. Schooner *America* wins the America's Cup, the trophy for a race around the Isle of Wight staged by the Royal Yacht Squadron.

1852

- Harvard and Yale oarsmen compete informally in the first intercollegiate competition.

1853

- Freehold Raceway opens at Freehold, New Jersey, with harness races.
- The Hippodrome, which seats forty-six hundred people, opens in New York City. Its shows feature acts such as acrobats, clowns, and chariot races.
- The state legislature authorizes New York City to buy land for a public park. The purchased 624 acres is bounded on the south and north by fifty-ninth and one hundred sixth Streets and on the east and west by Fifth and Eighth Avenues.

14 July Opening of the first U.S. world's fair in New York City. The Crystal Palace Exposition is modeled on the 1851 London Great Exhibition.

12 Oct. John C. Morrissey wins the boxing heavyweight championship, defeating Yankee Sullivan on a technicality.

1854

- A horse named Flora Temple breaks the 2:20 mile.

1855

- Fairmount Water Works is completed in Philadelphia. It will be the basis of Fairmount Park, the nation's largest urban park at 3,845 acres.

1856

- In the New York sporting paper *Spirit of the Times* baseball is called "the National game in the region of the Manhattanese."

1857

- Landscape architect Frederick Law Olmsted is appointed to supervise the construction of New York City's Central Park.

•	The first U.S. racing shell, *The Harvard*, is built for the Harvard Boat Club of Cambridge, Massachusetts.
May	At a convention called by the Knickerbockers, New York baseball clubs decide that nine innings, not twenty-one runs, should determine the length of a game.
8 July	The America's Cup is deeded to the New York Yacht Club as a prize for international races. The most coveted trophy in yacht racing will remain in the United States until 1983.
Fall	The first American Chess Congress begins in New York City. Twenty-year-old Paul Charles Morphy, a native of New Orleans, wins the competition. He will tour Europe the next two years and be recognized as the best player in the world.

1858

10 Mar.	Twenty-five New York baseball clubs meet to form the first amateur league, called the National Association of Base Ball Players.
20 July	Fans pay for the first time to see a baseball game. The fifty cents charged at the opening game of the National Association of Base Ball Players pays the cost of preparing the Fashion Race Course on Long Island for baseball. A crowd of fifteen hundred sees New York beat Brooklyn 22–18.
20 Oct.	U.S. boxing champion John C. Morrissey knocks out John C. Heenan, unable to answer the bell for the twelfth round of their title bout. Morrissey subsequently retires, and Heenan, claiming a moral victory, is named U.S. champion by default.

1859

•	Massachusetts establishes a 108-acre public garden in Boston.
30 June	Frenchman Charles Blondin (Jean François Gravelet) walks a tightrope across Niagara Falls.
1 July	The first intercollegiate baseball game is played in Pittsfield, Massachusetts. Amherst College defeats Williams 73–32 in twenty-six innings.

1860

•	U.S. sportsmen begin to wear plus fours, loose sports knickers made four inches longer than ordinary knickerbockers.
17 Apr.	A world boxing championship match is held between U.S. champion John C. Heenan and British champion Tom Sayers at Farnborough, England. After two and one-half hours the brutal fight is stopped; later, both men are awarded championship belts.

1861

- With the beginning of the Civil War, the number of New York baseball teams begins to drop, from sixty-two in 1861 to only twenty-eight at the end of the war in 1865.

- Thaddeus Lowe makes a record balloon voyage from Cincinnati to South Carolina, nine hundred miles in nine hours. He is briefly held as a Union spy. Lincoln later appoints him chief of U.S. Army aeronautics division.

1862

25 Dec.   A baseball game staged by the 165th New York Volunteer Infantry draws a crowd of forty thousand.

1863

- Saratoga Springs, New York, becomes the center of U.S. horse racing with the opening of its flat track.

- New Yorker James L. Plimpton invents four-wheeled roller skates. Roller-skating will become a fad not only in the United States but also in Europe.

- Eddie Cuthbert of the Philadelphia Keystones steals the first base in a game with the Brooklyn Atlantics.

10 Feb.   Huge crowds flock to the wedding of General Tom Thumb and Lavinia Warren, both thirty-two inches tall. P. T. Barnum had publicized the event heavily.

1864

- Congress passes a bill at the urging of Frederick Law Olmsted to preserve California's Yosemite Valley as the first national scenic reserve.

- Chicago names Lincoln Park, which will grow to encompass more than one thousand acres.

- A new baseball rule abolishes the practice of awarding an "out" when a fair ball is caught on the first bounce.

- Although baseball is still an amateur sport, gambling surrounds the games and star players are often paid surreptitiously. Al Reach, who draws a regular salary for a Philadelphia club, becomes the first openly professional player.

- The first running of the Travers Stakes is held at the Saratoga racetrack in New York.

1865

- With the end of the Civil War, soldiers return home. The foundation for the postwar expansion of baseball has been laid during the war as knowledge of the sport spread through both Union and Confederate ranks.

1866

- The annual convention of the National Association of Base Ball Players draws representatives from more than one hundred clubs.

- American Society for the Prevention of Cruelty to Animals is founded in response to various blood sports involving animals.

17 June   The New York Athletic Club is founded. The organization will build America's first cinder track and sponsor national amateur championships in swimming, boxing, wrestling, and track and field. Similar clubs will form in other cities.

1867

- The annual convention of the National Association of Base Ball Players draws representatives from 237 clubs, including more than one hundred from Ohio, Wisconsin, Illinois, and Indiana. The association officially bars blacks from membership.

- First running of the 1.5-mile Belmont Stakes in New York for three-year-old thoroughbreds. The winner is Ruthless, with a time of 3:05.

- Brooklyn pitcher William Arthur "Candy" Cummings invents the curveball.

July   The Nationals, an amateur baseball team from Washington, D.C., begin a 3,000-mile barnstorming tour of the country. The club often trounces the opposition, numbering among its victims the Cincinnati Red Stockings (53–10), the Indianapolis Western Club (106–21), and the Saint Louis Union Club (113–26).

1868

11 Nov.   The New York Athletic Club's first open indoor track-and-field competition is held at the Empire Skating Rink.

1869

- The Cincinnati Red Stockings become the first professional baseball team and achieve astounding success. They travel more than eleven thousand miles, beating almost every prominent club between California and Massachusetts, and appearing before more than two hundred thousand fans. They return to Cincinnati having won sixty-five games and tied one.

15 June   Mike McCoole is awarded the victory over Tom Allen in a nine-round fight in Saint Louis when Allen commits a foul.

6 Nov.   Rutgers defeats Princeton 6–4 in the first intercollegiate "football" game. The game is a soccer variant in which twenty-five men play on each side.

1870

- Massive hunting will reduce the buffalo population from four million to half a million in the next four years.

8 Aug.   In the first defense of the America's Cup, the American *Magic* defeats the English challenger *Cambria* in a race held in New York Bay.

14 June   After ninety-two games without a loss, the Cinncinati Red Stockings lose 8–7 in eleven innings to the Brooklyn Atlantics at the Capitoline Grounds in Brooklyn.

1871

- Ten-year-old Goldsmith Maid, a champion harness-race trotter, is bought by Harry N. Smith for $32,000. Instead of breeding her as he intended, Smith will continue to enter her in races. Goldsmith Maid will go undefeated until 1874, winning her owner about $100,000. In the course of her career the mare will win purses totaling more than $360,000.

- Former Union Army officers found the National Rifle Association.

17 Mar. In a meeting in New York City, representatives of ten teams agree to form the National Association of Professional Base Ball Players, the first professional league. One of the ten, the Brooklyn Eckfords, will find the ten-dollar entry fee too steep but will later replace the Fort Wayne Kekiongas, who will drop out in August.

4 May In the first game of the professional National Association, the Fort Wayne Kekiongas defeat visiting Cleveland Forest Citys, 2–0. It is the lowest-scoring game in the four-year history of the league.

Oct. The American ships *Columbia* and *Sappho* win two races each, defeating England's *Livonia*, 4–1, in the third America's Cup race.

1872

- The National Association of Professional Base Ball Players adds four new teams. Pitchers are allowed to use snap-and-jerk deliveries but must still throw underhand. The Boston franchise, which was plagued by injuries in the initial year of league play, claims the first of four consecutive pennants.

- The American Association of Oarsmen is organized.

1 Mar. Congress creates the nation's first national park, Yellowstone, a two-million-acre reserve in the Wyoming Territory.

1873

- In a rematch in Saint Louis, boxer Tom Allen defeats Mike McCoole in seven rounds.

- Parents in Witchita, Kansas, form a baseball club for young ladies.

- First running of the 1 3/16-mile Preakness Stakes race in Baltimore for three-year-old thoroughbreds. The winner is Survivor.

1874

- The first intercollegiate track-and-field meet is held. Its success leads to the formation of the Intercollegiate Association of Amateur Athletes of America and the first annual championship games in 1876.

Apr. Barnum's Hippodrome, a railroad depot remodeled by showman P. T. Barnum, opens at the north end of New York's Madison Square Park. In the winter Patrick S. Gilmore will buy and rename the structure Gilmore's Garden. It will eventually be known as Madison Square Garden, one of the country's most famous sporting venues.

14 May   Harvard defeats McGill in the "Boston Game" — the first intercollegiate contest that resembles American football. Each team fields eleven men and advance the ball by running with it as well as kicking it.

1875

- Harvard and Yale play the inaugural game of what will become the nation's longest-running football rivalry.

- President Ulysses S. Grant vetoes a bill that would protect the buffalo from extinction.

- The last year of play of the National Association of Professional Base Ball Players, which was losing fan support because of the uncontrolled influence of gambling.

May   The first running of the Kentucky Derby is held at Churchill Downs in Louisville, with Aristides, a chestnut colt, victorious in the 1.5-mile stakes race. In subsequent years, the length will be shortened to 1.25 miles. The Kentucky Derby, the Preakness Stakes, and the Belmont Stakes will later be recognized as the three jewels of the American Triple Crown.

1876

- Theodore Roosevelt enters Harvard, where he will box, row, and wrestle on interclass teams. As president he will symbolize the nation's belief in the character-building value of sports.

- Harvard, Yale, Princeton, and Columbia form the Intercollegiate Football Association to standardize rules. The rules are based on the rugby-style game played at Harvard rather than on the soccerlike game of Yale.

- A four-oared shell from Columbia University competes in England's Henley Regatta, inaugurating a long tradition of American participation in the event.

- Horace H. Lee of Pennsylvania sets a record in the one hundred-yard dash with a time of ten seconds.

- The Centennial Exposition is held in Fairmont Park in Philadelphia. Its 167 buildings hold some thirty thousand exhibits.

- New York City's 840-acre Central Park is completed.

- English fighter Joe Goss defeats Tom Allen in a twenty-seven-round fight in Kentucky.

- The trotter Hambletonian dies at age twenty-seven, having sired hundreds of offspring.

2 Feb.   Major League Baseball is born. In a suite of the Grand Central Hotel in New York City, Chicago businessman William A. Hulbert proposes the reformation of the National Association into the National League of Professional Base Ball Clubs. With Hulbert's reforms and solid structure, the National League will become an American institution.

1877

22 Apr. In the first game in National League of Professional Base Ball Clubs history, visiting Boston defeats Philadelphia, 6–5. Jim "Orator" O'Rourke makes the first hit; Tom McGinley scores the first run; Ezra Sutton commits the first error.

Aug. The U.S. defender *Madeleine* keeps the America's Cup, defeating the Canadian challenger *Countess Of Dufferin*, 2–0.

- The National League roster drops to six teams after the New York and Philadelphia clubs are expelled because of their refusal to make expensive western road trips. The season features the first prearranged schedule; previously, club secretaries were left to arrange the league games.

- The president of the Louisville club of the National League of Professional Base Ball Clubs, Charles E. Chase, suspends four of his players for life after they are found guilty of throwing games. League president Hulbert sustains the decision.

- Baseball catchers begin wearing masks and using lightly padded gloves.

- Swan Boats, designed to evoke Richard Wagner's *Lohengrin*, become a major attraction at Boston's Public Garden.

- Started by Pennsylvania clergyman Willard Parsons, the Fresh Air Fund brings deprived city children for a visit to his rural community.

May The inaugural Westminister Kennel Club dog show, held at Gilmore's Garden in New York City, attracts 1,201 entries.

OVERVIEW

Old Ways. The traditions of the past still defined recreations of most Americans in the 1850s through the 1870s, particularly in the years before the Civil War. Americans were flocking to cities, but in 1860 only six million, or one in five, lived in an urban environment. Old patterns of private entertainments, family amusements, and events such as cornhuskings, barn raisings, and country dances would continue to knit together the fabric of rural communities into the twentieth century. Throughout the nineteenth century, roles and recreations were largely dictated by one's sex. Although antebellum women, including Catharine Beecher and Lydia Sigourney, advocated physical exercise such as rowing, swimming, walking, and calisthenics, women generally engaged in domestic recreations, visiting neighbors and participating in quilting bees. Men spent much of their free time hunting and fishing and often gathered together for rougher amusements.

A Bloody Legacy. Entertainments that featured the shedding of blood lingered through the Civil War era and beyond. Men from all economic classes and races visited notorious "animal pits" where various kinds of creatures, often game cocks with razors affixed to their claws or ferocious dogs, would fight one another to the death. Blood sports flourished in cities in such sporting houses as Harry Hill's in New York and the Spanish Cockpit in New Orleans. Reformers opposed these sports because they thought them debasing to the men involved as well as being cruel to the animals. By 1866, the year of the founding of the American Society for the Prevention of Cruelty to Animals, twenty states had outlawed blood sports, but the spectacles continued clandestinely.

New Attitudes. Significant changes did occur during the period in the ways Americans thought about and enjoyed their leisure. In the first half of the nineteenth century many Christian Americans viewed sports with suspicion if not hostility, believing that too much emphasis on recreation distracted one from the proper attention to duty and God. But American culture was becoming more receptive to the idea of exercise for its own sake, and in the second half of the century a belief emerged that participation in sports could effect moral as well as physical benefits. Private athletic clubs sprang up in the city. Baseball, track and field, rowing, and football gained acceptance as part of college life. By 1869 the Young Men's Christian Association had built gymnasiums in San Francisco; Washington, D.C.; and New York City; in the subsequent twenty-five years the organization added more than 250 gyms.

Spectator Sports. As people were increasingly moving into the cities they were gradually growing more used to being entertained rather than contriving their own amusements. In antebellum America organized spectator sports were occasional events, but footraces, harness racing, and prizefights sometimes drew huge crowds and much gambling. Long distance footraces were held for purses ranging from a few dollars to as much as $4,000 and could draw crowds in the tens of thousands. Harness racing was immensely popular and probably attracted more fans than any other sport. In the 1850s there were about seventy tracks nationwide. Although illegal, bareknuckle prizefights attracted the same crowds—and the same disapproval—as the blood sports. While such events were a far cry from the regularly scheduled, commercialized products they would become, gamblers and promoters were finding it increasingly easy to turn any sort of contest into a massive crowd spectacle.

The Civil War and Sports. The Civil War was a watershed event in the development of American sports, particularly in the emergence of baseball on the national stage. All wars disrupt the routines of life, and the soldiers who survived the Civil War gained a new appreciation for sports as the result of the recreations of the camp. When not soldiering, the men on both sides of the conflict, among other leisure activities, participated in baseball, football, footraces, shooting matches, and boxing. Interest in baseball, which had reached a critical point of development in New York City before the war, spread among the Rebels as well as the Yankees. By the end of the war the sport was positioned to grow into a national pastime.

Professional Baseball. The evolution of baseball from a disorganized recreation into a regulated game and then into a professional sport is probably the most important development in sports in the nineteenth century. In its rise baseball had reflected all the schisms of class, gender, and ethnicity in American society, for the elite amateurs who had codified the game gave way to professionals, and women and ethnic minorities were excluded from participation. The success of professional baseball prepared the way for the development and professionalization of football, basketball, and a host of other sports that would transform American culture. With the creation of the National League, sport in America was well on its way to becoming a well-regulated, commercialized product. The professional athlete soon became an American icon, the figure little boys—and later, little girls—would dream of becoming.

TOPICS IN THE NEWS

AMERICA'S CUP

A Gentlemanly Rivalry. When the Earl of Wilton, Commodore of the Royal Yacht Squadron, heard of the New York Yacht Club's plan to show a vessel at the Great Exhibition in London in 1851, he wrote a welcoming letter to his American counterpart, Comm. John C. Stevens. Not mentioning a competition, he suggested he would be glad to learn "of any improvements in shipbuilding that the industry and skill of your nation have enabled you to elaborate." Stephens, a man who had introduced cricket to his countrymen, could read the Englishman's intent between the lines. In his reply he informed Lord Wilton that he would be crossing the Atlantic in *America*, a yacht that was then under construction, and raised the issue of a race: "We propose to avail ourselves of your friendly bidding and take with good grace the sound thrashing we are likely to get by venturing our longshore craft on your rough waters."

America. Despite his deprecating reply, Stevens and the other members of the syndicate—his brother Edwin, George L. Schuyler, J. Beekman Finlay, Col. James A. Hamilton, and Hamilton Wilkes—were confident of success. They had ordered "the fastest yacht afloat" from George Steers, an admired ship designer, and the builder, William Brown, had offered to forego his bill if *America* did not answer their needs. Although the new yacht was easily bested in a trial race with *Maria*, another of Stevens's yachts which had been designed for speed on smooth water, the ninety-three foot-*America*—with its sails tautly lashed to its booms and its long, hollow, sharp bow that gave it a wedge-shaped appearance—clearly combined seaworthiness with winning speed. Skippered by Capt. Dick Brown, *America* set sail from New York on 21 June, arriving on 11 July at Le Havre, a French port on the English Channel, to make final preparations.

The America's Cup

The yacht *America*, 1851 (Parker Galleries)

Showing Her Stuff. On its crossing of the channel on 1 August, *America* was discovered by one of its top English rivals, *Lavrock*. Stevens imprudently allowed his ship to show her speed in the informal race, thus spoiling the odds he could have gotten in wagers on his yacht. Upon docking at the port the Americans found that their ship had gained a formidible reputation. *The Times* likened its arrival at Cowes, a yachting port on the Isle of Wight, to the "appearance of a sparrow-hawk among a flock of woodpigeons or skylarks." When no individual matches could be arranged, it was decided that *America* would race in a Squadron regatta for the standard trophy, a cup worth one hundred guineas. After a poor start the Americans quickly forged ahead of the pack and led the field of fourteen other entrants around the Isle of Wight, finishing in ten hours and thirty-seven minutes, eight minutes ahead of their nearest competitor.

The Deed of Gift. The five syndicate members of *America* had no immediate intention of making the America's Cup an enduring legacy. The 134-ounce, 27-inch tall trophy—which is not really a cup at all as it has no bottom—was passed from one member to another and proudly displayed at social functions, but at one point the men considered melting it down to cast commemorative medals so each could have a keepsake. At length they acted on George L. Schuyler's suggestion

and on 8 July 1857 deeded the cup to the New York Yacht Club:

> It is to be distinctly understood that the cup is to be the property of the club, and not the members thereof, or owners of the vessel winning it in the match; and that the condition of keeping it open to be sailed for by yacht clubs of all foreign countries upon the terms laid down, shall forever attach to it, thus making it perpetually a challenge cup for friendly competition between foreign countries.

Although the intent of the deed was clear, "the terms laid down" were subject to interpretation.

The Ashbury Challenges. The first challenges for the America's Cup were made by James Ashbury, a businessman who aspired to be a member of Parliament, in 1870 and 1871. In a strained correspondence with the New York Yacht Club, Ashbury negotiated for a race to his liking. From the beginning he insisted that the word *match* implied a contest between two ships, a challenger and a defender, but the New Yorkers seemed reluctant to grant the point. In 1870 the negotiations ended with an ultimatum from the club—Ashbury would either forego his challenge or race for the cup with any and all club yachts that chose to enter. On 8 August, racing in a field of eighteen on the club's regular course in New York Harbor, Ashbury's *Cambria* finished eighth; *America*

The Red Stockings baseball team at the end of the 1869 season

placed fourth; and *Magic* carried the day. The next year Ashbury succeeded in his quest to race against a single opponent in a best-of-seven series of races, but the club claimed the right of choosing its champion for each race from among four defenders. The American yacht *Columbia* defeated Ashbury's *Livonia* in the first two matches but lost the third; *Sappho* was then chosen to defend the cup and won the fourth and fifth races to end the series. Ashbury, who believed he should have been awarded the second race because *Columbia* had rounded a stake boat incorrectly, claimed the sixth and seventh races by default and demanded the cup. The New York Yacht Club did not oblige.

A Centennial Challenge. Five years passed before the next challenge was made for the America's Cup, this time from Canada, and the New York Yacht Club was a good deal more complaisant than it had been in its dealings with Ashbury. Facing difficult times, with a declining membership and unstable finances, the club saw the defense of the cup in the country's centennial year as a means of boosting their sport. When the New Yorkers seemed to be holding out for a similar arrangement as that of the 1871 races with Ashbury, the leader of the challengers, Maj. Charles Gifford of the Royal Canadian Yacht Club of Toronto, protested that it was too much of an advantage for the defenders to be able to select a champion to suit the conditions of a particular day from among several yachts. The club eventually agreed to choose one defender, *Madeleine*, which easily handled the Canadian ship, *Countess of Dufferin*, in two August 1876 races. Despite their poor showing, the Canadians

had infused new life into the America's Cup races, putting the tradition of a single defender racing a single challenger on solid footing for the future.

Source:
Ian Dear, *The America's Cup: An Informal History* (New York: Dodd, Mead, 1980).

BASEBALL

Beginnings. Notwithstanding the myth that Abner Doubleday invented baseball in 1839 in Cooperstown, New York, the modern game is not the invention of an individual but the product of an evolutionary process. American children played various versions of the game now known as baseball as early as the eighteenth century. All such games—variously known as "barn ball," "four-old-cat," "base," and "base ball"—entailed hitting a ball with a stick, and most could trace their origins to the English games of rounders or cricket. The most popular version of the game in the northeastern states was derived from rounders and called "town ball," probably because it took place on town-meeting days. Towns or villages often played against one another, and the rules varied considerably with the circumstances and the players.

Town Ball. As few as eight or nine could play on a side, but some town ball games boasted as many as twenty or thirty men on a team. The most commonly used ball was made of string, stitched down to keep it from unraveling, or else of handsewn leather stuffed with wool, bits of rubber, or string. Town-ball players wore no gloves, but the soft handmade balls rarely hurt, no matter how hard they were thrown. The game was played on a square infield without foul lines. Since any hit was fair, a batter had only to make contact with the ball to put it in play. He then had to touch the poles staked at the bases in their proper order to score a run, but the runner was allowed to run into the outfield and wait until the opposition was distracted to continue his circuit—a tactic called "lurking." A runner could only be called out by being "plugged" or "soaked," that is, hit by the thrown ball. Sides changed whenever someone was thrown out, but scores often ran high. Although town ball had begun as a casual pastime, by the end of the 1830s the game was becoming more serious and more competitive.

The New York Game. An important step in the evolution of baseball, or the "New York game," as it was soon to be called, was taken in 1842, when nine prosperous businessmen and lawyers banded together to form the exclusive New York Knickerbocker Baseball Club. These men were dedicated to turning the sport into a "gentleman's" activity. They practiced seriously, wore similar clothing—blue trousers, white shirts, and straw hats—and, led by Alexander J. Cartwright, gradually changed and codified the rules. They decided that nine players would play on a diamond-shaped field and that three outs would constitute an inning. In an important change from rounders, Cartwright described how a baserunner must be tagged and wrote "that in no instance is a ball to be thrown at him." Other rules—such as the setting of twenty-one "aces" (runs) as the goal of the game, the requirement that the pitcher throw underhand, and calling a batter out if his hit ball was caught on the first bounce—would be changed as the game developed.

Elysian Fields. The Knickerbocker's first baseball game against another team was played on 19 June 1846 in a meadow in Hoboken called the "Elysian fields," where they lost 23–1 to the New York Nine. Gradually, other baseball clubs or fraternities formed in the city, composed mostly of clerks from banks, shops, and countinghouses, but there were also clubs of policemen, firemen, schoolteachers, bartenders, actors, doctors, and clergymen. Interest in the game grew as clubs began to schedule contests against rivals. In the years 1849–1851 teams began to create their own colorful and distinctive military-style uniforms. During the 1850s these baseball clubs also organized their own social activities, such as picnics, dances, and formal dinners.

Organization. The popularity of the game led the Knickerbockers to call a convention in May 1857, where it was decided that Cartwright's rules be modified so that nine innings rather than twenty-one runs determine the length of the game. A second convention on 10 March 1858 saw the creation of the sport's first league, the National Association of Base Ball Players. The twenty-five-member teams would become less and less exclusive as competition intensified and gambling on games became more widespread. The first game of the National Association, between rivals from New York and Brooklyn, was also the first occasion of fans paying to see a game. Some fifteen hudnred fans paid fifty cents apiece, the gate paying for the cost of preparing the field that was the Fashion Race Course for baseball.

Soldiers. The Civil War helped to nationalize the game of baseball as New Yorkers spread the gospel of their game. On Christmas Day 1862, for example, a game between two teams organized from the 165th New York Volunteer Infantry attracted forty-thousand spectators. Soldiers often played informal games while waiting in camp for their marching orders. One private from Ohio discussed the popularity of the game in the middle of war. "Over there on the other side of the road," he wrote home to his family, "is most of our company, playing Bat Ball and perhaps in less than half an hour, they may be called to play a ball game of a more serious nature." Southern prisoners of war learned the game in northern prisons, and Yankees brought baseball to Confederate prison camps, where they sometimes played with their captors.

Postwar Popularity. Both Confederate and Union soldiers brought the game back home with them after the end of the war and interest grew exponentially. The annual convention of the National Association of 1867 drew representatives from 237 clubs, many of them from mid western states such as Ohio, Wisconsin, Illinois, and Indiana. Baseball was gaining in popularity on college campuses as well, and even a few women began to play. "They are getting up various clubs now for out-of-door exercise," wrote home Annie Glidden from Vassar College in 1866. "They have a floral society, boat clubs and base-ball clubs. I belong to one of the latter, and enjoy it highly, I can assure you." Public disapproval soon led to the disbanding of such women's clubs.

Barnstorming. Although interest in baseball was becoming national, rivalries remained local because few amateur clubs had the resources or desire to travel beyond their regions. The first team to barnstorm the country was a group of government clerks and college students, who represented the Nationals of Washington, D.C. Leaving the capital in July 1867, they toured the Midwest, traveling some three thousand miles and trouncing many of the teams of the region. Washington suffered only one loss on the entire trip, to the Forest City Club of Rockford, Illinois. Pitching that day for Forest City was seventeen-year-old Albert G. Spalding, who had learned the game from a Civil War veteran.

The Red Stockings. One of the teams the Washington Nationals had humiliated on their tour was the Cincinnati Red Stockings. In 1869 a group of Cincinnati businessmen decided that the only way their city could have a team they could be proud of would be to field professional players. Although the practice of nominally amateur clubs surreptitiously paying a few players had been going on for years, the Red Stockings were the first avowedly professional team. Only Charles Gould, the first baseman, was from Cincinnati.

CONVENIENT TARGETS

The decimation of buffalo herds by white hunters, railroad crews, settlers, and soldiers is well recorded in the annals of American history. However, the rail passenger in the Great West also contributed to the destruction. Elizabeth Custer, wife of Lt. Col. George A. Custer, described one disturbing scene while traveling by rail in the late 1860s:

I have been on a train when the black, moving mass of buffaloes before us looked as if it stretched on down to the horizon. Everyone went armed in those days, and . . . [it] was the greatest wonder that more people were not killed, as the wild rush for the windows, and the reckless discharge of rifles and pistols, put every passenger's life in jeopardy. . . . I could not for the life of me avoid a shudder when a long line of guns leaning on the backs of seats met my eye as I entered a car. When the sharp shrieks of the train whistle announced a herd of buffaloes the rifles were snatched, and in the struggle to twist around for a good aim out of the narrow window the barrel of the muzzle of the firearm passed dangerously near the ear of any scared woman who had the temerity to travel in those tempestuous days.

Source: Geoffrey C. Ward, *The West: An Illustrated History* (Boston: Little, Brown, 1996), p. 261.

Cincinnati Reigns. The talented, well-disciplined Red Stockings were a revelation to the two hundred thousand fans who saw them that summer of 1869. They traveled nearly twelve thousand miles from coast to coast and played every prominent club without losing a game. The one blemish on their record resulted from their game with the Haymakers of Troy, New York, who quit in the sixth inning with the score knotted at seventeen because of an argument about a foul tip. When the Red Stockings returned to Cincinnati with a record of sixty-five wins and one tie, club president Aaron Champion declared, "I'd rather be president of the Cincinnati Reds than of the United States!" The Red Stockings continued their winning streak into the next season as they toured the deep South. It was finally snapped at ninety-two by the Brooklyn Atlantics, who beat them 8–7 in eleven innings—perhaps the first extra-innings game.

The National Association. The success of the Red Stockings created an appetite among fans for professional play. In a 17 March 1871 meeting in a New York saloon, the representatives of ten teams established the first professional league, the National Association of Professional Baseball Players. The original members included the Boston Red Stockings, Chicago White Stockings, Cleveland Forest Citys, Fort Wayne Kekiongas, New York Mutuals, Philadelphia Athletics, Rockford Forest Citys, Washington Nationals, and the Washington Olympics. The Brooklyn Eckfords, who had attended the meeting, on reflection decided that the new league was too unstable and not worth the $10 required for membership. However, when the Fort Wayne Kekiongas dropped out during the first season, Brooklyn replaced them. Each team was to schedule a best three-of-five series with the others, the team with the best record winning the honor of flying the championship streamer, or "whip pennant," at its ballpark for the next year. The National Association lasted five years, with the Boston Red Stockings dominating the last four seasons after the Philadelphia Athletics claimed the first pennant.

The National League. With the National Association fast losing public support because of gambling scandals, disreputable fan behavior, and its inability to enforce discipline on its member clubs, Chicago businessman William A. Hulbert saw an opportunity for reforming professional baseball. In 1875 Hulbert had accepted the presidency of the Chicago White Sox of the National Association and set about contracting the best players from the eastern clubs to play for his team, most notably Albert G. Spalding, then the star pitcher for Boston. In discussions with Spalding, Hulbert became convinced that the National Association was too undisciplined to survive and decided to propose a National League of Professional Base Ball Clubs, which could exercise much firmer control over the game. Calling a meeting of National Association teams at noon on 2 February 1876 at his suite in the Grand Central Hotel in New York City, Hulbert laid out his plans for a stronger, more disciplined organization: the entrance fee was raised from $10 to $100; membership was limited to cities with populations of at least seventy-five thousand to ensure adequate gate receipts; liquor and bookmaking were banned at ballparks; there would be no tolerance of players involved with gambling. The era of Major League Baseball had begun.

The Early Years. The first years of the National League were especially difficult ones. In the inaugural season the charter clubs—New York, Boston, Hartford, Philadelphia, Chicago, Saint Louis, Cincinnati, and Louisville—played a seventy-game schedule, with Hulbert's Chicago team taking the pennant. The stability of the league was threatened, however, when its biggest market clubs, Philadelphia and New York, refused to make the long road trips west to play return games with the clubs that had traveled east. Hulbert saw to it that both teams were expelled. In 1877 Boston won the championship. Four Louisville players were found guilty of taking bribes from gamblers and were suspended for life. Such strong actions ensured the credibility of the National League and its long-term survival. Professional baseball was on its way to becoming a permanent fixture of American life.

Sources:

Dean A. Sullivan, *Early Innings: A Documentary History of Baseball, 1825–1908* (Lincoln: University of Nebraska Press, 1995);

Circus parade in Michigan, circa 1860

Hy Turkin and S. C. Thompson, *The Official Encyclopedia of Baseball,* eighth edition, revised by Pete Palmer (South Brunswick & New York: A. S. Barnes, 1976);

Geoffrey C. Ward and Ken Burns, *Baseball: An Illustrated History* (New York: Knopf, 1994).

EVERYDAY ENTERTAINMENTS

A Simple Life. Most Americans in the nineteenth century lived relatively isolated lives in the country and had limited opportunities to see sporting events. Farm families found enjoyment in periodic trips to town, but for the most part they found their amusements close to home. Unless distance precluded visits, Americans dropped in on one another with great frequency. Women's diaries often record nearly daily visits from friends for tea, to help with projects, or just to sit and chat. During the Civil War women would get together to knit and sew for soldiers, write letters, or roll bandages.

The Parlor Table. In many homes the center table in the parlor, where family or neighbors would spend time together in the evening, was the spiritual and moral heart of the home. Family members would read to one another, sew, or talk. Their games included musical chairs and the charadeslike Dumb Crambo. Other activities included humorous or poetic recitations, singing, and "tableaux vivants," an elaborate entertainment in which participants create detailed costumes and sets to portray scenes from literature and poetry. These scenes were only shown for a few seconds; actual acting was considered improper for mixed company.

Hoedowns and Balls. Dancing was one of the chief social recreations of Americans of every class. Even some of the strictest Protestants, who disapproved of public entertainment and band music, would dance to songs if

The wedding of General Tom Thumb, one of P.T. Barnum's star circus attractions, 1863

U.S. Army officers and their families at a croquet party at Fort Bridger, Wyoming Territory, 1873

Long-distance footracing, or pedestrianism, came into vogue before the Civil War when the yachtsman John Cox Stevens offered $1,000 to any man who could run ten miles in under a hour. Between 1835 and 1860 footraces increased in number and size, and it was not uncommon to see events with fifty thousand spectators cheering on their favorite runners. While some prizes were as much as $4,000, most purses ranged from a few dollars to several hundred. Running could substantially supplement the income of any farmer, artisan, or laborer, especially in an age when $250 represented the annual wage of most workers. Some runners such as John Gildersleeve and William Howett even managed to live off their earnings from the races they attended in various cities.

While every major city in the country had pedestrian races by the 1850s, the sport developed the most in the New York City metropolitan area. Fans could watch the races at the Union Course on Long Island for a dime. The day was usually quite exciting, with the colorful uniforms of the runners and the intense drama of competition, drink, and good cheer adding to the festive air of the contest. However, like most mid-nineteenth-century sporting events, crowd control was a problem. Pickpockets, prostitutes, and professional gamblers were found at every race. Also, overcrowded stadium conditions and free-flowing alcohol lead to violence on more than one occasion.

Source: Elliot J. Gorn and Warren Goldstein, *A Brief History of American Sports* (New York: Hill & Wang, 1993).

there were no instrumental accompaniment. Most Americans knew how to do the figured, or "square" dances. Waltzes and polkas were also immensely popular. The interest in dance led to the publication of books such as *A Complete Practical Guide to the Art of Dancing* (1863), in which the etiquette advice of the author, Thomas Hillgrove, suggests that dancing was not just the pastime of the refined:

> Loud conversation, profanity, stamping the feet, writing on the wall, smoking tobacco, or throwing anything on the floor, are strictly forbidden. . . . The practice of chewing tobacco and spitting on the floor, is not only nauseous to ladies, but is injurious to their dresses. They who possess self-respect, will surely not be guilty of such conduct.

During the Civil War soldiers from both sides treasured the rare opportunites to dance with local girls. Charity balls were held in both the North and the South to raise funds for the war effort.

Clubs. As Americans moved into the anonymity of cities they often found that joining or creating clubs provided them the means of escaping the cares of the workaday world. While the most intense period of creating and joining clubs did not occur until the 1880s, the movement was clearly gaining momentum in the years after the war. Immigrant groups formed their own brotherhoods, such as the Irish Ancient Order of Hibernians and the German Sons of Hermann. Long-established groups such as the Freemasons and the Independent Order of Odd Fellows began to flourish in the late 1860s and 1870s. Other important groups included the Knights of Pythias, which formed toward the end of the Civil War, the Benevolent and Protective Order of Elks (1868), and the Ancient Arabic Order of the Nobles of the Mystic Shrine (now known as the Shriners), who organized during the early years of Reconstruction. Many

Members of the Cornell University crew in 1876

of these groups were dedicated to charity, but they were also social clubs whose members enjoyed throwing large parties, marching in elaborate parades, and wearing exotic costumes. Although most of these clubs and fraternities were representative of a wide range of social classes, they rigorously excluded African Americans.

Women Join Up. Women's clubs also flourished, particularly when they were tied to religious or temperance societies. Confederate women formed sewing circles known as "Thimble Brigades" to sew for soldiers, and Union women participated in Soldiers' Friends Associations and relief societies. Statewide and nationwide char-

Officers of the 114th Pennsylvania Regiment playing poker in camp during the Civil War

ity associations, temperance brigades, and woman suffrage groups gained many new members in the 1870s. There were also working-girls' clubs, formed to promote self-improvement and education.

Outdoor activities. As fresh air and exercise began to be seen as good for both health and morality, young people were encouraged to spend time outdoors in organized, respectable activities. Men and women enthusiastically participated in winter recreations, especially ice-skating and sleigh riding. Roller-skating became a national craze in the 1870s following the invention of the four-wheeled skate in 1863 by New Yorker James L. Plimpton. Americans flocked to popular seaside resorts such as Newport. Some of the more daring New York ladies took swimming lessons from instructors at the beach, where they wore the new bathing costumes, which consisted of a short dress over full "bloomers."

Central Park. In the 1850s New York City's wealthier merchants and bankers began to promote the idea of a central park that would serve as the "lungs of the city." Since many of these men owned lots along the upper east side, they hoped that such a park would not only improve public health and morals but also their own property values. In 1853 the New York state legislature set aside nearly seven hundred acres in upper Manhattan for an immense public park. The state ran a nationwide design competition, won by Frederick Law Olmsted. The nation's first landscaped, planned park opened to the public in 1858 but was not finished until 1876.

More Parks. By 1858 all major American cities had begun plans for similar public parks. In 1861 Philadelphia completed its "Fairmount Park," which was followed by parks in Baltimore, Brooklyn, Chicago, Hartford, and Detroit. The public park in Saint Louis included baseball fields and racetracks. Americans also began to become more aware of the importance of main-

A cockfight in New Orleans, illustration from *Every Saturday*, 15 July 1871

taining and preserving the country's natural heritage. Yosemite was formally created as the first state park in 1864 (it would become a national park in 1890), and Yellowstone was recognized as the first national park in 1872.

City Entertainments. City life offered Americans many entertainments beyond a day at the park. City dwellers of various classes frequented bars and hotels, which featured band music, dances, puppet and magic shows, and ventriloquists. Animal acts and menageries were always enormously popular. Minstrel shows, also a popular attraction at circuses, featured white actors in blackface attempting to imitate slave life and free black northern "dandies." One of the oddest of urban amusements was tightrope walking. Ropewalkers abounded in cities, and even a few daring ladies tried their luck at crossing streets on "slack" ropes strung between buildings. One man reported a memorable performance in Virginia City, Nevada, in which Miss Ella LaRue walked a rope before a crowd he estimated at fifteen hundred to two thousand people: "Bright moonlight, bonfire in the street, and red fire burnt at each end of the rope—beautiful sight. She was dressed in short frock, tights & trunks. . . . great 'shape'—more of it than I ever saw in any female. Immense across the hips—huge thighs."

The Circus. Along with spectator sports, mass entertainments were also on the rise. People in the country went to county fairs while residents of a few big cities could see circuslike exhibits at "museums," the most famous being Col. Joseph H. Wood's in Chicago and P. T. Barnum's in New York. The circus was probably the most popular occasional entertainment of the period. Barnum's circus was the best known. In the 1850s he brought Jenny Lind, the enchanting "Swedish Nightingale," to tour the United States, launching a nationwide craze. Little girls played with Jenny Lind dolls, ladies wore the Jenny Lind collar, and all gentlemen declared themselves madly in love with her, for she was pious, gentle, and virtuous. In the 1860s Barnum's shows became ever more marvelous, with their giantesses, dwarfs, bearded ladies, and mysterious Circassian beauties.

Sources:

Elizabeth Aldrich, *From the Ballroom to Hell: Grace and Folly in Nineteenth-Century Dance* (Evanston, Ill.: Northwestern University Press, 1991);

Foster Rhea Dulles, *America Learns to Play: A History of Popular Recreation, 1607–1940* (New York & London: D. Appleton-Century, 1940);

Daniel E. Sutherland, *The Expansion of Everyday Life: 1860–1876* (New York: Harper & Row, 1989).

HORSE RACING

Origins. Organized horse racing in the United States dates back to 1665, when Richard Nicolls, the royal governor of New York, authorized the first track at what is now Hempstead, Long Island. The first thoroughbred or purebred sire of record to reach the country was Bulle Rock, imported from England to Virginia around 1730. Thereafter scores of both sires and mares arrived, forming the foundation of the American racing stock, which by the 1860s was based on Diomed, the winner of the first English Derby, Glencoe, winner of the Two Thousand Guineas and Ascot Gold Cup, and others. During the colonial era horse racing was the favorite pastime of the Southern elite, especially the Virginian gentry. In the late 1820s track organizers in the United States standardized weights, planned yearly schedules, arranged the

Planet, one of the best racehorses in the United States before the Civil War (painting by Edward Troye, circa 1858; private collection)

settlement of bets, and fixed rules of entry. Local clubs increasingly charged admission, less to make a profit than to control the clientele, especially when only the wealthy could afford to own, maintain, and train thoroughbred racing horses. Most jockeys, in the South at least, were African Americans.

Popularity. By the 1830s horse racing had become a sensation in the United States, and remained so with each passing decade. The English traveler William Blane remarked that it roused more interest than a presidential election. By 1836 the sale of race horses amounted to more than $500,000 nationwide, and three years later there were 130 thoroughbred meetings in the country. Many of the races reflected the sectional issues of the day, pitting horses from the North against those from the South. In 1823 the race between the Northern champion Eclipse and the South's Sir Henry at Union Course, Long Island, attracted an estimated seventy thousand spectators, some of whom traveled five hundred miles to see the event. Eclipse won the prize, which amounted to $20,000. At least forty U.S. senators attended the 1842 match between Fashion (North) and Boston (South); grandstand seats at the event cost ten dollars apiece.

Civil War. The North-South challenges continued until the late 1850s. The Civil War, along with the Indian wars, helped promote the breeding of thoroughbreds—cavalrymen needed fast horses, and by 1861 most American horses were crossbreeds. As a result, Union officials during the Civil War steadily imported thoroughbreds from England. It was also at this time that the first major-stakes race occurred in the United States. (In a stakes or sweepstakes, the owner of each horse puts up money before the race, with the winner taking the full amount, known as a purse.) In 1864 John C. Morrissey, the former boxing champion turned businessman/pro-

fessional gambler, built a racetrack at Saratoga, New York. He chose the area because of the wealthy families who visited the nearby health resort in the summers. Incorporated the next year, the Saratoga Association for the Improvement of the Breed of Horses had socially prominent men on its board, including William R. Travers, John R. Hunter, and Leonard W. Jerome.

Three Classics. After the Civil War horse racing, like many sports, began to boom as other entrepreneurs followed Morrissey's lead. During this period the three American classic horse races began: the Belmont Stakes, Preakness Stakes, and Kentucky Derby. On 19 June 1867 the first annual Belmont Stakes was won by Ruthless, with a time of 3:05. The track was 1.625 miles long and was located at Jerome Park, New York. (In 1890 organizers moved the race to Morris Park, then in 1906 to Belmont Park.) The Maryland Jockey Club staged its inaugural meeting at Pimlico Racecourse, just outside of Baltimore, on 25 October 1870. The first stakes race, the two-mile Dinner Party Stakes, was held two days later, with the winner being a huge colt named Preakness. Afterward the duke of Hamilton purchased the horse and took it to England, where he killed the animal in a pique. Three years later the Jockey Club honored the great horse by naming a race for him and offering the Woodlawn Vase as a trophy. The Preakness Stakes had its first running on 27 May 1873, when the bay colt Survivor won the 1.187-mile race in 2:43. In 1875 the Kentucky Derby opened at Churchill Downs in Louisville, where a small chestnut colt named Aristides won the 1.5-mile stakes race. Local promoter M. Lewis Clark had modeled the track on the Derby Stakes at Epsom Downs, the Oaks, and other English classics. The stakes race for three-year-olds was later shortened to 1.25 miles, and is still held the first Saturday in May. The Derby is probably the best known of the three American classics, which today are called the Triple Crown.

Trotters. Another form of horse racing during this period was harness racing. By the 1850s there were seventy harness tracks nationwide, with seven in the New York metropolitan area alone. Most trotters in the mid nineteenth century traced their lineage to the stallion Hambletonian, the great-grandson of the English horse Messenger, who arrived in America in 1788. Harness racing appealed to Americans because it fostered egalitarianism: unhitched from its cart, any tradesman's horse could win at the track. Oliver Wendell Holmes in *The Atlantic Monthly* in 1857 observed: "Wherever the trotting horse goes, he carries in his train brisk omnibuses, lively bakers' carts, and therefore hot rolls, the jolly butcher's wagon, the cheerful gig, the wholesome afternoon drive with wife and child—all the forms of moral excellence." Nevertheless most good trotters were owned exclusively by prosperous businessmen, and the cost of the fine horses increased steadily from the 1850s to the 1870s. In 1869 Alden Goldsmith sold his eight-year-old mare Goldsmith Maid for $15,000; two years later, the

Horse-race spectators at the Metairie Course in New Orleans, 1867 (painting by Theodore Sydney Moise and Victor Pierson; from Alexander Mackay-Smith, *The Race Horses of America, 1832–1872: Portraits and Other Paintings by Edward Troye*, 1981)

new owner sold her for $32,000. By 1881 the mare had won a total purse of $364,200. The leading trotter owners were steamship magnate Cornelius Vanderbilt and newspaper owner Robert Bonner, whose rivalry was legendary. Although a devout Presbyterian who frowned upon racing, Bonner could not contain his competitiveness as he encountered Vanderbilt on the avenues of New York City. On 13 May 1862 they met at Fashion Course on Long Island. Bonner won the $10,000 bet, then quickly announced that he would make a "gift" of the money to anyone who could beat his time.

Sources:

Elliot J. Gorn and Warren Goldstein, *A Brief History of American Sports* (New York: Hill & Wang, 1993);

Ivor Herbert, ed., *Horse Racing: The Complete Guide to the World of the Turf* (New York: St. Martin's Press, 1981).

PRIZEFIGHTING

Crime or Sport? Boxing was the most noteworthy sport of the era in terms of crowds and newspaper coverage. American pugilism had its origins in England. In the mid nineteenth century contestants fought under the London, or Broughton, Rules, first devised by the boxer Jack Broughton in 1743. Opponents faced each other in the middle of the ring, toeing a mark called the "scratch." When the bell sounded, they proceeded to fight with bare fists. No hitting below the waist was allowed, and a fallen boxer could not be struck. A round ended as soon as a man went down; only thirty seconds separated each round. Moreover, there was no limit to the number of rounds in a fight. For example, the bout between John C.

Heenan and Tom Sayers on 17 April 1860 lasted for forty-two rounds (two hours and twenty minutes) by some accounts. Each boxer had seconds to assist, and referees supervised the bout. As may be expected, an individual needed to be in superb physical condition to engage in such activity; the average lifespan of a bare-knuckle prizefighter was forty-five years.

Manly Art. Although prizefighting was a bloody affair, it was far more than simple brutality. Boxing helped develop the manly virtues of physical conditioning, fair play, and athletic skill. The ring, it was said, taught a man "bulldog courage." In addition, bare-knuckle fighting nurtured the American notions of individualism and self-reliance. With the advent of heavy industrialization in the mid nineteenth century, urban centers throughout the country started to grow in size and population. City dwellers found boxing a welcome diversion from long hours at the factory and crowded living conditions. Moreover, many viewed the manly art as an opportunity to rise above poverty, and the boxers became ethnic and neighborhood heroes. Pugilists also served a useful purpose for urban politicians, becoming "shoulder hitters" on election day, roughing up the rival candidate's ballot-box stuffers and thugs. In return, politicians protected their muscular supporters whenever they were arrested (which was quite often).

Outcry. Boxing suffered from legal as well as religious opposition. Religious leaders opposed it on moral grounds, denouncing the violence and heavy gambling that accompanied the bouts. The *New York Tribune* de-

Various blood sports, imported from England and easily conducted in alleys and taverns, had great underground appeal in the United States since the colonial era. Although the contests were illegal, they occurred on a regular basis throughout the country, especially in such major cities as New York, Philadelphia, Baltimore, and Boston. The urban masses of the North enjoyed rat baiting. In the "classic" a fox terrier was placed in an eight-foot-long pit with one hundred rats. The object of the sport was for the dog to kill as many of the rodents as possible in a given time. The best trained terriers could dispatch all one hundred in twenty minutes. In the "handicap" a dog was timed in how long it took to kill its weight in rodents. Ratting occurred in saloons, livery stables, and private pits, with spectators paying twenty-five cents to $1.50 to see a handicap, and $5.00 for a classic. Sportsman's Hall in New York City, owned and operated by Kit Burns, could accommodate 250 spectators for such events.

Cockfighting pitted two specially trained roosters against one another. During this era at least two or three cockfights were held in New York City every week, and one breeder had at least seventy birds. While Southerners openly advertised gamecock matches in newspapers, Northerners relied on word of mouth or handbills to spread the news of upcoming events. One contemporary described the typical contest: "It is amazing to see how they peck at each other, and especially how they hack with their spurs. Their combs bleed terribly and they often slit each other's crop and abdomen with the spurs. There is nothing more diverting than when one seems quite exhausted and there are great shouts of triumph and monstrous wagers; and then the cock that appeared to be quite done for suddenly recovers and masters the other."

Source: Elliot J. Gorn and Warren Goldstein, *A Brief History of American Sports* (New York: Hill & Wang, 1993).

scribed a typical fight scene as follows: "Probably no human eye will ever look upon so much rowdyism, villainy and scoundrelism, and boiled-down viciousness, concentrated upon so small a space." *Frank Leslie's Illustrated Newspaper* was equally condemning: "A worse set of scapegallowses ... could scarcely be collected; low, filthy, brutal, bludgeon bearing scoundrels." The courts perceived prizefighting as a throwback to a less civilized

Constables trying to stop the boxing match between John C. Heenan and Tom Sayers (illustration from *Frank Leslie's Illustrated Newspaper,* 12 May 1860)

World boxing champion John C. Morrissey

McGrath. Rival betters then started to argue and in a few minutes five men had been shot, one of them fatally.

Champions. In 1850 one of the most popular American fighters was James Ambrose, an Irishman who came to the United States ten years previously after escaping from the penal colony at Botany Bay, Australia, and assumed the name "Yankee" Sullivan. In 1841 he fought Vincent Hammond for one hundred dollars, defeating him in eight rounds (ten minutes). The next year he battered Tom Secor in sixty-five rounds spread over one hour, earning $300. On 12 October 1853, Sullivan encountered John C. Morrissey in upstate New York. Morrissey won the match after Sullivan left the ring to slug a few hecklers between rounds; when the bell sounded to start the next round, he failed to get back into the ring in time. As the new champion Morrissey had no problem finding contenders. In fact the 1858 prizefight between Morrissey and John C. Heenan, the "Benicia Boy," was probably the most famous boxing match of the era. Both men trained for several weeks and then boarded a train from New York City to Buffalo, accompanied by thousands of fans, some from as far away as New Orleans. From Buffalo, boats took the crowd to Long Point, Canada. The fight was short; after eleven rounds Heenan was so exhausted that he could no longer throw punches. Morrissey, showing more "bottom," or endurance, knocked out his opponent. Some newspapers reported that in New York City alone more than $250,000 in bets changed hands. Another famous rivalry pitted Tom Allen against Mike McCoole. They fought on two separate occasions in Saint Louis, McCoole winning in 1869 and Allen in 1873. After 1877 John L. Sullivan, the "Boston Strongboy," would emerge as the new hero in the boxing world.

Sources:

Elliot J. Gorn, *The Manly Art: Bare-Knuckle Prize Fighting in America* (Ithaca & London: Cornell University Press, 1986);

Jeffrey T. Sammons, *Beyond the Ring: The Role of Boxing in American Society* (Urbana & Chicago: University of Illinois Press, 1988).

era, and classified it as an affray or a riot. As a result, promoters of the sport bribed and dodged police, holding events in wooded glades, barns, or on barges anchored in rivers and bays. Spectators of all ages and classes flocked to the events, their price of admission usually including boat or rail fare. At times, the violence spilled out into the audience. In 1863 at Virginia City, Nevada Territory, a thousand miners paid $2.50 each to watch Thomas Daly fight William McGrath. In the fourteenth round a disputed call of "foul" was leveled against

HEADLINE MAKERS

JOHN C. HEENAN

1835?-1873
CHAMPION BOXER

John Carmel Heenan was born in West Troy, New York, where he was apprenticed as a machinist after a minimal education. At the age of seventeen he followed the lure of easy money west, settling in Benicia, California, where he went to work for the Pacific Mail Steamship Company in the foundry. There he worked twelve hours a day swinging a thirty-two-pound sledge hammer and developing a formidable strength. By 1857 Heenan had a reputation as a saloon brawler, and vigilantes suggested that he had best fight elsewhere. Known as the "Benicia Boy" Heenan returned to New York, where backers arranged for him to fight American champion John C. Morrissey.

Bare-knuckle boxing was a disreputable sport. Many communities would not allow it, and contests often had to be held in hastily arranged locations. The sport was brutal, and it was conducted virtually without rules. A round lasted until one of the fighters was knocked off his feet, and a match lasted until one fighter could not continue. Fight fans tended to represent the most unsavory social element. Gamblers, thugs, pickpockets, and corrupt politicians followed the fights, and respectable citizens did not want to attract such people to their communities.

So it was that the Morrissey-Heenan fight was held on an island beach in Lake Erie on land that belonged to Canada on 20 October 1858. Backers of the fighters put up $5,000 each for the winner-take-all bout. Two rings were set up: one for the main event, another for contentious spectators. Fifty guards protected the fighters from rowdies in the audience. At 6'2" and 190 pounds, Heenan outweighed Morrissey by twenty pounds and was a clear favorite, despite his lack of experience. Heenan was not in top shape. He had an unhealed ulcer on his leg, and infection had sapped his strength. Nonetheless, he dominated the smaller champion, who scored his only points with vicious body shots. In the ninth round Heenan swung wildly and missed, hitting a ring post and breaking his right hand. Morrissey took advantage of the opportunity and decked Heenan for good in the eleventh round. It was the champion's last fight, and when he retired, Heenan, who claimed a moral victory in his one-handed attempt, was declared American champion by default.

Heenan was a celebrity in Manhattan. He worked as an enforcer for Tammany Hall politicians and married popular actress and writer Adah Isaacs Mencken. Together they ate and drank their way around the city, and Heenan's managers feared the bad influence of Mencken on their fighter as they arranged for him to fight the 5'8", 160-pound English champion Tom Sayers for the world championship. When Heenan's party left for England, the site of the fight, Mencken was left behind, where she promptly found other love interests.

The Heenan-Sayers fight was covered sensationally by journalists. Frank Leslie sent over a corps of woodcut illustrators to capture images from the fight for his *Frank Leslie's Ilustrated News*. *Police Gazette* sent correspondents. Even *The New York Times* observed that the fight overshadowed every other news story of the day. In London news reporters were fascinated by the contest, but moral crusaders were outraged. Heenan had to train in hiding as determined reporters tried to find him. On the day of the fight, the fighters wore disguises to a prearranged meeting place, where they traveled together to the site of the fight. Ticket holders, who had paid up to ten shillings for tickets, were instructed to gather at 4:00 A.M. at the London Bridge rail terminus; there they would be transported to the secret site of the battle by sixty-three railway carriages. The aristocracy was well represented among the passengers; novelists William Makepeace Thackeray and Charles Dickens were rumored to be in the crowd, which reportedly included as many as twelve thousand spectators.

On 17 April 1860 the railway cars traveled to rural Farnborough, where workers hastily fashioned a ring in the woods. Twenty-one professional fighters surrounded the ring to keep order. Peddlars sold refreshments, and betting was furious by the time the fight started at about 7:30 A.M. The first round took more than five minutes before Heenan wrestled his opponent to the ground. Heenan, six inches taller and thirty pounds heavier than his opponent, dominated the early rounds and disabled Sayers's right arm in the sixth. The eighth round lasted twenty minutes as the courageous Sayers attempted to hang on. The fight had been going on for about an hour, and both fighters, but especially Sayers, were battered by the ninth round, when the police showed up, but the enthusiasm of the crowd deterred them from interfering.

By the thirtieth round, Sayers, barely hanging on and fighting one-handed, had closed one of Heenan's eyes and had nearly blinded him in the other. Even though Heenan had seemed to be prevailing, at this point he looked far worse than his opponent, his face bleeding and swollen. At 9:30 A.M., in the thirty-seventh round of the fight, Sayers hit Heenan savagely in his barely open eye, and Heenan blindly grabbed at his opponent, catching him by the neck and pushing his head into the ropes. Sayers was choking to death when the managers, by mutual agreement, cut the ropes and the police finally stopped the contest. Accounts differ about which round ended the fight. The caption of the famous Currier and Ives print of the bout (which is not otherwise accurate) notes that the end came after two hours and twenty minutes in the forty-second round.

The fight was declared a draw, and both men were named world champions, but the adulation that they enjoyed immediately following was short-lived. Heenan left Mencken and went to Chicago with a girlfriend. Mencken divorced him, became a stage star in the 1864 production *Mazeppa*, and remarried.

Heenan went back to London and fought a series of exhibition fights, challenging any Englishman for a side bet of $10,000. He fought another championship bout in December 1863 against Englishman Sailor Tom King, and lost a contested decision in the twenty-fifth round. Heenan's handlers claimed he had been drugged. With that setback, the champion fighter, who had lost all three of his major fights, retired to become a bookmaker. After the Civil War he returned to the United States, but he was not welcomed warmly. When Boss Tweed was indicted in 1871 for corruption in New York, Heenan was charged along with him. Two years later the former champion was destitute and unknown. He died near Rawlings, Wyoming, before he was forty, an event barely mentioned in the news of the day.

Source:

Alan Lloyd, *The Great Prize Fight* (New York: Coward-McCann & Geohegan, 1977).

PAUL CHARLES MORPHY

1837-1884
CHESS MASTER

Paul Charles Morphy was born in New Orleans to a prosperous family. His father was a prominent attorney, and his family was socially secure. Young Morphy was taught the game of chess by his grandfathers, a Spaniard and a Frenchman, and within two years of first playing the game the boy was acknowledged as city champion. When he was thirteen, he played three games against J. J. Lowenthal, one of the foremost players of the day, winning two and drawing one.

Morphy was admitted to Spring Hill College at the age of thirteen, graduating with honors in 1854. He was a brilliant student who spoke French, Spanish, and German fluently. After a year of graduate study, he attended the University of Louisiana law school and graduated in 1857 at the age of twenty, a year after the death of his father. He was admitted to the bar with the qualification that he could not practice law until he reached an appropriate age. The chess community imposed no such restriction. Already his reputation as a young master of the game had reached New York, and he was invited to attend the first American Chess Congress there in fall 1857. He went to New York and stole the show. He played quickly and with enough eccentric genius to make his game entertaining to watch. He left New York after the congress acknowledged him as the most talented chess player in the nation. When he returned to New Orleans, the short, nattily dressed, well-mannered Morphy was a celebrity, and he played to the audience. That winter he began publically playing simultaneous games of chess blindfolded, and astonished chess aficionados by managing to win six games in one blind sitting.

In summer 1858 Morphy went on a chess tour of England and Europe. The British champion, Howard Staunton, refused to play him, and Morphy responded by soundly beating Lowenthal, who had recently defeated Staunton, and then playing eight of England's best players simultaneously while blindfolded: he won six of those games and played one game to a draw. In Paris he was similarly impressive. By the end of the tour he was acknowledged as the best chess player in the world, and he began to break under the pressure. He was unable to establish a career in law for himself in New Orleans, and increasingly he acceded to the wishes of his mother, who considered chess to be an interesting pastime but not a pursuit that should distract her son from serious work, which he seemed unable to undertake.

Morphy served as an editorial advisor for *Chess Monthly* late in the 1850s and wrote a column for the *New York Ledger* beginning in 1859, but in 1860 he began to withdraw from the chess community and from most other social contact. When the Civil War broke out, Morphy went to Havana and Paris with his mother and sister, playing arranged games under a low profile, avoiding publicity. After the war, he returned to New Orleans to live with his mother, and played only occasionally. His last recorded game was in 1869. It is generally thought that his career was ended by an emotional illness. He spent his last years obsessively preparing a lawsuit against the executor of his father's estate, and his mother attempted to commit him to a mental institution at one point. In 1875, he refused an invitation to play at the Centennial Exhibition of 1876. He died in 1884, less than three weeks after his forty-seventh birthday. He was the greatest chess player of his time.

Source:
David Lawson, *Paul Morphy: The Pride and Sorrow of Chess* (New York: McKay, 1976).

HARRY WRIGHT

1835-1895
FIRST PRO BASEBALL PLAYER

Harry Wright was born in Sheffield, England. His father, a professional cricket player, moved his family to the United States after Harry's birth. By the time he was twenty, Wright, following his father's model, was playing for the Saint George Cricket Club in Hoboken, New Jersey, but he enjoyed playing baseball as well, and in 1858, he joined the Hoboken Knickerbockers baseball team, playing the outfield.

Played exclusively by amateurs until after the Civil War, baseball had a reputation as a gentleman's sport, and it was very popular. Professional gamblers were quick to see betting opportunities, and they frequently arranged for skilled players in their employ to play for teams that attracted betting action. Amateur baseball was already becoming a money sport.

After the war Harry Wright, a jeweler by trade, traveled to Cincinnati with the intention of forming a professional cricket team. Baseball offered a better opportunity, and in 1868 he became the manager of the Red Stockings, one of two teams in the city. Wright decided to abandon the fiction of amateurism in the sport and announced in 1869 that he would pay his players. Wright paid himself $1,200 as manager and center fielder; he paid his brother George, the finest shortstop in the early era of the game, $1,400. Most regulars earned $800, and substitutes were paid $600. That year the Red Stockings won all of their sixty-six games but one, which ended in a tie when the opposing team quit. They traveled more than twelve thousand miles to play in their games, and they drew more than two hundred thousand spectators, who often paid 50 cents to see a game. The performance of the Red Stockings was a compelling argument for professionalism in the sport, and by 1871 there were enough teams to form the National Association of Baseball Clubs. But hometown fans in Cincinnati were unsupportive. The team folded in 1870, and Wright moved to Boston, where he spent the next eleven seasons. In Boston he won National Association pennants every year from 1872 to 1875, and in 1876 he organized the first tour of England by an American baseball team.

In 1881 Wright joined the Providence baseball team, and in 1883 he moved to Philadelphia, the team he managed until his retirement ten years later. Wright died in 1895, and he was elected to the Baseball Hall of Fame in 1953. Among the accomplishments listed on his citation was the feat of hitting seven home runs in a game at Newport, Kentucky, in 1867.

Source:
"Baseball's First Pro," *in The 50 Great Pioneers of American Industry by the Editors of News Front Year* (New York; Maplewood, N.J.; and Chicago: C. S. Hammond, 1964), pp. 59-63.

PUBLICATIONS

Athletic Sports for Boys (New York: Dick & Fitzgerald, 1866)—a handbook with descriptions of various sports;

J. T. Crane, *Popular Amusements* (Cincinnati: Hitchcock & Walden, 1869)—a description of games and other leisure activities;

Capt. Flack, *The Texan Rifle-Hunter* (London: J. Maxwell, 1866)—a handbook for Texas hunters;

Washington Gladden, *Amusements: Their Uses and Abuses* (North Adams, Mass.: J. T. Robinson, 1866)—the liberal clergyman argues for "sport, glee, fun, not the dismal, repressed, shamefaced variety, but the real hilarious, exuberant sort";

Thomas Hillgrove, *A Complete Practical Guide to the Art of Dancing* (New York: Dick & Fitzgerald, 1863)—which includes advice on matters of etiquette as well as dance;

Addison V. Newton, *The Saloon Keeper's Companion, and Book of Reference, for Saloon Keepers, Proprietors of Hotels, and Sporting Men* (Worcester: West & Lee, 1875)—includes a complete record of all sporting events up to 15 April 1875;

Charles A. Peverelly, *The Book of American Pastimes* (New York: The Author, 1866)—a description of leisure activities;

Caroline L. Smith, *The American Home Book of In-Door Games, Amusements, and Occupations* (Boston: Lee & Shepard, 1874)—a guide to home entertainments for the family;

William Wood, *Manual of Physical Exercises* (New York: Harper, 1867)—a guide to a variety of exercises, including gymnastics, rowing, skating, fencing, cricket, calisthenics, sailing, swimming, sparring, and baseball.

GENERAL REFERENCES

GENERAL

David W. Blight, *Frederick Douglass's Civil War: Keeping Faith in Jubilee* (Baton Rouge: Louisiana State University Press, 1989);

Avery Craven, *Edmund Ruffin, Southerner: A Study in Secession* (New York: D. Appleton, 1932);

David Herbert Donald, *Lincoln* (New York: Simon & Schuster, 1995);

Drew Gilpin Faust, *The Creation of Confederate Nationalism: Ideology and Identity in the Civil War South* (Baton Rouge: Louisiana State University Press, 1988);

Faust, *James Henry Hammond and the Old South: A Design for Mastery* (Baton Rouge: Louisiana State University Press, 1982);

Eric Foner, *Reconstruction: America's Unfinished Revolution, 1863–1877* (New York: Harper & Row, 1988);

George M. Fredrickson, *The Inner Civil War: Northern Intellectuals and the Crisis of the Union* (New York: Harper & Row, 1965);

William W. Freehling, *The Road to Disunion*, vol. 1: *Secessionists at Bay, 1776–1854* (New York: Oxford University Press, 1990);

Lori D. Ginzberg, *Women and the Work of Benevolence: Morality, Politics, and Class in the Nineteenth-Century United States* (New Haven: Yale University Press, 1990);

John McCardell, *The Idea of a Southern Nation: Southern Nationalists and Southern Nationalism, 1830–1860* (New York: Norton, 1979);

James M. McPherson, *Battle Cry of Freedom* (New York: Oxford University Press, 1988);

Phillip Shaw Paludan, *"A People's Contest": The Union and the Civil War, 1861–1865* (New York: Harper & Row, 1988);

David M. Potter, *The Impending Crisis, 1848–1861* (New York: Harper & Row, 1976);

Emory Thomas, *The Confederate Nation, 1861–1865* (New York: Harper & Row, 1979).

ARTS

Daniel Aaron, *The Unwritten War: American Writers and the Civil War* (New York: Knopf, 1973);

Kenneth A. Bernard, *Lincoln and the Music of the Civil War* (Caldwell, Idaho: Caxton, 1966);

Lawrence W. Levine, *Highbrow/Lowbrow: The Emergence of Cultural Hierarchy in America* (Cambridge, Mass.: Harvard University Press, 1988);

F. O. Matthiessen, *American Renaissance: Art and Expression in the Age of Emerson and Whitman* (New York: Oxford University Press, 1941);

David S. Reynolds, *Beneath the American Renaissance: The Subversive Imagination in the Age of Emerson and Melville* (New York: Knopf, 1988);

Lewis P. Simpson, *Mind and the American Civil War: A Meditation on Lost Causes* (Baton Rouge: Louisiana State University Press, 1989);

Marc Simpson, ed., *Winslow Homer: Paintings of the Civil War* (San Francisco: Fine Arts Museums of San Francisco, 1988);

Eric J. Sundquist, *To Wake the Nations: Race in the Making of American Literature* (Cambridge, Mass.: Harvard University Press, 1993);

Edmund Wilson, *Patriotic Gore: Studies in the Literature of the American Civil War* (New York: Oxford University Press, 1962).

BUSINESS

Alfred D. Chandler Jr., *The Visible Hand: The Managerial Revolution in American Business* (Cambridge, Mass.: Harvard University Press, 1977);

William Cronon, *Nature's Metropolis: Chicago and the Great West* (New York: Norton, 1991);

Alan Dawley, *Class and Community: The Industrial Revolution in Lynn* (Cambridge, Mass.: Harvard University Press, 1976);

Robert William Fogel, *Without Consent or Contract: The Rise and Fall of American Slavery* (New York: Norton, 1989);

David Montgomery, *The Fall of the House of Labor: The Workplace, the State, and American Labor Activism, 1865–1925* (Cambridge: Cambridge University Press, 1985);

George Rogers Taylor, *The Transportation Revolution, 1815–1860* (New York: Rinehart, 1951);

Gavin Wright, *The Political Economy of the Cotton South: Households, Markets, and Wealth in the Nineteenth Century* (New York: Norton, 1978).

CIVIL WAR

Bruce Catton, *The Centennial History of the Civil War*, 3 volumes (Garden City, N.Y.: Doubleday, 1961–1965);

Douglas Southall Freeman, *R. E. Lee: A Biography*, 4 volumes (New York: Scribner's, 1934–1936);

Mark Grimsley, *The Hard Hand of War: Union Military Policy toward Southern Civilians, 1861–1865* (New York: Cambridge University Press, 1995);

Herman Hattaway and Archer Jones, *How the North Won: A Military History of the Civil War* (Urbana: University of Illinois Press, 1983);

Gerald Linderman, *Embattled Courage: The Experience of Combat in the American Civil War* (New York: Free Press, 1987);

Robert E. May, *The Union, the Confederacy, and the Atlantic Rim* (West Lafayette, Ind.: Purdue University Press, 1992);

Reid Mitchell, *The Vacant Chair: The Northern Soldier Leaves Home* (New York: Oxford University Press, 1993);

Charles Royster, *The Destructive War: William Tecumseh Sherman, Stonewall Jackson, and the Americans* (New York: Knopf, 1991);

Fred A. Shannon, *The Organization and Administration of the Union Army, 1861–1865* (Cleveland: Arthur H. Clark, 1928).

COMMUNICATIONS

Richard N. Current, *The Typewriter and the Men Who Made It* (Urbana: University of Illinois Press, 1954);

Michael Emery and Edwin Emery, *The Press and America: An Interpretive History of the Mass Media*, seventh edition, revised and expanded (Englewood Cliffs, N.J.: Prentice Hall, 1992);

Peter T. Rohrbach and Lowell S. Newman, *American Issue: The U.S. Postage Stamp, 1842–1869* (Washington, D.C.: Smithsonian Institution Press, 1984);

Robert Luther Thompson, *Wiring a Continent: The History of the Telegraph Industry in the United States, 1832–1866* (Princeton: Princeton University Press, 1947).

EDUCATION

Frederick M. Binder, *The Age of the Common School, 1830–1865* (New York: John Wiley & Sons, 1974);

Lawrence A. Cremin, *American Education: The National Experience, 1783–1876* (New York: Harper & Row, 1980);

Charles Leslie Glenn Jr., *The Myth of the Common School* (Amherst: University of Massachusetts Press, 1988);

Jacqueline Jones, *Soldiers of Light and Love: Northern Teachers and Georgia Blacks, 1865–1873* (Athens: University of Georgia Press, 1980);

Carl F. Kaestle, *Pillars of the Republic: Common Schools and American Society, 1780–1860* (New York: Hill & Wang, 1983);

Michael B. Katz, *The Irony of Early School Reform: Educational Innovation in Mid-Nineteenth Century Massachusetts* (Cambridge, Mass.: Harvard University Press, 1968);

Edith N. MacMullen, *In the Cause of True Education: Henry Barnard and Nineteenth-Century School Reform* (New Haven: Yale University Press, 1991);

Henry J. Perkinson, *The Imperfect Panacea: American Faith in Education, 1865–1965* (New York: Random House, 1968);

David K. Schultz, *The Culture Factory: Boston Public Schools, 1789–1860* (New York: Oxford University Press, 1973);

David B. Tyack, *One Best System: A History of American Urban Education* (Cambridge, Mass.: Harvard University Press, 1974).

GOVERNMENT

Michael Les Benedict, *A Compromise of Principle: Congressional Republicans and Reconstruction, 1863–1869* (New York: Norton, 1974);

Daniel W. Crofts, *Reluctant Confederates: Upper South Unionists in the Secession Crisis* (Chapel Hill: University of North Carolina Press, 1989);

Paul D. Escott, *After Secession: Jefferson Davis and the Failure of Confederate Nationalism* (Baton Rouge: Louisiana State University Press, 1978);

Eric Foner, *Free Soil, Free Labor, Free Men: The Ideology of the Republican Party before the Civil War* (New York: Oxford University Press, 1970);

William E. Gienapp, *The Origins of the Republican Party, 1852–1856* (New York: Oxford University Press, 1987);

Michael F. Holt, *The Political Crisis of the 1850s* (New York: John Wiley & Sons, 1978);

Morton Keller, *Affairs of State: Public Life in Late Nineteenth Century America* (Cambridge, Mass.: Harvard University Press, 1977);

Phillip Shaw Paludan, *The Presidency of Abraham Lincoln* (Lawrence: University Press of Kansas, 1994);

Michael Perman, *The Road to Redemption: Southern Politics, 1869–1879* (Chapel Hill: University of North Carolina Press, 1984);

Kenneth M. Stampp, *The Era of Reconstruction, 1865–1877* (New York: Knopf, 1965).

LAW

Don E. Fehrenbacher, *The Dred Scott Case: Its Significance in American Law and Politics* (New York: Oxford University Press, 1978);

Lawrence M. Friedman, *A History of American Law*, second edition (New York: Simon & Schuster, 1985);

Morton J. Horwitz, *The Transformation of American Law, 1780–1860* (Cambridge, Mass.: Harvard University Press, 1977);

Horwitz, *The Transformation of American Law, 1870–1960: The Crisis of Legal Orthodoxy* (New York: Oxford University Press, 1992);

Harold M. Hyman, *A More Perfect Union: The Impact of the Civil War and Reconstruction on the Constitution* (New York: Knopf, 1973);

Hyman and William M. Wiecek, *Equal Justice Under the Law: Constitutional Development, 1835–1875* (New York: Harper & Row, 1982);

Thomas D. Morris, *Southern Slavery and the Law, 1619–1860* (Chapel Hill: University of North Carolina Press, 1996);

Mark E. Neely Jr., *The Fate of Liberty: Abraham Lincoln and Civil Liberties* (New York: Oxford University Press, 1991);

William E. Nelson, *The Fourteenth Amendment: From Political Principle to Judicial Doctrine* (Cambridge, Mass.: Harvard University Press, 1988);

G. Edward White, *The American Judicial Tradition: Profiles of Leading American Judges,* expanded edition (New York: Oxford University Press, 1988).

LIFESTYLES

John E. Bodnar, *The Transplanted: A History of Immigrants in Urban America* (Bloomington: Indiana University Press, 1985);

Michael H. Frisch, *Town into City: Springfield, Massachusetts, and the Meaning of Community, 1840–1880* (Cambridge, Mass.: Harvard University Press, 1972);

Eugene D. Genovese, *Roll, Jordan, Roll: The World the Slaves Made* (New York: Pantheon, 1974);

Peter Kolchin, *American Slavery, 1619–1877* (New York: Hill & Wang, 1993);

Leon F. Litwak, *Been in the Storm So Long: The Aftermath of Slavery* (New York: Knopf, 1979);

Anne C. Rose, *Victorian America and the Civil War* (New York: Cambridge University Press, 1992);

Lee Soltow, *Men and Wealth in the United States, 1850–1870* (New Haven: Yale University Press, 1975);

Kenneth M. Stampp, *The Peculiar Institution: Slavery in the Ante-Bellum South* (New York: Knopf, 1956);

Christine Stansell, *City of Women: Sex and Class in New York, 1789–1860* (New York: Knopf, 1986);

Daniel E. Sutherland, *The Expansion of Everyday Life: 1860–1876* (New York: Harper & Row, 1989).

RELIGION

Sidney E. Ahlstrom, *A Religious History of the American People* (New Haven: Yale University Press, 1972);

Jay P. Dolan, *The American Catholic Experience: A History from Colonial Times to the Present* (Garden City, N.Y.: Doubleday, 1985);

Ann Douglas, *The Feminization of American Culture* (New York: Knopf, 1977);

C. C. Goen, *Broken Churches, Broken Nation: Denominational Schisms and the Coming of the American Civil War* (Macon, Ga.: Mercer University Press, 1985);

Leon A. Jick, *The Americanization of the Synagogue, 1820-1870* (Hanover, N.H.: University Press of New England, 1976);

William McLoughlin, *The Meaning of Henry Ward Beecher: An Essay on the Shifting Values of Mid-Victorian America, 1840–1870* (New York: Knopf, 1970);

James Moorhead, *American Apocalypse: Yankee Protestants and the Civil War* (New Haven: Yale University Press, 1978);

Jon H. Roberts, *Darwinism and the Divine in America: Protestant Intellectuals and Organic Evolution, 1859–1900* (Madison: University of Wisconsin Press, 1988).

SCIENCE AND MEDICINE

Bonnie Ellen Blustein, *Preserve Your Love for Science: Life of William A. Hammond, American Neurologist* (New York: Cambridge University Press, 1991);

Robert V. Bruce, *The Launching of Modern American Science, 1846–1876* (New York: Knopf, 1987);

Thomas L. Haskell, *The Emergence of Professional Social Science: The American Social Science Association and the Nineteenth-Century Crisis of Authority* (Chicago: University of Illinois Press, 1977);

Reginald Horsman, *Josiah Nott of Mobile: Southerner, Physician, and Racial Theorist* (Baton Rouge: Louisiana State University Press, 1987);

Charles E. Rosenberg, *The Care of Strangers: The Rise of America's Hospital System* (New York: Basic Books, 1987);

Cynthia Eagle Russett, *Darwin in America: The Intellectual Response, 1865–1912* (San Francisco: W. H. Freeman, 1976);

Paul Starr, *The Social Transformation of American Medicine* (New York: Basic Books, 1982).

SPORTS AND RECREATION

Ian Dear, *The America's Cup: An Informal History* (New York: Dodd, Mead, 1980);

Elliot J. Gorn, *The Manly Art: Bare-Knuckle Prize Fighting in America* (Ithaca & London: Cornell University Press, 1986);

Gorn and Warren Goldstein, *A Brief History of American Sports* (New York: Hill & Wang, 1993);

Jeffrey T. Sammons, *Beyond the Ring: The Role of Boxing in American Society* (Urbana & Chicago: University of Illinois Press, 1988);

Dean A. Sullivan, *Early Innings: A Documentary History of Baseball, 1825–1908* (Lincoln: University of Nebraska Press, 1995);

Daniel E. Sutherland, *The Expansion of Everyday Life: 1860–1876* (New York: Harper & Row, 1989);

Hy Turkin and S. C. Thompson, *The Official Encyclopedia of Baseball,* eighth revised edition (New York: A. S. Barnes, 1976);

Geoffrey C. Ward and Ken Burns, *Baseball: An Illustrated History* (New York: Knopf, 1994).

Contributors

THE ARTS

MICHAEL MCLOUGHLIN
University of South Carolina

ROBERT MOSS
University of South Carolina

ANTHONY J. SCOTTI
Manly, Inc.

CAROLYN SHAFER
Wiregrass Museum of Art

BUSINESS & THE ECONOMY

FREDERICK DALZELL
*Maritime Studies Program of
Williams College & Mystic Seaport*

THE CIVIL WAR

ROBERT ZALIMAS
Ohio State University

COMMUNICATIONS

RICHARD LAYMAN
Manly, Inc.

EDUCATION

BRIAN KELLY
Brandeis University

GOVERNMENT & POLITICS

THOMAS J. BROWN
*Institute for Southern Studies,
University of South Carolina*

LAW & JUSTICE

THOMAS J. BROWN
*Institute for Southern Studies,
University of South Carolina*

LIFESTYLES, SOCIAL TRENDS
& FASHION

SILVANA SIDDALI
Harvard University

RELIGION

MARY ELIZABETH BROWN
Marymount College

SCIENCE & MEDICINE

SPORTS & RECREATION

KIMBERLY KELLISON
University of South Carolina

GEORGE P. ANDERSON
Manly, Inc.

ANTHONY J. SCOTTI
Manly, Inc.

SILVANA SIDDALI
Harvard University

INDEX1

![black bar divider]

A

Abbot, Francis Ellingwood   313
"Abdulla Bulbul Ameer" (French)   25
Abolitionism   26, 32–33, 40, 47, 48, 81,
    141, 143, 158
Ableman v. *Booth* (1859)   227, 248
Abortion   281
Academy of Music, New York City   25
Adams, Charles Francis   41, 61, 73, 83,
    190, 213
Adams, Charles Francis Jr.   23, 78–79,
    241
Adams, Charles Kendall   357
Adams, Henry   23, 41–42, 189, 336
Adams, John   41, 78, 189
Adams, John Quincy   41, 78, 189, 190
Adams, Samuel   217
Adler, Dr. Felix   146, 315, 321, 336
Adler, Samuel   319
Adventures of Huckleberry Finn (Clemens)
    36
The Adventures of Tom Sawyer (Clemens)
    25, 27, 36
Advertising agencies   54
Advisory Commission of Differential Rates
    259
African American actors   40
African American troops   89, 91
African American work songs   37
African Methodist Episcopal Church
    310, 334, 348
African Methodist Episcopal Church, Zion
    313, 334
African Zion Church   303
Agassiz, Louis   359, 363, 365, 369
The Age of Reason (Paine)   346
Agriculture   59, 60, 72, 83
Aiken, George L.   18, 26, 40
Akerman, Amos T.   255, 256–257
Akron Women's Rights Convention, 1850
    304
Alabama Baptist Convention   328
Alamo , Texas,   79
Albany Academy   376
Albert, Prince Consort of Great Britain
    273
Alboni, Marietta   39
Alcorn University   145

Alcott, Amos Bronson   30, 171
Alcott, Erastus B.   355
Alcott, Louisa May   23
Alcott family   30
Alemany, Joseph S.   347
Alford, John V.   166
Alger, Horatio   274, 276
All Soul's Unitarian Church, New York
    City (Mould)   19, 311
Allen, Tom   385–387, 402
Allen, William Francis   23, 38
Allston, Washington   47
Amana Society   310
The Ambassadors (James)   37
America (yacht)   382, 390–391
America's Cup   382–383, 385–386, 388,
    390–392
The American (James)   25, 27, 37
American Academy of Arts   359
American Academy of Arts and Sciences
    365
American Anti-Slavery Society   217, 261
American Association for the Advancement
    of Education   141
American Association for the Advancement
    of Science   359, 360, 365, 376
American Association for the Advancement
    of Social Science   229
American Association of Oarsmen   386
American Baptist Free Mission Society
    142
American Baptist Home Mission Society
    145
American Bar Association   245
American Chemical Society   358
American Chess Congress   383, 404
American College, Rome   310
American Emigrant Company   60
American Express   132, 136
American Forestry Association   358
American Journal of Education   157, 169
American Journal of Obstetrics   357
American Journal of Science   376
American Law Review   231
American Library Association   164
American Medical Association   360, 366
American Miners' Association   52
American Missionary Association   143,
    145, 165–166, 174, 313, 331, 333

American Museum of Natural History
    370
American National Baptist Convention
    334
American Party   221, 327
American Pharmaceutical Association
    354
American Public Health Association
    357, 368, 374
American Red Cross   374
American Renaissance (literature)   26,
    30–32
American Revolution   27, 99, 164, 188,
    206, 240, 252, 272
"The American Scholar" (Emerson)   30
American Social Science Association
    356, 370
American Society for the Prevention of
    Cruelty to Animals   385, 389
American Statistical Association   369
American Telegraph Company   130, 135
American Triple Crown   387
American Unitarian Association   309
American Woman Suffrage Association
    221, 257
American Womens' Education Association
    140
Ames, Oakes   186
Amherst College, Mass.,   341
Amish sect   329
Amman, Jacob   279
Anaconda Plan   86
Anagrams   382
Ancient Arabic Order of the Nobles of the
    Mystic Shrine   396
Ancient Fauna of Nebraska (Leidy)   363
Ancient Law (Maine)   235
Ancient Order of Hibernians   278, 396
Ancient Society (Morgan)   370
Anderson, Abram   55
Anderson, Robert   86
Andersonville [Georgia] prisoner of war
    camp   90, 209
The Andes of Ecuador (Church)   19, 20,
    25, 27, 35, 36, 37, 40, 44, 45
Andrew, John A.   89
Andrews, James O.   328
Andrews, Stephen Pearl   305

Mexican War   64, 87, 93, 99, 101,
    114–115, 191, 195, 199, 258
Michigan Military Academy   115
Michigan Central Railroad   71
Michigan Southern Railroad   50, 71
Michigan State University   164
Michigan, A History of Governments (Cooley)
    259
Milbank, Jeremiah   79
Milburn, Richard   19
Miles, Nelson A.   184
Military Reconstruction Act of 1867   185,
    211
Militia Act of 1862   105
Milk contamination   79
Mill Hill Fathers. *See* Society of Saint
    Joseph of the Sacred Heart
Miller, Elizabeth Smith   220, 300
Miller, Joachim   23
Miller, Samuel   255
Milligan, Lambdin P.   250
Milton Bradley board games   53
Mineral Land Act of 1866   54
Minié, Claude Étienne   94
Minié balls   94
The Minister's Wooing (Stowe)   20
Minneapolis Mill Company   51
Minstrel shows   19, 22, 38, 398
Mirror of Fashion   286
*Miss Ravenel's Conversion from Secession to
    Loyalty* (De Forest)   23, 33
Mississippi River Boom & Logging
    Company   56
Missouri Compromise of 1820   180, 183,
    191, 196–198, 202, 227, 242
Mitchell, James A.   173
Mitchell, Maria   356, 360
Mobile Medical Society   377
Moby-Dick (Melville)   18, 26, 31–32
A Modern Instance (Howells)   37
Mohun (Cooke)   33
Molly Maguires   57–58, 214, 233, 315,
    327
U.S.S. *Monitor*   87
The Monk (Innes)   24
Montgomery Ward and Company, Chicago
    55, 56
Mont-Saint-Michel and Chartres (Adams)
    41
Moody, Dwight   310–311, 313–314
Moore, Thomas O.   87
Morais, Sabato   308, 320
Moran, Thomas   26, 27, 43
Moravians   329
Morehouse College   145
Morgan, Charles H.   52
Morgan, E. B.   136
Morgan, J. P.   55, 81, 335
Morgan, John Hunt   90, 103
Morgan, Junius Spencer   51
Morgan, Lewis H.   370
Morphy, Paul Charles   383, 404–405
Morrill Act of 1862   144, 150, 163–164,
    203, 228, 350, 356
Morris Park, New York   399
Morrissey, John C.   382, 383, 399, 402,
    403

Morse, Samuel F. B.   130, 135, 371, 376
Morse Code   130, 376
Morse-Libby House, Portland, Maine
    (Austin)   22
Morton, Oliver P.   213
Morton, Samuel G.   369
Mosses from an Old Manse (Hawthorne)
    31
Motley, John Lothrop   19, 217
Mott, Lucretia   190, 220, 299
Mould, Jacob Wrey   19
Mount, William Sidney   29
Mount Auburn Cemetery   47
Mount Moran, Wyoming   27
Mount Washington Cog Railroad   356
Mountain Meadows Massacre   350
Mountaineering in the Sierra Nevada (King)
    24
Mountour Iron Works, Danville,
    Pennsylvania   65
Muhlenberg, William Augustus   309
Mullett, Alfred B.   23
Munn v. *Illinois*   58, 243, 260
Museum of Fine Arts, Boston (Sturgis and
    Brigham)   25
Music   37
Musical theater   38
Musical World   19
"My Old Kentucky Home" (Foster)   19,
    38
The Mystery (Delany)   215

N

N. W. Ayer & Son, Philadelphia   54
The Narrative of Sojourner Truth   304
Nasby, Petroleum V. *See* Locke, David
    Ross.
The Nasby Papers (Locke)   22
Nashville Convention of 1850   180
National Academy of Design, New York
    City (Wight)   21–22, 43
National Academy of Sciences   356
National Association   387, 393
National Association of Base Ball Players
    383–387, 393–394, 405
National Banking Act of 1863   53, 205
National Bankruptcy Act of 1867   230
National Board of Trade   54
National Congress of Penitentiary and
    Reformatory Discipline   231
National Education Association   170
National Educators' Association   145
National Emigration Convention   215
National Equal Rights League   261
National Era   32, 48
National Labor Congress of 1866,
    Baltimore   54
National Labor Tribune   60
National League of Professional Base Ball
    Clubs   387–388, 390, 394
National Mineral Act of 1866   212
National Rifle Association   386

National Teachers' Association   142, 144,
    160, 165
National Trademark Law of 1870   55
National Unitarian Conference   312, 313
National Woman Suffrage Association
    221, 305
Nature and the Supernatural (Bushnell)
    344
The Needs of the University   357
"Nelly Bly" (Foster)   38
Neumann, John Nepomucene   308, 311
New Apostolic Church   311
New Bowery Theater, New York City   40
New England Female Medical College
    379
New England Hospital for Women and
    Children   379
New England psalmody   37
New England Scenery (Church)   43
New School (Presbyterian) General
    Assembly   308
New School Presbyterians   310
New York, Albany and Buffalo Telegraph
    Company   135
New York & Harlem Railroad   82
New York and Mississippi Valley Printing
    and Telegraph Company   50, 135
New York Athletic Club   385
New York Central and Hudson River
    Railroad   83
New York Central College   141–143
New York Central Railroad   71, 82
New York Children's Aid Society   327
New York City   382–383, 386–388
New York Condensed Milk Company   79
New York Court of Appeals   228
New York Custom House   220
New York Herald   128
New York Hospital for Ruptured and
    Crippled Children   356
New York Infirmary for Women and
    Children.   355, 372, 379
New York Knickerbockers   382, 393
New York Ledger   405
New York Medical College   355
New York Mutuals   394
New York Nine   393
New York Obstetrical Society   377
New York Public Library   141
New York railroad commission   227
New York Sisters of Charity   313
New York Society for Ethical Culture
    315, 321
New York Society for the Promotion of
    Education Among Colored Children
    142
New York Society for the Suppression of
    Vice   347
New York State Charities Aid Association
    378
New York State insurance regulatory agency
    52
New York State Printing Telegraph
    Company   135
New York State Superintendent of Public
    Instruction   141
New York Stock Exchange   62, 73–74

Y

Z

INDEX OF PHOTOGRAPHS